Obituaries of Benton County Arkansas

Volume Seven
1923–1925

Compiled by
Barbara P. Easley

Edited by
Barbara P. Easley
and Verla P. McAnelly

HERITAGE BOOKS
2024

HERITAGE BOOKS

AN IMPRINT OF HERITAGE BOOKS, INC.

Books, CDs, and more—Worldwide

For our listing of thousands of titles see our website
at
www.HeritageBooks.com

Published 2024 by
HERITAGE BOOKS, INC.
Publishing Division
5810 Ruatan Street
Berwyn Heights, MD 20740

Heritage Books by the author:

Obituaries of Benton County, Arkansas:
Volume One, 1884–1898 to Volume Nine, 1928–1929

CD: *Obituaries of Benton County, Arkansas*

CD: *Obituaries of Washington County, Arkansas: Volumes One – Four, 1841–1912*

International Standard Book Number
Paperbound: 978-0-7884-0430-6

Table of Contents

Foreword

Previous books in this series:

Obituaries of Benton County, Ark., Vol. I, 1884–1898.

Obituaries of Benton County, Ark., Vol. II, 1899–1904.

Obituaries of Benton County, Ark., Vol. III, 1905–1909.

Obituaries of Benton County, Ark., Vol. IV, 1910–1913.

Obituaries of Benton County, Ark., Vol. V, 1914–1918.

Obituaries of Benton County, Ark., Volume VI, 1919–1922.

This book is number seven in the series Obituaries of Benton County, Arkansas. The records have been compiled from microfilm of Benton County newspapers. The microfilm was acquired from The Arkansas History Commission, One Capitol Mall, Little Rock, Arkansas.

In this book, each year is a separate chapter, and within each chapter the decedent is listed alphabetically. If a woman's maiden name it is given it is included. Each item is referenced to the paper and date in which it appeared. At times, the obituaries from two papers are combined and each paper is annotated.

This book is a treasure trove of information regarding the citizens of Benton County during the period 1923–1925. The information in the obituaries ranges from a brief report of death to an extensive biography of the decedent and often of his family, parents, grandparents, children and grandchildren. The date of death, the cause of death and the place of burial may be reported. Details about funeral services and church and lodge relationships are furnished. Candid accounts of the personality and the peculiarities of the individual are given in some obituaries. Indirectly, a mini–history begins to unfold of the development of the country, towns and churches . This book continues to offer many hours of interesting reading and study of the residents of Benton County, former residents and residents of other communities in neighboring or even in distant states. The paper may publish an obituary that appeared in a newspaper in another state. (continued)

Some surnames appearing in this volume are: Adams, Alfrey, Allen, Allred, Ammons, Anderson, Armstrong, Austin, Baker, Ball, Banks, Bates, Bell, Blackburn, Blake, Blevins, Bowen, Bowman, Boyd, Britt, Brown, Browning, Bryant, Buck, Burnett, Buttram, Callis, Campbell, Carl, Casey, Cavness, Chastain, Clark, Clement(Clements). Cole, Collins, Cook, Cooper, Covey, Crain, Crichlow(Critchlow), Cunningham, Daniel(Daniels), Darby, Davis, Dean(Deans), Deason, Dickson(Dixon), Douglas, Dunagin, Easley, Eden(s), Edwards, Ellis, Evans, Fair, Ford, Foster, Fox, Fraser(Frazer), Gailey, Gamble, Gilbert, Graham, Green(Greene), Guthary(Guthrie), Haley, Hall, Hammack(Hammock). Hardy, Harris, Hastings, Hayes(Hays), Handerson, Hendicks(Hendrix), Henry, Hickman, Hinds(Hines), Hinman, Hodges, Hoffman, Holcomb, Holland, Howard, Hull, Hunter, Hutcheson, Jackson, Jefferson, Johnson, Johnston, Jones, Keith, Kelley(Kelly), Kerr, Kirkpatrick, Knot(Knott, Knotts), Landers, Lawson, Lefors, Lemming, Lewis, Lindsey, Looney, Marr(s), Martin, Maxwell, McDaniel, McKenzie, McNeil(McNeill), Middleton, Miller, Mills, Mitchell, Moore, Morgan, Morris, Moser(Mosier), Murphy, Myers, Nance, Nichols, Oakley, Osborn(Osborne), Pace, Parker, Patterson, Patton, Pearson(s), Peel, Perry, Phillips, Pickens, Polk, Pollick(Pollock), Price, Puckett, Ragsdale, Rakes, Reed, Rice, Richardson, Robbins, Robinett, Robinson, Roller, Ross, Rouse, Ryan, Seamster, Sellers, Setser, Sharp, Shibley, Shields, Skaggs, Smith, Stater, Steele, Stringfield, Stroud, Tallman, Taylor, Thompson(Thomson), Trammel, Turner, Walker, Watson, Weaver, Wells, West, Whayne, White, Williams, Wilson, Womack, Woods, Woodward, Wright, Yeargain, Young.

Benton County, Arkansas Obituaries

from microfilm of Benton County newspapers

1923

ALEXANDER, Alta M. HINDS - Mrs. Willis Miller received a telegram yesterday morning announcing the death of her youngest daughter, Mrs. R.C. Alexander, at her home in Huntington, West Virginia. No particulars were given and we go to press too early to learn whether any further word had been received. The death was very sudden and came as a great blow to her mother who did not even know that she was ill. Mrs. Alexander is best remembered in Rogers as Miss Alta Hinds, one of our most popular and prettiest young women. She had not been in Rogers for a few years but many Democrat readers will remember her as the author of a number of most interesting articles telling of her experiences while traveling with her husband on business trips in Central and South America. She was a young woman of many talents and her untimely death is a great blow to the many friends. She is survived by her husband and a small son, one and a half years old. Mrs. Miller was in Rogers yesterday at the Hartley home. [Rogers Democrat 10/25/23]
Alta M. Hinds was born August 31, 1887 at Lincoln, Kas.; at the age of four years the family moved to Muskogee, I.T., her father being connected with the first U.S. Court established in the Territory. Her father lost his health there and the family came to Rogers to live. Alta was then eight years old. She attended the public school here and later Rogers Academy. She had croup when small and as she grew up it took the form of asthma, which caused her death. She tried different states and would find relief for a time. Spent several months at Columbus, Tenn. and was so well she sang in the choir and at Commencement time, at the Military Academy, but the trouble returned as soon as she came home. She took a business course at Fort Smith and became very proficient, holding positions at Sparks Memorial Hospital and Hunt & Jackson's wholesale house. Spent several years at her chosen work, all the time seeking better health. She worked in Birmingham, Ala. and Pensacola, Florida. She married R.C. Alexander at Dothan, Ala. in 1913, having known him previously at Rogers. They spent some time in Montgomery and she worked in the Capitol building. Later their work took them on extensive trips to South America. They spent almost two years at Havana, Cuba and rather than be idle she worked for an American hardware firm and on their trips did her husband's private secretarial work. During the late war, her husband having been a Yale student, they came from Cuba to Philadelphia to do his "bit." She especially enjoyed her stay in Philadelphia. They spent two years in New York and

then decided to rest from travel and bought a farm near Marshfield, Mo. but after a rest of two years, they wanted to get back in the old work and left the farm. While living on the farm a little son was born to them and she gave up her work and devoted her time to her baby. He is now one and a half years old. They had gone to Huntington, W. Va. where they hoped to locate permanently and have a home and she had been arranging the house when she gave way to a hard spell of asthma that was more than she could live through. She had written a long letter to her mother Sunday night and seemed to be well and Tuesday at 12:30 p.m. she passed away. She was buried at Huntington amid a host of friends and flowers. Her brother, Frank Hinds of Sapulpa, Okla.; her sister, Mrs. F.R. Ellett of Marshfield, Mo., attended her funeral. Her mother, Mrs. Willis Miller of Vaughn, this county, was in poor health and could not go. Tom Harvey and Tony LeBlanc, former residents of Rogers and Monte Ne, were two of the pall bearers. Besides her mother, sister and brother above mentioned, she is survived by a brother, Homer Hinds, of Monett, Mo., and many friends everywhere. [Rogers Democrat 11/1/23]

ALLEN, Mrs. E.J. - {from Oakley Chapel} Mrs. E.J. Allen, after suffering patiently as an invalid for 19 years, died at the home of her son, George J. Allen, last Monday night, January 22nd, and was buried at Oakley's Chapel Wednesday morning, the Rev. J. Wilson Critchlow conducting the funeral services. Grandma Allen, as she was affectionately called. was a sweet spirited woman and for more than 50 years a loyal member of the Baptist church. [Rogers Democrat 2/1/23]

ALLEN, Sarah Elizabeth STORM - Sarah Elizabeth Storm was born in Shelby Co., Ill. on Nov. 27, 1851. Departed this life at the home of her daughter, Mary Howard, on June 8, 1923, age 71 years, 6 months and 12 days. She was married to N.C. Allen on Sept. 26, 1869. To this union were born 15 children, 9 boys and 6 girls. The 5 eldest, all boys, dying in infancy. The living children are: Mrs. C.J. Richardson of Jane, Mo.; Mrs. R.E. Howard, Mrs. J.R. Puryear, Mrs. J.W. Kerr, W.C. Allen and D.R. Allen, all of Gravette; Mrs. Lot Banks and G.C. Allen of Hiwasse; Mrs. T.M. Hamilton of Cheraw, Colo. and B.N. Allen of Norborne, Mo. All of whom excepting B.N. Allen were with their mother during her last hours on earth. Besides these children and her husband she leaves to mourn her departure 21 grandchildren, two great-grandchildren, three sisters and many other relatives and friends. She united with the Church of Christ at about the age of 16 years and has lived a splendid christian life. Burial was held at Panill Cemetery. Services were conducted by Rev. O.T. Wilson of Anderson, Mo. at the Mt. Pleasant church. A Friend. [Gravette News-Herald 6/15/23]

ANDERSON, Elbert Clingman - {from Word} Died, at his home last Sunday morning, Mr. Cling Anderson. [Gravette News-Herald 3/9/23]
Elbert Clingman Anderson was born at Asheville, North Carolina Feb. 11, 1846 and died March 4, 1923, aged 77 years and 21 days. At the age of 18

years he joined the Confederate army and served more than two years, or till the close of the war, when he was honorably discharged. He married Miss Lena Holcomb in 1866. To this union were born eight children, all of whom survive him except two daughters who died in infancy. They are: J.H. Anderson, Mrs. Maggie Newman, J.W. Anderson, M.N. Anderson, Mrs. Mamie Stellman and Mrs. Ada Moore, all of whom live in Arkansas except Mrs. Mamie Stellman who lives in Idaho. In 1868 Mr. Anderson moved to Arkansas where he resided till the time of his death. He professed faith in Christ over 20 years ago but never united with any church. He lived an exemplary life. He was a kind husband, a good father, neighbor and citizen. [Gentry Journal-Advance 3/9/23]

ARMSTRONG, Mary - {from Prairie Creek} Mrs. Mary Armstrong, or Aunt Mollie as a number called her, died Monday night and was buried Wednesday afternoon at the Grimes cemetery southwest of Avoca. She was 77 years old and had lived here at her home, where she died, since her marriage. She leaves a daughter, Mrs. Hannah Williams, and five grandchildren, other relatives and many friends to mourn her loss. We extend our sympathy, especially to the lonely daughter and little grandchildren, who she has helped to care for from infancy. [Rogers Democrat 11/8/23]

ATKISSON, Mrs. J. Byron {SIKES} - Mrs. Atkisson, widow of the late J. Byron Atkisson, died Saturday afternoon at 1:20 o'clock at the home of her daughter, Mrs. A.M. Sherrill, in the south part of town. She had been seriously ill for several weeks and her death was not unexpected by the friends and family. Funeral services were held at the Central M.E. church Sunday afternoon at 2:30 and were conducted by the pastor, Rev. J.W. Crichlow. Burial was by the side of her husband who died May 19, 1920. Mrs. Atkisson was born in Benton county 56 years ago and was a daughter of Willis Sikes and a niece of Uncle Wade Sikes. She was married to J.B. Atkisson November 18, 1885 and most of their married life was spent in Rogers where Mr. Atkisson served for many years as city marshal, deputy sheriff, township constable, etc. Mrs. Atkisson is survived by seven children, three sons and four daughters: Mrs. H.A. Gordon of Rogers; C.C. Atkisson of Whittier, Cal.; Mrs. A.M. Sherrill of Rogers; C.L. Atkisson of Tulsa; Mrs. J.E. Webb of Miami, Okla.; Glen Atkisson and Miss Fay Atkisson. All of the children were with their mother at the time of her death and had been here for a week previous. The family have the sympathy of the entire community in their hour of bereavement and sorrow. [Rogers Democrat 1/11/23]

BAILEY, Iva - {from Pleasant Valley} Mrs. Iva Bailey, wife of Claud Bailey, died early Sunday morning at the B.A. Bailey home where she was brought Saturday night from her home in Kansas. Burial was made in the Coffelt cemetery Monday afternoon. [Gentry Journal-Advance 8/17/23]

BAKER, Annette Ruth - {from Larue} Annette Ruth Baker, the little daughter of Geo. Baker and wife, died Sunday night at the age of 10 months and 26 days. The little one had been sick for about four months. The remains were laid to rest in the Bland cemetery Monday evening. The bereaved parents have the heartfelt sympathy of their many friends. [Rogers Democrat 6/28/23]

BAKER, Naomi Katherine - Naomi Katherine Baker was born February 2, 1844 in Kataming, Mercer county, Penn. and died January 6, 1923 at the age of 78 years, 11 months and five days. She was married to William H. Baker in 1865. To this union was born ten children, her husband and six children having preceded her to the Great Beyond. Four sons are still living - Wilson B., John W., Harry C. and Tilden Baker. She was converted at an early age and united with the Cumberland Presbyterian church. The funeral services were conducted by Rev. B.R. Williams at the Methodist church at Seligman Sunday, January 7, at 1:00 o'clock, after which the body was laid to rest in the Seligman cemetery to await the Resurrection morn. We extend sympathy to the bereaved ones. [Rogers Democrat 1/11/23]

BALDRIDGE, Corda - Mrs. W.D. Baldridge and granddaughter, Miss Clara, have returned from their mission to Clayton, New Mex. for the benefit of the health of Clara's sister, Miss Corda Baldridge. The trip was in vain as Miss Corda died at Clayton on Saturday, Sept. 8, 1923. At first the invigorating western climate seemed to help her but tuberculosis had a fatal grip and she passed away. The relatives have the sympathy of many friends in their bereavement. [Gravette News-Herald 9/28/23]

BANKS, Herman - Herman Banks, whose death is reported from Hiwasse, was a nephew of James Banks of Gravette. [Gravette News-Herald 3/23/23]

Herman Banks, son of Mr. and Mrs. Will Banks, died at the home last Saturday morning, March 17, 1923, age 25 years, from flu. Herman had been an invalid the most of his life and was the only son. He is survived by father, mother, one sister and a host of relatives and friends. The body was laid to rest in Mt. Pleasant cemetery, Rev. Ragsdale of Bentonville conducting the funeral. Sympathy is extended the family. [Gravette News-Herald 3/23/23]

BARNETT, Mrs. Calvin {BARTON} - Mrs. Calvin Barnett, who with her husband have been victims of flu and pneumonia fever, died Tuesday at the home west of Gravette. Mrs. Barnett was a daughter of A.Y. Barton. Burial occurred Wednesday afternoon at the Dow cemetery following the funeral service. We failed to get other particulars. We also learn that Mr. Barton's sons, Calvin and Henry, are both down with pneumonia fever. [Gravette News-Herald 2/9/23]

BARR, Mary - {from Lowell} Mrs. Ellen Hathaway attended the funeral of Mrs. Mary Barr at Fayetteville Tuesday. Lowell residents were grieved to hear of the sudden death of Grandma Barr at the home of her son, Frank Barr, in Fayetteville Monday. She was on her way here to spend the summer with her daughter, Mrs. L.P. Davis. Grandma Barr was 93 years old and the mother of Mrs. L.P. Davis and J.H. Barr of this place. She visited here often and made many friends with her sweet smile and loving disposition. To know her was to love her and her many friends were looking forward with great pleasure to her visit. We extend heartfelt sympathy to the family in their hour of sadness. [Rogers Democrat 4/12/23]

BEAMAN, twin sons - {from The Grove, Okla. Sun} The twin boys of Mr. and Mrs. Frank Beaman, who live on the old Frank Pollan farm 2 miles east of Cayuga bridge, were burned to death about 1:00 o'clock Tuesday afternoon. The unfortunate children were from 12 to 15 months old. Another boy about 3 years old escaped from the burning house but was seriously burned on one hand and arm and his hair was singed. The 2 room house, as well as contents, was a total loss. The mother had gone to Mr. Pollan's about 200 yards away after water, leaving the smaller children on the bed. Pollan's barn stood between the two houses, shutting off the view from Pollan's house, so that the mother could not see the burning house until after she passed the barn on her return. [Rogers Democrat 2/15/23]

BEARD, E.C. - Friends throughout Northwest Arkansas were shocked to learn of the death of Rev. E.C. Beard, pastor of the Presbyterian church at Bentonville, at Chicago Saturday night in the Presbyterian Hospital where he had gone a few days previous for an operation. Memorial services were held Tuesday in the Presbyterian church at Bentonville and Reverend T.E. McSpadden of Rogers attended and was one of the speakers, as was also Rev. Gillespie of Fayetteville. Rev. Beard had been at Bentonville some two years or more and but few of his friends knew that his condition was serious or that an operation was contemplated. [Rogers Democrat 11/1/23]

BEARDSLEY, Charley - Charley Beardsley, an old-time resident of Gentry before going to Oklahoma some years ago, was found dead in his bed at a hotel in Drumright, Okla. last Sunday morning. Deceased was about 40 years of age and had been employed at Drumright by the Roxana Oil Co. Word from there by friends of the dead man said that no disposition for the burial of the body had been arranged up to Monday. His parents reside in Oberlin, O. but were unable to attend the funeral of their son, which in all probability occurred in Drumright. [Gentry Journal-Advance 2/9/23]

BELEW, Edna Irene - {from Hiwasse} Little Irene Belew died Sunday morning after a short illness, the result of inflammatory rheumatism. Funeral and burial Monday afternoon. [Gravette News-Herald 12/14/23] {from Pea Ridge} The many friends of Mrs. Sylvia Banks Belew of Hiwasse sympathize with her in the loss of her little girl, Edna Irene, on last Sunday morning. She was sick only a short time with pneumonia. She was an unusually bright, sweet child of past two years. Several of the relatives here attended the burial Monday. [Rogers Democrat 12/13/23]

BELKNAP, Jules - Dr. Jules Belknap, one of the best known physicians of Benton county, died at his home at Sulphur Springs Monday morning following a few days of illness from pneumonia. A week before the News Herald editor called Dr. Belknap to see his son, Wyric Lewis, and at that time the doctor said he had cared for 70 cases of flu in his own town. Two days later he developed the disease. Few people realize that many of our doctors make the supreme sacrifice in caring for their patients. Dr. Belknap had been at Sulphur Springs many years. He took pleasure in collecting curios and his office is a miniature museum. He leaves a wife and four children. [Gravette News-Herald 3/2/23]

BELL, Mrs. W.T. - Mrs. W.T. Bell died Monday at her home in Maple Grove Addition at 12:30. She was about 65 years old and had been an invalid for some time. The family came to Rogers six years ago from Jennings, La. and the body was taken to her old home there for burial, accompanied by the husband, W.T. Bell, and her son, J.A. Bell, of Rogers. She is survived by two other sons, W.C. Bell of Rogers and Geo. F. Bell of Tulsa. [Rogers Democrat 12/27/23]

BELL, Steve - Steve Bell, a farmer living west of Siloam Springs, died a week ago as a result of injuries sustained a few days previous when a fly wheel on a gasoline engine of a wood saw burst into a number of pieces and one struck him in the head, fracturing his skull. [Rogers Democrat 10/18/23]

BENNETT, Mr. - {from Pea Ridge} Mr. Bennett, who has been afflicted with cancer for quite a while, died Monday morning, the 10th, at 10:00 o'clock. He leaves a wife and six children to whom we extend our deepest sympathy. [Rogers Democrat 9/13/23]

BENTLEY, Clarence E. - Clarence E. Bentley was born in Hinsdale, N.Y. March 13, 1851 and departed this life March 15, 1923, aged 72 years and two days. At an early age he enlisted in the army and was sent to the Western Frontier during the 70's and 80's. He received an honorable discharge after thirteen years of faithful service. A character notation, "Excellent," is found on each of his discharge papers. On coming out of the army he took up his profession - that of carpentering and contracting. He was a skilled workman, one of the best in his profession. Many residences and business houses of Rogers are monuments of his skill and service. In 1904, February 29th, he married Mrs. Linnie Doan, who with her son, Charlie Doan, are the only known living relatives. He became a Christian thirteen years ago and was a faithful member of the First Christian Church, always present at the regular services when in town and able to go. Rogers has lost an asset in "Capt." Bentley, as he was affectionately called by his townsmen. At the time of his death he was a member of the school board. He was always interested in the school affairs of the city. He served for a number of years as president of the Board. The last time he was out of the house he attended a reception at the High School in honor of the Board. The funeral was held in the Central Methodist Church March 16th by Rev.

J. Watson Shockley, minister of the First Christian Church, and interment was in the city cemetery. Mrs. Bentley has the sympathy of the whole community in her great bereavement. [Rogers Democrat 3/22/23]

BEREMAN, Polly E. - Mrs. Polly E. Bereman, mother of Dr. F.A. Bereman, died Friday night at the home of the latter northeast of town. She was 77 years old and death was the result of paralysis. The remains were taken to Queen City, Mo. for burial. [Rogers Democrat 10/11/23]

BLACK, Dr. - {from Pleasant Grove} Dr. Black, who once lived in Pleasant Grove neighborhood, died a few days ago at Sulphur Springs. We extend thru the J-A heartfelt sympathy to Mrs. Black. [Gentry Journal-Advance 1/26/23]

BLACKBURN, Elbert - {from War Eagle} The death angel visited this community last week and claimed as its victim Elbert Blackburn. Mr. Blackburn has been confined to his bed since February. He took the flu and it affected his lungs and later he took the dropsy which caused his death. He has spent most of his life here and is well known and loved by all who knew him. He was a very patient sufferer and has gone to reap his reward. He leaves to mourn his loss a wife, four daughters and two sons: Mrs. Bertha Foust of Sonora; Mrs. Will Ingram of War Eagle; Mrs. Letha Whittaker of Slaten, Texas; Leta, who is still at home; Ottie Blackburn of this place and John Blackburn of Spring Valley, and a host of neighbors and friends. The family wishes to thank all who so kindly assisted them in his care during his sickness and death. [Rogers Democrat 7/12/23]

BLAKE, Barbray C. YOUNG - Barbray C. Young was born Oct. 25, 1845 at Vincennes, Ind., departed this life Feb. 1, 1923, aged 77 years, 4 months and 13 days. She came from Indiana in an early day and settled with her parents near Carthage, Mo. She was married to Henry A. Blake in 1864. To this union were born six children, two of which departed life at birth and one daughter after reaching womanhood. Three children and eight grandchildren survive her: Mrs. Frankie M. Quillian of Gravette, Ark.; Mr. Lee Blake of Jerome, Wash. and Mrs. Ida D. Williams of Walsenburg, Colo. Mrs. Quillian was with her mother when the summons came. "Mother" Blake, as she was lovingly called by her neighbors, united with the Christian church at Chetopa, Kan. some 36 years ago. She loved her Savior and was a loyal, true friend. Her son-in-law, A.R. Williams of Walsenburg, Colo., reached Decatur on Saturday and was present at the funeral which was held at the Baptist church and was conducted by Rev. Scroggins, assisted by the pastor and choir, at 2 p.m. Sunday. [Gravette News-Herald 2/16/23]

BLANCHARD, Mrs. Addison {GOWER} - Rogers friends received word Monday of the death of Mrs. Addison Blanchard on Saturday morning at Denver at the age of 80 years. She was ill only a week, death being the result of flu and pneumonia. Mrs. Blanchard is survived by her husband, Dr. Blanchard, and her sister, Miss C.A. Gower. Dr. and Mrs. Blanchard and Miss Gower were residents of Rogers for a number of years, leaving here and returning to Denver some six years ago, where he had for many years been a leader in the Congregational church of that state and a pastor of a number of the more important churches of that denomination. Mrs. Blanchard is remembered with much love and appreciation by the ladies of the Congregational and Presbyterian church and by the friends in the neighborhood where they resided here, on West Cypress street in the home now owned by A. Buttry. She was noted for her work among the poor and unfortunate and they were never turned away empty handed from her door. Dr. Blanchard and Miss Gower have the sympathy of their Rogers friends in their sad hour of great bereavement. [Rogers Democrat 2/22/23]

BLAND, Dewey - Dewey Bland, a son of Mrs. Andy Graham of Springdale, was struck by lightning May 3rd while working in the oil field near Bartlesville, Okla. and instantly killed. He was twenty-five years old and leaves a wife and a four-weeks-old baby. [Rogers Democrat 5/17/23]

BLAND, Ray Lee - {from The Springdale News} Mrs. Andy Graham, who was called to Bartlesville, Okla. several weeks ago by the death of her son, Dewey Bland, who was killed by lightning, received word this week of the death of her 8-year-old grandson, Ray Lee Bland, who was run over by a truck and killed near Tulsa. The lad was a son of W.H. Bland and wife. It is said the child stepped from behind a car which was stopped in the road, immediately in front of the approaching truck. The rear wheels of the heavy truck passed over the boy's body, killing him instantly. [Rogers Democrat 6/7/23]

BLEVINS, Mike - "Uncle Mike" Blevins, a former citizen of this section, died at his home in Williams, Calif. on Saturday, April 14 at the advanced age of 89 years. Mr. Blevins leaves several children. Among them are Mrs. B.F. Lindsey and Mrs. Rol Capehart of near Beaty, also Charlie Blevins of Williams, Calif. and Jim Blevins, who resided in Gravette a few years ago, now of Old Mexico. [Gravette News-Herald 4/27/23]

BOLAN, Frank - {from Pleasant Hill} Again the death angel has visited our community - this time calling Frank Bolan Sunday morning, July 29 at 7:30 o'clock. The funeral services were held at Little Flock Sunday at 6 o'clock p.m., conducted by Rev. Lark of Pea Ridge. He was 38 years old. Leaves a wife and two daughters to mourn his loss, also three sisters and a brother. Mr. Bolan had been affected for something over two years. Although his death was expected it came as a shock to the family. He was a Christian man and recently had united with the Methodist church. [Rogers Democrat 8/2/23]

BONE, Mrs. Lon - {from Elkhorn} The body of Mrs. Lon Bone, who died at her home at Avoca Tuesday, February 13th, was brought to Twelve Corners Wednesday for burial. Funeral services were conducted by Rev. George Berks. The bereaved family have our heart-felt sympathy. [Rogers Democrat 2/22/23]

BOWLIN, Wm. - {from War Eagle} News was received here of the death of Wm. Bowlin of Spring Valley. Mr. Bowlin lived many years near War Eagle and is well known by a number of War Eagle people who extend their heartfelt sympathy to the bereaved family. He had been sick for some time with the flu and took pneumonia which caused his death. He leaves a wife and five children. Mrs. Bowlin and three children have the flu and are yet seriously ill. [Rogers Democrat 2/22/23]

BOWMAN, Anna HALPAIN - Mrs. John Bowman, who has been sick for some time here at the home of her mother, Mrs. E.E. Mathews, died Saturday, June 16, 1923 at the age of 54 years. Miss Anna Halpain was born in Baxter county, Ark. She united with the Christian church at the age of 14 but more recently had been associated with the Holiness people. She leaves besides her husband, two children, Ollie and Clint; her mother, two brothers, Wm. Halpain, Pittsburg, Kan. and Henry Halpain of Gravette, and one sister, Mrs. J.W. Edwards, also of Gravette. The funeral was conducted by Mrs. Killingsworth Monday at 1 p.m. and burial was in Bethel cemetery. Sympathy is extended the bereft. [Gravette News-Herald 6/22/23]

BOX, Pleas - Pleas Box, aged 74, died last week at his home at Siloam Springs, where he had lived for many years. He was one of the pioneer settlers in that part of the county. [Rogers Democrat 3/22/23]

BOYD, infant - {from Lowell} The day old daughter of Mr. and Mrs. Dan Boyd died last Wednesday. [Rogers Democrat 11/8/23]

BRAMMER, Dot - Mrs. Dot Brammer of Rogers died Sunday at the home of her father in Kansas City. Her death was a great shock to the friends and relatives here for while she was known to be feeling poorly it was not understood that her condition was at all serious. Mr. Brammer joined her in Kansas City last week and they had expected to return to Rogers the first of this week. The funeral was held in Kansas City Tuesday. Mrs. Brammer is survived by her husband and three small children, one of whom was here with Mr. Brammer's mother, two being with the mother in Kansas City at the time of her death. [Rogers Democrat 10/18/23]

BROWN, Eugenia F. - Mrs. Eugenia F. Brown was born in Virginia Oct. 14, 1857 and died in Gentry, Ark. Jan. 9, 1923, age 65 years, 2 months and 25 days. She was married to Rev. S.F. Brown Sept. 30, 1879, ever filling the Methodist Parsonage with grace and ease in a way that only a consecrated Christian wife and companion can fill it. She accepted, as a part of her duties, co-labor with her husband in caring for the flock. Sister Brown was converted when but a child and was baptised and received into the Lutheran church by Rev. Hankins. Remaining in this church until she came into the Methodist church as the wife of the parsonage. She leaves to mourn her going away her husband, Rev. S.F. Brown, daughter, Mrs. Eula Woodward and husband, A. Woodward, S.C. Brown of Detroit, Frank, Lois, Anna Lee, Mildred and Charles Woodward, grandchildren, and a number of relatives in Virginia and friends who are numbered by her acquaintances. Her son, Ernest Hale Brown, preceded her in death. Funeral services were conducted at the Methodist church at 10:30 o'clock by Revs. Sherman and Martin Wednesday and Funeral director Ray Carpenter laid the body away in Gentry cemetery. [Gentry Journal-Advance 1/12/23]

BROWN, Tommie - {from Mountain View} Tommie Brown died November 22, 1923 at his home east of Avoca with dropsy. He was 78 years and a few days old. He was a member of the Christian church. Clarence Mitchell of Oklahoma preached the funeral. The body was buried at Tuck's Chapel on Friday. [Rogers Democrat 11/29/23]

BROWN, Yara RETHERFORD - {from Bestwater} Mrs. Yara Brown, a splendid young mother, has been called from earth to Heaven to live in that Holy City where she had prepared to make her eternal home. Yara Retherford, a daughter of John Retherford and wife, was born near Garfield, Ark. May 28, 1899 and died April 22, 1923 at Beaver, Okla. Age 23 years, 11 months and five days. In July 1917 she was married to Luther Brown and to this union was born two children, a son having died in infancy, a daughter being 15 months old. She accepted Christ as her Savior in 1915 and lived a faithful Christian life until her death. She leaves to mourn her loss a husband, daughter, father, mother, four brothers and four sisters, besides a host of other relatives and friends. The talk was made by Rev. Burks at Providence church and the body was laid to rest in the Snodderly cemetery. [Rogers Democrat 5/3/23]

BROWNING, James - {from Mt. Zion} James Browning died at his home Monday morning after a short illness. He had been a sufferer for some time but not bedfast until a few days ago. He was stricken and his last illness was of short duration. He was laid to rest in Falling Springs cemetery beside his wife and 4 children who had gone before. [Gentry Journal-Advance 11/16/23]

BRYANT, Amelia E. BOUTELLE - Mrs. C.M. Bryant died very suddenly Tuesday evening at her home on West Poplar street, supposed the result of a stroke of apoplexy. She had been lying on the bed reading and passed away as peacefully as tho she had fallen asleep. She has been in poor health for a number of years but there was no indication that she was any worse than usual and her death came as a great surprise to the family and friends. Funeral services will be held at the residence but the exact date and hour will not be decided until the daughter, Miss Winifred Bryant, arrives from Academy, S.D. where she is a teacher in Ward Academy, and word comes from the youngest son, Eugene G. Bryant, who is in Los Angeles. The only other son, C.S. Bryant, city recorder, lived here with his mother. Miss Bryant is expected Friday. Deceased had lived in Rogers since 1895 with the exception of a year or two in Lincoln, Nebr. and was well known to many of our people altho poor health had kept her close to her home in recent years. Miss Amelia E. Boutelle was born in Aztalan, Jefferson county, Wisconsin March 22, 1845, being 78 years, seven months and 28 days old at the time of her death. She was married to Colby M. Bryant at Aztalan March 27, 1867. To them were born three children, all of whom are living as mentioned above. The family lived in Iowa for many years, being pioneers in Monona county in the northwestern part of the state. The family came to Rogers from Dell Rapids, South Dakota in 1895. Mr. Bryant died here March 16, 1913 and Mrs. Bryant has since made her home with the children at the residence on West Poplar. Mrs. Bryant was for many years a faithful member of the Congregational church of Rogers. Besides her children she is survived by three sisters and two brothers, none of whom, however, live in this part of the country. The Democrat joins with the many friends in extending sympathy to the family in their hour of bereavement. [Rogers Democrat 11/22/23]

BUCHANON, M.L. - During the services of the "Fire Baptism" Holiness at the Carter building Wednesday night, M.L. Buchanon, aged 73, dropped dead just after he had testified and expressed himself that he would prefer death to participation in a church quarrel such as had been waged by parties. Funeral arrangements are not completed as we go to press. [Gravette News-Herald 4/13/23]

BUCK, Erastus A. - Erastus A. Buck, veteran educator who spent nearly 60 years in the public school room, died Sunday, June 24, 1923 at the age of 83 years, five months and 19 days. He leaves his companion, who is also past 80 years and who has been his constant co-worker for 61 years. Mr. Buck was born at Andover, Ill. February 5, 1840. He was married to Miss Marriam Baird at Andover Oct. 11, 1862. He leaves no children, however leaves several relatives, among them his nephew, Edwin H. Buck, on whose farm the elder Buck has resided since 1918 when he and companion moved here from Iowa. Mr. Buck had a national acquaintance among the educators, particularly in the north central states. He began teaching in the pioneer days when the conveniences and the remuneration was very light. He loved the school room however and devoted his life to it. He was a Civil war veteran, serving with the federal army for a time but had disregarded his right to a pension until about a year ago. He pursued an unostentatious life; and he and Mrs. Buck were much interested in the betterment of human life, etc., and here at Gravette have been active - even to the last weeks of his life - in a philanthropic work, scattering literature which disseminated pure thought, higher ideals, eugenics, Americanism, godliness, kindness to every living thing, humane treatment to animals, etc., and had support of prominent educators all over the land. Mr. Buck had formed a friendship with Editor Herb Lewis of the News Herald and just three days before Mr. Buck's death he wrote as follows: "Editor Lewis:- I may die, Should I do so I am asking you to make a little talk at my grave. I die honest. I believe in One God. Jesus Christ was a Good Man. All will be Happy Sometime; according to Natural law. Our spirit friends do come back. E.A. Buck." The funeral was held Monday afternoon, June 25th, Mr.

Lewis fulfilling Mr. Buck's request with a short talk and eulogy on the life of the veteran of the public school room who had devoted near 60 years, not only to teaching the text-books, but highest ideals, to American boys and girls. The speaker said: "If great monuments of stone counted for as much as do monuments of appreciation, this grave should indeed be marked with a tablet of pure bronze, bearing this inscription: 'He devoted his Life to the Great American Public School, the Bulwark of Our Liberty." Rev. G.T. Clark assisted in the services at the I.O.O.F. cemetery, where interment was made. Condolence is extended the bereaved ones. [Gravette News-Herald 6/29/23]

BURNS, Will - Will Burns of Bentonville died last week at the age of 45 years after an illness of several months. Funeral services were held at the Christian church Thursday afternoon. He is survived by his wife and two children, a son aged 14 and a daughter 18. He was a brother-in-law of Mrs. J.C. McSpadden and Mrs. Emmet Huffman of Rogers. He was well known here, having clerked here and having also been engaged for a year or two in the grocery business. He had lived in Rogers and Bentonville for 25 years. [Rogers Democrat 12/13/23]

BURROW, B.M. - Rogers friends have received word of the death of Rev. B.M. Burrow at the home of his mother at Altus, Ark. Rev. Burrow had been a helpless invalid for nearly two years. He was pastor of the Southern M.E. church here some fifteen years ago and his parents spent a year here with him. He was married after he left Rogers but his wife had been dead some years and he is survived by his mother and a brother. [Rogers Democrat 3/29/23]

BUTTRAM, Kit - {from Bestwater} Aunt Kit Buttram passed away July 8, 1923 after a long siege of sickness. She was 84 years old. [Rogers Democrat 7/19/23]

BYLER, Maggie M. POTTS - {from Providence} Maggie M. Potts was born at Harrisonville, Mo. October 10, 1865 and was married to James F. Byler February 20, 1884. To this union was born 11 children, four boys and seven girls, of whom nine are living. They are Harper Byler, Mrs. Mable German, Roy Byler, Mrs. Louise Park, Mrs. Vesta Easley, Miss Maggie Byler and Jim Byler, all of Garfield, Ark., and Mrs. Kitty McClain and Mrs. Beatrice McChessney, both of Bartlesville, Okla. All were at her bed-side when she passed quietly and peacefully away on March 6, 1923 at the age of 57 years, four months and 26 days. Besides her immediate family she leaves one sister, two brothers, a number of half brothers and sisters and 21 grandchildren. She moved with her family to Benton county in 1903 where she lived the rest of her life. She united with the Primitive Baptist church at Providence February 11, 1906 and was baptised by Elder W.J. Taylor and lived a faithful and consistent member until the death angel came to bear her soul away to a brighter world. Mrs. Byler had been in failing health for about two years and she was confined to her bed for several months but was never heard to complain. She never was heard to speak ill of anyone, just a kind and patient mother, much devoted to her family and ever willing to sacrifice for their comfort. [Rogers Democrat 3/15/23]

CALLIS, Orville - Orville Callis, aged 22, living about 8 miles east of Gravette, shot himself with fatal results. He was a son-in-law of G.W. Pitts. The cause was assigned to domestic troubles. [Gravette News-Herald 2/23/23]
Orville Callis, 23 years old, living five miles northwest of Centerton, committed suicide Tuesday afternoon by shooting himself with a .32 calibre revolver. The shot that killed him was fired directly through his heart. He had recently separated from his wife and it is supposed he became deranged while brooding over his troubles. Coroner A.D. Callison of Rogers was summoned to hold an inquest over the body. [Rogers Democrat 2/22/23]

CARL, infant - Word came Sunday from Clarence Carl of Little Rock of the death of their infant son. Their many friends here were grieved to hear of this sad occurrence. [Gentry Journal-Advance 12/21/23]

CARNATHAN, Mrs. Zack - Mrs. Zack Carnathan of Wister, Okla. died very suddenly in Rogers on Saturday morning at the A.C. Patterson home on North Second street. She came here early in the week with her husband to receive treatment for dropsy from local physicians. One daughter, Mrs. Troy Gardner, was also here and husband and daughter took the body back to their home at Wister on the noon train for burial. The deceased was 48 years old and leaves seven children. [Rogers Democrat 10/4/23]

CARR, Earl - Earl Carr, colored, was drowned last Thursday afternoon while swimming in White river near Fayetteville. His body was recovered by a companion. [Rogers Democrat 9/13/23]

CARROLL, Ab - Eureka Springs, Oct. 25.- Ab Carroll, age 35 years, committed suicide at his home on King river, five miles east of here Wednesday afternoon at four o'clock. He took a quantity of arsenic and walked in the room where his wife was and told her what he had wanted to do for a long time. He laid down on the bed and died before medical aid could be secured. He was a member of one of the oldest families in this section. His father, the late Captain John Carroll, was the first mayor of Eureka Springs. [Rogers Democrat 11/1/23]

CARROLL, Lewis H. - Our hearts were made sad Thursday when we learned that our old friend and neighbor, Lewis H. Carroll, had passed away. He had been sick for several months and his death was not unexpected. He spent most of his life near here and has an aunt, Mrs. T.E. Sager, and several cousins and many loving friends who mourn his early death. We extend our sympathy to his wife and three little boys and other relatives. [Rogers Democrat 6/28/23]
Understanding that an obituary of Lewis H. Carroll, who died Thursday, June 21st at No. 922 South Fourth street in this city, would be prepared and handed to the Democrat, we waited for same until it was too late to

secure the needed data for last week. Lewis was 39 years old, a son of the late Felix Carroll, and was born and raised on Prairie Creek, east of Rogers, where the family was one of the oldest and best known in this section of the county. He is survived by his wife who was Miss Maude Helterbran, a daughter of F.M. Helterbran, and by three young sons. He is also survived by one brother, Guy Carroll of St. Louis and two sisters, Mrs. Maude Mosley of Tulsa and Mrs. Bess Varnell of Kansas City, all of whom were here for the funeral which was held at the home Friday afternoon at three o'clock and was conducted by Rev. Barrett of the Baptist church. Mr. Carroll and family had been living in Rogers since last September, having returned here at that time from Paris, Texas where they made their home for several years. Mr. Carroll's untimely death is a great grief to the relatives and friends for he was a fine type of man and his passing is a loss to the community. [Rogers Democrat 7/5/23]

CASEY, Ira Carter "Pete" - I.C. {Pete} Casey, county clerk of Benton county, died suddenly Sunday night, or about 2 a.m. Monday, at his home in Bentonville. Mr. Casey was in his usual good health when he went home from town in the evening but had an attack of acute indigestion. A doctor was called and gave him treatment and he apparently recovered and spent the evening reading. About 1 o'clock he awoke from sleep with another attack and died in a few minutes. Clerk Casey was scheduled to be in Gravette this week Friday, as he had informed the News Herald by phone last week; but while man proposes he has no insight into the future. "Pete" Casey has figured in Benton County's official family for many years and was known to about everyone in the county. Following his death came the necessity of a successor and many county seat people at once espoused the appointment of Mr. Casey's daughter, who has been his deputy, to take his place, same being put up to the governor. Gravette was alert to secure this place for A.P. Dunagin, who ran second to Casey in the late election. We understand, however, that an appointment is only temporary and an election is required by law where a term of office is not half out. [Gravette News-Herald 5/4/23]

Word came from Bentonville Monday of the sudden death of I.C. Casey, county clerk of Benton county on last Sunday from acute indigestion. Mr. Casey had many friends over the county who will regret very much to hear of his untimely death. The Rogers Post of April 30 contains the following concerning Mr. Casey's death, which we reprint: County Clerk I.C. Casey died very suddenly this morning at about 3 o'clock of acute indigestion at his home in Bentonville. This news came as a decided shock to the county at large as Mr. Casey seemed to be in his normal health Saturday. Mr. Casey is a brother-in-law of our fellow townsman, W.T. Maxwell. Funeral arrangements have not been fully completed at this writing. A petition is being sent to Gov. McRae to appoint Miss Hoover Casey to fill out the unexpired term of the deceased. She has been acting as deputy clerk and is

familiar with all the details of the office, having served under the father for some time. There is no doubt but that Miss Casey is the logical one to receive the appointment from the standpoint of unruffled continuation of the work. [Gentry Journal-Advance 5/4/23]
{from The Bentonville Democrat} County Clerk I.C. Casey died very suddenly Monday morning at his residence in Bentonville of acute indigestion. He was 56 years old and was serving his fifth term as county clerk. This is his third successive term and he served two terms some years ago. He is survived by his wife, a son who is playing ball in Nebraska, and one daughter, Miss Hoover, who has been deputy since her father went in office. He was a brother-in-law of W.T. Maxwell of Rogers and has many relatives in the county. "Pete" Casey, as he was intimately known by his friends, was as popular and well known as any man in the county and his sudden and unexpected death came as a great shock. Governor McRae has been asked to appoint Miss Hoover Casey to fill out her father's unexpired term. [Rogers Democrat 5/3/23]
Ira Carter Casey was born November 16, 1866 near Carlyle, Ill. and died at his home in Bentonville April 30, 1923, aged 56 years, five months and fourteen days. He has been a resident of Arkansas since the year 1881 when with his parents he moved from his birthplace to the vicinity of Pea Ridge, a spot which he learned to love as he grew to manhood. With the exception of four years when he lived at Van Buren, Ark. and had charge of the Frisco express office there, he has been a continuous resident of Benton county. In August 1890 he was married to Addie P. Maxwell, who survives him, together with G.W. Casey of Rogers and A.S. Casey of Healing Springs. In the year 1900 Mr. Casey was elected county clerk of Benton county and served two terms in that office. In 1918 he was again honored by election to the same position and had served in that office since, having been elected to a third term in the fall of 1922 because of the esteem in which he was held by the electorate of Benton county. Mr. Casey had been for years a member of the M.E. Church, South, being an active member. For years he had been a member of the Masonic fraternity, being honored in that order by election to the various offices. He had served as worshipful master of the Blue Lodge and at the time of his death was secretary of the order of Knights Templar and worthy Patron of the Eastern Star. [Rogers Democrat 5/10/23]

CASEY, Walter - Harrison, July 17.- Walter Casey, a prominent business man and former U.S. deputy marshal, was shot and instantly killed Monday by John Sullivan, alias John Jackson, alleged highwayman, who snatched a pistol from Casey who was taking him back to jail from which he had escaped only a short time before. There was talk of lynching Sullivan but the officers prevailed and he will be given an early trial it is promised by the authorities. Sullivan was captured by auto tourists who he had attempted to hold up near Harrison. [Rogers Democrat 7/19/23]

CHAPIN, Cynthia Jane CULVER - Cynthia Jane Culver was born at North Collins, New York June 24, 1838, departed this life on June 15, 1923 at the home of her daughter, Mrs. Eva J. Maple in Gentry, Arkansas. Had she been spared nine more days she would have been 85 years old. On September 22, 1857 she was married to Burrell N. Chapin of Farmington, Illinois. On June 20, 1920 Mr. Chapin passed away, they having lived in happy wedlock almost 63 years. This union was blessed with four children: Mrs. Edith McClure of Knoxville, Ill.; Mr. Ora Chapin of Fort Myers, Florida; Ida Adell, who died in infancy and Mrs. Eva Maple of Gentry, Arkansas. Mrs. Chapin was a daughter of William and Susan {Kirby} Culver and comes of a long line of Mayflower, Colonial and Revolutionary ancestry. A lineal descendant of William and Susanna White of the Mayflower {1620}, who were parents of the first English child born in America. She has five known ancestors who fought for freedom in the Revolutionary War, she being a life member of the Daughters of the American Revolution and member of the society of Mayflower Descendants. Mrs. Chapin was a help-meet in the purest sense to her husband, a wife and mother of noble christian character, loving and self sacrificing to a degree. A woman of wonderful poise and fortitude, meeting the great sorrows and burdens with the same calm as the everyday trivialities of life. She has been a member of the Presbyterian church at Knoxville, Illinois for the past 45 years. Previous to her residence at Knoxville she was a member of the Congregational church at Farmington, Illinois and Galesburg, Illinois. The funeral services were conducted Sunday afternoon by Rev. Edward Parson at the home of her daughter, Mrs. Eva Maple. Mrs. Maple accompanied her body to Knoxville, Illinois where it will be laid to rest by the side of her husband. [Gentry Journal-Advance 6/22/23]

CHASTAIN, Mary - {from New Hope} Quincy Chastain was called to Bentonville on Saturday by the illness of his mother, Mrs. Mary Chastain. She was thought to be somewhat improved. On Monday between 11 and 12 o'clock Mr. Chastain went to a drug store to get her some medicine. He helped her to bed before he went as she had been sitting up most of the morning. He was gone probably fifteen minutes and when he returned she had passed away, having apparently not moved after he went out. It was a great shock to him although she was almost 85 years old. She had been a resident of Benton county for some 40 or 50 years, having moved here from Kentucky. Her funeral will be held today at the Baptist church in Bentonville with interment at the Temperance Hill cemetery, southwest of Bentonville. [Rogers Democrat 11/1/23]

CHURCHILL, Kate KIMBALL - {from The Nashua {Iowa} Reporter} Kate Kimball was born at Republic, Iowa Aug. 29, 1864. She passed away Jan. 11, 1923 at 11 p.m. at her home after many years of suffering, at the age of 58 years, 4 months and 14 days. Here she grew to womanhood and spent the greater part of her life with the exception of two years in Chicago and six years in Gentry, Ark. On October 18, 1888 she was united in marriage to Amitta Churchill of Plainfield, Iowa. There was no family from this union but in August 1916 Elizabeth Oviett was adopted and remains with her father. All through her foster mother's long illness Elizabeth was her constant nurse and was most untiring in her efforts to alleviate the pain of her mother. Deceased was a member of the M.E. church for the past several years. There remains of the relatives to mourn their loss, 4 sisters, Mrs. Eleanor Randall, Fredericksburg; Mrs. Augusta Adams, Emmetsburg, Iowa; Mrs. John Edison, West Union, Iowa; Mrs. Betsy Dodge, Fall Rock, Calif.; and two brothers, Ernest Kimball, Charles City and Samuel Kimball of Oelwein, and 15 nieces and 9 nephews. [Gentry Journal-Advance 1/26/23]

CLARRY, Mary Angelina BLAIR - Mrs. Mary Clarry, who has been confined to her room for many months at the home of her daughter, Mrs. A.M. McAllister, passed away last week Thursday morning, Dec. 13, 1923 at the age of 74 years, six months and three days. Mary Angelina Blair was born June 10, 1849 in Montgomery county, Ill., was married to George Clarry in 1864. To this union were born 8 children, four of which survive: Wm. F. Clarry, Alberta, Canada; John R. Clarry, Gravette; Mrs. Nannie E. Bond, Baker, Ore. and Mrs. Alice V. McAllister of Gravette, near Mt. Enterprise, where Mrs. Clarry united with the Baptist church. In 1913 Mr. Clarry died and since then she had lived with her daughter. The funeral was conducted at the residence Friday at 10:30, Rev. T.N. Norris officiating, and burial was in the Tinnin cemetery near Maysville. [Gravette News-Herald 12/21/23]

CLINE, infant - {from Ozark} Born to Albert Cline and wife August 22nd, a baby boy, It only lived a short time and was buried in the Ruddick cemetery Thursday afternoon, John Taylor conducting the funeral services. All join in extending sympathy to the bereaved family. [Rogers Democrat 8/30/23]

CLOW, Hattie APPLEGATE - {from Mt. View} Mrs. Fred Maskell received word of the death of her youngest sister, Mrs. Hattie {Applegate} Clow, which occurred at her home on December 17th near Albion, New York. She is survived by her husband and Frank Clow and two sisters and one brother. She had been sick for some time and death relieved her suffering. [Rogers Democrat 1/4/23]

COLLIGAN, Mathew Edward - {from The Siloam Register, Aug. 23rd} Mathew Edward Colligan, aged 58 years, died at the city hospital Tuesday afternoon following a long illness. The body was shipped yesterday morning by the McArthur undertaking establishment to Los Angeles, Calif. where interment will be made next Monday. [Gentry Journal-Advance 9/7/23]

COMPTON, David - David Compton was born at New Egypt, New Jersey Nov. 2, 1850. He was the direct descendant of the earliest settlers of New Jersey. His ancestor, Wm. Compton, was a member of Capt. Bowen's party which settled at Middletown in 1667. His close relations still live in the same community. In early life he became a school master. Graduated with high honors at Princeton University in the class of 1874 and completed a post graduate course at the University of Heidelburg in Germany. He was principal of the High Schools at Mt. Sterling, Illinois; Keokuk, Iowa and Dubuque, Iowa, where he removed from to Gentry, Ark. in 1895. Mr. Compton married in 1876 to Mary E. Heller. To them were born seven children; the four oldest sons preceding the father to the grave by many years. He is survived by his aged wife, sons David and William, and daughter, Mary. He was a member of the Protestant Church since the early 80's. He was 72 years, 9 months and 6 days of age. Funeral services were conducted by Rev. Sherman and the remains laid to rest Aug. 13, 1923 at Bozarth cemetery. [Gentry Journal-Advance 8/17/23]

CONLEY, Geo. - {from Mason Valley} Geo. Conley died at the home of his son, George, of this place Feb. 2, 1923. He leaves 3 sons and 1 daughter, Geo. and William of this place, Melvin Conley and Mrs. Bertha James of Watonga, Okla. who were at his bedside. Funeral services were conducted by Rev. Bradshaw of Vaughn at the Mason Valley church Sunday afternoon and the body was tenderly laid to rest in the Coffelt cemetery to await the resurrection morn. [Gentry Journal-Advance 2/16/23]

COPP, Mr. - {from Lowell} Lowell friends were grieved and shocked to hear of the death of Mr. Copp, father of Ben and Ab Copp. Mr. Copp was in Louisiana selling apples and fell dead on the streets. His body was taken to Kansas for burial. [Rogers Democrat 11/8/23]

COWEE, James S. - James S. Cowee dropped dead Tuesday morning while plowing in the garden of W.N. Pierce in the south part of town. While Mr. Cowee had not been in good health for several years his sudden death was unexpected and a great shock to the people of our city. Mr. Cowee was a native of Ohio and was born May 22, 1851 and was in his 72nd year at the time of his death. He had lived in and near Lowell for many years, removing to Rogers several years ago and worked at the carpenter trade until failing health made him give up that work. He was a faithful member of the Central Methodist church and attended Sunday school and preaching service every Sunday morning. Last Sunday night he felt well enough to attend the evening service, too, and this week he told one of his friends to be sure to attend the Friday evening Communion service. So he was faithful to the end. Mr. Cowee is survived by his wife, Mrs. Lyda J. Walden Cowee and three children - Mrs. Gladys Hays of Kansas City, Leon Leonard Cowee, who is now working in Iowa, and Opal Matilda, a child of ten years. All of the children are here for the funeral which will be conducted Friday afternoon at the Central M.E. church by the pastor, Rev. Crichlow. [Rogers Democrat 3/29/23]

CRAIN, Mrs. J.W. - Mrs. J.W. Crain, who left Gravette a few weeks ago, passed away Sept. 22, 1923 at her home near Merriam, Kans. after a lingering illness. She was born in Leo, Ind. July 11, 1865; came to Missouri when a child; grew to womanhood and was married to J.W. Crain at Rockville, Mo. on Jan. 11, 1883. The following survive her: the husband; 2 daughters, Mrs. John Dickinson, Merriam, Kans. and Mrs. Herman Bruno, Slater, Mo.; Rev. O.E. Crain, Holyoke, Mass.; C.M. Crain, Kansas City, Mo.; 3 brothers and 1 sister. She united with the Presbyterian church early in life and remained a faithful member. Burial was made at the old home town, Higginsville, Mo. on Monday, Sept. 24th, 1923. Gravette friends of the family offer sympathy to the bereaved. [Gravette News-Herald 10/5/23]

CRANE, George - George Crane, 80 years old, died last week at his home in Siloam Springs. He was the father of Stanley Crane, known in every printing office in Arkansas as a representative of the Mergenthaler Linotype Co. [Rogers Democrat 6/28/23]

CROWDER, David - David Crowder, 20 year old son of Mr. and Mrs. B.S. Crowder, died at his home on Friday, Jan. 5th, resulting from appendicitis. Funeral services were conducted by Rev. C.H. Sherman. [Gentry Journal-Advance 1/12/23]

DALE, J.H. - {from Heater Springs} Mrs. Grimes was called to Sulphur Springs Thursday on account of the death of her son-in-law, J.H. Dale. {Note: J.H. Dale, newspaper man, formerly resided at Gravette. His death was rather sudden, from lung trouble. [Gravette News-Herald 1/19/23]

DARBY, Ellen SMITH - Ellen Smith Darby, daughter of Edson F. and Sarah Hungerford Smith, was born in Elmwood, Ill. May 30th, 1848 and died at Wheaton, Minn.{sic} at the home of her daughter, Mrs. Nellie Petterson, Feb. 23, 1923. She finished the course of study in the local schools of Elmwood and then attended Knox College. After teaching in the home schools for a short time she was married to Henry Harrison Darby, also of Elmwood and a fellow student in the same college as herself. To this union were born three children, William Edson Darby and Henry Harrison Darby, Jr. who preceded her in death, and one daughter, Mrs. Benjamin Petterson of Wheaton, Ill.{sic}. She is also survived by five great-grandchildren and one daughter-in-law, Mrs. Darby of this city, and son-in law, Benjamin Petterson, of Minnesota. She was a member of the Woman's Relief Corps and order of Eastern Star of Rogers. She has been an active club woman, president of the Ladies Aid Society and for many years a devoted church member. She was an invalid for three years and was helpless for the last year. Funeral services were held in the Presbyterian church of Wheaton, Minn., after which her daughter accompanied her remains to Rogers, her home for many years, where she was laid to rest by the side of her husband and son. Funeral services were held in Rogers Tuesday afternoon at 2:30 o'clock at the home of her granddaughter, Mrs. Lloyd Patterson on West Oak, between Third and Fourth streets, conducted by Rev. T.E. McSpadden. [Rogers Democrat 3/1/23]

DAVIS, infant - {from Lowell} The 3-days old infant of Chas. Davis and wife died last Wednesday. [Rogers Democrat 2/1/23]

DAVIS, Mrs. B.B. - Dr. Thompson received word Tuesday night announcing the death of Mrs. B.B. Davis, aged 90 years, at Muskogee, Okla. Mrs. Davis was the grandmother of Dr. Thompson's children by his first marriage. [Gravette News-Herald 9/28/23]

DAY, James - James Day, ten-year-old son of Mr. and Mrs. O.F. Day, was instantly killed about five o'clock last evening by the kick of a horse. The blow struck the lad just over the heart and although he was taken at once to Love's Sanitarium, there was nothing that could be done for him. The Day family live on the old Howard Beale farm, just north of town, near the Grace Brezeale place. The family horse had gotten out of the lot into the corn and the mother sent the lad to drive it back to the lot. The horse has never shown any vicious traits and it is not known what caused it to kick at this time. Mr. Day is in Kansas with a threshing crew and his last known address was Haviland, that state. An effort was being made last night to reach him and although unsuccessful at our last report, has probably been found by this time. No announcement could be made as to the funeral until the father was heard from. [Rogers Democrat 8/30/23]

DEANS, Hiram King - {from Freedom} Hiram King Deans was born August 22, 1846 in Cleborne county, Tennessee, moved to Benton county, Arkansas with his parents when a child. He died November 15, 1923 at the age of 77 years, two months and 24 days. He leaves a wife and seven children to mourn his loss. We want to thank the neighbors and friends for their flowers and the kindness shown us through the sickness and death of our dear husband and father. [Rogers Democrat 11/22/23]

DENNEY, Davey - {from Fairmount} Word has been received here of the death of Davey Denney at Perryton, Texas of pneumonia fever. [Gentry Journal-Advance 1/23/23]

DICKSON, Dwight - {from The Bentonville Democrat} Bentonville friends were shocked Wednesday when it was learned that Dwight Dickson had succumbed to a short illness with meningitis, passing away at his home at 9:30 that morning. On Monday he had been about the offices of the Dickson Motor Co. in which he was senior partner, apparently in good health. That evening he became troubled with pains in his ear which gradually grew worse and despite every effort medical assistance was without avail. Funeral services were held Thursday afternoon with interment in the city cemetery. [Rogers Democrat 6/14/23]

DILLINGER, Mrs. John - Mrs. John Dillinger died at her home about 3 miles southeast of Gentry last week. She was buried Sunday in the Fairmount cemetery. Deceased was about 70 years of age and is survived by a husband, 3 sons and 2 daughters. [Gentry Journal-Advance 9/14/23]

DIXON, John T. - John T. Dixon died last week at Bentonville following an illness of several months. He was 73 years old, a native of Illinois and had lived in Bentonville since 1905. He was a contractor by occupation. [Rogers Democrat 3/15/23]

DOUGLAS, Sarah Burghart - Under date of September 10th the Democrat editor received the following note from Mrs. F.C. Burghart of Omaha, Neb.: "Mrs. Sarah Douglas died in Cortland, New York. Burial will take place in Missouri Valley, Iowa." Mrs. Burghart is a daughter-in-law of Mrs. Douglas, her husband being the only living child. Mrs. Douglas had been in New York several years assisting in caring for a nephew. So far as we know her only other living relative is a sister, Mrs. Clark of Independence, Ia. Mrs. Douglas was one of the early settlers of this section and came here some forty-five years ago. In those days her name was Burghart. After the death of her first husband she married a Mr. Douglas who died a good many years ago. Mrs. Douglas was one of the charter members of the Cumberland Presbyterian church of Rogers and was always especially active in the county fairs held here. She was a woman of education and vigor and she is remembered most kindly by her many friends and associates. [Rogers Democrat 9/13/23]

DUNCAN, Jasper - {from Bethlehem} Died Friday, Dec. 14, 1923, Jasper Duncan, at the home of his son, Eura. Bro. T.F. Jones conducted the funeral services. [Gravette News-Herald 12/21/23]

DUNN, B.S. - A double tragedy occurred last week at Anderson, Mo. when B.S. Dunn, a real estate dealer of that place, was shot and instantly killed by an old man, a Mr. Hester, who a short time later was found dead in a room in the hotel where he had taken his own life. Dunn was about 50 years old and Hester was close to 70 years old. There had been litigation between the two men but it was thought it had been satisfactorily adjusted. Hester met Dunn on the street and opened fire, killing him instantly. Dunn is survived by a wife and four children. Hester was a widower. [Rogers Democrat 10/11/23]

DURHAM, Ellen WEST - Mrs. Ellen Durham {nee Ellen West} died Feb. 24, 1923 at her home west of Maysville in Oklahoma. She was born Dec. 23, 1871 at Vandalia, Ill., was baptized and united with the Christian church about 1917. She leaves four sons, one daughter, four brothers and one sister. The funeral was held Monday, Rev. W.M. Shelton of Gravette conducting the same, and burial was in Tinnin cemetery at Maysville. The deceased was a sister-in-law of Mrs. Melvin Covey of this city. [Gravette News-Herald 3/2/23]

EASLEY, George - {from Providence} John Easley was called to Oklahoma last week on account of the death of his brother, George, who we understand committed suicide by hanging himself. He had been in very poor health a long time and we suppose he had become mentally unbalanced or he wouldn't have committed the act. He has many friends and relatives here who will be much grieved to learn of the sad affair. [Rogers Democrat 7/12/23]

EASLEY, Mary A. MITCHELL - {from Providence} Mary A. Mitchell was born in Knox county, Tenn. December 5th, 1853. Moved to Benton

county in early girlhood {in 1866} where she spent the remainder of her life. She united with the Primitive Baptist church at Providence near her home on September 8, 1883, was baptised by Elder Goad and remained a faithful member until death. She was married to John Easley November 28, 1883 and moved to their home on her birthday, December 5th, 1883 and remained in this same home until her death, living a devoted life to her husband and children, ever willing to make sacrifices for their pleasure. To this union was born six children, two dying in infancy. Those living are: Mrs. Ollie Mahurin, Clarence Easley and Hayden Easley, all of Garfield, Ark.; Mrs. Bertha Saunders of Cardin, Okla. All were present at the bedside when the end came. She contracted the disease on January 9th from which she suffered until death relieved her on March 6, 1923 at the age of 69 years, three months and one day. We extend heart-felt sympathy to the entire family, especially to Mr. and Mrs. Hayden Easley as they were called to the bedside of his mother and witnessed her passing away, then three hours later they were called to witness the death of her mother, Mrs. Byler. [Rogers Democrat 3/15/23]
{from Providence} Mrs. Rebecca Givens spent a few days last week with her brothers, W.J. and C.J. Mitchell, after attending the funeral of her sister, Mrs. John Easley. [Rogers Democrat 3/22/23]

EDENS, Ave Jennings - {from Ozark} Mrs. Ave Edens was buried at the Ruddick cemetery Saturday afternoon. Ave Jennings Edens was born August 22, 1845 in Washington county, Arkansas, moved to Benton county, Arkansas near Garfield with her mother when quite young where she spent the remainder of her life. Became a member of the Freewill Baptist church while yet in her teens. Married to Ap Edens on March 9, 1882. Three children were born to this union, one son and two daughters, Lee, Pearl and Nolia. Died at the home of her son, Lee Edens, April 6, 1923 at the age of 77 years, seven months and 16 days. The deceased was much loved and esteemed by all who knew her as a true loving mother, friend and neighbor. She leaves a son and a host of relatives and friends to mourn her loss. All join in sympathy for the bereaved family. The family wishes to thank the neighbors and many friends for their help and kindness during her last sickness and death. [Rogers Democrat 4/12/23]

ELLIS, Mrs. M.E. - Mrs. M.E. Ellis, aged 77, died last week at Bentonville at the home of her daughter, Mrs. Paul Chastain. She had been an invalid for many years. [Rogers Democrat 3/29/23]

ENLOE, Frank - {from Cloverdale} The many friends of Frank Enloe were shocked when the news came Thursday that he had passed away at his home on Pea Ridge. He had a stroke of paralysis from which he never recovered. Only a few weeks previous his wife passed to the great beyond. [Rogers Democrat 4/5/23]

ENLOE, Mattie - Mrs. Mattie Enloe died recently at her home west of Pea Ridge after an illness of several weeks. She is survived by her husband

and five grandchildren that she was raising in her home. [Rogers Democrat 3/15/23]

EUBANKS, infant - {from Ozark} The infant son of Earl Eubanks and wife was buried at the Ruddick cemetery Sunday afternoon. It was born Wednesday morning and died Sunday morning. Bro. I.D. Ames conducted the funeral services at the house. All extend heart-felt sympathy to the bereaved parents. [Rogers Democrat 1/11/23]

EVANS, Lucy - Miss Lucy Evans, who has been a victim of tuberculosis for some years, died Sunday at her home west of Gravette, aged 28 years, 9 months and 24 days. She leaves brothers and sisters. The funeral was conducted Tuesday, Feb. 27 by J.M. Haley and burial followed at the Russell cemetery. [Gravette News-Herald 3/2/23]

EVANS, Mrs. W.L. - {from Pea Ridge} Mrs. W.L. Evans died last Thursday and was buried Friday at the Hickman cemetery. She had been in bad health for quite a while. Mr. Evans is also in very bad health. His mind is almost entirely gone. [Rogers Democrat 6/14/23]

EVANS, William - William Evans, who died recently at the home of his son, R.C. Evans on Pea Ridge, was 80 years old and had lived in Benton county for more than seventy years. He was an ex-Confederate soldier. He is survived by four children, Robert C. Evans and Mrs. J.B. Blevins of Pea Ridge; Mrs. Albert Patterson of Trinidad, Colo. and Mrs. Dona Hall of Wichita, Kan. Mrs. Evans died three months ago. [Rogers Democrat 8/23/23]

EVANS, Winfield Scott - Winfield Scott Evans, prominent resident of Maysville vicinity, died at his home 3 miles south of that place on Saturday, March 3, 1923 following an attack of flu, aged 78 years, and had resided on his farm there over 60 years. He leaves his wife, three sons: Dr. Perry Evans, Hannah, Okla., Fred and Scott of Maysville, and three daughters: Mrs. Will Haley and Mrs. Henry Keith of Maysville and Mrs. Scott Yeargain of Miami, Okla. Mr. Evans was a Union soldier and for many years a member of the Baptist church. The funeral was conducted Sunday afternoon by Rev. T.F. Jones at Maysville Baptist church and the body was laid to rest in the Tinnin cemetery. The News Herald unites with friends of the family in offering sympathy. [Gravette News-Herald 3/9/23]

EVANS, Zoretta Vaniss - Zoretta Vaniss, the infant daughter of Mr. and Mrs. Charles M. Evans, {word left out?} Feb. 15th, 1923, died Monday, Feb. 19, 1923, being afflicted with flu. This baby girl was the thirteenth child of Mr. and Mrs. Evans. [Gravette News-Herald 3/2/23]

FAGALA, Mrs. Jess - {from Hebron} Our community was deeply shocked Wednesday when the news was circulated that Mrs. Jess Fagala was dead. Death was quick to take her without any warning. At six o'clock she told her husband to light the lamp, it was so dark, and before much help could be summoned her spirit had entered the other place. The most heartbreaking part is leaving a month old baby boy, also a little 6 year old girl. It breaks a happy home and leaves the husband in clouds of despair and lonesomeness. Words cannot express the sympathy we all feel for the bereaved ones. They are father, mother, one sister and eight brothers, the first beautiful flower to be transplanted from their home. Mrs. Fagala was a member of the Baptist church since early youth and lived a life to be a pleasure and profit to all her associates and died at the early age of 28 years. The body was tenderly laid away in the Pleasant Grove cemetery. May the bereaved ones look to the One who gives solace to aching hearts. [Rogers Democrat 2/15/23]

FAIR, Agnes Julia Ann WOMACK - Mrs. Agnes Julia Ann Fair died a week ago at her home at Centerton at the age of 72 years. She was born in Tennessee and her maiden name was Womack. She had lived in Benton county since 1855. [Rogers Democrat 2/8/23]

FELDT, Mrs. A.F. - Mrs. A.F. Feldt, after three months illness, passed away at a local hospital in Rogers last Friday morning. Her funeral was held from Callison's undertaking parlors on Saturday afternoon. Mrs. Feldt had only resided in this neighborhood about two and a half years and as she was of a very quiet, retiring disposition she had not made a wide circle of acquaintances. She leaves to mourn her early death {her age was barely 40 years} a devoted husband and two grown sons - Henry, who is now in the west and Edward of the home address. Mr. Feldt desires to thank the neighbors for their kindness and assistance during her long sickness and for the beautiful flowers. [Rogers Democrat 11/15/23]

FERRELL, Martha TUCK Rumley - {from Walnut Hill} Tuesday of last week marked the last milestone of one of our good old pioneer friends, Mrs. Martha Ferrell {nee Tuck}, born Dec. 14, 1848. When a young girl she was married to Bob Rumley and to this union was born 3 children, Jane Jackson, a daughter who has been dead some 30 years, and 2 sons, Bill and John Rumley of Bentonville, who were present at the funeral. She was left a widow while the children were small and married W.T. Ferrell on March 4, 1875. To this union was born 7 children: Martha E. Ferrell passed away Sept. 21, 1880; Mrs. Rosa German of Las Vegas, Nev. was unable to be at her mother's bedside; Mrs. Hattie Snoderly of Garfield; Mrs. Dovie Egan of Fall River, Kan.; Larkin Ferrell of Rogers; Albert Ferrell of Okmulgee, Okla. and Robert, who has cared for his mother for the past 10 years, were all present at the funeral. Mrs. Ferrell outlived her husband 10 years and had reached the ripe old age of 74 years, 6 months and 5 days. She also leaves to mourn her loss 2 sisters, Susan Reddick of Rogers and Sarah Walker of Salem, Ore. and 2 brothers, Joe Tuck of Seligman and Son Tuck of Tulsa. She leaves 8 children, 20 grandchildren, 10 great-grandchildren and a host of friends who join the relatives in their great sorrow. Mrs. Ferrell was converted while a young girl and joined the Baptist church of which she was a faithful member. She was stricken Sunday morning and passed away Tuesday evening. Bro. B.R. Williams conducted the funeral service, A.D. Callison of Rogers caring for the body. [Rogers Democrat 6/28/23]

FOLLETTE, child - The two-year-old child of Mr. and Mrs. Chas. Follette died yesterday at an early hour. Funeral services were held at the Callison Undertaking Parlors yesterday afternoon, conducted by Rev. J. Watson Shockley. [Rogers Democrat 1/25/23]

FORD, Ben - {from Tuck's Chapel} The funeral of Ben Ford of Rogers was conducted at this place Sunday at 2:30 p.m. [Rogers Democrat 7/5/23]

FORD, J.W. - Coincident with the sudden death of M.L. Buchanan at Gravette following the utterance of a prayer last week, Wednesday night, J.W. Ford dropped dead at the Bentonville Baptist church. [Gravette News-Herald 4/20/23]

FORSYTHE, Irwin - E.F. Jackson of the First National Bank received a telegram yesterday morning telling of the death of Irwin Forsythe, who formerly lived near Garfield, in a railroad wreck near Independence, Kan. on Tuesday. No particulars were given but it said the body would be shipped to Rogers for burial. Mr. Forsythe had a small account in the bank here and it is supposed a bank book or some other identifying correspondence was found on the body. The deceased was a man between 50 and 60 years old and had been separated from his wife for several years. It is understood he has a daughter in Nebraska but we have been unable to find anyone who knew her name or address. The morning papers report a wreck near Independence Tuesday in which five unknown men were killed and two others badly injured but no names were given. It said the men were stealing a ride. [Rogers Democrat 5/17/23]

L.T. Ferrell returned Saturday from Mound Valley, Kan. where he went to look after the body of Irwin Forsythe, killed Tuesday morning in a Frisco freight wreck a few miles from that place. The train consisted of ten tank cars of gasoline and several empty box cars. Seven men were stealing a ride in one of the empties, most of them headed for the Arkansas berry fields, and five were killed instantly and two were severely injured. The coroner's inquest said of the Arkansas man: "Irwin Forsythe, Rogers, Ark., identified by papers found on body. Apparently 50 years of age; slightly bald; slightly gray; eyes brown, five feet seven inches high; left ankle was crushed, ribs of left side crushed in; right wrist joint dislocated; deep cut below left ear, cut over right eye; cause of death, body crushed." Mr. Ferrell, who had known the deceased at Garfield, made arrangements for burying the body at Mound Valley where he bought a lot in the local cemetery and had the body embalmed so that it may be moved if the relatives desire. The personal belongings that were found on the body were turned over to Mr. Ferrell who brought them back and turned them over to the First National Bank where the deceased had an account. Only a few cents were found on the body. [Rogers Democrat 5/24/23]

FOSTER, Mrs. C.E. - Mrs. C.E. Foster, aged 51 years, died March 5th at her home at Pea Ridge. Her husband is a traveling salesman for the Inter-State Grocery Company of Joplin. [Rogers Democrat 3/15/23]

FOX, infant - Born Sunday to Mr. and Mrs. J.O. Fox, a boy and a girl. The little girl died within a few hours but the boy is still alive. Mrs. Fox is in a very serious condition and the worst has been feared for several days. [Rogers Democrat 1/25/23]
The infant children of Mr. and Mrs. J.O. Fox were buried Friday, the second of the twins, a boy, having died Wednesday. The condition of Mrs. Fox is now more encouraging and it is thought she will recover if there are no unforeseen complications. [Rogers Democrat 2/1/23]

FOX, Iris Valgene CUNNINGHAM - Mrs. Iris Valgene Fox, daughter of Mr. and Mrs. V.P. Cunningham, was born June 30, 1883 in Scotland county, Missouri. At the age of 19 she confessed her faith in Christ and was a devoted Christian to the end of her life. She was married October 4, 1911 to John O. Fox at Mountain Grove, Mo. and to this union were born three children, two boys and one girl. Those of her relatives surviving are: a father and mother, Mr. and Mrs. V.P. Cunningham, and a twin sister, Mrs. Vivian Holloway. The funeral was held in the First Christian Church with the minister, Rev. J. Watson Shockley, officiating. Interment was in the City cemetery. The deceased was held in high esteem in the church, social and lodge circles as was evidenced by the beautiful floral offerings. Her presence will be missed by the church, the Study Club and the Eastern Star. These organizations attended her funeral in a body. [Rogers Democrat 2/15/23]

FOX, John Stephen - John Stephen Fox was born in Tennessee in 1864 and departed this life at Little Rock, Ark. May 17th, 1923 at the age of 58 years, 5 months and 24 days. When about 10 years of age he moved with his parents to Washington county, Ark., later coming to Benton county to make his home. In 1884 he was united in marriage to Mattie E. Chastain. To this union was born eleven children, ten of whom are living; one having preceded his father in death about nine months. Mr. Fox professed religion about the age of 16 years and lived a faithful christian life ever after. He was a kind and loving husband and father, and a good neighbor. He was ever ready to lend a helping hand to those who were in need. He leaves to mourn his death a wife, ten children, three brothers, four sisters and a host of relatives and friends. [Gentry Journal-Advance 6/1/23]

FRAZER, William - In the death of William Frazer, which occurred Monday, August 27 at 4 p.m., a pioneer builder of Gravette has passed from the scene of action. Mr. Frazer, after nearly thirty years of steady application to a varied program of business affairs and untiring effort in behalf of Gravette, broke down last spring and except for a few days this summer has been confined to his home and his bed and his death was not unexpected. From Gravette's earliest existence Wm. Frazer had figured in every progressive step taken and when the town was incorporated became its first mayor, serving five consecutive terms, and was in later years re-elected to the same office. He has been engaged in various lines of business but for several years - perhaps 20 - has applied himself to real estate, abstracting and looking after important business of non-residents. He was a man of integrity and held the good will of everyone. For over 30 years, on farm and in town, he was a neighbor to the News Herald editor and we have known of no other more accommodating or public spirited citizen. He helped to build Gravette and has helped many a townsman when in financial straits. He never withheld contribution to any good cause. His death is our loss. William Frazer was born near Peoria, Ill. Oct. 12, 1852 and was aged 70 years, 8 months and 15 days. Was married to Miss Eliza Bales in Missouri in August 1879 and moved to Kansas. In 1882 they moved to Beaty, Benton county, Ark. In 1893, shortly after the town of Gravette was established, Mr. Frazer moved to this place. Besides his companion he leaves 5 brothers: Jasper of Yale, Okla.; Rev. James, Topeka, Kan.; J.W. of Austin, Colo.; D.E., Wellington, Kan.; Perry of Blackwell, Okla.; and three sisters: Mrs. Cora Worthington, Blackwell, Okla.; Mrs. W.H. Morris, Randle, Ore.; Mrs. Belle Mehaffy of Diamondville, Wyoming. Following the death of another brother, Samuel, and his wife at Yellville, Mr. and Mrs. Frazer took the children into their home. They survive and are: Mrs. Lillie Lopez, Sacramento, Calif.; Walter Frazer, Riverside, Calif. and Mrs. Vernon Crandall of Gravette. The funeral was held Wednesday at 2 p.m., the business houses being closed as a mark of esteem in which the citizenship held the deceased. Rev. S.S. Frazier conducted the services at the residence and burial followed at the I.O.O.F. cemetery. Relatives being present were Rev. James Frazer, Mrs. Cora Worthington, brother and sister of Mr. Frazer, and Mrs. Frazer's brother, M.F. Bales of Sand Springs, Okla. and his daughters, Miss Sarah and Mrs. Deborah Jacobs. The News Herald speaks the unanimous voice of sympathy which is extended the bereaved wife and relatives in their hour of sorrow. [Gravette News-Herald 8/31/23]

FULBRIGHT, Jay - Fayetteville, July 23.- Jay Fulbright, aged 54, local financier and leading business man, died at noon today after a week's illness. Funeral arrangements have not been announced but it is thought the body will be buried here. Surviving relatives include his wife, six children and a sister. Mr. Fulbright was rated as one of Arkansas' wealthiest men. He was president of the Arkansas National bank, president and chief owner of Phipps Lumber company, president of the Fayetteville Mercantile company, vice president of the Ozark Poultry and Egg company, principal owner of Fayetteville Ice company, of the Washington hotel and the Fulbright Wholesale Grocer company and the Fayetteville Democrat Printing and Publishing company, all of this place. He was a stock holder and director in the Citizens bank, Fayetteville; Bank of Winslow, Bank of Elkins, Bank of St. Paul, Citizens bank of Pettigrew, and a stock holder in the Ozark Grocer company, Fayetteville Lumber and Cement company in Fayetteville and the H.C. Bone Stave company, Stilwell, Okla., where he owns 12,000 acres of land. He was a founder and the president of the Washington County

Fair Association and chairman of the city water commission. He was a member of the board of directors of the Methodist assembly, a member of the Rotary Club and Chamber of Commerce. [Rogers Democrat 7/26/23]

GANNAWAY, Mrs. J.L. - Mrs. J.L. Gannaway, widow of Rev. Gannaway, who died here several months ago, died yesterday morning at the age of 74 years. Funeral services are being held at the First M.E. church this afternoon, conducted by the pastor, Rev. Lucke. [Rogers Democrat 1/25/23]

GIBSON, Marion - {from Monte Ne} Marion Gibson died here at 6:15 Monday morning from a stroke of paralysis sustained ten days ago. Mr. Gibson has resided at Monte Ne for several years and has been blind for nine years. Mr. Gibson was a Mason. Interment will be at Spring Valley Tuesday. He is survived by a wife and several children. [Rogers Democrat 6/7/23]

GILBERT, E.A. - Rev. E.A. Gilbert died last Wednesday, November 28th at his home in this city after an illness of several months. He was 79 years old, having been born December 18, 1844 at Tuscaloosa, Georgia. Funeral services were conducted by the pastor, Rev. Lucke, assisted by Rev. E.M. Dugger of Springdale, a former Rogers pastor. Rev. Gilbert made his home here with his daughter, Miss Rose Gilbert of the Mutual Aid Union force. Mrs. W.R. Nelson of Sedalia, Mo., a daughter, a former Rogers resident, was here for several weeks previous to her father's death. The deceased was an ex-Confederate soldier and had been a preacher for many years. He became a minister in the Arkansas Conference of the M.E. church in 1885 and was superannuated in 1908. A quiet God-fearing citizen, he leaves many acquaintances and friends throughout the state who will regret to learn of his answer to the final roll call. [Rogers Democrat 12/6/23]

GILMORE, Y.A. - Rev. Y.A. Gilmore of Conway, former pastor of the Gravette M.E. church and for years a citizen of Benton county, died suddenly Tuesday, probably from heart trouble. Rev. Gilmore was traveling in the interest of the Orphans Home of Little Rock and was found dead in bed at Ruddles where he had put up for the night. The burial occurs today - Thursday - at Oakley Chapel, near Rogers, the body having been brought to this county for interment. [Gravette News-Herald 3/27/23]
{from Oakley Chapel} Rev. Y.A. Gilmore of the M.E. church, South, whose home was at Conway, Ark., died Monday night at Ruddles, Ark. His remains were brought to Rogers Wednesday and funeral services were held at this place Thursday evening conducted by his son, Rev. O.T. Gilmore of Virginia, and Rev. Sherman of Gentry. He leaves to mourn his loss his wife and three sons: O.T. Gilmore of Virginia; Harlin and Charles Gilmore of Conway, Ark. He was at one time pastor at this place and his host of friends were sorry to learn of his death. [Rogers Democrat 5/3/23]
{from Oakley Chapel} Mrs. Y.A. Gilmore and son, who spent several days at the home of her brother, A.L. Spencer, returned home the first of the week. [Rogers Democrat 5/3/23]

GODARD, Mrs. T.M. - {from New Hope, written by request} Mrs. T.M. Godard, widow of Abel Godard, Senior, departed this life at her home in Baxter Springs, Kansas October 11, 1923. She was born at Pine Grove, Warren county, Penn. May 24, 1833, living to the age of 90 years, five months and seven days. She lived a devout Christian life, being a Seventh Day Adventist in belief. She leaves to mourn her passing two sons, S.H. Godard of Long Beach, Calif. and Abel Godard, Jr., who lived in Baxter Springs, Kansas and several grandchildren. She was, in her younger days, a devoted church and Sunday (look this up) school worker. She had many friends in Arkansas, having lived for many years in the Oak Hill and Oakley Chapel neighborhoods. Her remains were brought by auto hearse to the Oakley Chapel cemetery Saturday, October 13th and were laid to rest by the side of her husband who passed away several years ago. The family desire to thank all their old friends and neighbors for their kindness and assistance. [Rogers Democrat 10/18/23]

GOOD, Emma A. HUNTER - {from Ozark} Emma A. Hunter was born Dec. 25, 1874 and died September 6, 1923, aged 48 years, 8 months and eleven days. She was married at Cottage Hill, Kansas February 16, 1893 to Harry C. Good who survives her. To this union were born twelve children, three of whom died at the age of about four months each. The remaining nine were all present at the funeral. She was converted in early life and gave her heart to the Lord in true humble service. The many friends in the community offer heartfelt sympathy to the bereaved family. [Rogers Democrat 9/13/23]

{from Elkhorn} B.R. Williams was called to the Ruddick cemetery Saturday morning to conduct the funeral services for Mrs. Harry C. Good, who was found dead in her bed Thursday morning at her home north of Garfield. [Rogers Democrat 9/13/23]

GOSS, R.L. - R.L. Goss died suddenly Monday morning at his home at Avoca. He had been feeling in his usual good health the day previous but was stricken early in the morning and death occurred in an hour or so. Funeral services were held at the residence at Avoca yesterday afternoon at 2 o'clock and were conducted by Rev. Barrett of the Baptist church of Rogers. Mr. Goss was a native of Georgia where he was born Dec. 11, 1845. The family came to Avoca in 1916 from Colorado City, Texas, Mr. Goss having lived in Texas for more than 35 years where he engaged in farming most of the time. Mr. Goss is survived by his wife and 7 children: Tom Goss of Colorado City, Texas; George Goss of Fort Worth, Texas; Robt. Goss of Rochester, Texas; Mrs. Nellie Aaron, Fort Stockton, Texas; Mrs. Ollie Cole of Robert Lee, Texas; Marion Goss of Rogers and Mrs. Garland Davis of Avoca. Mr. Goss was a highly respected member of the community and Avoca has lost one of its best citizens by his death. [Rogers Democrat 3/22/23]

GRAHAM, infant - {from Lowell} The two weeks old infant son of Joe Graham and wife died last Tuesday night. [Rogers Democrat 3/1/23]

GRAHAM, Thine - {from Lowell} Mrs. Graham, better known as Aunt Thine, died last week in the Accident neighborhood. She was the mother of Jim and Joe Graham. [Rogers Democrat 7/5/23]

GRAVES, Dora - {from The Siloam Springs Herald Democrat} Dora Graves, 11-year-old daughter of T.N. Graves and wife in the Baptist Mission Settlement, died Monday after a week's illness with blood poisoning. The little girl was walking to school and in some manner got a gravel in her shoe which caused a bruise, resulting in blood poison. [Rogers Democrat 11/15/23]

GRAVES, T.H. - T.H. Graves died at his home in Gentry Monday night from appendicitis and was buried Wednesday morning at 10 o'clock. Deceased was about 50 years of age. [Gentry Journal-Advance 6/1/23]

GRAVETTE, Laura B. - We learned too late for last week's paper that Mrs. Laura B. Gravette, widow of E.T. Gravette, "father of the town of Gravette," had died on Saturday, Sept. 29, 1923 at the home of her daughter, Mrs. Tom Hughes, near Centerton. Mrs. Gravette had been in ill health for some time and was aged about 65 years. Mrs. Gravette and husband, E.T., were among the early settlers of this community, residing first at Old Town where Mr. Gravette established the "Old Chalk" distillery. The Kansas City Southern Ry., extending its lines south from Sulphur Springs, crossed Mr. Gravette's farm here and the town of Gravette was laid out on the farm. The family, except Ed M. Gravette, step-son of Mrs. Gravette, moved away some years ago, the elder Gravette dying in 1918. Mrs. Gravette leaves three sons, R.S. Gravette, Gold Spgs., Alberta; Will and Keet, and four daughters, Mrs. Hughes, Mrs. Fred Trout and Mrs. Frank Ernst of Centerton and Maud Gravette, Yuma, Ariz. Rev. W.J. Leroy of Centerton conducted the funeral and interment was made at Garfield, former home of the deceased. [Gravette News-Herald 10/12/23]

GREGORY, C.E. - Harrison, Jan. 16.- The body of C.E. Gregory, a striking railroad worker who resisted a posse of citizens probing sabotage on the Missouri and North Arkansas railroad, was found hanging from a railroad trestle here this morning. The posse visited all the strikers during the night investigating recent depredations. Gregory resisted the posse yesterday. Several shots were fired into his home and one of the posse was hit by a shot fired by Gregory. George W. O'Neal, a hotel man who went on the bond of the striking shop workers who were arrested for paralyzing transportation on the railroad by burning bridges, was taken from his home here in his night clothes shortly after the hanging last night and whipped by a mob of citizens. Twenty other strikers were rounded up and held in a hall by the mob where they were subjected to a vigorous questioning. The labor headquarters here were stormed and papers burned and furniture smashed. It was reported later today that the body of Pete Zenable, leader of the strikers, has been found hanging to a tree in an orchard near town. A delegation of deputies is investigating. Mayor J.L. Clute has resigned following a demand by the citizens. William Parr, city marshal, who was ordered to leave the community, has disappeared. [Gentry Journal-Advance 1/19/23]

GRIMES, James Clifford - James Clifford Grimes, son of Mr. and Mrs. Jas. W. Grimes of Rogers, died Saturday in St. John's Hospital, St. Louis, where he had been for a month receiving treatment. The body arrived in Rogers Sunday night and funeral services were held Tuesday afternoon at 2:30 o'clock at the First Baptist church. Services were conducted by Rev. Kline of the Christian church, assisted by Rev. McSpadden of the Presbyterian church and Rev. Austin of the Baptist church. Interment was in the Rogers cemetery. James Clifford Grimes was born at the home on Prairie Creek February 18, 1908 and died December 1, 1923. He was a member of the Sophomore class of Rogers High School and his class attended the funeral in a body. He was a very likable and popular boy and his death is a great grief to the many friends and relatives. [Rogers Democrat 12/6/23]

GUMM, Mrs. Clarence - {from The Madison County Record} Mrs. Clarence Gumm of near Clifty died Saturday from blood poisoning which resulted from an infected tooth. The deceased is survived by her husband and three small children. [Rogers Democrat 5/24/23]

GUTHRIE, William Arthur {Mike} - Arthur and Joe Guthrie, aged 19 and 17 years respectively, sons of Mr. and Mrs. Guthrie living near the old Flatt distillery, east of this city a few miles, were drowned in the Illinois river last night while in bathing, says the Siloam Daily Register of Aug. 9th. The boys and their mother were camping on the river east of here and had been fishing. Apparently the boys were in bathing about 6:30 p.m. and, being unable to swim, got in water over their depth and drowned. The nude bodies were found this morning about 6:30 close together in water six feet or more in depth. The mother who was left alone in camp, searched for the boys all night and this morning early spread the alarm. A large party assembled and the bodies were soon discovered. The clothing of the two boys was piled on the bank near where they were found. Coroner Petty and Dr. Maxwell were summoned to the scene this morning and the bodies were removed from the river. [Gentry Journal-Advance 8/17/23]
William Arthur {Mike} Guthrie was born near Siloam Springs, Ark. April 11, 1904 and died Aug. 8, 1923; age 19 years, 3 months and 27 days; Joe Cannon {Sandy} Guthrie was born near Siloam Springs, Ark. Oct. 27, 1906 and died Aug. 8, 1923, age 16 years, 9 months and 11 days; sons of Mr. and Mrs. W.F. Guthrie, were drowned in the Illinois river about six miles east of Siloam Springs, Ark. on the evening of Aug. 8, 1923. The boys and their sisters, Misses Millie and Manzie, had gone down to the river, the boys to fish and the girls to remain in the car to study and read. The girls heard the boys talking a few minutes before they were missing; one asked the other if he had any "bites" and he answered a few "nibbles." It was getting time to return home and the girls, after waiting longer than they had

expected for them to come to the car, went in search of them but could not find them. It was getting dark and they searched awhile and then went home for help and the search was kept up till about 3 a.m. but did not find the boys so began about daylight again and found them both drowned. Neither one of them could swim and no one knows anything about how they happened to be in the river as they had been very careful to not go in the river without their father being with them. Their clothing was found on the opposite bank from where the girls were. Sandy seemed to have had the cramps and it is supposed that Mike drowned trying to rescue his brother. They were near each other and Mike had his arm over a log and his head nearly out of the water with his face under the water and his upper teeth over his lower lip as tho' he was using every effort to save Sandy but no one knows just how it was. They leave a father, mother and two sisters besides a host of friends. H. Clay Griffin. [Gentry Journal-Advance 8/17/23]

HAAG, Edward - A letter from Mrs. Lua Pollock of Los Angeles, Calif. under date of February 19th, brought word of the death of Ed Haag, a former well known citizen of Rogers. She said he had died that morning at his home at Pasadena but no other particulars were given. The Haags went to California some years ago after having lived here for a number of years. They lived east of the Christian church, first door north of the G.L. Mays home. A clipping from the Pasadena Star News of Monday, February 19 says: "Edward Haag died this morning at his home, 1041 Maple street, at the age of 65 years. He removed here with his family from Long Beach last August. He is survived by his widow, Amanda R. Haag, and one son, William; also three sisters, who reside in Wisconsin. Funeral services will be announced later." [Rogers Democrat 3/1/23]

HAGLER, Jones - Rev. Jones Hagler died a week ago at his home in Centerton at the age of 84 years. [Rogers Democrat 5/10/23]

HALE, Edward E. - {from The Springdale News} Springdale people were called upon Sunday afternoon to perform the last rites for two of the oldest and best known citizens of the community - John L. McQuaid and Edward E. Hale. The former died Saturday morning at two o'clock at his home in the west part of town while Saturday afternoon, a few hours later, Uncle Ed passed away at his home a short distance east of town. The death of these two old citizens the same day has served to recall the friendship that has existed between the two for the past thirty-five years. When Mr. McQuaid and his family came to Springdale in 1887 they first made their home near that of Mr. Hale and family. One was a soldier of the North, while the other was a soldier of the South, and they frequently visited in each other's home, talking, among other things, of the days of the '60's and there grew a spirit of friendship which continued with them through the remainder of their lives. Both were splendid characters and it was not difficult for them to be friends, although having fought in opposing armies, for each recognized and appreciated the good qualities of the other. Mr. McQuaid was 80 years old last September and Mr. Hale was 83. [Rogers Democrat 4/5/23]

HAMILTON, Mollie HUNTER - {from Word} Died, at her home on Spavinaw Nov. 13, Mrs. Mollie Hamilton, very suddenly. Mrs. Hamilton had required the attention of a physician Tuesday morning and in the evening she prepared and ate supper and died at 7 p.m. Heart trouble was the cause. [Gravette News-Herald 11/23/23]

Mrs. Mollie Hamilton was born March 4, 1855 in Cedar Co., Mo.; died Nov. 13, 1923. When 15 years of age she moved to Arkansas with her parents. She married Frank Hamilton in 1881, who died Feb. 12, 1915. To this union were born ten children, five of whom survive. They are: Mrs. Minnie Wilmoth of Oregon; Mrs. Alice Tucker, Merwin, Mo.; Mrs. Ollie Rice, Van Buren, Ark.; Ed Hamilton, Decatur and Wm. Hamilton of California. Also two sisters and three brothers: Mrs. E.J. Allen, Mrs. William Summey, G.E., J.W. and J.D. Hunter. She was a faithful member of the Baptist church. [Gravette News-Herald 11/23/23]

HAMMACK, D.W. {Dock} - D.W. {Dock} Hammack died Monday noon, Oct. 22nd, at the home of his father, W.M. Hammack, on Spring Street as a result of tuberculosis. He was 29 years old and most of his life was spent in Benton Co. He was born near Elkhorn Tavern on Pea Ridge and had lived in Rogers until three years ago last summer when he went to Arizona for his health, returning here in May. Since his return he had been confined to his bed most of the time. Funeral services were held at the home Tuesday afternoon at two o'clock by Rev. Jack Deason and burial was in the Rogers cemetery. Mr. Hammack was married to Miss Colletta Sullivan of Rogers May 2, 1917 and they had one child, a son, who is two years old. He is also survived by two brothers, Mack and Bryan, of this city. [Rogers Democrat 10/25/23]

HANNA, Miles - F.M. Hanna received a telegram Monday morning announcing the death of his son, Prof. Miles Hanna, at his home at Salem, S.D. where he was principal of the schools. Prof. Hanna was known to many of our people as he had spent several summers here with his parents while he was attending college and played ball on the local teams. He has been very successful in his school work and his untimely death has cut short a most promising career. [Rogers Democrat 12/20/23]

HARGIS, Pink - Pink Hargis, 62 years old, died last Wednesday, June 6th at the home of Mrs. Becky Hays in Rogers from an attack of acute nephritis. The deceased was born and raised in the Twelve Corners community on Pea Ridge and was buried in the Rogers cemetery. He was cared for and buried by the county and was brought to Rogers from Pea Ridge some ten days before. He left no family. [Rogers Democrat 6/14/23]

HARRIS, James W. - Rev. James W. Harris, a former resident of Gravette and pastor of the Methodist church, died Monday, July 2, 1923 at an ad-

vanced age. He had been in ill health for some years and but recently he and Mrs. Harris had moved from Bentonville to the flatwoods north of Beaty where Mrs. Harris' brother, Mr. Shirley, resides. Rev. Harris was a brother of N.F. Harris of Beaty and an uncle of Luther Price of Gravette and leaves a host of relatives and friends in the county. The funeral was held today {Thursday} conducted by Rev. H.C. Hoy of Bentonville and burial was at Lee cemetery north of Beaty. [Gravette News-Herald 7/6/23]
Rev. J.W. Harris was born at Pea Ridge October 3, 1852 and died July 2, 1923 at Sulphur Springs at the home of his sister-in-law, Miss Shirley. Brother Harris has been in ill health for about eleven years. He was serving the Huntsville Circuit as pastor of the M.E. Church, South when he was suddenly stricken with paralysis from which he never recovered. During this period he was scarcely able to talk and hardly able to walk. He was very tenderly cared for by his family, especially his good wife. Brother Harris was married to Miss Iva Foster September 5, 1874. To this union were born five boys and two girls of whom three are living, namely Jim Harris of Bentonville; Mrs. M.H. Wright of Bentonville and Mrs. F.P. Tate of Illinois. His first companion was called to her reward and after several years he was united in marriage to Miss Kate Shirley February 12, 1901 who survives him. Bro. Harris became a Christian when twenty-one years of age. He united with the M.E. Church, South and was licensed as a local preacher and in due time ordained as a local elder, took regular work as a supply in the North Arkansas Conference which work he did for about nineteen years when he became afflicted and was no longer able to take work. Rev. Harris was a consecrated man and did efficient work as a Christian minister. He loved his church, family and friends. He was a good man indeed. He leaves to mourn him his wife, three children, twelve grandchildren and one great-grandchild. His life was well lived and will ever be a benediction to all who knew him. [Rogers Democrat 7/26/23]

HARRIS, Mrs. S.P. - Virgil Looney and wife were called to Wichita, Kansas Friday by the death of an aunt of the former, Mrs. S.P. Harris. [Rogers Democrat 7/5/23]

HARVEY, H.T. - {from Garfield} We are sad to state that Monday night about midnight the death angel hovered in our midst and took from us a friend and neighbor, H.T. Harvey. Mr. Harvey has lived in and around Garfield for some four or five years and we have learned to love him as a friend and neighbor. Mr. Harvey was in his car when he took sick near Mr. Spiker's east of town driving some folks in from the river. They phoned his son, E.H. Harvey, and he went and brought him home where he died about midnight the same night. We have not learned at this writing where the burial will be. [Rogers Democrat 5/31/23]

HENDERSON, Everette Chester - Little Everette Chester, 8 months old son of Mr. and Mrs. E. Lee Henderson of Memphis, Tenn. died in the Baptist Hospital of that city on May 30th and was buried in the Greenwood cemetery in Fayetteville June 1st. He was a grandson of Mrs. Belle Henderson of Rogers. [Rogers Democrat 6/7/23]

HENDERSON, Flavius J. - Mrs. Nott received a letter dated March 22, Rochester, New York from Mrs. L.W. Henderson which contains an account of the death of her husband, Flavius J. Henderson, of pneumonia in the hospital of the National Soldiers Home at Danville, Ill. Mr. and Mrs. Henderson are well known in Gentry, having lived here about fifteen years. They went to Kansas from here about six years ago. Mrs. Henderson is staying with her son in Rochester, N.Y. [Gentry Journal-Advance 4/13/23]

HENRY, Mrs. N.S. - Mrs. N.S. Henry died January 18th at Bentonville and had lived there all her life. Death was the result of a stroke of paralysis. [Rogers Democrat 1/25/23]

HEWITT, W.N. - W.N. Hewitt, a prominent business man of Elm Springs, 66 years of age, died recently, the result of a stroke of paralysis. He was for a number of years a resident of Springdale. [Rogers Democrat 10/25/23]

HICKEY, George - George Hickey is dead. George went to Caney, Kansas a few weeks ago to spend some time in that section with friends and the first intimation that anything was wrong with him was a telegram Friday to John W. Bryant announcing his death. In the case of George, one can not call his death sad or untimely for he was well advanced in years, poor in pocket, and had been a sorely deformed cripple from birth and there were a lot of queer kinks in his mind. And yet he will be missed by a great many people who for years have been accustomed to seeing him on the walk or in doorways on First street selling papers, pencils, gum, etc. George was never a man to bewail his infirmities. He accepted them as a handicap but never complained and was always the first to laugh at his awkwardness in getting about. He was always cheerful, always optimistic; things were always soon to be better for him. Suggestions to the effect that he be sent to the County Home were often made but he would not hear to it - he wanted to be his "own boss." The weather had to be extreme to keep him indoors or away from his beat. He will be missed by the editor for he had been bringing laughs into the Democrat office for some twenty or more years. Our acquaintance began when he lived with his widowed mother out on West Walnut street and sent in items from that neighborhood. George always had literary aspirations and was a frequent and voluminous contributor to the Democrat's waste basket. The non-appearance of his articles never worried George altho he frequently commented on the punk literary tastes of the editor. {A habit, by the way, that was not original with him.} The Democrat never had a more exacting critic. He was very near sighted but he used to spot mis-spelled words and incorrect statements {usually wrong initials or street locations} and take the editor to task at most inopportune times. George was no diplomat. But it was always such good natured "kidding" that we hate to realize there will be no more of it.

And those visits from George when he would return from one of his periodic swings through Oklahoma, Kansas and Arkansas. He was frequently arrested and often jailed for selling without a license but it worried him not a whit. It only meant free board and lodging and a welcome rest and when he tired of the jail fare or beds George would commence singing and keep it up day and night until they were glad to release him and hand him enough to pay his fare to the next town. He was the only person we ever knew who could sing himself into or out of jail with equal facility. He had no ear whatever for music but what he lacked in quality he more than made up in quantity. It was not an easy matter to tell where that childish innocence of his ended and where his mature shrewdness and intelligence began. He read much and had a wide range of general information and was far from being the half-wit that a lot of casual observers believed him to be. One never knew whether George believed those wonderful yarns he used to spin or was having fun in his own way with his hearers. But we know he dreamed great dreams and tried for years to put them into words in stories, books and more recently into moving picture scenarios. If he really lived in that make-believe world of his he was happier than most people; and if it was always only make-believe to relieve a drab and burdened life, and he knew it, he was a real philosopher. George Hickey goes into local history as one of the most interesting characters the Democrat editor has ever known. And the editor knows, too, that he has never had a more faithful friend and well-wisher. George Hickey was almost sixty years old and a native of Indiana. He is survived by two sisters and a brother. A sister, Mrs. L.E. Starrett and husband of Mariana, Ark., were here for the funeral which was held Sunday afternoon at the Rogers cemetery where he was buried by the side of his mother who died several years ago. [Rogers Democrat 8/16/23]

HICKS, Joe - {from Mt. Zion} Joe Hicks, who was sick with flu and other ailments, was buried Friday at Falling Springs cemetery. He left a wife and four children, an aged father and mother, and other relatives to mourn his departure. [Gentry Journal-Advance 2/23/23]

HIGGINBOTHAM, George Hunter - Philadelphia, Pa., Nov. 9.- Officials of the Marine Corps here are investigating the death of Private George H. Higginbotham, thirty-four years old, a member of the Marine Corps for twelve years, who was found dead on Thursday with a bullet hole in his chest. The marine was standing guard outside the court room at the Philadelphia navy yard when those attending the trial heard a shot. Investigating, they found Higginbotham lying on the floor in front of the door, face downward and a bullet hole in the right side of his heart. His automatic pistol was by his side, although officials of the navy yard refuse to say whether or not it contained an empty cartridge. Capt. Chas. King, commander of the company to which Higginbotham was attached, was emphatic in his praise of the dead marine. "Higginbotham was a good soldier and a fine example of American manhood," said Captain King. "I personally think he was accidentally killed by his own weapon. But it will be up to the board of inquiry to decide that. The dead soldier came to my outfit November 1. He came here from Cincinnati where he had been doing recruiting service. Previous to that he had fought overseas and was decorated at least twice for bravery. Private Higginbotham was born in Virginia April 28, 1889 but entered the service from Bentonville, Arkansas. he had been in the service for twelve years and in that time his service record had been absolutely perfect." [Rogers Democrat 11/15/23]

Bentonville, Nov. 12.- The body of Private George Hunter Higginbotham, U.S. Marine Corps, arrived at Rogers Monday morning and was taken to Oakley Chapel for burial, funeral services being conducted Monday afternoon by Rev. J.M. McMahen of the Bentonville Baptist church. Members of the Bentonville Post of the American Legion served as pallbearers and the casket was draped in the American flag. After serving in the Marine corps eight years he was out of the service four years but re-enlisted last August after a visit at his home near Bentonville. He was thirty-four, unmarried and is survived by his mother, Mrs. G.W. Higginbotham, and three brothers - Dr. M.H., J.D. and S.C. Higginbotham of Bentonville; six sisters - Mesdames M.L. Voyles and Edward Engstrom of Little Rock; C.L. Denny of Eads, Colo.; F.W. Hallock of Buffalo, Okla.; A.W. Fullerton of Neosho, Mo. and J.L. Cockrell of Fort Wayne, Indiana. [Rogers Democrat 11/15/23]

HIGHFILL, M.S. - On Monday evening September 10th at 7 o'clock occurred the death of Mrs. M.S. Highfill at the home of her daughter, Mrs. J.F. Mitchell. She was born in Perry Co., Tennessee Aug. 22, 1847. She was married to Hezekiah Highfill February 10, 1860 in Missouri. They moved to Benton county, Ark. in 1869, settling where the little town of Highfill now stands and there they made their home until the death of Mr. Highfill five years ago. She professed faith in Christ at the age of 13 and united with the Baptist church and ever lived a conscientious christian life. Mrs. Highfill had been confined to her room for nine months. She was a patient sufferer, never complaining, and ever thoughtful for those caring for her. She realized her condition was hopeless and that only a few more days were her's here on earth; but she had the faith that cast out all fear. She is survived by six children: Mrs. J.F. Mitchell of Gentry; Dr. J.E. Highfill, Cave Springs; C.D. Highfill, Ardmore, Okla.; Frank Highfill of Siloam Springs; Mrs. Sherman Lefors of Gentry and Mrs. J.N. Covey of Little Rock; also two brothers and one sister. Short services were held at her home Wednesday afternoon at 1:30 conducted by Rev. Collier of this place and Rev. J.A. Scoggins of Decatur. The remains were taken to Highfill where funeral services were held in the church where deceased had long held her membership and the body was laid to rest beside that of her husband, surrounded by a host of relatives and friends. [Gentry Journal-Advance 9/21/23]

HILL, Sarah - {from Lowell} Mrs. Nelson Bishop received word Monday of the death of an aunt, Mrs. Sarah Hill, who lived at Drake's creek, Madison county. [Rogers Democrat 7/26/23]

HINDS, Regina Beatrice FORWOOD - Mrs. Willis Miller received word Friday of the death of her daughter-in-law, Mrs. Homer Hinds, at Monett. A child was born several weeks ago and Mrs. Hinds had never recovered from the illness. She is survived by her husband and four children. She was a daughter of Reginald Forwood, a former well known Rogers citizen, by his first wife and was known to many Rogers people who regret very much to learn of her untimely death. [Rogers Democrat 111523]
{from The Monett Daily Times} Funeral services for Mrs. Homer Hinds who died Friday afternoon, November 9, were held at the St. Stephens Episcopal church Sunday afternoon, the rector, Rev. F.A. Foster of Carthage, officiating. Services at the cemetery were conducted by the local G.I.A. lodge of which Mrs. Hinds was a past president. Regina Beatrice Forwood was born August 11, 1886 at Wellsboro, Pa. Her parents were from Liverpool, England. When she was quite young her parents separated and each married again. Her mother died in February 1922 at Rochester, N.Y. Her father is in Toronto, Canada and as his address is not known here he has not been notified of his daughter's death but an effort is being made to find him. The deceased was a graduate of the high school at Wellsboro, Pa. She was married to Homer C. Hinds of Monett in 1909. They were the parents of four children - Howard Emmett, age 13 years; Richard Carl, 12; Homer Leonard, 6 years, and Wilma Joe, age 20 days. The death of this young wife is very sad, leaving, as she does, small children without a mother's care. [Rogers Democrat 11/22/23]

HINMAN, son - {from Hiwasse} The 3 year old son of Rev. and Mrs. Hinman died August 15 and interment was at Mt. Pleasant cemetery. [Gravette News-Herald 8/24/23]

HODGES, Ira M. - Ira M. Hodges, aged 69 years, died Monday, October 22nd at his home two miles north of Rogers. He was stricken down by paralysis while he was working in the orchard and lived only a few minutes after being taken to the house. Funeral services were held Thursday afternoon at 2:30 at the Callison Undertaking parlor and were conducted by Rev. T.E. McSpadden. Burial was in the local cemetery. The deceased had lived north of Rogers some eight or nine years, coming here from Frankfort, Kansas. He had never married and made his home with his sister, Miss Emma E. Hodges. A brother, George L. Hodges of Guyman, Okla., came for the funeral and is remaining for a few days while his sister decides what she will do. [Rogers Democrat 11/1/23]

HOLLIS, L.Y. - W.E. McGehee and family were called to Siloam Springs the last of the week by the death of Mrs. McGehee's father, L.Y. Hollis, at the age of 69 years. Mr. Hollis and wife made their home in Rogers last year on North Sixth street near Mr. McGehee but moved back to Siloam

Springs in December. He had been ill some time and died at the home of his daughter, Mrs. Clyde Inman, two miles north of Siloam Springs. [Rogers Democrat 2/22/23]

HOLT, Maud OAKES - Mrs. Maud (Oakes) Holt was born in southwest Missouri near Granby, Jan. 7, 1894, moved to Benton County, Ark. the fall of 1899 and was married to John E. Holt in the winter of 1909 and came to Florida to live in the fall of 1920; died Oct. 21, 1923 following the birth of a child. She leaves a husband, 3 sons, 3 daughters, a mother, 2 brothers and 2 sisters. She was a true Christian and loved to do God's will. Arthur E. Oakes, Zephyr Hill, Fla. [Gravette News-Herald 11/16/23]

HOSSMAN, Mrs. James - Mrs. James Hossman, aged 58, died at her home Tuesday, June 5. Burial was Wednesday at Bethel Cemetery. [Gravette News-Herald 6/8/23]

HOTT, D.G. - On May 20th, 1923 our town and community was made to sorrow from the going of our beloved brother and fellow citizen, D.G. Hott. Mr. Hott was not a native of this state but was born in Romney, W. Va. November 30, 1840 where he spent his boyhood days. He was married to Miss Harriet Jane Combs in 1865 to which union five children were born. Moving from there to New York state where he lived for a number of years. Leaving there for the state of Ohio where he lost his wife and 5 children who preceded him in death. In a few years he was married to Mrs. Mary Francis Walden who lived to mourn his going, together with the step-daughter and husband. He was a kind, loving husband and father. Mr. Hott has been a citizen with us about six years. He had proved to be a splendid citizen, standing for the things that were uplifting to the town, community and church. He was a member of the Baptist church of which church he had been a deacon for more than 40 years. He was a true and loyal soldier of his Lord as long as he lived. He was a member of the Odd Fellows of which organization he was a loyal and true member and was the last of the charter members to depart this world. Deceased was a confederate soldier and fought in the civil war. The funeral services was held in the home of his step-daughter after which his remains was carried to his old home in Ohio to be laid to rest with those of his family who preceded him in death. The funeral was conducted by Rev. Parsons, pastor of the Congregational church, and Rev. R.A. Collier, his pastor. [Gentry Journal-Advance 5/25/23]

HOUSTON, J.H. - (from Pleasant Hill) Again the death angel has visited our community, taking J.H. Houston. He was 46 years old and had been in declining health for over a year. He leaves a wife and four children to mourn his loss. While yet a young man he was converted and joined the Missionary Baptist church and lived a Christian life until his death June 1. The funeral services were held at the home Saturday morning by Rev. Crichlow of Rogers. Interment was made in the Meek's cemetery near Springdale. [Rogers Democrat 6/7/23]

HOWARD, M.R. - Mrs. W.L. Clark was called to Decatur last Friday on account of the death of M.R. Howard. Mrs. Howard is an aunt of Mr. Clark. Mr. Howard was the father of Mrs. Dewey Wagner of Kansas City and of Mrs. Walter Frazer of Riverside, Calif. He had been in poor health for some months. [Gravette News-Herald 8/31/23]

HUBBERT, Mrs. Geo. - Word was received Tuesday morning by Rogers friends of the death of Mrs. Geo. Hubbert of Neosho of flu and pneumonia. Mrs. Hubbert, who was the mother of Mrs. Horace Miller, was well known to many Rogers people and the news of her death was learned with much regret. The Hubbert family at one time owned the orchard west of Rogers later owned by M. Wheatley and for many years known as the Hubbert farm. [Rogers Democrat 2/8/23]

HUDSON, Eugene - Fayetteville, July 26.- Lightning struck and instantly killed little Eugene Hudson, 3-year-old son of Geo. Hudson and wife, tenant farmers on the place of Judge Ernest Dowell here, burned down the family's two room house and left Mrs. Hudson in a dazed and serious condition late Wednesday afternoon. The child was sitting near an open window when struck. His clothing and the room of the house immediately became enveloped in flames which attracted the attention of a neighbor who went to the rescue. A wire clothes line attached to the house is thought to have attracted the lightning to the dwelling. Mrs. Hudson, who is 22 years old, was alone with her two children in the house, the husband being at work on a farm four miles away. The children, Eugene, and a little girl two years old, were in one room and the mother in an adjoining room when the bolt struck. When help arrived the mother had taken the little girl out of doors and placed an umbrella over her to protect her from the rain. She had not touched the body of the little boy and seemed to be suffering from the shock. The dead child was brought from the house by Ernest Swaggerty just as the roof fell in. During the same storm several workmen were shocked and a mule was killed on the Carl Ownbey farm, eight miles north of here. [Rogers Democrat 8/2/23]

HUFFMAN, John R. - The veteran printer-editor, John R. Huffman, who established the Sulphur Springs Speaker over 30 years ago, "laid down on his couch" and entered the mystic realm Monday at his daughter's home at Sulphur Springs. Mr. Huffman was past 80 years of age. [Gravette News-Herald 1/5/23]

INGRAM, Frank - {from Lowell} Frank Ingram, who made his home with his daughter, Mrs. Claud Nail, east of town, died last Thursday. Burial was in the Danford cemetery on White river. [Rogers Democrat 6/21/23]

JAY, Charlie - When Charlie Jay was down town a week ago Monday friends could not have believed that on Friday night following he would depart this life. But following an attack of pneumonia, such was the case and Friend Jay passed away Friday night, January 5, 1923 at the age of 62 years. Mr. Jay was born in Sheridan, Iowa Dec. 6, 1861. He was married to

Miss Clara J. Matterson May 8, 1884 and moved soon after to Frontier county, Neb. About this time he united with the M.E. church, being a faithful member until 1908 when Mr. and Mrs. Jay came to Gravette and placed their membership with the M.E. Church, South and have ever contributed very liberally, both of finances and personal work, to the cause. With plenty of the world's goods, Mr. Jay busied himself here only with insurance work, devoting much time to fraternal work, being a Mason and Modern Woodman, and for years as Sunday school superintendent. No appeal of merit to Charlie Jay was turned but met with prompt response accompanied by his perpetual smile. No wonder the church would not accommodate the throng that attended the funeral Sunday morning, for everyone enjoyed his friendship and jovial disposition. The funeral was conducted by Presiding Elder Oliver, assisted by the pastor, Rev. W.M. Shelton, and in a memorial to Mr. Jay, A.C. Davis, in behalf of the citizens, and Joel F. Smith, representing the Masons and Woodmen, paid high tribute to the departed fellowman and W.A. Patton eulogized Mr. Jay as a fellow churchman. Besides the wife Mr. Jay leaves one sister, Mrs. John C. Kuhns of Chicago; one uncle, Evan Jay, and one cousin, Louie Jay of Fort Scott, Kansas, all of whom were present at the funeral. The body was taken to Bertrand, Neb. Sunday night, Mrs. Jay and Evan Jay accompanying the same to its last resting place. The community unites with the News Herald in offering condolence to the bereaved ones. [Gravette News-Herald 1/12/23]

JEFFERSON, Tom - J.H. Black, who was born in Benton county eighty years ago but who has lived in Oklahoma for many years, has been visiting at Bentonville and other points in the county. He was born east of Bentonville in the Jefferson neighborhood and has many interesting stories of conditions before the Civil War. He went to school to Uncle Wade Sikes of Rogers, who is still living. It is seldom that a pupil and teacher, of 80 and 93 years respectively, meet and exchange stories of school time days. Mr. Black served in the Confederate army and was in the company under command of Captain Tom Jefferson, who was killed during the war. [Rogers Democrat 8/23/23]

JOHNSON, Tillie MUSE - {from The Rock Island Journal} Mrs. J.A. Johnson, aged 68 years, wife of J.A. Johnson, deputy county recorder, died at 1 o'clock Jan. 16 in Siloam Springs, Ark. following an illness of several years. She had been at Siloam Springs since June last for her health. Mrs. Johnson, who was formerly Miss Tillie Muse, was born on Carr's Island near Milan July 11, 1854. She was a student in Eaglewood Normal school and afterward a teacher in the public schools in Milan and Moline, and Washington, Kans. She had been a resident of Rock Island practically all of her life. Surviving are the widower, J.A. Johnson, Rock Island, a daughter, Mrs. Stella Witherill, teacher in the state school for the deaf at Baton Rouge, La.; two brothers, James A. Muse, Rock Island and Will F., Mason City, Iowa, and a sister, Miss Ada Muse, teacher in the Kemble school,

Rock Island. ***** The deceased is well-known by many friends in and around Gentry, having spent part of the time the last few years on their farm on Flint creek and part of the time here in town. [Gentry Journal-Advance 1/26/23]

JOHNSON, William T. - William T. Johnson of the Vaughn neighborhood, died Tuesday, March 13th at the home of his son, Dick Johnson, on North A street. Funeral was held Wednesday afternoon at 3 o'clock, conducted by Rev. Barrett of the Baptist church, with interment in the Rogers cemetery. [Rogers Democrat 3/15/23]

JONES, Mr. and Mrs. Frank - {from Hiwasse} The community much regrets the death of Mr. and Mrs. Frank Jones, he dying March 2 and she, March 4th. These good people had resided here many years; were members of the Christian church, the pastor of which conducted the funerals on Sunday and Tuesday, following the death. Burial at Mt. Pleasant. [Gravette News-Herald 3/16/23]

KENT, sister - {from War Eagle} B.B. Kent received a message last week of the death of his sister in Oklahoma but the message reached him too late to attend the funeral. [Rogers Democrat 11/8/23]

KING, Arch - Crazed by worrying over domestic troubles, very largely of his own making, Arch King committed suicide Sunday morning by swallowing a dose of strychnine. He was under arrest at the time and had made his escape from Deputy Sheriff Bob Wells, who was taking him to Bentonville to place him in the county jail, by jumping from the automobile several miles west of Rogers on the Walnut street road. There is small doubt but that the thought of suicide had been in King's mind for some time for the poison was secured from a Rogers drug store early that morning, just after he had arrived from Kansas City on the morning train and before he attempted to see his wife or before he had been threatened with arrest, although he knew that he faced the latter when he returned to Rogers. The charge against him was not serious enough to warrant such a desperate act to escape the law and his suicide appears to have been a premeditated step to wind up his earthly troubles should he fail to secure the children or effect a reconciliation with his wife. King, who was a trifle over 28 years old, was born and raised in Benton county and was a son of Sam King. He was married and leaves a wife and 3 daughters, the oldest about 8; the youngest, 3. His wife is a daughter of John Matthews and wife of Rogers and she and the girls had been living with them since King was arrested about July 4 and fined on the charge of assaulting and cursing his wife. Other warrants were issued on various charges and King was under bond for the September term of circuit court. Deputy Wells also had a warrant for his arrest for breach of the peace. King left the state, going to Kansas City where he found work and was staying with his sisters, Mrs. W.L. Cromwell and Mrs. Bessie Myers, both formerly of Rogers. According to the sisters King was anxious for his wife and children to come to him in

Kansas City and blamed all the trouble upon his wife's parents, Mr. and Mrs. Matthews. They say he wrote to Rogers asking his wife to join him and when he received no answer, worried himself almost sick and finally decided to come to Rogers, saying that he would at least bring the children back with him. He arrived in Rogers Sunday morning but before going to the Matthews home bought a small bottle of strychnine. He called twice at the place but his wife was not there and he did not see her. In the meantime Mr. Matthews notified Deputy Wells that King was back and feared that he meant to make trouble. King was placed under arrest and Wells, accompanied by Matthews, started with their prisoner for Bentonville. He was very abusive of his father-in-law, declaring him to be the cause of his arrest and of all his troubles. About two and one-half miles west of town King sprang from the car which was making about fifteen miles an hour, and before it could be stopped had regained his feet and started across the field on the run. Several men in that neighborhood joined in the chase and he was overtaken after a run of a mile or so. Wells took him back to the car and they proceeded on the trip to Bentonville. Before they arrived King became violently ill and was hurried to the office of the sheriff and physicians hastily summoned. It was too late however to give him any relief and he died within a few minutes. Funeral services were held at the City Cemetery yesterday afternoon at 2:30 o'clock and were conducted by Rev. J.L. Barrett of the Baptist church. His sisters were here from Kansas City as well as his father and other relatives, for they have many relatives in and around Rogers. Mrs. Henry Goodhart of Rogers is an aunt and Burr Potts an uncle of the deceased. [Rogers Democrat 8/30/23]

KUEBLER, John - The Decatur Herald reports the death of John Kuebler, well known fruit shipper of Decatur, his death occurring at Tampa, Fla. Oct. 30th. [Gravette News-Herald 11/9/23]

LANPHERE, Stiles - A telegram was received here Tuesday evening telling of the death of Stiles Lanphere at his home in Wisconsin. Mr. Lanphere and family came to Gentry with the Seventh-day Baptist colony about 22 years ago and resided here about seven years. He was a brother-in-law of D.E. Maxson and Dan Ricketts of this place. [Gentry Journal-Advance 1/23/23]

LAUDERMILK, Mrs. Hal - Mrs. Hal Laudermilk died Saturday at her home in this city and funeral services were held Sunday afternoon at the Christian church at two o'clock, conducted by the pastor, Rev. H.B. Cline. The deceased is survived by her husband and two-year-old child. She was 19 years old. [Rogers Democrat 9/27/23]

LEACH, Everett - Everett Leach, age 11 years, son of Mr. and Mrs. Frank Leach, died Monday night from a complication of diseases and was buried Tuesday. [Gentry Journal-Advance 6/1/323]

LEFORS, Eliza A. JANUARY - Mrs. Eliza A. Lefors was the daughter of Joseph January. She was born Feb. 20, 1841 near Nashville, Tenn. and died at her home near Gentry June 9, 1923, age 86 years, 3 months and 20 days. Miss January came to Benton County with her parents before the Civil war. Here she married Thomas M. Lefors. To this union three sons were born: Thomas, William and Joseph, all of whom survive her. Her husband died during the Civil war. Funeral services were conducted at the home Saturday June 9 at 4 p.m. by Revs. Martin and Sherman and she was laid to rest in the Bozarth Cemetery. [Gentry Journal-Advance 6/15/23]

LeGRAND, Rosa GRAVES - {from an Anaheim, Calif. newspaper} Rev. Leon L. Myers received a message recently conveying the sad news of the death of Mrs. John H. LeGrand, wife of the noted evangelist, whose passing comes as a shock to the many local friends and persons with whom the couple were acquainted. Death came on the operating table. Rev. and Mrs. LeGrand are remembered as having conducted a most successful revival meeting over Southern California last winter and during their stay in Los Angeles many Anaheim persons heard them. Mrs. LeGrand was a talented vocalist and directed the big chorus. They were dated for a series of meetings in Santa Ana beginning April 1. ***** Deceased was well known in Gentry, having resided here several years ago when she was Miss Rosa Graves. [Gentry Journal-Advance 3/2/23]

LEIB, W.H. - W.H. Leib, former Gravette citizen and Joplin's foremost professor of music, died at his home in Joplin, Mo. at the age of 81 years following an attack of heart trouble. Prof. Leib had many friends in Gravette. He was one of America's foremost singers and teachers of music. The funeral will be held Friday in charge of the Scottish Rite Masons. [Gravette News-Herald 5/4/23]

LEWIS, Lucy E. Brown - Mrs. Lucy E. Lewis, wife of Jacob Lewis, died Thursday, Oct. 11, 1923 at the home west of town, aged 70 years. She was born in Iowa. Mrs. Lewis had been in ill health for some years and had been in the hospital at Wichita, Kan. for treatment until a short time ago. Besides the husband Mrs. Lewis leaves one son, Ernest Brown, by a former marriage. The son was in Oklahoma at the time of her death and was not located until Wednesday this week, at Quapah, hence the funeral was delayed awaiting his return. As we go to press funeral arrangements are not yet made. [Gravette News-Herald 10/19/23]

LINCOLN, George T. - {from The Bentonville Record} Captain George T. Lincoln, one of the best known fruit men in Northwest Arkansas and Southwest Missouri, died at 5 o'clock Wednesday morning, January 24th, 1923 at St. Petersburg, Florida of pneumonia. Captain Lincoln was 86 years old and has been in ill health for some time. The remains will be brought back to Bentonville for burial. In 1916 he married Mrs. Mary Luther of Wingo, Ky. and has made his home in that city ever since, making annual visits back to Bentonville and spending his winters in Florida. Besides his widow he is survived by one son, George Morton Lincoln. Mr. Lincoln was born near Liberty, Mo. in 1836. He was educated in Kentucky and at the

William Jewell College at Liberty, Mo. He was married in 1859 to Virginia W. Pryor, to whom was born one son, G. Morton Lincoln. The mother died in childbirth. He served in the Confederate army under General Forrest and was in a number of important battles. At the close of the war he was married in Mississippi to Miss Ellen Sikes. Captain Lincoln came to Arkansas in 1884 and engaged in the mercantile business with J.C. Arthur. Later he became interested in fruit growing and purchased the Bunch farm and orchard west of town. He devoted a great deal of attention to his fruit farm and the Lincoln Orchards became noted throughout this section. With the organization of the Ozark Fruit Growers Association in 1904 he became one of its first directors and at the annual meeting in January 1906 was unanimously elected president of that organization and held this position until 1917 when he refused to serve longer. [Rogers Democrat 2/1/23]

LOCKE, James Thomas - While our people knew that Prof. Tom Locke was ill and that he had been compelled to retire from his work in the High School several months ago, very few save his most intimate friends realized the seriousness of his condition and the news of his death last Friday evening about six o'clock came as a most unwelcome shock to practically the entire community. Death came as a result of complications of asthma and heart trouble. He died at his home on West Persimmon street in the northwest part of town. Funeral services were held at the Central M.E. church Saturday afternoon at three o'clock and were conducted by the pastor, Rev. Crichlow. Members of the school board acted as pall bearers and the pupils of the Eighth grade, which he taught in the High School building this year, attended the services in a body. Burial was in the Rogers cemetery. James Thomas Locke was born in Shelbyville, Tenn. April 18, 1865. He came to Benton county when a young man and has taught in the county schools continuously ever since, over a period of thirty-five years. He had taught in the country schools most until he moved to Rogers, where he served as principal in the days before there was a regular high school, in the Fairground Addition school, and for the past seven years has been at the head of the city grammar school. In October of this year failing health compelled him to give up his work after having served this community faithfully and well for nearly his entire working life. [Rogers Democrat 12/20/23]

LONG, Robert - {from Maysville} Robert Long died Wednesday, Oct. 10 at the National Soldiers' Home in Wisconsin. The body was sent here for burial. Rob was a soldier in the World war and had been in poor health for the past year. Interment was made in Tinnin cemetery Monday, Oct. 15. He leaves several brothers and sisters and many friends who mourn his departure. [Gravette News-Herald 10/19/23]

LYNN, Mary BANKS - Mary Banks Lynn was born in Tennessee Feb. 23, 1848 and passed away August 2, 1923 at the home of her daughter, Mrs. John Patton, aged 85 years, 5 months and 8 days. Other than this daughter she leaves seven grandchildren, one brother and many other relatives and friends. Another daughter, Isabel Brown, preceded her to the better world. Mrs. Lynn was a Banks, related to the several Banks families at Hiwasse, also was an aunt of James Banks and Mrs. J.S. Steward of Gravette. Mrs. Lynn, better known as "Aunt Mary," accepted Christ as her Savior early in life and was a sweet Christian character. Rev. W.M. Shelton conducted the funeral at Mt. Pleasant Friday, Aug. 3 and the body was laid to rest in the cemetery close by, a large gathering of relatives and friends being present. [Gravette News-Herald 8/10/23]

McANALLY, James K. - James K. McAnally was born July 5, 1881, died March 3, 1923 at his home west of Gravette, age 41 years, 7 months and 28 days. Mr. McAnally was converted 20 years ago and united with the Pleasant Home Baptist church, was baptized and endeavored to live a Christian life. He leaves mother, 4 brothers and 3 sisters. His youngest brother and twin sister, Mrs. Martha Gilbert, were with him during his illness and death. Burial was at McCraw cemetery, Elder John West conducting the funeral. Sympathy is extended the bereaved family. [Gravette News-Herald 3/9/23]

McBRINN, R.J. - John W. Nance received a telegram Monday morning telling of the death of his brother-in-law, R.J. McBrinn, the previous night at his home in Oklahoma City. Mr. Nance left for Oklahoma City at once to attend the funeral which was held on Tuesday. Mrs. McBrinn is a former well known Rogers girl and is best remembered here as Miss Bonnie Nance, a daughter of Mrs. R.L. Nance, now of Fayetteville. [Rogers Democrat 3/29/23]

McCLINTON, Lela May - {from Lowell} Lela May McClinton, daughter of Theo. McClinton, south of Springdale, died Monday night of pneumonia fever. The McClintons lived for many years south of Lowell and have a host of friends who sympathize with them in their sad hour of bereavement. [Rogers Democrat 4/12/23]

McCOMBS, Eddie - {from Hiwasse} Eddie McCombs died at his home east of town Tuesday morning and was laid to rest in the Mt. Pleasant cemetery Wednesday afternoon. [Gravette News-Herald 12/28/23]

McCOY, Mattie - {from Oakley Chapel} Hugh Britt and wife, Cy McSpadden and wife, Lee Britt and wife and daughter and Mrs. Sarah Britt attended the funeral of Mrs. Sarah Britt's cousin, Mrs. Mattie McCoy, of Elm Springs Sunday. [Rogers Democrat 5/17/23]
{from Fairmount} Rev. Sherman, who was to have preached at Fairmount Sunday, May 13, was called to Elm to attend the funeral of his wife's aunt, Mrs. McCoy. He will preach here next Sunday, the 20th. Everybody invited. [Gentry Journal-Advance 5/18/23]

McCOY, Mrs. - {from War Eagle} Angus McCoy was called to Oklahoma Sunday by the death of his mother. Mrs. McCoy had lived near War Eagle for several years and had many friends here who will be grieved to learn of her death. She leaves a daughter and two sons to mourn her loss. She had been an invalid for several years and has lived with her daughter in Oklahoma for the past two years. We extend our sympathy to the bereaved family. [Rogers Democrat 10/25/23]

McKINZIE, Chas. - {from Lowell} Chas. McKinzie, living east of town, died Saturday morning after an attack of typhoid fever. He was born in Tennessee and was 50 years old at the time of his death. He and his wife came to Lowell 2 or 3 years ago and he has been engaged in the carpenter trade. He made many friends during his short stay here and was held in the highest esteem by all who knew him. Funeral services were conducted at the home Sunday afternoon by Rev. Marmon. Burial in Goad Springs cemetery. He leaves a wife to mourn his loss. [Rogers Democrat 6/7/23]

McMILLEN, Nancy Louiza JONES - Nancy Louiza Jones was born Oct. 25, 1853 at Bellfountain, Iowa and died at her home one half mile east of Gentry Jan. 19, 1923. She was united in marriage to S. McMillen May 25, 1871. To this union was born 7 children, all of whom are living. Mr. McMillen passed away August 6, 1921. Mrs. McMillen has been for many years a faithful member of the Congregational church. In her life she was unobtrusive, kindly and christian. She lived out the days appointed her and then fell asleep in Jesus. The funeral was conducted by Rev. Edward Parsons at the Congregational church Sunday afternoon, Jan. 21. [Gentry Journal-Advance 1/26/23]

J.M. McMillen and wife of Enid, Okla. attended the funeral of the former's mother, Mrs. Nancy McMillen, here last Sunday. [Gentry Journal-Advance 1/26/23]

MABRY, child - {from Lowell} The 3-year-old child of Mr. and Mrs. Colonel Mabry died Monday after a lingering illness. The little fellow got a bad fall some time ago and had never been well since. The community extends their heart-felt sympathy to Mr. and Mrs. Mabry in their hour of bereavement. [Rogers Democrat 3/1/23]

MAGGI, Ardis - J.V. Maggi of Rogers was called to Sherman, Texas last week by the death of his five-year-old granddaughter, Ardis Maggi, daughter of E.F. Maggi and wife, former residents of Rogers. The little girl was struck by an automobile and the driver is in jail charged with negligent homicide. [Rogers Democrat 11/29/23]

MARLIN, Mellissa E. MERRITT - Frank M. Marlin left last evening for Kansas City where he had been called by a telegram announcing the death of his mother, Mrs. J.W. Marlin, who died in that city Tuesday at the home of her son, Cal A. Marlin, at the age of 83 years. Burial will be at Adrian, Mo. beside her husband who died just six years ago while living at Exeter, Mo. Mrs. Marlin's maiden name was Mellissa E. Merritt and she was born in Knox Co., Ohio, marrying J.W. Marlin in 1861. They came to Benton county in 1893 from Audubon county, Iowa and lived here for nearly twenty-five years. [Rogers Democrat 12/20/23]

MARSH, Elizabeth M. FERGUSON - Mrs. Elizabeth M. Marsh, who has been afflicted for some time at the home of her daughter, Mrs. W.H. Hoffman, passed away Sunday morning Feb. 25, 1923. Elizabeth M. Ferguson was born at Brownsville, Mo. {later called Sweet Springs} May 18, 1856; was married to John W. Marsh Oct. 3, 1875 at Richomnd, Ky. Mr. Marsh died Dec. 22, 1907. There were three children: Richard T. Marsh, who died Jan. 19, 1909 and two daughters who survive, Mrs. Myrtle M. Hoffman and Miss Gladys Marsh, also one granddaughter, Mary Elizabeth Hoffman, all of Gravette, two brothers and one sister. Deceased was a daughter of Capt. Richard Lee Ferguson, at one time member of the Missouri state legislature. The body was taken to Kansas City Sunday where the funeral was held and she was laid to rest on Tuesday beside her husband and son in Forrestville cemetery. Gravette people unite in extending the bereaved ones condolence. [Gravette News-Herald 3/2/23]

MARSHALL, Mr. and Mrs. - {from Bozarth} We are sorry to announce the death of Mr. and Mrs. Marshall. They were nice people and will be much missed in the neighborhood. [Gentry Journal-Advance 1/19/23]

MARTIN, Joe - Joe Martin, living at Rock House in Madison county, not far from Huntsville, committed suicide Saturday by shooting himself with a rifle. He was 45 years old. No motive is known. [Rogers Democrat 4/12/23]

MATTHEWS, Paul E. - {from The Beaumont, Texas Daily} The body of Paul E. Matthews, infant son of Mr. and Mrs. Fred Matthews, 1125 Wall Street, was buried Wednesday afternoon following services at the residence. Interment was in Magnolia cemetery. ***** Fred Matthews is a former Rogers boy, a son of Mr. and Mrs. Zeke Matthews and a nephew of Mrs. Frank Matthews of this city. [Rogers Democrat 2/15/23]

MAXWELL, J.H. - J.H. Maxwell, a well known business man of Kingston, Madison Co., died very suddenly last week of heart failure. He was engaged in the drug business. [Rogers Democrat 8/16/23]

MIDDLETON, Mary Israel - {from New Hope} Mrs. J.C. Key, who lives in Rogers, reports the death of her only aunt, Mrs. Mary Middleton, which occurred at Lawton, Okla. February 26th on her 76th birthday at the home of her daughter, Mrs. Annie Brown. Mrs. Middleton lived for many years on Prairie Creek and had many relatives and friends in Arkansas who will be sorry to hear of her death for she was a good Christian woman. She will perhaps be remembered best as Mrs. Mary Israel. She visited Mrs. Key and other Benton county relatives three years ago. [Rogers Democrat 3/22/23]

MILLER, son - {from Monte Ne} We all sympathize with Mr. and Mrs. Miller in the loss of their little son who died last week and was buried at Stony Point cemetery. [Rogers Democrat 4/5/23]

MILLER, Billy - Billy Miller, 69 years of age, died last week at the Benton County Home. He at one time conducted a watch repair shop in

Bentonville but suffered a stroke of paralysis and was taken to the Home. [Rogers Democrat 3/1/23]

MILLER, Morgan - Word has been received by relatives that Willis Miller failed to reach the side of his son, Morgan Miller, at Chippewa Falls, Wis. before he passed away Saturday night, June 9. Mr. Miller was delayed in leaving and did not succeed in getting thru until Monday. Loy Miller left here earlier in the week and reached his brother before he died. [Rogers Democrat 6/14/23]

Morgan Miller, son of Willis Miller, was born at Templeton, Iowa April 5, 1889 and died at Chippewa Falls, Wis. June 9, 1923. He came to Arkansas with his parents while a small boy and grew to manhood in and near Rogers. He spent 18 months overseas and came home in Division 9 with Pershing and spent a time in Washington, D.C. in the parades of that division. Morgan and his brother, Steve, were Shorthorn stock raisers in Iowa before the war several years and after his return they decided to go into a new country where they could have more land so moved to upper Wisconsin and built homes and started in a very pleasant though hard life of building up a new country. Morgan was one to have friends as acquaintances and all went well until health failed. He was laid to rest in his new home land among friends. He leaves a wife and son, a father, Willis Miller, three brothers, Steve of Chippewa Falls, Wis., Frank of Southwest City and Loy of Prairie Creek. [Rogers Democrat 6/21/23]

MILLER, Mrs. - W.H. Miller of the Miller Motor Co., arrived home Friday morning from Waverly, Mo. where he had been at the bedside and burial of his aged mother. Mrs. Miller was one of the oldest and most beloved residents of Waverly as evidenced by the memorial services in all of the public schools during the funeral hour. She was near to 93 years of age. [Gentry Journal-Advance 2/2/23]

MILLIGAN, Arthur Augustus - Dr. A.A. Milligan died at an early hour last Friday morning, February 8th, at his home north of Rogers. He had been ill for some time and his death was not unexpected. Funeral services were held at the home Friday afternoon and were conducted by Rev. R.C. Lucke, pastor of the First M.E. church, of which the deceased was a member. The body was taken to Indianapolis, Ind. for burial. Dr. Milligan and wife came to Rogers from Eureka Springs some ten years ago and until recently he maintained an office in town where he practiced as a specialist in tubercular troubles, but lived on his farm north of town. He was of a quiet and retiring nature and his circle of friends outside the First M.E. Church was perhaps not especially large but he was held in the highest esteem by all who knew or were in any way associated with him and his death is learned by all with deep regret. Arthur Augustus Milligan was born at Portland, Ind. October 25th, 1859, being 62 years, three months and fifteen days old when he died. He was married to Nancy Weaver October 28, 1890. He united with the M.E. church at San Antonio, Texas in

1896. He entered college at the age of nineteen at Valparaiso, Ind. and for some years engaged in teaching school. He then began to read medicine and graduated from a medical college in Cincinnati, Ohio in 1883, which profession he followed until two years ago when failing health compelled him to abandon it. [Rogers Democrat 2/15/23]

MINOR, M.M. - M.M. Minor, age 73, a well known farmer residing near Huntsville, Madison county, was instantly killed Sunday when he was struck by a falling tree. He was riding through the woods on horseback, on his way home from a visit to a neighbor when a tree, which had been partly burned in a small forest fire, was felled by the wind, crushing both horse and rider beneath it as it struck the ground. [Rogers Democrat 4/5/23]

MITCHELL, George - Henderson Mitchell received a telegram early Monday morning informing him of the death of his brother, George Mitchell, in Vinita, Okla. Deceased was 72 years old and is survived by 6 brothers and 2 sisters. The funeral was held at 3 o'clock Wednesday afternoon. Mr. and Mrs. N.H. Mitchell and Zack Mitchell attended the funeral. [Gentry Journal-Advance 1/19/23]

MONROE, Melvin M. - M.M. Monroe, one of the pioneer residents of Gentry, died at his home in this city Tuesday morning after an illness of several months. Funeral services were held from the residence Thursday and interment in the Gentry cemetery. [Gentry Journal-Advance 7/27/23] Melvin M. Monroe was born Oct. 28, 1848; died at his home in Gentry, Ark. July 24, 1923, age 74 years, 8 months and 24 days. He was born in Ohio and moved with his parents to Allen county, Indiana when a child. On February 26, 1871 he was united in marriage to Flora A. Ireland at Richland Center, Indiana. To this union six children were born: E.M. Monroe of Springfield, Mo.; O.E. Monroe of Monte Vista, Colo.; Mrs. O.W. Feemster of Gentry, Ark.; A.J. Monroe of Quincy, Ill.; A.W. Monroe of Springfield, Mo.; and Sadie Monroe of Gentry, Ark. Besides his wife and six children he leaves one sister, two brothers, 14 grandchildren and two great-grandchildren to mourn his death. He united with the Christian Church at Coburntown, Indiana when a young man and has lived a quiet and consistent life ever since. He moved with his family to Gentry, Ark. in June 1894. He was a member of the Christian church in Gentry until it disbanded some years ago; later he united with the Congregational Church. He was instrumental in organizing the first Sunday School in Gentry and was its first superintendent. Mr. Monroe was an affectionate husband and father, a faithful and loyal member of the church, a good citizen, kind and charitable to all. He was not so much a man of words as of deeds. To him pretense was abominable. He loved the genuine and true, which virtues were exemplified in his character. His memory will always be held in esteem by those who knew him as a man of unquestionable integrity and uprightness of character. [Gentry Journal-Advance 8/3/23]

MORGAN, Mary B. - {from War Eagle} Mary B. Morgan was born at Logan, Mo. September 14, 1869 where she was reared to womanhood. At the age of 18 was converted and lived a consistent Christian life until death. She was married to Dr. D.C. Morgan of Marionville, Mo. After living at this place 11 years they moved to Durham, Ark. and in 1905 moved to War Eagle where they lived until her death at 5 o'clock Monday morning, May 14, 1923 at the age of 53 years, eight months. To this union were born six children, four boys and two girls. The two girls preceded their mother to the great beyond many years ago. The four boys: John Morgan of Wewoka, Okla.; Claud Morgan of Newton, Kansas; Joe Morgan of Bentonville and George Morgan, the baby boy, who was yet at home. They were at her bedside through most of her sickness and with a host of friends are left to mourn her loss. Mrs. Morgan was a kind and loving woman and loved by all who knew her. A host of friends join in extending their heartfelt sympathy to the bereaved ones in their sad hour. [Rogers Democrat 5/17/23]

MORGAN, Sarah A. HAYNES - Mrs. Sarah A. Morgan died at her home in Rogers on Saturday, October 6th at 10:30 p.m. on East Walnut street. Sarah A. Haynes was born October 8, 1836 and joined the Baptist church when quite young. Was united in marriage to James S. Morgan in 1856. They raised a large family of children, ten of whom are living to mourn her passing away. They are Wm. and James Morgan of Colorado; Mrs. C.W. Basham of Kansas; Mrs. George Moore of Oklahoma; Ed Morgan of Missouri; Mrs. J.E. Stocking, Mrs. W.C. Coghill, Mrs. E.S. Neil, Tom and Harvey Morgan of Rogers and a large number of grandchildren. She has gone from us to join her loving companion who passed away twenty years ago. [Rogers Democrat 10/11/23]
Mrs. Ras Neil, who was called here by the illness and death of her mother, Mrs. Morgan, returned the last of the week to her home at Pharr, Tex. [Rogers Democrat 10/18/23]

MORRIS, Carrie - Mrs. Carrie Morris, wife of R.H. Morris, former Gravette citizens, died at the home of her son, Winlock Morris, April 3, 1923 in Miami, Okla. aged 82 years past. The body was brought thru here to Bentonville where the funeral was conducted on Wednesday by Rev. H.C. Hoy. Burial at Bentonville cemetery. [Gravette News-Herald 4/13/23]

MORRIS, John - John Morris, a farmer living northwest of Bentonville, died on New Year day at the age of 81 years. He was a native of Scotland. [Rogers Democrat 1/11/23]

MULLENS, Mrs. John - {from Mt. Zion} Mrs. John Mullens, who died in Oklahoma last week of flu and pneumonia, was brought to Falling Springs and laid beside her husband who had gone before her several years ago. [Gentry Journal-Advance 2/23/23]

MULLINS, Mae - {from Monte Ne} Mrs. Ruth Pullum and Charley Brewer attended the funeral of their niece and sister, Mrs. Mae Mullins, at Cherokee City Saturday, February 10th. [Rogers Democrat 2/22/23]

MURPHY, infant - {from Providence} We extend sympathy to S.T. Murphy and wife in the loss of an infant baby on Wednesday of last week. The little body was laid to rest in the Walnut Hill cemetery, making six little graves there for them. [Rogers Democrat 3/22/23]

MYERS, daughter - Word reaches Gravette in a letter to B.M. Simpson from A.C. Veach, Newkirk, Okla. to the effect that Mrs. Veach had been called to Kansas City on account of the death of the baby of their daughter, Mrs. W.A. Myers, but we do not learn further particulars. [Gravette News-Herald 11/16/23]

NEAL, Ross - Ross Neal, son of S.D. Neal of Cherokee City and who at one time resided near Gentry, died last Monday in Denver, Colo. of diabetes, aged 33 years. Deceased was buried at Wray, Colo. Tuesday. [Gentry Journal-Advance 9/7/23]

NEELY, J.H. - {from Larue} J.H. Neely was born in Coweta county, Georgia August 31, 1839. Soon afterwards his family moved to Campbell county, Georgia where he lived until the outbreak of the Civil war at which time he enlisted in the Southern army, 35th Ga. Infantry of Volunteers, and served under General Lee and General Jackson throughout the war. At the close of the war he went back to his old home and widowed mother. On Dec. 27, 1865 he was married to Feriba Elizabeth Humphries. In 1860 they emigrated to Mise county, Texas where he lived until 1888 when he came to Benton county, Arkansas where he resided until death, May 20, 1923. The remains were laid to rest in the Bland cemetery Monday evening. Uncle Henry, as he was commonly called, was a man of many friends and no known enemy. Four of his children live here and were all present at the funeral. He had one daughter in California and one son in Oklahoma who did not get to visit him during his illness. The family have the sympathy of the community. [Rogers Democrat 5/24/23]

NEILSON, Mrs. Kenneth - A week or so ago Mrs. Frank Brammer of Rogers was called to Newburg, Mo. by the serious illness of her father. All of the children had been called home and on Thursday Mrs. Brammer and daughter were out driving in a car with a sister, Mrs. Kenneth Neilson of California, and several children. Mrs. Neilson was driving. Descending a hill the car got beyond the control of the driver and was overturned, throwing out the passengers. Mrs. Neilson's neck was broken but no one else was injured save for cuts and bruises. Mr. Brammer went to Newburg Saturday to attend the funeral of Mrs. Neilson. [Rogers Democrat 3/15/23]

NOEL, Grace - {from Bestwater} Mrs. J.H. Buttram and Mrs. Albert Tiner went to Pineville, Mo. Sunday in answer to a message telling of the death of Mrs. Grace Noel, who died very suddenly with hardening of the arteries. [Rogers Democrat 10/18/23]

O'BRYANT, J.H. - Rev. J.H. O'Bryant, a former well-known pastor of the M.E. Church, South of Rogers, died Sunday at his home at Earle, this state, of heart trouble and the body was brought to Rogers Tuesday morning for burial beside the grave of a daughter who died during his pastorate here. Funeral services were held at the Central M.E. church in Rogers Tuesday morning at 10:30, conducted by Rev. J.J. Galloway of Arkadelphia; assisted by Rev. Fred Lark of Van Buren, Rev. Ira Brumley of Springdale and the Rogers pastor, Rev. J. Wilson Crichlow. The entire official board of the Central M.E. church was at the train to meet the funeral party, as were also a large number of the former members of the congregation of the deceased minister, one of the most popular pastors the local church has ever known, not only among his own denomination but in the city as well. Rev. O'Bryant is survived by his wife and four children - one son, W.E. O'Bryant of Hoxie, and three daughters - Mrs. Kyle Fraser, Springdale, Mrs. Craig, wife of Rev. R.B. Craig of Tuckerman, and Miss Eunice O'Bryant of Earle. The deceased was 54 years old and had been preaching in Arkansas for more than 30 years. He was a native of Mississippi. [Rogers Democrat 9/20/23]

OAKLEY, H.A. {Berry} - Word was received Friday morning of the death of H.A. {Berry} Oakley in Chicago the previous evening after an illness of several years. The body arrived in Rogers Sunday morning from Chicago, accompanied by Mrs. Oakley and son, Raymond, who were met here by the oldest son, Sidney Oakley, of Henryetta, Oklahoma. Funeral services were held in the Central M.E. Church here Sunday afternoon at three o'clock and were conducted by the pastor, Rev. Crichlow. The deceased had been a member of this church for many years. Burial was in the Oakley Chapel cemetery where so many of his kinfolks have preceded him. Mr. Oakley was one of the early settlers of this section and was for many years one of the best known citizens of Rogers, holding numerous positions of trust and importance, and engaging in various lines of business. For a number of years most of the family have been in Chicago and Mr. Oakley, who had been traveling for a commission house, joined them there when his health began to fail. He was a native of Bedford county, Tenn. where he was born May 20, 1854, coming to Benton county with his parents at the age of fifteen. At the time of his death he was 60 years, three months and ten days old. The family located west of the present site of Rogers and Oakley Chapel received its name from the family. While living in that neighborhood he married Miss Mollie Horsley, who survives him, and to them were born seven children, five daughters and two sons. All of the daughters are now living in Chicago - Mrs. Myrtle Buttry, Mrs. Mabel Hall, Mrs. Fray Fergus, Misses Lelia and Maurine. The sons are Raymond and Sidney Oakley. Mr. Oakley was a brother of Mrs. C.E. Smith and Bud Oakley of Oakley Chapel neighborhood; Ben Oakley of California, and Tom Oakley of Park Hill, Okla. Another brother, D.A. Oakley, father of O.A.P. Oakley of Rogers, died some years ago. The deceased was a life long Democrat and served as postmaster of Rogers during the first Cleveland administration, always taking an active interest in the political matters of the city, county and state. He was for a time cashier of the Citizens Bank; was secretary and treasurer of the Rogers Lumber Co.; was engaged in the grocery business for a time and then became a representative of northern commission houses, a business in which he spent the last fifteen years of his life. His memory is held in respect and esteem by the older residents of our town who remember him as a good citizen, a kind neighbor and a loyal friend and associate. [Rogers Democrat 9/6/23]

ODEN, Franklin Carl - Franklin Carl Oden was born in a Methodist home at Rogers, Arkansas July 24, 1893. When he was only five years old his mother was called home to be with God. From that day his father and older brothers and sisters became a mother to Frank, as they lovingly called him, the baby boy. His boyhood days were spent at Rogers where he went to school at the academy. Later he took a commercial course. When America entered the great World War Frank offered his services to his country, being among the very first to volunteer. He was among the first to reach France, his contingency landing in April 1918. Here while doing service in the supply department of the aviation corps he contracted influenza, followed by pneumonia, which developed into lung trouble from which he was suffering when he received his honorable discharge in Little Rock in June 1919. Seeking health he went to California, Arizona and New Mexico and then to the Grace Lutheran Sanitarium in San Antonio, Texas where he died at 10 o'clock in the morning, March 23, 1923. He is survived by his father, August Oden of Pace's Chapel; four brothers, Wm. S. Oden of Jonesboro, Walter L. Oden of Rogers, Warren A. Oden of Delaware, Okla. and Elza Oden of Fort Smith and two sisters; Mrs. Dora Hendrix of San Bernardino, Calif. and Mrs. Ethel Farley of Pace's Chapel. The funeral was conducted Monday afternoon at Pace's Chapel, the Rev. J. Wilson Crichlow and the American Legion having charge of the services. [Rogers Democrat 3/29/23]

Elza Oden of Fort Smith was here Monday to attend the funeral of his brother, Frank Oden, as were also Mr. and Mrs. John Goodman from Springfield. Mrs. Goodman was an aunt of the deceased. [Rogers Democrat 3/29/23]

ORTLEIB, Mrs. Leon - Fayetteville, April 30.- Mrs. Leon Ortleib, aged 33, and her daughter, Eileen Freeda, aged seven, drowned in Hickory Creek, 11 miles from here late yesterday. The bodies were both recovered and sent to Kansas City for burial. Mrs. Ortleib and daughter had been visiting a Farmington friend Saturday afternoon and started home following a heavy rain. They stopped at the house of a friend but refused to stay the night, laughing at the statement that they could not cross the swollen stream. Their team was found Sunday hitched to a tree near a gully on the side of the creek and a searching party found the bodies shortly afterward, some distance apart where they had been washed up a quarter of a mile down stream. It is believed the couple tried to wade the stream and were overcome by the strong current. [Rogers Democrat 5/3/23]

OSBORNE, Lloyd Eldon - The Death Angel has again been in our midst and taken from us one of our dearest and brightest little boys. Lloyd Eldon Osborne was born July 18, 1908 about three-quarters of a mile south of Clantonville and resided there until January 22, 1923 when death claimed as a ransom his precious life, his age being fourteen years, six months and four days. His suffering was intense, his death being caused by spinal tubercular trouble, but it was not as one without hope, he being converted and baptized about two years ago, and has been a bright and shining light, not only in the home of his parents, Mr. and Mrs. W.J. Osborne, and his sister, Zilla, but the community as well. [Rogers Democrat 2/1/23]

PARKER, Amanda Elizabeth - {from Hiwasse} Mrs. Amanda Elizabeth Parker died Thursday night, Oct. 4, 1923 at the home of her daughter, Mrs. Sarah Jane Pendergraft, in Hiwasse, aged 95 years. [Gravette News-Herald 10/12/23]

PARKER, Billy - {from Hiwasse} Uncle Billy Parker, one of the oldest residents of this part of the county, died Friday, July 20, 1923 and interment was made Saturday in Mt. Pleasant cemetery. [Gravette News-Herald 7/27/23]

PARKER, G.W. - Funeral services for G.W. Parker, who lived one mile east of Avoca and who died December 27th, were held December 28th at Tucks Chapel and were conducted by Rev. F.M. Seamster of Rogers. He leaves an aged wife and seven children - four girls and three sons, and a host of friends to mourn his loss. He was 75 years old. He was buried by the side of the three children who preceded him, two sons and one daughter. [Rogers Democrat 1/4/23]

PARKER, Georgia Anna - {from Mountain View} Georgia Anna Parker, infant daughter of Jim Parker and wife, died the 21st of August, having lived only two weeks and one day. All was done that loving hands could do for the little girl. She leaves her father and mother, two sisters and two brothers, to mourn her loss. She was buried at Tuck's Chapel. Friends of the family extend their sympathy to the family. [Rogers Democrat 8/30/23]

PARKER, William - William Parker, who died July 20th south of Hiwasse, this county, was credited with being 105 years old, having been born in 1818 in East Tennessee. He had lived in Arkansas since childhood. [Rogers Democrat 8/2/23]

PARKS, Samuel - Sam Parks, a well known citizen of Gentry, and who had been confined to his bed for the past several months, died at his home last Saturday morning and was buried the same day. Rev. R.A. Collier of the Baptist church held a short service at the grave. [Gentry Journal-Advance 4/27/23]

In our last issue we had a short notice of the death of one of our citizens, Samuel Parks, not knowing the particulars of his death we make the correction. Mr. Parks died on Friday night, April 20th at 8:50 o'clock and was buried on Saturday, April 21st at 5 o'clock. He was born at Conlington,

Indiana on March 18, 1866, being 57 years of age at the time of his death. He leaves an aged father who resides at LaJunta, Colo. and as far as known this is all the relatives he had. Sam, as he was familiarly known, was a good man, unassuming in his character, but strictly honest, and we do not believe he owed any one a penny when he died. With the passing of this man Gentry loses a good church member, a kind neighbor and a good friend to all. [Gentry Journal-Advance 5/4/23]

PARMER, Mary E. - {from Pleasant Hill} Again the death angel has visited our community, this time to summon Mrs. Mary E. Parmer on March 1, 1923. Age 70 years and 26 days. Mrs. Parmer's home was at Springdale. She came here a year ago to visit her granddaughter, Mrs. Moreland. She had been here only two days when she was stricken with paralysis which rendered her an invalid until death called her. Her remains were shipped to Bartlesville for interment. Mr. and Mrs. Moreland accompanied the body. [Rogers Democrat 3/15/23]

PEARCE, Etta DOLLAR - Mrs. Etta Pearce, wife of Dr. N.J. Pearce, died Monday evening at nine o'clock at the home at 428 Spring street. Funeral services were held at the cemetery Tuesday afternoon at three o'clock and the funeral was conducted by the A.D. Callison Undertaking Co. The deceased, who was a daughter of J.L. Dollar, is survived by her husband and a little boy eight years old. She was 32 years old. She is also survived by three sisters, Fanny, Ruth, and Minnie Dollar. [Rogers Democrat 7/26/23]

PEARSONS, C.Z. - The attached obituary of the late C.Z. Pearsons came to the Democrat office through the mail and we do not know what Missouri paper it is from so we can not give proper credit. Mr. Pearsons was for a number of years a well known resident of Benton Co. and lived for a time southeast of Rogers on the old Monte Ne hill road. We had not heard of his death until the notice came to hand and it was a surprise to the editor as it will be to his old friends here, for he was a man we all held in high esteem. - C.Z. Pearsons was born Sept. 9, 1850 at Wales, Erie county, N.Y. He was reared to manhood in that town. He was married August 24, 1870 to Julia Hubbard. To this union were born O.J. Pearsons and R.D. Pearsons. Later with his family he moved to Duke Center, Pa., where Mary D. Pearsons, now Mrs. H.N. Weaver, was born. After living there for some time he moved to the state of Kansas where C. Arthur Pearsons was born. He came to Seligman about 17 years ago. All the children are living and were present. The father is the first of the family to cross over. He was converted some 18 years ago and had lived faithful to his Lord until the end. He received injuries from a fall which resulted in his death on July 5, 1923 at the age of 72 years, 9 months and 27 days. He leaves a host of relatives and friends who mourn his departure. [Rogers Democrat 7/26/23]

PERRY, William Waters - W.W. Perry died yesterday afternoon about four o'clock at his home two and one-half miles north of Rogers in the Pleasant Hill neighborhood. Death was the result of a stroke of paralysis suffered several months ago while driving in his car. The stroke was a very severe one and there has been no hope for recovery and death came as the only possible solution for his sufferings. The body will be taken this evening to his old home at Rolla, Mo. for burial in the family lot. Mr. Perry came to Rogers about fifteen years ago from Waco, Texas where he had been engaged in the manufacture of cigars, and his venture on the farm here was the first experience he had in farming. That he has been successful was due to the great interest he took in the work and to the fact that he was ever on the alert for modern methods. William Waters Perry was born at Rolla, Mo. December 1, 1866, being at the time of his death 56 years, nine months and four days old. He is survived by his wife and three sons, John and Ed of Kansas City, and Robert, the youngest, who is still at home. All of the boys have been at home since their father's illness. Funeral arrangements are under the direction and care of the A.D. Callison Undertaking Co. [Rogers Democrat 9/6/23]

PITTS, Goldie ROLLER - {from Central} Word came on Monday of the death of Mrs. Joe Pitts of Harrison, Ark. Mrs. Pitts was known as Miss Goldie Roller and was well known and respected in this community. The family have our deepest sympathy. [Rogers Democrat 5/10/23]

POE, Mrs. John - {from Garfield} Mrs. John Poe departed this life last Saturday morning after a long siege of illness. Mrs. Poe had the flu over a year ago from which she never fully recovered. Other diseases gripped her and at last she was relieved by death. Everything was done for Mrs. Poe that loving hands could do. She has left vacant a place in her home that never can be filled. She was 69 years old. She was married to John Poe of this place in 1881 and to this union were born nine children - seven of whom are still living. All were with their mother in her last hours and at her bedside when she died. She was laid to rest at the Reddick cemetery and Rev. Martin of Rogers conducted the services. [Rogers Democrat 9/6/23]

POOLE, Nelley - Fayetteville, June 28.- Nelley Poole, 17-year-old son of Clarence Poole of near West Fork, this county, was drowned in Clear Creek, near Wolsey, shortly after 7 o'clock last night, according to information reaching here today. Young Poole had gone to the Wolsey bridge in company with his small brother, Johnny, and both prepared for a swim in the creek, just south of the bridge. Nelley was seized with an attack of cramps while in midstream and went under. When he failed to rise his brother spread the alarm but a rescue party failed to arrive in time to save the older boy whose body was soon found. [Rogers Democrat 7/5/23]

POTTS, John H. - John H. Potts, aged 37 years, 3 months and 28 days, died at the home of his sister, Mrs. Wm. Woody, near Gentry Friday afternoon at 6:20. The body was taken in charge by the McArthur Undertaking parlors at Siloam until Saturday when it was taken to Mrs. Woody's home where funeral services were held at 3 p.m. followed by interment in Flint

Creek cemetery. Mr. Potts died following an attack of meningitis, probably caused by being severely shaken in riding a bucking horse over a month ago. [Gentry Journal-Advance 5/25/23]

PUCKETT, Beulah HALL - {from Twelve Corners} Hugh A. Hall attended the funeral of his sister, Mrs. Beulah Puckett, of Rogers Tuesday, March 6th. She leaves a husband, one child and three brothers and a host of friends to mourn her loss. [Rogers Democrat 3/15/23]

PUCKETT, Mattie - Mrs. Gertrude Veach, Mrs. A.C. Chandler and Mrs. Nelle Austin attended the funeral of Mrs. Mattie Puckett, well known past president of the State Rebekah Assembly, at Siloam Springs Sunday. Mrs. Puckett was widely known and very popular with the order all over the state. She died suddenly on Friday last, the result of a paralytic stroke. Many friends here regret her departure. [Gravette News-Herald 1/12/23]

RAGAN, William - William Ragan of Siloam Springs, the young son of W.H. Ragan, lost his life last week while visiting with a sister in Tulsa. He was overcome by gas while in the bath room. [Rogers Democrat 5/24/23]

RAGSDALE, Mrs. Joe {LEWIS} and infant - {from Stony Point} The body of Mrs. Joe Ragsdale and a new born baby was brought to the home of her father, Uncle Billy Lewis, Saturday from some point east of Fayetteville. Funeral services were held at the Lewis home Sunday afternoon and burial was at Pleasant Grove. She is survived by her husband, four children, a married daughter by a former marriage, 2 grandchildren, an aged father, a brother and two sisters besides numerous other relatives. We extend heartfelt sympathy to the family in this sad hour. [Rogers Democrat 3/15/23] {from Monte Ne} We are very sorry to hear of the death of Mrs. Ragsdale. She is the niece of Aunt Ruth Pullum. She is the second niece of Aunt Ruth's who has died in the last month. [Rogers Democrat 3/15/23]

RAINEY, Mrs. G.W. - Mrs. G.W. Rainey of Huntsville died last week at the age of 95 years and the Record says she was perhaps the oldest citizen of Madison county. Her father was 100 years old when he died and a sister died a few years ago at the age of 96. She had no children of her own but had raised nine orphan children in her home during her long and useful life. [Rogers Democrat 2/8/23]

RANKIN, Margaret E. WILSON - Margaret E. Wilson was born Sept. 29, 1840 and died July 15, 1923, aged 82 years, 10 months and 16 days. She was married Dec. 1, 1858 to Dr. David W. Rankin in Morristown, Tenn., making their home in that state until April 1881 when they moved to Viney Grove, Washington Co., Ark.; soon afterwards they moved to Bloomfield, Benton county, Ark.; coming from that place to Gentry about the year of 1895 where she spent the remainder of her life. To this union thirteen children were born; the husband and five children preceded her in death. There remains: Mary A. Raum of Marietta, Okla.; Laura I. Carl of Gentry, Ark.; Catherine V. Tallman, Gentry, Ark.; Mariah T. Varney, Kansas City, Mo.; Margaret M. Collins, Greenville, Tex.; Lela A. Stroud, Newton, Kans.;

Robert A. Rankin, Gentry, Ark.; and Ralph W. Rankin of St. Joe, Mo.; all of whom were present except Lela, who was absent on account of sickness in her home. She also had twenty-two grandchildren and three great-grandchildren. Sister Rankin has been a consecrated christian woman; always interested in the work of the Kingdom of God. She attended church and her presence was an inspiration to the preacher. The funeral services were held July 17 from the residence of her son, R.J. Rankin, conducted by Rev. C.H. Sherman of the Methodist church. The remains were laid to rest by the side of her husband in the Bloomfield cemetery. [Gentry Journal-Advance 7/20/23]

RATLIFF, infant - The two-month-old daughter of E.F. Ratliff and wife died Friday of spinal meningitis. Funeral services were held at the home Saturday. [Rogers Democrat 2/22/23]

RAYMER, A.V. - Miss Willis and Mrs. A.H. Hull advise us of information received from Drexel, Mo. that A.V. Raymer, who moved from Gravette to that place a few years since, had died, the result of cancer of the stomach, and the funeral was held Saturday, Jan. 13. Mr. Raymer was a good citizen and Gravette people will regret to learn of his death. [Gravette News-Herald 1/19/23]

REDLINGER, Grace - Another kerosene tragedy was recorded Wednesday morning when Grace Redlinger, 16 years old, who lived with her parents in the Plank neighborhood just this side of Decatur, used kerosene to kindle a fire in a stove. The can exploded and her clothing was burned off and her body was so badly burned the flesh was sloughed in places. She was conscious when the doctor arrived but died a few hours later. The house and all its contents were destroyed. Grace was the youngest child of a large family and her tragical death was a shock to the entire community, who deeply sympathize with the grief stricken family. [Gentry Journal-Advance 7/20/23]

{from The Bentonville Record} Grace, the 14-year-old daughter of Will Redlinger and wife, living on the E.N. Plank property, one and one-half miles southwest of Decatur, died of burns received when she was caught in her burning home about 11 o'clock Wednesday, July 18th. The little girl had poured coal oil on the fire in the kitchen stove and in some manner the can of oil exploded, throwing the oil over the child and enveloping her in flames. Though the mother was sitting in the yard and men were working in a field across the road from the place, the house was destroyed before they could reach it. The child lived nearly two hours after she was removed from the ruins. [Rogers Democrat 7/26/23]

RICE, Mrs. Rollie M. {PUCKETT} - {from Bestwater} Mrs. Rollie Rice passed away Monday morning at an early hour after years of suffering. Funeral will be held at Buttram's Chapel some time Tuesday. [Rogers Democrat 7/19/23]

A number of Rogers relatives attended the funeral of Mrs. R.M. Rice at

Buttram's Chapel Monday afternoon. Mrs. Rice was a sister of J.W. and Hugh Puckett, Mrs. T.E. Sager and Miss Sallie Puckett of Rogers, and a sister-in-law of Dr. C.A. Rice. She had been an invalid for many years. [Rogers Democrat 7/19/23]

RICE, R.S. {Rufe} - Dr. R.S. {Rufe} Rice died last night at 7:00 o'clock at his home on South Second Street. Funeral services will be held at the Central M.E. Church Friday afternoon, March 23rd at 2 o'clock. [Rogers Democrat 3/22/23]

One of the largest funerals ever known in the history of Rogers was that of last Friday afternoon at the Central Methodist church when the body of Dr. R.S. Rice was escorted to its resting place by hundreds of friends and neighbors. As briefly stated in the Rogers Democrat of last week, Dr. Rice died at his home on South Second street at 7:30 o'clock Wednesday night, March 21st at the age of 59 years, 11 months and 16 days. He had been in failing health for several years but his condition had not been considered critical until a few weeks ago. For several days previous to his death it had been feared the end might come at any time. The Central M.E. Church was crowded with many standing and many unable to gain entrance, for the deceased was one of the most popular and best known men on this side of Benton county and friends came from many miles around to pay the last tribute to his memory. Services were conducted by the pastor, Rev. Crichlow. The Masonic orders attended in a body and besides the Rogers members there were many visiting brethren. The medical fraternity of Rogers were also present in a body. Practically all of the business houses of Rogers were closed during the hours of the funeral, 2:30 to 3:30 o'clock. Rogers people who have only known Dr. Rice during the last few years, especially since he began to fail in health, can have no idea of the important part he played in the history of Rogers for a quarter of a century. He was one of the first men of the town with whom the Democrat editor became acquainted and the friendship formed then has always continued. He was interested in everything that interested his friends, but his real loyalty was to the children - first, last and all the time. It seemed that every child in Rogers and for miles around knew him and called him by name. Especially did he father the poor and the neglected tots, and hundreds of them will remember the red letter days when he extended a helping hand by buying them necessities of life, slipped them into the shows when he found them hanging around the door on the outside, lined them up at the ice cream and candy counters, picked them up along the roadside as he was answering country calls and sympathized over their woes, be they real or imaginary. He was big and deliberate, and that easy drawl used to irritate the fellow who wanted to do something right now but the doctor never went off half-cocked and the safe plan was to allow him to do a thing in his own time and way. We shall also miss him now for while we had not seen him much during the last year or two, there was always the hope that he would eventually regain his old health and again take his place among our most active professional men and citizens. The following sketch is taken from Fay Hempstead's History of Arkansas, written in 1911, and we quote verbatim: "Dr. Rice represents one of the pioneer families of Benton county - a family, some of the members of which have become leading professional men, while others have kept to the vocation of their ancestors, that of agriculture, and all of them, no matter to what they have devoted their energies, have contributed a royal citizenship to the commonwealth in which they were reared. Dr. Rice was born in Fayetteville, Washington county, April 4, 1863, his parents having moved to that place during the War of the Rebellion. The father, although Southern in sympathy and conviction, acted as storekeeper for the Federal commissary for a time during the progress of the war period. When Rufus S. was but a child his parents returned to their first home on Pea Ridge and there their large family of children was reared. The farm on Pea Ridge came into the hands of Dr. Rice's father, Chas. W. Rice, in 1859, at which date he brought his family from McMinn county, Tennessee. This certain section was destined to acquire a pathetic and historic interest, for within three years after Mr. Rice acquired the farm it became the scene of one of the chief battles of the Civil War, namely the battle of Elkhorn, or Pea Ridge, and since that time the locality has remained a point of historic interest. Upon that spot and amid the memories which fired the blood of the high spirited youth, Rufus S. Rice reached the years of young manhood. The fulfillment of the various duties of the farm gave him breadth of frame and vigor of constitution, and the Academy at Pea Ridge afforded him his literary training. Like so many men who have eventually entered the professions he began his career as a wage earner in the honorable capacity of a school teacher, serving this for a short time. In 1883 a resolution as to his future life work materialized and he took up the study of medicine in the Missouri Medical College, but before he finished the course, which was the goal of his ambition, he engaged in medicinal practice at Brightwater, Ark., near his home. Hungering for all the available knowledge in his particular field, as soon as possible he returned to its pursuit and entered the college of Physicians and Surgeons, St. Louis, from which institution he graduated. Shortly thereafter Dr. Rice came to Rogers, his identification with the place dating from 1890, and in the ensuing decade this has been the scene of his practice. His connection with various important societies of a professional nature and the various public offices which have been entrusted to him are an eloquent testimony of the high regard in which he is held by the community. He is a member of the Benton County and the Arkansas Medical Societies; he is a member of the United States Pension Examining Board for Benton county, having also served in the same capacity during the Cleveland administration; for several years he was one of the medical examiners for Benton county and he is at the present time president of the Rogers Board of Health and of the Benton County Board of Health.

He served several terms on the Rogers school board. Dr. Rice comes from a family of tried and true Democrats and is himself imbued strongly with devotion to the principles of that faith. He has no interest in politics for himself but his desire for the success of personal friends whom he believes capable of good public service, often draws him into a conflict. He is orthodox in his religion and a member of the Southern Methodist Episcopal church. His Masonic connection is one of the big things in his life and includes membership in the Pea Ridge Blue Lodge and the Bethany Commandery of Bentonville. He is also a Woodman of the World and a Maccabee. On Dec. 15, 1887 Dr. Rice was united in marriage to Miss Dorinda Puckett, a daughter of A. Puckett, who came from Tennessee to Benton county before the war. Mrs. Rice was born here and received her education in Rogers Academy and was a teacher previous to her marriage. This worthy woman passed away August 31, 1904, the mother of two daughters, Misses Pearl and Grace Rice {Mrs. Pearl Ball and Mrs. Tom McNeil, both of Rogers}. On April 29, 1911 Dr. Rice was married to Miss Katharine Carr, a native of Mississippi. Dr. Rice's father, Chas. W. Rice, died in 1893 at the age of 76 while his mother lived until 1910, dying at the advanced age of 84. The children were as follows: Miller B. Rice of Pea Ridge; James A. Rice, who died at Bentonville in 1910; Mrs. I.M. Mitchell, who died in Rogers; Wilford C. Rice of Madison county; Thomas M. Rice of Avoca; Timothy S. Rice of Pea Ridge; Dr. Thomas C. Rice of Avoca; Dr. Rufus S. Rice, the subject of this sketch; Charles M. Rice, an attorney of Bentonville; Dr. Clinton A. Rice {then at Gentry but now a resident of Rogers}; and Roland M. Rice, living near Brightwater." {All of the brothers were here for the funeral Friday with the exception of Miller Rice, who has been ill for some time with the flu and could not attend.} [Rogers Democrat 3/29/23]

ROBBINS, Jim - {from Highfill} Jack Robbins attended the funeral of his brother, Jim, who died Feb. 15 at his home west of Centerton. He was buried in the Barron cemetery and leaves a wife and three children, mother, brother and sister. [Gentry Journal-Advance 3/2/23]

ROLLER, John - {from Central} This community received a great shock when the news came that John Roller died very suddenly at his home on last Thursday night, supposed to have been from heart failure. [Rogers Democrat 12/6/23]

ROOKS, Dort - {from Mason Valley} Mrs. Robert Rooks left Thursday morning for Pittsburg, Kan. to attend the funeral of her son, Dort Rooks, who died Thursday at Piedmont, Mo. of flu and pneumonia. The remains were brought to Pittsburg for burial. He leaves a wife and 3 children, a father, mother, two brothers and two sisters. [Gentry Journal-Advance 2/2/23]

ROSS, J.K. - J.K. Ross, the "Uncle Matt of Dewey Bald," of Harold Bell Wright's books, died at Springfield, Mo. Monday. [Gravette News-Herald 7/13/23]

ROSS, James Franklin - Rev. J.F. Ross died very suddenly Saturday afternoon while speaking at the meeting of the fruit growers that was being held in the Campus Park. He was standing by one of the benches addressing the chairman when he suddenly faltered, stopped speaking and then fell forward into the arms of friends who were seated near him. Physicians were called but death was evidently almost instantaneous. Rev. Ross was 87 years old and death was the result of the oppressive heat and the infirmities of old age. He was carried across the street to the home of his daughter, Mrs. T.A. Winkleman, where he had visited that morning and had mentioned the fact that he planned to speak at the afternoon meeting. He was very much interested in fruit growing and despite his advanced age made a point of attending such meetings when possible. Funeral services were held Sunday afternoon at the First M.E. Church and were conducted by the pastor, Rev. R.C. Lucke. Services at the cemetery were under the auspices of the Odd Fellows, Rev. Ross having been a member of that order for more than 66 years and he took great pride in his long membership. James Franklin Ross was a native of Erie, Penn. where he was born January 20, 1836 and where he grew to manhood. He was married September 21, 1875 to Phoebe Jane Halstead and to them were born four children, two of whom survive their father: W.A. Ross of Wichita, Kan. and Mrs. T.A. Winkleman of Rogers. Their mother died March 13, 1913. In April 1914 Rev. Ross married Mrs. Mary E. Rhoades who survives him. The deceased served four years in the Union army during the Civil War, a member of Co. D, 1st Michigan cavalry, holding a commission as second lieutenant when the war closed. Rev. Ross began his ministerial work in 1855 when he was but nineteen years of age in the Methodist Episcopal church and he served many circuits and pastorates during his long term of service in the states of Michigan, Louisiana, Missouri, Oklahoma and Arkansas where his work was crowned with a success of which his relatives and friends may well feel proud. For a man of his age and seemingly frail physique Rev. Ross was very active and took a working interest in every civic and religious movement in Rogers. He had often expressed the desire that his death might come suddenly and without sickness, and all who knew him realize that the end was such as he would have chosen. The following were called here for the funeral of Rev. Ross: Ed Sample and family of Westfork, Ark. and Will Sample of Kent, Okla., both sons of Mrs. Ross, and Chas. Green of Ada, Okla., a son-in-law. Also Mrs. J.J. Bowman of Neosho, Mo., a friend of the family. Mrs. Ross will close the home at 222 North 3rd Street for the present at least and go to the home of her son, Ed Sample, at Westfork. [Rogers Democrat 8/9/23]

ROSS, Mrs. J.K. - Mrs. J.K. Ross, known in Harold Bell Wright's novel, "Shepherd of the Hills" as "Aunt Molly," died at her home at Garber, Mo. last week. Her husband, Mr. Ross, was known as "Old Matt" in the book. [Gravette News-Herald 3/30/23]

ROTRAMMEL, Lucinda Jane ROBISON - Mrs. Lucinda J. Rotrammel, wife of Henderson Rotrammel, died Saturday night, July 28th, 1923, aged 82 years, at the home of her daughter, Mrs. J.H. Daniel. Mrs. Rotrammel has resided in this community since 1857. The funeral was conducted by Joe Fair of Centerton and burial was in Mt. Pleasant cemetery Sunday afternoon. The News Herald joins with the community in extending sympathy to the bereaved relatives. [Gravette News-Herald 8/3/23]
Lucinda Jane Robison was born in Macon county, N.C. Dec. 14, 1840; came with her parents to Benton county Nov. 1857, residing near Sulphur Springs until 1864 when the family went to Texas and stayed about two years then came back and settled the home where she lived until about 15 months ago when she moved in with her daughter to be cared for. She was married to R.H. Rotrammel Jan. 24, 1871. To this union were born two children, Sallie and Altha. She accepted Christ as her Savior in her girlhood and united with the M.E. church. She lived a Christian life, was a faithful wife and mother and always ready to help her neighbors when in need. She departed this life July 28, 1923. Besides her invalid husband she leaves one daughter, Mrs. Sallie Daniel, four grandchildren, Stella and Terry Daniel, and Guy and Louemma Barlow, all of Gravette, Ark., and a foster son, H.C. Frazier, of Whitney, Tex. and a number of relatives and friends. One daughter, Mrs. Altha Barlow, and three grandchildren preceded her to the world beyond.- S.C. [Gravette News-Herald 8/17/23]

ROUSH, L.C. - Mrs. J.P. Roush died March 13th at her home after a brief illness. Her family were all with her - her husband, J.P. Roush, and their three children, W.W. Wetzel of Kansas City, Mo., Mrs. Lester C. Mudge of Salina, Kans. and Mrs. A.M. Schaeffer of Gentry, Ark. It was Mrs. Roush's request that the funeral be private - limited to members of her family. The family desires to express their sincerest appreciation of the expressions of sympathy from the many good friends and neighbors who lived Mrs. Roush so dearly. [Gentry Journal-Advance 3/16/23]
Mrs. L.C. Roush, wife of J.P. Roush, our well-known fellow-townsman and lumber dealer, passed away at her home about 4 o'clock last Tuesday afternoon from a complication of diseases. She was surrounded by her children, two daughters and a son, and her husband, who were at her bedside when the end came. Funeral services were held from the family home Thursday morning at 10 o'clock, Rev. Edward Parsons of the Congregational church having charge of the services. Burial was in Gentry cemetery. Mr. Roush and relatives have the sympathy of the entire community in their bereavement. [Gentry Journal-Advance 3/16/23]

RYAN, Milton M. - {from The Ft. Smith Times-Record} Prof. Milton M. Ryan, 63 years old, of Spiro, Okla. and an educator of Oklahoma for many years, died at 12:45 Friday {Jan. 5, 1923} in a Fort Smith hospital where he was brought for an operation Thursday. He leaves his wife, 5 daughters: Mrs. Flora Park, Spiro; Mrs. W.E. Adams, Wichita, Kansas; Miss Lois Ryan,

McCloud, Okla.; Miss Reba Ryan, Muskogee, Okla.; Miss Lucy Ryan, Spiro, Okla.; four sons: Leonard and Modie Ryan, Kansas City; Robert Ryan, Dayton, Ohio; and Berkley Ryan, Spiro. He is also survived by four brothers, Judge J.L. Ryan, Claremore, Okla.; Joe Ryan, Walla Walla, Wash.; and John and Sterling Ryan of Gravette, Ark. Prof. Ryan had resided in Spiro 20 years. He represented La Flore county in Oklahoma legislature in 1912. He was a member of the W.O.W. and Baptist church at Spiro. Burial will take place at Spiro. [Gravette News-Herald 1/12/23]

SAMUEL, Cornelia J. - {from War Eagle} The sudden death of Cornelia J. Samuel will come as a great shock to her many friends here and elsewhere, which occurred Sunday morning at 10 minutes of 1, caused by heart trouble. She was sick only about 5 minutes. She was born in Natchez, Miss. Sept. 24, 1842 and quietly passed away Dec. 16, 1923 at the age of 81 years, two months and 22 days. She was married to Fielding Samuel Feb. 22, 1865; to this union were born eight children, four of whom have preceded her to the great beyond. The four living are: Will of Springdale, Mrs. Fannie Capps of Holdenville, Okla.; Mary, who is yet at home, and Otho of this place. Mrs. Samuel, with her husband and children, moved from Holdenville, Okla. to War Eagle some five years ago where she has made a host of friends to extend their sympathy to the bereaved in their dark hour of sorrow. She leaves an aged husband, 13 grandchildren, 16 great-grandchildren, two sons and two daughters to mourn her loss. Mrs. Samuel lived a consistent Christian life, having professed Christianity at the early age of 13, and was a member of the Missionary Baptist church of War Eagle. Interment was in Clifty cemetery on Tuesday, Dec. 18, Rev. Bean officiating. [Rogers Democrat 12/20/23]

SANDERS, Carl - {from Providence} Little Carl Sanders, son of Roy Sanders and wife, was born July 14th, 1920 near Garfield, Ark., died October 27, 1923 at Cardin, Okla. Physicians thought he provably suffered a stroke of paralysis or acute indigestion. The sudden news of his death was indeed a sad shock to relatives here as he was taken seriously ill only one hour before death came. The little body was laid to rest in the City cemetery at Miami, Okla. and his spirit has flown to God. He was a child of exceptionally bright intellect and of a kind, loving disposition. Many friends here extend sympathy to the bereaved parents who were reared in this community, also the grandparents, Mr. and Mrs. Wiley Sanders and John Easley, and other relatives residing here. [Rogers Democrat 11/8/23]

SAVAGE, Mrs. E.L. - {from Pleasant Valley} Mrs. Geo. Marrs received news Monday of the death of her youngest sister, Mrs. E.L. Savage, who passed away Thursday, March 8th at her home at McKinney, Texas after an illness of two weeks of flu and pneumonia fever. [Gentry Journal-Advance 3/16/23]

SAWREY, Edith RHEA - Word was received in Rogers yesterday of the death of Mrs. Virgil Sawrey on last Saturday night at her home in Long

Beach, Calif. She will be remembered in Rogers as Edith Rhea, a daughter of John Rhea, former Rogers residents. They have been at Long Beach for a number of years and Rogers friends have kept in close touch with the family through the medium of Pacific Coast visitors. She is survived by her husband and several children who have the sympathy of the many Rogers friends. [Rogers Democrat 6/8/23]
A card from a former Rogers resident of Long Beach, Calif. says the death of Mrs. Virgil Sawrey was caused by infection, induced by the scratch of a pin. [Rogers Democrat 7/5/23]

SCHMALL, Johnny - {from The Siloam Springs Herald and Democrat} It was only a fortnight ago that Johnny Schmall left here and the report comes to us that he died on board ship and was buried at sea. Uncle Johnny got the notion that he would like to go back to the Fatherland before he died and as he was getting old and feeble he disposed of most of the property he had left and started back. For many years he lived around Siloam Springs and was a good citizen and industrious farmer. Several children survive him, one son living here. [Rogers Democrat 6/14/23]

SCHMIDT, W.J. - W.J. Schmidt, who resided on the Lamberson farm near Beaty, died Wednesday morning the result of tuberculosis, at the age of 48 years. Deceased was a native of Germany. He leaves a wife and three small children. The interment was made this Thursday a.m. in Gravette I.O.O.F. cemetery, Rev. W.M. Shelton officiating at the grave. Sympathy is extended the family. [Gravette News-Herald 2/23/23]

SCROGGINS, Willard Guy - Willard Guy Scroggins died at his home east of Gravette Tuesday, August 28, 1923, aged 23 years. He was born June 10, 1900. [Gravette News-Herald 8/31/23]

SETSER, Daniel Cecil - Daniel Cecil Setser, youngest son of Mr. and Mrs. Dan M. Setser of Tulsa, Okla., died at Lawrence, Kansas May 30, 1923 of cerebromeningitis, aged 18 years. He had just completed his second year at the University and was preparing to start home when he took sick. His mother and brother, Winfred, were at his bedside when he passed away. He was a member of the First Baptist Church of Tulsa. Services were held at his fraternity house at Lawrence and the funeral was conducted at the First Baptist church of Tulsa by the pastor and the DeMolays, of which he was a member, and the body laid to rest in the Rose Hill Cemetery. Mr. and Mrs. Setser and family have a host of friends at Gravette who regret to hear of their son's death and who offer sincere sympathy. [Gravette News-Herald 6/8/23]

SETSER, Veda Elma GATTON - Mrs. T.E. Setser, who has been in ill health for several months, died Sunday, June 3, 1923 at her home northeast of Gravette, aged 36 years, 7 months and 2 days. Veda Elma Gatton was born in Lawrence Co., Mo. Oct. 31, 1886 and came to Arkansas with her parents when a child. Was married to T.E. Setser Dec. 23, 1904. Five children were born to the union, Beulah, Mary, Leo, Woodrow and James, all of whom, with the husband, survive. She also leaves her father, J.W. Gatton, and three brothers, J.G. and L.D. of Baxter Springs, Kansas and C.H. Gatton of Gravette. The funeral was conducted Monday afternoon by G.W. Tuttle and burial was in the I.O.O.F. cemetery. The community sympathizes with the bereaved ones. [Gravette News-Herald 6/8/23]

SEWARD, Stephen H. - S.H. Seward died at his home on Rust avenue in Gentry Tuesday at 10:30 o'clock. Funeral was held on the evening of the 4th. Mr. Seward is a member of the G.A.R. and was a man who was universally respected. [Gentry Journal-Advance 7/6/23]
In loving remembrance of Stephen H. Seward, died July 3, age 76 years, 11 months, 8 days. {A poem follows.} [Gentry Journal-Advance 8/3/23]

SEWELL, Mrs. N. - Word was received here the first of the week of the death of Mrs. N. Sewell, which occurred at her home at Tecumseh, Oklahoma on Saturday, February 10th. Mrs. Sewell was one of the first residents of Gentry, her husband being one of the pioneer doctors of this place. They moved from here to Oklahoma about twenty-two years ago. Mrs. Bob McKinney of this place is a daughter of Mrs. Sewell and helped care for her during her illness. [Gentry Journal-Advance 2/16/23]

SHARP, Ed - {from War Eagle} The many friends of Ed Sharp will be grieved to learn of his death which occurred last Thursday night at 11:40 o'clock. Mr. Sharp has been quite ill for several months and his death was not a great shock to the people of War Eagle and his immediate family. He has grown to manhood in War Eagle and has made a host of friends who mourn his loss. He was forty-three years and eight months old. Funeral services were conducted at the home of his parents, Nimrod Sharp and wife, by Mr. Bean of Springdale. Interment was in the Austin cemetery. We extend our sympathy to the bereaved family. Besides his mother and father he leaves three sisters and two brothers to mourn his loss. [Rogers Democrat 11/29/23]

SHOOK, Mr. and Mrs. Ike - {from Hebron} Mr. and Mrs. Ike Shook near Cave Springs died of flu-pneumonia - he died Wednesday morning - Mrs. Shook died on Wednesday the week before. They leave a family of eight children, the oldest girl being 19 years of age and the baby is two years old. [Rogers Democrat 2/15/23]

SHUTTS, Mrs. Frank {TALLMAN} - Word was received Saturday of the death of Mrs. Frank Shutts at the home of her daughter, Mrs. Harry L. Clark, at Downs, Kans. The deceased was the only sister of W.H. and Arthur Tallman of this place and her home for the past twenty-five years has been at Woodston, Kans. She leaves a husband, one son and a daughter. W.H. Tallman left Sunday morning and arrived at Woodston Monday to attend the funeral services. [Gentry Journal-Advance 2/23/23]

SKAGGS, infant - {from Wet Prairie} The two weeks old baby daughter of Mr. and Mrs. Edgar Skaggs died Thursday, Jan. 18, 1923. [Gravette News-Herald 1/26/23]

SLINKARD, Wm. U. - Wm. U. Slinkard died recently at his home near Caverna, Mo. at the age of 63 years. He was well known in Benton county and had numerous relatives here. [Rogers Democrat 3/29/23]

SMITH, Ethel May MORRIS - Ethel, wife of Joel F. Smith, passed away on the morning of Wednesday, Jan. 24, 1923 after several days illness from pneumonia fever of very severe type. She was aged 29 years and about 8 months. Mrs. Smith was the daughter of Dr. and Mrs. W.L. Morris and grew to womanhood in Gravette. Besides her husband and two little boys, Morris and Alvis, she leaves one brother, Joe P. Morris, and one sister, Mrs. Millie Foster, all of whom were with Mrs. Smith during her last illness. This is a sad blow to the family as well as to friends, particularly of the Christian church and Bible school where Mrs. Smith has been an untiring worker and teacher for several years. The funeral is to be held this Friday at 2:00 o'clock p.m. at the Christian church, C.D. Purlee of Siloam Springs officiating; the burial will be at I.O.O.F. Cemetery. Profound sympathy is extended the bereaved ones. [Gravette News-Herald 1/26/23]
Ethel May Morris was born May 3, 1892 at Siloam Springs, Mo., the elder daughter of Dr. and Mrs. W.L. Morris. Moved to Gravette, Ark. at the age of 4 years; united with the Christian church at the age of 16 years and has ever been a faithful worker therein. On August 9, 1911 she was married to Joel F. Smith. Two children were born to them: Morris, now aged 9, and Alvis, aged 3 years. She died Jan. 24, 1923, aged 30 years, 8 months and 21 days, leaving husband and children, her parents, one brother, J.P. Morris, and one sister, Mrs. Millie Foster. Funeral services were held Friday, Jan. 26, 1923 at the Christian church with a host of sympathizing friends present. Eld. C.D. Purlee of Siloam Springs, who baptised Mrs. Smith some 14 years ago, delivered the funeral discourse, paying a high tribute to the departed and the body was laid to rest in the I.O.O.F. cemetery. [Gravette News-Herald 2/2/23]

SMITH, J.G.W. - {from Lowell} J.G.W. Smith died suddenly Thursday afternoon. He had bought a hog and was helping to fix a pen when he sank to the ground and was dead in a few minutes. Funeral services were conducted by Elder Joe English. Mr. Smith had lived in and near Lowell for a good many years. He was 76 years, seven months and eight days old. He is survived by his wife, Mrs. Lucy E. Smith, two daughters, Mrs. Elizabeth Sanders of Little Rock and Mrs. E.P. Roy of Stuttgart, Ark., and two sons, W.B. Smith and Triplett Smith, both of St. Louis. [Rogers Democrat 10/4/23]

SMITH, Joseph M. - Joseph M. Smith was born on a farm in Switzerland county, Indiana February 5, 1839, died in Rogers, Arkansas January 29, 1923, lacking a week of being 84 years old. In early life he was a Baptist but upon his family moving to a community where there was no Baptist church he became a Methodist and for some 68 years he lived a Christian life in that church that lasted seven days every week. In the 37 years that the writer has known him, most of the time very intimately, he has never heard it even asserted that he ever wronged any person in any way. In 1860 he was married to Miss Lutherie Smith, who remained a faithful wife to him for 60 years, her death occurring in October 1920. Of their three children, the son died in infancy; Mrs. F.H. Duff, the younger daughter, passed away in February 1917; and Mrs. E.J. Linton, the elder daughter, preceded her mother by six months. In the Civil war he was for three years a Union soldier. In 1884 he moved from Indiana to Kansas where he resided until coming to Benton county in the spring of 1893. Since that time he has resided in or around Rogers until the time of his death. Excepting two grandsons, now in California, the entire family now sleep in the family lot in Rogers cemetery. All were faithful Christians and all looked to him who has now gone for counsel and courage. May his good works live long and help many. [Rogers Democrat 2/8/23]

SMITH, Mary J. McCANDLESS Beringer - Mary J. McCandless was born in Venango county, Penn. July 27, 1839 and died in Joplin, Mo. March 5, 1923 at the home of her daughter, Mrs. J. Lawson, at the age of 83 years, 7 months and 8 days. She was married to John Beringer in Pennsylvania in 1856 who died in 1867. She then moved to Kansas where she married B.F. Smith in 1873 and who died in 1895. She was the mother of six children, only two of whom survive her to mourn her loss: J.W. Beringer, Nowata, Okla. and Mrs. Jennie Lawson, 208 N. Connor, Joplin, Mo.; also ten grandchildren, three great-grandchildren and a host of friends. She had served the Lord since a child and was many years a member of the Free Methodist church. She had suffered for years yet was always patient and uncomplaining. Funeral services were conducted in the home, sermon preached by Rev. Balameir of the Nazarene church. She was laid to rest in the family lot in Fairview cemetery. [Gentry Journal-Advance 3/16/23]

SNIDER, Martin A. - For several years M.A. Snider and family resided in this community and enjoyed the friendship of a large circle of citizens. The following announcement of Mr. Snider's death is from the Glenwood {Iowa} Opinion: Martin A. Snider was born at Gallatin, Mo. Dec. 25, 1848 and departed this life Oct. 5, 1923, being about 75 years of age. He was united in marriage to Alice McGee at the age of 27 years at Quitman, Texas. To this union were born seven children: Mrs. Miller Rockwell of Everett, Wash.; Mrs. Carrie Bogher, Pine Bluff, Ark.; Mrs. Bessie Brown of Thornton, Ark.; Roy and Fred Snider {twins} of Glenwood, Ia. and Oregon, Mo.; Wilfred Snider of Tulsa, Okla.; Glenn Snider of Glenwood. His early home was mostly in Missouri where his occupation was that of farming. He united with the Christian church in early manhood. For the past two years Mr. Snider had been in poor health, the result of a bad case of influenza. With his wife he was preparing to go south for the winter and was making a short visit at the home of his son, Roy, just north of Glenwood, when the old trouble made a new attack and with the age of many years the body gave way. The good wife and all the children survive the husband and father. Services were conducted from the residence of his son, Roy, Saturday, Oct. 6 by Rev. D.S. Thompson. Interment was made in the Glenwood cemetery. [Gravette News-Herald 10/19/23]

SNOW, Margaret Isabella BOZARTH Stout - The funeral of Mrs. Margaret Snow, who died at the home of her sister, Mrs. Nancy L. Bunt, on February 28, 1923, was held at Wet Prairie on Thursday and burial was in the Wet Prairie cemetery. Miss Margaret Isabella Bozarth was born May 22, 1849 in McLean county, Ill., moving with her parents to Iowa in 1854. On October 29, 1868 she was married to William Stout. To this union were born five children. Mr. Stout died and some years later, Dec. 3, 1879, she married J.F. Snow and two daughters were born to this union. Mrs. Snow also leaves three sisters, Mrs. Bunt and Mrs. Jane Hale of Gravette, Mrs. McIntosh of Iowa, and three brothers, J.C. of Kansas and Samuel and Ira Bozarth of Missouri. Mrs. Snow had been a member of the Baptist church for many years. [Gravette News-Herald 3/9/23]

SNYDER, H.C. - {from Pleasant Grove} H.C. Snyder died at his home Thursday, Nov. 22. Mr. Snyder was a member of our school board and will be sadly missed in this neighborhood. We extend our sympathy to the bereaved family. [Gentry Journal-Advance 11/30/23]

SOOTER, Myrtle HOLT - Mrs. Henry Sooter, formerly Myrtle Holt, died at her home at Blue Jacket, Okla. Monday, June 11, 1923 after two months sickness, aged 46 years. She was a daughter of Henry Holt and she leaves her husband, 4 children, father, 3 brothers and 4 sisters. The body was conveyed to Gravette by Undertaker Haywood Wednesday and burial was held at Bethel cemetery, Rev. J.T. Butler of Southwest City conducting the funeral. Sympathy is extended the family. [Gravette News-Herald 6/15/23]

SPENCER, Minnie - {from Cherokee City} Mrs. Minnie Spencer died in a hospital at Drumright, Okla. March 2 and was brought back to the home of her mother, Mrs. Geo. Sullivan, Sunday. She was buried Monday at the Bloomfield cemetery. She leaves a host of friends and relatives to mourn her loss. [Gentry Journal-Advance 3/9/23]

STATER, M.O. - M.O. Stater died quite suddenly Sunday morning at his home on Chestnut street after an illness of only a day or two. Funeral services were held Tuesday afternoon at the Christian church, conducted by the pastor, Rev. J. Watson Shockley. Mr. Stater was 75 years old but was unusually active in spirit and body and had been actively engaged in the real estate business since coming to Rogers some four years ago. He is survived by his wife and three children, two sons, P.E. Stater of Oklahoma City and B.A. Stater, who lives a couple of miles north of town, and one daughter. [Rogers Democrat 4/12/23]

STEPHENSON, Charles Willis - {from Tuck's Chapel} Little Charles Willis Stephenson, 20 month old son of Cloe Stephenson and wife, died Wednesday night, October 17th. The funeral was held at Tucks Chapel by

Rev. Jackson Deason Friday morning at ten o'clock. Charles Willis was a dear little fellow and was dearly loved by every one that knew him. The grief stricken parents and little sister have the sympathy of the entire community in their sorrow. [Rogers Democrat 10/25/23]

STEVENS, Margaret M. - Margaret M. Stevens was born Dec. 13, 1863 and died March 18, 1923. She was born in Salina, Kans. making this her home until 1900 when she and her husband F.G. Stevens, moved to Oklahoma, remaining there until they came to Arkansas five years ago. She has been a member of the Methodist church since early in life. She had unmistakable knowledge of Christ as her personal Savior. She never lost an opportunity to do good. She was in her highest realm when serving others. She answered freely every call. As a companion she was loving, tender and kind; as a neighbor, always considerate of others; as a leader few could excel her; as a Christian she studied to show herself approved of God. The Methodist church, of which she was a member; the Methodist Missionary Society of which she was president; the Sunday School Class of which she was teacher; the Union Missionary Society of which she was a member, together with her circle of friends, all join in one prayer that God will give of His riches of grace to the family in this sad hour. Funeral services were conducted at the Methodist church by the pastor, Rev. C.H. Sherman. The body was taken to Arkansas City, Kans. for burial. [Gentry Journal-Advance 3/23/23]

STRINGFIELD, William Harrison - Under date of November 2nd, the Humboldt {Nebraska} Standard tells of the death of William Harrison Stringfield, 83 years old. who passed away at the country home of his daughter, Mrs. T.G. Atwood, Saturday, October 27th. Mr. Stringfield and wife were residents of Rogers for several years and lived on North 5th street, going to Nebraska a year ago last July. One son, E.P. Stringfield, lives near Rogers and another son for a time clerked here in the Sample Shoe Store to be with his parents. We quote from the Standard as follows: "W.H. Stringfield was born Sept. 30, 1840 in Edmondson county, Kentucky and moved with his parents to Missouri in 1843, thence to Iowa in 1863. He enlisted in Co. A, 4th Iowa cavalry September 4, 1861 and served four years and 28 days. After the war he came to Nemaha Falls, south of Falls City, in 1865. He was married to Pamelia Brown July 4, 1867 to which union was born seven sons and two daughters. There are left to mourn his demise, besides his aged wife: E.P. Stringfield, Rogers, Ark.; C.C. Stringfield, Ewing, Neb.; W.S. Stringfield, Humboldt; F.S. Stringfield, Oakley, Idaho; R.C. Stringfield, Randolph, Neb.; J.L. Stringfield, La Grande, Ore.; Mrs. T.C. Atwood of Humboldt and Mrs. W.E. Wheeler, Shickley, Neb." [Rogers Democrat 11/8/23]

STROUD, Marjorie - Marjorie, the 14-year-old daughter of Mr. and Mrs. Thomas Stroud, died Friday night at their home in the southeast part of town. She had been ill for some months. Funeral services were held at the home Sunday afternoon and interment was in the Rogers cemetery. The family came to Rogers from Cave Springs. [Rogers Democrat 4/12/23]

SUMNER, Henry C. - {from War Eagle} Henry C. Sumner was born in Lawrence county, Illinois October 19, 1846 and died at his home here on Monday, November 19, 1923 at the age of 77 years. He was married to Permelia Robison. To this union was born eight children, six boys and two girls - all of whom were here at the time of his death except one daughter, Mrs. Lizzie Easley, of Wan, Okla. Dick Sumner and Bert Sumner, his two sons, have also lived here for several years. Grandpa Sumner and wife moved here some six years ago and have made many friends who extend their heartfelt sympathy to the bereaved wife and children. [Rogers Democrat 11/22/23]

SWAGGERTY, Ellen - Fayetteville, May 30.- Mrs. Ellen Swaggerty, aged 70, was instantly killed this morning when she stepped in front of a Ford coupe driven by Mrs. Nina Braymer of this place. No blame is attached to Mrs. Braymer. The accident, the only serious one marking Memorial Day, occurred on the Greenland road where Mrs. Swaggerty was walking with her daughter, Mrs. Alice Terhune. An approaching car caused Mrs. Swaggerty to swerve immediately in front of the Braymer car, coming behind her. Her neck was broken in the impact. [Rogers Democrat 6/7/23]

TEASDALE, Mrs. Robt. - Mrs. Robt. Teasdale, mother of Mrs. Carl Cannon of this city, died Saturday night at her home in St. Louis and the funeral services were held Monday afternoon. Mr. and Mrs. Cannon had been with her two weeks previous to her death. The Teasdales had visited frequently in Rogers and the death of Mrs. Teasdale was learned by friends here with much regret. [Rogers Democrat 8/9/23]

TETRICK, infant - {from Pea Ridge} The five-weeks-old baby of Chas. Tetrick and wife died last Saturday afternoon at 3 o'clock of whooping cough. Rev. Carnahan conducted the funeral services at the residence Sunday afternoon after which the little body was laid to rest in the Pea Ridge cemetery. We extend sympathy to the bereaved ones. [Rogers Democrat 7/19/23]

TEVEBAUGH, A.J. - A.J. Tevebaugh was born May 7, 1847, died Nov. 21, 1923, age 76 years, 6 months and 14 days. In early life he was united in marriage to Martha Winn near Springfield, Mo., spending most of his married life in East Arkansas. To this union was born 13 children; 7 boys and 6 girls; 11 of whom are still living. Some 20 years ago he professed religion and joined the Missionary Baptist church and was baptized at Oaks, Okla. and lived a faithful member until his death; expressing willingness to go but regretting to leave his children, his wife had preceded him 12 years; they having lived together happily for 43 years and raised their family to womanhood and manhood. [Gentry Journal-Advance 11/30/23]

THOMAS, Suzanne - Attorney H.E. Funk Tuesday received a telegram from Pasadena, Calif. announcing the death of Miss Suzanne Thomas of that city, a former well known Rogers resident. Death was the result of an accident Sunday when Miss Thomas was struck by an automobile and suffered concussion of the brain. She died early Monday morning without recovering consciousness. The telegram said the body would be taken to the birthplace of Miss Thomas at Stowe, Vermont for burial. Miss Thomas lived with her mother, Mrs. Jennie R. Thomas, who has been in poor health for a long time; it is not presumed she was able to make the long trip east. Mrs. Thomas and daughter, Miss Suzanne, came to Rogers from the east a number of years ago to be with the former's sister, Mrs. Sarah Bailey, who is now with her daughter, Mrs. Kate Prickett, at Glendale, Calif. They moved to California some eight years ago for the benefit of the health of Mrs. Thomas and Miss Suzanne has for a number of years been an instructor in the commercial and business department of the Pasadena high school. She was a woman of education and ability and had a great many friends in Rogers who regret most deeply to learn of her untimely death and extend to the bereaved mother their heartfelt sympathy. Mr. Funk has for a number of years looked after the business interest of the family here. [Rogers Democrat 10/4/23]

THORNTON, William M. - {from Beaty} W.M. Thornton, after a long illness, died Sunday, May 13, 1923 at the home of his brother, G.C. Thornton. The body was taken to Nebraska City for burial, accompanied by Mr. and Mrs. G.C. Thornton. [Gravette News-Herald 5/18/23]

{from The Daily Press, Nebraska City, Neb., May 15, 1923} William Thornton passed away at his home at Beaty, Ark. Sunday afternoon according to a message received by his brother, Fred Thornton, of this city. Paralysis was the direct cause of his death. The body will arrive here this morning and will be taken to the home of his brother, Fred, southeast of the city where funeral services will be held at 3 p.m. He was born at Monticello, Ill. Oct. 14, 1872 and came to Nebraska in June 1880 with his parents. He attended the schools of this community and in the early nineties, in company with Jerome Vaughn and Geo. Dole, drove overland to Caldwell, Kan. and registered for the opening of the Cherokee Strip. They shipped across to Orlando and made a run on horse back; drove his stake and held his claim but gave it up later and took a claim in the Standing Rock reserve in South Dakota. He engaged in farming several years until failing health compelled him to go to Arkansas. About two months ago he suffered a stroke of paralysis from the effects of which he passed away at the home of his brother, Gilbert Thornton, at Beaty. He was well known and highly esteemed in this community and has hundreds of friends here who will regret to learn of his death. The funeral will be conducted by Rev. Hall of the Christian church, of which body Mr. Thornton has been a member since 1894. He is survived by his mother, Mrs. J.W. Thornton, three brothers and three sisters. [Gravette News-Herald 5/25/23]

TINDALL, Grandpa - {from Meadow Brook} Grandpa Tindall, father of Mrs. J.H. Fuller, grandfather of Mrs. F.A. Clark and great-grandfather of Ted Bruce, died March 28 at the home of his son in Custer Co., Okla. Many News Herald readers knew him when at home here several years with Mrs. Fuller. [Gravette News-Herald 4/6/23]

TOMLIN, Grandpa - {from War Eagle} Grandpa Tomlin of Larue died last week and was buried in the War Eagle cemetery Thursday. We extend our sympathy to the bereaved family. [Rogers Democrat 8/30/23]

TROUT, Bill - "Uncle" Bill Trout, 73 years old, one of Bentonville's best known and most respected colored citizens, died a few days ago. He had worked for the late James A. Haney and his family for more than fifty years. [Rogers Democrat 6/28/23]

TRUE, Bettie - {from Pleasant Valley} Aunt Bettie True, formerly a resident of this vicinity but who has made her home for some time with Uncle John Wright and wife of Springtown, passed away Thursday and was buried Friday in the Springtown cemetery. [Gentry Journal-Advance 5/18/23]

VAN KIRK, Anna Jane - Mrs. Anna Jane VanKirk died last Thursday night at the home of Mr. Anderson at 113 East Maple Street at the age of 84 years. She had lived in Rogers for many years and was well known to our older citizens. Her husband, who died many years ago, was once a practicing physician here. She is survived by one daughter, Mrs. Lillie Harmon, of Paris Texas. [Rogers Democrat 11/8/23]

VICK, B.C. - B.C. Vick died last evening at his home on West Walnut street after a very brief illness. He was on the street Saturday and Sunday was attacked by the flu. He grew worse with surprising quickness, pneumonia developing at once. He was 63 years old and had seemingly been in very good health. He was born at Bay, Ark. He came to Rogers three years ago from Beggs, Okla. where he had lived for sixteen years. He is survived by his wife and four children: Mrs. Ella Kimble and Mrs. N.O. Brand of Clayton, New Mexico; Joe B. Vick, who is in college at Conway, this state, and Hoyt G. Vick of Beggs. He was a brother of Mrs. J.A. Isbell of Rogers. The body will be taken to Beggs for burial, but at the time of our closing the paper last night the funeral arrangements had not been fully decided, awaiting replies from telegrams from relatives. Mr. Vick was a prominent member of the Central M.E. church of Rogers and undoubtedly Rev. Critchlow will have charge of the service here but we do not know whether they will be at the church or at the house. His untimely death will be learned by the many friends with great surprise and deep regret for only a few had as yet learned of his illness. [Rogers Democrat 3/8/23]

VON NETHEN, Anna - Mrs. Anna Von Nethen died last week at the home of her grandson, Ed Thiessen, northwest of Rogers, at the age of 80 years, ten months and five days. She was a native of Germany. Brief funeral services were conducted at Callison's undertaking parlors by W.F.D. Batjer and the body was taken to Lanham, Nebraska for burial. [Rogers Democrat 11/22/23]

WALKER, Jack - Hon. Jack Walker, aged 53, internal revenue collector for Arkansas during the Wilson administration, died very suddenly last Wednesday at his home in Fayetteville. Death was the result of neuralgia of the heart. He was not married. All of his life was spent in Fayetteville save during his term as collector and he was buried there by the grave of his father, Hon. Dave Walker, an early United States senator from Arkansas. He had served a term in the legislature, as mayor of Fayetteville, and two terms as circuit clerk of Washington county. He is survived by his brothers, Dr. Dave Walker of Little Rock, Vol and J. Wythe Walker of Fayetteville and a sister, Miss Sue Walker, Fayetteville. [Rogers Democrat 9/6/23]

WALLACE, Mr. - {from Pleasant Grove} The friends of Mr. Wallace will be sorry to hear of his death at Wichita, Kans. Nov. 15. The family left here a few weeks ago hoping Mr. Wallace would be better in the north. He lived here several years and was respected by all. [Gentry Journal-Advance 11/30/23]

WARD, Anzell - {from Fairmount} Anzell Ward, a former resident of this community, died of flu and pneumonia at Dodge, Okla. Thursday night and was buried at Fairmount Friday afternoon. [Gentry Journal-Advance 1/23/23]

WATKINS, W.L. - W.L. Watkins, who was one of the early business men of Rogers and who had made his home here for thirty-five years, died Tuesday noon at his home on South Fourth street at the age of eighty-six years. He had been an invalid for many years and because of his confinement to his home in recent years had dropped out of the knowledge and fellowship of most of our people. His funeral was held yesterday afternoon from the home and was conducted by Rev. Critchlow of the Central M.E. church. It was noticeable that the men present to pay a last tribute to the memory of Mr. Watkins were those who had lived here for at least a quarter of a century or more. Hundreds of our citizens have never even heard of him but when the editor came to Rogers he was one of the best known men in town. Burial was in the Rogers cemetery. W.L. Watkins was born in New Madrid, Mo., August 15, 1837. He came from a distinguished family, his father being one of the most eminent lawyers of southeast Missouri. As a boy Mr. Watkins was associated with his father as his private secretary. When the Civil War broke out he entered the Confederate army. During most of the war he was a prisoner. After the war he married Miss Maggie Brown who survives him. They came to Rogers in 1888 and for many years was engaged in the grocery business, a large share of the time in partnership with E.W. Dawkins. Also with A.J. Duckworth. He was compelled to retire from business a number of years ago because of failing health and in more recent years an invalid under the constant, loving care of his faithful wife. Besides his wife he is survived by a brother, William Blackburn Watkins; a nephew, Harry C. Watkins; and two nieces, Mrs. Maude Stubbs and Miss Susie A. Watkins. [Rogers Democrat 12/20/23]

WATSON, Joe - Joe, the 24 year old son of Mr. and Mrs. W.A. Watson of Springdale, Ark., took his own life by swallowing strychnine. The act was well planned and took place in an abandoned farm house two miles northeast of that place. That Watson repented of his action, or attempted to notify persons of his deed, seems certain from the position of the body, which was found early Saturday morning by neighbors, only a short distance from a telephone in the house. He had connected a switch which had been disconnected by persons leaving the house but the rapid effect of the poison prevented the use of the phone. Despondence over a love affair is given as the only probable cause. He is survived by his parents and four brothers and three sisters. [Gentry Journal-Advance 7/13/23]

WEBB, Sarah J. SCOTT - {from Larue} Sarah J. Scott was born May 5th, 1855. Was married to John W. Webb December 2, 1877; to this union nine children were born - 5 girls and 4 boys; Elizabeth and Thomas dying in infancy, Rebecca Kelly dying at the age of 33, two girls and two boys were present with her when she departed this life August 1, 1923. She was a member of the Church of Christ, obeying the Gospel several years ago under the preaching of John T. Hines at Wesley, Ark. The remains were laid to rest in the Webb cemetery August 2, 1923, Rev. G.C. Bland conducting the funeral services. [Rogers Democrat 8/9/23]

WEBSTER, Kathleen JENKINS - Mrs. W.H. Webster died at her home two and three quarter miles southwest of Rogers on Wednesday, June 27th at 8:50 p.m. Funeral services were held at the home Saturday, June 30th at two o'clock at the residence and were conducted by Rev. Barrett, pastor of the Baptist church of Rogers. Burial was in the Oakley Chapel cemetery. Kathleen Jenkins was born in Franklin County, Ky. March 12, 1853; was united in marriage to W.H. Webster Dec. 22, 1872. They were then living in Owen county, Ky.; from there they moved to Kansas; in 1888 they moved to Arkansas where they had since made their home. To this union were born eight children - six of whom are living. Besides her husband she is survived by six children - Mrs. Lucy Volk, Mrs. Rena Johnson, Mrs. Florence Phillips, Mrs. Della Ingersoll and J.D. Webster of Siloam Springs; Mrs. Effa Baker of Joplin, Mo. Also eleven grandchildren and four great-grandchildren. In her young days she united with the Baptist church, her membership at the time of her death being in the Baptist church of Rogers. [Rogers Democrat 7/5/23]

WETZEL, infant - The infant of Mr. and Mrs. Claude Wetzel died the first of the week at Tulsa, Okla. and the body was shipped back for burial at Maysville. Mr. and Mrs. G.C. Tinnin and Mr. and Mrs. Claude Queen went to Joplin, Mo. Wednesday to meet the Wetzels. Mesdames Queen and Wetzel are daughters of Dave Edwards. [Gravette News-Herald 6/15/23]

WHITESIDE, Mabel Marie - Mabel Marie Whiteside, daughter of Mr. and Mrs. Will Whiteside, was born Aug. 3, 1918 and died Nov. 22, 1923 at the age of 5 years, 3 months and 19 days. Her twin sister died in infancy.

She leaves father, mother, three brothers and one sister to mourn for her. Mabel was the youngest of five children, all being at home. Heaven's gain is our loss. She will be greatly missed in the home and by everyone that knew her. [Gentry Journal-Advance 11/30/23]

WHITLOW, L.E. - L.E. Whitlow, a brother of R.H. Whitlow of this city, died Tuesday in a Fort Smith hospital. The body was taken to Springdale for burial, that being the home of two daughters of the deceased, Mrs. R.H. Mitchell and Mrs. Minnie Rogers, where services were held yesterday afternoon and were conducted by Rev. J.W. Shockley of this city. The deceased was 63 years old. [Rogers Democrat 1/11/23]

WILCOXTON, Clay - Clay Wilcoxton, a 12-year-old boy from Fayetteville, died in the Frisco hospital at Springfield Friday night, the result of injuries received in Rogers that morning when he fell under the wheels of a Frisco freight train. In company with several youthful companions. Young Wilcoxton had beat his way to Rogers Thursday night on a freight train and was attempting to board a south bound freight train in the south end of the local yard when he slipped, or was thrown by the speed of the train, under the car wheels. His right leg was crushed below the knee so that amputation was a very evident necessity, while the calf of the left leg was torn and mangled and the foot crushed. The accident occurred about nine o'clock Friday morning and the lad was rushed to the office of Dr. Curry where first aid treatment was given by Drs. Curry and Moore. Passenger No. 4 was held until the wounded boy could be taken aboard and then, accompanied by Dr. Curry, he was taken to the hospital. The examination at the hospital revealed that the boy was even more seriously injured than at first anticipated and he was unable to survive the combined shock of the injury and wounds, and died on the operating table. He was a son of Tom Wilcoxton of Fayetteville and we understand that his mother is dead. We presume there is little use of calling the attention of boys in Rogers in particular, and of everywhere in general, to the dangers that are resultant of the habit of "hopping the trains." Each boy is supremely confident that he knows more about it than the fellow who got hurt or killed and that no accident can happen to him. The number of accidents of this kind that are being daily reported is evident that "hopping trains" is really a most dangerous pastime. [Rogers Democrat 7/19/23]

WILKERSON, Leola COFFELT - A sad message reached the many friends here of Clarence Wilkerson Wednesday morning announcing the death of his young wife which occurred about midnight Tuesday, Feb. 20, 1923. Mrs. Wilkerson underwent an operation for appendicitis about three weeks previously and seemed to be doing nicely but developments necessitated a second operation after which the patient gradually declined until the hour of death. Mrs. Leola Wilkerson was the daughter of Mr. and Mrs. W. Coffelt of Aurora, Mo. and was married to Clarence Wilkerson Aug. 1, 1920. She leaves besides husband, parents and other near relatives, one little son, A.B. Wilkerson, Jr. The funeral was to be held this Thursday morning at Aurora and interment made in the cemetery there. This is indeed a sad blow to the husband and other relatives as well as a shock to a host of friends here who held Mrs. Wilkerson in high esteem. The condolence of all is extended the bereaved ones. [Gravette News-Herald 2/23/23]

WILLIAMS, Elizabeth FRANCIS - Elizabeth Francis was born in Auburn, Cannon county, Tennessee May 27, 1848; was married to Wm. Williams in 1870. He preceded her to the great beyond August 29, 1895. To this union five children were born: Etta and Lillie {deceased}; Joe A. in San Francisco, Calif. and was unable to attend the funeral; John F. and Wm. H. were with her at the time of her death, Nov. 28, 1923. She united with the Baptist church in Tennessee while in her youth. After moving to Arkansas in 1867 she placed her membership at Pond Springs. Although unable to attend church for a number of years she remained ever faithful to her God and church. She was very devoted to her home and family, never tiring in administering to their needs. She was among the pioneers of Rogers. her father, with his family, settled near Oakley Chapel in 1867. She leaves besides her children, one sister, Mrs. Henry Williams, who resides in Rogers, and a brother, J.A. Francis at Pace's Chapel, other relatives and many friends to mourn her departure. Funeral services were conducted at the home by Rev. J.W. Shockley Thursday afternoon. Her remains were laid to rest in the Guyll cemetery by the side of her husband to await the coming of our Lord. [Rogers Democrat 12/6/23]

WILLIAMS, John W. - The many friends of J.W. Williams will regret greatly to learn that he is seriously ill at the country home of his daughter, Mrs. J.W. Walker, east of Rogers, and that the physicians can give but little hope for his recovery. He is suffering from an attack of blood poisoning, induced by age and the breakdown of some of the vital organs. He is 77 years old and has been in rather feeble health all summer although able to be around. Mr. Williams was for many years one of the leading business men of Lowell and well known throughout the entire county. For several years he has been living here with his daughter, Miss Lucy Williams, just north of the Christian church. The children and relatives have been notified that his condition is considered very serious, although of course so long as there is life they will not give up hope of his recovering. [Rogers Democrat 7/19/23]

A phone message just as we go to press this morning tells of the death of J.W. Williams at 8 o'clock at the country home of his daughter, Mrs. J. Wythe Walker. Funeral services at the Presbyterian church in Rogers Friday afternoon. [Rogers Democrat 7/19/23]

Northwest Arkansas lost one of its most interesting characters by the death last Thursday morning of John W. Williams, who passed away at the country home of his daughter, Mrs. J. Wythe Walker, east of Rogers, at the age of 78 years, after a brief illness. He had been a resident of Benton county for more than half a century and had taken an active part in the religious and political activities of her people during practically all of that time. Related to many of the leading families of the east end of the counties, both by birth and marriage. "Uncle John," as he was familiarly known to friends and relatives, was for years a leader in his neighborhood, south of Bentonville, and later in the little town of Lowell, where he was engaged in the general mercantile business from 1887 until he came to Rogers some two or three years ago. He was a man of strong convictions with the courage to stand for whatever he believed to be right. It could truly be said of him that he never betrayed a trust, never deserted a friend, and never took a mean advantage of an antagonist. Funeral services were held at the Presbyterian church in Rogers Friday afternoon at three o'clock and were conducted by the pastor, Rev. T.E. McSpadden, assisted by Rev. Peter Carnahan of Bentonville, a life-long friend and associate of Mr. Williams. Burial was in the Rogers cemetery. John W. Williams was a native of Lawrence county, Missouri where he was born April 21, 1845. He was a member of a family of sixteen children. Two brothers were killed during the Civil War and Mr. Williams himself served in the Confederate army in Company A, Third Missouri. Two brothers lived until a comparatively few years ago, Wash Williams dying about 1915 and Ceph Williams dying a few years earlier. Four sisters survive Mr. Williams: Mrs. L.E. Cox of El Reno, Okla.; Mrs. Cy McSpadden of Oakley Chapel; Mrs. Dave B. Huffman of Verona, Mo.; and Mrs. M.D. Duval of Ventura, Calif. Mrs. Duval, before her second marriage, was Mrs. John Droke. Mr. Williams came to Benton county in the fall of 1866, his father dying during the trip. His mother and children settled three miles south of Bentonville where they took a homestead. In 1869 Mr. Williams married Miss Nanny Pace, an aunt of Lon Pace of Bentonville. To them were born 3 daughters: Mrs. Lena Walker and Miss Lucy Williams of Rogers; Mrs. Zelda Thomas of Carrollton, Ill.; and 2 sons, Will and Earle. Will died several years ago in Michigan and Dr. Earle Williams is living at San Antonio, Texas but was unable to come to his father's bedside because of illness. Mrs. Williams died in 1882. In 1883 Mr. Williams married Mrs. John Oakley who died in 1909, leaving one daughter, Miss Nina, who has been teaching the past year at Ardmore, Okla. and who was called home for the funeral. Mr. Williams left the farm in 1887 and moved to Lowell, where he was for years its best known citizen and a leader in most of the activities of the little town. He was a member of the Cumberland Presbyterian church and an elder in that denomination for many years and one of its most influential laymen. He organized and was instrumental in building the Presbyterian church at Lowell. When the C.P. Church merged with the Presbyterian Church, U.S.A. Mr. Williams gave the new church the same wholehearted support he had his first choice and served as an elder both at Lowell and in the Rogers church where he had been one of the most faithful attendants. He was a life-long Democrat and he fought the political battles of his day with all the vim and enthusiasm that he could muster. There was never the slightest trouble in telling just where and for what and for whom Mr. Williams stood. The family and the entire community will miss his kindly presence but will rejoice that he left a private and public life worthy of emulation. [Rogers Democrat 7/26/23]

WILLIAMS, Lester - Lester, six-year-old child of Lee Williams, died recently at the home near Bentonville, death being the result of tetanus, following an injury received when a horse stepped on the child's foot. [Rogers Democrat 9/6/23]

WILLIAMS, Mr. and Mrs. J.M. - Mrs. and Mrs. J.M. Williams, aged parents of Mrs. Dr. F.G. Eubanks, both died at Decatur last week, he passing away Wednesday and she on Thursday, the result of flu and infirmities. These venerable people at one time resided in Gravette. The bodies were both laid to rest on Saturday. [Gravette News-Herald 2/23/23]

WINKLER, Mrs. - {from Fairview Chapel} Mrs. Winkler died Sunday morning after a long illness. She leaves several children, her husband and many friends to mourn her departure. Burial was in Lee cemetery Monday, Nov. 26. [Gravette News-Herald 11/30/23]

WINTON, Mrs. Martin - Bentonville, July 6.- Mrs. Martin Winton, 87 years old, member of a pioneer Benton county family, died at her home, Winton Place, on Pea Ridge yesterday morning. Mrs. Winton is survived by two daughters, Mrs. James A. Rice and Miss Minnie Winton, both of Winton Place, and by a number of grandchildren. The Winton home, which is in the historic Pea Ridge section made famous by the battle of Pea Ridge, has one of the most beautiful locations in this section and is one of the show places of the county. [Rogers Democrat 7/12/23]

WOMACK, James W. - James W. Womack died last Wednesday morning at his home at Centerton at the age of 74 years. He had been a resident of Benton county for many years and the family is one of the best known in the state, for the children include Prof. J. Pitts Womack, superintendent of the public schools at Jonesboro; Prof. R.E. Womack, a member of Hendrix Academy faculty at Conway; Rev. W.B. Womack, pastor of the M.E. Church, South at Forrest City; Rev. A.J. Womack, pastor of the M.E. Church at Fayetteville; Miss Stella Womack of Pueblo, Colo., a deaconess; Mrs. Frank Marr, Warrenburg, Mo.; Mrs. Hugh Good, Centerton and Mrs. Robert Lee, Missouri. [Rogers Democrat 9/6/23]

WOOD, Margaret - Mrs. Margaret Wood died last week at her home at Bentonville at the advanced age of 90 years and 10 months. She was the mother of Misses Maggie and Nana Wood. [Rogers Democrat 1/25/23]

WOODEN, Harvey M. - Harvey M. Wooden, for forty years a resident of Benton county, Ark., died at his residence west of Gravette on the morning of Jan. 30, 1923 at the ripe age of about 87 years. At his request the burial was made on his farm, about 250 yards west of the house in which he had lived so long. The funeral was conducted by Rev. W.M. Shelton of Gravette.

Mr. Wooden was born in Indiana about the year of 1835 or 36. When he was three years old his parents moved to north Missouri where he grew to manhood. In 1856, at about the age of 20 years, he professed faith in Christ and united with the Methodist church. The date of his marriage is not known but about the time he had reached his majority, marrying Miss Mary Jane Smith. To this union were born eight children. Three of the children were at his burial which was largely attended by friends and neighbors, to whom the family wishes to express appreciation for the great kindness shown. [Gravette News-Herald 2/9/23]

WOODS, Dave H. - Dave H. Woods, one of the pioneer business men of Bentonville, died last Thursday afternoon at the home of his son, Loyd C. Woods, east of Bentonville. He was 78 years old and had been in feeble health for some years. [Rogers Democrat 8/2/23]

WOODS, Edna JEFFERSON - Mrs. Allie P. Woods died Wednesday afternoon February 7th at 3:30 o'clock at the home three miles northwest of Rogers, the result of pneumonia fever, after a short illness. Mr. Woods was seriously ill at the same time and the disease and the strain were too much for her. Funeral services were held at the Woods home Friday afternoon at 2:30 o'clock, the services conducted by Rev. Barrett, pastor of the Baptist church of Rogers. Interment was at the Jefferson cemetery, two miles east of Bentonville. Miss Edna Jefferson was a daughter of the late S.A. Jefferson and was born April 9, 1883 at the home place east of Bentonville where she grew to womanhood. She is survived by her husband and two little sons. Also by four sisters, Mrs. C.C. Huffman, Mrs. Mary Landers and Misses Mollie and Pearl Jefferson of Bentonville, and three brothers, B.A. Jefferson and Tom Jefferson of Pea Ridge and C.O. Jefferson of Dublin, Texas. Her untimely death is a great blow to the family and relatives and they have the sympathy of their large circle of friends and neighbors. [Rogers Democrat 2/15/23]

WOOLSEY, Harriett - Mrs. Harriett Woolsey, 81 years of age, for more than fifty years a resident of Bentonville, died last week at Sulphur Springs at the home of her daughter, Mrs. Dice Anderson. [Rogers Democrat 5/3/23]

WORTHY, Mrs. Tom - {from Hebron} Mrs. Tom Worthy died of cancer at her home in Cave Springs Sunday morning and was buried at Hebron Monday afternoon. She had lived to the age of 66 years, 6 months and had spent 31 years of the time in Arkansas, had lived in this neighborhood until three years ago when her and her husband moved to Cave Springs. She was a good, kind woman and was always cheerful, had been a member of the Methodist church for years. She leaves two daughters, Mrs. Maud Trent and Mrs. Bob Ratliff; two sons, Tom and Barney, and a number of grandchildren and one great-grandchild and an aged husband to mourn her loss. [Rogers Democrat 3/29/23]

WORTHY, Tom - Death has again called in this neighborhood and taken Uncle Tom Worthy in his keeping Saturday morning at 8 o'clock at the age of 78 years and nine months. This is certainly a sad time for the Worthy children as their mother died just two weeks before their father did. He was stricken Tuesday with pneumonia and soon passed away. Uncle Tom, as he was called by everyone, was a grand old man and faithfully kept the Golden Rule and never spoke aught of his fellowmen. He had been a member of the Methodist church for a number of years. After a short funeral sermon by Rev. Brogan he was laid to rest in the Hebron cemetery by the side of his life companion. [Rogers Democrat 4/12/23]

WYATT, T.M. - Bentonville, Aug. 21.- The fiery cross of the Ku Klux Klan was in evidence for the first time at a Bentonville home Friday night when one of the emblem in electric lights burned all night on the front porch of the home of the late Dr. T.M. Wyatt, whose death occurred here Friday morning. The watchers at the bier of Dr. Wyatt, said to have been a member of the Klan of early days, included members of the local organization, it is said. [Rogers Democrat 8/23/23]
Dr. T.M. Wyatt, 81 years of age, died last Friday morning at Bentonville after an illness of many months. He had lived at Bentonville for some thirty years and was a dentist by profession. [Rogers Democrat 8/23/23]

YEARGAIN, Pearl - Pearl Yeargain died at his home on the McCaffree farm east of Sulphur Springs Thursday, April 5, 1923, the result of a stroke of paralysis. Mr. Yeargain was aged 34 years. He leaves his wife and one son, Ernest, and one daughter, Fern; also two brothers, Marion and Charlie of Sulphur Springs vicinity. The funeral and burial took place on Friday, April 6, interment being made at Mt. Pleasant cemetery, east of Gravette. The family has the sympathy of all in their bereavement. [Gravette News-Herald 4/13/23]

YEOMAN, G.G. - Word was received the last of the week of the death of Rev. G.G. Yeoman in a hospital at Kansas City. Death was the result of cancer of the stomach and he had been very low for the past month or two. Rev. Yeoman was a former pastor of the First M.E. church of Rogers and was very popular here and the news of his illness and death was learned with much regret. Rev. Yeoman was a native of Iowa and his father and uncles were at one time among the Democrat leaders of that state. E.M. Funk of the Democrat knew his father, Col. F.G. Yeoman, when he was editor of the old Des Moines Leader and was also well acquainted with his uncles. [Rogers Democrat 6/28/23]

YOUNG, Riley - Monday morning two lives were lost by fire at Beaver, the summer resort on White river between Seligman and Eureka Springs. The victims of the flames were Riley Young, 54, and his 7-year-old grandson, Jack Barnes. When rescued from the ruins of the house both were so badly burned they died a short time after being hurried to the Huntington Hospital in Eureka Springs. Mr. Young was attempting to start a fire with coal oil and an explosion scattered the flames over the room and on his clothes. The little boy was in a room on the ground floor and evidently was unable to open the door or the flames and smoke overcame him before he had a chance to escape. An 18-year-old son was sleeping upstairs and was forced to jump from a window. The flames destroyed another cottage close by but the Riverside Hotel was saved after a hard fight. The father of Jack Barnes was killed two years ago at Beaver by falling from the bridge one dark night and his mother was in Kansas City. Mrs. Young died three months ago. [Rogers Democrat 2/15/23]

ADAMS, Ella - Mrs. Ella Adams was born in Wood county, Ohio January 26, 1852 and died April 12, 1924 at the age of 72 years, two months and 17 days. On June 17, 1872 she was married to William Adams who died in 1907. To them were born six children, all of whom are living: Mrs. Emery Johnson of Rogers; Mrs. Charlie Lenon of Rogers; Mrs. T.O. Mann of Pittsburg, Kansas; Charlie and Earl Adams of Rogers and Lynn Adams of Haswell, Colo. She has twenty grandchildren living and five dead. Also two great-grandchildren living. From Ohio Mr. and Mrs. Adams moved to Kansas and lived there until 1890 when they came to Rogers. Mrs. Adams has a brother and sister living in North Baltimore, Ohio. She was a member of the First M.E. church and lived a consistent Christian life. Services were conducted at the First M.E. church by the pastor, Rev. R.C. Lucke, on Tuesday afternoon at 2:30. Interment was in the Rogers cemetery. [Rogers Democrat 4/17/24] [Rogers Daily Post 4/16/24]
Mr. and Mrs. Fein Johnson of Oskaloosa, Mo. arrived this morning to attend the funeral of Mrs. Ella Adams. Mr. Johnson is a grandson of Mrs. Adams. Other relatives who came to attend the funeral were Mrs. Adams' son, Lynn, who arrived last night from Haswell, Colo. and Mr. and Mrs. P.O. Marr and children from Pittsburg, Kans. Mrs. Marr is Mrs. Adams' daughter. [Rogers Daily Post 4/15/24]

ADAMS, Stephen Hays - {from Rogers} Rev. S.H. Adams, a retired minister, died at his home south of Rogers Sunday following an attack of pneumonia. He leaves a wife and five grown children. [Benton County Record 2/29/24]

ALFREY, Mrs. J.S. {GUNTHER} - {from The Siloam Springs Daily Register, Oct. 3.} Mrs. J.S. Alfrey was probably fatally injured when she was struck by an automobile near her home yesterday about five o'clock. It seems that Mrs. Alfrey had made a visit to one of her neighbors and was returning home when the accident happened as she started to cross the street. According to eye witnesses Mrs. Alfrey had just started to step down from the bank on the side of the street as the car came along. The driver, Miss Maud Harwood of north of the city, saw Mrs. Alfrey standing there and signalled to her with the horn but Mrs. Alfrey evidently became confused from the nearness of the car, lost her balance and stumbled in front of the car which had no opportunity to stop, knocking her down and running over her. The ambulance was called immediately and she was moved to the City Hospital where an examination was made to determine the extent of her injuries. It was learned that she suffered a fracture of the base of the skull and there was no hope given by the doctors last night for her recovery. Her condition this morning is reported to be about the same. It is understood that Miss Harwood is prostrated from the shock and is in a critical condition at her home on Flint creek. She is not held responsible for the accident. ***** Mrs. Alfrey died in the hospital Saturday night without regaining

consciousness. Funeral services were held at the Presbyterian church Monday afternoon. Mrs. Alfrey was a Gunther before marriage. She leaves three children: Curtis Alfrey of Siloam Springs; Jim Alfrey of Bentonville and Mrs. Claude Pickens of Tulsa. [Rogers Democrat 10/9/24]
Funeral services were held in Siloam Springs Monday for Mrs. J.S. Alfrey who died Saturday from injuries received on Thursday when she was struck by an automobile driven by Miss Maud Harwood of the Harwood Stock Farm, north of Siloam Springs. Miss Harwood was prostrated by the accident and was taken to Kansas City and placed in a hospital for medical attention. Mrs. Alfrey was about 55 years of age and was well known to many Bentonville people. She leaves, besides her husband, two sons: James Alfrey, Jr. of Bentonville; Curtis Alfrey of Siloam Springs and Mrs. Claude Pickens of Tulsa, Okla. [Benton County Record 10/10/24]

ALFREY, Mrs. W.T. - Mrs. W.T. Alfrey died at the family home east of Bentonville on Monday, June 9th, 1924 at the age of 67 years. While she had been ill for some time it was not until the past few days that her condition was thought to be serious. The funeral, which was largely attended, was at the home on Wednesday afternoon, the Rev. J.M. McMahen conducting the services. Interment was made in Mt. Eden. Mrs. Alfrey was born in White county, Ind. in 1857. Her parents both died when she was quite young and she came here when a child with an aunt. In 1877 she was married to W.T. Alfrey. She has been an active member of the Baptist Church and leaves a host of friends and relatives to mourn her loss. Besides her husband she is survived by four sons - Lester, who lives west of Cherokee City; Albert of Siloam Springs; Harry of Blocker, Okla. and Walter Alfrey of Baxter Springs, Kansas; also four daughters - Mrs. Pres Marrs, Jane, Mo.; Mrs. Amos Cavness, Bentonville; Mrs. O.E. Arnett, Afton, Okla. and Mrs. Will Lighart of Newton, Kansas. [Benton County Record 6/13/24]

ALLEN, Ed - Ed Allen, constable of Esculapia township and proprietor of the Ozark Garage on South First street of this city, was instantly killed at a late hour Sunday night when an automobile he was driving was struck by a runaway horse and buggy. The accident occurred east of Rogers on the road to the Panorama, about a mile north and west of the old Carl Starck place. The tip of the buggy shaft struck Mr. Allen just over the heart, breaking several ribs and although he was a large man of unusually strong physique, the shock was so terrific that he never spoke and it is thought death must have resulted practically at once. Mr. Allen, in company with Jack Napier, who works in the garage, and Winfred McDaniels, left Rogers about nine o'clock Sunday night to raid a place east of Rogers, supposed to be the gathering place of gamblers and bootleggers. They found the house dark and were returning home shortly after ten o'clock when they saw a horse and buggy approaching them. Mr. Allen, who was driving a Chandler car, turned out to give the buggy half the road but found too late that the horse had no intention of giving up any of the right-of-way. As he attempted to pull the car to the right far enough to allow the horse and buggy to pass, the left front buggy wheel caught inside the left front wheel of the car, demolishing both the car light and the buggy wheel. The shaft, torn loose from the buggy, swing around and just missed the windshield, was thrust through the side curtain with terrific force and struck Mr. Allen on the left side. The force of the blow and the tight grip on the wheel, combined in such a wrench that the steering wheel was torn loose. As the horse jerked with full weight on the shaft the harness was torn loose and the animal proceeded home with only the collar. As the accident happened almost in front of the Wm. Bly farm house Napier and McDaniels phoned from there to Rogers for a doctor and the body of the unfortunate man was carried there. Dr. Curry was soon at the Bly home but there was nothing he could do. An examination showed that the skin had not been broken by the blow as the body was protected by the coat and overcoat, but the bruised area and crushed ribs testified to the force with which the sharp shaft had hit him. Sheriff George Maples and Deputy Joe Gailey had also been notified at Bentonville and were soon on the grounds and made a careful examination of the car and surroundings. There have been many weird rumors on the street regarding the accident but the officers found no reason for not accepting the story of the collision and death as it has been give here. The horse and buggy belonged to Lamont Graham, son of Albert Graham of Monte Ne, who was visiting at a home some distance down the road. The horse had managed to slip his bridle and started for home in a hurry. Young Graham had heard the noise of the disappearing horse and buggy and was in pursuit when he arrived at the scene of the collision. No blame attaches to Graham and the accident was just one of those unforeseen tragedies that seemingly cannot be avoided. Mr. Allen had been a resident of this section for many years and was one of our best known citizens. For a number of years he was foreman of the White Lime Company plant at Limedale and also owned a farm near there. Some twenty years ago he married Miss Ora Hummel, a daughter of Al Hummel, and besides his wife he is survived by five children, two daughters and three sons. Ruth, the oldest daughter, is president of the Senior class of the Rogers High School; Burt, 17 years, the oldest son, worked in the garage with his father. The other children are Tony, 15; Roy, 8 and May, 2. Sunday was Mr. Allen's 47th birthday and the family spent the most of the day in Bentonville at the home of his brother, Lee Allen. He also leaves two brothers and two sisters in Missouri. The deceased was always known as a hard-working, energetic citizen and business man and had been making good as constable in every way. He did not know the meaning of the word fear and was held in respect by every law breaker in this part of the country. As the news of his death spread among our people Monday morning, and also in the big crowd at the opening day of court at Bentonville, it was surprising to learn how wide was his acquaintance and how sincere the expressions of regret at his unfortunate and untimely death. The funeral was held yesterday afternoon at the First M.E. church and in spite of the very inclement weather the church was crowded by the many friends of the deceased, quite a number coming from the country. Had it been a nice day many would have been unable to get in the church. The service was conducted by Rev. Lucke. [Rogers Democrat 3/20/24] [Benton County Record 3/21/24] [Rogers Daily Post 3/17/24]

ALLEY, Tom - Tom Alley, a resident of Siloam Springs for over 50 years and well known in Benton county, died last Saturday. [Benton County Record 2/15/24]

ALLRED, J.B. - {from Prairie Creek} The relatives and friends were shocked when they heard of the sudden death of J.B. Allred about 8 o'clock in the evening. While his daughter, Orpha, was reading to him he quietly passed away while sitting in his chair, almost without a struggle. He had been to Rogers that day and seemed to be feeling unusually well and talkative. J.B. Allred was born in Randolph county, North Carolina in 1843 and died May 13, 1924, having lived to the ripe old age of 81 years, 1 month and 23 days. He was married to Miss Sarah A. Griffith October 21, 1873 and to this union four children were born, three dying in infancy. One boy is living in Checota, Okla. The wife and mother also died. He was again married in 1883 to Miss Anna Gibson and eight children were born to this union and two died in babyhood. This wife preceded him to the great Beyond a number of years. The children were all present at his funeral but Frank, whose address is unknown. Miss Orpha Allred lived with him. Allison Allred of San Antonio, Texas, Oscar Allred of Wichita, Kansas, Clebourne Allred of Coffeyville, Okla.{?} and Mrs. Lillian Allred of Rogers, Ark. He also leaves 16 grandchildren, two brothers and two sisters, His early life after leaving North Carolina was spent in Indiana and Kansas. He moved to Arkansas in 1887 to the farm where he died, having lived there 37 years. He united with the M.E. church at an early age in North Carolina. After moving to Arkansas he united with the M.E. church at Pace's Chapel where his membership remained till death. He lived a consistent Christian life. The funeral services were conducted by Bro. Chas. Edwards at Pace's Chapel at 2 o'clock Friday afternoon. The remains were laid to rest by the side of his wife in the little cemetery near Pace's Chapel to await the resurrection. We wish to extend our heart-felt sympathy to the bereaved children and grandchildren and other relatives. Our whole community will miss him. [Rogers Democrat 5/22/24]

ALLRED, James - James Allred, aged eighty–three, living on the White river, died Tuesday following a stroke of paralysis. [Benton County Record 5/16/24]

ALLRED, Jerome - Jerome Allred, living near Puckett's Ford, died last night at 8 o'clock from a stroke of paralysis. He was 83 years old and was transacting business in Rogers yesterday. [Rogers Daily Post 5/14/24]

AMOS, Ava Catherine MASON - Mrs. Ava Catherine Amos was born on May 17th, 1897 at Mason Valley, Benton county, Ark. Graduated from the Miami, Okla. high school in May 1916. Married to Don L. Amos on May 16th, 1921 at Elk City, Okla. Died on May 4th, 1924 at El Paso, Texas. Her remains were sent to the home of her grandparents, Mr. and Mrs. Joshua Mason of Mason Valley, in which home services were conducted by Rev. W.J. LeRoy of Centerton and Rev. F.A. Bradshaw of Vaughn, after which the body was laid to rest in the Coffelt cemetery. {Her mother, Mrs. Minnie C. Mason, died August 15th, 1898.} The deceased is survived by her husband, Don L. Amos, a little daughter two years old, Mary Jo; Charles Mason, her brother; Helen and Dorothy Mason, sisters, of El Paso, Texas; O.F. Mason, her father, of Miami, Okla.; Mrs. Martha Wetzel, Mr. and Mrs. Joshua Mason, grandparents, and many other relatives and friends. [Benton County Record 5/30/24]

ANDERSON, infant - {from Pea Ridge} Mrs. O.F. Anderson received word this week that her great-grandson had died on April 7th of pneumonia. He was the infant son of Alva Anderson of Weaubleau, Mo. [Benton County Record 4/18/24]

ANDERSON, Robert P. - Robert Anderson, a well-known farmer, living two and one-half miles southeast of Vaughn, committed suicide sometime after 10 o'clock Tuesday night and 7 o'clock the following morning by shooting himself in the head with a 16-gauge shotgun. Mr. Anderson was a widower and lived with his son, Albert, and wife. Neither one was home when the deed was committed. When found the dead man was lying on the bed with the shotgun across his body. Since the death of his wife several years ago he has not been the same and has brooded over her death a great deal. For some time he has acted strangely and both his son and daughter-in-law were afraid of him. Monday he drove into Vaughn in his buggy with a pair of big spurs fastened to his boots. Tuesday morning conditions became such that Mrs. Anderson left and went to her parents in Springdale. Her husband drove her down there and upon returning home that evening was abused by his father and ordered to bed. A little later, it is stated, the father came in from an adjoining room with a shotgun in his hand. Albert became frightened and ran out of the house. He spent the night at the home of his employer, A.M. Smith, in Vaughn. Wednesday morning Albert returned home accompanied by Mr. Smith, Sid Rice, Tom True and Jim Mason. On reaching the house they knocked at the door and later, on opening it, found Robert Anderson lying dead. Mr. Smith, who is justice of the peace of Anderson township, phoned for Coroner Callison in Rogers. Upon his arrival a jury, composed of John Gross, Jim Mason, C. Warren, J.B. Kerr, Walter Crabtree, Rich Murray, Whitley Kerr, Chas. Henderson, P. Hutchinson, M. Kirby, Mr. Dunham and Cal McSpadden, was empanelled by the coroner. After hearing the testimony of witnesses the jury returned a verdict of "Death by his own hand by a shotgun during Tuesday night

after 10 o'clock and 9 o'clock Wednesday morning." Funeral services were conducted by Rev. F.A. Bradshaw, pastor of the Vaughn Presbyterian church at the old Anderson home. The funeral was largely attended. The body was buried in the Anderson cemetery near by. Robert P. Anderson was born in 1858 on the old Anderson farm south of Vaughn which his grandfather homesteaded in 1830. The Anderson spring on this farm is one of the noted springs in the county. He was the son of Ollie I. Anderson, a well to do and highly respected farmer. He was married to Miss Laura Purcell to whom one son was born - Albert Anderson. Besides his son he is survived by two brothers - Hugh Anderson of Tulsa and Dick Anderson, who lives in Idaho; also four sisters - Mrs. Kate Crum and Mrs. Billie Bratton of Springdale; Mrs. Annie Jackson of Tulsa and Mrs. Pearl Crawford of Phoenix, Ariz., also two nephews - Sam Anderson of Centerton and Allen Anderson of Tulsa. [Benton County Record 5/23/24] [Rogers Daily Post 5/21/24]
Robert P. Anderson, about 66 years old, a son of the late O.I. Anderson, one of the oldest settlers of Benton county and one of the prominent families of Northwest Arkansas, committed suicide Tuesday night near Osage Mills in Anderson township by using a shotgun. Mr. Anderson was a brother of Hon. W.A. Anderson, deceased, and also a brother of Mrs. Sid Jackson. He leaves a son and many other relatives in this part. [Rogers Democrat 5/22/24]

APPLEBY, Almira STANFIELD - Mrs. John T. Appleby died in Fayetteville last Friday after a short illness. She was the mother of Charles and George Appleby, the well-known fruit growers and canners. Had she lived a few days longer she would have been 88 years of age. Mrs. Appleby was born in Washington county in 1836 and was one of its noted pioneer women and her life was filled with stirring events. Her parents, Mr. and Mrs. Alexander Stanfield, and Mr. and Mrs. Hezekiah Appleby, the parents of Mr. Appleby, both came to Washington county in 1830 from Eastern Tennessee. [Benton County Record 4/25/24]
Fayetteville, April 19.– Mrs. Almira Stanfield Appleby, who would have been 88 years old next Wednesday, died at the home of her son, Chas. Appleby, here Friday at 9:15 a.m. Death came after a very critical illness. Mrs. Appleby was born in Washington county on the Appleby farm and spent all of her life in this immediate section. She was the daughter of Mr. and Mrs. Alexander Stanfield. Surviving her are two sons, George and Charles, both of Fayetteville, Mrs. Charles Stearns, Mrs. C. Cunningham and Mrs. E.M. Freyschlag, all of near Fayetteville. Funeral service will be held Saturday with interment at Mount Comfort. [Rogers Daily Post 4/19/24]

ASBURY, William Henry - William H. Asbury, 94 years old, died last week at the home of a grandson, P.N. Waters, near Bentonville. He was a veteran of the Civil War, enlisting from Wisconsin in Co. I, 25th Infantry. [Rogers Democrat 4/10/24]
{from Valley View} William Henry Asbury died Sunday morning at 2 o'clock and was buried Sunday afternoon. He was an old man - 94 years, two months

and 23 days. He lived with his grandson, Perry N. Waters. [Benton County Record 4/4/24]
Wm. H. Asbury, one of the oldest residents in this section, passed away Sunday morning at the home of his grandson, Perry N. Waters, three and one-half miles northeast of Bentonville. He was 94 years of age and one of the oldest residents of the county. Mr. Asbury was born in Westmoreland county, Va. in 1830. He came west with his parents in 1842 when they drove from St. Louis to Texas with a team. They passed through Benton county, following the old military, or wire, road between these two points. The old trail passed through an edge of Mr. Waters' farm. The following year his parents moved back to Arkansas and settled east of Fayetteville on the Middle Fork of the White river where his father took up a homestead. Later they moved to Illinois where Mr. Asbury married. He moved to Wisconsin and when the Civil War broke out he enlisted in the 25th Wisconsin and served under General Wm. T. Sherman. In 1894 he again decided to make Arkansas his home. His last four or five years have been spent with his oldest grandson, Perry N. Waters. Seven sons and three daughters survive him; one only, Henry Asbury, living south of Bentonville, lives in this state. Funeral services were held Sunday afternoon with interment in the City Cemetery. [Benton County Democrat 4/3/24] [Benton County Record 4/4/24]

ATKISSON, Almyra DEASON - {from Walnut Hill} On Wednesday night after Mr. and Mrs. J.L. Atkisson had retired for the night, somewhere near 10 o'clock, Aunt Myra, as we all loved to call her, awoke Uncle Jim saying someone was wanting him on the phone. It proved to be J.W. Stroud of Rogers and when Uncle Jim came back in the room Aunt Myra said "I can't breathe," so a doctor was hastily called but before one could reach her she quietly passed away. Almyra Atkisson, nee Deason, was born November 1, 1856 one mile east of Rogers on Prairie Creek and spent her entire life in Benton county. She was married to J.L. Atkisson April 6, 1897. She professed a hope in Christ in 1875 at what was known as the Droke school house, at a revival meeting. She never united with any church but lived a faithful Christian life and was a loving companion and mother to his orphan children. She was a member of one of the pioneer families of Benton county, being a descendant of the Deasons and Sikes. Her passing breaks up a home that will be missed as much or more than any in Garfield township. She had lived in Walnut Hill, Providence and Garfield districts and her presence in the sick rooms and needy places in her neighborhood was well known and is still remembered. No one of our acquaintance has made more personal sacrifices to cheer sad homes and relieve suffering. She was always preparing some dainty dish to tempt the fevered appetite, or to turn a scorching pillow into a cool place of rest. She was a willing worker in all enterprises in our community to make it a better place in which to live. It is said that we become a part of all we meet and we know that our communities have been made better by her having lived among us. The only members of the Atkisson family present were Mrs. Jim Dye, Mrs. H.D. Snodderly of Garfield and Mrs. Sid Murphy of Springfield, Mo. A large number of relatives and friends, among them her only living uncle, J. Wade Sikes of Rogers, attended the funeral services held at the cemetery south of Avoca near the Bill Allred farm. Services were held by George Williams and Elder John Taylor. - Written by request by Mr. and Mrs. George Williams. [Rogers Democrat 9/11/24]

AUSTIN, Ellis Maxwell - Ellis Maxwell Austin, son of Mr. and Mrs. A.D. Austin, died at his home north of Bentonville September 19, 1924. He was 28 years old and was born at Norwood, Mo. May 8, 1896. He moved to Wichita with his parents when he was five years old where he received his education in the public schools. In 1913 he entered Milled Business College but was unable to finish the course because of ill health. He moved to Bentonville with his parents in January 1920 in hopes of regaining his health. Ellis was a member of the M.E. Church, South of Bentonville. He was loved and respected by all who knew him and more so among the old people. He leaves to mourn their loss besides his parents, one sister, Mrs. W.N. Sherrick, and husband, and intended wife, Miss May Presley, and a host of friends and relatives. [Benton County Democrat 9/26/24]

BAKER, infant - {from Larue} A daughter was born to Mr. and Mrs. George Baker last Friday and died the same day. She was buried late that afternoon at the Bland cemetery. [Rogers Democrat 7/31/24]

BAKER, Joe - {from Decatur} Joe Baker died Saturday night of stomach trouble. Burial was made in the Coffelt cemetery near Vaughn the following day. He was about 67 years old and is survived by his widow and several children. [Benton County Record 6/13/24]

BARRON, John Kitzmiller - John Kitzmiller Barron was born near Jonesboro, Tenn. July 7, 1866 and departed this life August 12, 1924 at the age of 58 years. He was married December 10, 1893 to Miss Kate Mills of Vaughn. To this union was born eight children, seven of whom survive him and were all present in his last days. They are: Mrs. Clarence Odle of Springdale; Roy and Paul of Tulsa, Okla.; Mrs. Will Piercy of Osage Mills; Mrs. Dewey Porter of Huntington Beach, Calif.; Mrs. Anne Aaron of the home address. The deceased was converted at the age of twenty-two years and united with the M.E. Church, South of Centerton, Ark. in 1890 and his dying testimony was that he was ready and willing to go. The funeral was conducted at the home two and one-half miles southwest of Springdale by F.A. Bradshaw Wednesday at 9:30 a.m. Interment was made at the Barron cemetery at Vaughn. [Benton County Record 8/22/24]

BARTEL, E.J. - E.J. Bartel, secretary of the Taxpayer's League and a prominent fruit grower west of Centerton, died on Sunday, February 2nd, 1924 at the home of his sister, Dr. D.B. Nicholl, in Topeka, Kansas where Mr. and Mrs. Bartel were visiting. Besides his widow he is survived by two daughters. Mr. Bartel was about 50 years of age and died of kidney trouble after a short illness. Mr. Bartel moved to Benton county from Kansas about eight years ago and bought a large fruit farm in the Edgewood neighborhood southwest of Centerton. He became an enthusiastic fruit grower and by a liberal use of money and hard work built up a splendid orchard. Ill health caused him to retire from his farm last fall and he moved to Rogers where a daughter, Miss Frances, was attending high school. In the death of Mr. Bartel the editor loses a particular friend who, with hundreds of others, will sadly miss him. [Benton County Record 2/8/24]

BASSINGER, Jake - {from Prairie Creek} Mrs. Pierce Farley received the news recently of the death of her father, Jake Bassinger. He was a resident of this community a number of years and lived within a few miles of here most of his life. He moved with his family to Texas a few years ago where he lived at the time of his death. He has many friends and neighbors who were grieved to learn of his death and sympathize deeply with the bereaved wife and children. [Rogers Democrat 3/27/24]

BATES, Cleo BROWNING - Mrs. Cleo Bates died Sunday at the home of her parents, W.C. Browning and wife, four miles west of town, at the age of twenty-two years, four months and twelve days. Funeral services were held at the Church of Christ in Rogers Monday afternoon at 2:30 and were conducted by Rev. W.T. Hines. Interment was in the Rogers cemetery. Mrs. Bates is survived by her husband, Earl Bates, who is in Texas, and by two small sons. Mrs. Browning was a sister of Mrs. Eugene Dale and Walter Browning, both of Rogers. [Rogers Democrat 5/1/24]

BATES, George M. - George M. Bates, a pioneer resident and merchant of Bentonville, died at his home in Leavenworth, Kansas Thursday, January 24th, 1924 at the age of 72 years. He died from the effects of a three weeks attack of the flu and a complication of other diseases. Mr. Bates was born near Greenfield, Dade county, Mo. on July 8th, 1851. He came here with his parents in 1867 and located on a farm about a mile east of town. He lived here over 50 years and was engaged in the grocery business. A few years ago he moved to Leavenworth, Kansas where he again entered the grocery business. He is survived by his widow, Mrs. May Bates, and seven children - Seth Bates of this city; Barney C. Bates of Little Rock; John Bates of Fort Smith; Mrs. Birdie Johnson of Rogers; Mrs. Georgie Carter, residing in Missouri; Mrs. Frankie Smith and Miss Sallie Bates, of Leavenworth, all of whom were present at the funeral. Also one brother, A.J. Bates, of this city, and one sister, Mrs. Nora Woods, of Edgar, Montana. Burial was made in the city cemetery at Leavenworth. [Benton County Record 2/1/24]

BATES, Mrs. Earl {BROWNING} - Mrs. Earl Bates, daughter of Mr. and Mrs. Browning living four miles north of Rogers, died yesterday at the home of her parents. The funeral was held this afternoon at 2:30 at the Church of Christ. Interment was in the City Cemetery. Mrs. Bates was 21 years old and leaves besides her husband, two boys, one two years old and the other 4 months old. Especially sad is this to the family since Mr. Bates is in New Mexico, their old home, with his parents, a victim of pneumonia and was unable to attend the funeral. They came from that place last fall and Mr. Bates returned expecting to send for his wife and babies as soon as he had secured a home for them. Mrs. Bates is a sister of Walter Browning who is in the employ of the Harrison and Dale Meat Market. [Rogers Daily Post 4/28/24]

BAUTTS, John - John Bautts, aged about fifty–five years, and one of the best known farmers in this part of the county, was instantly killed last Thursday by a fall from the roof of an old berry shed which he was repairing at his home southwest of town, just west of New Hope. Mr. Bautts was alone at the time of the accident so there is no direct testimony as to the time but the body was found at noon when his little daughter was sent to call him in to dinner. A physician was called but an examination showed that the neck had been broken and that Mr. Bautts had undoubtedly died instantly. A pole supporting the roof had broken and Mr. Bautts was hurled headlong to the ground. He struck the back of his head on a pole with such force that his neck was broken and he also received a number of bruises but not of sufficient extent to have seriously injured him. Funeral services were held at the home Saturday afternoon at 2:30 and were conducted by Rev. R.L. Austin, pastor of the Baptist church. Mr. Bautts had lived here for many years and was a highly respected citizen. He was a successful farmer and owned several good places. In the death of Mr. Bautts the neighborhood and county has lost one of its best citizens. He is survived by his wife, three sons and four daughters. Of the sons, Deck and Ed Bautts work for the American Express Company and Ed{?} Bautts is a mail carrier; of the four daughters, Mrs. Clarence Boyd lived in Rogers, Misses Agnes and Jennie were at Helena, Ark. and the youngest, Katherine, was at home. [Rogers Democrat 7/3/24]

BAXTER, B.B. - B.B. Baxter, a resident of this section for over 40 years, died at the home of his daughter, Mrs. E.B. Jackson, west of Bentonville, on Wednesday, April 16th, 1924 at the age of 81 years. He had been ill only a short time. Funeral services were held at the home on Thursday afternoon and were conducted by Rev. Lester Weaver of the M.E. Church, South in Bentonville and Rev. W.J. LeRoy, pastor of the Centerton Community Church. He is survived by three daughters, Mrs. E.B. Jackson and Mrs. J.M. Jackson, both of Bentonville and a daughter in Colorado; also by one son who lives out of the state. Mr. Baxter was born in Eastern Tennessee in 1843 and served during the Civil War in the Union army. He came to Benton county about 40 years ago and located on a farm just west of Bentonville. [Benton County Record 4/18/24]

BEANE, H.A. - H.A. Beane, a brother of the late Mrs. J.G. Bailey and for several years a resident of Rogers, passed away at his home in

Ladysmith, Wisconsin on Jan. 11, 1924. Death was caused by a general breakdown due to his advanced age. He was born in Warner, New Hampshire July 27, 1839. At an early age he went to Wisconsin and it was there that his life was spent with the exception of the few years that he lived in Rogers. During his active years he was engaged in lumbering and affiliated industries. Since retiring from business life several years ago he has made his home with one of his daughters, Mrs. E.F. Pies, of Ladysmith, Wisconsin. He is survived by his widow and two daughters, Mrs. Pies and Eunice Beane of Chicago. Funeral services were held at the home in Ladysmith on January 14th with Reverend Richard Evans of Wausau as officiating clergyman, assisted by Reverend Grant Clark of Ladysmith. [Rogers Democrat 1/24/24]

BEASLEY, Noble Penfield - Mrs. Ann Beasley of Hiwasse received a telegram yesterday {Thursday} from the commanding officer of Kelly Field, San Antonio, Texas stating that her son, Lieutenant Noble Beasley, was killed on that field at 9:40 o'clock Thursday morning in an airplane accident. Further particulars were not given. The body will be returned to Hiwasse for burial. Besides his mother he is survived by two brothers, Sam and Joe Beasley of Bentonville, and two sisters, Hattie Beasley, who is postmistress at Hiwasse, and Esther Beasley, of the same address. Lieutenant Beasley, since his graduation from West Point, has been at Kelly Field studying aviation. Lately he was promoted to the aviation corps and evidently met his death while flying. He was 24 years of age. This is the second Benton county boy who was killed in the aviation service at Kelly Field, the other one being Field Kindley of Gravette, who met his death there early in February 1920. [Benton County Record 5/30/24]
Impressive funeral services for the late Lieutenant Noble P. Beasley, who was killed in an airplane accident at Kelly Field, San Antonio, Texas last Thursday, were held at the home of his widowed mother, Mrs. Ann Beasley, in Hiwasse Sunday afternoon. Probably no funeral ever held in Benton county was so largely attended. Hundreds of people and nearly three hundred automobiles surrounded the little home and listened with bared heads to the touching services and paid their last respects to the dead soldier boy. The services were conducted by Reverend Stephen Morton of Bentonville, assisted by Rev. W.J. LeRoy of the Centerton Community Church. Owing to the immense throng of people the services were held on the porch. Rev. Morton's funeral address was a splendid effort and he paid a touching tribute to those who die in the service of their country. The choir was composed of the following Bentonville singers: Mr. and Mrs. E.C. Pickens, Mr. C.M. Bullock and Dr. R.O. Pickens, with Miss Pauline Wheat as accompanist. The pallbearers, composed of members of the American legion, were Ernest Alfrey, Vol T. Lindsey, Jeff R. Rice, John Applegate, D.W. Peel, Jr., of Bentonville, and A.R. Dunagin of Gravette. After the service the body was taken to the Mt. Pleasant cemetery, two miles west of town,

followed by a cortege that reached the whole distance. At the grave a squad of American legions from Siloam Springs fired a farewell salute over his grave and Bugler Stockburger sounded taps. Loving hands placed the many beautiful floral wreaths over the fresh-covered grave and Noble Penfield Beasley was laid to rest. Lieutenant Noble Penfield Beasley, youngest son of Mr. and Mrs. B.F. Beasley, was born near Hiwasse, Ark. October 29, 1898 and died at Kelly Field, San Antonio, Texas May 29, 1924 at the age of twenty–five years and eleven months. After completing his grade school course at Hiwasse he entered the Bentonville School and graduated in May 1918. He then entered the University of Arkansas at Fayetteville and became a volunteer member of the Student Army Training Corps from 1918 until the end of the World War, leaving the University to enter the United States Military Academy at West Point. In June 1923 he graduated from this institution with a commission of lieutenant in the air service. After spending his three months furlough at home he was assigned to duty in the Primary Flying School at Brooks Field, San Antonio, Texas. He graduated from here April 7, 1924 and was transferred to the Kelly Field Advanced Flying School where he was on duty at the time. Funeral services with full military honors were held in San Antonio Friday, May 30. The services were conducted by the chaplain of Kelly Field and ended with Lieutenant Beasley's classmates singing the West Point Alma Mater. After the services the body was accompanied by military escort to the station where four of his classmates stood guard until the departure of the train. Lieutenant J.M. Fitzmaurice, who was Lieutenant Beasley's closest friend and roommate at West Point and at Kelly Field, was assigned to the sad duty of accompanying the body home, reaching Hiwasse Saturday night. In a letter from Noble Beasley to his brother, Joe, in Bentonville, dated May 25, 1924, he wrote: "If I get through the chances of transferring to another branch are very slim. I wish you would get the idea out of your head that it is suicide to fly. Of course there is always a chance of an accident but since one dies doing his duty in the service of his country, what difference does it make when he dies? This work has to be done and someone has to do it. Love, Noble." Lieutenant Beasley was killed while making his daily practice flight in a De Haviland airplane. He was practicing 180 degree landings. In this maneuver the engine is cut off while flying at an altitude of about eight hundred feet over a certain point. The pilot then circles around and lands on this point with his plane headed in the opposite direction. This is an important maneuver and is taught students to aid them in making forced landings on cross-country flights. As Lieutenant Beasley was circling over the flying field while making the descent, the ship slipped in the air and lost its forward speed and nosed downward and struck the ground. Hundreds of officers and men witnessed the accident and rushed to the spot but he was evidently killed instantly when the plane hit the ground. [Benton County Record 6/6/24] [Gravette News Herald 6/6/24]

1924

BEDDOWS, Mrs. W.R. - Mrs. W.R. Beddows died at her home east of town last Monday morning of pneumonia. Sunday a message came saying that Mr. Beddows, who is in the soldier home in Kansas, was not expected to live but a few hours. The remains of Mrs. Beddows were held here pending developments there, until Thursday afternoon, when it was laid at rest in the city cemetery. [Gentry Journal–Advance 2/1/24]

BELTON, Percy - Mr. and Mrs. W.M. Belton, living in the Valley View community northeast of Bentonville, received the sad news last Thursday of the death of their son, Percy, in an automobile accident at Chehalis, Washington. The particulars of his death were not given in the message. He was about thirty years of age and left Bentonville a few years ago to make his home in the Pacific Northwest. The body arrived from Chehalis Wednesday and after the funeral services, which were conducted at the City cemetery by Rev. W.F.D. Batjer of Fayetteville and W.D. Wheat of Bentonville, the body was interred in the family lot. [Benton County Record 7/18/24]

BENEDICT, O.R. - Word was received here Monday of the death of O.R. Benedict which occurred Sunday night about eight o'clock at Mena, Ark. at the age of 85 years and burial took place at Courtland, Nebraska. Mr. Benedict was sergeant in Company A. 3rd Regiment, Wisconsin Volunteer Cavalry. He came to Rogers in 1892 and, with the exception of a short while they lived in Fayetteville while Miss Julia went to school, they made their home here until they went to Mena in 1910. At the close of the Civil War he was married to Martha L. Dodge, sister of the late J.H. Dodge of this city, and to them were born five children, all dying in infancy. In later years they took a niece, Miss Julia Benedict, to raise and who now lives in Kansas City. His wife died in Mena about ten years ago. Several years later he was married to Mrs. Susie Porch who survives him. [Rogers Democrat 5/22/24]

BERRY, Mr. and Mrs. E. - Mr. and Mrs. E. Berry, who suicided under peculiar circumstances near Pierce City Saturday last, operated the restaurant in the McDaniel building here a few weeks last summer. Their bodies were found in Clear Creek, both with their hands tied behind them. The couple left Colorado a year ago with $1400 cash but met with hard luck everywhere they went and a few days ago landed in Southwest City with only $50. They started out one day last week stating that they were going to borrow money and return. It is however believed they had decided to end their troubles. An old family Bible left at Southwest City helped to identify the couple. [Gravette News Herald 3/14/24]

BILLINGTON, Mr. - Friends have received word of the death at Hobart, Okla. of a Mr. Billington who last winter, with his wife and five grandchildren, lived in Rogers for a few months. They came to Rogers from a farm near Vaughn but owing to failing health they had to go to a daughter at Hobart. Mr. Billington was about 75 years old. [Rogers Democrat 4/10/24]

BLACKBURN, W.T. (Tom) - Rogers relatives and friends were surprised and shocked when a telegram was received Saturday night bringing word of the sudden death of W.T. (Tom) Blackburn who fell dead Saturday in Little Rock while on his way home from the sash factory where he was working. Mrs. Blackburn has been in the hospital in Little Rock for several months in a very serious condition and the first thought was that a mistake had been made in the telegram but later word confirmed the correctness of the first message. The body arrived in Rogers Monday morning and funeral services were held at the Central M.E. church that afternoon at two o'clock, conducted by the pastor, Rev. J. Wilson Crichlow, with the Masonic order in charge. Burial was in the Rogers cemetery by the graves of two children who had died a number of years ago. The body was accompanied to Rogers by Clifford Stringfield Blackburn who is attending the University of Arkansas. Mr. Blackburn had not resided in Rogers for many years, having left here in 1897 and had for twenty or more years been a resident of Danville, this state. He had been working in Little Rock for the last two years and Mrs. Blackburn had been at their home in Danville until she was stricken several months ago and taken to the hospital in Little Rock. Both Mr. and Mrs. Blackburn were born and raised in Benton county and were representatives of several pioneer families of this section. Mr. Blackburn was a son of Josiah Blackburn, oldest son of Sylvanus Blackburn who settled at War Eagle in the early '30s, coming from Tennessee. He was born at War Eagle and was 65 years, five months and three days old when he died. In 1883 he married Miss Lula Stringfield, a daughter of J.K.P. Stringfield and a granddaughter of Peter Van Winkle, founder of the Van Winkle settlement on War Eagle. The Van Winkles, Blackburns and Stringfields were the lumber kings of Northwest Arkansas in their day and have many descendants in every town in this country. To Mr. Blackburn and wife were born three children, only one of whom is living, Prof. Clifford Blackburn, who has taught several years at Danville and attended the U. of A. between terms there. Mr. Blackburn is survived by two sisters, Mrs. F.C. Roberts of War Eagle and Mrs. Louisa Robertson of Logan, Utah and one brother, J.N. Blackburn, of this city and is a cousin of Mrs. Arthur Miller and Mrs. Ed Kruse. Practically all of his life was spent in some branch of the lumber business and he was a sawmill and planing mill specialist, a fine machinist, a carpenter and builder. He had been a Mason for years and stood high in the degrees of that order. When he left Rogers he was one of the best known men of the city and while he is remembered now only by relatives and older residents, his death has brought back to them a rush of memories of an upright character and a good citizen. [Rogers Democrat 5/15/24]

BLAINE, Ben - Ben Blaine, 46 years old, who had resided in Rogers most of his life, committed suicide Saturday afternoon at the home of his sister, Mrs. L.B. Lutz, by shooting himself through the head with a .22

target rifle. Ill health is given as the probable cause. Since the death of his wife some six years ago Blaine has lived at the home of his sister, Mrs. L.B. Lutz, No. 225 North C street. Two daughters, one 14, the other 18, also made it their home. Saturday afternoon Blaine asked the youngest girl, Jessie, to borrow a .22 target rifle from a neighbor, saying that he wanted to shoot some birds that were eating the chicken feed in the back yard. When he secured the rifle Blaine suggested that the women stay in the house as he was afraid they would scare the birds away. A few minutes later Mrs. Lutz and her niece heard a shot followed by the sound of a falling body on the back porch. They rushed out to find the body of Blaine on the porch and a bullet hole in his left temple. Death was practically instantaneous. An inquest was held by Coroner A.D. Callison and the verdict was that the death was the result of a "Bullet wound, self inflicted." Blaine had been in ill health for some time and it is thought this was the cause of the act. Mr. Blaine's father, one of the oldest residents of Rogers, was killed here several years ago when struck by the southbound morning Frisco passenger train at the Walnut street crossing. Funeral services were held at the Lutz home Sunday afternoon. [Rogers Democrat 9/25/24] [Benton County Record 9/26/24]

BLANCK, Elizabeth SAYRE - Mrs. Elizabeth Sayre Blanck, wife of the late Charles A. Blanck, architect and builder, died at her home in Bentonville on Saturday morning, December 13th. Funeral services, conducted by Rev. J.L. Evans of the M.E. Church, South, were held Monday and interment was made in the city cemetery. Elizabeth Sayre was born in Madison, New Jersey in 1852 and was a member of one of the most prominent families in that state. She grew up in Madison and married C.A. Blanck in Elizabethtown, New Jersey in 1860. She came west to Illinois with her husband in 1870, coming to Bentonville in 1887 where they have made their home since that time. She is survived by four children - Mrs. Harry Martin of Bentonville; Mrs. A.A. Armstrong of Colorado; F.A. Blanck and C.S. Blanck of Stilwell, Okla., all of whom were with their mother at the time of her death. [Benton County Record 12/19/24]

BLANSETT, Chester Archale - Chester Archale Blansett, aged two years, three months and thirteen days, son of Mr. and Mrs. Arch Blansett of Garfield, died Friday afternoon and was buried at the Liberty cemetery. The Daily Post extends its sympathy to the parents. [Rogers Daily Post 1'2/7/24]

BLEVINS, Jesse - Jesse Blevins, a resident of Bentonville for nearly fifty years, died at the home of his son, Arthur Blevins, on Thursday, December 18th, 1924 at the age of about 84 years. Mr. Blevins has been blind for many years and for some time has been gradually failing. He was, in his younger days, quite a prominent farmer. He also engaged in the nursery business for many years. He originated a valuable seedling apple which was named the Blevins. [Benton County Record 12/19/24]

BLOOMQUIST, baby - {from Decatur} The nine-month-old baby of Mr. and Mrs. Bloomquist, living on the Jack Donnely place west of town, died suddenly last week and the funeral was held Saturday. [Benton County Record 4/11/24]

BODINE, Billie - {from a Quanah, Tex. newspaper} Uncle Billie Bodine, aged 72, a former resident of Quanah, Texas for some 38 years, died at Kingsville Tuesday, Dec. 18, 1923 and was brought here for burial this afternoon at 5 o'clock or tomorrow morning. The W.O.W. will have charge of the funeral services. It was not definitely known who would preach the funeral sermon Wednesday night and it was understood that interment would be made Friday afternoon. Uncle Billie, as he was known to all, was a native of Ohio and had lived near and in Quanah for 38 years before moving to east Texas. He was a Methodist and a good consecrated Christian man. He leaves many friends and relatives to mourn his demise. It was not known that he was seriously ill until word was received that he had passed away. ***** Deceased was a brother to J.W. and J.D. Bodine of Gentry. Jack attended the funeral of his brother at Quanah. [Gentry Journal–Advance 1/11/24]

BOGGS, Camilla BROGDEN - Mrs. Camilla Brogden Boggs, formerly of Bentonville, died at the home of her son, Henry Boggs, in Fayetteville on Tuesday morning, Feb. 5th, 1924 at 9:10 o'clock at the age of 78 years. Camilla Brogden, daughter of a Southern planter, was born in Sumpter county, South Carolina in 1845. She grew to womanhood in that country and after the close of the Civil War, in 1869, she was united in marriage with Rev. D.C. Boggs, a chaplain during the war. That same year they moved to Bentonville, Ark. where Rev. Boggs held the pastorate of the South Presbyterian Church for 28 years, during which time the present Presbyterian Church building was erected. After the death of her husband she stayed in Bentonville for about four years after which she moved to Fayetteville where she has made her home with her children for the past 15 years. She is survived by two children - Henry Boggs and Miss Lucy Boggs, both of Fayetteville. The body was brought back to Bentonville Wednesday morning and the funeral services, conducted by Rev. Paisley of Fayetteville and Rev. Wheat of Bentonville, were held in the church which she and her husband helped to build. Here her old friends and neighbors gathered to pay their last tribute to their dear friend. Interment was made in the city cemetery. [Benton County Record 2/8/24]

BOGLE, Charlotte MABERRY Putman - Mrs. Charlotte Bogle was born December 16, 1843 and died March 16, 1924 at Crowley, Texas. Charlotte Maberry was born in Wilson county, Tenn. Here she grew up to womanhood and in 1866 confessed her faith in Christ and united with the Twelve Corners Baptist church and to the end of life lived consistent with the confession. She was united in marriage with William L. Putman October 27, 1863 and to this union was born one daughter, Margaret Lee, who died in infancy,

John J. and J.M. Putman of Pea Ridge, Ark. and William H. Putman of Athens, Tex. Her husband died November 11, 1868. Mrs. Putman was then married to Mr. James M. Bogle August 20, 1870. To the latter marriage were born three daughters, Leora, who died in infancy, Mrs. Ida Clements and Mrs. Ada Evans of Crowley, Tex., four sons, Denna Bogle of Crowley, Tex., Curry Bogle of Loganport, La., Luther Bogle of Mansfield, La. and Edgar Bogle of Bentonville, Ark. All of the children, living, were present at the funeral, her seven sons acting as pall bearers. Mrs. Bogle possessed an unusually cheerful and happy disposition and uncomplainingly met the ordeal of life. Funeral services were held at the Presbyterian church at Crowley, Tex. March 18, 1924, conducted by the pastor, and the pastor of the Baptist church, after which she was laid to rest in the Crowley cemetery until the Great Day when the trumpet shall call from the dust the sleeping bodies of the just. [Benton County Democrat 4/3/24] [Rogers Democrat 3/27/24]

BOHRN, Willie Pearl - Willie Pearl Bohrn, the two-year-old daughter of Mr. and Mrs. C.W. Bohrn, living north of town near the state line, died Monday morning. [Benton County Record 12/19/24]

BOLES, Clifford D. - Clifford D. Boles died at his home in Hindsville, Ark. last Saturday at the age of 67 years. Funeral services were held Monday afternoon in Fayetteville and interment made in the Evergreen Cemetery in that city. Mr. Boles came to Washington county over 50 years ago and has been there practically all his life. Three sons survive him, including Ashleigh P. Boles, formerly of Bentonville and now field horticulturist of the University of Missouri. [Benton County Record 10/3/24]
Clifford D. Boles died a week ago at his home at Hindsville, Madison Co. where he had lived for several years. He was for most of his life a citizen of Fayetteville where he was county clerk several terms and held other local offices. He was father of Ashleigh Boles of Columbia, Mo. and Chalmers Boles of Chicago, both of whom have many Rogers friends. [Rogers Democrat 10/9/24]

BOMBACK, Mrs. Fred - {from Pleasant Hill} O.J. Bomback received a message Friday from a brother, Fred Bomback, stating the death of his wife at a hospital in St. Paul, Minn. O.J. and wife left for Memphis, Tenn. to attend the funeral and interment which will be at that place. [Rogers Democrat 9/18/24]

BOND, William - {from Centerton} Will Bond, living west of the Marr's Hill schoolhouse, died last Wednesday after a lingering illness. [Benton County Record 2/8/24]
{from High Top} Wm. Bond died at his home last week at the age of about 74 years. He had been in bad health for some time. Burial was made in the Gamble cemetery. [Benton County Record 2/8/24]

BOWEN, William - William Bowen died Saturday morning, February 16th at 10:15 a.m. after an illness of a year, at the age of twenty-four years, six months and two days. He had worked for the Rogers Building Supply Company and for the Dyke Lumber Company for some eight years. The funeral services were held at the home on North Ninth street Sunday afternoon and were conducted by Rev. R.M. Seamster. The deceased was born at Rolla, Mo. August 18, 1899 and had lived in Rogers for a number of years. He is survived by his mother, Mrs. John T. Bowen, a sister, Miss Alice Bowen, who is teaching in the high school at Gravette, and a brother, John Bowen, who is clerking at Puckett's grocery store. His father and sister, Miss Maude, died several years ago. [Rogers Democrat 2/21/24]

BOWMAN, Lee - {from Pleasant Valley} Lee Bowman, who lived here for some few years, died in Blackwell, Okla. a few days ago. [Gentry Journal-Advance 9/19/24]

BOWMAN, William - William Bowman was born in Rolla, Missouri Aug. 18, 1899 but moved to Rogers with his parents when he was a youth and received his education in the schools of this city. He worked for the Merril Lumber Co. and was retained by the Merril-Dyke Lumber Co., for eight years, until his sickness. He passed away at the home of his mother last Saturday morning and was buried Sunday afternoon. At his request the services were conducted by Judge E.F.M. Seamster, father of J.W. Seamster, who is a cousin by marriage. He was laid to rest beside his father who preceded him eight years ago and his sister, Maude, whom he had tenderly nursed during her illness two years ago. William was known as "Bill" to his many friends. He was of a retiring disposition and spent his spare time with his mother and nearest friends and relatives. His virtues were many, perhaps the greatest was his love for his sick sister and tender solicitude for his mother and "he is not dead who lives in the hearts of others." [Rogers Daily Post 2/19/24]

BOYD, Ed - {from Mt. Pleasant} Mrs. Jas. Boyd received news of the death of her son, Ed, who died in Idaho Dec. 27th, the result of appendicitis. [Gravette News Herald 1/18/24]

BRADLEY, Cornelia ANDERSON - Mrs. C.M. Bradley died on Friday, December 12th, 1924 at the home of her brother, W.T. Anderson, east of Bentonville, at the age of 76 years. Funeral services were conducted at the Anderson home and the remains were shipped to Glasgow, Ky. where the body was laid to rest beside her husband who passed away in 1919. Since that time she has made her home with her brother, W.T. Anderson, and his family. Rev. Evans, pastor of the M.E. Church, South conducted the services and the choir of that church sang her favorite hymns. Cornelia Anderson was born in Glasgow, Ky. in 1848 and was married to C.M. Bradley in 1897. She united with the M.E. Church, South at the age of 17 years and was for a time a teacher in the Jefferson Community Sunday School. Both old and young who knew her loved her. [Benton County Record 12/19/24]

BRAITHWAIT, William Minter - William Minter Braithwait died at his home north of Bentonville on Sunday, March 23rd, 1924 at the age of forty–three years. He had been in ill health for some time. He is survived by a widow, two sons and three daughters. Funeral services were conducted on Tuesday afternoon by Rev. O.M. Campbell and interment was made in the New Home cemetery. [Benton County Record 3/28/24]

BRAY, Muncy Elizabeth CARTER - {from Walnut Hill} Mrs. Muncy Elizabeth Bray {nee Carter} was born September 11, 1885 in Benton county near Old Liberty church. Was married to R.R. Bray Nov. 9, 1902. Born to this union, five children, one of whom died in infancy, one daughter and three sons survive their mother. Mrs. Bray passed away January 29th, 1924 after a long illness. She was converted when young and united with the Free Will Baptist church at Old Liberty and lived a true faithful Christian life. She leaves, besides her family, two sisters and a brother to mourn her loss. She was laid to rest in the Old Liberty church yard after a brief talk by George Williams. A host of friends join in sympathy in this sad hour. [Rogers Democrat 2/7/24]

BREWER, Fannie{sic} E. GARNER - Mrs. Fannie E. Brewer died a few minutes after midnight Sunday morning at the home of her son, George W. Brewer, of the Benton County Hardware Co., four miles north of town, at the age of 79 years, ten months and 29 days. She had been ill for some time and her death was not unexpected. Funeral services were held Tuesday afternoon at 2:30 o'clock at Alpine Cemetery on the J.M. Crismon place, east of Prairie Creek, and she was buried there by the side of her husband, G.F. Brewer, who died some six years ago. Miss Frankie{sic} Garner was born in Laclede county, Missouri August 29, 1844 and came with her parents to Benton county when a small child. They settled in the east side of the county where she married G.F. Brewer, one of the early settlers of the Larue neighborhood, where they lived until his death. To them were born eight children, seven of whom are still living: W.D. Brewer, Salina, Okla.; Mrs. Eliza Boydstun, Burkburnette, Texas; Jas. F. Brewer, Pryor, Okla.; Mrs. J.H. Wilder and George Brewer of Rogers; Mrs. John Caldwell, Baker, Montana; Mrs. John Butler, Carrollton, Ill. [Rogers Democrat 7/24/24]

BROWN, Curtis - {from Sulphur Springs} Mr. and Mrs. W.J. Brown returned Monday evening from Tulsa, Okla. where they were called by the death of their son, Curtis. Mr. and Mrs. Arthur Brown accompanied them home. [Benton County Record 8/22/24]

BROWNING, Rice - Rice Browning, 35, a farmer living three miles west of Grove, Okla. was instantly killed when struck by lightning near his home Monday. [Benton County Record 6/13/24]

BRUEN, Rose MORGAN - We have received word of the death of Mrs. Rose Bruen, who was the daughter of Mr. and Mrs. P.C. Morgan, which occurred at their home on Jan. 3, 1924. Mrs. Bruen was aged 35 years, 4 months and 29 days. She had been confined to her bed four months suffering greatly but was patient and died in the faith. She leaves three children: Mrs. Fred McMurray, Ponca City, Okla.; Juanita and John Paul; one brother,

Frank Payton, Cardin, Okla.; and three sisters, Gladys Morgan and Mrs. Jesse Keith, Marland, Okla. and Mrs. Frank Strome, Caruthers, Calif. and her father and mother. All relatives except Mrs. Strome were present at the last rites which were conducted by Rev. Gemplin of Billings, Okla. Interment was in Blackwell cemetery. [Gravette News Herald 1/18/24]

BRYANT, son - {from Gravette} The little son of Walter Bryant, who lives in the neighborhood of the Georgia church, died Sunday night of measles. [Benton County Record 1/11/24]

BUCK, Amelia - Mrs. Amelia Buck, a former resident of Bentonville, died at her home in Roosevelt, Okla. April 6th. The remains were brought to Bentonville for burial and funeral services were held at the Presbyterian church Monday afternoon. Mrs. Buck was born in Macon county, Missouri in 1855 and grew up there. She was married to Mr. Buck in 1877 and moved to Oklahoma in 1903 where she has lived since with the exception of one year in Bentonville. She is survived by her husband, a daughter and granddaughter. [Benton County Record 4/11/24]

BULL, Mattie SANFORD - Mattie Sanford, daughter of Mr. and Mrs. James B. Sanford, was born in Michigan July 2, 1840 and died May 29, 1924. She was married to Jas. M. Bull in 1861 with whom she lived happily until the day of his death 14 years ago. She was converted in early life and lived a consistent Christian until the end came. She was a member of the Methodist church and was always present at the regular services, and the different institutions of the same, when she was able to get there. She was one of a large family of 12 children, 7 of whom preceded her to the spirit world and, me thinks, were waiting anxiously for her arrival. Five are still of this side of the river and soon will join her at their eternal home where parting will be no more. She was carefully cared for by loving relatives and friends to the end. Her remains were brought to Gentry for interment. This was her home for a number of years. Her life was a benediction to our town and to all who knew her. Her husband was converted near the middle of life, joined the Methodist Episcopal church, and soon after felt the call to preach and became one of the great scholars as well as evangelists of his church. They have both left us for a higher realm while their bodies sleep side by side in our beautiful cemetery, waiting their Lord's call. Funeral services were conducted by B.L. Harris and S.F. Brown preached the sermon. [Gentry Journal–Advance 6/6/24]

BULLARD, W.P. - {from Gravette} W.P. Bullard, an old gentleman about 68 years of age, died at the home of his nephew on the old Stahl farm last Friday. The cause of his death was given as hardening of the arteries. Mr. Bullard had never married and had been living with his nephew for some time. The funeral was conducted by Jeff Finch and interment made in Bethel cemetery Saturday. [Benton County Record 1/18/24]
W.P. Bullard, single, a long-time resident of this vicinity, died at the age of 68 years at his nephew's home on Spavinaw Jan. 11, 1924. Mr. Bullard was

a brother of Mrs. Newt Williams who died about a year ago. Jeff Finch conducted the funeral and burial was at Bethel. [Gravette News Herald 1/25/24]

BUMP, Horace J. - Horace J. Bump was born in Meigs county, Ohio 78 years ago and died at his home near Jacket, Mo. on September 20, 1924. He had been sick for several months before the final call came but through all his sickness he was never heard to complain. Forty-eight years ago he united with the Christian Church and was always a faithful and diligent worker for the Lord. The many friends and relatives that gathered to see him during his last illness and to pay their respect to his remains gave ample proof of the love and esteem in which he was held by all, for to know Granddaddy Bump was to love him. He leaves to mourn his loss his wife and eight children, a number of great-grandchildren. Mrs. John Alfrey, east of town, was his oldest child and Ernest Alfrey of Bentonville was a grandchild. [Benton County Record 9/26/24]

BURCH, Jim - {from Lowell} Jim Burch, after a long illness and much suffering, passed peacefully away Wednesday evening. His funeral was preached by Rev. McSpadden of Rogers at the Presbyterian church Thursday. Interment, under auspices of Masonic order, was held at Silent Grove cemetery. Mr. Burch was 57 years old, the father of eleven children, nine of whom, with the mother, are left to mourn his loss. [Benton County Democrat 4/3/24]

{from Lowell} Mr. Burch, who has been low so long, passed away Wednesday night at 9 o'clock. Funeral services were conducted by Rev. T.E. McSpadden at the Presbyterian church of which the deceased had been a member for many years. Interment was in the Silent Grove cemetery in charge of the Masonic lodge. Mr. Burch was 57 years, 6 months and 10 days old. He leaves, besides the heartbroken wife, nine living children to mourn his loss. He was the constable of this place for many years and leaves a host of friends who sympathize with his family. [Rogers Daily Post 4/1/24]

BURDICK, Carey L. - Carey L. Burdick, a well-known citizen and lawyer of Stillwater, Okla., was found dead in his summer home two and one-half miles north of Bentonville on Tuesday afternoon of this week. The discovery was made by Roy and Ray Cunningham. The brothers immediately notified the sheriff's office and Deputy Sheriff Gailey went at once to the home. The doors were all locked and on breaking in they found the lifeless body on the floor near the head of the bed. A number 410 shotgun lay on the bed and there was an ugly wound in his neck. A piece of bailing wire was found around his neck and a chair and box stood upon the bed and it is thought that he first contemplated suicide by hanging. Coroner A.D. Callison of Rogers and his partner, Whitley Kerr, arrived shortly afterward and stated the deed had been committed several days previously. No inquest was necessary they thought. A note found pinned on his coat told of the step he was about to take and from the character of the note it showed that he had planned the step he had taken. The body was shipped to his old home in Stillwater where he is survived by a mother, a wife and 3 children. Mr. Burdick was 45 years of age and was at one time reputed to be quite wealthy. He enjoyed a large law practice and during the World War was prominently connected in putting over many of the government loans. Under the strain of overwork he broke down and gave up his practice and entered a hospital for treatment where he remained until pronounced cured. Afterwards he traveled and while here visiting his sister, Mrs. O.E. Young, he fell in love with the country and purchased a 40-acre farm north of Bentonville. This he visited from time to time and a few months ago he returned here. He appeared very despondent and wanted to be alone. He was last seen alive on Thursday of last week and when his sister called on him the following day she found the door locked. Mrs. Young left then for a visit in Tulsa, Okla. and while there her women's intuition told her all was not well with him. She wrote to the Cunningham boys and to E.C. Pickens asking them to call on him. This they did and the tragedy was discovered. [Benton County Record 2/22/24] [Rogers Daily Post 2/20/24]

CALDWELL, Mrs. W.W. - Mrs. W.W. Caldwell, an old resident of this section, died suddenly at the home of her son, E.T. Caldwell, in Vernon, Texas at the age of 82 years. Mr. and Mrs. Caldwell left here a little over a week ago to make their home with their sons in Vernon, Texas. They arrived in Vernon last Saturday and Mrs. Caldwell seemed to be in good health but a little tired after a three days drive from Bentonville to Vernon. That night she was taken suddenly ill and died Sunday morning. She was buried in the cemetery at Vernon. Mrs. Caldwell was a woman of splendid qualities and a lifelong member af the Baptist Church. Besides her husband she is survived by three sons, E.T. Caldwell and J.R. Caldwell of Vernon, Texas and W.M. Caldwell of Post, Texas. [Benton County Record 9/12/24]

CAMPBELL, James K. - On Tuesday, December 25th, 1923 J.K. Campbell, aged 71 years, one month and 23 days, was "called Home." The end came peacefully after a period of suffering and his death was made triumphant in his desire to go and be at rest. The funeral services were conducted at the home on Wednesday afternoon, December 26th by Rev. T.M. Morris of Gravette assisted by Rev. F.A. Bradshaw of the Vaughn church and a quartet, Elmer Pickens, Judge W.A. Dickson, Mrs. R.O. Pickens and Mrs. Arch Wright, from Bentonville. After the services the body was transferred by Messrs. Kerr & Callison to the Hart cemetery, five miles west of Rogers, where it was laid to rest to await the "resurrection morning." He was born near Adairville, Ky. November 13th, 1852 and came as a young man to Benton county in 1872, locating on a farm seven miles south of Bentonville where he lived until his death. On January 3rd, 1878 he was married to Miss Rosa Glover with whom he lived happily until October 24th, 1884 when the "Death Angel" called her home. To this union there were born three sons - V.J. of Portales, N.M.; W.M. of Billings, Okla.;

and J.S. of Dallas, Texas. On December 22nd, 1885 he was married to Miss Sarah Ellen Hall and with her he was permitted to live and build a home which was as the last lingering trace of paradise and a foretype of heaven until October 31st, 1915 when God called her to her reward and to the plaudit, "Well done." To this union were born nine children, two of whom died in infancy; the seven living were with him in his last illness and at the time of his death. They are: Mrs. Breck Burgin, Route 2, Bentonville; Mrs. Roy Blevins of Rogers; Misses Ethel, Mabel and Grace, at home; Archie of Joplin, Mo.; and Raymond, at home. Aside from his children he is survived by an aged aunt, Mrs. J.H. Burns of Bentonville. Mr. Campbell was one of the oldest residents of this section and was well known in Bentonville and throughout the county and was highly esteemed by all who knew him. In 1877 he united with the Temperance Hill Baptist church, continuing a member thereof until the time of his death. As a church-man he was vitally interested in the welfare of the church in all of its activities, devoting much time to the study of the Bible and to teaching in the Sunday school. He abounded in liberality, giving cheerfully and freely to the church causes and never turned a deaf ear to any one in need or distress. His character was marked by piety, firmness of conviction, gentleness and humility. He is missed by his church, his family and by the community in which he lived. He has gone from us but has entered the rich inheritance that God has prepared for his saints and his influence will live throughout the coming years. [Benton County Record 1/11/24]

CARL, John R. - {from The Oklahoma City Oklahoman} Despondent because of business reverses, J.R. Carl, about 50 years old, former vice president of the C. & A. Drug Co. here, committed suicide at 10 o'clock Saturday morning in Oklahoma City at the Masonic Temple by drinking poison. Attracted by the sounds of suffering Tom Holwell, employed as a janitor in the temple, found Carl a few moments after he had swallowed the contents of a 2 ounce vial of the poison. Carl died, however, before an ambulance reached the hospital. The body was taken to the Hahn Undertaking Co. here. A.T. Early, Justice of the Peace and coroner, announced that the death was suicide and that no investigation would be made. Carl lived at 423 East Sixth street with his wife and son, Fred Carl. He also is survived by a niece, Mrs. Claud Aikman, 329 West 22d street. Mrs. Carl was prostrated when informed of her husband's death and was not questioned but friends of the family said Carl had been despondent for several weeks. Last Monday he is reported to have told Edward Sneed, a porter at the temple: "I would end all this trouble by taking my life if I didn't think so much of my family and the boys here at the temple." He referred to the members of the lodge of which he was an enthusiastic member. The drug company of which Carl was vice president and one of the principal stockholders, went into bankruptcy several months ago. It operated the store at 3rd street and Broadway now owned by Roscoe Hadley, and two stores outside the downtown district. Carl had lived here for more than 7 years. He came to Oklahoma City from Frederick, Okla. Burial was at Lawton, Okla. Tuesday. ***** John R. Carl was the son of J.J. and M.J. Carl and was born at the home of his grandfather who owned the J.B. Whiteside farm 1½ miles northwest of Gentry, Ark. on the 8th day of Nov., 1866, was raised on a farm joining north. Was educated in the common schools of the country. Later graduating in banking and bookkeeping in a business college in Lexington, Ky. His brother, R.H. Carl, of the Gentry Hardware Co., left immediately for Oklahoma City last Saturday upon receipt of a telegram informing him of his death. [Gentry Journal–Advance 5/9/24]

CARLOCK, Jasper - Jasper Carlock, one of the best known citizens of Huntsville, died at his home there last week at the age of 45 years. He was the oldest son of the late State Senator Nelson Carlock. [Rogers Democrat 1/3/24]

CARTER, Adam - Adam Carter, an old Union soldier, dropped dead Monday at his home in West Fork, Ark. He was over 80 years of age. He was buried in the National Cemetery at Fayetteville. [Benton County Record 3/21/24]

CAVNESS, Amos Jarm - Amos Jarm Cavness died at his home in Bentonville early Saturday evening, Feb. 9, 1924, aged 54 years and five days. His death was the result of illness from which he had suffered for several months. Born on Pea Ridge, this county, February 4, 1870, he spent practically his whole life in this section and was known to and sincerely liked by a great number of people. He and his family moved to Bentonville in November 1906. For sixteen years, and until stricken with severe illness last July, he had been in the employ of K.C. Campbell and will be greatly missed from his old place there. In September 1897 he was married to Miss Gertrude Alfrey, a member of a pioneer Benton county family. Besides his wife he is survived by three daughters, Miss Lucille, Mrs. Zelma Woodruff and Miss Hazel Cavness, his aged parents, one sister, Mrs. Belle Bogle, all of Bentonville, two brothers, Henry of Bentonville and Reagon of Wichita, Kan. and other relatives including a much loved small niece and nephew, children of Mrs. Cavness' sister, who since their mother's death several months ago have been at the home of their "Daddy Amos." To these children he was devoted. "Amos," as he was best known to hundreds of friends and acquaintances, will ever be remembered as one unusually devoted to his family, who bore his sufferings and troubles uncomplainingly, who appreciated his friends, and who, if he had ill feeling against any man, did not burden others with such complaints. Funeral services at the residence Monday afternoon were conducted by J.M. McMahen, pastor of the Baptist church. Interment was at the City Cemetery, a host of friends paying a last tribute to his life and memory. [Benton County Democrat 2/14/24]

CAVNESS, Amos Jarmore - Amos Jarmore Cavness died at his home in Bentonville Saturday, February 9th, 1924 at the age of 54. His illness has extended over a period of eight months. Funeral services were conducted at the family home on Monday, the Rev. J.M. McMahen officiating. The funeral was largely attended. Besides his widow, Mrs. Gertrude Cavness he is survived by three daughters, Lucille and Hazel Cavness and Mrs. Zelma Woodruff. Also by his aged father and mother in Bentonville; two brothers, H.C. Cavness, of this city, and R.D. Cavness of Wichita, Kansas, also one sister, Mrs. E.D. Bogle of Bentonville. Amos Cavness was born on Pea Ridge in 1870 and grew to manhood there. He was the son of Joseph and Laura Cavness. In 1897 he married Miss Gertrude Alfrey and in 1904 they moved to Bentonville where they have since made their home. Mr. Cavness was a barber by trade and had many friends. Kit Campbell, his employer, states that he had worked for him 16 years and in all that time never missed the Saturday's work. [Benton County Record 2/15/24]

CAWTHER, infant - {from Elm Springs} The six-months old son of Mr. and Mrs. Jess Cawther died one day last week. The funeral services were held at the Methodist church and the babe was laid to rest in the Elm Springs cemetery. [Benton County Record 2/15/24]

CHANCELLOR, George - George Chancellor, a well known resident as well as one of the early settlers of Osage Mills community, died at his home one mile north of that place on Wednesday, July 2nd, 1924 from an illness of about three months. A cancer is said to have caused his death. Mr. Chancellor was born near Parkersburg, W. Va. September 8th, 1840. When a small child he moved with his parents to North Missouri. He came to Arkansas in 1870 and homesteaded 40 acres of land in the Osage Valley where he lived continuously until his death. He became acquainted with Miss Laura Wilson, daughter of James and Rachel Wilson, soon after locating here and the two were married in September 1874. To them were born six children, two of whom died in infancy. Two sons, Frank Chancellor of Fullerton, Cal. and Henry Chancellor who lives in Louisiana and two daughters, Mrs. Minta Walls and Mrs. Mable Walls, both of Fullerton, and his widow survive him. Mr. Chancellor was converted in 1895 and has been an active member of the old Temperance Hill Baptist church since that time. He was an old Confederate soldier and spent four years in the army. Funeral services were conducted Thursday by Rev. Rice of Springdale with burial in the Temperance Hill cemetery. [Benton County Record 7/11/24]

CHAPMAN, S.P. - {from Stony Point} S.P. Chapman, father of Mrs. Harry Smelser, departed this life some time early Friday morning. His wife arose and prepared breakfast, believing he was resting well but when she tried to wake him found he was dead. He was 88 years and one day old. The body was taken to Muskogee Sunday for burial. Two daughters arrived from Muskogee Sunday and his son on Sunday morning and they all accompanied the body to the burial place. We extend sympathy to the family in this sad hour. [Rogers Democrat 8/21/24]

CHASE, Jonathan - Jonathan Chase passed away suddenly Sunday morning at his home in Bentonville while Mrs. Chase was attending services at the M.E. Church, South. He was alone at the time and his wife left him in apparently good health. When she returned she found him dead in his chair. Heart failure is said to have been the cause of his death. Mr. Chase comes from old New England stock, his ancestors moving to New York State in the early part of the last century. He was born at Batavia in the western part of New York in 1849. When about 16 years of age his parents moved to Council Bluffs, Iowa. Here he grew to manhood and married Miss Charlina Mary Barnett. Later they moved to Weeping Water, Nebraska where he was engaged in several business enterprises. Seeking a warmer climate they went to Dallas, Texas where he engaged in the furniture business. In 1918 Mr. Chase retired from business and moved to Bentonville where he purchased a fine fruit farm just west of town - the one now owned by W.H. Heath. This he later sold and moved to Bentonville. Besides his widow he is survived by five sons - Jack B. Chase of Bentonville; Frank, George and Nathan Chase of Louisville, Ky.; James Chase of Dallas, Texas; and one daughter, Mrs. Webster Evoy of Houston, Texas - all of whom were present at the funeral. The funeral services were held at the M.E. Church, South Tuesday afternoon with Rev. Lester Weaver officiating, assisted by Rev. Harry C. Hoy, his former pastor, now located at Searcy. Both of these ministers paid a glowing tribute to the character and life of the deceased. [Benton County Record 2/1/24]

CHASTAIN, Mrs. Bud - {from Vaughn} Mrs. Bud Chastain, after a lingering illness from flu followed by pneumonia, passed to her heavenly reward on last Saturday night and was buried in the Barron cemetery Sunday afternoon, Rev. Billy Sears of Cave Springs conducting the service. [Benton County Record 2/1/24]

CHASTAIN, Nancy J. - Mrs. Nancy J. Chastain died in Kansas, Okla. early last Monday morning at the age of 82 years, 7 months and 2 days. She had reared a large family of children and they were all at her bedside when death came except D.H. Chastain who lives in Washington. She leaves a large circle of relatives and friends who mourn her going. The remains were brought to Fairmount cemetery and laid at rest Wednesday afternoon at 2:30. Funeral services were conducted by Rev. J.S. Spises of Watts, Okla. [Gentry Journal–Advance 1/18/24]

CHRISTIAN, Goldie - {from Mason Valley} Word has been received here that Goldie Christian, a well known girl here and in the Edgewood vicinity, died this last week of heart trouble at her home near Centralia, Oklahoma. She leaves a husband and a little son under a year old, father, mother, brothers. sisters and a host of friends to mourn her loss. [Benton County Record 2/29/24]

CHURCH, Charles F. - {from Sulphur Springs} The largest funeral ceremony in the history of Sulphur Springs occurred Sunday following the death of Charles F. Church, pioneer citizen, who passed away Saturday morning after several days illness attending a paralytic stroke. Mr. Church suffered the stroke last week, Tuesday, while talking on the porch of the Sulphur Springs hotel and never regained consciousness. He was 58 years of age, one of the town's oldest residents, well-known in this and neighboring counties. He has figured in many local enterprises. The funeral service was conducted by Rev. W.B. Hart and burial was at the Butler creek cemetery. As a Mason, the remains were accorded full rites and honors of the fraternity, members from far and near participating. Hundreds from neighboring towns and counties attended. Among relatives present were: Ross Church;, Joplin; Felix Church, Miami; Vol Lindsey and Mrs. L. Majors, Bentonville; Frank Lindsey, Dodge; Jim Lindsey, S.W. City and others. A son, Victor Church, failed to arrive from California. Universal sympathy is offered Mrs. Church and family. [Gravette News Herald 5/9/24] [Benton County Record 5/9/24]

CLANCEY, W.D. - W.D. Clancey, who resided a few miles southwest of town, died last week and was buried Saturday, aged 61 years. Funeral services were held in Gentry from the Methodist church. [Gentry Journal–Advance 3/28/24]

CLARK, Mr. - {from Valley View} Niles Clark received the sad news of the death of his brother in Chicago last week. [Benton County Record 9/12/24]

CLARK, Maude CROWDER - Mr. and Mrs. George Crowder received the news of the sudden death of their daughter, Maude Crowder Clark, at Caldwell, Kansas about 8 o'clock Saturday evening as the result of heart trouble. They left two hours later in their car for Vinita where they took the train for Caldwell. [Benton County Record 5/9/24]

CLAUSSEN, John - {from New Hope} Word has been received of the death of John Claussen at Buffalo, N.Y. the first of April. Mrs. Claussen brought the body to Marysville, Kansas for burial and later will come here to look after the farm. Mr. Claussen and wife left here in February for Buffalo where he had a position as millwright. [Rogers Democrat 4/10/24]

CLEGG, Joseph T. - Dr. Joseph T. Clegg, one of the best known citizens in Benton county and its oldest practicing physician, died at his home in Siloam Springs on Sunday, October 19th, 1924 at the age of 74 years after an illness of several weeks. Funeral services, which were held Tuesday afternoon, were largely attended, the Masons having charge of the funeral. Many representative citizens from all parts of the county were present. He is survived by two sons, John Clegg of Siloam Springs and C.B. Clegg of Amarillo, Texas; also one daughter, Mrs. A.M. Turner of Portsmouth, Ohio. Dr. Clegg was born near Pine Bluff in 1850 and when a young man took up the study of medicine, graduating from the University of Nashville when

23 years of age. He came to Benton county in about 1876 at the little town of Hico which is now Siloam Springs. He has made his home ever since at this place. Dr. Clegg was one of the best read men in the county and was familiar with most every important subject brought up. He was one of Siloam Springs' best boosters. In his passing the county loses one of its most distinguished citizens. [Benton County Record 10/24/24]

CLEMMER, J.G. - {from The Springdale News, Aug. 15th} J.G. Clemmer, 82 years of age, a long time resident of Springdale, died suddenly Thursday morning at his home on Thompson street. He has not been feeling well for some time but was up as usual, having voted Tuesday and was down town Wednesday. Thursday morning he went down into the basement at his home for some articles for breakfast and on ascending the stairs sank down on the back porch. He was carried into the house but soon passed away, death being due to apoplexy. Funeral services will be held at the Lutheran church Saturday morning at 10 o'clock. Mr. Clemmer had long been a resident of this community, for many years making his home on a farm north of town where his children were reared. Several years ago he and Mrs. Clemmer moved into town. Deceased is survived by the widow and four sons and three daughters. The sons are John of Ranger, Texas; Will of Tahlequah, Oklahoma; Dr. Joe of Gentry and Elbert of Illinois. The daughters are Mrs. Oma Gore of DeQueen; Mrs. M.A. Miller of Oklahoma and Mrs. Ella Ewalt of Springdale. Mr. Clemmer was a good citizen, thoroughly conscientious in all his acts and deeds. [Gentry Journal–Advance 8/22/24]

COCKEREL, Emily - {from Prairie Creek} Mrs. Emily Cockerel, who lived near Willow Springs, died Friday and was buried at Pace's Chapel cemetery on Saturday afternoon, Rev. Jeff Hendrix having charge of the funeral services. Mrs. Cockerel lived to some eighty years of age. She united with the M.E. church at an early age. She leaves two daughters, Miss Francis Cockerel and Mrs. Will Agnew, and a number of grandchildren to mourn her loss. We extend our sympathy to them. [Rogers Democrat 2/21/24]

CONAWAY, John - John Conaway died Tuesday at the home of his daughter, Mrs. C.M. Compton, one mile west of town, at the age of 93 years. The body was sent to Barry, Illinois for burial and was accompanied by Mrs. Compton, C.E. Conaway of Rogers and W.A. Conaway of McPherson, Kansas. A daughter, Mrs. W.J. Anderson, Great Bend, Kan. was called here by the illness and death of her father but was not able to accompany the body to Barry where the deceased was buried by the side of two daughters and his wife, who died some 45 years ago. Mr. Conaway was a native of Ohio. He came to Rogers from McPherson some seven or eight years ago. [Rogers Democrat 2/28/24]

The funeral of John Conaway was held Wednesday at the home of a daughter, Mrs. C.M. Compton, and the body was shipped to Barry, Illinois for interment. Mr. Conaway was born in Scio, Ohio August 7th, 1830, being nearly 94 years old when he died. He was married to Elizabeth Hendricks January 4, 1854. To this union 8 children were born: W.A. Conaway, McPherson, Kans. who passed away at 22; Mrs. Wm. Evans, living in Washington; C.E. Conaway and Mrs. C.M. Compton, both living in Rogers; Mrs. A.J. Compton, living in Mason, Iowa {only 5 named}. Mr. Conaway enlisted in the beginning of the Civil War in the 84th Illinois infantry, Co. E. He joined the M.E. church when a young man and at the time of his death was a member of that church in McPherson, Kansas. The funeral was conducted at the home of Mrs. C.M. Compton Wednesday, Feb. 27 by Rev. R.C. Lucke, pastor of the First M.E. church. [Rogers Daily Post 2/28/24]

CONE, Sally Hannah CITERLY - Sally Hannah Citerly, daughter of Abraham and Julina Citerly, was born in New York state April 24, 1845 and died near Gentry, Ark. Nov. 4, 1924, aged 79 years, six months and 11 days. When she was six years old her parents moved to Perry, Lake county, Ohio where, in sight of the placid waters of Lake Erie, she grew to womanhood. At about 15 years of age she was converted and joined the United Brethren church, of which she was a faithful and consistent member about 65 years. October 9, 1861 she was married to Oscar D. Cone. To this union three children were born: one daughter and two sons. A few years after their marriage her husband felt the call to preach the gospel and entered the ministry of the United Brethren church. In the fall of 1879 the family moved to Unadilla, Neb. where her husband continued his work in the ministry until called to his reward in June 1885. Her two sons died some years ago leaving the daughter, Mrs. E.F. Stoner, living northwest of Gentry, the only surviving member. She also leaves seven grandchildren and nine great-grandchildren. The funeral services were held at the home Thursday afternoon conducted by her pastor, Rev. A.F. Powell. Friday morning Mrs. Stoner started for Unadilla, Neb. with all that was mortal of her mother to lay it by the side of her father. [Gentry Journal–Advance 11/14/24]

COOK, Glen - Grove, Okla., Oct. 21.— Glen Cook, 17 years old, son of Mr. and Mrs. Isaac Cook of Cleroa, died from a result of self-inflicted injuries Sunday night according to announcement made by the coroner's inquest Monday morning. The lifeless body of the youth was found hanging from a limb of a tree near the family home early Monday morning and examination revealed evidence that led to the belief that the youth had met his death at his own hand, it was said. [Rogers Daily Post 10/21/24]

COOPER, Francis - {from Sulphur Springs} Carl D. Fisher left Tuesday morning for his home in Arkansas City, Kansas in response to a message that Francis Cooper had been killed in an automobile accident Monday night. No particulars have reached Sulphur Springs friends except that the car that he was driving, a powerful sport model Cadillac, had turned over three miles out of Winfield, Kansas. Francis, with his father, mother, two brothers and sister-in-law, had spent the past month in Sulphur

Springs, returning to their home in Kansas about a week ago on business. His parents, with Mr. and Mrs. Owen Cooper, were going from there on a motor tour through the north of Canada. Francis planned to return Thursday to Sulphur Springs to spend the summer. The family has a cottage at Bella Vista and spend a great deal of time there and at Sulphur Springs. He was a splendid young man 21 years old and has a host of friends here who are sincerely grieved to hear of his death. [Benton County Record 6/20/24]

COOPER, Matthew - Matthew Cooper, aged 82 years, an old and respected citizen of Gentry for the past two years, died at his home last Saturday from heart trouble. He leaves a wife and sons to mourn his loss. The remains were shipped to Olathe, Kansas Sunday night by Carpenter Bros. for burial. [Gentry Journal–Advance 8/1/24]

COVEY, Cora Dell DURHAM - Mrs. J. Melvin Covey died at 3 a.m. Wednesday at the home on the Keltner farm, aged 47 years and 14 days, following several weeks of illness which became serious last week. Besides her husband Mrs. Covey leaves three children, John and Truman, and Mrs. Pete Williams of Southwest City, Mo. John, the eldest son, arrived from Topeka, Kans. where he was attending the school of telegraphy, in time that his mother recognized him. Two of Mrs. Covey's brothers from Grove, Okla. were gone after in the night, Tuesday, by Dean Covey. The funeral is being held this Thursday, forenoon, at the Christian church of which Mrs. Covey was a member, Dr. W.A. McDonald conducting the services. Interment will be made in the family plot at Maysville. The husband, children and other relatives have the profound sympathy of the community in their untimely bereavement. [Gravette News Herald 4/18/24]

Cora Dell Durham was born April 2, 1877 at Aurora, Mo., being one of five children. Three brothers and one sister survive her. She was married to J.M. Covey Jan. 17, 1897. To this union were born five children: Terry, Olin, John and Truman, and one girl, Anna Dora, now the wife of Pete Williams of Southwest City. Terry and Olin passed to the home beyond in early childhood. The husband, Mrs. Williams and John and Truman, grandchildren and a host of relatives and friends remain to mourn her departure. Mrs. Covey united with the Church of Christ in 1912 and lived a faithful life. She was a true wife and mother and a kind neighbor. She died April 16, 1924. The funeral was conducted by her minister, W.A. McDonald, on Thursday April 17 at the Christian church and interment was made at Maysville. [Gravette News Herald 4/25/24]

CRABAUGH, Luther - Jess Crabaugh received the sad news Tuesday morning of the death of his brother, Luther Crabaugh, in Berryville, of tuberculosis. Mr. and Mrs. Crabaugh and Mrs. Bessie Lee Murphy drove over Tuesday afternoon to attend the funeral. [Benton County Record 7/4/24]

CRAIG, George T. - Charles R. Craig received the sad news Sunday of the death of his nephew, George T. Craig, who died in Beaumont, Tex.

Saturday following an operation for appendicitis. He was the son of Mr. and Mrs. George Craig and was born in Bentonville 32 years ago. [Benton County Record 6/6/24]

CRAIG, Grandma - {from Rocky Comfort} Grandma Craig departed from this earthly life last Wednesday morning at 5 o'clock. She is sadly missed by her daughter, Mrs. Cassie Grammer, with whom she has been making her home for the past few months, and by her many friends. She was laid to rest Wednesday afternoon at 2:30 at the Stults cemetery at Springdale. [Benton County Record 9/5/24]

CRAWFORD, Sarah Jane - Mrs. Sarah Jane Crawford died at her home near Healing Springs on Sunday, June 29th, 1924. It was the 44th anniversary of her wedding, being married to J.H. Crawford on June 29th, 1880. Mrs. Crawford was born September 18th, 1863 and is survived by eleven children, six boys and five girls, all of whom were present during her last hours excepting three who live in Texas who were unable to come. She was converted to Christianity in 1910 and lived the remainder of her life a devoted Christian. She was faithful as a companion, as a mother and as a neighbor. Her last testimony was that all was well and the future bright. Funeral services were conducted at the Mission in Cave Springs, Rev. W.B. Brogan officiating. Interment was made in the Cave Springs cemetery. [Benton County Record 7/11/24]

CRISTY, Call - Mrs. W.C. Wills received word that her brother, Call Cristy, fell dead Sunday morning at his home in Welch, Okla. Death was assigned to goitre. Mr. Cristy was quite well known to many people here. [Gravette News Herald 4/11/24]

CROWDER, Clara HUMPHREY - Mrs. George M. Crowder, a well known local writer and social worker of Bentonville, died at her home at the Park Springs Hotel on Saturday morning, December 13th, 1924. She was formerly Clara Humphrey and was born in Jamesport, Ky. on March 17th, 1860. She moved with her family to Carlinville, Ill. where she spent her girlhood, uniting with the Presbyterian church when quite young. She completed her education at the Blackburn College in Carlinville and married George M. Crowder on December 12th, 1876. To this union was born three children - Mrs. Guy Clark, Caldwell, Kansas, who died last May; Mrs. A.J. Vasey, Fort Worth, Texas and George T. Crowder of Bentonville. Mrs. Crowder came to Bentonville eleven years ago from Emporia, Kansas. She was a member of the Authors and Composers Society of Arkansas and the United Daughters of the Confederacy. Until her death she was a prominent club woman and a great worker along all educational lines. Two years ago she was appointed by Governor McRae to visit and inspect all rural schools for an educational report of the district. She was an artist of ability, her pictures having taken prizes in the Middle States Contest in Chicago. She was an author and a story from her pen was awarded the Arkansas Federation prize last year. Her poem, the "Arkansas Birth," is well known over Arkansas. Mrs. Crowder is survived by her husband, two children and four grandchildren, besides a host of friends in the community and in the state who will mourn her loss. [Benton County Record 12/19/24]

DALTON, Jas. H. - Jas. H. Dalton died April 12, 1924 at his home three miles east of Rogers of dropsy, aged 76 years and 6 months. Mr. Dalton was born in Illinois. He lived in Kansas for several years and has been a resident of Benton county for 37 years. He was married to Miss Lynn and to them eight children were born, six of whom are living. Mr. Dalton was a Baptist. He was well known in this locality and had a host of friends. The funeral was held at Ozark school house, east of Rogers, at 4 o'clock Sunday, conducted by Rev. Robt. Thompson and burial was in the Ozark cemetery. [Rogers Daily Post 4/16/24]

DAMRON, Ida May OSBORNE - The different communities west of Bentonville were shocked and grieved at the sudden death of Mrs. Joe Damron which occurred early Friday morning, November 7th and in her going a daughter of one of Benton county's pioneers started on the long, long trail. Mrs. Damron had been in apparently good health and arose that morning with her usual good spirits and energy. The first signs were when she told her husband that she felt dizzy and faint and in a very short time she passed away. Ida May Osborne, the daughter of George and Lucy Osborne, was born in Benton county in the Little Flock neighborhood, four miles east of Bentonville, on August 26th, 1875. She married Joe N. Damron on January 27th, 1895. To this union was born four children, one having died when a child. She professed faith in the Christian religion when a young girl and with her husband united with the Bethlehem Missionary Baptist church three years ago. She was a faithful member and had attended the service there only a few hours before she answered the hurried call of her Master. Besides her husband she is survived by her children: Mrs. Dora Edmonson, Nampa, Idaho; E.E. Damron, Dalhart, Texas; E.G. Damron, Texola, Okla.; by her mother, Mrs. Lucy A. Myers, Wheeler, Ark.; a sister, Mrs. Dora Lovelace, Rogers, Ark. and a brother, W.L. Osborne of Thomas, Okla., all of whom were present at the funeral. Services were held Wednesday afternoon and interment was made in the Barron cemetery. [Benton County Record 11/14/24]

DANIELS, Robert - Robert Daniels, a Cherokee Indian, died at his home west of Grove, Delaware county, Oklahoma last week at the age of 103 years. When the Cherokees were removed from Georgia in 1836 Daniels was one of the number. [Benton County Record 1/18/24]

DAVID, Laura - {from Cave Springs} Mrs. Laura David, one of the oldest citizens in this community, died at her home southeast of Cave Springs Friday morning and was buried in the Hebron cemetery Sunday afternoon. Bro. Tom Pattishall conducted the funeral service. She leaves several children and a number of friends to mourn her loss. [Benton County Record 1/25/24]

DAVIES, Victor - {from Cloverdale} Mrs. Sherwood returned Saturday from Bartlesville, Okla. where she was called to attend the funeral of her little grandson, Victor Davies, who underwent an operation from which he never recovered. [Rogers Democrat 4/24/24]

DAVIS, Lou WEISER - Mrs. Roy Davis died Tuesday morning at her home, the Hotel Main, after a protracted illness caused by malignant cancer from which she had suffered for several years. She had refused to give up however and was up and around the hotel for a portion of each day until a very short time before her death. The body was taken to her old home at Milford Center, Ohio for burial beside the grave of her only child, Mrs. Mabel Brown, who died in 1914. The body was accompanied by Mr. Davis and Mrs. Walter Staley and little daughter of Harrison. They left Rogers yesterday morning and the funeral services will be held at Milford Center Friday. They were accompanied as far as Monett by Frank Weiser of Haskell, Okla., a brother of Mrs. Davis. Mrs. Davis, whose maiden name was Lou Weiser, was born at Milford Center Feb. 2, 1869. She married Roy Davis when she was fifteen years old and they had but the one child, Mabel. They came to Rogers in 1901 and took over the Commercial Hotel which they conducted until 1921. A little later they opened the Davis Cafe on First street, giving it up last year to take over the management of the Hotel Main. Mrs. Davis was one of the best known hotel women in the state for she has always been actively identified with her husband in the management of the hotels and restaurant. The Democrat editor had known her ever since the family came to Rogers and there was not a bigger hearted, more charitable woman in the country. No person suffering from hunger was ever turned away from their door and no one will ever know how many boys and women she helped in a financial way. She was a friend and counselor in time of need to many a wayward boy of Rogers and vicinity and often as the editor dropped in for a late lunch he found her advising boys {and girls, too} to get off the street and go home. There are hundreds of men and boys scattered over this broad land who would have been glad to have lightened her last days by a message of cheer and appreciation had they been given the opportunity. [Rogers Democrat 10/9/24] [Rogers Daily Post 10/7/24]

DAVIS, Thomas C. - Thomas C. Davis, aged 84, passed away on Friday, February 22nd, 1924 at the home of his daughter, Mrs. Wilmot Clark, in Bentonville. He had been an invalid for a number of years. Funeral services were held Sunday afternoon at the M.E. Church, Rev. E.M. Dugger of Springdale officiating. The services were largely attended and the floral offerings beautiful. Interment was made in the City Cemetery. Mr. Davis was born in Deersville, Ohio in 1839 where his early life was spent. Later he moved to McLean county, Ill. where in 1860 he was united in marriage with Mary Eleanor Hauer. To this union six children were born. In 1913 Mr. Davis and family moved to Arkansas and bought a farm west of

Bentonville and followed his vocation of farming until ill health compelled him to give up farm life and since then he and Mrs. Davis have made their home with their children. Besides his wife, Mrs. Mary E. Davis he is survived by three daughters - Mrs. Wilmot Clark and Mrs. John Neuenschwander of Bentonville and Mrs. Etta Winters of Saunemin, Ills. When a young man he joined the M.E. Church but after coming to Arkansas transferred his membership to the Centerton M.E. Church. Mr. Davis was a man who loved his home, a faithful husband and loving father and a God-fearing citizen. [Benton County Record 2/29/24]

DEAN, Helen Christine - Helen Christine Dean, eight year old daughter of Mr. and Mrs. Walter Dean, died Sunday at their home in the northeast part of town, east of Sunnyside School. She was taken ill Sunday about noon and died that night. Owing to the fear that the disease might be contagious, although the cause was not fully determined, the funeral, which was held from the chapel of the Callison Undertaking Co., was private. It was conducted by Rev. Crichlow of the Central Methodist Church Monday afternoon and interment was in the city cemetery. The sudden death of this bright little girl was a great shock to the family and friends and they have the sympathy of the entire community. [Rogers Democrat 12/18/24] [Rogers Daily Post 12/15/24]

DEASON, Thomas Newton - Thomas Newton Deason died yesterday morning at 9:15 at his home at 1106 South Fourth street. Death was the result of a cancer from which he had suffered a year or more and had been confined to his bed for a month past. Funeral services will be held at the First Baptist Church this afternoon at 3:00 o'clock and will be conducted by the pastor, Rev. R.L. Austin. Burial will be in the Oakley Chapel cemetery. Mr. Deason was born June 19, 1874 in the Pleasant Hill neighborhood and some of the older people still refer to the Deason school and church at Pleasant Hill. Most of the life of the deceased was spent within a few miles of his birthplace. He was married in 1895 to Miss Maud Rodecape of near Grove, Okla. who survives him, together with four children - Mrs. J.R. Heffner, Miss Madge Deason and Clyde and Glen Deason. Also two brothers, Robert and Will Deason, and one sister, Mrs. Ellen Maxwell of Miami, Okla. Mr. Deason was a popular and well-known resident of Rogers and had a wide circle of friends and acquaintances who will deeply regret to learn of his death. [Rogers Democrat 8/28/24]

DeBORD, Flossie - {from Stony Point} The following death notice is taken from the Simila {Colo.} News-Echo: "Mrs. Flossie DeBord, wife of Ralph DeBord, passed away at Beth El hospital in Colorado Springs Thursday, October 16th. Age 30 years. Mrs. DeBord had been a sufferer from tuberculosis for several years and was removed to the hospital three days before her death. Funeral services were held at Alta Vista conducted by Rev. Higgins and burial was in the Calhan cemetery." We extend sincere sympathy to this family in their loss. They lived in this neighborhood several years and were well liked by everybody who will be grieved to learn of the passing of this good woman and young mother. [Rogers Democrat 10/30/24]

DICKSON, Dwight - After a long and painful illness, Dwight Dickson died at the home of his son, Russell D. Dickson, in Bentonville, Ark. on Monday, August 18th, 1924 at 1:20 o'clock p.m. at the age of 65 years, two months and 16 days. Mr. Dickson was born in Bentonville, Ark. on June 2nd, 1859 and has lived on and near the place of his birth all his life. He was the youngest member of the family of Uncle Jimmie and Aunt Mary Dickson who were among the earliest settlers of this country and who were of that sturdy pioneer stock that blazed the way for the present civilization and caused the wilderness to blossom as a rose. On January 21st, 1885 Dwight Dickson and Madeline Jefferson, daughter of Mr. and Mrs. John J. Jefferson, another one of the pioneer families of Benton county, were united in marriage and to this union two sons were born - Bennett and Russell Dickson. Bennett Dickson departed this life on June 6th, 1923. Thus with the death of the loving father Russell Dickson is the only surviving member of this once most happy and contented family and the sincere sympathy of the entire community goes out to this sole survivor who has been so sorely bereft. About 12 years ago Mr. Dickson happened to an accident which broke his leg and after about a year of suffering, and in the meantime making every effort to restore the broken member, it became necessary to amputate the limb. For a time thereafter Mr. Dickson seemed to regain some of his lost vitality but it seemed fate was against him for it was not very long until he suffered a stroke of paralysis and from that time on a gradual decline set in which never abated until his spirit was released from his pain-wracked body and took its flight to that eternal home where all is peace and joy and love. In his younger days Mr. Dickson was an exceedingly energetic man, an indefatigable worker with a keen intellect and good business discernment and he succeeded in accumulating a liberal amount of this world's goods. He was fair, honest and generous in all his dealings with his fellowman and a splendid provider for his own household. For many years he was one of the members of the board of directors of the First National Bank of Bentonville and has been identified with numerous business enterprises of this city. In early life Mr. Dickson united with the Cumberland Presbyterian Church and remained true to that faith even until the end. He was a Christian in the true sense of that term and never faltered in the faith. Besides the only surviving son he leaves five grandchildren Dwight Bennett, Lon Russell and Marguerite McGill, children of Mr. and Mrs. Bennett Dickson; Dee Ruth and Madeline Susan, children of Mr. and Mrs. Russell Dickson. He also leaves two sisters - Mrs. Frank Kindley of Graham, Texas and Mrs. James Black of Oklahoma City, Okla. and a great number of kindred and friends who will sorely miss him. Funeral services were held at the home of his son on Tuesday afternoon at 3 o'clock conducted by Rev. Stephen A. Morton of the Christian Church, assisted by Rev. Peter Carnahan. After the services the body was laid to rest in the City Cemetery beside his companion in the presence of a large number of sorrowing relatives and friends who came to pay their last respects to the memory of one whom they loved. [Benton County Record 8/22/24]

DICKSON, Madeline JEFFERSON - {A Memorial} Madeline Jefferson was born in Bentonville, Arkansas on May 14th, 1867. She was the oldest of eight children of John J. and Cynthia Woods Jefferson. Her childhood days were spent in and around Bentonville. She was always a kind and obedient child. On January 21st, 1885 she was married to Dwight Dickson. To them were born two children, Dwight Bennett and Dee Russell. Bennett, the eldest, passed into the great beyond on June 6th, 1923. Mrs. Dickson was a very devoted wife and mother and her life was spent in making her home happy and caring for her family and relatives. She professed religion in November 1893 and united with the Cumberland Presbyterian Church and remained true to the faith the remainder of her life. On the morning of December 19th, 1923 at 3:15 a.m. she departed this life. She is survived by her devoted husband, Dwight Dickson, one son, Russell Dickson, four grandchildren, Dwight Bennett and Lon Russell {the twins}, Dee Ruth and Marguerite McGill Dickson; two sisters, Mrs. Edgar Carnahan and Mrs. Perry Arthur, and one brother, John Jefferson, all of whom were present at the funeral except her brother. J.M. McMahen. [Benton County Record 1/25/24]

DILLARD, child - {from Oakley Chapel} Mrs. W.D. Bassett was called to Dewar, Okla. Friday evening to the home of her sister, Mrs. Jack Dillard, whose child had died of spinal meningitis. [Rogers Democrat 2/7/24]

DILLINGER, Mrs. - {from Oakley Chapel} Mrs. W.C. Bassett left for Durant, Okla. Sunday. She received a telegram stating the death of her sister, Mrs. Dillinger. Mrs. Bassett was called to her sister's home four weeks ago for the burial of her nephew. [Rogers Democrat 3/6/24]

DIVEN, Mary Jane EDMISTON - Mrs. Mary Jane Diven died at the family home between Bentonville and Rogers on Saturday, April 12th, 1924 after an illness of some time. Old age and a complication of diseases caused her death. Funeral services were held Sunday. Among those who attended from Decatur were Mr. and Mrs. George Edmiston, Mr. and Mrs. Clyde Edmiston, Mr. and Mrs. Mack Peek and Mr. and Mrs. Charles Adkins. She is survived by one brother, George Edmiston of this place, a daughter, Nancy Diven, and two grandchildren, Earl and Hubert Diven, with whom she made her home. Mary Jane Edmiston was born in Washington county, near Viney Grove, 85 years ago. In 1856 she was married to M.A. Diven and later moved to Benton county. She was a member of the M.E. Church, South for over 40 years. She began to fail rapidly about a month ago and Mr. Edmiston has spent a great deal of time with her during these declining days of her life. [Benton County Record 4/18/24]

Mary Jane Edmiston was born near Viney Grove, Ark. April 18, 1924 {1839?} and died April 12, 1924 at her home near Rogers at the age of 84 years, 11 months and 24 days. About 40 years ago she was converted and joined the First M.E. church South and has lived a consistent christian life ever since. She was united in marriage Sept. 25, 1856 to M.A. Diven. To this union was born two children, James Diven, who died Jan. 10, 1917 and Nancy Diven, now living. She leaves one brother, George A. Edmiston of Decatur and two grandsons, Hubert and Earl Diven, who made their home with her, and a large number of relatives and friends to mourn her loss. [Rogers Daily Post 4/14/24]

DIXON, Walter - {from Maysville} Johnnie Poindexter received a telephone message telling him of the death of his nephew, Walter Dixon, at Cherokee City. Mr. Poindexter attended the funeral last Monday. Have not learned the cause of the death. [Benton County Record 8/15/24]

DONELSON, Mrs. ?. C.W. - (This item is a little garbled.) Mrs. ?.C.W. Donelson died this the home 607 Electric Street at 2:30 Monte Ne. Mrs. Donelson has been ill for a year or more and her death came as a relief from intense suffering. The body will be taken to the old home in Elgin, Kansas for burial. Mrs. Donelson is survived by her husband and by Mrs. E.H. Reynolds of Wichita, Kansas who has been caring for her mother for some time and by Lieut. Commander J.F. Donaldson(?) of Hampton Roads, Virginia. [Rogers Daily Post 12/4/24]

DRAKE, Albert - {from The Madison County Record} Albert Drake, age 20 years, son of Jake Drake, a former citizen of this county, was accidentally killed recently while working in the oil fields near La Habra, Calif. and his body and also that of his sister, Maud, who died about a year ago, were shipped back to Fayetteville for interment in the Evergreen cemetery, the double funeral and burial Saturday being attended by relatives from Huntsville and Drake's Creek. [Rogers Democrat 5/8/24]

DRUMMOND, Anna Hubbard - Mrs. Anna Drummond died Sunday at the home of her daughter, Mrs. Fred Landers, the result of a paralytic stroke suffered a week or two ago. Funeral services were held at the Landers home Monday and were conducted by Rev. F.M. Seamster. Mrs. Drummond was 80 years old and had lived in Benton county for twenty years, coming here from Missouri. Her husband died some years ago and she is survived by five children. Mrs. Brinson Dean of Prairie Creek is a daughter of the deceased, and Ernest Massey, a grandson. [Rogers Democrat 3/20/24]

Mrs. Anna Hubbard Drummond was born in Nebraska and died at the home of her daughter, Mrs. Fred Landers, March 16, aged 80 years, 2 months and 9 days. She spent the most of her life in Missouri and came to Arkansas 20 years ago living near Avoca until the death of her husband after which she came to Rogers. She was the mother of nine children, 5 of whom are living and all were present during her recent illness. which was caused by a paralytic stroke a few weeks ago. Mrs. Brinson Dean, living on

Prairie Creek, is a daughter and Ernest Massey, employed at the Ford service station, is a grandson. The funeral was conducted yesterday at the Landers home by Judge F.M. Seamster; the interment was at the City Cemetery. [Rogers Daily Post 3/18/24]

DRUMMOND, Esther Ann HUBBARTT - Esther Ann Hubbartt was born in Indianapolis, Indiana January 7, 1844. She was married to P.W. Drummond October 9, 1863 in Gallia Co., Ohio. They spent several years in Ohio, later going to Nebraska where their children grew up, the winters being so cold they came to Arkansas to spend their declining years. March 16th she passed to the great beyond to be with the loved ones gone before - one son, three daughters, with the husband having preceded her to the better land. Grandma Drummond, as she was known, was loved by one and all. Those in trouble could always find a word of cheer from her. She had been a member of the Methodist church since childhood and was a diligent worker in her younger days. As she grew older and her sight became dimmed her son, W.F. Drummond, of Cuba, New York, presented her with a large type Bible that she could more easily study God's holy work. Since the death of her son a few years ago she had made her home with her youngest daughter, Mrs. Fred Landers of Rogers. Her children were all with her when that peaceful sleep began: Mrs. R.J. Shuck of Franklin, Nebraska; W.F. Drummond of Cuba, New York; Mrs. Geo. Boley, Oklahoma City, Okla.; Mrs. B.F. Bridgford, Mrs. Brinson Dean and Mrs. Fred Landers, all of Rogers. She was laid to rest by the side of loved ones in the Rogers Cemetery to await the resurrection. [Rogers Democrat 3/27/24]

DUDLEY, Virginia JACKSON - Virginia Jackson, daughter of Judge James Jackson, was born July 30, 1847 about three miles west of Bentonville. On January 9th, 1868 she was married to J.L. Dudley, having until that time remained in the home with her parents. To this union were born two sons: W.T. Dudley and James Dudley, the latter of whom passed to his reward Dec. 17, 1899. Mr. and Mrs. Dudley, after their marriage, settled on a farm southwest of Bentonville where they continued to reside until the death of their son, James. Soon after this bereavement they moved into Bentonville where they both spent the remaining years of life. Early in life Sister Dudley united with the Cumberland Presbyterian Church of which she was a consistent member until the union of this church with the Presbyterian Church, U.S.A. She did not identify herself with the new organization. She dearly loved the church and faithfully attended the services as long as it was reasonably possible. Her husband, for some 25 years of his later life was an invalid, being seriously afflicted with rheumatism. During these years of suffering, true to the sacred vows of marriage, she patiently waited with him and tenderly cared for him until in June 1916 when he was called to his reward. Sister Dudley enjoyed fairly good health until about three years ago she had a fall which fractured her hip. Since that time her strength has gradually failed and on Lordsday,

December 7th, at 8:20 p.m. she peacefully fell asleep at her home on West A street, next door to her surviving son, W.T. Dudley. She was a good woman - a faithful and true wife and one of the very best and dearest of mothers. The funeral services were conducted from the home by Stephen A. Morton, minister, Christian church, 2:30 p.m. December 8th after which the remains were taken to the cemetery at Centerton for interment. Stephen A. Morton. [Benton County Democrat 12/11/24]
Bentonville, Ark., Dec. 10 - Mrs. Virginia Jackson Dudley, widow of the late Liberty Dudley, died at her home Sunday night at the age of 77 years. Mrs. Dudley was the daughter of James Jackson, pioneer of Benton county and was born at the Jackson homestead near Bentonville and lived here all of her life. She is survived by one son, W.T. Dudley, of Bentonville Cash Store and member of the city council, and one grandson, Burkes Dudley of Bentonville. Among the nephews and nieces surviving her are J. Mack Jackson, John Jackson and W.E. Jackson of Bentonville, Mrs. Belle Knott of Little Rock, Mrs. John Blansett of Rogers and Mrs. George P. Jackson of Bentonville. [Rogers Daily Post 12/10/24]

DUNCAN, Mrs. Horace - {from Rocky Comfort} Mrs. Elsie Crain received the sad news of the death of her brother's wife, Mrs. Horace Duncan of Manhattan, Kansas. [Benton County Record 7/18/24]

DUNN, L.M. - Mrs. C.M. Bullock has received the sad news of the death of her father, L.M. Dunn which occurred last Monday at his home in East Tennessee. Burial took place in the family cemetery at Abington, Virginia on Wednesday, May 21st. [Benton County Record 5/30/24]

EARLEY, W.J. - W.J. Earley, a prominent farmer who resides one-half mile east of town, committed suicide last Saturday night about 9:30 o'clock at his home by taking strychnine and died within fifteen minutes from the effects of the poison. His wife was away from home at the time but a doctor was called and he was dead before the physician arrived. Mr. Earley left a letter to the family giving details as to how to handle the property and other matters. His rash act was caused by ill health as he had been ill for several days and it seemed to dishearten him that he had to be sick and he had told a friend a few days previously that it was the first time he had had a doctor in 40 years. He seemed to think that he would never get well. Mr. Earley was about 60 years of age and leaves a widow, two sons and three daughters to mourn his demise. Funeral services were conducted by Rev. B.L. Harris of the Methodist church Tuesday at 2:30 o'clock. Mr. Earley was in the house alone with one of his daughters. He called his daughter into his room at about 9:30 and told her what he had done and gave her a letter he had written. The girl immediately sent for her mother and Dr. Clemmer but he died a half hour later. [Gentry Journal–Advance 7/25/24]

EARLY, Whitmer James - Whitmer James Early, son of Mr. and Mrs. Edward Early, was born in Jasper county, Iowa Feb. 22, 1865. Bro. Early was one of a fine family of six children and the one brother and four sisters survive him. At the age of sixteen he, with his father's family, moved to Kansas where he lived for 36 years until 7 years ago he came to this state and lived among us until the time of his death which occurred about 10 p.m. July 19th, 1924. Converted early in life he united with the Presbyterian church but coming to this state he united with the Congregational church, then later the Methodist church. He was active in our church work and at the time of his death was teacher of the Adult Bible Class and was loved and respected by all. He was also an honored member of the Woodmen of the World. He will be missed by these organizations and will be much thought of. On Nov. 28th, 1899 he was married to Miss Callie Brown. To this union was given five children, all of whom, with the mother, survive him and these with a large circle of friends, with deep heart break, mourn his sudden departure. Your Pastor, B.L. Harris. [Gentry Journal–Advance 8/1/24]

EASLEY, Rosetta - Rosetta Easley was born in Benton county, Arkansas on August 11th, 1885 and died on May 6th, 1924 at the home of her parents, Mr. and Mrs. W.P. Easley, east of Centerton. At the age of 16 she was united in marriage with Fred Jones in Benton county, Ark. To this union two children were born - Grace and Kenneth. On March 1st, 1905 this union was divided and the custody of the children given to the mother. Rosetta Easley and children made their home with her parents until death came upon her. Rosetta Easley leaves to mourn her death her mother, Mrs. Sarah Jane Easley; two children, Grace {Easley} Mauler and Kenneth Easley, of Benton county, Ark.; three sisters, Mrs. Ella Swindle of Wilson, Okla.; Mrs. Florence Miller of Southwest City, Mo. and Mrs. Esther Edwards of Centerton, Ark.; and four brothers, Steve Easley of Missouri; Jim Easley of Hiwasse, Ark.; W.E. Easley and Seth Easley of Bentonville, Ark. Rosetta Easley was laid to rest on May 7th, 1924 in the Gamble cemetery. [Benton County Record 5/23/24]

ECKART, Richard J. - Richard J. Eckart, brother-in-law of C.C. Beall, died Friday night at his home in St. Louis. Mrs. Beall left last night for St. Louis while Mr. Beall, who was on business in the south part of the state, was located by long distance telephone and was expected to start at once for St. Louis. [Rogers Daily Post 12/14/24]

EDEN, infant - {from Monte Ne} We are very sorry to report the death of the infant daughter of Mr. and Mrs. Chas. Eden. Interment in the Frisco cemetery. [Rogers Democrat 4/17/24]

EDMISTON, Geo. W. - Geo. W. Edmiston, well known in western Benton county, and one of the early settlers near Decatur, died at his home there Sunday evening about 7 o'clock. Mr. Edmiston has been in ill health for some time, suffering from a complication of diseases which finally resulted in his death. Funeral services were held Monday afternoon and were attended by a large number of old friends and relatives. Besides his widow he is survived by four married children, all of whom live at Decatur. These are Clyde C. Edmiston, Mrs. Chas. Adkins, Mrs. Mack Peek and Mrs. Andy Wilmoth. [Benton County Record 12/5/24]

EDMONSON, infant - {from Vaughn} The infant child of Mr. and Mrs. Arthur Edmonson was buried on Monday afternoon. These parents have the sympathy of the entire community. [Benton County Record 12/5/24]

ELIFF, Mrs. Jess - {from Gravette} Word was received here Monday of the death of Mrs. Jess Eliff at her home in Anderson Sunday. Mrs. Eliff was well known to many people here. [Benton County Record 6/6/24]

ELLIS, George W. - George W. Ellis departed this life January 30, 1924 at the Bernett Sanitarium, Fresno, Calif. where he had undergone an operation for cancer of the stomach only the day preceding. He was born in Ash Grove, Shelby county, Illinois May 1, 1857. When a boy he, with his parents, moved to Benton county, Arkansas, near Garfield, where he lived for many years. He married Miss Eliza Jane Cox who is left to mourn the loss of a devoted husband. To this union were born eight children: Mrs. Della Brown, Mrs. Fleeta Carmichael, Clee and Loyd of Selma, Lester of Aurora, Mo. and Mrs. Myrtle Whitaker of Pryor, Okla. Two children, Ernest and Frank, preceded the father to the better world. He had 15 grandchildren and one great grandchild and one sister, Mrs. Sarah Poe, of Fresno, Calif.; two brothers, John of Garfield, Ark. and Will of Tulsa, Okla. and many other relatives and friends. He with his family came to Selma about three years ago where he engaged in the mercantile business. He was well respected, just and honest in all his dealings and will be greatly missed by his family, relatives and a host of friends. He was laid to rest in the I.O.O.F. cemetery February 1, 1924. The I.O.O.F. lodge of Selma had charge of the services. A Friend. [Rogers Democrat 2/14/24]

ELLISON, Emily - Miss Emily Ellison, sister of Mrs. Frank Saunders, died last night at nine o'clock. The funeral will be held tomorrow at 10 o"clock from the residence on Third Street, conducted by Rev. Lucke. Burial will be in the city cemetery. [Rogers Daily Post 12/26/24]

ENNIS, Mrs. John {EDENS} - {from Monte Ne} We are sorry to report the sad death of Mrs. John Ennis who committed suicide by taking carbolic acid last Friday morning. She had been in poor health for quite a while which affected her mind. She is survived by a husband and a two months old baby girl. Also her parents, Mr. and Mrs. Johnse Edens, two sisters, Mrs. Herbert Davis of Rogers and Mrs. Dunlap of Texhoma and Pet and Huston Edens, who live here. Interment in the McDaniel cemetery. We tender our sympathy to the bereaved family. [Rogers Democrat 8/21/24]
Mrs. John Ennis, aged 25, committed suicide early last Friday morning at the home of her parents, Mr. and Mrs. John Eden, at Monte Ne by drinking carbolic acid. Death is thought to have been caused by undue excitement in connection with the birth of a daughter about two months ago. Her home life is said to have been unusually pleasant and the young husband and parents, as well as her many friends at Monte Ne and Lowell, were shocked

at her tragic end. During a spell of despondency she arose early Friday morning and went to her husband's store and procured a bottle of carbolic acid and after drinking its contents started for home. The poison acted quickly and she fell to the ground as she entered the yard of her home. Medical aid was summoned but she died in agony two hours later. Funeral services were conducted at the home of her parents Saturday afternoon by the Rev. I.H. Burgess, pastor of the Christian church in Springdale, in the presence of a large number of loving friends. Interment was made in the McDaniels cemetery north of Lowell. Mrs. Ennis was born near Lowell in 1899 and was married to John Ennis a few years ago. Besides her husband and parents she is survived by 2 sisters and 3 brothers. [Benton County Record 8/22/24]

EVANS, Manda - {from Hiwasse} Aunt Manda Evans died at her home near Hiwasse Sunday morning and was buried in the Daniels cemetery Monday evening. She had been an invalid for several years and recently underwent an operation. [Benton County Record 5/9/24]

EVANS, Newton - {from Larue} Newton Evans, who was a well known citizen of Sedalia, became ill on Monday, the first, and died on Wednesday, the third. He was buried the next day at the Woodruff cemetery. Reverend Thompson conducted the funeral services. He leaves a sister, seven brothers and three minor children to grieve and mourn his loss. [Rogers Democrat 9/11/24]

FAIR, C.V. - Hugh Fair received the sad news of the death of his brother, C.V. Fair, which occurred Wednesday, Oct. 22 at Los Angeles, Calif. C.V. Fair was aged 47 years and was reared in Benton county, Ark. He leaves a widow. Interment was made at Glendale, Calif. last Friday. [Gravette News Herald 10/31/24]

FAIR, Joseph A. - Joseph A. Fair, a resident of Benton county for more than 60 years, died at his home in Centerton on Wednesday, March 26th, 1924 at the age of 78 years. Death was due to apoplexy. While Mr. Fair had been in ill health for several years it has only been during the past week that his condition was considered serious. Funeral services, conducted by Revs. Weaver and Campbell, were held at the M.E. Church in Centerton on Thursday morning and the body was taken to the Bethel cemetery, south of Gravette, for interment. The funeral was largely attended. Uncle Joe Fair, as he was commonly called, was born in Sullivan county, Tenn. in 1845. He came to Benton county in 1859 and located on the Spavinaw southeast of Gravette. He served with distinction in the Southern army and on his return from the war married Miss Martha Russell in 1865 - who died in 1899. In 1901 he married Miss Parolee Collier who survives him. He is also survived by eight sons. Mr. Fair was a conscientious Christian and has been a church member for 55 years. He was ordained a preacher in 1884 and was pastor of the Centerton church for 40 years. [Benton County Record 3/28/24] [Benton County Democrat 4/3/24]

Ellis Fair of Kingsville, Tex.; Dick Fair of Duenweg, Mo. and Wiley Fair of Whitesboro, Tex. departed for their respective homes Saturday morning after having attended the funeral of their father, J.A. Fair, which was held at Bethel Thursday last. [Gravette News Herald 4/4/24]
Joseph A. Fair was born in Sullivan county, Tennessee June 21st, 1845; departed this life March 26, 1924, aged 78 years, 9 months and 5 days. He came to Benton county in November 1859; became a Christian in early manhood and for 55 years was a faithful worker in the M.E. church which he dearly loved. He was ordained as a local minister in 1884 and no doubt conducted more funerals than any other minister in the county. He was married in 1869 to Martha A. Russell, she having passed on in June 1899. He was again married Jan. 13, 1901 to Miss Parolee Collyer, who with eight sons by his first wife, are left to mourn his departure. Father was a Mason and was the last charter member of the Bethel lodge. He served three years as a soldier in the Southern Confederacy. He has lived a long and useful life. He was very kind to everyone, always charitable, even to those who persecuted him. He suffered greatly in his last days yet was patient, kind, his hope never wavering. The funeral sermon was held at the Community Church, Centerton, conducted by the Revs. Weaver and Campbell of Bentonville after which the body was conveyed to the Bethel cemetery where another service was conducted by Rev. Boyles, assisted by Rev. Harris. Lovingly and tenderly submitted by his son, Hugh L. Fair. [Gravette News Herald 4/11/24]

FARISH, Emma - {from Elm Springs} Mrs. Clem Glover has made several trips to see her sister, Mrs. Emma Farish, near Tontitown during the last week. Mrs. Farish died Sunday. [Benton County Record 2/22/24]

FARRAR, D.D. - D.D. Farrar, a prominent and highly respected farmer living between Cave Springs and Elm Springs, shot himself in the temple with a 22 caliber rifle at 4 o'clock this morning, dying about 7 o'clock. There is no known reason for the act. It is known that he was worrying over some recent business deals but so far as can be learned the worry was more due to a state of mind or habit than to any business misfortune. Mr. Farrar owned a splendid farm near the Osage river and was well fixed financially. He was 35 years old and had six children. It is said he had been troubled with restlessness at night. When he could not sleep he would get up and sit by the fire. Last night he was particularly restless and spent most of the fore part of the night sitting up. When his wife asked if he was ill he said that he was alright and told her to go to sleep. But during the conversation he told his wife how much he thought of her and the children. Reassured, Mrs. Farrar retired and went to sleep. About four o'clock Mr. Farrar stretched out on the floor, placed the muzzle of a 22 caliber rifle to his temple and pulled the trigger. The rifle was found by his side. It is said that a few days ago Mr. Farrar called on a neighbor for a visit and at that time went over his financial affairs. There were some small details worrying him but on the whole his affairs seemed to be in good shape. It is said he was quite well to do. He was always overly considerate of his family, a good husband and father. He had a wide circle of friends in Benton and Washington counties, enjoying a wide popularity. His father was formerly in business in Springdale. Mrs. Will Stroud of Rogers is a cousin. Mrs. Farrar was a Pattishall before her marriage, her parents live near Cave Springs. Both families are highly respected and they have the sympathy of the entire community in their bereavement. [Rogers Daily Post 12/27/24]

FERRY, Dora - Mrs. Dora Ferry, wife of C.N. Ferry, died at her home in Pea Ridge on Saturday morning, May 31st, 1924 from paralysis from which she had been afflicted for the past six years. She seemed to be getting better but a few days ago she became worse and death came to her relief. Funeral services were conducted Sunday at the M.E. church by Revs. Carnahan, Lark and Hall. She was laid to rest in the Pea Ridge cemetery. Mrs. Ferry was born in Ohio in 1860. She is survived by her husband, four sons and four daughters, all of whom were present at the funeral excepting one daughter. She was a kind mother and faithful companion and leaves a host of friends to mourn her loss. [Benton County Record 6/6/24]

FINCHER, Grace – Grace, a daughter of Mr. and Mrs. Hiram Fincher, former residents of this county, passed away at her home in Ennis, Texas last Saturday. The body was shipped to Rogers where it was met by Mr. Tom Maxwell of Gentry, uncle of the deceased, and taken to the family burying ground near Gentry by the Carpenter Undertaking Co. The deceased leaves a husband and three small children. [Rogers Daily Post 4/15/24]

FLETCHER, A.B. - A.B. Fletcher died Sunday, February 17th at his home on West Poplar street at the age of 83 years, three months and sixteen days. Funeral services were held at the residence Monday morning at ten o'clock and were conducted by Rev. Lucke of the First M.E. church, interment being in the Rogers cemetery. Mr. Fletcher had been a resident of Rogers for many years and was a very familiar figure on our streets. He was a veteran of the Civil War, having served in Co. C, 11th Cavalry in the Union army through the war. He was born in Illinois November 1, 1840. He was married to Nancy Gregg September 6, 1868 and to them were born eight children, five of whom are living - Robert, Henry and Fred, Mrs. A.H. Truax and Mrs. Fred Coe. The mother died in 1906. Mr. Fletcher was married to Mrs. Sarah Lyons September 3, 1906 who survives him. [Rogers Democrat 2/21/24]

FLOYD, William Hugh - A most distressing accident happened to little William Hugh Floyd, fourteen months old son of Mr. and Mrs. Hugh Floyd, formerly of Bentonville, at their home in Okmulgee, Okla. Sunday when the little one pulled a kettle of beets from the stove, the scalding water blistering him. He died from the effects of the burns about four hours later. The accident happened while Mr. Floyd and his two little daughters were at Sunday School. Mrs. Floyd was out of the room at the time and little Hugh was in the kitchen alone. The remains were shipped by rail to Fayetteville where Undertaker Whitley Kerr met the body and brought it to Bentonville for burial Monday. All Bentonville extends to the bereaved parents their deepest sympathy. [Benton County Record 7/11/24]

FLYNN, Net - {from Elm Springs} Aunt Net Flynn, who resided west of town, was found dead in bed Saturday. Funeral services were held at the M.E. church Sunday afternoon. The body was laid to rest in the Elm Springs cemetery. [Benton County Record 2/15/24]

FORD, Oscar William - {from Valley View} Oscar Ford of Webb City, Mo. died Sunday night at 10:30 o'clock. He was a nephew of Melvin and Harve McCurdy. He was taken back to Webb City on the 3 o'clock train. [Benton County Record 6/6/24]

Oscar William Ford, 34 years old, died suddenly Sunday night at 10:30 o'clock at Bentonville where he was visiting. He has been visiting with friends and relatives for the last two weeks in Rogers and Bentonville. Short services were conducted in Bentonville yesterday but the funeral will be held at the home of his parents at Webb City. He is survived by his wife and two small daughters, Nadine and Caroline, his parents and two sisters, Miss Rosa Ford and Mrs. Lula Dows, all of Webb City, Mo. He is a nephew of Mrs. W.P. Beshears, Mrs. J.H. Ricketts, Mrs. F.O. Mackey and Mr. D.E. Ford of Rogers. [Rogers Daily Post 6/4/24]

FOREMAN, Clara Belle - Clara Belle, the eleven year old daughter of Mr. and Mrs. W.C. Foreman, died in Rogers Monday, August 4th. She has been an invalid for half her life and for five years has been confined to her bed. Funeral services were held Monday with interment in the city cemetery in Bentonville. [Benton County Record 8/8/24]

Clare, 11-year-old daughter of W.C. Foreman, died Monday morning at their home on North Seventh St. after several years of suffering, the result of an attack of infantile paralysis. Funeral services were held at Bentonville Tuesday morning at the cemetery where the little girl was laid to rest by the side of her mother who died a number of years ago. [Rogers Democrat 8/7/24]

FOULKS, R.A. - R.A. Foulks, who resided on Sulphur Springs R.F.D. No. 3, between Gravette and that city, died last week Thursday, we are informed by Eld. W.S. Houchins, who recently leased the Foulks farm. The funeral was held in the M.E. church at Sulphur Springs and burial was in I.O.O.F. Cemetery at Gravette. Mr. Foulks left but one member of his family, a son, R.A., Jr. of New York City who is the general domestic and foreign agent of the American Express Co. The elder Foulks had retired to the Ozarks some time ago. [Gravette News-Herald 2/15/24]

FOUTS, Frank F. - Frank F. Fouts, born March 3, 1856 at Ellisville, Fulton county, Ill.,was the eldest of the eight children of George and Eliza Fouts. Died December 6, 1924 at the home of Mr. and Mrs. Geo. R. Jenkins.

The early part of his life was spent in and around Ellisville, Ill., moving to Herrington, Kan. in 1902; also lived several years in Oklahoma and in Neosho, Mo., coming to Gentry, Ark. three years ago. He was a member of the Odd Fellows Lodge for 47 years, still holding his membership at Neosho, also a member of the K.K.K., counting his membership in both lodges as sacred as vows to the church. He followed the occupation of farming all his life; was an honest, upright, conscientious man, having the respect of all who knew him. He had been in poor health for years. He leaves to mourn his loss two brothers, Geo. W. Fouts, Lewiston, Ill. and Sherman Fouts, Ellisville, Ill.; two sisters, Emma L. Kuter, Keokuk, Iowa and Flora B. Jenkins, Gentry, Ark. His parents and three sisters have gone before. Mr. Fouts never married, having made his home for 32 years with his youngest sister and brother-in-law, Mr. and Mrs. Geo. R. Jenkins. The funeral was held at the Gentry M.E. church Sunday afternoon, conducted by Rev. S.F. Stevens of Neosho, Mo., assisted by Rev. F. Villines, the regular M.E. pastor. Services at the cemetery were conducted by the Neosho Odd Fellows, assisted by brothers from Decatur, Gravette, Siloam Springs and Gentry. [Gentry Journal–Advance 12/19/24]

FOX, Bert - {from Gentry} Mrs. S.P. Griffith received a message from Washington telling her of the death of her brother-in-law, Bert Fox. Bert Fox resided near Gentry until about eighteen years ago. [Benton County Record 9/26/24]

FOX, Edward W. - Rev. Edward W. Fox, one of the oldest citizens in Benton county, died at his home in Bentonville on Friday, May 16th, 1924 at the age of 92 years. Old age and a general breakdown of his once rugged constitution was the cause of his death. Mr. Fox was born in Albany, New York in 1832 and was a direct descendant of George Fox, the noted Quaker who was banished from England for his religious views and settled in America. His ancestors also served in the Revolutionary and Mexican Wars and Mr. Fox was also a veteran of the Civil War. He has been a resident of Bentonville for about 10 years. For the past 21 years he has been a minister of the gospel. Mr. Fox was also one of the oldest, if not the oldest, Mason in the state, having been a member of that order for over 70 years, as well as a member of the M.E. Church for this same period. In the Record for March 28th will be found a lengthy and interesting biography that was written just after he had passed his 92nd birthday. His funeral, held at the M.E. Church, South last Saturday was largely attended, Rev. Lester Weaver conducting the services. The Masonic lodge also held services at the cemetery. [Benton County Record 5/23/24]

Rev. Edward Fox of Bentonville celebrated his 92nd birthday on Wednesday, March 26th. Rev. Fox is probably one of the oldest Masons in the state, having joined the Masonic Lodge in 1854. He has also been a member of the Methodist Episcopal Church for 71 years - two memberships of unusual length. He was born in Albany county, New York in 1832 on the site over which the state capitol now spreads. He was the son of Steadman Fox, a pioneer of Sullivan county and a colonel in the Mexican War. His education began in a district school where the three "R's" were the extent of the teacher's knowledge. After finishing this school he worked to earn money to carry him through a thirteen weeks session of an academy in Albany. This money was earned by digging potatoes at 35 cents a day. Following the fourth term at this academy he spent one season as cabin boy on the river mail boat plying between Troy and New York City. He rode on the second railway in the United States, running between Schenectady and Albany. As a young man he learned the trade of carpenter and millwright. The latter included building the mills which were numerous in that state and installing machinery and making the necessary parts. Seven years were spent in building and operating tanneries. Being too old to be drafted in the war he enlisted in the 56th regiment of New York volunteers of which his good friend, Charles Van Wyke, was colonel. He later joined the construction corps and helped to rebuild the Bull Run bridge. He was wounded at the battle of Honey Hill and just before the assassination of Lincoln he was taken home seriously ill and on account of his illness he was not told until late fall of the tragic death of the man he so loved. He has no knowledge of receiving a discharge from the army. He was married to Miss Mary McIntosh who died 19 years ago, a short time before their golden wedding. Rev. Fox is a descendant of the Quaker, George Fox, who was sent from England by King George on account of his religious views. His great-grandfather and great-grandmother spent the winter at Valley Forge with General Washington and were present on the occasion of the first flag-raising when Old Glory was made the national emblem. His grandfather was a soldier in the War of 1812 and carried the same gun which was carried by his father during the Revolution. When a boy Mr. Fox had a wonderful comradeship in the person of his grandfather and often together they used this famous gun when hunting squirrels. He moved his family to Kansas about 1910 and lived in the Sunflower State for about five or six years, after which he moved with his children and grandchildren to Bentonville and settled in the outskirts of the town. Mr. Fox was pleased with the climate and the way in which he regained his health. As he was the oldest member of his family, he cared for his brothers and sisters and now he is caring for his great-grandchildren. Mr. Fox said that his life's pathway had indeed been strewn with flowers but they were human flowers. There is nothing that so pleases this old gentleman as the prattle of little children. In politics he joined the Democratic party though not always voting a straight ticket as he believes that not all Republicans are bad. His first vote was cast for Franklin Pierce of Vermont and he remembers the slogan at that time: "Pierce and King, Shout and sing, And triumphant in November." He has been a minister of the Gospel for the past 21 years. [Benton County Record 3/28/24]

FOX, James H. - James H. Fox, son of Henry W. and Sarah Fox, was born in Greene Co., Tenn. on the 8th day of July in the year 1861 and died at his home in Gentry, Ark. March 25th, 1924. He was converted and joined the M.E. church, South in early childhood and lived a consistent Christian life until death. On Nov. 4th, 1888 he was married to Miss Mildred Jane Whiteside and this union was blessed with five children, four of whom survive him, but one child with the wife, preceded him into the glory land. Bro. Fox leaves to mourn his loss four children, four sisters, two brothers, many relatives and a large host of friends. Funeral services were conducted on March 26th at the M.E. church, South at two p.m. by the pastor, Rev. B.L. Harris. Interment was made in the city cemetery. B.L. Harris. [Gentry Journal–Advance 4/4/24]

FOX, Joe - "Uncle Joe" Fox, one of the best known Cherokee Indians, who lived on Honey Creek below Southwest City, Mo., died last week. [Gravette News Herald 6/20/24]

FRENCH, Virginia - Virginia, the 15-month-old daughter of Mr. and Mrs. Will French, died at the family home in the southwest part of town Thursday morning of spinal meningitis. The funeral services were held Thursday afternoon. [Benton County Record 8/15/24]

FULLERTON, infant - Friends in this city will be sorry to learn that Mrs. J.R. Fullerton, formerly Miss Marsh Holmes, is in a Tulsa hospital where she is seriously ill. Her day-old baby died last Thursday. [Benton County Record 5/2/24]

GAILEY, Louisa Frances YEARGAIN - Mrs. Frances Gailey, wife of G.W. Gailey, died at the family home near Logan on Sunday, December 14th, 1924 at the age of seventy–six years. She had been ill but about ten days. Funeral services were conducted at the home Monday by Rev. Wm. Downum in the presence of a large number of her old friends and neighbors. Burial was made in the Douglas cemetery at Highfill. Besides her aged husband she is survived by five sons - Joe Gailey of Bentonville; Owen of Caverna, Mo.; Arthur of Rocky Comfort, Mo. and Amzi and John, who live near their parents at Logan; also two sisters - Mrs. Belle Smith of Bentonville and one living near Watts, Okla. Three brothers - James Yeargain of Maysville; Tom Yeargain of Tahlequah, also survive her. Louisa Frances Yeargain was born in Tennessee on May 23rd, 1848. She came to Benton county with her parents in 1855, who settled in Gordon Hollow, north of Hiwasse, or, as it was then called, Dickson. Here she grew to womanhood and married G.W. Gailey, a neighbor, in 1866. Nine children were born to them. Later they moved and settled in a valley north of Logan where they have since resided. Mrs. Gailey united with the M.E. Church, South in 1868 and has lived the life of a true Christian, a devout mother and a loving wife. Her departure will greatly be missed by her friends and neighbors in the community that has been her home for over half a century. [Benton County Record 12/19/24]

Mr. and Mrs. George Maples and daughter, Beatrice, attended the funeral of Mrs. G.W. Gailey in Highfill Monday. [Benton County Record 12/19/24]

GALLAGHER, Samuel - {from Sulphur Springs} Samuel Gallagher, aged 83 years, died at his home on Black avenue Wednesday morning. He had been in ill health for several years but had been confined to his home only a few days. Mr. and Mrs. Gallagher came here about three years ago from Dodge City, Kansas for the benefit of his health. The body was taken to Dodge City for burial, accompanied by Mrs. Gallagher and a brother. [Benton County Record 3/14/24]

GALYEAN, Elizabeth AUSTIN - As we go to press we learn that Mrs. E.W. Gallagher, sister of Jody Austin, died Wednesday night at her home near Centerton, the result of heart trouble. [Gravette News Herald 6/27/24]
In the Ozarks, near Gravette, Ark. in the "seventies" resided William Bryant Austin with his companion, Mary Jane. Inured to the hardships and toil of that early day there was little to divert their minds from the irksome daily duties. But in the month of May 1875 the monotony was agreeably broken by the advent of a girl baby into the home whom they called Elizabeth. Elizabeth, or "Bettie," as she was usually called, brought sunshine and gladness into the home of her father and mother. Her parents died when she was a child after which she made her home with her brother, Jody Austin. When she reached young womanhood she decided to be queen of her own home. She was united in marriage with E.W. Galyean August 27, 1893. To this union two sons were born, namely, Auda E. of Sulphur Springs and Clifford A. of Centerton. Sister Galyean is survived by her husband, two sons, one brother, Jody Austin of Gravette, and one sister, Mrs. Nancy Wilkins of Idaho, and a number of other relatives, all of whom realize they have sustained a great loss in her death. She numbered her friends by her acquaintances. She professed faith in Christ about 1895 and soon after joined the Mt. Pleasant Missionary Baptist church where she retained her fellowship until about 1908 when she and her husband transferred membership to Bethlehem Baptist church and remained an orderly member of this body until she fell asleep in Jesus June 26th, 1924. After the funeral services were held the body was planted in the earth in Bethel Cemetery to await the resurrection of the Just. T.F. Jones. [Gravette News Herald 7/11/24]
Mrs. E.W. Galyean died at her home 2 1/2 miles south of Centerton early Thursday morning, June 26, 1924 of heart failure. She has been suffering from this disease for the past year and has had several dangerous spells. Funeral services were conducted by Rev. T.F. Jones last Friday with interment in the Bethel cemetery south of Gravette. Besides her husband she is survived by 2 sons, Clifford Galyean, who lives near Centerton, and Auda Galyean of Sulphur Springs. Mrs. Galyean was the youngest daughter of Mr. and Mrs. Wm. Bryant Austin and was born on the old Stahl farm south of Gravette {now better known as the Limekiln Farm} 49 years ago.

Her parents died when she was quite young and she was cared for and raised by Mr. and Mrs. Jody Austin. Later she married E.W. Galyean and has lived nearly ever since on their farm near Centerton. Mrs. Galyean has long been a member of the Baptist Church and lived a life that has made her many friends who will sadly miss her. [Benton County Record 7/4/24]

GARVIN, John - {from War Eagle} The friends of John Garvin will be grieved to learn of his death which occurred last Wednesday. He has lived near War Eagle for many years and is well known here. He leaves an aged widow and other relatives and friends to mourn his departure. [Rogers Democrat 5/29/24]

GIGER, Charles N. - Charles N. Giger, a well known resident of Centerton, passed away Wednesday night, May 28, 1924 at the age of 63 years. Death was due to a complication of diseases which followed a severe attack of the flu. He is survived by a wife, three sons, Jess and Roy Giger of Centerton, and Ben Giger of California. Also three daughters, Miss Lucy Giger of Centerton, Mrs. Mamie Conner of Sapulpa, Okla. and Mrs. Lama Coker, who also lives in Oklahoma. Mr. Giger was born in Fairfield, Ill. in 1861 and came to Benton county from Granby, Mo. about 40 years ago. He was one of the leading citizens in the Centerton community and was highly thought of by all who knew him. [Benton County Record 5/30/24]

GILBERT, Egbert Eubey - Egbert Eubey Gilbert was born in Medina county, Ohio Feb. 4, 1852. Departed this life April 4, 1924, age 72 years, 2 months. Moved with his parents when a small boy to Michigan. Moved from Michigan to Texas Dec. 1910. Came to Arkansas in 1917. Married to Lois Dorman in 1878. To this union 2 children were born, Willie Morgan and Baby Earl, who died in infancy. The wife was called away in 1886. Remarried to Eva McLown in 1889 at Sparta, Mich. To this union was born 1 child, Clara Arvesta Knowles of Cisco, Texas. Was converted and united with the Missionary Baptist church in 1914 and lived a consistent Christian life until the end came. Bro. Gilbert had 4 brothers and 2 sisters, all preceding him in death. He leaves behind to mourn his departure a wife and one son and daughter. The daughter was present with her father when he was called to his reward. Funeral was conducted at the Christian church Saturday afternoon, April 5, at 2:30 and the body was laid to rest in the city of the dead at Gentry, Ark. to await the resurrection morn. Funeral conducted by the writer. Eld. W.A. Watson, Pastor. [Gentry Journal–Advance 4/11/24]

GIPPLE, John Herbert - John Herbert, four-year-old son of Herbert Gipple and wife, and a grandson of H.W. Gipple of Appledale Farm, was killed Saturday afternoon at their home six miles west of Rogers when he was struck by an automobile driven by his uncle, Donald Gipple, as the car was being backed from the garage. At the first examination by a physician it was not thought the little fellow had been injured beyond a few minor bruises but later it developed he had suffered serious internal injuries and he died several hours later. Funeral services were held at the home Sunday afternoon, conducted by Rev. A.E. Carnahan of Pea Ridge and were largely attended by friends from Rogers, Bentonville and Pea Ridge. The Gipple family is one of the best known in the county and the news of the sad accident brought grief to an unusually large circle of friends and acquaintances. The little boy was a nephew of Mrs. Forest Larimore of this city. [Rogers Democrat 4/17/24] [Benton County Record 4/18/24] [Rogers Daily Post 4/14/24]

GLICK, Charles - The body of Charles Glick, the young man who was killed in the gun battle at Springdale Thursday night, was shipped to his home at Rockridge, Illinois on No. 6 Saturday night. The boy's mother is a widow. Murphy, who was wounded and is in custody at Bentonville, is said to be resting well. Reports from Marshall Odle at Springdale say he is not in a dangerous condition. Sheriff Maples questioned the injured boy for more than an hour late Friday. He duly related the story of their beginning of crime. He said the three boys were pals, joining in Fort Collins, Colo. only a few weeks ago. He said, according to Sheriff Maples, that they stole an automobile at that place November 27, last, and after driving twenty-two miles became frightened and abandoned the machine. They next went to Longmont, Colo., stole another car and proceeded with several store robberies in the surrounding towns and territory of Longmont. He told of entering and burglarizing one store and escaping with eleven automatic pistols, seven of which, the boys said, were in their possession when they stole the machine at Bentonville Thursday night, according to the officer. Other hi-jacking stories which the boy related during the questioning included a burglary in which the trio escaped with approximately fifty dollars in cash and other merchandise. He also told of robbing a Colorado filling station of several dollars and a tank of gasoline. After the robbery he said they forced the filling station owner to accompany them for several miles. He was then left by the roadside. The boys drove a stolen car to Coffeyville, Kan., according to confession of the youth, Maples said, and from there stole still another automobile after they had abandoned the Colorado car. They drove this machine to Bentonville and "exchanged" it for the sedan that resulted in their capture, Carroll said. Sheriff Maples found the deserted car, which was driven by the youths from Coffeyville near this town Friday. He communicated with the owner at Coffeyville and the description of the abandoned car was duplicated, Maples said. Carroll assisted officers in locating the parents of the dead boy. In answer to the slain youth at Rockbridge, Ill. county officers were notified to place his body in charge of an undertaker. A formal charge had not been placed against the surviving youths late Friday night. "We are waiting to gather more information before filing charges," Sheriff Maples said. [Rogers Daily Post 12/7/24]

GLOVER, Garnette KELLEHER - Mrs. Garnette Glover, wife of T.J. Glover, died Sunday night, October 26 at her home in Dallas, Texas, the result of an operation for appendicitis. Her mother, Mrs. M.L. Kelleher of this city, was with her when she died, having been called to Dallas the last of the week. Funeral services were held in Rogers yesterday afternoon at the Central Methodist church at 2:00 o'clock, conducted by the pastor, Rev. Wilson T. Crichlow. Mr. Glover and Mrs. Kelleher accompanied the body from Dallas. Burial was in the Rogers cemetery. As Garnette Kelleher, second daughter of Mr. and Mrs. M.L. Kelleher of Rogers, she is remembered as one of the prettiest and most talented young women who ever graduated from the Rogers high school, being a member of the Class of 1915. She was born at Monett, Mo. March 5, 1897 but the family came to Rogers when she was less than a year old so that she was distinctly a Rogers girl until her work took her into other fields, but she had visited here often {her last visit only a few months ago} and had retained her large circle of friends. After her graduation she taught for two years in Oklahoma and then attended business college in Muskogee. She served as a Yeomanette in the Ladies Naval Reserve at Washington during the war and at the close was given her discharge but retained for civil service work if needed. In 1920, July 17, she married Thos. J. Glover of New York City. Two years ago they moved to Dallas where she has worked for the U.S. Veterans Bureau. Her husband is an interior decorator and salesman for the Anderson Furniture Co. of Dallas. Mrs. Glover is survived by her parents of this city and by two sisters, Mrs. F.S. {Marjorie} Borum of Buffalo, N.Y. and her youngest sister, Miss Eva, who has been in Buffalo and who arrived home yesterday morning. Mrs. Borum could not come. An uncle, D.G. Galloway, of Oklahoma City and Al Geister and wife of Monett, old friends of the family, were here for the funeral. [Rogers Democrat 10/30/24] [Rogers Daily Post 10/30/24]

GOODWIN, Lavada DAVIDSON - {from The Siloam Springs Daily Register} Mrs. Lavada Goodwin, wife of L.J. Goodwin, died at the family home three miles northeast of town today {Monday, Feb. 4th} aged 49 years. She leaves her husband and 4 children. Funeral services will be conducted in Oak Hill cemetery. ***** Mrs. Goodwin was born at Gravette; was a sister of Assistant Postmaster Harley L. Davidson and half-sister of Willie Davidson of Gravette. Mr. Goodwin is a nephew of Dennis Conneway of our city. Relatives from here attended the funeral Wednesday. Mrs. Goodwin has been afflicted with cancer of the liver for several months. The family has many sympathizers at Gravette. [Gravette News Herald 2/8/24]

GORUM, F.M. - F.M. Gorum, brother of C.A. Gorum of Gentry, died at his home in Petty, Texas last Friday. He was 60 years of age and leaves a wife and 4 children. [Gentry Journal–Advance 12/12/24]

GOULD, Nannie A. EDRINGTON - Mrs. Nannie Gould died Monday at the home of her daughter, Mrs. Earl Adams, No. 1101 South Fourth St., after an illness of several months at the age of 68 years. Funeral services were held at the residence Tuesday afternoon at 2:30 o'clock and were conducted by Rev. Ben Moore, pastor of the Presbyterian church. Burial was at Oakley Chapel by the side of her husband, L.C. Gould, who died twenty-three years ago. Nannie A. Edrington was born in Trigg Co., Ky. January 21, 1856 and lived there until 1870 when the family moved to McCracken county, that state. In 1876 the family came to Arkansas and she had lived here ever since. January 5, 1876 she was married to L.C. Gould who passed away January 22, 1901. Mrs. Gould united with the M.E. Church, South at the age of 18 years and lived in that church until she united with the Presbyterian church to be with her husband and daughter. She passed away at her home in Rogers Monday, Oct. 20, 1924 at the age of 68 years, eight months and 20 days. She leaves one daughter, Mrs. Earl Adams of Rogers and one granddaughter, Bettie Earlene Adams. She leaves one sister, Mrs. B.T. Oakley of Covina, Calif. and two brothers, J.L. Edrington, Norwalk, Calif. and R.H. Edrington, Azusa, Calif. and numerous other relatives. Two nephews, Earl Gould, wife and daughter of Cane Hill, Washington county, and Ora Huffman and wife of Monett, were here for Mrs. Gould's funeral. [Rogers Democrat 10/23/24]

GRAHAM, Adelaide Price DARLING - {from The Monmouth (Ore.) News} Mrs. James Graham died at her home in this city at 8:15 Wednesday morning after a lingering illness. Funeral services are to be held in the Evangelical church Sunday, January 20th with Rev. Louis C. Kirby officiating. Burial is to be in the K.P. cemetery south of this city. Adelaide Price Darling was born in Sterling, Iowa December 26, 1855. On her 22nd birthday she was married to James Graham who, with two sons and one daughter, survives her. The children are W.J. Graham of Herrin, Ill., W.R. Graham of Monmouth and Miss Bessie Graham of Portland. The Grahams came west in 1904, settling first at Hood River. Later in the year they moved to Independence and three months later, in the early days of 1905, to Monmouth which has since been their home. Mrs. Graham, when able to go, was a regular attendant at the Evangelical church. Her kindly ways endeared her to many who will mourn her departure. [Gravette News Herald 2/1/24]

GRAHAM, Ben F. - {from Lowell} Ben F. Graham died Sunday morning after a two weeks illness of pneumonia fever. [Benton County Record 3/14/24]

B.F. Graham, 55 years old, died March 9th near Springdale in the same locality in which he was born and had spent practically all his life. [Rogers Democrat 3/27/24]

GRAHAM, James - We are informed that James Graham, one-time Gravette citizen, died on Nov. 17th, 1924 at his home at Monmouth, Ore. His son, W.R. Graham, resides at Monmouth. Mr. Graham was a highly respected citizen and many will regret to learn of his death. [Gravette News Herald 12/5/24]

GRAVES, James - James Graves, 83, of Springdale, dropped dead last week while engaged in raking leaves in his yard. Death was the result of heart failure. [Rogers Democrat 12/4/24]

GREEN, Lester - Lester Green, son of Mr. and Mrs. F.M. Green, living north of Decatur, died Monday morning of tuberculosis at the age of twenty-two years. He had been ill for about a year. Funeral services were held Tuesday with burial in the Word cemetery. Besides his parents he is survived by three sisters, Mabel, Pearl and Genevieve. [Benton County Record 1/11/24]

GREENE, Richard - Word was received of the death of Richard Greene on Saturday November 9, 1924 who had made his home, together with his parents, Mr. and Mrs. Haskel M. Greene, near Bakersfield, Calif. The boy's father is the son of Mr. and Mrs. J.R. Greene, now living near Centerton, and a brother to Mrs. M.C. Dana of Bentonville. Death resulted from the premature explosion of a torpedo used in oil field practice. The torpedo, used for shooting oil wells, was the invention of Richard's father. Death came instantly to the sixteen year old lad. Although he was taken in his youth let us hope that he was faithful unto death and has received a crown of life. He leaves many relatives and friends to mourn his sudden death.- Contributed. [Benton County Democrat 11/20/24]

GREGORY, sister - O.L. Gregory was called to Honey Grove, Texas last week by the death of a sister. [Rogers Democrat 2/14/24] [Rogers Daily Post 2/8/24]

GRIFFITH, father-in-law - Mrs. Earl Griffith, who was called to Salina, Kan. several days ago by the death of her father, returned home last Sunday. Mrs. Griffith reached her father's bedside in time to see him alive. [Gentry Journal–Advance 2/22/24]

GRIFFITH, Samuel J. - Samuel J. Griffith, a resident of Mason Valley for 40 years, died at the home of his son, Sam Griffith, Jr., east of Gentry on Monday May 19th, 1924 at the age of 80 years. Death was due to a complication of diseases. Funeral services were held the following day and were conducted by Rev. John Scoggin of Decatur in the presence of a large number of old friends and neighbors. Interment was made in the Coffelt cemetery. Mr. Griffith was born in Iowa in 1843 and came to Arkansas when a young man. He was in the Civil War and was wounded at the battle of Prairie Grove. For a number of years he taught school and later served as a justice of the peace in Mason Valley. He was also an active member and Sunday school superintendent of the Mason Valley Baptist church. Owing to ill health in late years he has been forced to give up these activities. He is survived by two children - Samuel Griffith, Jr. with whom he made his home, and one daughter, Mrs. Roy Schreier of Centerton. [Benton County Record 5/30/24] [Gentry Journal–Advance 6/6/24]

GRIMES, Fern - {from Walnut Hill, for last week} The sad news was received that Miss Fern Grimes, who was reported last week as being low with measles and pneumonia, died the 8th and was buried at Kansas City. [Rogers Democrat 2/28/24]

GUTHRIE, John Samuel - John S. Guthrie, a resident of Bentonville for nearly 35 years, died at his home south of Springdale Monday, June 9, 1924 at the age of 74, where he has lived for several years. He has been in ill health for the past six months. Funeral services were held Wednesday afternoon, the Rev. W.B. Brogan of Healing Springs officiating. The remains were shipped back to Eminency, Ky., his former home, for burial. John Samuel Guthrie was born in Shelby county, Ky. in 1850. He joined the Baptist Church at the age of 13 and has been a member of that denomination ever since. In 1875 he was married to Miss Sallie R. Goods who died in Bentonville in 1918. Later he married Miss Dollie Spotts who lived south of Bentonville and survives him. For many years he was engaged in the lumber and coal business and had his yards south of the Massey Hotel. Mr. Guthrie will be remembered as a good and kindly man as well as a splendid citizen. [Benton County Record 6/13/24]
Three old citizens of Springdale died within the last week or two: J.S. Guthrie, 74, who before going there four years ago was for 35 years in the lumber business at Bentonville; W.H. Kelson, 88 years old; Thomas Chambers, 71 years old, who was born and raised near Springdale. [Rogers Democrat 6/19/24]

HAGLER, Mrs. Lindsey BUTTRAM Lasater - Mrs. Lindsey Hagler died a week ago at her home at Centerton, the result of a recent stroke of paralysis. Mrs. Hagler was a Buttram and before her marriage to Mr. Hagler was a Mrs. Lasater. [Rogers Democrat 6/19/24]
Mrs. Lindsey Hagler died at her home in Centerton Sunday morning following a second stroke of paralysis that occurred a few days ago. She suffered her first stroke about two years ago and has been ill ever since. Funeral services were held Monday with interment in the Centerton cemetery. She was about 65 years of age and is survived by her husband and a married daughter, Mrs. Mamie Lee, of Bernice, Okla. Mrs. Hagler was born and grew to womanhood on Pea Ridge and was married to Kas Lassiter in 1874. Mr. Lassiter died about 10 years ago. In 1920 she was married to Lindsey Hagler and has lived in Centerton since. [Benton County Record 6/13/24]

HAIRE, L.J. - {from Hebron} Mr. Haire died at his home in Cave Springs Friday and was buried in the Cave Springs cemetery Saturday. He has been afflicted with cancer for the past year and death at last released him from intense suffering. [Rogers Democrat 2/21/24]
L.J. Haire, a resident of Cave Springs for many years, died last Thursday afternoon from cancer. Funeral services were conducted at the Mission on Saturday. Besides his widow he is survived by two daughters, Miriam and Marjorie Haire of Oklahoma City. Both were present at the funeral. The attendance was large and the floral offerings many. Mr. Haire came to

Cave Springs from Waldron, Ark. about 15 years ago and engaged in the hardware business until about a year ago when his health compelled him to retire. [Benton County Record 2/22/24]

HALL, Mary Ellen CUNNINGHAM - Miss Mary Ellen Cunningham was born May 9th, 1862 in Pulaski county, Ind. Moved to Ames, Iowa in 1880. She was united in marriage to S.E. Hall in November 1881. To this union was born nine children. All of her children are still living. She leaves, besides her children, her husband, S.E. Hall, to mourn their loss. Sister Hall had been in declining health for several years but for the past few days she went down rapidly until the end came on January 30th at 5:30 p.m. She came to Bentonville with her family four years ago from and has lived here ever since. She was converted early in life and ever afterwards lived a consistent Christian life. She was a member of the local Church of the Nazarene here. Sister Hall was a devoted wife and a kind and loving mother. She was laid away in the Bentonville cemetery to await the first resurrection of the dead. I.D. Farmer, Her Pastor. [Benton County Record 2/8/24]

HAMMACK, Florine JACKSON - Mrs. Bryan Hammack died very suddenly last Friday noon at her home in this city and the unexpectedness of her passing away made the loss the more tragic. She had been suffering from her teeth but it is thought this was only one of several complications that caused her death. She was sleeping when her husband went home for dinner Friday noon and he did not disturb her but when he went to rouse her before he returned to the store he found that she had quietly passed away some time before. Funeral services were held at the Central Methodist church Sunday afternoon and were conducted by the pastor, Rev. Wilson Crichlow. Burial was in the Oakley Chapel cemetery, near her former home west of Rogers, where she had lived before her marriage six years ago. Floreine{sic} was the oldest daughter of Mr. and Mrs. J.D. Jackson of the Droke neighborhood and was born at Fort Smith August 20, 1898, being just twenty-six years and two days old when she died. She united with the Central Methodist Church of Ft. Smith when nine years old and was ever a faithful worker in that denomination. She is survived by her husband, Bryan Hammack, who clerks for the Deason Grocery Store, and by three small children: Roberta, aged five years; Jacksene, aged three, and John Bryan, who is but ten months old, and her death means the breaking of the happy circle of a loving home at the most vital point. She is also survived by a brother and sister. Mrs. Hammack was always a general favorite wherever she lived and her sad and untimely death has brought great sorrow, not only to the home where the father and motherless children mourn in vain for the touch of the mother's hand and the mother's smile, but to a very large circle of friends and relatives. [Rogers Democrat 8/29/24] Mrs. Bryan Hammack of Rogers, daughter of Mr. and Mrs. J.B. Jackson of the Droke neighborhood, died at her home in Rogers on Friday, August

22nd, 1924 and was buried at Oakley Chapel on Sunday. Mrs. Hammack, who was Miss Florine Jackson, was born and reared in this community and had many friends here who regret the passing of this lovable woman. She leaves, besides her parents, one sister, Miss Margaret Jackson, and one brother, Kelton Jackson, of Kansas City, her young husband and three small children, who have the sympathy of the entire community. [Benton County Record 8/29/24]

HAMMOCK, Martha Jane WILLIAMS Vandergriff - Martha Jane Williams was born September 27, 1857 and was converted and joined the Baptist church at Twelve Corners in 1872 of which she is still a member. She was married to Thomas Vandergriff in 1879. To this union two children were born - Charlie and Lee Vandergriff, now of Picher, Okla. Mr. Vandergriff died in 1882. Five years later, in 1887, she was married to W.M. Hammock. To this union five children were born, three boys and two girls, one girl dying in infancy, and Docia dying in 1915 and Dock dying in 1923, Mack and Bryan, who reside in Rogers. She also leaves a husband, a mother 87 years old, one brother, seven step-children, 13 grandchildren and a host of other relatives and her friends were numbered with her acquaintances. Mrs. Hammock passed to the Great Beyond May 20, 1924 at the age of 66 years, seven months and 23 days. Mrs. Hammock, with her family, lived in Rogers 15 years and with the exception of a short while at Southwest City, her whole life has been spent in or near Rogers. All the children were present at the funeral except Lee Vandergriff of Picher, Roy Hammock of Joplin and Gene Hammock of Southwest City. Funeral services were conducted at the home on Spring street Wednesday afternoon at two o'clock by Reverend Jack Deason, pastor at Twelve Corners. Interment in Rogers cemetery. [Rogers Democrat 5/22/24]

HARDAGE, Claudia Jane ALFORD - Mrs. C.W. Hardage, who has been afflicted for the past two years and who has been quite low for the past two weeks, passed away at the family home on East Main St. Monday evening, Sept. 8th, 1924, aged 52 years, 10 mos. and 17 days. Claudia Jane Alford was born Oct. 21, 1871 at Social Hill, Ark. Was married to C.W. Hardage Oct. 7, 1892; was mother of five children who survive as follows: Mrs. I.O. Kile, Coalgate, Okla.; Mrs. Lloyd Nichols, Kansas City, Mo.; Mrs. Morriss, Chicago, Ill; Bert Hardage, Kansas City, Mo. and Louis Hardage, Gravette, Ark. She also leaves her husband and her father and mother, Mr. and Mrs. J.R. Alford, also of Gravette. All were present when death came. Under direction of Undertaker Tom Haywood the body was conveyed to Social Hill where the funeral took place Wednesday at 11 a.m. and burial in the cemetery near by. [Gravette News Herald 9/12/24]

HARDY, Florence PACE - Mrs. Florence P. Hardy, a well-known resident of Bentonville, died at the home of her daughter, Mrs. Jennie Derreberry, in Eureka Springs on Saturday, January 26th, 1924, aged 70 years. The remains were brought to Bentonville for burial and services were held at the cemetery on Sunday. She is survived by one son, Claude Hardy, and three daughters, Mrs. Clara Whayne and Mrs. Wm. Jackson of Bentonville and Mrs. Josephine Derreberry of Eureka Springs. Mrs. Hardy was one of Benton county's pioneer daughters and was born in 1854 northeast of Bentonville on what is now known as the old Kindley place. Later her parents, Mr. and Mrs. Christopher Pace, moved to Maysville where they lived until the close of the Civil War when they returned to Bentonville where she later married John Hardy. About 15 years ago they moved to Oklahoma and at the death of Mr. Hardy four years later she returned to Bentonville to make her home. For the past four years she has been spending the summers in Bentonville and the winters in Eureka Springs. Mrs. Hardy was loved by all who knew her. She was a member of the old Cumberland Presbyterian Church and bore her affliction with true Christian fortitude. [Benton County Record 2/1/24]

HARGIS, infant - The one-day-old daughter of Mr. and Mrs. F.L. Hargis, living near the Park Springs Hotel, died Monday. [Benton County Record 6/20/24]

HARLAN, H.E. - Died on June 27th at his home near Oakley Chapel, H.E. Harlan, an old and highly respected citizen. Mr. Harlan was about 65 years of age and had made his home with his daughter since the death of his wife several years ago. [Benton County Record 7/11/24]

HARPER, Dave - {from Gravette} Dave Harper, who lived here a number of years ago, died at his home in Southwest City Monday of tuberculosis. He was half-brother to W.H. Austin and Squire Lige Austin. [Benton County Record 12/19/24]

HARRAL, Leman - Leman Harral, age 93 and a resident of Benton county for over 50 years, died at the old home place in the Hightop neighborhood northwest of Centerton on Saturday, August 2, 1924. Funeral services were held Sunday with interment in the Gamble cemetery near Centerton. Mr. Harrel{sic} came to Benton county from Tennessee over a half century ago and located on the land that has been his home ever since. He has been in a feeble condition for some time and his nephew, Harvey Bishop, and wife have lived with him. One son, Chas. Harrel, living in the west, and two daughters, Mrs. Wm. Easley, of the Hightop neighborhood, and Mrs. Mattie Stroud, of Neosho, survive him. [Benton County Record 8/8/24]

HARRIS, Wiley L. - Wiley L. Harris, living one and a half miles north of Cave Springs, died Thursday night without regaining consciousness after a fall from a load of hay that afternoon. He had gone to the barn to assist in putting the hay in the barn and was working on the hay wagon while his son, Tom Harris, and a helper were in the barn loft stowing the hay away. When he failed to release the fork the men investigated and found him lying on the ground unconscious. Physicians were called and it was found his skull was fractured and a shoulder badly bruised by the force of the

fall. Whether he was overcome by the heat or a stroke of apoplexy and fallen from the wagon, or whether he had slipped and the injuries were the result of the fall and the shock, could not be determined. Funeral services were held Saturday morning at ten o'clock at the Barron cemetery near Vaughn and were conducted by Rev. Norris from Gravette, an old friend and former pastor. Mr. Harris was 67 years old and had lived in Benton county for some fifty years. He was a native of Jasper county, Mo. He is survived by his wife and six children: W.B. Harris, Bentonville; Mrs. Pearl Blevins of Springfield, Mo.; Walter Harris, Osage Mills; J.C. Harris of Rogers; and Tom and Ruby Harris, who lived at home. He was a brother of John R. Harris, a former well known Fayetteville business man, and Jim Harris of Springdale. He was an uncle of Riley Berry of this city and had many relatives in the county. He was a fine type of Christian citizen and farmer and was highly respected in his community. [Rogers Democrat 7/3/24] [Rogers Daily Post 6/27/24]
{An almost identical article in The Benton County Record of 7/24/24 identifies his widow as the former Miss Florence Crank.}

HARRY, Madison - {from Gentry} Rev. M. Harry died very suddenly Tuesday morning. His wife found him dead in his chair supposedly a victim of heart trouble. Mr. Harry is an old resident of Gentry and was well known all around in this part of the county. Only the day before his death Rev. Harry was down town and seemed in his usual health. [Benton County Record 10/3/24]
Madison, son of Jacob and Susana Tobey Harry, was born Feb. 3, 1845 about 10 miles west of Dayton, Ohio and died very suddenly at his home in Gentry on the morning of Sept. 30, 1924, aged 79 years, 7 months and 27 days. His family left Ohio when he was ten years of age, living for a year near Jefferson City, Mo., later moving to Coles county, Ills. where he grew up and lived until about 32 years of age. He graduated from the United Brethren College at Westfield, Ills. at the age of 25. During his college life Bro. Harry was converted and united with the United Brethren church of Westfield, Ills. Later he was ordained to the ministry by this denomination and preached for this people several years. In 1872 he was united in marriage to Miss Sarah Davis of Bour{this article ends here}. [Gentry Journal–Advance 10/17/24]

HART, John - {from The Cassville Democrat} Rev. John Hart of the New Salem neighborhood near Seligman, died at his home one night last week at the age of 81 years. He left three sons and three daughters surviving him. He was a member of the Holiness church. The remains were taken to Bentonville, Ark. for burial. [Rogers Democrat 12/4/24]

HARTLEY, James Dixon - J.D. Hartley died Sunday morning, November 9th at 10:45 at his home in this city at No. 322 North Second St. Funeral services were held at the residence Monday afternoon at 2:30 and were conducted by Rev. R.C. Lucke of the First M.E. Church. Interment was in the Rogers cemetery. James Dixon Hartley was born at Sullivan, Indiana Feb. 23, 1843 and died at the age of 81 years, eight months and sixteen days. He was raised by his grandfather and while attending business college at Terre Haute, Indiana was married to Miss Cintha Gilkerson. He had served some time in the Union army during the civil war and in his first years, being too young to be in the ranks, had served as a messenger boy for General Grant. He came to Rogers when the Frisco was completed this far and was for some time a foreman in the car repair department at the local roundhouse. He was transferred to Monett when the Frisco division was moved to that point and served there for nineteen years in one office. He then retired from railroad work and came to Rogers to make his home. He was in business in Rogers for several years, giving it up when his wife's health failed, to devote his entire time to her care. She died December 16, 1918. He later married Miss Lucy McHenry who survives him as also does a sister living in Texas. He was always ready to help in the upbuilding of every community in which he lived and leaves a large circle of friends. [Rogers Democrat 11/13/24]

HASTINGS, J.R. "Pete" - J.R. "Pete" Hastings, older son of Mr. and Mrs. Yell Hastings, who was born on Batie Prairie west of Gravette 50 years ago, died in the Baptist hospital at Miami, Okla. on Friday, July 18th, 1924. Mr. Hastings was related to Mrs. B.C. Phillips of Gravette. [Gravette News Herald 8/1/24]

HAWTHORNE, J.O. - {from Larue} J.O. Hawthorne died at his home near Larue December 11, 1924. Funeral services were conducted by Rev. G.C. Bland at Bland cemetery December 11 at 3 o'clock. Uncle Ollie, as he was most familiarly known, was born November 27, 1834 in South Carolina, being more than 90 years at the time of his death. He was married to Hannah Huff December 27, 1865. To this union eight children were born, four of which had passed on before him. Two sons and two daughters and his aged widow still survive him. Mrs. J.W. Allred and Mrs. J.S. Garrison were the only children present. He leaves 18 grandchildren and 15 great-grandchildren and a host of friends to mourn their loss. He joined the Confederate army and served as a true soldier until captured and served 18 months in soldier's prison, received an honorable discharge, returned to Alabama at close of war and later moved to Kansas, then to Arkansas some 40 years ago. Served several terms as Justice of the Peace in Walnut township, thereby being well known in Benton county quorum court some few years. Uncle Ollie professed a hope in Christ in 1868 and lived a true member to the Freewill Baptist church until death, being a deacon in his church at the time of his death. He was a man of his word, good for his contracts, good to visit the sick, kind words to those he chanced to meet. Although he had been kept at home of late years on account of his age, he will be sadly missed by many relatives and friends. A Friend. [Rogers Democrat 12/18/24]

HAYWOOD, George - George Haywood, senior member of the Peoples Hardware firm and for several years a highly respected citizen of Gravette, died at his home in Gravette Saturday, January 19, 1924 at the age of 73 years, 8 months and 14 days. Mr. Haywood has been in ill health for some months and for several weeks confined to his home and bed. He was born near Worcester, England May 5, 1850. At the age of 19 years he came to Pennsylvania and later moved to Fremont, Nebr. and there was united in marriage to Sarah Conrad who survives him. To this union were born three children: Mrs. Guy Houchen of Neosho, Mo.; Mrs. Fern Luebker of Prague, Okla. and T.H. Haywood, who was associated with him in the hardware store. He also has one sister living, Mrs. Eliza Yapp of Worcester, Eng. Twenty-seven years of his life were spent in Arkansas, formerly at Stuttgart from whence he moved to Gravette with his family. He was a Christian and church member since early manhood and was loyal to God, his church and his fellowman. The funeral services were held at the Presbyterian church Sunday at 2 p.m. in the presence of a host of people, Rev. G.T. Clark conducting the same. Interment was made in the I.O.O.F. Cemetery. Owing to illness in their families, neither of the daughters were able to come but their husbands, Guy Houchen and Joe C. Luebker, were present as was also Tom Conrad, brother of Mrs. Haywood, who had been a faithful watcher at the bedside for two months. [Gravette News Herald 1/25/24]
{An almost identical article in The Benton County Record of 1/25/24 gives the place of residence in Nebraska as Kearney. Ed.}

HEARTAGE, Caldra Jane ALVORD - {from Gravette} Mrs. Caldra Jane Alvord Heartage, who has been ill for the past three years, died at her home on East Main Street Tuesday afternoon at the age of 52 years. The body was shipped to Malvern, Ark. for burial. Besides her husband, John Heartage, she is survived by her parents, Mr. and Mrs. J.R. Alvord, southeast of town, and five children. [Benton County Record 9/12/24]

HEASLEY, Fannie Bowen - The many friends of Mrs. Fannie Bowen Heasley were shocked to receive the news of her sudden death at her home in Blytheville, Ark. on Wednesday evening, February 6th at 6 o'clock following a stroke of paralysis at 10 o'clock that morning. Mrs. Chas. Heasley, better known to the people here as Mrs. Fannie Bowen, was a former resident of Bentonville for many years and had many friends who were grieved to hear of her death. She was a faithful member of the M.E. Church, South and was loved by all who knew her. She is survived by two sons - Sam Bowen and Russell Bowen, both of Luxora, Ark. [Benton County Record 2/8/24]

HEINS, infant - The infant son of Mr. and Mrs. Orval Heins died Saturday night. The funeral services were held Sunday afternoon at 3:00 o'clock at the Church of Christ and burial was in the Rogers cemetery. The number of friends present at the funeral was a testimony of their sympathy with the young couple in their bereavement. [Rogers Democrat 9/25/24]

HEMPHILL, J.J. - Mrs. Jay Dalton was called to Partridge, Kansas the last of the week by the death of her sister's husband, J.J. Hemphill, who married Mrs. Frankie Updyke of this city in 1910. [Rogers Democrat 4/24/24]

HENDREN, Richard A. - The six months old baby son of Mr. and Mrs. N.B. Hendren died Tuesday night at their home southwest of Gravette following several days illness from bronchial pneumonia. The funeral will be conducted today, Thursday, by Rev. G.T. Clark and burial at the I.O.O.F. cemetery. The family has the sympathy of their many friends. [Gravette News Herald 1/25/24]
{from Gravette} Died Tuesday morning, January 22d, Richard A. Hendren, infant son of Mr. and Mrs. N.B. Hendren, living southwest of town. Interment of the little body was made in the I.O.O.F. cemetery on Wednesday. [Benton County Record 1/25/24]

HENDRIX, Edward Frank - {from Prairie Creek} E.F. Hendrix, better known to the community as "Uncle Frank," was born in Tennessee March 31, 1843 and died at the home of his son, Marion Hendrix, on Prairie Creek Sunday morning, August 17th at the age of 81 years, four months and sixteen days. He came to Benton county with his parents when a child and they settled in the neighborhood where he died. He had lived on the home farm where he died for more than sixty years and was one of the best known men in this part of the county. In recent years he wore a gray Confederate uniform when on the street in Rogers and was a very familiar figure. He enlisted in the Confederate army under General McCulloch. "His General" fell in the battle of Pea Ridge and he then was placed in the command of General Price. He was discharged in Mississippi for being under age but returned to Benton county and enlisted under the famous Indian leader, General Standway. He held the rank of lieutenant when discharged at the close of the war. He was a member of the Masonic order which he loved. He professed a faith in Christ but never united with any church. Mr. Hendrix leaves five children, 17 grandchildren, 13 great-grandchildren, many other relatives and a host of friends. His children were all with him during his last days, his son, Walter, from San Bernardino, Calif. arriving just a few days before his death. Mr. Hendrix was married three times. Just after the close of the war he married Miss Perry Lee Keltner, who lived only a few months. He was married again in a few years to Miss Jane Baker and to this union four children were born, three of whom are living: Mrs. S.B. Skaggs of Rogers, Mrs. Isom Porter of Prairie Grove and W.E. Hendrix of Rogers. The wife and mother died while the children were small and he later married Miss Rebecca Roller, who died in July 1917. Four children were born to this union, two dying in infancy and two living, Walter Hendrix of San Bernardino, Calif. and Marion Hendrix of Rogers. Funeral services were held at the home Monday afternoon and were conducted by Rev. Clark Bland of Larue. The body was taken to the

Rogers cemetery for interment and there the Masonic order had charge of the services. [Rogers Democrat 8/21/24]
{from Valley View} Lee Roller attended the funeral of his brother-in-law, Frank Hendrix, near Rogers Monday. [Benton County Record 8/22/24]

HENRY, Sidney GATLIN, Mrs. - Mrs. Sidney Gatlin Henry, widow of the late Dr. James Taylor Henry, died at her home here early Saturday morning. Though Mrs. Henry has been seriously ill for a month her condition had so greatly improved that her family and friends were hopeful of her recovery and her death, which took place a few hours after a stroke of apoplexy, was a shock to the entire community. Mrs. Henry was born near Lisbon, in Union county, August 20th, 1852 and spent her entire life in Arkansas. Her family, and that of her husband to whom she was married in 1874, were pioneers in South Arkansas and were identified with the early history and development of the state, both families being splendid representatives of the ideals and culture of the Southern plantation. Dr. Henry was one of the state's leading physicians and his large property interests and success in business in many lines gave him high standing in the business circles of his section. Mrs. Henry was loved wherever she was known and during the past few weeks friends in all parts of the state have shared in the anxiety of her loved ones gathered at her bedside. The family came to Bentonville fourteen years ago, moving here from Eagle Mills for the benefit of Mrs. Henry's health, and at once became identified with the life of this community. She is survived by one son, Dr. Hugh Henry, of Eagle Mills; by five daughters: Mrs. O.F. Wyman of Trout, La.; Mrs. W.A. Utley of Benton; Mrs. Henry D. Wharton of Warren and the Misses Pearl and Beryl Henry of Bentonville; and by five grandchildren, Hugh and Marjorie Wyman, Miss Elizabeth and James Henry and Sidney Wharton. All were present at her funeral as were Mrs. Hugh Henry and Messrs. Wyman, Utley and Wharton. A sister, Mrs. W.A. Elliott, of Fordyce, and two nieces, Mrs. T.W. Juniel of Mansfield, La. and Mrs. C.W. Watson of Russellville, also came to be with the family. Funeral services were held at the M.E. Church, South Sunday afternoon by the Rev. Lester Weaver, assisted by the Rev. F.N. Brewer of Benton. At the close of Rev. Brewer's eulogy he made a special prayer for the comfort of Miss Pearl Henry, who has been privileged to be so closely associated with her mother since her father's death six years ago and who has cared for her mother with such devotion and tenderness. After the service the body was taken to the Bentonville cemetery and placed beside that of Dr. Henry in the mausoleum. R.D.B. [Benton County Record 8/8/24]

HENRY, William Claybaugh - William Claybaugh Henry, 24 years a resident of this community, died at his home between Gravette and Decatur on July 24, 1924, aged 68 years, 8 months and 10 days. He was born near Bloomington, Ind. Nov. 15, 1855 where he grew to manhood. He graduated from the State University at that place. He united with the United

Presbyterian church at the age of 17. Mr. Henry was married to Miss Florence B. Todd Sept. 1, 1875 and to the union were born nine children: two - Herman and Robert - preceding him in death. He is survived by his wife and the following seven children: Mrs. Lula Watson and Theodore Henry of Chetopa, Kans.; Mrs. Mable Mathis, Wichita, Kans.; Lee of Manteca, Calif.; Curtis of Pratt, Kans.; Mrs. Dee Andrews of Topeka, Kans. and Glen of Reedley, Calif. There are also seven grandchildren and one great-grandchild. In 1875 he moved to Robinson, Ill. In 1883 the family moved to Chetopa, Kans. and in 1900 to the homestead near Decatur, Ark. The funeral was held at Decatur Tuesday, July 29, conducted by Rev. E.L. Boyles of Gravette and interment was made in the Decatur cemetery. [Gravette News Herald 8/1/24] [Benton County Record 8/1/24]

HIEK, Christy - {from New Salem} Word was received here Sunday of the death of Christy Hiek of St. Louis, Mo. Mr. Hiek was a son-in-law of W.R. Wise. [Benton County Record 6/27/24]

HIGHFILL, infant - The friends of Mrs. Dorothy Highfill {foster child of Mrs. A.H. Hull} will regret to learn the baby son born to Mr. and Mrs. Highfill at Idabel, Okla. died on March 19th. [Gravette News Herald 3/28/24]

HILL, Bernice N. KETCHUM - Following a long period of ill health Mrs. W.E. Hill died at the family home here at 6 o'clock Sunday morning, April 13th, 1924. Miss Bernice N. Ketchum, only child of the late Mr. and Mrs. L.L. Ketchum, who, from 1880 until their deaths were residents of Bentonville, was born June 28th, 1879 in Howard county, Missouri. Coming to Bentonville with her parents when only a year or so of age, she grew to womanhood, lived and died among Bentonville friends. On August 20th, 1902 she was married to W.E. Hill and proved a true and faithful wife and devoted mother to their two sons. Of a retiring disposition she loved to be at home but was a good and faithful friend and neighbor, always solicitous of the welfare of friends and loved ones and always true to the Baptist church of which she had become a member when only twelve years of age. Besides her husband she is survived by two sons, Lee, aged 20 and Erle, 16, other relatives and a host of friends and acquaintances. A daughter, Virginia Elizabeth Hill, died in infancy. At the funeral service at the home, conducted by Rev. J.M. McMahen, pastor of the local Baptist church, a large gathering of friends and many beautiful flowers marked the love and respect in which the memory of Mrs. Hill and her family are held. Interment was made at the City Cemetery. [Benton County Record 4/18/24]

HILLIARD, Hattie WILLIAMS - Hattie Williams was born May 14, 1860 and died April 17, 1924, making her stay here 63 years, 11 months and three days. She was married to W.J. Hilliard December 7, 1879 and to this union was born four children. Mrs. Della Mahurin died last January. The following are living and were at her bedside when death came - Mrs. Myrtle Scott, Mrs. Mary Galyon, James Hilliard. Mrs. Hilliard was born in Illinois but was reared to womanhood and spent most of her life near the home where she died. She leaves a large circle of friends and the ones that knew her best are the ones who loved her most. Besides her husband, children and grandchildren she leaves three sisters and one brother, Mrs. Amanda Staniford, Mrs. Clara Staniford, Mrs. Sarah L. Marler of Garfield and Frank Williams of Rogers. Funeral services were conducted by Rev. Burt of Rogers and attended by a large crowd. [Rogers Democrat 4/24/24]

HINMAN, Arabella Lindsey - Mrs. G.B. Hinman, a resident of Bentonville for more than 30 years, died at the family home on West Fourteenth Street early Monday morning. She was ill but a week and on Sunday morning she collapsed while walking in the house and never regained consciousness. Eight children survive her - four sons, A.B. Hinman, Lewiston, Idaho; Will Hinman, Oakland, Cal.; Fred Hinman, Greeley, Col and Frank Hinman, Shreveport, La.. Also four daughters, Mrs. Maude Conine, Nowata, Okla.; Mrs. Mary Bachelor, Cuba, Kans.; Mrs. Lena Young, Bentonville and Miss Annie Hinman, with whom she lived. Mrs. Arabella Lindsey Hinman was born in Hardin county, Kentucky December 24th, 1841. In 1862 she was married to G.B. Hinman in Griggsville, Ill. Four years later they moved to Ray county, Mo. and in 1892 the family came to Bentonville and purchased farming property just west of Bentonville that is now known as Fairview Heights. He built the brick house now occupied by Harry Hays, which formerly was a part of the Hinman farm. Mr. Hinman passed away in 1906. Funeral services will be held at the home on Friday afternoon at 2:30 o'clock. The services will be conducted by Rev. W.J. Robinson of Fort Smith, her former pastor. Mrs. Hinman was a member of the Baptist Church. During her long residence in Bentonville she made many friends who will sadly miss her. [Benton County Record 6/13/24]

HOBBS, L. - L. Hobbs, formerly of Bentonville, died at the home of his brother, Geo. Hobbs, in Miller, Mo. on April 2nd, 1924. Mr. Hobbs had been in ill health for the past two years which caused his death. He is survived by his wife and three children - Mrs. Grace Hamon of Bentonville, Ark.; Mrs. W.H. Holmes of Tulsa, Okla. and Alpha Hobbs of Bentonville. Funeral services were conducted by Rev. Proctor at the Baptist Church of Miller Friday afternoon at 2 o'clock and interment was made in the Grove cemetery at Miller, Mo. [Benton County Record 4/11/24]

HODGES, Howell - Howell Hodges, one of the pioneer citizens of Northwest Arkansas, died yesterday morning in this city at the home of his son, Dr. T.E. Hodges, at the age of 94 years, one month and four days. Funeral services will be held this morning at Cane Hill in Washington county where he will be laid by the side of his wife who died there November 1, 1915. Services will be conducted by Rev. A.E. Carnahan of Pea Ridge whose family had been a neighbor and friend of the deceased for many years. Howell Hodges was born March 19, 1830 in East Tennessee but came to Arkansas with his parents in 1835. The trip as far as Van Buren was made on a flat boat on the Arkansas river and from that point they came on to Washington county where they settled on a farm six miles east of Cane Hill where most of his life was spent. In 1850 he joined the great crowd of fortune seekers in the gold fields of California and he remained in the west for seven years. Shortly after his return home in 1857 he married Martha Jane Morrow and to them were born five children, four daughters and one son, three of whom are still living: Miss Hodges is matron of the Presbyterian school at Durant, Okla.; Mrs. Lillian Jones of Fort Worth, Texas and Dr. T.E. Hodges of Rogers. Mr. Hodges lived on the farm until 1904 when he moved to Cane Hill. After the death of his wife in 1915 Mr. Hodges came to make his home with his son. He had been in failing health for some time and unable to often get away from the house. His condition had been serious for several weeks and his death was not unexpected and brought to a peaceful end a long and useful life. He was the grandfather of Dr. Guy Hodges and Howell Hodges of this city. [Rogers Democrat 4/24/24] Howell Hodges was born March 19, 1830, Washington county, East Tennessee. Died at the home of his son, T.E. Hodges, Rogers, Arkansas April 23, 1924 at the ripe old age of 94 years, 1 month and 2 days. He was the father of one son and three daughters: Mrs. Lillie Jones, Ft. Worth; Mrs. Jennie Kline, Tahlequah; Miss Maggie Hodges, Blackmore, Okla. Two daughters died years ago. He was the grandfather of Dr. Guy and Howell Hodges of this city. His wife passed away in 1915 at Cane Hill where he had made his home since he was 10 years old with the exception of seven years spent in hunting gold in California which is a story full of interest and is best told in his memoirs which he wrote for his friend, Rev. A.E. Carnahan, who preached his funeral sermon at Cane Hill last Thursday where he was laid to rest beside his wife and children. "In 1850 I joined a train, or company, bound for the gold fields of California. The company formed at Cane Hill and consisted of about 12 men, including Isaac Spencer, Lon Kisson, Anson Hodges (cousin), Jas. Hagood, Henry Allen, Jonathan Allen, Isham Burrow, Lon Latto, Jack Latto, Eli Latto, Frank Shannon, Robert Cox and William Grey. We left Cane Hill April 10. Our captain was Jonathan Allen. At Carthage we stopped ten days waiting for grass to grow. Corn then cost fifteen cents a bushel. From there we went to Fort Laramie on the Platt river and on to Salt Lake. At this point we were joined by another company from Arkansas under Jack Holt. The two companies united. We were one day and night crossing the desert, starting at nightfall and traveling through the night and the day following reaching Carson river at the close of day. Two old people and two small children, a boy and a girl, who were unable to cross the desert were overtaken by this company. The children were taken forcibly from the old couple and taken on to California. Later the girl was married in California. The boy returned to Arkansas and settled in Benton county, near Maysville. We were four months on the trip and gone from Arkansas seven years. On the return trip we took ship from San Francisco on the mail steamer Golden Gate, going by way of Panama. Crossed the isthmus on the railroad. The fare was 55 cents for 25 miles. From there on to Cuba and from Cuba to New Orleans on the Philadelphia. The entire trip cost $300 in gold." Mr. Hodges speaks of having heard Brigham Young at Salt Lake City. Mr. Hodges joined the Haupt regiment, 31 Texas, Co. Y under Capt. Ellis of the Confederate army. He was in the battle of Newton, Mo., Grove, Ark., Mansfield, La., Pleasant Hill, Mo. and was mustered out at the close of the war under Col. E.S. Strum at Ft. Smith. He was a farmer for many years until tiring of hard work he moved in Cane Hill and spent his time happily and quietly. He was a member of the Cane Hill Presbyterian church and was active in church work. He was temperate in his habits and actively believed in "early to bed and early to rise." He smoked a pipe and often joked about smoking shortening one's life. He was respected by his many friends and his relatives made the last years of his life as comfortable and happy as was possible for them to do so. His daughter-in-law, Mrs. T.E. Hodges, who cared for him as tenderly as a child the past ten years says of his character and life: "He lived by the side of the road and was a friend to man. Having been in the family for 35 years and having him in my home for ten years, I know whereof I speak. Gentle, kind and patient, and always cheerful seeing the bright side of life and saying good of everyone he knew. All who knew him well will bear me out in saying his life was worth living. He studied and practiced the real things in life." [Rogers Daily Post 4/29/24]

HOEL, Florence TAYLOR - John V. Taylor received the sad intelligence last Friday of the death of his sister, Mrs. Florence Hoel, her son, Frank, and her little granddaughter, Frances Grubb, the result of an auto accident at their home city, Montezuma, Ohio. No further particulars have as yet been received. Some Gravette people will remember the visit here, over a year ago, of Mrs. Hoel and the little granddaughter. Bro. Taylor has the sympathy of his many Gravette friends in this tragic bereavement. Later: Miss Lucile Hoel, who also visited Gravette, was injured. Their auto was struck by an interurban car. [Gravette News Herald 2/8/24]

HOFFMAN, Charles J. - Mrs. W.H. Hoffman and daughter, Mary Elizabeth, returned Tuesday night from Tulsa, Okla. where she was called on account of the death of Mr. Hoffman's brother, Charles J. Hoffman, which occurred last week Wednesday. The deceased was terribly injured a few days previous when he was hit by several sheets of plate-glass at their factory. He leaves his wife and three grown children. Funeral was Saturday and burial in Rosedale cemetery at Tulsa. The deal falls heavily upon our townsman, W.H. Hoffman, joint owner of the glass factory with his brother and who lost his son a short time ago. [Gravette News Herald 7/11/24]

HOFFMAN, R. Roy - R. Roy Hoffman, son of W.H. Hoffman of Gravette, died at the age of 42 years at the Fort Smith hospital Friday night, Feb. 15, 1924 following an operation for appendicitis, which had been troubling him for some time. Like his father, who is engaged in glass factory work at

Tulsa, Okla., Roy was connected with the Harding Glass Company at Fort Smith. He leaves a wife and three children, Ruth, Leona and Fay. The funeral was conducted Sunday at Fort Smith and interment was made in Forest Park cemetery there. His father, W.H. Hoffman, went immediately to Fort Smith and following the funeral came to Gravette and is spending a few days here with his family. The family have the sympathy of their many friends in their bereavement. [Gravette News Herald 2/22/24]

HOLCOMB, Bruce - Fayetteville, Dec. 24.- Bruce Holcomb, pioneer citizen, former banker and prominent lumberman, died here at 12:40 o'clock Tuesday morning. Death followed an illness of several weeks, the last three weeks having been spent in the City Hospital. Holcomb, who was about 52 years of age, was manager of the Fayetteville Lumber and Cement Company here and was very prominent in business. Surviving are his wife, Mrs. Daisy Holcomb, and three children, Crawford of Memphis, Tenn. who arrived here Friday to be at his father's deathbed, and a daughter, Mary, by his first wife; and Richard, a young son by his second marriage. A brother, George, and two sisters, Mrs. E.F. Ellis and Miss Jobelle Holcomb, the latter of the U. of A. faculty, also survive. Holcomb was the son of Joseph Holcomb, a pioneer here of Civil War days, and was born at Springdale. He spent practically all of his life in Northwest Arkansas and was one of Fayetteville's most prominent citizens. The funeral will be held Wednesday afternoon at 2 o'clock from the First Presbyterian Church with Rev. M.L. Gillispie officiating. [Rogers Daily Post 12/24/24]

HOLDER, Claude Earl - Earl Holder, 24 years old and an ex-service man, died Tuesday noon at his home west of town. Death was caused by a cancer on the face which grew from a bruise or scratch on the lip. He has made a hard plucky fight for life and while death has relieved him of much suffering he was ever hopeful of recovery to the very last. [Rogers Democrat 8/7/24]

Claude Earl Holder, only son of W.H. Holder and wife, was born May 5, 1891 at Wichita Falls, Texas and died August 5, 1924 at the home of his parents in the west part of Rogers. He was an ex-service man, having been a member of the 360th Inf., 90th Division, and serving more than a year in the A.E.F. He joined his parents in Rogers about three and one-half years ago. Death was the result of a cancer and he was a patient sufferer for many months. The funeral services were held at the home on Thursday afternoon, August 7th, at three o'clock and were conducted by Dr. A.W. Young of the Christian church. Burial was in the Rogers cemetery. The deceased is survived by his parents and three sisters: Mrs. Anna Magee of Electra, Texas; Mrs. Geo. W. Lee of St. Louis and Miss Willie Mae Holder of Rogers. [Rogers Democrat 8/14/24]

HOLLOWAY, Bob - Bob Holloway, a well-known young farmer and baseball player, died at his home near Hiwasse on Saturday following an operation the day before for appendicitis. Funeral services were conducted by his grandfather, Rev. Holloway of Bentonville, with interment in the Mt. Pleasant cemetery. He was a single man and about 24 years of age. A mother and other relatives survive him. Bob was well known in Bentonville where he was for two seasons one of the most popular ball players on the Bentonville team. He was sick only a week, suffered intensely, but was conscious until the very last. He expressed his preparedness and willingness to meet his Savior and his last words were a comfort to the sorrowing mother, brothers and sister he has left behind. The large number that attended the funeral and the beautiful flowers told of the many friends he had. [Benton County Record 4/11/24]

HOOD, Zerrelda - Mrs. Zerrelda Hood, 71, died at her home northwest of Bentonville Tuesday after a long illness. She had lived in Benton county 40 years. [Rogers Democrat 7/17/24]

HOWARD, Noah Hampton - Following out the last wishes of N.H. Howard, the Centerton druggist who died last Thursday, the body was taken to Kansas City Sunday night by his widow, Mrs. Ida Howard, and a brother of Mr. Howard's from California, where it was cremated according to his wishes. What disposal of the ashes will be made is not known at present. Mr. Howard has been in the drug business in Centerton for the past seven years and has been in ill health for nearly two years. About two months ago he became worse and gradually became weaker every day. His death was due to cancer of the stomach. Noah Hampton Howard was born in Carthage, Mo. in 1855 and was nearly seventy years old. He located in Benton county first in Siloam Springs where for many years he ran a drug store. Later he sold out there and purchased another one in Gravette. This he sold also, purchasing one in Centerton where he has since made his home. Mr. Howard was a quiet unassuming man and thought to be eccentric by some but those who knew him best regarded him as a good friend and loyal citizen. [Benton County Record 8/1/24]

HOWSER, George J. - Miss Ella Denton, well-known former resident of Gravette and community, sends the following notice of the death of her sister's husband, which occurred at Santa Cruz, Calif.: George J. Howser, who was stricken with paralysis two weeks ago yesterday, died this morning at 6:30 at his home, 169 North Branciforte Avenue. Mr. Howser was born in Sutter County, May 11, 1862. On April 3rd, 1891 he was married to Miss Kate Denton and in January 1915 came to Santa Cruz. Mr. Howser leaves a wife, Mrs. Kate Howser, of 169 North Branciforte; a sister, Mrs. Paul Smith of Alameda; a brother, Henry Howser of Marysville; a sister-in-law, Miss Ella Denton of 169 North Branciforte; a niece, Miss Ella Denton, and a nephew, J.W. Denton, of 160 Fairmount Avenue; great nephews, F.E. Denton of Loomis, Calif., W.H. Denton and Leland D. Denton of Oakland. Mr. Howser for a number of years was an active deacon of the First Baptist church of this city. The funeral services were held at the Chase undertaking parlor Saturday afternoon at 1:30, conducted by Rev. J.N. Hoover. Burial was in the Odd Fellows' cemetery. [Gravette News Herald 12/12/24]

HULBROK, Lena DICKMAN - Mrs. August Hulbrok died at the family home on South Main Street, Bentonville, on Monday, October 27th, 1924 in her 68th year after a lingering illness. She is survived by her husband and two children, Paul of Springfield, Mo. and Mrs. Fred M. Phinney of Bentonville. The entire family were with her at the time of her death. The funeral services were held at the Presbyterian church Wednesday afternoon at 2:30 and were conducted by Dr. Harry R. McKeen, her former pastor and family friend, assisted by Rev. W.C. Wheat and Rev. A.M. Henderson. The services at the grave were conducted by the Rebeccas, of which Lodge she had been an active member for many years. Mrs. Hulbrok's maiden name was Lena Dickman. She was born in Horn, in the Province of Dedmold, Germany and came to America in 1884. A year later she married August Hulbrok at Sommerville, Ind. Later they moved to Bentonville. She confessed Christ and joined the United Brethren church at the age of 14. On coming to Bentonville she affiliated with the Cumberland Presbyterian church. She was a devoted wife, mother, friend, church and lodge member, cheerful in disposition, earnest and sincere in her friendships and devoted to her home. She will live in the lives of those fortunate to have known her intimately in family circle, lodge room and church society. [Benton County Record 10/31/24]

HULL, Henrietta KELLY - Henrietta Kelly was born in Morrow county, Ohio on January 14th, 1842 - being 82 years and one month old at her death. She united with the Bryan Zion Baptist Church when 12 years of age, later in life uniting with the Presbyterian Church, her father and grandfather both being deacons in the Baptist church until their death. When a young woman she finished her education in a seminary in Mansfield, Ohio. On February 2nd, 1865 she was united in marriage with Henry Hull in Mansfield, Ohio, her uncle, a Baptist minister, performing the ceremony. She was the mother of four children, Ralph C., who lives in Montana, was unable to come. The daughters, Mrs. Anna Pharris and Mrs. Mary Howard, were both here. The youngest daughter, Henrietta, passed away in childhood at the age of six years. In 1889 the family came to Arkansas, settling on a farm northwest of Bentonville, the husband and father dying in a few weeks after coming to his country. After spending 25 years in Benton county she moved to Kansas City, Mo. and was there stricken ten months ago by disease that wore her out. She passed away at 9:20 p.m. on February 15th, 1924. The funeral services were held at the Presbyterian Church in Bentonville on Monday afternoon and interment was made in the city cemetery. [Benton County Record 2/22/24]

HULL, Mr. - We extend the sympathy of this neighborhood to the Hull family in the sickness and death of their father, Mr. Hull. Hence one more Civil War Veteran to pass over. [Rogers Daily Post 12/27/24]

HUST, John H. - John H. Hust, one of the oldest residents in Benton county, died at the family home north of Vaughn on Saturday evening, February 2nd, 1924 after a long, lingering illness. He had lived to the ripe old age of 91 years and was respected and loved by all who knew him. He accepted Christ at an early age and was a member of the Centerton M.E. Church. Funeral services were held at the Hazel Glen Presbyterian Church, conducted by Rev. W.J. LeRoy and assisted by Rev. F.A. Bradshaw of Vaughn. Interment took place in the Barron cemetery. He is survived by four sons - Dr. Reuben Hust of Albuquerque, N.M.; Harry Hust of New York City; Arthur and Matthew Hust of Calif.; and three daughters - Mrs. Arthur Henderson, Mrs. Arthur Motley and Mrs. Annie Keller, all of the Vaughn community. Those attending the funeral from a distance were Mrs. Harry Hust, Mrs. Mattie Kelton, Mrs. Dr. Hathcock of Fayetteville, Mr. and Mrs. John Holland and Misses Beth and Emily Henderson of Tahlequah, Okla.; Mr. and Mrs. E.K. Hale and Wm. Dudley of Bentonville. Mr. Hust was born in 1832 in Montgomery county, Tenn. He married Miss Frances Harris in 1854. Two children were born to them. Mrs. Hust died in 1862. His second wife was Miss Caroline Dixon, to whom nine children were born. He moved to Benton county about 50 years ago and located north of Vaughn where he spent the best years of his life. [Benton County Record 2/8/24]

HUTCHESON, Frank - It is with sorrow we announce the death of Frank Hutcheson, which occurred at his home in Highfill Wednesday morning, March 5, 1924. Frank was born in Benton county October 9, 1889. He was united in marriage to Miss Bertha Foster September 9, 1920 and to this union was born one son, Coy, two and one-half years old. Frank's parents came to this country in early childhood and David Hutcheson, Frank's father, was married to Sallie Edwards about 50 years ago. To this union were born seven children, Mrs. Ella True, Dick Hutcheson, Susie Cavness, Charlie Hutcheson, Roof Hutcheson and Walter Hutcheson. Frank's mother passed to the Glory land in his infancy and his father and Mrs. Cavness passed to Glory land while Frank was overseas. Frank leaves a host of relatives and friends to mourn his loss. A Friend. [Rogers Democrat 3/13/24]

HUTCHESON, Hurley - Hurley Hutcheson, the fourteen-year-old son of Mr. and Mrs. Lee Hutcheson of Bentonville, died on Friday morning of last week after three weeks of suffering from a broken neck and paralysis. Funeral services were held the same afternoon with interment in the Oak Grove cemetery. Death was due to injuries received when diving in a shallow pool in Sugar creek on Sunday, August 24th. [Benton County Record 9/19/24]

HUTCHINGS, Gracie Maud FINCHER - Gracie Maud Fincher, only daughter of H.W. and Alice Fincher, was born on the 13th day of December 1889 near Bentonville, Arkansas. She spent her early life in Washington county, going with her parents to Missouri in 1903. On March 14, 1913 she was married to Luther G. Hutchings. To this union three children were born, Maxwell, 7 years old, Jenelle, 2 and a tiny babe 3 days old. She died in Ennis, Texas on April 12, 1924, being 34 years and 4 months old. Besides her husband and children she leaves a father, mother, one brother, Grandpa Fincher, Grandma Maxwell, and many relatives and friends to mourn. She was converted when a girl and later joined the Baptist church and lived a consistent Christian life until death. Funeral services were conducted at the home of T.J. Maxwell on April 15th by Rev. B.L. Harris, pastor of the Methodist church and interment made at the cemetery in Gentry, Ark. [Gentry Journal–Advance 4/25/24]

HUTCHINSON, Frank - Frank Hutchinson, aged 34, died at his home in Highfill last Wednesday of tuberculosis. He leaves a wife, a small child and four brothers. Burial was made in the Barron cemetery Thursday. [Benton County Record 3/14/24]

JACOBS, W.A. - W.A. Jacobs, a former resident of Bentonville, died at his home in Commerce, Okla. on Sunday morning, March 9th, 1924 at 9:45 o'clock at the age of 46 years. He made Bentonville his home for a number of years and was in the photography business here. He is survived by his widow. The remains were brought here Thursday morning and funeral services were held in the afternoon, conducted by Rev. J.M. McMahen. [Benton County Record 3/14/24]
{from The Commerce, Okla. News} Mr. W.A. Jacobs died at his home on Main Street Sunday, March 9, 1924. Death was caused by a heart attack but he had been in poor health from a chronic ailment several months. Mr. Jacobs was born in Battle Creek, Mich. May 31, 1887. He came to Commerce, Oklahoma during 1915 from Bentonville, Ark. and has conducted a photograph {apparently a line or two omitted here} first Boy Scout Troop here and has been Scout Master ever since, accomplishing much good work with the boys of the town. He was a member of the Baptist church and with his wife were active church workers, specializing in Missionary work. He also belonged to several lodges. He is survived by his wife, who will continue the work here, and some relatives in distant states. In recognition of the place Mr. Jacobs held among the boys and community work in general, Mayor O'Brien published a proclamation asking all business places be closed during the hour of the funeral. The funeral service, which was largely attended, was held at the Baptist church Wednesday afternoon at 2:30, the Rev. J.F. Phillips of the Baptist church, Rev. Wm. LeMay of the Christian church and Rev. R.E. Burt of the M.E. church officiating. [Benton County Record 4/4/24]

JAMES, James - News was received today of the death of James James in the Old Soldiers home in Virginia and the body is being taken to Dodge City, Kansas for burial. Mr. James was an old resident of Rogers and the estate still has property here. [Rogers Daily Post 5/15/24]

JANUARY, Mary Martina PARKHURST - {from Pleasant Grove} Mrs. Nute January died at her home one mile south of the Fairmount schoolhouse

on June 1st. Funeral services were held at the residence and interment at Flint cemetery. [Gentry Journal–Advance 6/6/24]
Mary Martina Parkhurst was born near Effingham, Ills. April 7, 1861. She departed this life June 1 at her home near Fairmount, Ark. She was united in marriage with Newton January in Nov. 1877. To this union nine children were born, three of whom with her husband survive her: Thomas Jefferson January of Locust Grove, Okla., Charles N. January of Picher, Oklahoma and George Chester January of Gentry, Ark. [Gentry Journal–Advance 6/13/24]

JEFFERSON, Eva Lee WOODS - {from Pea Ridge} Eva Lee Woods was born August 29, 1902 at Pea Ridge and died Friday, November 7, 1924 at her home in Rogers at the age of twenty–two years, two months and eight days. She was converted at the age of fourteen years and united with the M.E. church, South at Pea Ridge and was a member of that church at the time of her death. She was united in marriage to Pierce R. Jefferson July 26, 1919 and to that happy union was born two children, Louise and Betty Jane, who with their father, two sisters, Mrs. W.C. Deason of Rogers and Mrs. L.N. Martin of Pea Ridge; two brothers, Claude of Bentonville and Raymond, at home at Pea Ridge with her father and mother, Mr. and Mrs. E.E. Woods, survive her. There has never been a larger funeral at this place than that of Mrs. Eva Jefferson Sunday for her friends were only numbered by her acquaintances. [Rogers Democrat 11/13/24]
Mrs. Eva Woods Jefferson, wife of Pierce Jefferson, died at her home in Rogers on Friday, November 7th, 1924 following a months illness from typhoid fever. She was twenty–two years of age. The funeral services, which were held at the M.E. Church in Pea Ridge, was one of the largest ever held at that place. Only about one-third of the people present could gain admittance to the church. The services were conducted by Rev. J.A. Crichlow of Rogers, Rev. A.E. Carnahan of Pea Ridge and Rev. Denton Woods of Drumright, Okla. There was a large number of friends and relatives present from Bentonville and Rogers. Relatives from a distance who were present at the funeral were: Mr. and Mrs. N.P. Stipp and Mrs. W.M. Guthrie of Neosho; Rev. and Mrs. Denton Woods and family of Drumright, Okla. and George Woods of West Fork, Ark. Mrs. Eva Jefferson was the daughter of Mr. and Mrs. E.E. Woods, one of the oldest and most prominent families on Pea Ridge, and was born on August 29th, 1902. Here she grew to womanhood and in July 1919 was married to Pierce Jefferson, son of Mr. and Mrs. Thos. Jefferson. About four years ago they moved to Rogers where Mr. Jefferson became connected with M.V. Deason in the grocery business. Besides her loving parents and husband she is survived by two little daughters, Louise, three years of age, and Betty Jane, six months old; also two brothers, Claude Woods of Bentonville and Raymond of the home; also two sisters, Mrs. L.N. Martin of Pea Ridge and Mrs. W.C. Deason of Rogers. [Benton County Record 11/14/24]

JEFFERSON, Thomas W. - Hardly had the residents of Pea Ridge recovered from the shock of the death of Mrs. Pierce Jefferson last Friday when the sad news traveled through the little town Sunday morning of the sudden death of her father-in-law, Thomas W. Jefferson, who was found dead in his bed when neighbors called early that morning to learn his wishes about digging the grave for the dead wife of his son. None of his family were home at the time. His death was due to hemorrhage of the brain it is stated. Funeral services were held at the Presbyterian church Tuesday morning with Rev. John Hall and Rev. A.E. Carnahan officiating. The church was filled to overflowing with friends and relatives of this well-known citizen, kind neighbor and friend of all who knew him. Besides his faithful wife, Mrs. Alice Jefferson, he is survived by three sons, Pierce Jefferson, Fred Jefferson and Walter Jefferson, all who now live in Rogers; and one daughter, Mrs. Frank Foster, of Neodesha, Kansas; also two brothers, B.A. Jefferson of Pea Ridge and C.T. Jefferson of Dublin, Texas. Four sisters also survive him, Mrs. C.C. Huffman and Misses Mollie Jefferson and Pearl Jefferson of Bentonville and Mrs. Tom Landers of Rogers and a host of relatives in this section of the country. Thomas W. Jefferson was born on the old Jefferson homestead just east of Bentonville in 1869 and was fifty-six years of age and was the son of S.A. and Joeann Neal Jefferson. In 1894 he was married to Miss Alice Joyner of the Jefferson neighborhood. He engaged in farming for many years until about 15 years ago when he moved to Pea Ridge which has since been his home. [Benton County Record 11/14/24]

JESSE, David L. - David L. Jesse was born November 6, 1842 at Mexico, Mo. and died June 20, 1924. He was married to Mary E. Read September 17, 1865. To this union eleven children, nine daughters and two sons, were born, of whom nine are living. Five daughters, Mrs. J.A. Pace, Mrs. Frank Lefors, Mrs. S.J. Whiteside, Mrs. J.E. Stump and Mrs. E.C. Thrasher, were at his bedside when death came. He professed faith in Christ early in life and lived a devout Christian. He showed his faith by his words, as he served many years in the offices of deacon, Sunday School superintendent, class teacher and choir leader in the Missionary Baptist church. Following the death of his wife on January 15, 1906 he married Mrs. Elizabeth Spangler of Maysville in July 1909. He moved with his family from Mexico, Mo. to Benton county, Arkansas in 1881, living first near Siloam Springs and later moving near Maysville where he made his home. He had been afflicted for the past seventeen months. Much of this time he was bed-fast at the home of his daughter, Mrs. J.A. Pace. Funeral services were conducted Saturday, June 21 by Bro. Lierly, pastor of the Maysville Baptist church. The casket was lowered to its last resting place in the Tinnin cemetery north of town. Those of his children not present are: Ray Jesse, Heber, Calif.; Mrs. Jarvis L. Fox, Spokane, Wash.; and Mesdames E.S. and E.T. Gibbs of Mexico, Mo. [Gravette News Herald 7/18/24]

JESSEE, David L. - {from Maysville} David L. Jessee died at the home of his daughter, Mrs. Allie Pace, on Friday, June 20th at 3 p.m. Mr. Jessee was in his 82nd year. He had been a devout Christian the larger part of his life and was loved by all who came in contact with him. The bereaved ones have the heartfelt sympathy of the whole community. [Benton County Record 6/27/24]

JOHNSON, Van - {from Walnut Hill} Charley Johnson of Grove, Okla. and Dan Johnson of Muskogee, Okla. attended the funeral of their father, Van Johnson, at Walnut Hill Tuesday, January 29th. Their father was nearly 90 years old. He lived many years at Walnut Hill but for the past few years had lived in Rogers. [Rogers Democrat 2/7/24]

JOHNSON, W.F. - James J. Johnson of Decatur received a message last Saturday announcing the death of his son, W.F. Johnson, of Golden, Colo. He had been a sufferer for several months of a cancer of the face. Mr. Johnson has many friends who will sympathize with him in the loss of his only son. [Gentry Journal–Advance 12/19/24]

JOHNSTON, Maidson - Maidson Johnston was born in Jackson county, Ill. April 23, 1854. He united with the Christian church at Gramhorn, Texas in 1879; was married July 1, 1883 to Iva Richardson at Montage, Texas. Died July 17, 1924 at his home near Maysville, in Oklahoma, where he had resided for 30 years. He was ready to meet his God. He was a good husband. He leaves four brothers and one sister, also his companion to mourn his death. Rev. W.H. McCarroll of Gravette conducted the funeral Friday at 2:30 p.m. and interment was made in the Tinnin cemetery near Maysville. [Gravette News Herald 7/25/24]

JONES, Columbus L. - C.L. Jones, manager of the Fair Store, died at his home in Bentonville on Monday, January 7th, 1924 following an illness of nearly three months. While his recovery has been doubtful for some time pneumonia set in last Saturday and owing to his weakened condition he died two days later. His death was a shock to our city. Mr. Jones was taken ill last fall with typhoid fever after returning home from a business trip. The fever was of a baffling nature and one that physicians could not seem to check. Funeral services were held at the Christian church Wednesday and the pastor, Rev. S.A. Morton, paid a splendid tribute to the fallen member of his church. Out of respect to Mr. Jones the business houses closed during the funeral hour and the church was filled to its capacity by his many friends who had gathered to pay him their last tribute. Columbus L. Jones was born in Limestone Valley in Newton county, Arkansas on May 15th, 1872. When 15 years of age his parents moved to the Northwest and after staying there only eight days concluded that Arkansas was the best place after all and moved back, settling in Western Grove in the same county. Later Mr. Jones opened a general merchandise store in Western Grove and afterwards located in Harrison. About six years ago he became connected with the Fair Store Corporation and became manager of the

Berryville house. Three years ago when this company opened its Bentonville store Mr. Jones came here to manage it. In 1892 Mr. Jones married Miss Maggie Truitt of Western Grove. To them was born seven children - two sons, Reuel of Oklahoma City and Bernard, who has managed the store during his father's illness; also five daughters, Esther, Agnes, Lillian, Gladys and Irene, all of whom live at home. He is also survived by four brothers - D.C. Jones of this city; J.K. Jones of Harrison and W.R. and J.N. Jones of Ashland, Okla., and one sister, Mrs. Sarah Chambers of Woodward, Okla. Mr. Jones was a true Christian and practiced it in his every day life. He was chairman of the board of the Christian church of this city and a member of the city council which passed a resolution of respect at its meeting Tuesday night. In the death of Mr. Jones Bentonville has lost one of its best citizens and the family a kind and loving husband and father. The bereaved ones have the sympathy of the entire community. [Benton County Record 1/11/24]

JONES, Earl - Earl Jones, a resident of Bentonville and vicinity for the past 25 years, died at his home in the north part of town on Saturday, December 29th, 1923 of meningitis. He was about 54 years of age and had been ill but a few days. He is survived by his widow and several children. The funeral services were conducted by Rev. Lester Weaver with interment in the Hickman cemetery on Pea Ridge. [Benton County Record 1/4/24]

JONES, Wm. H. - Wm. H. Jones, or perhaps better known to his many friends as Bud Jones, died at his home one mile south of Maysville last Thursday after a lingering illness. He was about 67 years of age. Funeral services were held last Friday with interment in the Fairmount cemetery near where he formerly lived and where many of his relatives are buried. The Masons had charge of the funeral. The earlier years of Mr. Jones' life were spent on the old Jones homestead near Felker and is now known as the Coburn Orchards. In 1895 he married Miss Lydia Comer in Elm Springs. When a young man he taught school in several districts in that vicinity. County Assessor George Gearhart was a pupil of his at one time and states that he was an excellent teacher. After selling his farm and orchard to Mr. Coburn he bought a farm near Maysville where he has since made his home. Besides his widow he is survived by three children, all of the home place. One son, Frank Jones, and two daughters, Edith and Kate Jones. He also leaves two brothers - Frank Jones of Dodge, Okla. and G.A. Jones of Amoret, Mo. - and a host of friends and relatives to mourn his loss. [Benton County Record 8/1/24]

JORDAN, Florence E. - C.O. Mitchell and Chas. Foster of the Bentonville Marble Works returned the first of the week from Kansas City where they secured an order for a $1,400 monument to be placed in Mt. Washington, Kansas City's most beautiful cemetery. The order was given them by G.C. Jordan of Independence, Mo. and the monument will be placed over the graves of his two daughters, Miss Florence E. Jordan and Ada Jordan Oakes, who was the wife of E.F. Oakes, a former Bentonville resident. Mrs. Oakes died in 1920 and was buried in the city cemetery. Last week the remains of Mrs. Oakes and her sister, who was buried in Illinois, were taken up and sent to their beautiful new resting place. The monument that will cover their new resting place will be of Georgia granite and carved and polished from the rough stone here in Bentonville. Both Mr. Mitchell and Mr. Foster have a right to feel proud of this order secured in competition with Kansas City marble works with their large stocks and low freight rates. [Benton County Record 8/29/24]

KEHELEY, Joseph G. - Joseph G. Keheley, father of M.W. Keheley, died at the home of the latter in this city last Thursday at the age of 75 years. Funeral services were held Friday at the Baptist church and were conducted by Rev. Crichlow. He had lived in Rogers for about three years, coming here from Guthrie, Okla. [Rogers Democrat 11/6/24] [Rogers Daily Post 10/30/24]

KEIGLEY, son - The little 2-year-old son of Mr. and Mrs. Frank Keigley died at the home on Main street last Monday morning of pneumonia. Burial was in Coffelt cemetery. [Gentry Journal–Advance 12/5/24]

KEITH, Thomas Richard - Thomas R. Keith, a native son of Benton county and one who helped make history along the western border of this county, died in Gravette on Saturday night following a short illness. He was 77 years of age. Funeral services were held Monday at the home of his son, R.M. Keith, and were conducted by Rev. W.A. McDonald and the Masonic Lodge at the grave. Burial was made in the Odd Fellows' cemetery by the side of his wife who preceded him to the grave a number of years ago. He is survived by three sons - R.M. Keith of Gravette; John Keith of Joplin; and Claude Keith of Walsenburg, Col.; two daughters - Mrs. Herbert Witty of Independence, Kansas and Mrs. Paull of Helena, Montana. A sister, Mrs. Dave Victor, of near Maysville also survives him. Thomas Richard Keith was born at Maysville in 1847 where he lived for over 30 years. In his early years he operated a large hardware store when that town was about as wild and woolly as they make them. Later Mr. Keith conceived the idea of starting a new town as a rival to this important trading post about a mile south of the present town of Maysville. This he called "Rome City." Here he erected a fine brick building, the bricks being made on his own farm there. Mr. Keith operated his hardware in this new town for a number of years. When the Kansas City, Pittsburg & Gulf Railway built through the county and established the town of Gravette Mr. Keith saw the passing of Rome City and Maysville and took down his building, brick by brick, and moved to this promising new town. Here he built a new and substantial brick business block that is now known as the Buffington Hotel. In this building he engaged in the hardware business for quite a number of years before retiring. For over 30 years Mr. Keith was a resident of Gravette and in his death Saturday another of our sturdy pioneers passes on. [Benton County Record 12/5/24]

Thomas R. Keith, who has been in feeble health for some time, died at the home of his son, R.M. Keith, Nov. 29, 1924. He was born near Maysville, Ark. Sept. 8, 1849 and has resided in this part of the county most of his life. He was married to Miss Ollie Lewis in November 1872. Seven children were born to them, five of whom survive: Mrs. Gertrude Paull, Helena, Mont.; Mrs. Beulah Witty, Independence, Kan.; Claude Keith, Walsenburg, Colo.; John Keith of Joplin, Mo. and R.M. Keith of Gravette. There are also several grandchildren. Mrs. Keith died June 24, 1912 at Heavener, Okla. where they made their home for a short time after returning from Texas. Brother Keith obeyed the gospel 50 years ago and was a charter member of Gravette Christian church, serving as elder, teacher of the Book, and for many years was a power in the church. The church and friends as well as the family feel a loss in his departure. Mr. Keith moved to Gravette from Maysville about 27 years ago, erecting the building known as Hotel Buffington and Gravette Produce house, conducting a hardware business in the latter building and later at the Kirkpatrick stand. He was a loyal, highly respected citizen, whose life of service will live on in the community. A large crowd of people attended the funeral at the R.M. Keith home Monday, which was conducted by Dr. Wm. A. McDonald. Burial was in the I.O.O.F. cemetery. [Gravette News Herald 12/5/24]
All of Thomas Keith's children except the eldest daughter were here to attend the funeral, including R.M. Keith and family at whose home he died; Claude Keith and family, Walsenburg, Colo.; Mrs. Herbert Witty and family, Independence, Kan. and John Keith and family of Joplin, Mo. Claude made the 800 miles auto trip to Gravette in about 36 hours. [Gravette News Herald 12/5/24]

KEITH, Thos. W. - {from The Salina {Ok.} News Herald} Rev. Thos. W. Keith, for 60 years a Baptist minister, died at Adair last week at the age of 85. For many years he lived near the Oklahoma-Arkansas border and was pastor of the Baptist church at Cherokee City. His son, P.O. Keith, still lives in that community and is one of the county commissioners of Delaware county. An impressive funeral sermon was preached by Rev. Guy Carr of Salina. The editor of the Salina News Herald was born near the old home of the Keiths. [Gentry Journal–Advance 4/18/24]

KELLEHER, Mrs. Garnett - {from Rogers} The remains of Mrs. Garnett Kelleher, a former resident of this city who died last week in Dallas, Texas following an operation for appendicitis, were buried here Wednesday after funeral services that were held at the Central M.E. Church. [Benton County Record 10/31/24]

KELLY, V.P. - {This article is obviously taken from another paper but credit is not given by The Democrat. Ed.} V.P. Kelly, familiarly called "Uncle Puce" by his friends, a resident of this vicinity since 1894 and a well known and highly respected citizen, passed away at his home in this city at 1:20 o'clock this morning, Feb. 7, 1924. He had the flu five years ago and never seemed to fully get over it and had two attacks of the same disease since that time. He has been confined to his bed or room most of the time the past year and the past month his health and strength failed rapidly. Though the end was not unexpected his death has caused sorrow and sadness throughout the community. Mr. Kelly was born in West Point, Tenn. and would have been 73 years old on the 12th day of March. He lived in his native county until he moved to this section thirty years ago. He was a farmer all his life until the last few years when he had to give up the work on account of his health. Fifty-three years ago he married Miss Bettie Caperton and of their ten children, two died in childhood. His wife and eight children survive, namely: Jas. C. Kelly, mayor of Davis and assistant cashier of Oklahoma State Bank; B.E. Kelly, business man of Yakima, Wash.; C.H. Kelly, cashier of the Drovers National Bank at Kansas City; Payne Kelly, manager of Mays Lumber Co. at Davis; four daughters - Mrs. E.E. Bagwell of Humble, Tex.; Mrs. D.R. Johnson of Los Angeles, Calif.; Mrs. Claude Hardy of Great Falls, Mont. and Mrs. Alex Anderson of Parsons, Kans. All were present at his death except Mrs. Johnson and Mrs. Hardy. A brother, Ed Kelly, resides at Wetumka and a sister, Mrs. Lizzie Campbell, resides in Tennessee. Mr. Kelly was a man of high character and had a host of friends. He possessed strong moral courage and was ever on the side of morality and good government. He was a life-long Mason and the Masonic fraternity conducted its ritual burial service at his funeral. For many years he has been a member of the Presbyterian church and he lived an upright, christian life. The funeral was held at the Presbyterian church Friday. Dr. H.O. Moore conducting the services. Interment was in Green Hill cemetery. ***** Mr. Kelly will be remembered by older residents as a citizen of the county seat some sixteen or eighteen years ago. At the time a son-in-law, E.E. Bagwell, was principal of the Baptist seminary on the present site of the high school. [Benton County Democrat 2/14/24]

KENDALL, Amos G. - Rev. Amos G. Kendall, age 83 years, one of the best known preachers of Northwest Arkansas, died last week at his home at Berryville and was buried at the cemetery at Alabam. [Rogers Democrat 3/20/24]

KENDRICK, infant - {from Lowell} The infant son of Lafe Kendrick and wife passed away Thursday night after a lingering illness of pneumonia and whooping cough. Interment was in the Goad Springs cemetery. [Rogers Daily Post 3/19/24]

KERR, Katherine - Miss Katherine Kerr, 28 years old, the daughter of Mr. and Mrs. W.N. Kerr of Fayetteville and mathematics instructor in Fort Smith High School, died at the city hospital in Fayetteville soon after 5 o'clock Tuesday afternoon, November 11th as the result of fatal injuries received in a motor accident 17 miles south of Fayetteville on the state highway to Fort Smith Saturday night. The accident occurred when the car in which Miss Kerr was riding with Mr. and Mrs. John T. Laws, Miss

Stella Coker, Miss Amy Pires and Clyde Herbert, all of Fort Smith who were returning from attending the Homecoming Day football game in Fayetteville, struck a large stone in the newly graveled road, skidded through the guard rail of the bridge and crashed into the dry creek bed below. The other five persons were able to crawl from under the wrecked machine but Miss Kerr was removed unconscious and taken to Fayetteville in an ambulance to the city hospital where she passed away, never regaining consciousness. Miss Kerr was a Fayetteville girl and a graduate of the University in 1919. She taught mathematics in Two Rivers, Wis. one year and at Tana, Ill. two years and then was instructor in the Fort Smith High School. Funeral will be held Friday afternoon from the Springdale Baptist church at 2 o'clock and interment will be made in Bluff cemetery. She is survived by her parents, Mr. and Mrs. W.N. Kerr of the home address; two sisters, Olive Mae Kerr and Elizabeth Kerr, of Mertzon, Texas and two brothers, Jack Kerr of Coronado, Cal. and Sam Kerr of Fayetteville. She has a host of relatives and friends who mourn her tragic death. Bentonville people will know her as the niece of Mr. and Mrs. Whitley Kerr. [Benton County Record 11/14/24]

KIFER, Lena Tucker - {from Centerton} Mrs. Lena Tucker Kifer died at her home in Cane Hill last week. She was one of the oldest native born residents in Washington county. She was born near that place in 1856. [Benton County Record 2/22/24]

KIRKPATRICK, Annette - Mrs. J.W. Seamster received a message from John Kirkpatrick of Springfield, Mo. advising her of the sudden death of his sister, Miss Annette Kirkpatrick, who was visiting relatives in Indiana. The body is being shipped to Rogers for interment beside her mother and will arrive Wednesday night or Thursday morning, when arrangements for the funeral will be made. The Kirkpatricks were former well known residents of Rogers, Mr. Kirkpatrick having built two houses on Fifth and Maple streets. He lived in one and his sister and mother occupied the other. They have many friends here, a very near one being Mrs. Seamster, who will go to Springfield tonight and return with the family. [Rogers Daily Post 3/31/24]

Miss Annette Kirkpatrick, born at Rushville, Ind. Sept. 17, 1868, died at Rushville, Ind. March 30, 1924. Her father died in 1910 and her mother in 1917 at Rogers. Miss Kirkpatrick came to Missouri from Indiana in early childhood and lived near Pierce City, Mo. until her father's health failed then moved to Rogers to be near Mr. John Kirkpatrick, but before the new house was completed the father died, leaving Miss Annette to care for her sweet frail mother and when the mother passed away Miss Anna lived with a brother, John Kirkpatrick, who had moved to Springfield from Rogers and helped care for his family. At her death she was spending the winter with an invalid aunt. So one can see that Miss Anne has spent her life in caring for others. She was the only daughter in a family of five, one brother,

Ed, died three years ago and three brothers, John at Springfield, Frank at Pierce City and Will of Cashmere, Washington, survive her. Mr. and Mrs. Frank Kirkpatrick, Mr. John Kirkpatrick and family, Arthur and Helen, and Mr. and Mrs. Frank Webb; Mrs. Ed Kirkpatrick of Oklahoma City, Mr. and Mrs. John Stevens of Springfield, Mr. and Mrs. F. Spurgeon of Ft. Smith and Mrs. May Sicle of Aurora, attended the funeral. Miss Kirkpatrick was a member of the Christian church and had many friends. A life like her's, though quiet, was well spent in service. The funeral services were conducted yesterday at the Christian church of this city, Rev. Martin of the First Christian church at Bentonville officiating. [Rogers Daily Post 4/4/24]

KNOTTS, mother - Mr. and Mrs. Chas. Baldwin received a message last night of the death of the mother of Mrs. H.H. Knotts of Neosho and who is also an aunt of Mrs. Corine and Mrs. Drake at Bentonville. Mrs. Knotts has visited here several times at the Baldwin home and has many friends who will be grieved to know of her loss. [Rogers Daily Post 3/22/24]

KOST, Laura S. HALE - Laura S. Hale, daughter of Mr. and Mrs. John Hale, was born in Michigan Nov. 18, 1842 and died October 26, 1924. She was married to David L. Kost in 1879. She was converted in early life and lived a consistent Christian until the end came. Mrs. Kost had been confined to her room for almost eight years. Sitting there in her wheel chair, day after day, she was a patient sufferer, never complaining, ever thoughtful of those caring for her. She is survived by her husband and four children, also two sisters and one brother. A short service was held at the home Tuesday afternoon at 2:30 after which the body was taken to the Congregational church where deceased had long held her membership. Her funeral services were held by the pastor. While the sun was slowly going down the western horizon the body was laid to rest, surrounded by relatives and friends. [Gentry Journal–Advance 11/7/24]

LAWRENCE, Mrs. {Ferrin} - {from Decatur} Mrs. Lawrence, mother of H.N. Ferrin, died Sunday afternoon at the home of her son at the age of 83 years. [Benton County Record 6/6/24]

LAWSON, son - {from War Eagle} The small son of Lester Lawson and wife, who has been sick for a few days with membranous croup, died last week and interment was in the Berk Shed cemetery. It was a twin baby and the other one died about a year ago. It was indeed very sad and their many friends extend their deepest sympathy. [Rogers Democrat 4/10/24]

LAWSON, R.B. - R.B. Lawson of Sun Prairie, Mont. died in the hospital at Havre, Mont. recently after an illness of about 7 weeks. He was 74 years of age. He is survived by a son, Robert Lawson, and daughter, Mrs. Georgia Wilson, both of Sun Prairie. Mr. Lawson was a resident of Bentonville for over 25 years and left here about 16 years ago. He will be remembered by many of our older settlers. He was a barber and made a tonsorial artist out of Kit Campbell, proprietor of the Elkhorn barber shop. Later he worked in Mr. Campbell's shop for many years. [Benton County Record 10/17/24]

LAWSON, W.A. - W.A. Lawson, an old resident of Bentonville, died Wednesday morning, June 18, 1924 following an illness of over three years. W.A. Lawson was born October 12, 1846 in Roane county, Tenn. He was married to Miss Elizabeth Mead in 1865. To this union was born twelve children, four of which died in infancy. He leaves to mourn his death his widow and eight children: Mrs. A.P. Smith of Orient, Iowa; W.O. Lawson of Trinidad, Colo.; Tom Lawson of Compton, California; Harden Lawson of Monett, Mo.; Mrs. Lue Asbell, Mrs. Jess Herman, Mrs. C.A. Herman and Ben Lawson, all of Bentonville. He also left a host of grandchildren and seven great-grandchildren and many friends to mourn his death. He was converted in the Christian faith when a young man. At the time of his death, June 18, he was 77 years, eight months and six days old. Funeral services were conducted at the home Wednesday, Rev. I.D. Farmer officiating. Interment was made in the City cemetery. [Benton County Record 6/20/24]

LAYMAN, Anna Elizabeth DAVIS - Anna Elizabeth Davis was born in Warsaw, Gallatin Co., Ky. Dec. 26, 1844 and while still a very small child her parents moved to Switzerland Co., Ind. where she grew to young womanhood. Later they went to Jasper Co., Ill. where on Sept. 1, 1868 she was married to William Layman. To this union were born five children: W.C. Layman of Standard, Calif.; Rev. M.F. Layman, Everton, Ark.; Mrs. W.J. Sears of Stockton, Calif.; Mrs. B.F. Bryant and Mrs. Belle Henderson of Rogers, all of whom were with her during her last days. She is also survived by thirteen grandchildren and four great-grandchildren, two brothers and one sister. In 1885 the family moved to Rogers where they have since made their home. Mrs. Layman joined the church when eight years old and a better example of a consistent Christian would be difficult to find. She was devoted to her home and family and was always ready to do a deed of kindness to a neighbor or friend and it is no wonder that the children tried in every way to make the remaining days of their mother as pleasant as possible. Only the day before her passing away she seemed so much better and joined in one of the most pleasant visits that had been had in several years since all the children arrived. Easter was the last Sunday she was permitted to be at church and she quietly slipped away at the beginning of Mother's Day, May 11th. Funeral services were held at the First M.E. church Monday afternoon at 2:30 May 12th and was conducted by her pastor, Rev. R.C. Lucke, with interment in the Rogers cemetery. [Rogers Democrat 5/15/24] [Rogers Daily Post 5/14/24]

LAYMAN, William - William Layman was born at Litchfield, Ky. September 16, 1842 and died at Rogers, Ark. June 1, 1924 at the age of 81 years, 8 months and 15 days. He served in the Civil War in Co. K, Illinois Volunteers Infantry and marched with General Sherman to the sea. This experience was cherished by him as one of the outstanding features of his life. On September 1, 1868 he was married to Miss Anna Davis and to this union were born five children, all of whom are living, and with the exception of one, Mrs. W.J. Sears of Stockton, Calif., were present at the funeral. The children are: Mrs. B.F. Bryant and Mrs. Belle Henderson, Rogers; W.C. Layman, Standard, Calif.; Mrs. W.J. Sears, Stockton, Calif.; M.F. Layman, Everton, Ark. Just three weeks ago his wife passed away and one may consider it a peculiar experience when it is made known that his parents passed away in a similar way as also did a brother and his wife. Mr. Layman was very familiar with Rogers citizens, having lived here for many years and his passing away is just strengthening the bond in the Eternal Home. Funeral services were conducted by Rev. Lucke at the First M.E. Church Monday afternoon and interment was in Rogers cemetery. [Rogers Democrat 6/5/24] [Rogers Daily Post 6/3/24]

LEACH, Mrs. J.A. - {from Robinson} Mrs. J.A. Leach died at her home at Siloam Springs Saturday, March 22, the body being kept until the arrival of a son, Nathan, from California. Funeral services were held in the Christian church at Robinson on Wednesday, interment being made in the Yell cemetery. [Benton County Democrat 4/3/24]

LEE, Mary E. - Mary E. Lee, an old resident of Pea Ridge, passed peacefully away Thursday, September 18, 1924 at 2:00 o'clock p.m. at the age of 73 years. She leaves to mourn her loss one son, two grandchildren, one brother and four sisters and a host of friends. We wish to thank the many friends and neighbors for their many acts of kindness and sympathy during the illness and death of our dear mother and sister. We also wish to thank Dr. Greene for his efforts to relieve her pain. Mr. and Mrs. W.P. Hileman and children, Josie and Rachel Lee, Mr. and Mrs. J.H. Lee, Mr. and Mrs. M.B. Rice, Mr. and Mrs. J.A. Francis. [Benton County Record 9/26/24]

Aunt Mary Lee was born in Tennessee on October 30th, 1850 and on Sept. 18, 1924 passed to her reward from her home near Pea Ridge, where she had lived the most of her life of seventy–four years in the companionship of her two loving sisters. To her marriage in 1868 a son was born who, though now the father of a family of grown children, has had the coveted privilege of being close to his mother all his life; in early years to receive training at her hands, in the strength of his manhood, while still listening to her words of counsel and wisdom, finally to her stay in her infirmity and weakness. In early life she was converted and joined the Methodist Episcopal Church, South and was a faithful member until death. Because of feebleness of body she was permitted seldom to attend the services at the house of God but she nevertheless had an abiding interest in the things of the kingdom. By the testimony of a life well lived and her last words of assurance that it was well with her soul, the son, two grandchildren and two great-grandchildren and four sisters, one brother and many other relatives and friends, all are consoled and urged to lives of greater faith in God and a larger service for humanity that their end may be like hers. The funeral was held the 20th at ten a.m. at the home of her son, conducted by the writer, assisted by her grandson, and then the body was taken to the Pea Ridge cemetery for burial. M.L. Lark, Pastor. [Benton County Record 10/17/24]

LEUDER, Henry - Henry Leuder, aged 60, of Galesburg, Ill. was killed by a southbound Frisco freight train south of Garfield last Saturday night. For two days the body lay in the morgue of the Callison Undertaking Company in Rogers awaiting identification. Thursday night R.S. Leuder of Indianapolis arrived in Rogers and identified the body as that of his father who left his home about a week ago. It is stated that the dead man was a retired capitalist but through an unfortunate investment had lost all his wealth, amounting to about $30,000. It is thought that the man worried so over his loss that his mind became unbalanced and that he chose this manner of ending it all. The remains were shipped back to Galesburg for burial where he is survived by his wife and several children. [Benton County Record 11/7/24]

LIEBHART, Mrs. - {from Hebron} Mrs. Liebhart died at her home near the Liberty school house Thursday last and was buried at Oakley Chapel Saturday afternoon. She was 80 years old and had lived in our vicinity but a short time. She leaves an aged companion and several children. [Rogers Democrat 8/28/24]

LILLARD, Bradley Louis - {from Elm Springs} Funeral services were held at the Methodist Church Sunday afternoon for Bradley Louis, the five-month-old son of Mr. and Mrs. Austin Lillard of Spring creek. Interment was made in the Elm Springs cemetery. [Benton County Record 11/28/24] An obituary of Bradley Louis Lillard, infant son of Mr. and Mrs. J. Austin Lillard, born June 18, 1924, died November 22, 1924, was received but owing to its length and the fact that we were compelled to get out a day early, we could not publish it. [Rogers Democrat 11/27/24]

LILLARD, Mary Catherine - {from Hebron} The stork visited Mrs. Ervin Lillard the 6th and left a two-pound daughter who was named Mary Catherine but death claimed the baby in seven hours and the body was interred in Hebron cemetery. [Rogers Democrat 3/13/24]

LONE, J.A. - Funeral service for J.A. Lone who died Friday at the home of a daughter at Ash Grove, Missouri, were held Sunday afternoon at the Presbyterian church in Rogers, being conducted by the pastor, Reverend T.E. McSpadden. Burial was in the Rogers cemetery by the side of his wife who died here a number of years ago and his son, Wiliford Lone, a former well known Rogers man. Mr. Lone was eighty–eight years old and had lived in Rogers for a number of years previous to the death of his wife. He was the father of E.C. Lone of this city and had been here often at the home of his son. The deceased is survived by a daughter and two sons. [Rogers Democrat 6/12/24] [Benton County Record 6/13/24] [Rogers Daily Post 6/6/24]

LONG, George Johnsey - Johnsey Long, who has been very poorly at the home of his brother, J.W. Long, for several weeks, passed away Sunday night, August 3, 1924 aged eighty–four years and five days. George Johnsey Long was born July 29, 1840 in Knox County, Tenn., moving the same year with his parents to Camden County, Mo. He resided there until 1862 when he moved to Arkansas, residing many years in the Pea Ridge region. In 1861 he enlisted with a Missouri regiment of the Civil army and six months later became attached to the Blocker Battery Battalion of Arkansas and served throughout the war, rising to the rank of Sergeant Major. He had been captured and was in the Union military prison when the war closed, being paroled therefrom. Mr. Long was never married. He was of that sturdy Daniel Boone type of manhood who knew what pioneering meant. He was a great hunter and he had a record of killing one hundred six wild deer in his day when such game was plentiful. He obeyed the Gospel in 1888, was studious of the Bible and a devoted Christian the rest of his days. The past thirty–four years he has made his home with his brother, J.W. Long, and wife. He also leaves several nephews and nieces. The funeral was conducted at the house Monday afternoon by Rev. W. McCarroll and burial was made in the I.O.O.F. cemetary following the services. [Gravette News Herald 8/8/24]

McCLINTON, D.W. - The body of D.W. McClinton, a former well known Rogers citizen, arrived here Friday from Stigler, Okla. where he had lived for many years. Funeral services here were conducted by Reverend Crichlow of Central M.E. church. The family lived here for several years and were in the grocery business. [Rogers Democrat 3/6/24]
The body of D.W. McClinton, who died at Stigler, Okla., will arrive here Friday morning on No. 4. The funeral service will be at nine–thirty at the cemetery with Rev. I. Wilson Crichlow conducting the services. Mr. McClinton was an old Rogers business man, having, with his son, conducted a grocery store on West Walnut street. A son, F.H. McClinton, lives in Fort Smith at the present. [Rogers Daily Post 2/28/24]

McCOOL, Tennie MITCHELL - {from The Bentonville Democrat} Mrs. Tennie McCool, wife of John McCool, died at 4:30 a. m.Monday, August twenty–fifth at the family home six miles northeast of Bentonville, aged sixty–eight years. She had been ill for some time. Funeral services, conducted by Rev. Carnahan of Pea Ridge, were held at the home at three o'clock Monday afternoon and interment made in the Pea Ridge cemetery. Mrs. McCool, whose maiden name was Miss Tennie Mitchell, was born on the same place where she died, on the property which originally belonged to her parents. Besides her husband she is survived by a number of children and other relatives. [Rogers Democrat 9/4/24]

McCORMICK, daughter - {from Vaughn} Rev. F.A. Bradshaw was called to Prairie Grove on Sunday to preach the funeral sermon for the daughter of Mr. and Mrs. Graem McCormick who died at their home in Springdale on Saturday morning, December sixth, 1924 and was buried at Prairie Grove Sunday afternoon, December seventh. [Benton County Record 12/12/24]

McHENRY, Sadie A. MILLER - Mrs. W.A. McHenry died Tuesday morning at 10:30 o'clock at the Home Hospital following an operation which had been performed a few days previous as a last resort to save her life. She had been in poor health for a long time and in a serious condition for some months with but little hope for recovery. She was given every possible care but it proved of no avail. Funeral services were held at the McHenry home at No. 133 North Second street Wednesday morning at ten o'clock and were conducted by her pastor, Rev. Richard C. Lucke of the First Methodist Episcopal church. Burial was in the Rogers cemetery. Sadie A. Miller was born in Fond du Lac county, Wisconsin January 25, 1860 and was married to Doctor W.A. McHenry at Winona, that state, July 25, 1883. To them were born six children, five of whom are still living:Mrs. Milton Brown and Misses Maude and Edith McHenry of Rogers; P.W. McHenry of St. Louis and Dr. Ray R. McHenry of Seligman. She is also survived by her husband; one sister, Mrs. Edith Harris of Bellingham, Wash.; and two brothers, William A. Miller of Rochester, Minn. and H.A. Miller of Havre, Montana. The family came to Rogers from St. Louis some eighteen years ago and for sixteen years have lived in their present home and neighborhood. Mrs. McHenry had been a member of the First Methodist Episcopal church of this city since 1906 and while poor health has prevented her from taking an active part in the work of the church she has given much to the community through the influence of the members of her family. [Rogers Democrat 1/3/24]

McKINLEY, Mr. - Mrs. G.M. Farabough was called to Alma, Michigan the first of the week by a telegram announcing the death of a brother, a Mr. McKinley. The children are staying with Mrs. J. Dalton who is now quite recovered from injuries received a short time ago when she fell and injured her hip. [Rogers Democrat 9/4/24]

McMAHEN, Ben F. - Ben F. McMahen, judge of the chancery court of this district, died Tuesday morning, March 25th, 1924 at his home in Harrison after an illness of nearly a year. He has been very low for the past week and his friends have doubted his recovery for some time. Funeral services were held yesterday afternoon in that city. The funeral was largely attended. Judge McMahen was born in Boone county about 55 years ago and succeeded Judge Humphreys six years ago. He was considered one of the best chancellors in the state. [Benton County Record 3/28/24]

McNEIL, D.D. - {from Gentry} D.D. McNeil died late Tuesday night following an illness of nearly five years. Funeral services were held Wednesday with interment in the Gentry cemetery. Mr. McNeil has resided here for about six years. He is survived by his widow, Mrs. Dora McNeil. [Benton County Record 7/25/24]

McNEIL, David D. - {from Gentry} David D. McNeil died on July 22nd, 1924 after a lingering illness of over five years. He was a single man and leaves only nieces and nephews. Rev. Hughes conducted the funeral services at the Gentry cemetery. [Benton County Record 8/1/24]

McNEILL, Dave - Dave McNeill died at the home of his sister-in-law, Mrs. John McNeill, a week ago last Tuesday night. He had been ailing for some time and was blind. Mr. McNeill was the first barber that Gentry had and he was well liked by all. [Gentry Journal–Advance 8/1/24]

MABRY, Eurie - {from Lowell, for last week} The body of Eurie Mabry who died last Thursday in Tulsa, the result of injuries received in an automobile accident Christmas eve, was shipped to Springdale for burial. [Rogers Democrat 1/17/24]

MAFFITT, Mrs. - John W. Irelan was called to Springfield the first of the week by the death of his sister, Mrs. Maffitt, a former Rogers resident. [Rogers Democrat 1/10/24]

MAHURIN, Nancy - Mrs. Nancy Mahurin died at her home in Bentonville about 5 a.m. Monday, March 3rd, 1924. Burial was made in the City Cemetery that afternoon. Mrs. Mahurin was born in Benton county 67 years ago and had lived here all her life. [Benton County Record 3/7/24]

MARBERRY, Mayme WEAVER - {from Gravette} Mrs. Mayme Marberry died at the home of her parents, Mr. and Mrs. W.W. Weaver, in south side, on January 6th. She was born on February 27th, 1889. She is survived by five sisters and one brother. Funeral services were held at 2 o'clock p.m. Tuesday at the Methodist church conducted by Rev. W.J. LeRoy of Centerton. Burial was made in the I.O.O.F. cemetery under the auspices of the Eastern Star. [Benton County Record 1/11/24]

MARBURY, Mayme Alice WEAVER - Mrs. Mayme Alice Weaver Marbury died Sunday night, Jan. 6th, 1924 at the home of her parents, Mr. and Mrs. W.W. Weaver, south of town, the result of a cancer. Mrs. Marbury was born near Marion, Ill. and was aged 34 years, 10 months and 10 days. She came to Arkansas in 1905 and has been active as a teacher and a prominent Home Demonstration agent in Clark and Yell counties. She was married to Leonard Marbury at Rene, Colo. in 1919. He died two years ago. Mrs. Marbury leaves her parents and five sisters: Mrs. Luther A. Baughn, Gravette; Mrs. Coy of Lindsey, Okla.; Mrs. Pledger of Shreveport, Tex.; Misses Ruth and Esther Weaver and one brother, Wallace Weaver, now in the University of Pennsylvania in Philadelphia. The funeral was conducted at the M.E. Church Tuesday, 2 p.m. by Rev. W.J. LeRoy of Centerton and burial was in the I.O.O.F. cemetery. Sympathy is extended the family. [Gravette News Herald 1/11/24]

MARLAR, Jeff - {from Garfield} Jeff Marlar, who has been a victim of tuberculosis for several long months, passed away at the home of his mother Thursday, May 1 and was laid to rest in the Walnut Hill Cemetery on Friday. [Rogers Daily Post 5/7/24]

MARLER, Helen Mae - {from Pine Log} Relatives and friends here of Mr. and Mrs. Wallace Marler were very much grieved Friday when the news came telling of the death of their little daughter, Helen Mae, on May 30th at Tulsa, Okla. at the age of four years and ten months. She was brought back here for burial, the party arriving Saturday night and was taken to the Henry Marler home. The funeral was preached Sunday afternoon by Rev. Clark Bland and the little baby laid to rest in the Ruddick cemetery in the presence of a large crowd. She leaves a father, mother and one little sister and other relatives to mourn her loss. [Rogers Democrat 6/5/24]
{from Ozark} Wallace Marler and wife brought the body of their baby daughter back from Tulsa Saturday evening and she was buried in the Ruddick cmetery Sunday afternoon. Helen May Marler was born July 26, 1919 and died May 30, 1924. The family had moved to Arizona the first of January and had remained there until a few days ago when they had started back thinking to get better medical assistance but got no farther than Tulsa where the child died. Bro. Clark Bland preached the funeral sermon. All join in offering the deepest of sympathy to the sorrowing family. One little daughter is still living. [Rogers Democrat 6/5/24]

MARR, Mrs. Frank {WOMACK} - {from Centerton} Death came to Mrs. Frank Marr Tuesday morning after several years illness from tuberculosis. The funeral, which was held Wednesday afternoon, was largely attended. Rev. W.J. LeRoy, her pastor, conducted the services. Besides her husband she is survived by several grown children, also by four brothers, Rev. John Womack, presiding elder of the Fayetteville District of the M.E. Church, South; Elwood Womack, Pitt and Vance Womack; also one sister, Miss Stella Womack. [Benton County Record 11/14/24]
A host of Gravette people will regret to learn of the death of Mrs. Frank Marr which occurred Tuesday, Nov. 11, 1924 at their home this side of Bentonville. The Marr family for years were residents of Gravette and were held in general esteem. Mrs. Marr has been in ill health for some years. Besides the husband she leaves three sons and two daughters, all prominent in educational work, and one sister, Stella Womack, and four brothers, Presiding Elder J.A. Womack, Pitts, Vance and Elwood Womack. Rev. W.J. LeRoy of Centerton conducted the funeral and interment was made at Centerton on Wednesday afternoon. The bereaved family have a host of sympathizers at Gravette. [Gravette News Herald 11/21/24]

MARRS, Mildred Vera - Mildred Vera Marrs, daughter of Cleveland and Anna Marrs, was born Feb. 23, 1914. Her father passed away when she was a small child and she was reared by her grandparents, Wm. T. and Fanny Marrs, being continuously cared for by her grandmother since she was 11 months of age. She passed away between 8 and 9 a.m. on Monday, October 20, 1924 after an illness of about 20 days in which she suffered intensely. Besides the aged grandparents, by whom she was cared for, she leaves to mourn her departure her mother, one sister, another grandmother, Mrs. Abbott, and a host of relatives and friends. Funeral services were conducted by Eld. J.L. Chastain and the body was laid to rest in the Springtown cemetery. [Gentry Journal–Advance 10/31/24]

MARTIN, Albert F. - {from Rogers} Albert F. Martin, living north of town, died last Thursday at the age of 84 years. He came here a good many years ago and at one time was a prominent fruit grower. He leaves a wife and two grown sons. [Benton County Record 6/13/24]
The funeral of Albert F. Martin, who died Thursday at his home three miles northwest of Rogers aged 84 years, 8 months and 28 days, was held this afternoon at 2:30 at the home, Rev. Lucke conducting the services. Mr. Martin was a native of New York and a man of splendid education. He came to Arkansas several years ago, settling on a fruit farm and was one of the foremost in progressive development of an Arkansas orchard so far as his age and physical ability permitted. He is survived by his aged wife, two sons, W.W., who has been managing the farm, whose home is in Trinidad, Colorado, and a daughter, Mrs. Fred Barnett of Rogers. The funeral was in charge of the Callison mortuary. [Rogers Daily Post 6/6/24]

MASONER, Katherine - A number of friends went to Springdale yesterday to attend the funeral of Mrs. Katherine Masoner, mother of Mrs. John Willingham who lives on North Sixth street. Mrs. Masoner was 80 years old. She was a native of Tennessee but has made her home in Springdale for more than 30 years. She is the mother of eight children, seven of whom survive and all were present at the funeral. Two girls and three boys live in Springdale, a son lives in Monett, Mo. and a daughter in Rogers. The services were conducted by the two local Methodist ministers with special music and a wealth of floral offerings covered the casket. Mrs. Masoner was buried beside her husband who passed away 20 years ago. [Rogers Daily Post 6/23/24]

MAYBRY, Uriel - {from Hebron} The Mr. Uriel Maybry we mentioned two weeks ago in our notes, died and was brought home and buried in the Spring Creek cemetery. The first word his parents received was that he had been injured in a car wreck but he regained consciousness before he died and told his father that a negro hurt him. He said he came by where some negroes had a wreck in a truck and they asked him to assist them and one of them struck him with a spoke from the demolished wheel and broke his hand the first blow and crushed his skull and succeeded in taking $50 of money from him. It is a sad death as he was a young man in the flower of life and such a shock for his relatives. He leaves a young wife and a number of brothers and sisters. [Rogers Democrat 1/17/24]

MEINEN, Iris Gregg GRAMMER - Mrs. Iris Gregg Meinen, wife of J. Fred Meinen, passed away Monday evening, July 21st, 1924 at the home of her parents, Mr. and Mrs. J.A. Grammer. Funeral services were held at the Grammer home Wednesday morning at ten o'clock, the Reverend

Stephen A. Morton conducting the services. Interment was made in the City Cemetery. Mrs. Meinen was born in Bentonville on November 18th, 1884 and grew to womanhood in this city. In 1912 she was married to J. Fred Meinen in Muskogee, Okla. To this union was born one daughter, Thelma, aged 11, who, with the father and her parents, survives her. Mrs. Meinen has been an invalid for the past ten years, the last four of which she has been confined to her bed. During this time she has borne her affliction with true Christian fortitude. Kind friends and neighbors have also helped to brighten her life with many acts of kindness. [Benton County Record 7/25/24]

MENDENHALL, Mrs. O.S. - {from New Hope} We are sorry to report the death of Mrs. O.S. Mendenhall which occurred at an Old Ladies Home near Cincinnati, Ohio about March 10th. Mrs. Mendenhall was a resident of this neighborhood for several years and as long as her health permitted took great interest in the New Hope Sunday school and church. Her friends were numbered only by her acquaintances who will greatly regret to hear of her passing. [Rogers Democrat 4/10/24]

MIDDLETON, Phoebe B. TANKERLY - Mrs. John Middleton {nee Phoebe B. Tankerly} was born in the state of Ohio on the 2d day of March 1862 and died at the age of 61 years and 11 months. She was married about 20 years ago to John Middleton with whom she lived devotedly until his death which occurred eight years ago. She was converted in early life and united with the Methodist church and was active in the organized woman's work in the Ladies Aid and Missionary Societies. As the wife of a Union soldier, like her husband, her heart was warm for the flag of our country. She was true to her husband, her country, her church and loyal to her Christ. Sister Middleton spent the last year of her life in the home of her niece, Mrs. Alice Waddell, of Bartlesville, Okla. where she received the best of love and care in the last miles of her life's journey. Our prayers and sympathy are extended to her niece and her many friends in this sad, but we trust, victorious hour, for the last enemy that shall be destroyed is Death. B.L. Harris. [Gentry Journal–Advance 1/11/24]

MILLER, child - {from Hiwasse} Mrs. Tobe Parker had a letter Thursday from her brother, John Miller, with the sad news of the death of their youngest child. [Benton County Record 10/3/24]

MILLER, F.M. - F.M. Miller, living on the old Brunskog place north of town, died in Texas last Friday of cancer. Mr. Miller left here for the Lone Star State about three weeks ago. [Benton County Record 5/16/24]

MILLER, Mattie Francis BRIDGEWATER - Mattie Francis Bridgewater was born March 14th, 1870; died at her home in Gentry, Ark. March 26th, 1924, at the age of 54 years, 12 days. She was born in Pettis county, Missouri and moved with her parents to Saline county, Mo. when a child. She was converted and united with the Baptist Church at Mr. Zion, Mo. at the age of twelve years and has lived a faithful Christian life ever since. She was united in marriage to William M. Miller at Waverly, Mo., Lafayette county, May 13, 1890. To this union four children were born: Leon W. Miller of Gentry; Mrs. W.S. Statler of Orange, Tex.; Ricel N. Miller and Lula N. Miller of Gentry. Besides her husband and four children she leaves three brothers: J.R. Bridgewater of Hopkins, Mo.; G.W. Bridgewater of Olympia, Wash. and J.N. Bridgewater of Waverly, Mo. and also one grandchild. She moved to Gentry, Ark. October 28th, 1920, uniting with the Baptist church here. Mrs. Miller was a devoted wife and mother, a loyal member of the church, kind and charitable to all. She was not so much a woman of words as of deeds. She loved the genuine and true, which virtues were exemplified in her character. She was quiet and unassuming in all that she did. Her memory will always be held in esteem by those who knew her. Funeral services were conducted from the home Friday morning by Rev. C.H. Sherman and burial was made in the city cemetery by the O.E.S. of which she was a member. [Gentry Journal–Advance 4/4/24]

MILLER, Mrs. J.F. - Mrs. J.F. Miller died very suddenly yesterday morning at her home on West Walnut street. She underwent an operation two weeks ago at the Home Hospital and was thought to be getting along nicely. A son and his wife from Hutchinson, Kansas, who had been called here by her serious condition, decided she was doing so well that they started on the home journey in their car Tuesday. At our last report last evening all efforts to reach the son had been unavailing owing to the bad weather and the uncertainty of where it had caught him. [Rogers Democrat 3/20/24] The body of Mrs. J.F. Miller, who died last week following an operation of a week previous, was sent Saturday to their former home at Van Buren, this state, for burial. [Rogers Democrat 3/27/24]

MILLER, Mrs. J.L. - Mrs. J.L. Miller, who was operated on at the Home Hospital a week ago, died late last night. No arrangements will be made for the funeral until word has been received from her son, L.E. Miller, who has been with his mother since the operation and left yesterday for his home in Hutchison, Kansas. He thought his mother was recovering when he left but she became worse about 6 o'clock last night and passed away. Mrs. Miller is survived by her son and husband. They had lived for several years on West Walnut St., near the McClain farm. [Rogers Daily Post 3/18/24]

MILLER, R.W. - {from Centerton} Word has been received here of the recent death of R.W. Miller in Crescent City, Cal. Mr. Miller left here last fall with his nephew, R.W. Miller of the Centerton Hardware Company, and Claude Callis. They planned to engage in mining on a tract owned by the elder Mr. Miller. [Benton County Record 11/21/24]

MILLIGAN, Rebecca McDONALD - Mrs. R. Milligan died Friday, September 12th at her home in Rogers on South Fourth Street, at the age of 85 years, seven months and twenty-three days. She suffered a stroke of paralysis some six months ago and had been confined to her bed since that time. Funeral services were held at the Milligan home Saturday afternoon at 2:30 and were conducted by Rev. Ben Moore, pastor of the Presbyterian church. Burial was in the Rogers cemetery by the side of her husband, Joseph Milligan, who died here some nineteen years ago. Rebecca McDonald was born January 30, 1839 at Blue Springs, Mo. She married Joseph Milligan November 19, 1857 and they moved to Southwest City, Mo. in 1869. Later they moved to Fayetteville, coming to Rogers in 1881, the year the town was started, and had made her home here ever since. She was a charter member of the Cumberland Presbyterian church of Rogers and in her younger days was very active in that body. Eleven children were born to Mr. and Mrs. Milligan, seven of whom are now living: J.A. Milligan, Vaughn, Ark.; Mrs. W.R. Moore, Mrs. Leon B. Powell and C.E. Milligan of Rogers; Mrs. A.V. Manning of Pineville, Mo.; A.F. Milligan of Stella, Mo. and Dr. W.S. Milligan of Miami, Okla. She is also survived by ten grandchildren and eleven great-grandchildren. [Rogers Democrat 9/18/24]

MISER, Frank A. - Word has been received of the death of Frank A. Miser, a former resident of Pea Ridge who died very suddenly in Fortuna, California on August 31st. He had been seriously ill for some time and was thought to be improving. He leaves a heart-broken wife and an aged mother, Mrs. M. Patrick. He is also survived by one sister, Mrs. John Foster of Fortuna, Calif.; also by three brothers, Dwight Miser and Robert Patrick of Eureka, California and Wm. Patrick of Grizzly Bluff, California. Frank Miser was the son of the late John Miser, an old resident of the Pea Ridge country. He left this section a good many years ago for the west. [Benton County Record 10/24/24]

MISNER, Maria PARKER - Word was received here Saturday of the death of Mrs. Maria Parker Misner at the home of her brother, Porter Parker, at Marine, Ill. at the age of seventy--three years. She was buried at Marine Sunday, May 17th. Her passing marks the going of one of Rogers' oldest citizens and many of our people will remember her. She came to Rogers with her parents in 1885 and lived here thirty-three years, during which time she was married to Capt. Misner, who died here several years ago. She left Rogers about six years ago and has since made her home with her brother at Marine. She was a cousin of H.R. Sackett who lived here several years but is now deceased and an aunt of Andy Parker who conducts a rooming house on West Walnut street. [Rogers Democrat 5/22/24]

MITCHELL, Henry Lee - Henry Lee Mitchell died at his home west of Sulphur Springs on Thursday, Oct. 2, 1924 at the age of 18 years. His death was due to typhoid fever. Interment was made in the Lee cemetery. He was the son of Mr. and Mrs. R.T. Mitchell. [Benton County Record 10/10/24

{from Fairview Chapel} Lee Mitchell, son of Mr. and Mrs. Roy Mitchell, died Oct. 2d and was buried in Lee Cemetery Oct. 3d. The community sympathizes with the family. [Gravette News Herald 10/10/24]

MITCHELL, Marenda - {from Sassafras}W.L. Patterson and children attended the funeral of Mr. Patterson's grandmother, Mrs. Marenda Mitchell, Sunday afternoon. Mrs. Mitchell spent most of her life here. She was loved and honored by all who knew her. The body was laid to rest in the Twelve Corners cemetery. [Rogers Democrat 4/24/24]

MONEYHEN, Mrs. Ben {JOHNSTON} {from Hiwasse} Mrs. H. Johnston received a message Saturday that the body of her niece, Mrs. Ben Moneyhen, of Olathe, Kansas would be shipped to Springdale for burial at that place Sunday. Mrs. H. Johnston and N.A. Johnston accompanied them and returned to Hiwasse Sunday night. Mrs. Ben Moneyhen was a daughter of Mr. and Mrs. H.W. Johnston of Olathe, Kansas. [Benton County Record 5/23/24]

MOREHEAD, Harry Duncan - Harry Duncan Morehead died Nov. 10 at Seaside, Ore., aged about 44 years. Interment was made in Astoria following the arrival of his sister, Mrs. E.B. Harrington, of Gravette on November 12. Harry's father, "Uncle Billie," was of the Morehead family to be honored by giving the state of Kentucky a governor; his mother was a teacher in a Kentucky seminary who died at his birth in McLean county, Illinois. Mr. Morehead was an Odd Fellow, serving for a time as treasurer of Elmwood Lodge, Kansas City, Mo. He was jailer at police headquarters and also for years connected with the Kansas City water works department, resigning as superintendent of meter setters on coming to Gravette. He went to Oregon a few months ago where he became afflicted and died. Mrs. Harrington of Gravette, his sister, was his only near living relative. [Gravette News Herald 11/28/24]

MORGAN, Martha Ann PENDERGRAFT - Martha Ann Pendergraft was born June 7th, 1849 and departed this life October 9th, 1924. In 1867 she was married to Sam. Watson Morgan and to this union were born nine children; five of whom survive, namely: Ola Prigmore of Arlington, Texas; Cinda Beavers of Austin, Texas; Jane Austin of Kansas City, Missouri and Pearl Gwartney and Reuben Morgan of Gravette, Arkansas. Early in life she was converted and joined the Methodist church. Grandma, as she was often called, was a hard worker, noble woman, true mother and grandmother and a good neighbor. She will be greatly missed by all, especially by grandchildren who she loved tenderly. Her life and influence will be missed in the community. Funeral services were conducted by the writer after which her body was laid to rest in the Mt. Pleasant cemetery by the side of her husband to await Resurrection Morn. Roy E. Daugherty. [Benton County Record 10/24/24]

MORRISON, Nancy HEGWOOD - {from Larue} We were sorry to learn of the death of Aunt Nancy Morrison who has been in failing health for more than 12 months who died on the 19th of March. She was a sister of Uncle John Hegwood who departed this life seven years ago. Rev. Thompson officiated at the funeral services. [Benton County Democrat 4/3/24] {from Glade} Aunt Nancy Morrison departed this life March 25th aged 76 years. She leaves to mourn her loss seven children, four boys and three girls and a number of grandchildren. [Benton County Democrat 4/3/24]

MORRISON, Naoma HARTLEY - Miss Naoma Hartley was born April 12, 1903 and died at the home of her mother, Mrs. S.H. Hartley, on East Oak street May 29, 1924 at the age of 21 years, one month and 17 days. She was married eighteen months ago to Edward Morrison of Rogers, who with a few days old baby daughter, survive. Her passing away was a great shock to her many friends and the love and esteem in which she was held was evidenced by the unusually large number of friends who accompanied her remains to the cemetery. The funeral service was conducted by Rev. John Hines of Bentonville and burial was in Rogers cemetery. The husband and other relatives have the sympathy of the entire community. [Rogers Democrat 6/5/24]

MOSER, Marion Lee - {from Hebron} Baby Marion Lee, the month old son of Mr. and Mrs. Marion Moser, died Monday morning at 6 o'clock and the little body was laid to sleep in the Hebron cemetery. The little fellow made a brave effort for life but death released his sufferings. A number of friends attended the funeral. [Rogers Democrat 4/10/24]

MULVEY, Margaret Francis CHAPMAN - A long and useful life came to a close yesterday noon when Mrs. O. Mulvey passed quietly away at her home on South Third street. She had been very low for some days but was conscious until the last minutes when she slipped peacefully and painlessly across the border line between life and eternity. She was 87 years old. Funeral services will be held at the Baptist church Friday afternoon at 2:30 o'clock and will be conducted by Rev. Wilson Crichlow of the Central M.E. Church, the Baptist church being at present without a pastor. Interment will be in the Rogers cemetery. Margaret Francis Chapman was born June 25, 1837 at Madison, Indiana where she lived until after her marriage in September 1862 to Oliver Mulvey. From Madison they went to Jackson, Michigan where they spent ten years and then moved to Wichita, Kansas where they lived until they came to Rogers some twenty-two years ago. Since then their time had been spent between Rogers and the lower Rio Grande Valley at Mercedes. To Mr. and Mrs. Mulvey were born three children: Mrs. Geo. S. Freeman of Rogers, with whom they have been living; Miss Florence Mulvey, a teacher in the Wichita schools who arrived this morning; and a son, Jim Mulvey, who died in 1915 in the Argentine Republic of South America where he was engaged in building and equipping an astronomical observatory for that government. The sympathy of the entire community goes out to the bereaved husband. [Rogers Democrat 10/30/24] [Rogers Daily Post 10/29/24]

MURPHY, Michael P. - M.P. Murphy died last Tuesday morning at his home on Rust avenue at the age of 87 years. About a week ago he fell and broke his left limb just below the hip and following that he developed double

pneumonia, all of which resulted in his death. Funeral services were held at the Methodist church Wednesday afternoon. [Gentry Journal–Advance 12/19/24]
Brother Michael P. Murphy was born Oct. 24, 1837 near Serval, Serval Co. {Sevierville, Sevier Co.?}, Tenn. He moved to this state in 1880 and settled first at Cincinnati, spending a number of years in the vicinity of this place, later moved to Oklahoma and spent some eighteen or twenty years in that state, then moved to Arkansas about six years ago, locating in Gentry where he lived until his death. He married Miss Rebecca Cusick who died January 3, 1859. One child, Andrew Murphy, was born, who died four years ago. He was married to Miss Malinda H. Perry December 14, 1860. She died September 14, 1862. Two children were born, Mrs. Fannie Lyman, now living in Upland, Calif., and John T. Murphy, now living in Delaware, Okla. His third wife was Miss Martha Ellen Shadden. Eight children were born, six of whom are living, two girls having died in infancy. He was converted early in life and spent seventy years in the service of the Lord. Until recent years he was a very active Christian worker but for some time he had not been able to attend services because of failing health. He was a local preacher, also had other official places in the church. He died on the morning of Dec. 16, 1924 at his home in Gentry. [Gentry Journal–Advance 12/26/24]

MYERS, Mrs. Earl - Friends of the Earl Myers family here regret to hear of the death of Mrs. Myers which occurred in the hospital at Joplin Sunday morning, June 15th, following an operation. The burial, we are informed, was at Lewisburg, Kansas where the family lived before they came to Gravette. Their present residence is in Galena, Kans. [Gravette News Herald 6/20/24]

NANCE, Lula Ellen BRAME - Mrs. Lula Ellen Nance, widow of the late Hon. R.L. Nance of Rogers, died Saturday night at Fayetteville at the home of her daughter, Mrs. A.M. Harding. Mrs. Nance had been in poor health for some time and it was realized that her condition was serious but the end came so suddenly that it was a shock to friends and relatives. Funeral services were held Tuesday afternoon at 2:30 at the home of her son, John W. Nance, south of Rogers, and were conducted by Rev. Ben H. Moore of the Presbyterian church. Interment was in the Oakley Chapel cemetery by the side of her husband who died February 9, 1909. Lula Ellen Brame was born in Bedford county, Tennessee July 19, 1857. She was married in that state to R.L. Nance and came to Northwest Arkansas with her husband and her sisters, Mrs. D.A. Oakley and Mrs. W.A.O. Jones, in 1879, 2 years before Rogers was organized as a town. They were farming in those early days but Mr. Nance came to Rogers in its infancy and was actively identified with its business and civic growth until the time of his death 15 years ago. Mr. and Mrs. Nance were the parents of 11 children, 7 of whom are still living: R.S. Nance and Mrs. Bonnie McBrinn and Mrs. M.G. McGehee, all of Oklahoma City; Mrs. A.M. Harding of Fayetteville;

John W. Nance of Rogers; James C. Nance of Walters, Okla. and Will L. Nance, who is in a federal hospital at Legion, Texas. She is also survived by one sister, Mrs. W.A.O. Jones of Rogers. O.A.P. Oakley of this city is a nephew of the deceased. [Rogers Democrat 11/6/24]

NELSON, A.R. - {from Pleasant Ridge} Bro. A.R. Nelson passed away Monday, May 12th after several weeks illness which he bore without a murmur. He leaves a wife and seven children, also an aged mother that lived with them, a sister, Mrs. Martin, who lives near White river, a brother, John, at Iola, Kansas and a brother, Willie, who lives near War Eagle. He assured them he had finished his mission on earth and was ready to go at the Lord's command. He lived in our community from early manhood until a few years ago. He had many friends in this community. The family have our sympathy in the bereavement. [Rogers Democrat 5/22/24]

NELSON, Albert Nora - Albert Nora Nelson was born October 6, 1883 and died May 12, 1924 at the age of 40 years, seven months and six days. He was married to Louise Mullens December 2, 1907 and to this union were born seven children. He leaves his wife, those children, a mother, one sister and two brothers to mourn his loss. He professed a hope in Christ September 1907 and joined the South M.E. church and lived a devoted Christian life. He leaves a number of friends to mourn his loss and they wish to thank his many friends for their kindness during his illness. [Rogers Democrat 5/22/24]

NICHOLS, infant - {from Hiwasse} Mrs. Juniper Nichols' baby, only two days old, died Sunday and was laid to rest in the Mount Pleasant cemetery Monday. [Benton County Record 8/1/24]

NICHOLS, Claude - Claude Nichols died last Thursday of appendicitis at the old Nichols homestead near Hiwasse where he was born about 38 years ago. Funeral services were held on Friday with burial in the Gamble cemetery west of Centerton. Besides his mother, Mrs. Allison Nichols, he is survived by three sisters - Mrs. J.H. Willey of Bentonville; Mrs. Robert Sooter of Hiwasse and Mrs. Ellen Burcham of Gravette. The deceased was highly thought of by all who knew him and he leaves a host of friends to mourn his loss. [Benton County Record 1/18/24]
{from Hiwasse} Claude Nichols died at the home of Elza Galyean Thursday morning and was laid to rest in Gamble cemetery Friday afternoon. [Gravette News Herald 1/18/24]
{from Hiwasse} Claude Nichols, who died Jan. 10th at the Elza Galyean home, had underwent an operation for appendicitis Jan. 6th. He was born and raised here and was aged 42 years. He is survived by his aged mother, Mrs. Laura Nichols, three sisters: Mrs. Robert Sooter, Mrs. Willie and Mrs. Ellen Burcham. Rev. Gift conducted the funeral and burial was in the Gamble cemetery. [Gravette News Herald 1/25/24]

NICHOLS, Margaret TODD - Conley Banks informs us of the death of Mrs. Ora Nichols, formerly Maggie Todd, at Hiwasse Wednesday. The funeral will be at Mt. Pleasant today, Thursday. [Gravette News Herald 9/5/24]

Mrs. Margaret Todd Nichols, wife of Ora Nichols, died at Hiwasse Wednesday, Sept. 3, 1924, aged 30 years, 7 months, 13 days. She leaves her husband and three children. The funeral was held at Mt. Pleasant church on Thursday, conducted by R. Gift, and interment was made in the Mt. Pleasant cemetery. Sympathy is extended the sorrowing ones. [Gravette News Herald 9/12/24]

NICHOLS, Meta - {from Decatur} Miss Meta Nichols died at the home of her mother, Mrs. E.J. Nichols, last Friday afternoon at the age of 46 years. Funeral services were conducted by Rev. Phillips of Westville Saturday afternoon. Interment was made in the Decatur cemetery. Besides her mother she is survived by two half-brothers - M.L. Nichols of this place and G.B. Nichols of near Eldorado Springs, Mo.; also by a sister-in-law, Mrs. M.L. Nichols of Kansas City, who was present at the funeral. [Benton County Record 11/7/24]

NOTSON, mother - R.L. Notson received a message Tuesday morning announcing the death of his mother in Hamburg, Iowa early Tuesday morning. She was 87 years old and her husband preceded her in death four weeks ago. This makes three deaths in Mr. Notson's family in the past six weeks, his aunt, Mrs. Irving, being the first. [Gentry Journal–Advance 2/15/24]

NUNNALLY, Sam - Sam Nunnally, a former deputy income tax collector and well known in Benton county, died at his home in Fayetteville Monday morning. He was 54 years of age. A wife and two sons survive him. Mr. Nunnally was born at Huntsville, Ark. in 1870. He was long identified with the banking business in that town besides having considerable farming interests in Madison county. [Benton County Record 2/15/24]

NYE, H.L. - A somewhat belated news story came to the Democrat editor's attention this week. It was an account of the death of H.L. Nye, a former Rogers citizen, who was drowned in the Oklahoma City flood in October. His home was washed away in the same flood. Mr. Nye and family lived here twenty-five years ago and more, and owned the farm on Prairie Creek which is now the home place of Jas. Grimes. He leaves two daughters - Mrs. Hallie Weaver of Pueblo, Colo. and Mrs. Rose Harnage of Tahlequah, Okla. and a son, Neil, in California. The body was buried in Belle Plaine, Kansas by the side of his wife. [Rogers Democrat 1/3/24]

ONEAL, Fred L. - Fred L. Oneal, a former well known Rogers boy and the oldest son of R.M. Oneal, was instantly killed Friday evening while working on a high tension electric wire at Purdy, Mo. A careful examination of the pole and wires fails to show just how the accident occurred. Fred had the reputation of being one of the most careful men in the business and his death was a great surprise to all who knew him as well as a great shock to the family and many friends. Funeral services were held at Monett Tuesday afternoon, the funeral being delayed to await the arrival of the two brothers of the deceased, Harvey Oneal of Globe, Ariz. and Lloyd Oneal of East Orange, New Jersey. Services were jointly conducted by Rev. T.E. McSpadden of the Presbyterian church of Rogers; Rev. Gillespie of the Presbyterian church at Fayetteville; Rev. Ward of the Presbyterian church at Tahlequah, Okla. and Rev. McKee of the Presbyterian church at Monett - all pastors of the churches to which Mr. Oneal had belonged in recent years. Interment was in the cemetery at Monett. Fred Oneal was born in Kansas 34 years ago and came to Rogers with his parents when just a boy. He graduated from Rogers Academy in 1909 and from the electrical department of the University of Arkansas in 1913. For several years he was manager of the Fayetteville Light & Power Co., going from there to Tahlequah and a year ago moving to Monett where he engaged in the electrical supply business with his father, R.M. Oneal, who moved there from Rogers. Nine years ago he was married at Fayetteville to Miss Lena Henshaw who survives him and they have one child, a daughter of about seven years. Fred was a general favorite wherever he has lived for he was of the very highest type of clean-cut, energetic, enthusiastic worker and citizen and his death is a real loss. [Rogers Democrat 6/19/24] [Rogers Daily Post 6/16/24]

OWENS, George W. - Mrs. W.M. Fritts, living on the old J.W. Stroud farm south of Pea Ridge, identified Monday the body of the unknown man that was found in the woods south of Gravette on Saturday, November 22nd, as that of her father, George W. Owens, of Los Angeles, Calif. Mr. Owens came last July to visit his daughter and remained at the Fritts home until nearly the middle of November when he left for home. While at the home of his daughter he appeared very depressed and melancholy at times, due to brooding over the loss of his wife who died about two years ago. Mrs. Fritts thinks that upon leaving for home he became more depressed and after wandering around for a few days took his own life by severing an artery in his left wrist with a razor. The body was removed from the undertaking rooms of the People's Hardware Company in Gravette on December 2nd and taken to the mortuary of A.D. Callison in Rogers to await identification. Mrs. Fritts had supposed that her father, who was about 74 years old, had reached his home in safety but upon hearing that he had not arrived she became worried and learning of the unknown dead man at Callison's she came to Rogers Monday and stated at once, after viewing the body and clothing, that the corpse was that of her father. Mrs. Fritts was prostrated by the discovery. Funeral services were held Tuesday at Pea Ridge where burial was made. [Benton County Record 12/19/24] [Rogers Daily Post 12/15/24]

PARKER, Cash M. - Rogers friends will regret to learn of the death of Cash M. Parker, sixty–nine years old, who died last Saturday in Fort Smith. For many years he had been with J. Foster & Company as stock keeper and was regarded as one of the best grocermen in the city. He retired from active service a year ago owing to poor health. Mr. Parker is survived by his wife, one son, Tony Parker, who is in South America, and one daughter, Mrs. Earl Marcus. Cash Parker was a resident of Benton county in the early days and has often told the Democrat editor how, as a barefoot county boy, he saw the first train roll into Rogers and how that same year he saw his first circus here. He was gone for many years, returning here about 1902. He worked in a local grocery store for some time and at the special election in May 1903 was elected marshal at the first election after Rogers became a city of the second class by special act of the legislature. He served for two years and then in 1905 moved back to Fort Smith where he had lived before and where he has since made his home. He was a well– known member of the Odd Fellows and the W. O. W. [Rogers Democrat 3/27/24]

PARKER, Tom H. - Tom Parker, aged 56, who for many years lived near Vaughn, met death in an automobile accident Monday afternoon at Ritzville, Washington where he has lived for some time. Further particulars were not stated in the telegram received by his brother-in-law, Andy M. Smith, of Vaughn and his aged mother, Mrs. Parker, who makes her home with Mr. and Mrs. Smith. The day turned pleasure into sorrow for Mrs. Parker who celebrated her 81st birthday Monday. Mr. Parker was a native son of Benton county and was born in 1865 near Vaughn. He left Benton county many years ago but has made frequent trips back and forth during this time. A sister and her husband, living in Montana, went at once to the scene of the accident and will bring the body here for burial, leaving there Wednesday and arriving in Rogers some time Saturday. The funeral services will be held at Vaughn Sunday afternoon at 2:30 and interment will be made in Barron cemetery. Mr. Parker has many friends in this section and each of them offer their sympathy to the bereaved mother, Mrs. Sarah Parker, the brother, C.M. Parker, the sisters, Mrs. A.H. Smith and Mrs. J.H. Mosier. The funeral services will be under the Hazel Valley Lodge, F. and A.M. of which he was a member and all neighboring lodges are invited to send representatives. [Benton County Record 8/22/24] from Rocky Comfort} Jim Wilson received the sad news of the death of his nephew, Tom Parker, of Spokane, Washington. [Benton County Record 8/22/24] Few funerals in Benton county have been so largely attended as that of T.H. Parker last Sunday, whose tragic death in Washington was announced last week. T.H. Parker was born near Vaughn, Ark. October 14th, 1869. Here he spent his childhood days and those of young manhood. In 1898 he went West and had made his home in and near Spokane, Wash. On Monday afternoon, August 18th, he, with a cousin, Dan Callis, also of Benton county, were driving from Spokane to Ritzville when, in passing another car, the one in which they were riding was overturned and Mr. Parker was caught underneath the car. He survived the accident only a few minutes. He died at the age of 55 years, 10 months and 4 days. His sister, Mrs. E.H.

Smith, of Libby, Mont. was notified of his death and arrived at the scene of the accident very soon and took charge of the body and with the assistance of the Masonic Order had the body prepared, by embalming, to be sent back here for burial. The body arrived in Rogers on Saturday noon via the Frisco and was met by relatives and friends of the deceased and was borne to the home of Mr. and Mrs. A.M. Smith at Vaughn where resides Mrs. Sarah Parker, the mother of the deceased. Here the body rested until Sunday afternoon when at 2:30 it was borne by members of the Hazel Valley Lodge, F. & A.M. to the Barron cemetery, followed by a large number of relatives and a host of friends. The deceased is survived by his mother, Mrs. Sarah Parker, 3 sisters, Mrs. A.M. Smith of Vaughn, Mrs. J.H. Moser of Lowell and Mrs. E.M. Smith of Libby, Mont.; and a brother, M.C. Parker of this place. Mrs. E.M. Smith accompanied the body from Washington to the former home of the deceased and was met at St. Joseph, Missouri by A.M. Smith and M.C. Parker. The funeral sermon was preached by F.A. Bradshaw under the auspices of the Masonic Lodge. The funeral rites of the Lodge were conducted by Past Grand Master L.P. Kemper of Siloam Springs, and other members from the Lodge. [Benton County Record 8/29/24]

PARKS, Elfie - Miss Elfie Parks, sister of Misses Mary and Laural Parks, died Monday afternoon at their home on West Poplar street after a long illness with cancer. Burial was from the home Tuesday morning. [Rogers Democrat 11/6/24]

PARMALEE, Helen - Mrs. J.C. Parmalee returned last night from Ft. Smith where she had attended the funeral of her grand-daughter, Helen Parmalee, who died last Monday. Helen was a niece of Mrs. Chas. Applegate after whom she was named. The father, H.C. Parmalee, was a former resident of Rogers, leaving for Ft. Smith about 12 years ago. [Rogers Daily Post 3/6/24]

PARMER, William - Thomas A. Haley, a former Gravette boy who left here in 1904 and moved to near Clifty in Madison county, Arkansas where he still lives, found one day in 1908 a boy tramp by the roadside dangerously ill. He carried him to his home, nursed him back to health and took care of him. William Parmer, the boy's name, enlisted in the World War and was sent overseas. He took out a $10,000 life insurance policy in favor of his benefactor. He was later killed in action but the government refused to pay the insurance because Parmer was not related by blood to Haley. The case was placed in the hands of an attorney who convinced the government that the claim was a lawful one. The government reconsidered the case and sent Haley a check for $10,000. Haley came to Gravette with his parents when he was young. His father's name was Elmer Haley. The boy had been in a fire when a little child and one arm was burned off. His face was also disfigured. This family was not related to the Haleys who live in Maysville. [Benton County Record 5/30/24]

PATRICK, Martha FOSTER - Mrs. Martha Patrick, aunt of W.D. Foster, died at Eureka, Calif. last week at the age of 88 years. She had lived there in Humboldt county since 1860. The California newspaper reports that she was a member of the O.E.S. and was known for her sweet and loving character. She leaves three sons and one daughter and was the last remaining member of Dr. Foster's father's family. [Gravette News Herald 12/5/24]

PATTERSON, Mrs. L. - I.C. Patterson, manager of the Farmers Trust Company, was called to Sedalia, Mo. last week by a telegram announcing the death of his mother, Mrs. L. Patterson. He was accompanied by his wife and daughter, who returned home the last of the week and L. Patterson came with them. Mr. Patterson went on east on a business trip and Monday he attended the Rotary luncheon at Rutland, Vermont. He is expected home Sunday. In connection with the death of Mrs. Patterson, Sr. it is noted that just a short time before her death she attended the Golden Wedding of a brother of Mr. Patterson, the fourth brother to celebrate such an event. Mr. and Mrs. Patterson celebrated their own Golden Wedding some nine years ago. [Rogers Democrat 1/17/24]

PAYNE, Thos. A. - Thos. A. Payne died Sunday morning at his home in the west part of town and was buried Monday in the Cherokee City cemetery. Deceased had been in poor health for some time. [Gentry Journal–Advance 8/22/24]

PEARSON, I. - {from Centerton} Word has been received here of the death of I. Pearson who passed away June 14 at his home in Mt. Vernon, Washington. Mr. Pearson is remembered by many of our old residents. He formerly lived near George Gearhart in Mason Valley and came to this country from Kansas in the early seventies. He moved to Washington about fifteen years ago. [Benton County Record 8/15/24]

PEEL, Lon C. - Lon C. Peel, a prominent and well known young business man of Bentonville, died at the family home just south of town on Tuesday afternoon, May 13th, 1924 at the age of 45 years after an illness of over a year. For the past two weeks death has been expected any time. Funeral services were held at the home Wednesday afternoon in the presence of a large number of old friends. As a mark of respect to the deceased the business houses were closed during the services. Rev. Stephen Morton conducted the services, assisted by Rev. W.C. Wheat. Services at the cemetery were held under the charge of the Knights of Pythias of which he was a prominent member. Lon C. Peel was born in the old Eagle Hotel, where the Hotel Massey now stands, in Bentonville on April 6th, 1879. As a young man he studied pharmacy and became a registered pharmacist in 1902. He was also in the drug business here for a number of years. He later became a traveling salesman for the John Schapp Wholesale Drug Company of Fort Smith and was with them for 13 years, resigning to organize the Peel Motor Company with which he has been connected ever since. Besides his father,

Joe H. Peel, he is survived by two brothers, Will Peel of Cabin Creek, W. Va. and Robert Peel of this city; also one sister, Mrs. Walter Haxton of the home address. [Benton County Record 5/16/24]

PEEL, Samuel W. - "Col. Sam W. Peel is dead." Such was the news that passed from mouth to mouth shortly after one o'clock on Thursday afternoon December 18th, 1924. The end came quietly and peacefully after a sinking spell that came upon him Wednesday. Ninety-three years and three months had been his privilege to live on earth and when the call came he was ready. Coming from a family of pioneers who settled in the Territory of Arkansas before the birth of the state, his life was one fraught with toil and hardships. Col. Peel was a self-made man. His education was secured in the school of hard knocks. The positions that he attained, either in peace or in war, were gained through his own efforts. His enemies were few and his friends many. Although his passing was to be looked for at any time it could not help but cast a shadow of sorrow over our community. Samuel W. Peel was a native son of Arkansas, being born in Independence county on September 13th, 1831. When a boy his father, J.W. Peel, and his family moved to Carrollton, then the county seat of Carroll county. Here he grew to manhood and clerked in his father's store. He was appointed deputy county clerk and later elected county clerk in 1858 and 1860. Col. Peel was married in Carrollton, Ark. in 1852 to Miss Mary E. Berry, a sister of U.S. Senator James H. Berry. To this happy marriage was born nine children, eight of whom are now living: D.W. Peel, Bentonville; Frank W. Peel, Fayetteville; Mrs. Fannie Clark, Bentonville; Mrs. L.H. McGill, Bentonville; Mrs. J.W. Banks, Peirce City, Mo.; Mrs. W.E. Anderson, San Benito, Texas; Mrs. Preston Davis, Vinita, Okla. and Mrs. N.E. Bowden, Atlanta, Ga. Funeral services will be held at the Presbyterian church, of which he was a member, on Sunday afternoon at 3 o'clock with interment afterwards in the city cemetery. When the war broke out he entered the Confederate army and owing to his bravery was soon made a captain. He was promoted to major and finally made the colonel of a regiment. He served all through the war and was in that memorable battle of Wilson's creek near Springfield. On returning to Carrollton at the close of the war he found their property destroyed and moved with his family to Hindsville in 1866. The following year he moved to Bentonville which has since been his home. Here he studied law and engaged in farming. He was also one of the first prominent apple growers in this section. He served as prosecuting attorney of this district in 1873 and 1874. When the present courthouse of Benton county was built in 1873 he secured the contract for the brick which were burnt on his property west of town. Col. Peel made the race for congress in 1880 but was defeated by T.M. Gunter. He was successful two years later and served ten years as a congressman from this district. He played quite a prominent part in congress and for many years was chairman of the committee on Indian Affairs. He was a colleague of the late President McKinley and was

always a great admirer of him. After returning from congress he retired to his beautiful country place and occasionally practiced law in the federal courts. In 1894 Col. Peel suffered a light stroke of paralysis which gradually impaired his health. This and old age told on him and he has been confined to his bed most of the time for the last year and a half. In the passing of this noted character Northwest Arkansas has lost its most distinguished citizen with the exception of the late Senator James H. Berry who also made Bentonville his home. [Benton County Record 12/19/24]
Bentonville, Dec. 18.- Colonel Samuel W. Peel, 93 years old, prominent in the affairs of both state and nation, died at his home in Bentonville Thursday at one o'clock. Col. Peel had been ill for more than a year but was not considered serious up to the time of his death. Samuel W. Peel, a citizen of Bentonville since 1867, was born in Independence county, near Batesville, Arkansas September 13, 1831. His father, John W. Peel, came from Kentucky to Arkansas at the age of nine and his grandfather, Richard Peel, was the first county judge of Independence county. Colonel Peel's family moved to Carroll county when he was a child and in his young manhood he served as deputy clerk of Carroll county under his father. In 1858 and again in 1860 he was elected circuit clerk of Carroll county. At the beginning of the war between the states he enlisted as a private in Pittman's company and was elected major of the Third Arkansas regiment under Colonel Dave Walker. He took part in the battle of Wilson's Creek and other engagements and on the reorganization of troops after being mustered into the Confederate service, he was elected colonel and served as colonel of the Fourth Arkansas until the close of the war. He had seven brothers and brothers-in-law in the Confederate service and of the number Colonel Peel was the only one to go through the war without being wounded. After the war he began the practice of law at Carrollton and after his removal to Bentonville he was appointed prosecuting attorney in 1873 by Governor Baxter and after serving two years was elected to the same position. In 1880 he was defeated for congress by Tom Gunter of Fayetteville but two years later was elected without opposition, serving ten years. Becoming interested in Indian affairs during his service in congress, at the expiration of his last term he formed a law partnership in Washington which specialized in Indian cases and for many years had a large and lucrative practice. Colonel Peel's country home, "The Oaks," with its 100-acre orchard, was for many years one of the show places of the county, but he sold it some years ago and built a handsome home in Bentonville where he has had for many years large banking and property interests. He had always the greatest interest in public and political events and worked untiringly for the election of his friend, Governor Thomas C. McRae. Colonel Peel was married in 1853 at Carrollton to Miss Mary E. Berry, sister of the late Senator James H. Berry. She died in 1902 and some years ago he was married to Mrs. Willie Peel, who survives him. He is also survived by two

sons, D.W. Peel of Bentonville and F.W. Peel of Fayetteville, and by six daughters, Mrs. Alice Vance of Peirce City; Mrs. W.H. Anderson of San Benito, Texas; Mrs. Minnie Davis, Vinita, Okla.; Mrs. Ruby Bowdish of Atlanta, Ga.; Mrs. Fannie Clark and Mrs. L.H. McGill, both of Bentonville. Funeral services were held at the First Presbyterian church of Bentonville Sunday afternoon at three o'clock and burial was in the city cemetery. [Rogers Democrat 12/25/24]

PENNOYER, O.A. - O.A. Pennoyer, one of the oldest residents of Rogers, died at an early hour Tuesday morning. He had been failing for some time and his death was not unexpected by family and friends. Funeral services were held at the Baptist church Wednesday afternoon at 2:30 and were conducted by the pastor, Rev. R.L. Austin. Burial was in the city cemetery and was under the auspices of the Masonic order. The deceased was a native of Canada where he was born Nov. 21, 1833 and at the time of his death was 90 years, one month and 18 days old. He had been a resident of Rogers for more than thirty years and a member of the Baptist church for about the same length of time, having been converted when he was sixty years old. He was married to Miss Cordelia C. Jewett August 6, 1874 who died in May 1900. They had but one daughter, Mrs. Sebra Deason, wife of M.D.C. Deason, and it was at her home on South Fourth street that Mr. Pennoyer died. The deceased was one of Rogers' best citizens and while a man who took little part here in public or civic affairs and therefore not known to many of our people, was always held in high esteem by his friends and associates. [Rogers Democrat 1/10/24]

PERRY, W.T. - W.T. Perry, aged 80, died recently at his home near Springdale and the body was sent to his former home at Ellis, Kansas for burial. [Rogers Democrat 3/27/24]

PETERS, Cora - {from Valley View} Mrs. Cora Peters, mother of John Peters of Osawatomie, Kansas, died last week and was buried Wednesday at Paola, Kansas. Mrs. Peters formerly lived in Valley View. [Benton County Record 8/15/24]

PHAGAN, James R. - James R. Phagan was born Aug. 21, 1865 in Benton Co., Ark. and lived there all of his life and died April 23, 1924. He was married in 1891 to Miss Barbara Goode and this union was blessed with 4 children, 2 boys and 2 girls, all of whom are living. The children are Morris F. Phagan of New Mexico; Mrs. L.J. Curtis of Gunnison, Colo.; Miss Margaret and Bruce who live near Gentry, Ark. Besides his wife and 4 children he leaves one brother, J.C. Phagan, and 2 sisters, Mrs. J.F. Clegg and Mrs. A.R. Wilson, to mourn his departure. He was a Mason and Odd Fellow and as a member of these fraternal orders he proved true and devoted. He was a man of strong personality, devoted to his family and friends and loyal to his fraternal orders. Funeral services were conducted at the family residence by Rev. F.L. Harris of the Methodist church. [Gentry Journal–Advance 5/23/24]

PHELENT, Mary Jane KENDRECK - {from Fairview} Mary Jane Kendreck died Sunday April 6, 1924 at the age of 87 years and some months. She was married to A. Phelent and to this union was born two boys, 10 girls. Only three were here. She leaves eight children and a host of relatives and friends to mourn her loss. Funeral services were conducted at Pleasant Grove Monday, April 7th by Rev. Johnson of Lowell. Burial in Pleasant Grove cemetery. [Rogers Democrat 4/10/24]

PHILLIPS, Clarence McClelland - Mrs. C.M. Phillips arrived on Wednesday night of last week from Orlando, Florida with the remains of her husband for interment here. Mr. and Mrs. Phillips lived here a number of years ago and the many friends here sympathize with her in her bereavement. The remains were laid to rest in the city cemetery surrounded by sorrowing friends. Mrs. Phillips will make her home in Gentry. [Gentry Journal–Advance 9/5/24]

Clarence McClelland Phillips, youngest son of Miner N. and Roxana Clark Phillips, was born in Clarence, Iowa July 6, 1861. He was married to Miss Edith M. Means on March 24, 1909 in Cincinnati, Ohio, with whom he lived in perfect accord during the ensuing 15 years. He bore his long, painful illness with patient and christian courage equaled by few and excelled by none. His many sleepless nights were filled with intercessions and prayers to God to help him bear his burdens. He was one of God's gentle men. His love for his mother and his high regard for womanhood in general were an outstanding characteristic. He went from his bed of pain to his Heavenly reward Wednesday, August 20 at 2 p.m. His wife, Edith M. Phillips. [Gentry Journal–Advance 9/12/24]

PHILLIPS, Nora Johnson - Mrs. Nora Johnson Phillips was born May 2d, 1889 and departed this life March 27th, 1924 at the age of 34 years, 10 months and 23 days. She was married to Clarence Phillips March 29th, 1911. To this union was given 7 children, all of whom survive her. She leaves a husband, 7 children, father, 2 brothers and 3 sisters and a large circle of relatives and friends to mourn her departure. She was converted at the age of 15 and united with Lone Elm church. She remained a true Christian until death. She was a devoted wife and a kind and loving mother. Funeral services were conducted by Rev. B.L. Harris. A Friend. [Gentry Journal–Advance 4/4/24]

PHIPPS, John W. - {from Walnut Hill} John W. Phipps died Tuesday, April 8th at the age of 81 years, two months and one day. Funeral services were held in the Old Liberty Church and were conducted by George Williams and Rev. Martin of Rogers. John W. Phipps was born January 31, 1843 in North Carolina and went to Tennessee with his parents at the age of four years, where they remained until 1870, going to Texas where he resided only one year. He settled in Benton county in 1871 where he lived on one farm for nearly half a century. He was married to Mary Ruddick January 25, 1876 and to this union was born eight children, all living except one daughter, Ettie May, who passed away at the age of three. The sons and daughters are widely scattered: Thomas W. Phipps, Garfield; Arthur N. Phipps, Springfield, Mo.; Ella Harlin, Vials, Colorado; Cora Phipps, Oklahoma City, Okla.; Mrs. H.B. Couch, Topeka, Kansas; Mrs. R.L. Deitrich, Wichita, Kansas; Isa Phipps, New York City. All the children were at the funeral but three daughters - Miss Isa being so far away and Mrs. Harlin and Mrs. Couch being unable to come. Besides leaving an aged widow, seven children and a number of grandchildren, no man in Benton county left more real friends who feel an interest in the loss of a friend and neighbor than did Uncle John Phipps. He was the purest man in word and deed that it has been our good fortune to meet in life. He established one of the first commercial orchards in east Benton county and was very successful in orchard and small fruit culture. He was baptized a number of years ago by Marion Clanton and always had a high estimate of true religion but was a man with utter contempt for pretentious goodness. The family join in thanks for the kindnesses during the sickness and death of our husband and father and for the many floral tokens of love and good will. Written by request by Mr. and Mrs. George W. Williams. [Rogers Democrat 4/17/24]

PICKENS, Anna LAWRENCE - Funeral services were held Sunday afternoon at the Baptist Church for Mrs. Anna Pickens who died at her home west of Decatur on April 12th, 1924. The pastor, Rev. John Scoggin, conducted the services. The church was completely filled with old friends and relatives of the departed one. Interment was made in the Decatur cemetery. Besides her husband, Thomas Pickens, she is survived by one brother,Tom Allen, of Phoenix, Arizona. Mrs. Pickens was the daughter of Col. and Mrs. C.L. Lawrence and was born in Madison county, N.C. in 1853. The family moved to Benton county about 40 years ago and settled about two miles west of where Decatur now stands. Her father was a colonel in the Confederate army during the Civil War and was also a judge of the circuit court in North Carolina. [Benton County Record 4/18/24]

PIERCE, Levi - Mr. C.W. Boyer went to Siloam Springs today to attend the funeral of his sister's husband, Mr. Levi Pierce, who died yesterday from the result of a stroke of paralysis occurring last week. [Rogers Daily Post 5/7/24]

POLK, John B. - John Polk, a former resident of Healing Springs and Rogers, died last week in Riverside, California where he has been for the past year for his health. Mr. Polk was nearly 70 years old and was for a long time the Healing Springs correspondent for the Record. He leaves many friends in Benton county who will regret to hear of his death. [Benton County Record 6/13/24]

{from Rocky Comfort} Mrs. Minnie Casey received the sad news of the death of her father, John B. Polk, at Riverside, Calif. Mr. Polk has a host of friends at Rogers and Healing Springs who will mourn his loss. He will also be remembered in this and other vicinities as a music teacher. He was about the most accomplished musician that this community has ever had. [Benton County Record 6/20/24]

It was with much regret that the Democrat editor learned upon his return home the first of the week of the death at Riverside, Calif. of our old friend and former well known Benton county citizen, John B. Polk. Mr. Polk had been a subscriber and correspondent of the Rogers Democrat during the entire twenty-eight years that it has been under the present management - and we know not for how many years before that. Mr. Polk always took a great interest in small fruits and wrote often on that topic. In late years he spent much time visiting with his children in various parts of the west and his letters from these places were always read with much interest. He is survived by his wife and several children and his death will be a matter of regret to friends all over the country who, while they liked to joke with John anent his proclivity for wandering, always held him in high esteem. [Rogers Democrat 6/12/24]

John B. Polk was born June 29th, 1851 in Macon county, Tenn. and died at Riverside, Calif. May 30, 1924, being 72 years, 11 months and one day old. When a small child he went with his parents to Illinois and there grew to manhood. In 1876 he went to Arkansas where he married Miss Virginia T. Wardlaw and to this union were born twelve children as follows: Ernest Polk of Avoca, Ark.; Luvenia F. Shook, who departed this life in January of 1923; Mrs. Cora C. Barton of Hood River, Oregon; Jas. K. Polk of Riverside, Calif.; Mrs. Martha E. Hamlin, Cristobel, Canal Zone; Mrs. Minnie A.V. Casey of Healing Springs, Ark.; C.C. Polk of White Plains, N.Y.; Mrs. Leona B. Brigham, North Bend, Oregon; Mrs. Dollie Slutz, Riverside, Calif.; Homer E. Polk, who died at Camp Funston, Kansas during the World War, and Jewel E. Polk, who died when 6 years old at Arlington, Wash. 17 years ago {only 11 named}. Mrs. Polk, his widow, lives at Riverside, Calif. Mr. Polk came west with his wife in May 1923 and in June of that year settled at Riverside. He thought the climate of Southern California would benefit his failing health but since last August he had been steadily growing worse and some two months ago his mind failed and he could not remember much of the past. He passed away peacefully at 7:30 on the morning of May 30th. Mrs. John B. Polk. [Rogers Democrat 6/19/24]

News came this morning of the death at Riverside, California of John B. Polk, who lived in Benton county nearly all his life, having married Miss Virginia Wardlow near fifty years ago. These two being the parents of 10 children, the oldest son living in Avoca, a daughter, Cora, married a man named Barton and lives in Hood River, Oregon, another daughter is some where in Europe with her husband who is an expert on manufacturing airplanes, two sons James and Christ live in New York, being connected with the street car company, another daughter, Mrs. Minnie Casey, lives at Healing Springs, Ark. A son, John, lives in Riverside, California. Then came a pair of twins to this couple whose name, the boy, Homer, and this one (sic) sleeps in the Rogers cemetery; it was at the home of the other twin, Mrs. Ross Slutz, that the father passed away last Friday morning. Another daughter, Jewell, lays at rest near the Columbia river in Washington. Mr. Polk had a wide acquaintance in Benton county and had traveled over the greater part of the United States occasionally sending back letters to the local papers of his impressions of the country and the people, it being through these letters that he kept in touch with his many friends in northwest Arkansas. [Rogers Daily Post 6/4/24]

PRAY, Beatrice Evelyn - Mrs. M.L. Kirk received a telegram Monday announcing the sad news of the death of her little niece, Beatrice Evelyn Pray. She was run over by an automobile Sunday and died early Monday morning at her home in Eldorado, Ark. [Gentry Journal–Advance 5/30/24]

PRESLEY, A.C. - A deplorable story comes from the office of Coroner Callison this morning regarding the death at 3:30 yesterday afternoon of a Mr. A.C. Presley, the father of ten children living on a farm about 15 miles to the northwest of Bentonville. From the testimony at the inquest it seems that Mr. Presley and two of his neighbors and J.D. Hurley of Bentonville were all sitting out in the barn lot and that Mr. Presley and Mr. Hurley were talking of trading farms and that there was no quarrel of any kind is the testimony of the two neighbors, but Mr. Hurley, who had been whittling on a shingle, suddenly jumped to his feet and reaching over toward Mr. Presley slashed him twice with his knife, severing the jugular vein and in a second, before anyone could interfere to prevent or to help, Mr. Presley sank to the ground unconscious. The coroner was notified and upon his arrival a jury was impaneled and they brought a verdict of death at the hands of J.D. Hurley. Miss Nixie Presley, a daughter of the deceased, is living in Rogers at 100 West Maple and went home as soon as she heard of the death of her father. [Rogers Daily Post 2/4/24]

PRESLEY, Centers - Centers Presley, a farmer living fifteen miles northwest of Bentonville, near Hiwasse, was killed last Sunday afternoon by J.D. Hurley, a well-known citizen and barber of Bentonville. Presley's throat was cut twice with a pocketknife, severing the jugular vein. He died about ten minutes later. The murder occurred on Hurley's farm which joins Presley's. After the killing Hurley drove back to Bentonville and, after changing his clothes, told his wife of what he had done, walked to the sheriff's office and gave himself up. Mrs. Hurley was prostrated with grief. Both men had always been good friends and were on the best of terms up to the moment of the killing. Hurley was given a preliminary hearing before Justice of the Peace Whitley Kerr on Wednesday afternoon. The courthouse was filled with spectators from all parts of the county, particularly from that section northwest of Bentonville who had come to hear of the cause and justification of the murder. Hurley was represented by Attorneys Vol Lindsey, and Wythe Walker of Fayetteville while Assistant Prosecuting Attorney Joe Beasley represented the state in a very able manner. Two eyewitnesses to the crime, J.S. Walter and James Harris, were examined. The testimony of each was practically the same. Mr. Walter, the first witness, is well known in Bentonville and leased the Hurley farm last year where he now lives. In his story to the court he testified that Hurley drove out to the farm about ten o'clock Sunday morning and that the two looked over the farm. Presley and Harris came later and the four gathered and talked and joked in the barnyard. Hurley, Walter and Harris had their pocketknives out and were whittling. The talk drifted to land. Hurley and Presley each had a forty-acre tract of land the other wanted. Hurley had previously offered Presley one hundred and fifty dollars for his but he wanted more money. Walter suggested the price of either tract be left to Harris and him to decide. Both agreed and the two went behind the barn to discuss the value of the land. They decided that $200 was a fair price for either forty and returned to where Hurley and Presley were sitting. On hearing the price decided upon Presley said: "Hurley, you have bought something." "No," said Hurley, "I've got the first say," and asked Walter if it was not so. Walter stated nothing was said about who should have the first say. After arguing somewhat, in which Harris and Walter both testified that neither was angry, Presley said something that he did not hear. Harris testified that Presley said "I will have nothing to do with it." Hurley, in his testimony, said Presley called him a foul name and reached toward his pocket. Hurley then jumped to his feet and cut Presley twice across his throat with his pocketknife. Presley walked about twenty–five steps and picked up an old buggy hub. Hurley, it was stated, told him to drop it or he would get his gun from the car and kill him. Presley died a few moments later and Hurley walked to the spring, washed his hands and came back to where Harris and Walter were standing over the dead man. Hurley told them not to go back on him as they knew he had to do it. At the inquest held by Coroner Callison, no revolver or weapon, excepting a closed pocketknife, was found on Presley. Presley was about 50 years of age and leaves a wife and ten children. He was regarded by his neighbors as a peaceful and law-abiding citizen. Although Hurley, Harris and Walter testified that none of them had been drinking, a bottle of moonshine was found, at the inquest, sticking out of the front righthand overall pocket of the dead man. Walter stated at the hearing that Presley fell on his face and that when he turned him over he did not see any bottle. Harris stated that he had been with the murdered man nearly all day but did not see any bottle on him. He also testified that after the killing he had seen Hurley go to the car and get a bottle which he carried in his hand through the house. Hurley, it was stated, afterwards was around the body. How did this bottle get into Presley's pocket, or was it there all the time? At the close of the hearing Justice Kerr ordered Hurley bound over to the grand jury on the charge of murder in the second degree. In the absence of Judge Dickson, Hurley was taken before County Judge David Compton who fixed his bail at $5,000. He was then taken back to jail. At 3 p.m. yesterday {Thursday} he had failed to raise his bond. [Benton County Record 2/8/24] [Gravette News Herald 2/8/24]

PRESLEY, Ceph - Ceph Presley, a farmer living 14 miles NW of Bentonville was killed Sunday evening by J.P. Hurley, a barber of Bentonville. The weapon used by Hurley was a pocket knife and he struck Presley in the throat, severing the jugular vein. Death resulted in a few minutes from the loss of blood. The assault was so sudden and unexpected that no resistance was made by Presley and there was no opportunity for interference on the part of the other 2 men who were present and saw the killing. Hurley lived in Bentonville but owns a farm adjoining that of Presley. He came out to visit the farm and in company with C.W. Walters, who lives on the place, was walking over it when they met Presley and a brother-in-law, Harris. According to the testimony of Walters and Harris at the coroner's inquest, the men discussed the sale of a tract of land and while there was no complete agreement there was no quarreling and no sign of anger on the part of either, but without warning Hurley rushed at Presley and struck him in the throat with a pocket knife. Hurley came back to town in his car and went at once to the office of Sheriff George Maples and surrendered, saying he thought he had killed a man, but refused to give any particulars or say anything as to the cause. The result of the inquest was that Hurley was ordered held in jail without bail until after the preliminary hearing. It is stated that a bottle of whiskey was found in the pocket of the dead man but friends claim he had not been drinking and that the bottle was placed there after the killing. There seems to have been no evidence that Hurley had been drinking either. The men had always been friends and so far as known there has been no trouble of any kind between them. Hurley is 45 years old and has a wife and 1 son. He came to Bentonville several years ago from Texas. Presley was about 50 years old and leaves a wife and 10 children, and Coroner Callison said the scene at the home Sunday night when the inquest was held was heartbreaking. The scene of the killing was in what is known locally as Gordon Hollow, near the Missouri line, and about 2 miles from Caverna. [Rogers Democrat 2/7/24]

PRICE, Carl - Carl, only child of Luther Price, died Monday afternoon, December 1, 1924 at his home in the west part of town following several days of illness from typhoid fever and pneumonia which had just developed. Carl was born in Gravette 20 years ago in September and grew to young manhood here, graduating from Gravette high school with the class of 1922 and was popular in the young people's circle. His mother died 2 years ago in July. The funeral was held Wednesday at 10 o'clock at the home, conducted by Rev. E.L. Boyles. Young men friends acted as pallbearers. The body was conveyed to Pea Ridge where it was laid to rest beside his mother. The sorrowing father and other relatives have the sympathy of friends. [Gravette News Herald 12/5/24] [Rogers Daily Post 12/7/24]

QUIGLEY, Laura CASE - M.L. Case and J.J. Quigley received a message Monday afternoon announcing the death of Mrs. W.J. {Laura} Quigley, which occurred that day at Vinita, Okla. Mrs. Quigley was a sister of Mr. Case and the wife of Jay Quigley's brother. Mr. and Mrs. Quigley have been in Colorado for about two years for the benefit of Mrs. Quigley's health and had just returned to Vinita. Deceased leaves three brothers, M.L., James and Lincoln, and three sisters, Mrs. Harriet Johnson, Anderson, Mo.; Mrs. Wallace Austin, near Decatur and Mrs. M.E. Johnson of Vinita. M.L. Case left Monday night for Vinita to attend the funeral. [Gravette News Herald 3/14/24]

RAGSDALE, John Baxter - John Baxter Ragsdale died Friday, February 1st at Batesville, Ark. at the home of a nephew. The body was brought home for burial and funeral services were had here Sunday at the Church of Christ, corner of Chestnut and Second streets, at 2:30 o'clock, being conducted by his pastor, T. Park Burt. Interment was in the Oakley Chapel cemetery. Mr. Ragsdale, who traveled for the Ozark Candy Company of Joplin, left Rogers some three weeks ago for his first trip of the new year. He was taken ill while at Calico Rock and went to the home of a nephew at Batesville. When it was realized that his condition was serious the family here was notified and Mrs. Ragsdale and youngest son, Albert, left at once for his bedside. Later they were joined by all the children save the youngest daughter and they were with him when he died Friday, February 1st. John Baxter Ragsdale was born February 12, 1868 in Blount county, Tenn., being 55 years, eleven months and 19 days old at the time of his death. On March 11, 1888 he was united in matrimony with Miss Martha Jane Arnold and to this union were born eight children, five sons and three daughters. The family came to Missouri twenty-three years ago and have owned a farm west of town since then. Mr. Ragsdale is survived by his wife, four sons and two daughters, as follows: William B. Ragsdale of Morrillton; J. Arthur Ragsdale of Southwest City, Mo.; Chas. E. and Albert F. Ragsdale, Mrs. W.S. Thompson and Mrs. Herbert Hawkins, all of Rogers. On the first Lord's day in September 1923 Bro. Ragsdale "Obeyed from the heart that form of doctrine being then made free from sin, he became the servant of righteousness." Bro. Ragsdale was a great friend of mankind and while his life as a Christian was of only a few months duration yet his entire life as a husband, father and citizen is said to have been clean. [Rogers Democrat 2/7/24]

Wm. Ragsdale and wife of Conway, Ark. and Arthur Ragsdale and wife of Southwest City, Mo., came in Saturday night to attend the funeral and burial of their father. [Rogers Daily Post 2/8/24]

RALSTON, Albert - {from Silent Grove} Our community was shocked Saturday morning to learn of the death of Albert Ralston which occurred Friday night at his home in Springdale. The funeral was held Sunday afternoon and interment was made in the Hulsey cemetery. He leaves a wife, three small daughters, father, mother, two brothers, four sisters, other relatives and many friends to mourn his death. [Benton County Democrat 4/3/24

RALSTON, G.C. - G.C. Ralston died at his home in Sulphur Springs on August 17th at the age of 81 years. "Dad," as he was called by his many friends, had been in ill health for some time. For many years he was proprietor of the Windsor Hotel and after selling that he engaged in the restaurant and mercantile business on Spring Street but his failing health caused him to sell that about a year ago. He is survived by his wife, Mrs. Mary Ralston, and son, Jack Ralston, of Kansas City. The bereaved ones have the sympathy of the community. [Benton County Record 8/22/24]

RAMBO, Mrs. Charley (LYNCH) - Mrs. Charley Rambo dropped dead in her home at 615 West Maple street Tuesday evening. She was alone at the time and was discovered by a neighbor who chanced to call. Her husband was notified and a physician called but there was nothing that could be done. Death had evidently been instant. The Rambo family have lived in Rogers for many years and Mrs. Rambo, who was a Lynch before her marriage, was 54 years old. She is survived by her husband and two children, George, who is working for Gregory vinegar plant at Paris, Texas, and a daughter, Miss Nellie, who is with the Bell Telephone Company at Tulsa. Both of them arrived home yesterday. The funeral is being held this morning at 11:00 at the cemetery and will be conducted by Rev. Lucke of the First M.E. Church. [Rogers Democrat 3/13/24] [Rogers Daily Post 3/12/24]

RAMSDILL, Emma Priscilla SHEPHERD - Mrs. O.E. Ramsdill, nee Emma Priscilla Shepherd, daughter of Ashbul and Abigail Williams Shepherd, was born in Ft. Wayne, Ind. Feb. 13, 1851 and passed to her eternal reward on Oct. 5, 1924 at 11:35 a.m., age 73 years, 7 months and 22 days. Her only brother, Louis Shepherd, preceded her some years ago. Sister Ramsdill was married on August 28, 1872 to O.E. Ramsdill with whom she lived 52 devoted, happy years. Over four of these years have been spent in our city where she made many friends who deeply sympathize with Brother Ramsdill in his great loss. To this marriage were given four children. Two of these died in infancy. One daughter, Mrs. Chas. Van Scoyk, died about seven years ago. Mrs. Clara L. Gunsaulas, the only surviving child, lives in South Dakota and she, with the husband and five grandchildren, remain to miss mother's love. Sister Ramsdill was a member of the Eastern Star and as long as her health permitted was a most faithful attendant of same. Funeral services were held from the Methodist church Monday at 3 p.m., conducted by Rev. Harris. The Gravette and Gentry Eastern Stars attended in a body and conducted their beautiful service at the grave and the remains were laid to rest in the City cemetery. [Gentry Journal–Advance 10/10/24]

RATLIFF, Mrs. T.J. - Mrs. T.J. Ratliff of Bestwater died March 24th at the age of 85 years and two months and seven days. She was born in

Missouri but came to Arkansas in 1866. She was a good Christian mother. She leaves a host of friends to mourn her loss. She was buried at Pace's Chapel beside her husband and several children. Funeral services were conducted by Rev. F.M. Seamster. [Rogers Democrat 3/27/24] [Rogers Daily Post 3/24/24]

Mrs. T.J. Ratliff departed from this life March 23rd at 1:30 p.m. She was 85 years, 2 months and 22 days old. She became a christian in her early days and was an active church member until she sprained her limb several years ago. She was always ready to help any who went to her. She will be especially remembered by some of the grand children, by her kindness and care she gave them, especially one, Lonnie Goodart, whom she had raised from a baby. When she was almost past speech she called Lonnie and they sent for him. When he came in she held out her left hand and said, "Lonnie, I'm going, be a good boy and meet mother." She is survived by a sister, seven children, Mrs. J.D. Deans of Texas; Mrs. Stephen Hays of Carthage, Mo.; Jack Ratliff of Bestwater; Alec Ratliff of Macon City, Mo.; several grandsons, seven of whom attended for their grandmother. They were the at the services and acted as pall bearers: Frank Goodart, Odes Goodart, Harry Arendale, Lonnie Goodart, Todd Goodart, Lewis Ratliff and Frank Ratliff. [Rogers Daily Post 3/28/24]

REED, John Riley - John Riley Reed was born in Barry county, Mo. near the Arkansas line January 23, 1854 and died July 12th, 1924, being 70 years, five months and nineteen days old. He lived all his life on the place where he was born and was never further south than Ft. Smith or further north than Peirce City, Mo. Many Benton county people knew Uncle John. He was married to Miss Nannie Long about 43 years ago. His wife, five children, three brothers, three sisters and several grandchildren survive him. The children living are: Andy, Jess and Austin Reed, Mrs. Alice Mills and Mrs. Velma Nesbit. He professed a hope in Christ over fifty years ago and united with the Church of Christ where he lived faithfully until death came to relieve his suffering. His illness extended over a period of two years and the family wish to thank everyone who assisted them in any way during his illness and death. [Rogers Democrat 7/24/24]

RICH, Rebecca Bond Moore - {from Walnut Hill, for last week} Our people were thrown into sadness Monday when they learned that Mrs. Tim Rich of Bestwater had died some time after midnight Sunday. She was 62 years old and had never had a doctor called to treat her in her long life and died without the family knowing of her ailments. She will be remembered as Mrs. Joe Moore of Mountain View some years ago. An unusually large crowd attended her funeral at Walnut Hill Christmas day at 2:00 o'clock. After a brief funeral service by George Williams the remains were laid to rest in the Walnut Hill cemetery. [Rogers Democrat 1/3/24]

{from Mountain View} Christmas was very sad owing to the death of Mrs. Rebecca Rich of Bestwater. She lived in this neighborhood until two years ago. She died Monday morning and was buried Christmas day. Her daughter, Mrs. L.A. Slinkard, and her son, Bart Bond, lived here. One son, John Bond, lives in Kansas City and the other son in California. She was a good Christian woman and will be missed in her church work and she was so good to wait on the sick. She leaves her husband, T.M. Rich, of Bestwater and a granddaughter, Gladys Buckmaster, besides her children and a host of friends to mourn. [Rogers Democrat 1/3/24]

RICHARDSON, Charles - Fayetteville, Dec. 22.- Dr. Charles Richardson, editor of the Fayetteville Democrat, founder of the national Sorority of Chi Omega, and pioneer of Fayetteville, died here tonight. Death followed a severe attack of double pneumonia followed by complications. Dr. Richardson was stricken with pneumonia more than two weeks ago and in spite of a weak heart and kidney trouble, survived the crisis. Wednesday night he was pronounced practically out of danger and his brother, E.R. Richardson of New York, left his bedside and went to Virginia to the bedside of a second brother, John Richardson of Richmond, who died there Thursday night. Dr. Richardson has lived in Fayetteville for more than 35 years, coming here in 1889 when he set up in dentistry. He was a charter member of the Kappa Sigma fraternity, the first Greek letter organization on the Arkansas campus, which he secured in 1890. In 1895 he founded Chi Omega, a fraternity for women, which now has over 60 chapters in universities and colleges of the U. S. with thousands of members. In 1922 Dr. Richardson gave up his profession of dentistry and assumed the editorship of the Democrat of which he was co-partner with the late Jay Fulbright. Dr. Richardson also was a director of the Arkansas National bank, a director of the Chamber of Commerce, a Rotarian, an Elk, and belonged to other organizations. He is survived by his brother, E.R. Richardson, of New York and 2 sisters, Mrs. C.M. Shannon of Blueville, Va. and Miss Ella Richardson of Saltville, Va. who was with him when he died. Dr. Richardson will be buried in Fayetteville it was decided tonight. The time for the funeral was not set. It was at first planned to take the body to Saltville, Va., the family home, but his wish to be buried here in the surroundings where he found his greatest joy in life, was respected. Services will be held from the Chi Omega house, the national sorority of which he was founder. [Rogers Democrat 12/25/24] [Rogers Daily Post 12/23/24]

RICHEY, Hodge - {from Tuck's Chapel} Little Hodge Richey, 3 year old son of Emmon Richey and wife, passed away Tuesday night, Feb. 5 after a 2 days illness. The little fellow was kicked in the stomach by a horse last Sunday which caused his death. He is survived by his parents, 3 sisters and 6 brothers. Funeral services were held at the church Thursday afternoon at 2 o'clock by Mr. Nelson and interment was in the Tuck's Chapel cemetery. [Rogers Democrat 2/14/24]

ROBBINS, Albert M. - Albert Robbins died at his home in the northwest part of Bentonville on Thursday morning, July 3rd of tuberculosis of the

bowels. Funeral services will be held Friday afternoon at 2 o'clock at the home with interment in the cemetery at Dug Hill. He is survived by his widow of 3 months, Mrs. Winnie Johnson Robbins. [Benton County Record 7/4/24]
Albert M. Robbins died at his home in Bentonville July 3, 1924 and was laid to rest in the Dug Hill cemetery Friday, July 4th. He was born in Benton county January 17, 1893 and lived in this vicinity all his life. He gave his life to the master in his early boyhood and has been a loyal Christian and an active church worker ever since. At the age of seventeen he was elected Superintendent of the Dug Hill Sunday school. Last August he transferred his membership to the M.E. Church at Bentonville. His father and two sisters preceded him in death. He leaves a wife and five brothers and a host of friends to mourn his early departure. [Benton County Record 7/25/24]
Albert Robbins died at his home in the northwest part of Bentonville on Thursday morning, July 3rd of tuberculosis of the bowels. Funeral services will be held Friday afternoon at 2 o'clock at the home with interment in the cemetery at Dug Hill. He is survived by his widow of 3 months, Mrs. Winnie Johnson Robbins. [Benton County Record 7/4/24]

ROBERTS, Wm. - {from Hebron} Will Roberts died at his home at Hiwasse Thursday, the 24th, and the body was brought to the Hart cemetery and was buried near his parents. He was 45 years of age - we may say in the prime of life, but death has no regard for age and reaps both young and old alike. Mr. Roberts spent most of his life on a farm in this vicinity and had many friends here. He was married when 19 years of age to Miss Grace Gillmore who lived on a farm near his father's home. 6 children were added to this union and were all present at the funeral except Howard who lives at Trinidad, Colo. Mr. Roberts had been a member of the Baptist church for years. Rev. McMann of Hiwasse conducted a funeral service at the home and at the cemetery. Many friends were present at the funeral and beautiful flowers were banked on the grave. Those to mourn his departure from life are his companion, children, grandchildren, 2 brothers, Alfred and John Roberts, and 1 sister, Mrs. Joe Giddens. [Rogers Democrat 5/1/24]

ROBINSON, Dan - {from Robinson} Uncle Dan Robinson, who had been making his home with his niece, Mrs. Bill Beaver, died Monday, 24th, after a brief illness of pneumonia and was laid to rest in the Elm Springs cemetery Tuesday afternoon. [Benton County Democrat 4/3/24]

ROBISON, Mary - {from Fairview Chapel} On June 20, 1924 Aunt Mary Robison died at the home of her son, Mike Robison, north of Beaty. She leaves 2 sons, 3 daughters and several grandchildren. Funeral services were conducted by Rev. Fomby of Southwest City then the body was laid to rest in Lee cemetery. [Gravette News Herald 6/27/24]

ROGERS, Ella - {from Pine Log} Mrs. Davy Bowman received a telegram Wednesday telling of the death of her daughter, Mrs. Ella Rogers, who was at Douglas, Ariz. She leaves two children, Hoyle and Izella, who were with her at the time of her death. Her husband died several years ago. Friends and relatives are sorry to hear of her death. [Rogers Democrat 5/15/24]

ROLLER, son - {from Sassafras} Word comes from Kansas City that Cleo Roller and wife's oldest little boy had died with typhoid fever. Friends here extend their deepest sympathy to the parents in their hour of sorrow. [Rogers Democrat 9/18/24]

ROLLER, J.M. - {from Clantonville} J.M. Roller was born in 1871; died February 11, 1924. Jim was the oldest son of N.J. Roller and wife. He was born and raised in Benton county and lived with his parents 4½ miles southeast of Seligman until about 28 years old when he went out into the world to make his own way, part of the time working in the mines and while there contracted a weakness of the lungs from which he never recovered and was the cause of his death. His home in late years has been at Mt. Vernon, Mo. and at that place he has been in the sanitarium for some time. His wife preceded him to that great beyond a year and one day. He leaves his father, mother, four sisters and one brother besides a host of relatives and friends to mourn. Funeral services were conducted by Rev. A.W. Roller and his remains were laid to rest in the Roller cemetery Wednesday, Feb. 13. [Rogers Democrat 2/21/24]

ROLLER, Julia Ann - Julia Ann Roller was born January 6, 1848 and died May 4, 1924 at the age of 76 years, three months and 28 days. She lived a life of usefulness for she was devoted to her parents, her relatives and her friends. Her home was where her services were most sorely needed. She was the chief servant and nurse of her sister and many relatives who have gone before her. In her last suffering, so long as conscious, she importuned with her Savior for relief and to take her to her home in the fair beyond. We, her relatives and friends who survive her, may confidently believe that while her body is now molding in its parent dust, her soul is blooming in eternal day. [Rogers Democrat 5/8/24]

ROUSE, John A. - Rogers friends received word a few days ago of the death at Kansas City of J.A. Rouse, a former well known Benton county citizen who lived for many years northwest of Rogers on the old Bentonville road. The Rouse family is well remembered by the older residents. Mr. Rouse had lived in Kansas City for a number of years but visited Rogers several times. [Rogers Democrat 5/8/24]

{The following is clipped from a Kansas City paper. The deceased is a former Rogers resident} John A. Rouse, age 74, passed away Thursday night at the home, 2400 East Ninth. Survived by wife, Mrs. Julia Rouse; six sons, Albert Rouse, Perry, Okla.; Walter Rouse, Indianapolis; Lawrence and Lewis Rouse, Los Angeles; Arthur Rouse, Oxford, Neb.; Theodore Rouse, Fairmount Park; two daughters, Mrs. William Gibson, Gainesville, Texas; Mrs. C.A McCleary, Los Angeles; three brothers, Burnam, H.T. and Marion Rouse; four sisters, Mrs. J.L. Sublett and Mrs. Susan Jeffries of Hallsville,

Mo.; Mrs. B.P. Owing of Cope, Colo; Mrs. Fannie Kelley of Roseville, Cal. Funeral services at Mrs. C.L. Forster's chapel Monday, 2 p.m. Burial in Mt. Washington. [Rogers Daily Post 5/6/24]

RUDDICK, Pearl Louise MANN - {from Central} Pearl Louise Mann was born near Brightwater, Ark. on July 6th, 1885. Departed this life March 23, 1924 at the age of 38 years, 8 months and 17 days. She was married to Thomas Ruddick on Sept. 18, 1901 and to this union were born seven children, three boys and four girls, all of whom were with her during her last illness and death. She was converted at the age of 16 years and united with the Methodist church and lived a consistent member until God bade the angels to bear her spirit into the haven of everlasting peace and joy. She leaves seven children, two sisters, one brother and a large number of other friends to mourn her death. Mr. Ruddick preceded her in death in 1920. The family wish to thank the many friends who were so kind in assisting to help care for the loving one who has gone, during her sickness and death. [Benton County Democrat 4/3/24] [Rogers Democrat 3/27/24] An especially sad obituary notice comes from Central neighborhood recording the death of Mrs. Pearl Ruddick, aged 38 years, 8 months and 17 days, leaving seven children, three boys and four girls, leaving them without either parent, the father, Thomas Reddick{?} having passed away March 4, 1920. She is also survived by her mother, two sisters and one brother. She was born near Brightwater, Ark. [Rogers Daily Post 3/28/24]

RUMLEY, baby - {from Walnut Hill, for last week} George Williams said he expected to put in 52 Sundays at Sunday school the past year and he kept his promise well until the last Sunday when he was called to Walnut Hill in the forenoon to make a grave for Bud Rumley's baby and to Liberty in the afternoon to conduct a funeral for Bill Myers' baby. [Rogers Democrat 1/10/24]

RUSSELL, Marie - Mrs. Marie Russell, wife of Frank Russell, living 6 miles northwest of Bentonville on the Sweaney place, died Tuesday of last week of leakage of the heart. She passed away while sitting in a chair which she had been compelled to occupy for the past 8 weeks. Burial was made in the Miller cemetery. Mrs. Russell was about 50 years of age and is survived by her husband and 3 children. [Benton County Record 3/21/124]

RUTHERFORD, Mrs. N.C. - Mrs. N.C. Rutherford, mother of Mrs. Alice Hartwick of this city, died at the home of a sister in Greenwood, Ark. Wednesday morning. Death was due to a fall which Mrs. Rutherford received in Fort Smith about two weeks ago. She was 80 years of age and is survived by eight children. Rev. James Robinson of Fort Smith and formerly pastor of the Baptist church here, conducted the funeral services yesterday in Greenwood. [Benton County Record 3/28/24]

SAGER, William - {from Prairie Creek} T.E. Sager received the sad news that his brother, William, died the 5th at the home of his son, Henry, at Muskogee, Okla. [Rogers Democrat 2/14/24]

SANDERS, Byrd HENDREN - Mrs. Byrd Sanders, daughter of Joe Hendren, died in St. Louis last week and the body was taken to Southwest City for burial. Mrs. Sanders was a niece of Fate and N.B. Hendren and Mrs. W.H. Austin. [Gravette News Herald 3/21/24]

SANDOE, Calvin - Calvin Sandoe, living near Sulphur Springs, who was well known at Gravette, died on Sunday, Sept. 21 at about the age of 75 years. [Gravette News Herald 10/3/24]

SATTERFIELD, Mary YOUNG - Death has again entered our midst and taken the much beloved wife of James Satterfield who died at her home on Sunday evening, Jan. 25 about 5:30. She fell peacefully asleep. Mary Young was born Aug. 20, 1859 in Gilmore Co., Georgia. She was united in marriage to James Satterfield July 18, 1876 at Summerville, Ga., Chattanooga Co. and was permitted to live a happy married life for about 48 years. Aunt Mary, as she was familiarly called, gave her heart to God when quite young and lived a consistent christian life. Two children were born to this union, also she reared two grandchildren, Ernest and Oma Dodson, whom they had cared for since they were quite small. Oma is married and living in Oklahoma while Ernest stayed with them and helped to care for them in their declining years with the exception of while he served in the world war. To know this good woman was to love her, she always had a smile and kind word for all and made friends with all she met. She leaves a husband and two children, Allie Satterfield of Highfill and Mrs. Monroe Fritz of Oklahoma, and ten grandchildren. One sister, Mrs. William Harris of Highfill, who have all through their lives been permitted to live close together and great love existed between these sisters, more than common. Funeral services were conducted by Rev. A.L. Sapp of Mason Valley Tuesday afternoon then she was tenderly laid to rest in the Douglas cemetery to await the resurrection morn. A Friend, Anna F. Mallory. [Gentry Journal–Advance 2/15/24]

SAWREY, Clinton A. - Clinton A. Sawrey, world war veteran who died in the veterans hospital at Fort Line, Colo., was buried Sunday with military honors in the national cemetery at Fayetteville where his wife and two children live. The deceased was a younger brother of Virgil Sawrey, a former well known Rogers boy who is now in Long Beach, Calif. [Rogers Democrat 12/18/24]

SCHELL, Robert - Robert Schell died at his home near the Donovan Schoolhouse, six miles northeast of Gravette Monday morning, succumbing to injuries received when he fell from the barn loft last Thursday. His back was injured and the injuries were fatal. He is survived by his widow and three grown children. Burial was made at Mt. Pleasant Tuesday. [Benton County Record 1/4/24]

SCOTT, Joseph W. - {from Gentry} Joseph W. Scott died at his home in Gentry on Sunday evening, April 6th, 1924 at the age of 65 years. The immediate cause of his death was sclerosis coronary arteris. The body was

shipped to Broken Bow, Neb. for burial. Broken Bow was his former home before coming to Gentry. Mr. Scott had been in the feed business in Gentry but sold out the first of the year. [Benton County Record 4/11/24]
J.W. Scott died Sunday night at his home here. Mr. Scott had been in failing health for some time but his condition was not considered as so serious. He died rather suddenly and unexpectedly at this time. He leaves a wife to mourn his loss and had made a multitude of friends during his residence in Gentry. Short funeral services were held a the home Tuesday morning by Rev. Watson and the remains were shipped to Broken Bow, Neb. for burial. Mrs. Scott and her daughter, Miss Edith Baker, accompanied them. [Gentry Journal–Advance 4/11/24]

SCOTT, Mrs. J.C. {CAMPBELL, Wright} Mrs. Walter Wright, Misses Flora and Bobbie Blake and M.C. Cunningham motored to Fayetteville Thursday to attend the funeral of Mrs. J.C. Scott. [Benton County Record 2/29/24]
Mrs. J.C. Scott, formerly of Bentonville, died at her home in Fayetteville on Tuesday, February 19th, 1924 at the age of 76 years. She is survived by her husband, J.C. Scott, and one son, A.D. Wright, besides a brother, Frank Campbell, postmaster of Fayetteville, and a grandson, Bobbie Wright. Funeral services were held at the Methodist Church in Fayetteville on Thursday afternoon and interment was made in the cemetery there. Mrs. Scott lived in Bentonville a number of years ago and has many friends who will regret to hear of her death. [Benton County Record 2/29/24]

SEAMSTER, Francis Marion - F. Marion Seamster, one of the best known citizens of Benton county and a justice of the peace for over thirty years, died suddenly at his home in Rogers Thursday, June 5, 1924 at the age of 77 years. Death is said to have been caused by heart failure. Mr. Seamster was apparently in good health that morning. Just before noon he came into the house and fell to the floor, dying shortly afterwards. Funeral services were held at Tuck's Chapel, west of Avoca, Saturday afternoon where he had preached for many years. Rev. Stephen Morton preached the funeral while the Masonic services were conducted by George Miser of Bestwater and R.F. Renfro of Avoca, two old members of that organization, with which Mr. Seamster had been connected for over 50 years. The attendance at the funeral was one of the largest ever gathered in this section. Francis Marion Seamster was born in Lancaster, Mo. in 1847. When a young man he moved to McDonald county, Mo. where he taught school and was county superintendent, a position he held for a number of years. Dr. W.D. Foster of Gravette, who taught school when a young man, received his first license to teach from Mr. Seamster. It was while following this occupation that he met Miss Amanda Dunagin, the daughter of Rev. Jasper Dunagin, a well known preacher in the early days who homesteaded the land where the town of Avoca now stands. The two were married in 1872 and located on a farm just west of the Dunagin farm.

Five children were born to this union, all of whom survive him. These are John Seamster of Rogers; Robert Seamster of Osawatomie, Kansas; George Seamster of Wichita, Kansas; Mrs. Cora Snodgrass of Pineville, Mo. and Mrs. Carrie Massey of Kansas City. Also four brothers, Dr. Lee Seamster, Mineral Wells, Texas; B. Seamster, Afton, Okla.; B. Seamster, Caverna, Mo. and M.L. Isaiah Seamster, Hiwasse and two sisters, Mrs. Amanda Campbell of Bentonville and Mrs. John Headrick of Kansas City. Also one half sister, Mrs. James Jamison of Phelps City, Mo. Mrs. Seamster died in 1899. She was a sister of John R. Dunagin of Gravette. Later he married Miss Mollie Allred, who survives him. Mason, a son of this marriage, lives in Kansas City but was unable to come to the funeral. Three small children and the widow survive the husband and father. Mr. Seamster, while being a substantial farmer, also devoted quite a little time to preaching. He was one of the pioneer berry growers in Benton county and lived to see this industry grow until whole train loads of strawberries were shipped from this section annually. In 1907 he was elected to the state legislature where he served with great credit to his county. He also served as a justice of the peace for 30 years and always took a prominent part in the work of the levying court and could always be found on the progressive side of every measure. In his passing Benton county has lost one of its worthy citizens and noble men. [Benton County Record 6/13/24] [Rogers Democrat 6/12/24] [Rogers Daily Post 6/5/24]
Mr. and Mrs. Alvin Seamster and Mr. and Mrs. Jess Seamster attended the funeral of their uncle, F.M. Seamster, at Tuck's Chapel west of Avoca last Saturday. [Benton County Record 6/13/24]

SEDWICK, Ben Frank - {from The Fayetteville Democrat} Ben Frank Sedwick, aged 34, graduate of the College of Engineering, University of Arkansas, class of 1911, and first assistant to the chief engineer of the Baltimore and Ohio railroad, who died at Chicago Sunday, will be buried Wednesday at Baltimore. Mr. Sedwick was one of a family of five brilliant brothers and two sisters and was the son of Mr. B.W. Sedwick of this place. His mother, who resides at 342 St. Charles street, was called to his bedside in Chicago at the home of his brother, Tom Sedwick, a short while ago. Meager information has been received of the death or funeral arrangements. Tom Sedwick, also a graduate of the University of Arkansas, 1902, is now second vice-president of the Rock Island System with headquarters in Chicago, and with his mother, accompanied the body to Baltimore. Jim Sedwick, a second brother and field agent for the Midland Valley railroad, Fort Smith, is expected to attend the funeral services as is a sister, Mrs. Ben Harden of Little Rock, formerly Miss Bess Sedwick of Fayetteville. The fourth brother, Richard Sedwick, holding a government position in Panama, will be unable to be present but Mrs. Fred Shuber, Kansas City, will probably join the family funeral party. Mr. Sedwick is a nephew of Miss Minnie Dunlap of this place and a nephew of Louis Dunlap of Monett.

***** Mr. Sedwick, who is survived by his wife and the relatives mentioned above, is well remembered in Bentonville where he spent much of his boyhood. [Benton County Democrat 4/3/24]

SHAILER, W.H. - W.H. Shailer, a former resident of Sulphur Springs, died at his home in Mound Valley, Kansas July 4th. He was well advanced in years and a Civil War veteran, having served in the Union army. Mr. Shailer was a Delaware Indian and a prominent member of his tribe. [Benton County Record 7/11/24]

SHARP, George W. - George W. Sharp, who resided near Row, Okla. died June 19th, 1924, the result of the accidental discharge of a revolver. Mr. Sharp was living alone and that night he started to take the bed covers to lie down near a door when the firearm fell to the floor and discharged. The bullet hit him in the leg and ranged upward to the abdomen. His shouts brought assistance and he was hastened to Siloam Springs but died before the hospital was reached. W.A. Sharp of Maysville and another brother were with him when he died. Mr. Sharp was born Dec. 19, 1873; married to Miss Nina Lamm in 1899 and had three children. Dr. W.A. McDonald of Gravette conducted the funeral and burial was in Ward cemetery near Maysville June 20th. [Gravette News Herald 6/27/24]

SHARP, Mollie J. - Mollie J. Sharp, a well known resident of Bentonville, died at her home on West A Street early Tuesday morning, July 29th following a second stroke of paralysis that occurred last Wednesday. Since that time she has been unconscious. The first stroke occurred about a year ago and she has been gradually getting worse since that time. She was born in Marion county, Ark. on Dec. 26th, 1846 and came to Bentonville about 50 years ago. For a number of years she and her sister, Mrs. R.D. Steward, ran the Globe Hotel, which stood at the time, 1878, on the site of the U.S. Weather Bureau. When this was built, about 20 years ago, the hotel was moved to the lots east. This was the leading hotel in this section for many years and was called for many years the Texas House. The post office was also located in this building at one time when "Sheep" Davis was postmaster. Aunt Mollie, as she was familiarly called, is survived by one daughter, Mrs. Dora Yoder, of the home address, and two sisters, Mrs. R.D. Steward of Eufala, Okla. and Mrs. George Bennett of Catale, Okla., both of whom were present during her last illness. Mrs. Willie Cline, living east of town on the Jack Bates farm, is a niece. Funeral services, which were conducted from the house Tuesday afternoon, were largely attended. She leaves a large number of old friends who will miss her. During the earlier days of her life it was filled with acts of kindness to both the needy and afflicted. During cases of severe illness it was Aunt Mollie who was sent for and who nursed them back to health. [Benton County Record 8/1/24]

SHARP, Wm. Edward - Wm. E. Sharp died Sunday, June 15th at his farm southwest of Rogers near Colville. He was 72 years old and had lived on the place where he died for the past three years. The family came here

from Texas and the body was sent to El Paso, that state, by the A.D. Callison Undertaking Co. where funeral services will be held and interment made. The deceased is survived by his wife, Mrs. Margaret Sharp, two sons and one daughter: I.C. Sharp, Wm. Edward Sharp, Jr. and Miss Drury Sharp, all of El Paso, Texas. [Rogers Democrat 6/19/24]
Mr. Wm. Edward Sharp, beloved husband of Mrs. Margaret Sharp, entered into rest on the 15th of June, 1924 at 1:30 a.m. at his home near Colville, where he has lived the past three years, at the age of 72 years. Mr. Sharp is survived by two sons, Mr. I.C. Sharp and Mr. Wm. Edward Sharp, Jr. and by one daughter, Miss R. Drury Sharp, all of El Paso, Texas. The funeral and interment will be held at El Paso and the arrangements will be in charge of A.D. Callison Undertaking Company. [Rogers Daily Post 6/16/24]

SHAW, W.B. - {from Clantonville} A telegram was received Saturday night that W.B. Shaw, Mr. Baker's son-in-law, was accidentally killed in Kansas City. [Rogers Democrat 7/24/24]

SHELL, John - John Shell, a farmer residing near Mt. Pleasant, fell from his hayloft last Friday while feeding his stock and sustained a broken back. He was found in a helpless condition from which he never recovered, dying Sunday night. Mr. Shell leaves a family. Burial was made in Mt. Pleasant Cemetery Tuesday afternoon. [Gravette News Herald 1/4/24]

SHELTON, Annie VINCENHELLER - {from The Whitesboro {Tex.} News Record} Mrs. W.M. Shelton, wife of Rev. W.M. Shelton, was found dead in bed Saturday morning, November 8, 1924. Altho Mrs. Shelton had been in failing health for some time she retired Friday night in good spirits and seemed to be feeling better than usual. Her husband, rising before her and preparing breakfast as usual, on calling her had no response and on investigation found that she had passed to the beyond. Mrs. Annie V. Shelton, the daughter of Geo. and Elizabeth Jean Vincenheller, was born in Jeffersontown, Ky. Jan. 23, 1848. Here she was reared and educated and grew to womanhood. She never knew any other home till her marriage. Her early training and environment were most favorable to the development of both mind and heart and under these conditions she grew into a well rounded Christian character and was well equipped for the place she was destined to fill in her life work. On October 10, 1877 she was married to Rev. W.M. Shelton. To this union four children were born, two dying in infancy. The other two, Will Shelton of Bonham and Paul Shelton of Sherman, survive her. The funeral services were conducted at the M.E. Church by Revs. D.F. Fuller of Grand Prairie and F.B. Wheeler of Royse City, assisted by Revs. Jones and Alderson of this city. Besides her husband and two sons she leaves seven grandchildren to mourn her loss, also one sister, Mrs. W.T. Cox of Eureka Springs, Ark. Interment took place at Oakwood Cemetery where she was laid to rest under a mound of flowers. ***** A host of people at Gravette and Decatur will regret to learn of Bro. Shelton's bereavement. He writes that on the evening before her death

Mrs. Shelton asked him to read the News Herald to her first, out of several papers he had just received. Mrs. Shelton did not die, says Bro. Shelton, "She just went to sleep here and awoke in glory land." [Gravette News Herald 11/21/24]

SHIELDS, Silas Morton - Silas Morton Shields was born in Indiana June 7, 1861; died November 25, 1924 at the home of his niece, Mrs. Roberts, southwest of Gravette. He was married to Mary McAmama and nine children were born to them, four of whom survive. They are Murtie Malone, Drumright, Okla.; Will Shields of Decatur, Ark.; Elmer Shields of Enid, Okla.; Jesse Shields of Pawhuska, Okla. One brother, Joe Shields, resides at Gravette. The funeral was conducted by Mrs. Killingsworth and burial was in Dow cemetery. [Gravette News Herald 12/12/24]

SHORES, Nancy J. - In the death Thursday, June 26th of Mrs. Nancy J. Shores, wife of John F. Shores, another old pioneer has gone. She came to Arkansas half a century ago, settling on a farm two miles south of Bentonville where she lived continuously until three years ago when she moved to Rogers, on Spring street, and has been lovingly cared for by her daughter, Miss Maud. Also she enjoyed the pleasures of three great-grandchildren, the children of Ray Blevins, an employee at the Ford service station, and three others. Mrs. Shores was a native of Missouri. She was married at the age of sixteen and was the mother of twelve children. She has known sorrow too, having given four of them back to their Maker, in one month, from a contagious disease. The others are grown and have been assets to the communities in which they lived, reflecting the wonderful influence and counsel of a mother who lived and toiled and taught and loved in so doing, her work of rearing a splendid family of men and women, the personnel being: Mrs. Ferrestine, Bartlesville, Okla.; J.E. Shores, Walla Walla, Wash.; Mrs. W.W. Hedges, Oklahoma City, Okla.; C.A. Shores, Sun Prairie, Mont.; Lewis A. Shores, Cave Springs; J.M. Shores and Mrs. F.R. Blevins, Bentonville and Miss Maud Shores, Rogers. All except the two in Montana and Washington have kept loving vigils during her last illness of several months and were present at the funeral services Friday at the Church of Christ conducted by J.H. Martin, an old friend of the family. The interment was in the Hart cemetery by the side of the father who passed away on Christmas Day seventeen years ago. Grandmother Shores, as she was known to all her friends, is at rest but the memory of her long useful life of 81 years will long remain and will be worthy of emulation. [Rogers Democrat 7/3/24] [Benton County Record 7/4/24] [Rogers Daily Post 6/27/24]

SICKLIN, L.W. - Springdale, March 24.- L.W. Sicklin, who was sixty-five years old, committed suicide on his farm two miles north of Springdale Monday afternoon by tying a rope around his neck and jumping from a stack of hay, his neck being broken in the fall. His body was found by an employee that evening. Mr. Sicklin had sent his wife to Fayetteville about noon to do some shopping. She returned at three o'clock and failing to find her husband, sent the hired man in search of him. The body was found suspended from a rafter in the barn. Failing health and worry over financial affairs is believed to have been the cause of the tragedy. Two weeks ago Mr. Sicklin left a note in the house saying that he was contemplating suicide. Mr. Sicklin owned considerable property in this vicinity. He came here five years ago from Moberly, Mo. He is survived by his wife and a son who lives at Cleveland, Ohio. The funeral will be at Moberly. [Rogers Democrat 3/27/24]

SIMPSON, Mr. - R.J. Simpson received a message Tuesday morning announcing the death of his brother in Eureka, Ill. Monday night. He was 83 years old and was the oldest boy of the family. Mr. Simpson did not go to Illinois as he could not possibly get there in time for the funeral Wednesday afternoon at 2:30. [Gentry Journal–Advance 2/15/24]

SITTON, Wiley C. - Wiley C. Sitton died on October 16th, 1924 on the old homestead, near Decatur, where he had lived continuously for the past 45 years, coming to this country from Georgia in 1874. He was born in that state on May 22nd,1846 - being at the time of his death aged 78 years, four months and 24 days. He taught school for a number of years when a young man, Esquire E. Austin being one of his pupils. He was married in 1876 to Sarah E. Fair, who died in 1904. He was a member of the M.E. Church. Funeral services were held at Bethel Friday, conducted by Rev. McCarroll. Burial was made at 3 p.m. beside his wife. A good man and neighbor, an upright and honorable citizen is gone. Just before his death he called in his lifelong friend and neighbor, Lige Austin, to make his will and act as administrator. [Benton County Record 10/24/24]

Wiley C. Sitton, following a stroke of paralysis, died Thursday, October 16, 1924 at his home south of Gravette. He was born in Georgia May 22, 1846 and was aged 78 years. He came to Arkansas in 1876 and was married to Sarah E. Fair in 1876. This wife died in 1904 and Mr. Sitton again was married in 1908 to Lonnie Dye. To the latter union were born two daughters, Mrs. Alva Ford and Miss Irene Sitton. Mr. Sitton was a pioneer resident of this region, active as a teacher and farmer, and he leaves quite an estate. Many years he maintained what was known as Clementine postoffice at his farm, the same being discontinued when rural mail service started. Mr. Sitton was a member of the Methodist church. His funeral was held at Bethel Friday, Oct. 17th, Rev. W.H. McCarroll conducting the same. Burial was in Bethel cemetery. [Gravette News Herald 10/24/24]

SIVER, J.L. - J.L. Siver died at his home in Bentonville Saturday, August 2, 1924 at the age of 84 years. The body was taken to Decatur for burial Sunday. He is survived by his widow, Mrs. Mary G. Siver. Mr. Siver was born in New York state in 1839 and served as a soldier in the Union army. He has been a resident of Bentonville for about three years. [Benton County Record 8/8/24]

SKAGGS, Alonzo A. - A.A. Skaggs, who became afflicted with what was diagnosed as pellagra three weeks ago, died at his home in Oldtown last Friday, Aug. 29th, 1924 at 10:15 p.m. aged about 57 years. Alonzo A. Skaggs was born near Raleigh, Marys county, Mo. June 7th, 1868, the son of Mr. and Mrs. Elijah J. Skaggs. When eight years of age he moved with his parents to this community and except for a few trips to Texas spent his life in or near Gravette. The past few years he has conducted a barber shop and had a host of customers and friends. On Aug. 15, 1894 he was married to Miss Effa E. Wilson. Three children survive: George Skaggs of Kansas City; Mrs. Tisha Martin, Tulsa, Okla. and Bonita of Gravette. Mrs. Skaggs died Sept. 29, 1917. On Oct. 27, 1920 Mr. Skaggs and Mrs. Bessie Barnett were married. The wife, step-son, Leslie Barnett, his three children, his parents, now at Pawhuska, Okla., two brothers, Marion of Gorman, Tex. and Charlie of Pawhuska and other relatives, survive. The funeral was conducted by his pastor, Rev. T.M. Norris, at the Baptist church Saturday afternoon and burial took place in the I.O.O.F. cemetery. The relatives have the sympathy of everyone in their bereavement. [Gravette News Herald 9/5/24]
In the obituary of A.A. Skaggs, for lack of information, we omitted the fact that Mr. Skaggs leaves two sisters, Mrs. Stella Berry of Tulsa, Okla. and Mrs. Etta Palmer, Carrol, Ida. [Gravette News Herald 9/12/24]

SKELTON, Henry - Henry Skelton of Seligman was instantly killed Tuesday morning when a truck he was driving was struck by northbound Frisco passenger train No. 4. Skelton was thrown 75 feet, falling on the track and the train passing over the body before it could be stopped. The wagon was completely demolished but the team escaped injury we are told. Skelton was about 35 years old and most of his life had been spent in or near Seligman. He was a member of the transfer company of Skelton Bros. of Seligman. He is survived by his wife, who is a niece of Mrs. George Cline of Rogers, and a daughter fourteen years old. Mrs. Skelton was in Rogers recently for an operation and was completely prostrated by the shock of the accident. [Rogers Democrat 9/25/24] [Benton County Record 9/26/24]

SMARTT, Essie Catherine PYLES - On February 17th, 1831 at the little town of Abbeville, South Carolina, an infant daughter made her advent into the home of Mr. and Mrs. Lewis Pyles and was christened Essie Catherine. Her parents, being among the most influential in the community, gave her every advantage possible so that as the years went by the unfolding petals of a true Christian character developed and gave forth its influence to the world which will bloom more abundantly in eternity. In girlhood she gave her heart to God and ever after to the close of life was a true Christian. She was the eldest member of the Bentonville Presbyterian Church and when she was able to do so was regular in attendance upon its services. In 1848 she was happily married to Dr. John Smartt, who preceded her to the grave some twenty-five years, leaving her to brave life's battles alone. But she faltered not along life's way and trusting in Him who had promised strength and grace for every day until the 27th day of January 1924 when her spirit flew to realms beyond - and her loved ones said "she is gone." She leaves two daughters, Mrs. Sue A. Terry and Mrs. W.A. Burks, of this place and two sons, L.P. Smartt of Vinita, Okla. and A.P. Smartt of El Paso, Texas. Some of these have "silver threads among the gold," reminding them that they, too, are nearing life's sunset. She also leaves eight grandchildren and ten great-grandchildren. More than half a century of her busy and useful life has been spent in Bentonville. Her battles have been fought and a faithful service rendered to the community. To her the struggles and burden-bearing of earth are ended and we trust that like one who awakes from a troubled dream, she has awakened to see life's endless morning break and know herself at home with the blest. And so, with bated breath and hearts bereft we bow above the bier and in benedictions soft and low, breathe that sad, sweet name, "Mother!" W.A. Burks. [Benton County Record 2/1/24]

SMITH, A.T. - Dance, Bad Whiskey, Man Killed - These five words tell the tale of a tragedy that happened at a country dance in the eastern part of Madison county Saturday night. Here is the story as reported: John Cummings and his cousin, A.T. Smith, got into a quarrel at the home of a farmer, W.J. Lawson. Both had been drinking moonshine, it is stated, and after more words Cummings drew a revolver and shot Smith. The wounded man was taken to the hospital in Fayetteville where he died Sunday night. His murderer escaped and has not been captured. [Benton County Record 11/14/24]

SMITH, Alfred Thomas - Alfred Thomas Smith died Sunday at his home at Springdale at the age of 63 years. He was born in Hindsville, Madison county and his life had been spent in Northwest Arkansas. He is survived by his wife and ten children. [Rogers Democrat 9/4/24]

SMITH, Don D. - Don D. Smith, a former Bentonville boy, died at Fort Sam Houston federal hospital, near San Antonio, Texas Tuesday, March 18th, 1924 following a lingering illness. He was 22 years of age and had grown up in Bentonville. Up until a year before his death he had been in splendid health and had been active and interested in farming but had enlisted in the army in 1922. He is survived by his mother, Mrs. T.M. Burrows, one brother, George Smith, and three sisters, Mrs. Lydia Banks of the home address, Mrs. Bert Spencer of Waggoner, Okla. and Mrs. Wm. Watkins of Webb City, Missouri. Funeral services were held at the M.E. Church at 10 o'clock Saturday morning and interment was made in the City Cemetery. [Benton County Record 3/28/24]

SMITH, J.W. - J.W. Smith, father of Earl Smith, former demonstration agent of Benton county, dropped dead at his home in Fayetteville on Saturday afternoon. Death was due to heart failure. Mr. Smith was about 60 years of age and was well known in Benton county. For many years he has been an agent for the Guardian Life Insurance Company. He was born in Marion county, Ark. in 1863 and has lived for the past 15 years in Fayetteville. Besides his widow he is survived by two sons - Earl of Muskogee, Okla. and Dallas Smith of Dallas, Texas. [Benton County Record 3/14/24]

SMITH, Margaret - Miss Margaret Smith, daughter of W.H. Smith who lives south of Vaughn, was born September 20th {no year given} and died October 9th, 1924. Her mother died December 1914. For three years she had been under the care of a physician, spending sixteen months of this time in the sanatorium at Booneville, this state. From this institution she returned to the home of her father early this past spring where she remained until the time of her death. She was a member of the Baptist Church at Mason Valley and a consecrated Christian girl. Surviving her are four brothers: Hugh of Portland, Oregon; Allen and Beryl of Ojai, Calif.; Spofford of Springfield, Missouri and two sisters, Mrs. Opal McBee and Lottie of Vaughn. Services were conducted by her pastor, Rev. L.F. Rice of Springdale, at the Barron Cemetery. In accord with her wishes the following young ladies, former classmates, acted as pall-bearers: Bethel Douglas, Leon Gholson, Esther Gholson of Mason Valley; Fern Grimsley, Grace Turner and Ruby Rice of Vaughn. The father of the young lady and the surviving members of the family wish to express their sincere thanks to all their friends for their kindly ministrations during the death and burial of their loved one, also during her long illness. [Benton County Record 10/17/24]

SMITH, Mr. and Mrs. Lew - A double tragedy occurred at Noel, Mo., five miles north of Sulphur Springs, Sunday when Lew Smith, aged 74, shot his young wife, 36 years of age. Mrs. Smith was shot three times and died about 20 minutes later. After the shooting Smith turned his revolver on himself. The shot grazed the side of his head. Not being successful in taking his own life in this manner, he drew a knife and cut his throat. This proved unsuccessful also so he went out to the barn and after securing a rope hanged himself. No particulars have been obtained as to what lead up to the killing. Smith and his wife had been married about 15 years and have a son 14 years old. They separated some time ago and Mrs. Smith sued for a divorce. Smith, who has been absent from Noel for some time, returned home Friday. He called at his wife's home Sunday evening and after being there a short time a shot was heard. Mrs. Smith came running out of the house and her husband again shot her. Smith is an old resident of Noel and is well known. He was formerly a saloon keeper. [Benton County Record 8/22/24]

SMITH, Mrs. Albert - The body of Mrs. Albert Smith, a former Rogers resident, arrived Tuesday night from Chelsea, Okla. and was interred yesterday afternoon in the Rogers cemetery by the side of her husband, Albert Smith, who died some six or seven years ago. The body was accompanied by Miss Zada Jones and a nephew, Floyd Rayburn, both of Chelsea. Mrs. Smith has no living relatives and had been living with her husband's people. Brief services were conducted at the cemetery by Rev. R.C. Lucke. [Rogers Democrat 8/21/24]

SMITH, Thorn - Fayetteville, Nov. 10.- Thorn Smith, 36 years old, victim of a shooting at a country dance hear the Madison county line shortly before midnight Saturday, died at the city hospital here Sunday night at 9:30 after an emergency operation had been performed in an effort to save his life. The trouble in which Smith was shot arose at a dance at W.J. Lawson's home, which is, according to officers, in the extreme west part of Washington county, only about 100 yards from the Madison line. Following the shooting Smith's assailant, whose name is Cummings, disappeared into Madison county. No arrests have been made. Cummings is a brother-in-law and also a cousin of Smith. Two shots were fired, one taking effect through the abdomen, perforating the intestines several times. Smith was rushed to the hospital but was too seriously wounded to rally. He is a Madison county man, the son of Lee Smith, a well known farmer. He is survived by his wife and two children, a daughter two years old and a son four years old. [Rogers Democrat 11/6/24]

SOOTER, Matilda Cougar - Mrs. Matilda Sooter, a resident of Benton county for over 50 years, died at her home in Hiwasse on Thursday, July 3rd, 1924 at the age of 83 years. Although she has been ailing for the past year it was only the last week her condition was serious. Heart trouble was the cause of her death. Mrs. Sooter was born in Illinois in 1841 where she married Alex Cougar. They moved to Arkansas about 1870 and located near Bethel on the Spavinaw. After the death of Mr. Cougar she was married to Elisha Sooter, a well known resident of the Gravette neighborhood and a Confederate veteran. He died about 11 years ago. Mrs. Sooter was a kind and loving neighbor, a good mother and a true Christian. She is survived by five children - Miss Nellie Cougar of the home address; Mrs. Laura Hastings of Fayetteville; Mrs. Larkin Ford of New Mexico; Mrs. Jessie Bagby and Mrs. Sturgeon of Oklahoma. The funeral was largely attended, the Rev. E.L. Boyles of Gravette officiating. Interment was made in the Bethel cemetery. [Benton County Record 7/11/24]

SPARKMAN, J.M. - Springdale, August 2.- Dr. J.M. Sparkman, 68 years old, died at 7:00 o'clock Friday morning at his home in Springdale. Funeral services were held at the residence Saturday afternoon, conducted by Reverend M.L. McDowell, pastor of the First Baptist Church, and burial was in the Roller cemetery near Seligman. Dr. Sparkman was born January 20, 1856 in Warren county, Tenn. He was a practicing physician for many years in Barry county, Missouri, coming to Springdale about sixteen years ago. He had been ill for several months. [Rogers Democrat 8/7/24]

SPENCER, Mrs. - {from Lowell} W.H. Cowan and Stanley Martin were called to Elkins Friday to attend the funeral of Mrs. Spencer who died on the morning of their leaving. Mrs. Spencer was the mother of Mrs. Cowan. [Benton County Record 5/23/24]

STALLCUP, Eliza - Mrs. Eliza Stallcup, wife of Los Stallcup, died at her home just east of the old Bethel Church early Monday morning at the age of 65 years. Funeral services were held that afternoon with interment in the Bethel cemetery. Besides her husband she is survived by two daughters, Mrs. Henry Halpain and Mrs. Tom Mathews of Oklahoma. Mrs. Stallcup was one of the oldest residents in this section and has lived here nearly 50 years. [Benton County Record 9/19/24]

STANLEY, W.R. - W.R. Stanley died on May 4th, 1924 at the age of 83 years, five months and two days. Mr. Stanley was well known throughout this and Washington county, having made his home for the last 30 years at the old Stanley farm which lies between Cave Springs and Elm Springs. He has left to mourn his loss a host of friends - one sister, Mrs. Sallie Tiles of San Antonio, Texas; five daughters and four sons - Mrs. Dollie Parr of Grinnell, Kansas; Mrs. Anna Oakes of Oakley, Kansas; Mrs. Mary Honest of Doretta N.M.; Mrs. Nellie Woodell of Elm Springs, Ark.; Mrs. Laura Skinner of Springtown, Ark.; H.C. and J.C. Stanley of Gans, Okla.; S.T. Stanley of San Francisco, Cal.; Charles Stanley of McComb, Ill. and 31 grandchildren. In 1853 he was united in marriage with Miss Anna Moore of Illinois, who departed this life 27 years ago. He served with great distinction during the Civil War, having enlisted at the beginning and stayed with the ranks of the Gray until the close of this great struggle. Owing to the poor state of health which fell upon him last fall he was compelled to leave his old home, which was so dear to his heart, and go to Grinnell, Kansas where he remained with his daughter, Mrs. Parr, until his death. The funeral services were conducted at the Community Church at Grinnell, Kansas and the remains were lovingly laid to rest in the cemetery at Oakley, Kansas. [Benton County Record 5/23/24]

STARR, Mrs. Harvey - Mrs. Harvey Starr, who spent some time here last fall for her health and drinking the water of Kidney Springs, died recently in Eureka Springs where she was spending the winter. An attack of flu, which developed later into pneumonia, was the cause of her death. The body was sent back to her old home in Frankfort, S.D. for burial. [Benton County Record 3/14/24]

STEVENS, Mrs. J.K. - {from New Hope} We were sorry to hear of the death of Mrs. J.K. Stevens, which occurred August ninth at the home of her son-in-law, F.R. Nash, near Cassville, Missouri. She was buried beside her husband at Purdy, Missouri. Mrs. Stevens was a former well known Rogers lady and lived for many years on South Fourth street and her many friends were only numbered by her acquaintances. [Rogers Democrat 8/28/24]

STEINBECK, Willis E. - Willis E. Steinbeck died yesterday at his home near the green house after several weeks illness, having been stricken with paralysis. His funeral was held this afternoon at 2:30, conducted by the Rev. J. Wilson Crichlow, the interment being in the City cemetery. Mr.

Steinbeck was born in Iowa but spent the greater part of his life in South Bend, Ind.. He was 68 years old and is survived by his wife and no children. He is best known by his love for flowers, many homes on the South side being made cheery by gifts of them which he raised when he and his wife lived in the little cottage that was located on the lot between the Applegate's home and where he raised such beautiful specimens that friends passed that way especially to admire them, which exemplifies his character, his love for all things in nature. [Rogers Daily Post 3/17/24]

STINEBECK, W.E. - W.E. Stinebeck, who had been confined to his home for several weeks following a paralytic stroke, died Sunday morning, March 16th at 12:10. Mr. Stinebeck and wife came to Rogers twelve years ago from Buchanan, Michigan, first occupying the cottage on West Poplar, now the home of Mr. and Mrs. Lockwood Searcy. At the time of his death they were living at 410 West Willow street and this place, as well as their former home, always attracted much attention and admiration because of the great variety of beautiful flowers Mr. Stinebeck delighted in raising. Funeral services were held Monday afternoon at 2:30 o'clock at the parlors of the Callison Undertaking Co., Rev. Crichlow of the Central Methodist church officiating. Interment was in the Rogers cemetery. Mr. Stinebeck was a native of Iowa where he was born January 21, 1859. Besides his wife he is survived by his mother, one sister and two brothers. [Rogers Democrat 3/20/24]

STITES, William R. - William R. Stites, a well-known farmer and old resident, died at his home near Siloam Springs on Sunday at the age of 80 years. Mr. Stites had been in ill health for several months. A few days ago pneumonia set in which resulted in his death. Funeral services were held from the home on Tuesday afternoon. [Benton County Record 2/22/24]

STOVER, William Riley - William Riley Stover died Friday at his home in Rogers on South Third street after a prolonged illness. He was 37 years old and leaves a wife and several children. [Rogers Democrat 8/21/24] {from Rogers} W.R. Stover died last Friday of tuberculosis and was buried Saturday afternoon. He was about 30 years of age. [Benton County Record 8/22/24]

STRACK, Carl - Miss Anna Hardwick of Gravette was married to Mr. Carl Strack at East St. Louis, Ill. on May 6th and her husband, who was a telephone lineman, was accidentally killed while at work on June 25th, only a month after the wedding. Mrs. Strack is in St. Louis this week closing up her affairs there to return to Gravette. [Gravette News Herald 7/11/24]

STRAIN, John A. - John A. Strain, a former resident of near Decatur, died suddenly at his home in Mason Valley on December 27th, 1923 at the age of 54 years. He was born in Polk county, Mo. on October 29th, 1969 where he grew to manhood. At the age of 37 he married Miss Addie Coffman, who died in 1898. In 1919 at Aldrich, Mo. he married Mrs. Sallie Williams. He engaged in business here a number of years and was also postmaster in that town. Later he moved to Arkansas and located on a farm near Decatur. He is survived by his wife, four brothers and three sisters. Burial was made in the Coffelt cemetery with Rev. R.F. Jones officiating. Mr. Strain confessed Christ at an early age and lived a faithful Christian life. He leaves behind him a host of friends and relatives to mourn his death. [Benton County Record 2/1/24]

STREETER, Judson H. - Judson H. Streeter, well known in this community, passed away on September 4, 1924 at Hamilton, Mo. at the home of his daughter after a lingering illness of four months. He was 80 years old on March 15, 1924. He was a veteran of the Civil war, belonging to Co. A, 6th Missouri Cavalry. He joined the Harker post at Gentry Oct. 1920. [Gentry Journal–Advance 10/10/24]

STRINGFELLOW, Granville - Granville Stringfellow died Thursday last, January 10th, at his home on North Fifth, No. 615, after a year or two of illness. He was 67 years, 11 months and 22 days old and had been a resident of Rogers since last fall when he built the home where he died. Funeral services were held at the First Christian church Friday afternoon at three o'clock, conducted by Rev. Harry Byrd Kline. The body was taken to the former home of Mr. Stringfellow at Rosehill, Iowa for burial. Mr. Stringfellow was a native of Iowa, having been born near Osceola. He was married to Florence Bacon in 1880 and to them were born four children, two of whom with the mother died some years ago. Two children are living, Mrs. Martha E. Moore of Garlington, Okla. and Prof. E. Stringfellow of Drake University, Des Moines, Iowa. In 1919 he married Mrs. Kittie Dunn at Fayetteville. She was a former Rogers citizen and owned property here and last year they decided to move here from Oklahoma to make this their home. [Rogers Democrat 1/17/24]

STROUD, Wilma - {from Hebron} W.C. Davis and wife and the Moser family attended the funeral of Wilma Stroud in Rogers Wednesday. She was the youngest daughter of Mr. and Mrs. Tinker Stroud and was their second girl to die in the past year. Each was afflicted with diabetes and it is very, very sad for the family. [Rogers Democrat 5/1/24]

STURDY, Eliza - {from Pea Ridge} Again death has called another of our old-time citizens. Mrs. Eliza Sturdy passed away on Wednesday, April 2nd, 1924 at the age of 76 years. She was ill but a short time. The funeral services were conducted by her pastor, Rev. M.L. Lark, assisted by Revs. John Hall and A.E. Carnahan. Interment was made in the Pea Ridge cemetery. Mrs. Sturdy was one of the oldest residents on Pea Ridge and has been a devoted member of the M.E. Church since childhood. [Benton County Record 4/11/24]

{from Pea Ridge} Edgar Fields, a representative of the Mutual Aid Union of Rogers, was here Tuesday and paid $1,000 to W.J. Sturdy on an insurance policy in the Union carried by his wife who died recently. [Benton County Record 5/16/24]

STURGIS, Mrs. William R. {DOUGHERTY} - Mrs. William R. Sturgis died very suddenly Monday afternoon at the home on North Fourth street. She is survived by her husband and two small children, one five years old and one three. Mrs. Sturgis was a daughter of J.O. Dougherty and wife, the present manager of the Martin Bros. Music Store of this city, and had lived here a year or so. Mr. Sturgis is a piano tuner. The body was taken to her former home at Hugo, Okla. for interment. [Rogers Democrat 7/17/24]

SULLIVAN, John L. - Mrs. Mell Sullivan received the sad news Saturday night of the death of her brother-in-law, John L. Sullivan of Kansas City. Mell Sullivan, who was with his brother three weeks and had returned home only a few days when he received a call to return and was with his brother when he died. John Sullivan spent many months with his brother in this community in an effort to regain his health and will be remembered by many people here. [Benton County Record 11/14/24]

SUMNER, Eliza Jane Yates Hunt - Word was received by the Democrat editor yesterday of the death of Mrs. Eliza Jane Sumner on April 30th at the home of her daughter, Mrs. Kate Hopwood, at Indianapolis, Ind. after a short illness of a few weeks at the age of 78 years and nine months. She was born in Roanoke county, Virginia August 23, 1845. She was a resident of Rogers and Benton county for nearly forty years, going to her daughter's in Indianapolis only a few months ago. She is survived by nine children, six sons and three daughters and also by three sisters. Interment was in the Crown Hill cemetery in Indianapolis. She was for years a member of the Christian church. Mrs. Sumner was married several times and is perhaps best remembered in Rogers as Mrs. Hunt, mother of Tom Hunt. Her first husband's name was Yates. For a number of years she had made her home at Gentry but returned to Rogers upon the death of Mr. Sumner. [Rogers Democrat 5/8/24]

SUTTLE, Florence McCUMBER - Mrs. Florence Suttle, wife of Wm. S. Suttle of Ketchum, Okla., died Saturday afternoon about 2:30 in a hospital in Vinita, Okla. following injuries received a few hours before by being kicked in the face by a horse as Mrs. Suttle and her husband were driving from their home to Vinita. The two left home that morning to visit her brother in that city and as they were entering Vinita part of the harness became unbuckled in some way, allowing the buggy to run up on the horse. The horse, which was one they had raised from a colt and perfectly gentle, became frightened and kicked backwards, Mrs. Suttle receiving the full blow of the kick, made more severe by the steel shoe, direct in the face. The force of the kick was so hard as to leave an imprint of the shoe on her face. Mrs. Suttle was hurried to the hospital where she never regained consciousness. Funeral services were held Sunday at Ketchum, Okla. and were largely attended. Mrs. Suttle was about 31 years of age and besides her husband is survived by three little daughters - Mildred, Enola and Geraldine; a brother, G.A. McCumber of Vinita; her mother, Mrs. Walter

Waker of Buxton, Oregon; and two sisters, Mrs. Lark Cloe and Mrs. Leslie Brown of Centerton. Mrs. Suttle was the daughter of Mr. and Mrs. W.A. McCumber and was born at Forestburg, S.D. Nov. 3rd, 1893. At an early age she was converted at a revival conducted by Rev. Y.A. Gilmore and Rev. Duggins at the old Center Point church. Her tragic death has left a pall of sorrow around her home and at Centerton as well. [Benton County Record 10/31/24]

TALLMAN, Arthur Gabriel - Arthur Gabriel Tallman, a well known resident of Gentry for the past 27 years, where for 25 years he was editor of the Journal-Advance, died very suddenly yesterday at about 5 o'clock while on duty in the J-A office. Mr. Tallman had not been in the best of health for several years, in fact since he sold out to the present management 2 years ago, but had not complained of feeling bad. He was cheerful and seemed in the best of health up to within a few minutes before his death and it was a severe shock to his wife, relatives and friends. Arthur Tallman was a good, conscientious Christian man, a loving father to the little girl they raised and a good husband. We will publish his obituary next week. [Gentry Journal–Advance 1/11/24]

Arthur Gabriel Tallman died suddenly Thursday afternoon about 5:15, January 10, 1924 while working in the Journal-Advance office. At the time of his death he was 56 years, 10 months and 25 days old. The news of the death of Mr. Tallman came as a severe shock to his relatives and a very large circle of friends. He was born near Pontiac, Illinois February 16, 1866, being the youngest son of Isaac and Elizabeth Tallman, both of whom preceded him to the Better World Feb. 8, 1903 and July 14, 1899, respectively. On April 27, 1904 he was united in marriage to Miss Catherine V. Rankin, daughter of Dr. and Mrs. D.W. Rankin of this city. To this union no children were born. However for a number of years past and until recently they had in their home a little girl, known as Katherine Tallman, to whom they gave affectionate care, the same as if she were their own daughter. This little girl went to her mother a few months ago and now lives in Brooklyn, New York. Mr. Tallman has two brothers and one sister. Walton Tallman, the eldest child of the family, has made his home with Arthur for many years and is the only surviving one. His brother, Albert, died in Kansas about three years ago and his sister, Mrs. Alice Tallman Shutts, died in Kansas last February. In his younger days he took up the profession of newspaper publishing and engaged in that work for nearly forty years. He was devoted to his profession and as an editor and writer he was very successful. He was ever ready to encourage all good and progressive works and spared no pains to make his paper a means of help to the entire community. Coming to Arkansas about 37 years ago he located in Prairie Grove, Washington county, where he established a newspaper and published same for a number of years. Later he moved to Decatur and established a paper which he published for a while and 27 years ago he came to Gentry and began publishing the Journal-Advance, which he published for nearly 25 years. Two years ago last November he sold the Journal-Advance to the present editor and, being in ill health, spent a few months in Hot Springs, returning to Gentry in the fall of 1922. Since his return to Gentry he has worked in the J-A office, assisting with the press work of last week's edition when he fell,to rise no more. Years ago Arthur joined the Methodist church and ever since has lived a true and faithful christian life. Recently he purchased the newspaper at Prairie Grove and contemplated moving there to assume charge of same in a few weeks. Funeral services were held from the Methodist church Saturday afternoon at 2:30, conducted by Rev. B.L. Harris, his pastor, and assisted by Rev. C.H. Sherman, former pastor and close personal friend. The remains were laid at rest in the city cemetery. [Gentry Journal–Advance 1/18/24] [Benton County Record 1/25/24]

TATE, Robert - {from Clantonville} Robert Tate, who has been in real bad health for some time, died the 27th of February and funeral services were held at the Roller cemetery on the 28th. [Rogers Democrat 3/6/24]

THOMSON, Malinda WYNINGER - Malinda Wyninger was born in Virginia Feb. 25, 1844. Died April 30, 1924, aged 80 years, two months and 5 days. Father, Jacob Wyninger, mother, Jennie Wyninger, 4 brothers and 4 sisters, all preceded her in death. Moved to Kansas in early days and to Arkansas in 1887. Married to Hans Thomson Feb. 27, 1873. To this union were born 4 sons, A.T. Thomson, Los Angeles, Calif.; E.C. Thomson, Tucumcari, N.M.; R.M. Thomson, Gentry, Ark. and one who died in infancy, also three daughters: Mrs. Fannie Wilson, Gentry; Mrs. Hattie Brown, Denver, Colo. and one who died in infancy. Ten grandchildren survive her. Her husband preceded her, dying in 1901. Mrs. Thomson was converted to the Christian faith in her girlhood and joined the Methodist church in which faith she consistently lived and died. Rev. S.F. Brown conducted the services at the grave and a large crowd of people attended the funeral which was in Gentry cemetery Thursday afternoon. [Gentry Journal–Advance 5/9/24]

TINKER, Ivan - Ivan Tinker of Perry, Okla. died Thursday night from heart trouble after a days outing with friends. There was apparently nothing wrong with Mr. Tinker when he and his wife returned home Thursday evening but when Mrs. Tinker arose Friday morning she found him dead. Mr. Tinker was 23 years old and was employed for the past two years by the Comar Oil Co. He is survived by his wife, his father, Henry Tinker of Gentry, Ark.; his mother, Mrs. Sarah E. Tinker of 217 West Oak street and two brothers, William J. Tinker and R.H. Tinker, both of Enid. [Gentry Journal–Advance 8/1/24]

TIPPINS, Leta - Mrs. Leta Tippins, mother of Mrs. Owen Gailey of Caverna, died at her home in Westville Saturday at the age of 87 years. [Benton County Record 12/19/24]

TRAMMELL, Lonnie E. - Gentry experienced an awful tragedy on Monday night about 9 o'clock on Main street when A.O. Siegmann shot and killed Lonnie Trammell with a 12-gauge single barrel shot gun in the Farmer Jones Cafe at which place he conducts a restaurant. It seems that Siegmann and his wife had been having more or less trouble for the past several months and she had threatened to leave him and on Monday had gotten out papers before Justice of the Peace Ellis to put him under a peace bond but the papers were not signed by her for some reason. Monday night Siegmann was seen abusing his wife in the restaurant by her father, Mr. Stout, and two or three men on the opposite side of the street, one of them being Lonnie Trammell, who together with the other men, immediately rushed into the restaurant to protect the woman when Siegmann, who had the gun sitting in the corner, grabbed it and fired a shot, the charge taking effect in Trammell's stomach on the left side. Siegmann immediately reloaded the gun and was going to shoot again when his wife placed her hand between the hammer and breech of the gun and prevented him doing so. After this happened she threw the gun outside into the yard. Dr. Clemmer was called and administered to the injured man as best he could, but advised them to take him to the hospital at Siloam for an operation. Trammell lived only a few minutes after he was put on the operating table. He realized that he was going and told the boys present what to do and to be sure and take care of his mother. Siegmann was taken to Bentonville by Sheriff Maples, who had been sent for in the meantime, and lodged in jail. It is reported that Siegmann had previously threatened the lives of his wife, father-in-law, S. Stout, and brother-in-law, O.B. Crites, and it is thought that he was insanely jealous of Mrs. Seigmann. Lonnie Trammell was 38 years of age and was born and reared in Benton county, served a year in the world war, part of the time in the trenches, and was gassed. Deceased is survived by 3 brothers and 2 sisters and many relatives and friends to mourn his loss. [Gentry Journal–Advance 5/16/24]

Dona Trammell and wife of Granby, Mo. arrived here Tuesday morning to attend the funeral of his brother, Lonnie Trammell. [Gentry Journal–Advance 5/16/24]

Lonnie Trammell, a well known young man of Gentry, was shot and killed by Arthur Seigman{sic} in the latter's restaurant about 9 o'clock Monday evening. Trammell died an hour later in the City Hospital in Siloam Springs. He was about 35 years of age and the son of Mrs. Margie Trammell, a widow. The day before, so it is stated, Seigman quarreled with his wife and beat her. The quarrel was resumed Monday and Mrs. Seigman was preparing to return to her father's home. Seeing her at the door Monday evening her father, S. Stout, went in the little restaurant and asked Seigman, "What's the trouble?" "There is no trouble," said Seigman. It is then reported that Seigman struck his father-in-law and started to choke him. Thinking the old man was about to get badly treated, several men who were standing outside the door, including Trammell and Hugh Carl, came in to separate them. Seigman started for the kitchen which is divided from the front room by a wooden partition and the doorway covered by a curtain. A cloth screen stood in front of the doorway. While Seigman went around this screen, followed by Carl and others, Trammell went through the screen. As he did so Seigman grabbed a shotgun, which he had loaded that day, and shot Trammell. So close was Seigman to him that Trammell's clothing caught fire. As Trammell fell, shot in the stomach, Seigman broke the gun to reload it, His wife, who is a little woman, weighing only about 90 pounds, grabbed the gun and threw it out the back door. The murderer was arrested by Constable Bill Collins and Sheriff Maples and Deputy Gailey phoned for. Dr. Clemmer was called and dressed the wound and ordered the wounded man taken to the hospital in Siloam Springs. The Carpenter Brothers made a record time in taking him down. Trammell, who realized that his end was near, told them it was useless to take him there and asked that his brothers take good care of his mother. He died within 15 minutes after arriving at the hospital. When Sheriff Maples and Deputy Gailey arrived they found an angry mob of people gathered around the restaurant. Mayor Pitkin and the city council, who were meeting across the street, had been quieting the crowd until the officers arrived. Fearing violence against the prisoner, Maples and Gailey rushed Seigman to their car and hurried away. As one Gentry citizen told the Record representative, only the drop of a hat was needed to start the crowd into making short work of Seigman. The prisoner, who is in the county jail in Bentonville, has so far not been inclined to talk. Gentry citizens take the killing to heart as this is the first murder that has ever occurred in that little city since it was built. Funeral services for the dead man were held at the M.E. Church on Wednesday afternoon and was one of the largest funerals ever held there. The services were in charge of the Masons and about 75 members of this order were present from surrounding towns. Lonnie Trammell was about 37 years of age and was born about three miles north of Gentry. He was the son of Mr. and Mrs. D.K. Trammell, his father dying about six years ago. At the breaking out of the World War he volunteered and was sent to France. He was badly gassed at the fight at Chateau-Thierry. He was a quiet and peaceful young man and did not know the meaning of fear. He was highly thought of by all who knew him. Besides his mother he is survived by two children - a daughter aged 14 and a son 12 years old; 3 brothers, John Trammell of Granby, Mo.; Henry Trammell of Mt. Vernon, Wash. and Jay Trammell, who lives in Wash.; two sisters, Mrs. Will Whiteside of Gentry and Mrs. Arrie Fox in Montana. A host of relatives and friends are left to mourn his loss. Seigman was the son of Charles Seigman, who came to Benton county years ago and took up a claim in Tanyard Hollow north of Bentonville. He moved to Oklahoma about 30 years ago. Arthur Seigman and his brother returned to Benton county and bought a farm on Flint creek a few years ago. Last fall he moved to Gentry and bought the Farmer Jones restaurant owned by Bob Grimmett. [Benton County Record 5/16/24]

Lonnie E. Trammell, son of L.K. and Margaret Trammell, was born near Gentry, Ark. March 18, 1888 and died May 12, 1924, age 36 years, 1 month and 24 days. He volunteered for military service in Billings, Mont. and entered the U.S. Army during the late World war and saw service over seas for 12 months with Co. B, 9th M.G. Batt. While in the front line trenches as a member of the machine gun company he was wounded and gassed, so felt and saw the real tragedy of the most horrible war known in the world's history. After the close of the war, having received his honorable discharge, he returned to his home town and place of his boyhood days and here as a worthy pensioner spent the remaining short years of his life. He was a member of the American legion and of the Masonic Lodge. He is survived by his aged mother, 2 sisters, Mrs. Will Whiteside of Gentry, Ark. and Mrs. Tom Fox of Idaho, 3 brothers, Jay Trammell of Bellingham, Wash., Henry Trammell of Mt. Vernon, Wash. and Jonah Trammell of Granby, Mo., also 2 children, a boy and a girl, and a large circle of other relatives and friends. Funeral services were conducted by Rev. B.L. Harris and the Masonic order from the Methodist church May 14th at 3 p.m. and interment was made in Flint Creek cemetery. [Gentry Journal–Advance 5/23/24]

TRAMMELL, Tom W. - {from Decatur} Tom W. Trammell, for many years a resident of Decatur and a former postmaster, died at his home in St. Joseph, Mo. Feb. 22nd at the age of 60 years. Death was due to paralysis. Besides his widow he is survived by two sons and three daughters. Three brothers of the deceased, William, Van and James Trammell live near Gentry. [Benton County Record 3/7/24]

TRAXEL, Herbert Eugene - Herbert Eugene, 4 months old son of Mr. and Mrs. Ernest Traxel, died in the night Sunday, probably from a weak heart and pneumonia which was developing. The parents found the baby dead in bed. The child was born September 26, 1923. Burial was at Mt. Pleasant Monday afternoon, Rev. G.T. Clark conducting the funeral. Sympathy is extended the bereaved ones. [Gravette News Herald 1/25/24]

TRIBBLE, Allen Yell - Allen Tribble, one of the pioneer residents of Rogers, died Saturday afternoon at the home on South Third street after a long illness. Funeral services were held at the home Monday afternoon at 2:30 and were conducted by Rev. J. Wilson Crichlow of the Central M.E. church, assisted by Rev. Austin of the Baptist church. Interment was in the Rogers cemetery and the Masonic order, of which he had been a member for many years, conducted impressive services at the grave. The following sketch of the life of the deceased was prepared by his pastor, Rev. Crichlow: Allen Yell Tribble was born near Shelbyville, Tenn. February 4, 1854 and died at his home in Rogers April 26th at the age of 70 years, two months and 22 days. His father, Patrick Henry Tribble, was a brave Confederate soldier who gave his life for the Southland in the battle of Chickamauga and thereby made Tennessee doubly sacred to his son. After the death of his father Allen and his sisters and brothers lived with their mother at the home of their grandfather, Nimrod Burrow. Here, at Shelbyville, he spent his boyhood days and here, January 26, 1879 he married Martha Letitia McFarlin, the faithful wife and loving companion of two score and five years. Soon after the marriage, in fact the very first year that the Frisco railroad passed through here {1881} and the town of Rogers was begun, Mr. and Mrs. Tribble moved to this city. At first Mr. Tribble engaged in the fruit business but by profession he was a carpenter and all over this town you can find the good work of his hands. In 1895, during the revival at the Central Methodist church that year, he gave his life to Christ. He has ever been upright in his principles and fair in his dealings with his fellow men. For two years Mr. Tribble had not been well. For the past four months he has been confined to his bed. The last meal he ate with his family was on Christmas Day. Mr. Tribble is survived by his wife and three children - Mrs. J.F. Pace of Grove, Okla. and Miss Sadie L. Tribble and Henry Tribble of Rogers; one grandson, Elmo Pace, of Center College, Danville, Ky.; two sisters, Mrs. T.M. Hendrix of Lewisburg, Tenn. and Mrs. J.P. Wallis of Shelbyville, Tenn. and one brother, C.R. Tribble, of Bell Buckle, Tenn. [Rogers Democrat 5/1/24] [Rogers Daily Post 4/29/24]

TROXEL, Herbert Eugene - {from Gravette} Died, Herbert Eugene Troxel, baby son of Ernest and Mary Troxel, on Sunday, January 20th, aged three months and 25 days. The babe died of pneumonia. Burial was made in Mt. Pleasant cemetery. [Benton County Record 1/25/24]

TRUEBLOOD, Charles W. - Charles W. Trueblood, age 63, a well known citizen of the county, died at his home mid-way between Centerton and Hiwasse Sunday night after a week's illness. Funeral services were held at the family home on Tuesday and again at the Christian church in Rogers, of which he was a member. The body was laid to rest in the cemetery in that city. Besides his widow he is survived by five children: Mrs. Dave Looney of Rogers, Mrs. G.W. Daniels of California and Lester, Bennie and Grace Trueblood of the home. Mr. Trueblood was born in Illinois in 1861. In 1892 he moved with his family to Rogers and located on a farm east of town. A few years ago he bought the Rucker fruit farm northwest of Centerton where he has since resided. [Benton County Record 10/31/24] Chas. W. Trueblood, a former well-known Rogers citizen, died October 26 at his home nine miles west of Bentonville at the age of sixty-three years, seven months and ten days. Funeral services were held at the First Christian church of Rogers Tuesday afternoon at 2:45 by Rev. R.M. Thompson. Mr. Trueblood leaves two children by his first wife who died in 1894 - Mrs. David Looney of Rogers and Lester Trueblood, who is in Nebraska. In 1900 he married Miss Adah Headley who survives him and three children by this marriage - Mrs. Ruth Daniel of Orange, Calif., Benjamin and Grace, who are still at home. For years he lived east of Rogers on a farm now owned by O.A.P. Oakley and later came to town and built the C.R. Latto house. [Rogers Democrat 10/30/24]

Charles W. Trueblood was born in Illinois March 16, 1861 and died Oct. 26, 1924 at his home nine miles west of Bentonville at the age of 63 years, 7 months and 10 days. His boyhood days were spent in Indiana, Illinois and Missouri but later moved to Kansas where he was married to Miss Alice Weaver in 1887. To this union were born four children, two of whom are still living, Mrs. David Looney of Rogers and Lester Trueblood at present in Nebraska. In 1892 Mr. Trueblood moved to Arkansas on a farm east of Rogers known for many years as the Trueblood farm. About two years after locating on this farm his first wife died. Six years later in 1900 he married Miss Adah Headley who survives him. To this last union three children were born, Mrs. Ruth Daniel of Orange, Calif., Benjamin and Grace still at home. He also leaves two sisters, Mrs. C.B. Daniel and Mrs. Robt. Daniel, both of Calif. Mr. Trueblood was a prosperous farmer and fruit grower but in 1912 decided that he could do better in Rogers as a carpenter. He built a nice residence in the east part of Rogers, proving that he was not only a successful farmer but a first class mechanic. He then went to Fort Smith but it was not long until he returned to Benton county, this time on a fruit farm near Hiwasse and he soon added two more farms to his homestead. He took great pride in raising the best of products and wanted them in the nicest pack, which accounts for the good prices and leading prizes at both Arkansas and Oklahoma fairs. He was a hard worker and never idle but in spite of a strong constitution his health began to fail about 2 years ago. He never did give up, even attending the Bentonville fair when he should have had a physician. Strong nerve power can defy the lurking ills of humanity for a long time but sooner or later this earthly body must succumb. Charlie, as his many friends called him, put up a brave fight and yet he won. He won in the hearts of his neighbors by his honest and upright dealings. He was always kind and generous to them, full of sympathy for their troubles; in fact he was better to his neighbors than to himself. He was a member of the Christian church and while living in Rogers was a deacon in the First Christian church. Neighbors and friends will long remember him and join his relatives in their bereavement. [Rogers Daily Post 10/29/24]

TRULL, Bert - {from Tuck's Chapel} Clarence Trull received a message Friday morning stating that his brother, Bert, who lived in Elgin, Ill., had died suddenly. He left that night to attend the funeral. Mr. Trull made annual visits to Arkansas to visit his brother and family; his last visit was last Christmas when he came down and spent a week here. [Rogers Democrat 8/14/24]

TUCKER, Ella Jane - {from Lowell} Ella Jane Tucker, wife of James Tucker, died Sunday night at her home after a lingering illness of cancer. Funeral services were held at the home Monday afternoon by Rev. Bates of Fayetteville. Burial was in the Pleasant Grove cemetery. Grandma Tucker was loved by all who knew her for her loving and patient disposition. She was a consecrated Christian and was not afraid to die. Loving and tender care was bestowed upon her by her faithful children during her long illness. Seven children and a host of grandchildren and friends are left to mourn her loss. [Rogers Democrat 12/11/24]

TUCKER, Nancy EDEN - {from Monte Ne} We are sorry to report the death of Mrs. James Tucker who passed away Wednesday evening after a short illness. She had been quite ill with a complication of diseases and died suddenly from heart failure. Mrs. Tucker will probably be better remembered as Miss Nancy Eden, youngest daughter of James Eden. She was 36 years old and is survived by a husband and six daughters, one son, one granddaughter, four brothers and two sisters. She was held in high esteem by all who knew her and the entire community extends sympathy to the bereaved family. [Rogers Democrat 12/4/24]

TURNER, Mrs. John - Mrs. John Turner, 85 years old, died Saturday at the home of her son, Lewis Turner, four miles west of Rogers on Walnut street. The family came here from Texas some five years ago. The funeral services were conducted by Rev. Austin of the Baptist church at Oakley Chapel. [Rogers Democrat 9/25/24]

TYGART, Mary Jane - Mrs. M.F. Tygart died last Monday afternoon at 5:30 at her home in the south part of town after several weeks illness from a paralytic stroke. The funeral was held from the home Wednesday afternoon at 2 o'clock conducted by Rev. T.A. Martin of Fayetteville and interment was made in Flint creek cemetery. The bereaved family have the sympathy of the entire community in their bereavement. [Gentry Journal–Advance 6/20/24]

Mrs. Frank Tuttle of Chanute, Kansas was called here several days ago on account of the illness and death of her mother, Mrs. M.F. Tygart. [Gentry Journal–Advance 6/20/24]

Mrs. Clarissa Gibson had been here for several days with her mother, Mrs. M.F. Tygart, before she passed away Monday evening. [Gentry Journal–Advance 6/20/24]

Mary Jane Tygart was born April 25, 1843. Departed this life June 16, 1924 at her home in Gentry, Ark. She was married to Martin F. Tygart December 13, 1860. To this union ten children were born, eight of whom are now living: Mrs. G.W. Hogan, Mrs. Clarissa Gibson, Mrs. B.F. Tuttle, Mrs. Claud Coffelt, Cooper and Vic Tygart. All were with their mother during her last illness. Mrs. Tygart was true and faithful in her relations to all through her life, to her husband, her children, her friends and neighbors. She was modest and reticent, a lover of house and home associations. Though she has gone to her heavenly home she will be lovingly remembered by all who had the pleasure to know her. [Gentry Journal–Advance 6/27/24]

UMHOLTZ, infant - {from Fairview} Born Tuesday, March 3rd to Mr. and Mrs. Harry Umholtz, an 8½ pound daughter who died Saturday, March 8th at at 8:00 o'clock. She was laid to rest in the Pleasant Grove cemetery Sunday at 10 o'clock. [Rogers Democrat 3/13/24]

UNKNOWN - The body of an old man was found Saturday afternoon on the Buxton farm southwest of town by Hugh Harris and the Cravens boys who were hunting. The man was about 70 years old and had been seen on the streets here Thursday. There seems to be disagreement as to cause of death; however there was a deep wound in the wrist which Undertaker Tom Haywood says severed the artery. There are also deep bruises on the face and skull which may have been the result of falling, the body being found with the head on a rock. There seems to have been no motive for murder. The authorities were notified, the body brought to the Peoples Hardware Undertaking rooms and Acting Coroner Foster impanelled a jury. Dr. J.T. Powell examined the body and was inclined to think the wound on the skull sufficient to be fatal. There appeared to be some indications of a scuffle on the hillside where two razors and a purse containing 14¢ were found. The coroner's jury in the case decided Monday that the man had come to his death by suicide by cutting the artery in his wrist. The man had gray hair and mustache, blue eyes, weight about 160. He wore a blue coat, slouch hat and was rather shabby. The body was embalmed and held at the undertaking rooms awaiting possible identification. There were no letters or any means of identification found on the body. [Gravette News Herald 11/28/24] [Rogers Daily Post 12/2/24] A letter has been received from P.L. Bearden, City Clerk of Tuscumbia, Alabama inquiring about the body now being held at the Callison mortuary awaiting identification. Mr. Braden is seeking an uncle whom he has not seen since 1898. According to his description it is hardly probable that the body being held is that of his uncle. [Rogers Daily Post 12/3/24]

WAGNER, Mrs. - {from Pea Ridge} Mr. Priest received a message Friday containing the sad news of the death of his wife's mother, Mrs. Wagner, which occurred at Topeka, Kansas. Mrs. Priest and Mrs. Watson were with her at the time of her death. [Benton County Record 12/5/24]

WAKEFIELD, Louisa HAINES - In the death of Mrs. Louisa Haines Wakefield, who passed away on Tuesday, July 22nd, 1924, another of Bentonville's oldest citizens has gone beyond. Death was due to old age and a complication of diseases. She died at the home of her daughter, Mrs. Sam B. Maxwell, where she has made her home for some time past. The funeral services, which were largely attended Wednesday afternoon, were held at the Maxwell home, the Rev. O.A. Fortune, pastor of the M.E. Church, officiating. Interment was in the City Cemetery. Mrs. Wakefield is survived by three children - a son, J.C. Wakefield of Ozark, Ark. and two daughters, Mrs. Sam B. Maxwell and Mrs. J.S. Black, both of this city. Louisa Haines was born in St. Clairsville, Ohio in 1847. The family later moved to Fairplay, Missouri, where she later married J.H. Wakefield. Mr. and Mrs. Wakefield and their three children moved to Bentonville in 1884 which has since been their home. Mr. Wakefield died about 20 years ago. Mrs. Wakefield was a devout Christian and a member of the M.E. Church to which organization she was ever faithful even to the end. Being possessed of a very bright mind and a most kindly and lovable disposition she endeared herself to everyone who had the good fortune of her acquaintance. She spoke no ill of anyone and none spoke of her except to praise her noble qualities. Surely "a mother in Israel" has gone from us and entered into the joys of eternal life. [Benton County Record 7/25/24]

WAKEFIELD, Philetus - Dr. Philetus Wakefield died yesterday morning at his home in this city, the first residence north of the Mutual Union Building, on South Second Street, at the age of 74 years, one month and two days. The body was taken to his old home at DeWitt, Illinois for burial. The body was accompanied by his son, George Wakefield, who arrived last night and left on the northbound train this morning. Dr. Wakefield and wife came to Rogers in 1901. [Rogers Democrat 2/7/24]

WALRAFF, William - William Walraff died Wednesday, Feb. 13, 1924 at the home of his daughter, Mrs. J.H. Shields, west of Gravette. Mr. Walraff was born in Germany Nov. 26, 1837 and was aged 86 years, 2 months and 17 days. He came to America in 1845, settling in Illinois. Later he moved to Fort Lupton, Colo. where his parents died, both at the age of 88 years. The body was shipped to Mound Valley, Kans. for burial. [Gravette News Herald 2/22/24]

WALTER, Martha McCULLISTER - Mrs. Martha Walter, wife of J.S. Walter, died at her home fifteen miles northwest of Bentonville on Wednesday night after a two weeks' illness from a complication of diseases resulting from erysipelas. She was sixty-six years of age. Martha McCullister was born in West Virginia in 1858 and when grown to womanhood was married to J.S. Walter. To this union was born eleven children, nine of whom are now living - Alonzo, Lawrence and Arthur Walter and Mrs. Lizzie Odell, who live at the family home; Edwin of Garden City, Kansas; Mrs. Myrtle Shiever of Howard, Kansas; Mrs. Dora Fyock of Douglas, Kansas - all of whom were present during their mother's last hours. Two children - Chas. Walter in Montana and Mrs. Faye Frazee of Belle Plains, Kansas were unable to come. Funeral services were held at the home yesterday afternoon and interment made in the Bentonville cemetery, Rev. Lester Weaver conducting the services. [Benton County Record 10/24/24]

WARDLAW, David Dickie - The report reached Maysville this morning that D.D. Wardlaw, who lived east of Maysville, died last night, January 15th. Mr. Wardlaw had not been feeling well for a few days but he was feeling much better yesterday and ate a hearty supper. About two o'clock a.m. some of the home folks went to his room to see if he was resting and found him dead. Mr. Wardlaw had been living on the farm for several years and everyone knew him and the community extends sympathy to the bereaved family. Besides his widow he is survived by four children, two sons and two daughters. [Benton County Record 1/18/24]

Word was received last week by relatives of the sudden death of Dick Wardlaw at his home near Maysville. He has numerous relatives on this side of the county as he was raised near Avoca and has a sister, Mrs. John B. Polk, at Riverside, Calif. [Rogers Democrat 1/24/24]
A gloom of sorrow came over the home of Mr. David Dickie Wardlaw and spread over the entire community when they learned of his sudden death on Tuesday morning, January 15th, 1924, the result of heart failure. Mr. Wardlaw was born near Brightwater, Ark. on May 28th, 1861, spending the earlier part of his life there and on Pea Ridge engaged in farming. He was married in 1887 to Frances T. Webb of Pea Ridge, Ark. To this union was born six children, two dying in infancy. In 1906 he moved near Maysville to the farm that he occupied at the time of his death. He leaves his wife; Robert and Everett Wardlaw of Gravette; Mrs. Connely Primrose of Maysville; Mrs. Barney Thomason of Westville, Okla. and a host of friends to mourn his loss. He was a member of the Cumberland Presbyterian Church 28 years and lived a Christian life. He was a devoted husband and a kind and loving father. He was always striving to make the pathway of life smoother for those who should follow him. No task was ever too large, no days were ever too long; he kept faithfully moving toward the goal, and by his earnest and diligent work he accumulated wealth. Mr. Wardlaw's life was an open book to all who knew him. During the many years that I have known him as a neighbor I never knew him to tell an untruth; I never knew him to do a dishonorable act and he has always drawn a line on everything that was impure and unclean. Funeral services were conducted at the Presbyterian Church in Maysville by Rev. Sade of Southwest City, Mo. and the body interred in the Tinnin cemetery. A Friend. [Benton County Record 1/25/24] [Gravette News Herald 2/1/24]

WATTS, infant - The infant daughter of Mr. and Mrs. Jess Watts, living near the high school, died last Wednesday. Interment was made the following day in the city cemetery. Rev. S.J. LeRoy of Centerton conducted the funeral services. [Benton County Record 5/9/24]

WEED, Wm. - Wm. Weed, uncle of W.G. Check, died at Sulphur Springs Jan. 23 and was buried in Lee cemetery near the home of his sister, Mrs. X.S. Check, Jan. 25. [Gravette News Herald 2/1/24]

WEEDMAN, Ona - Ona Weedman, Odd Fellow, who died at Sulphur Springs Wednesday, will be laid to rest in Gravette I.O.O.F. cemetery today. [Gravette News Herald 6/6/24]

WELLS, Moses John - Moses John Wells was born December 30th, 1859 in Freestone county, Texas. Departed this life April 8th, 1924. He came to Yell county, Ark. and lived one year then moved to Benton county. He professed faith in Christ in the fall of 1886 while in the field at work and joined the Mt. Pleasant Baptist Church and lived a true Christian life until death. He was married on Dec. 2nd, 1897 to Edna L. Galyean, who with nine children are left to mourn his departure - one daughter having passed away January 16th, 1917. He was only sick eight hours and his wife was the only one with him at the time of his death. Ola Barnwell of Row, Okla.; Lue Callis of Grove, Okla.; Berzilda Hendren of Miami, Okla.; Alex Wells of Fortescue, Mo. and Herman Wells of Gravette were present at the funeral. Caire Wells of Spokane, Wash.; Jessie Holt of Mt. Vernon, Wash.; Eva Hatcher of Clarkfort, Idaho and Docia Allen of Hamburg, Iowa did not get here. He also leaves one own sister and a half-sister and many other relatives and friends. The funeral was conducted at the Mt. Pleasant church on Thursday, April 10th by Rev. Roy Daugherty. The body was laid to rest in Mt. Pleasant cemetery. [Benton County Record 4/18/24] [Gravette News Herald 5/2/24]

Mrs. Bert Douglas was in Hiwasse Thursday where she attended the funeral of her uncle, John Wells, who died Tuesday. [Benton County Record 4/11/24]

WELLS, Robert W. - Robert W. Wells died Thursday, December 4th at the home of his daughter, Mrs. C.A. Walton, on Electric street, and funeral services were held from the home Friday afternoon at 2:30. The services were conducted by Rev. J. Wilson Crichlow, pastor of the Central Methodist church, followed by interment in the Rogers cemetery. Mr. Wells was born in Mercer Co., Missouri September 20, 1870. When only a youth he came from his native state to Rogers where most of his life has been spent. He was married to Polly Ann Breeze September 18, 1891. To this union were born 5 children, 4 daughters and 1 son; all survive him. The children are Mrs. C.A. Walton and Mrs. Fred Stophlet of Rogers; Mrs. Lee R. Lemming of Holden, Mo.; Mrs. James P. Ocheltree of Hood River, Oregon and William Edward Wells of Rogers. Also 2 grandchildren, Polly Lou Lemming and Bobby W. Stophlet. Mr. Wells was well known throughout NW Arkansas, having served the people as an officer for more than fifteen years. He was elected township constable at the October election, a position he had filled with honor a number of terms. In his official capacity he was always loyal, and self sacrificing. Rogers loses one of its most loyal citizens. After an illness of two months, during which time he suffered greatly, he has passed to his reward. [Rogers Democrat 12/11/24] [Rogers Daily Post 12/5/24]

WEST, L.B. - L.B. West, one of Gravette's oldest citizens, died at his home Sunday night, June 15th, 1924 at the age of 86 years. Mr. West has been in very poor health for some time and became much worse last week. Funeral services, conducted by Rev. T.F. Jones of Burgin Valley, were held Tuesday with interment in the local cemetery. Mr. West was born in Indiana in 1838 and came to Arkansas in 1901 and located on a farm west of Sulphur Springs. He has resided with his wife in Gravette for the past six years. Besides his widow he is survived by one daughter, Mrs. W.G. Check. [Benton County Record 6/20/24]

L.B. West, one of our highly respected citizens, died at his home in Gravette Sunday, June 15th, 1924 at the age of 85 years, 9 months and 21 days. Mr. West had been in ill health for some time. He leaves his aged companion, one daughter, Mrs. W.G. Check, and an adopted daughter, Miss Mae West, and many relatives and friends. The funeral was conducted at the home by Eld. T.F. Jones Tuesday morning and burial was in the I.O.O.F. cemetery. Obituary later. [Gravette News Herald 6/20/24]

L.B. West, whose death occurred in Gravette June 15, 1924, was born in 1838 near Crawfordsville, Ind. When 13 he moved with his parents to Iowa, later to Northwest Missouri, then to Kansas. When the civil war began he was among the first to enlist, in Co. I, 2nd Regiment, and served his country until his health failed him; was honorably discharged, to enlist again as soon as health would permit. At the age of 14 he was converted and joined the Baptist church, remaining a faithful member until death. He was married to Miss Margaret West Sept. 15, 1863; to this union were born 4 children: Arvilla M. {now Mrs. W.G. Check}, Simeon E., Cora F., Eloise E. The 3 youngest died in infancy. He leaves to mourn his departure his aged wife, the daughter and an adopted daughter, Miss Mae West, and a host of relatives and friends. He was a brother of Rev. J.W. West who died here a few years ago and like the latter was a citizen and neighbor held in esteem by all who knew him. [Gravette News Herald 6/27/24]

WETZEL, Martha C. - The following is a brief obituary of "Grandma" Wetzel who died at the home of her granddaughter, Mrs. G.C. Tinnin, at Maysville June 6th, 1924 at the age of 84 years. Martha C. Wetzel was born in Georgia July 2, 1840. Soon after the Civil War she moved to what is now Oklahoma and lived there until her death. She was married to D.K. Wetzel in 1864. To this union were born 8 children, 3 of whom survive and besides her own children she reared 4 grandchildren. She united with the Christian Church when 16 years old and has shown her faithfulness to the cause by her consistent Christian life and her willingness to aid the cause in every way possible. Funeral services were conducted by Dr. W.A. McDonald of Gravette and the body laid to rest in Worel{Word?} Cemetery Tuesday. The family has many friends who join in sympathy for the bereaved ones. [Gravette News Herald 6/20/24]

WHITE, infant - The infant son of Mr. and Mrs. Harry White, born Wednesday night at the Home Hospital, died Thursday night. Dr. A.W. Young of the Christian church conducted services at the Rogers cemetery Friday afternoon. [Rogers Democrat 8/21/24]

WHITE, C.W. - C.W. White, one of the oldest residents in Fayetteville, died Monday. He was 88 years old and was born and raised in that city. [Benton County Record 1/11/24]

WHITE, John Calvin - John Calvin White, aged 85 years, passed away at 8 o'clock the morning of Monday, February 4th at the home of his son, W.C. White, 303 North 3rd street. The A. D. Callison Undertaking Co. prepared the body for shipment to Harvine, Neb. His son, E.C. White, of Akron, Colo. accompanied the body to the place of burial. [Rogers Democrat 2/7/24]

Fayetteville, Ark., Dec. 30.- J.C. White, 71 years old, president of the Citizens bank and prominent business man here, died at his home here Sunday morning after a lingering illness of many months. Mr. White, a citizen of Fayetteville for more than 25 years, was born and reared near Dutch Mills, this county, the son of one of the oldest pioneer families in Northwest Arkansas and was a graduate of the old Cane Hill Academy, long since discontinued. In his section of the county he was a successful business man and mercantile store director before coming to Fayetteville. Surviving are two daughters, Misses Pearl and Eddie White, and a son, Sloan F. White of Wilkesborough, Pa. The son arrived here Christmas day. Two sisters, Mrs. W.M. Bush of Fayetteville and Mrs. C. Evans of San Antonio, also survive. [Rogers Daily Post 12/30/24]

WHITE, Martha J. ROBISON - Martha, wife of "Uncle" Frank White, died last Wednesday, Feb. 13 at the family home west of Gravette. Martha J. Robison was born Aug. 3, 1847 in Fairfield, S.C. and moved to Georgia with her parents at the age of ten years; was married to W.F. White Feb. 8, 1874 and moved to Arkansas 45 years ago. To this union were born five boys, two dying in infancy - Edgar of DeKalb, Mo.; Loy of Santa Ana, Calif. and John with whom she lived near Maysville, he being the only one at her bedside when death came. Her husband also survives. Mrs. White united with the Methodist church at an early age and lived a consistent Christian life. The funeral was conducted Friday by Rev. G.T. Clark and interment was made in Bethel cemetery, south of Gravette. The bereaved family have the sympathy of all and especially old neighbors at Gravette where the family resided many years, at the big spring southeast of town. [Gravette News Herald 2/22/24]

Mrs. M.J. White was born in Fairfield, S.C. Aug. 3, 1847; departed this life Feb. 13, 1924. Moved to Cherokee county, Ga. before the Civil War. There she lived with her parents until grown. United with the Methodist South when quite young. Married to W.F. White Feb. 8th, 1874; moved to Carthage, Mo. in 1878 and lived one year. Moved to Benton county, Ark. with husband, father and mother in 1879, residing here until her death. To her marriage with W.F. White were born 5 boys, the second and third dying in infancy. She leaves her husband, three sons and 14 grandchildren to mourn the loss, one brother and one sister in Georgia. She was ever ready to help the needy and visit the sick. Only one son and family and brother and family were able to attend the funeral. Her oldest son lives in Missouri and the youngest in California. Her Husband. [Gravette News Herald 2/29/24]

WHITE, Sadie A. BATTERSON Manwaring - Sadie A. White, wife of Robert R. White, was born at Angola, Ind. April 12, 1848, the daughter of Henry and Harriet Batterson, and died at Gravette, Ark. May 10th, 1924 following several years of ill health, aged 76 years and 28 days. The funeral was conducted Sunday, May 11, 2 p.m. at the Methodist Church, South by the Rev. N.E. Wood of the M.E. church of Sulphur Springs, attended by a large number of friends and relatives. Interment was in the I.O.O.F. cemetery beside her former husband, J. Manwaring, who died here in 1905. Besides her husband, Mr. White, other relatives present were Mrs. Etta Manwaring, Miami, Okla. and Mrs. May Reniker of Independence, Mo., sisters-in-law, and one nephew, Leland Batterson of Lawrence, Kan. Mr. and Mrs. Manwaring came to this region from Larned, Kansas over 30 years ago, residing at Maysville, also on their farm west of Gravette, now known as the Bamberry place; locating in Gravette over a quarter century ago. Mr. Manwaring was a prosperous stockman and owned much property, bank stock, etc. She was married to Robert R. White of Indianapolis, Ind. June 23, 1913 and continued residence in Gravette and during her long illness has had the kindest care and attention of her husband in her affliction. Sympathy is extended those bereft. [Gravette News Herald 5/16/24]

WHITE, W.F. - We regret to report the death of our venerable friend, W.F. White, which occurred Sunday at the home of his son, John, west of town. Mr. White, aged about 90, was feeble and a fall hastened his death. John came for the funeral which was conducted by Rev. Boyles Tuesday at Bethel, where interment was made. Obituary next week. [Gravette News Herald 10/17/24]

W.F. White was born Dec. 18, 1834 in Spartanburg, S. Carolina. Moved to Georgia when about 15 years of age; married Martha J. Robinson Feb. 8, 1874; moved to Carthage, Mo. in 1878, then to Benton county, Ark. in 1879, residing here until his death. Mrs. White preceded him in death just 8 months. Five boys were born to them, two dying in infancy, the remaining sons being Edgar of DeKalb, Mo.; Loy of Santa Ana, Calif.; and John, with whom he made his home and being the only one present when death came. There are 15 grandchildren. Mr. White was converted 69 years ago, uniting with the Baptist church but later with the Methodist church and was a devout Christian, always looking for a nobler, higher life in everyone. He was a man of broad mind, always active in good works, having said "I am not going to sleep my life away." He was a great reader and the knowledge imparted to others was based on wisdom and justice. His motto, marked in his Testament was "Have communion with few, Be intimate with one; Deal gently with all, And speak evil of none." Mr. White was a Civil war veteran - he was in 7 days of battle around Richmond and other places. The funeral was conducted at Bethel by Rev. E.L. Boyles where on Oct. 14th the body was laid to rest in the cemetery close by. [Gravette News Herald 10/24/24]

WHITE, Wesley - Sulphur Springs relatives have received word of the death of Wesley White which occurred at his home in Los Angeles, California Wednesday, October 1st. He was reared in Sulphur Springs and is well known by all the older residents of the town and community. He was married fourteen years ago to Miss Grace Alderson, also a resident of Sulphur Springs. They moved to Clarksdale, Arizona and later to Los Angeles. He had been in poor health for about three years but death came suddenly at the last. He is survived by his wife, his mother, Mrs. Rose Davis of Mayer, Arizona, and one brother, James White, one sister, Mrs. L.H. Edgerton, both of Los Angeles. Their many Sulphur Springs friends extend sincere sympathy to the bereaved ones. [Benton County Record 10/10/24]

WHITE, Wm. Franklin - {from Maysville} Died, Wm. Franklin {Grandpa} White, at the home of his son three miles north of town the 13th of this month. Mr. White fell against a wagon last week and died from the effect of the fall on Monday morning at 2:30. He was known and loved by almost everyone in the entire community. He was a devout Christian and lived in the love of God. Had Mr. White lived until December he would have been 90 years old. [Benton County Record 10/17/24]

WHITMORE. Edward - Joint resolution adopted by the Masonic Lodge {Pea Ridge Lodge No. 119} and Eastern Star Chapter {Starlight Chapter No. 457}, of which he was a member, in honor of Brother Edward Whitmore, who was found on the morning of January 25th in his last long sleep. [Rogers Democrat 2/21/24]

WILKS, daughter - {from Garfield} Word was received this morning, Tuesday, that a daughter of Charlie Wilks, near Seligman, Mo., was dead and will be buried at Bayless cemetery this evening. Charlie Wilks is a brother to R.M. and Esta Wilks of this place. [Rogers Democrat 7/17/24]

WILKS, Lucy A. - Mrs. Lucy A. Wilks died here Saturday morning at the home of her son, Tom J. Wilks, at 822 West Walnut street, with whom she had lived for some time. She was 89 years old. The body was taken to her old home at Hindsville, Madison county for burial and the funeral was held there Sunday. [Rogers Democrat 3/6/24] [Rogers Daily Post 3/1/24]

WILLIAMS, Della GARVIN - {from War Eagle} The funeral services of Mrs. Williams was held here Monday evening at the N.P. Sharp home. Interment was in Cottage Hill cemetery. Mrs. Williams was Della Garvin before her marriage and her many friends here and elsewhere will grieve to learn of her death. She leaves a small baby and her husband to mourn her loss, with other relatives and friends. She grew to womanhood near War Eagle and is well known. She has a large circle of friends who mourn her departure. [Rogers Democrat 4/10/24] [Rogers Daily Post 4/8/24]
{from Cloverdale} Miss Della Garvin was born in Benton county, Arkansas September 28, 1902; departed this life April 5, 1924. She was married to Floyd Williams a little over three years ago. To this union was born one little son who is left in his babyhood without a loving mother's care. Mrs. Williams was stricken a year ago with tuberculosis and everything that could be done was done for her but medical aid and loving care failed and after long months of patient suffering God called her home. She was ever kind and thoughtful for others, doing many little acts of kindness that will ever be bright in their memory. She leaves besides her father and mother, Mr. and Mrs. Will Garvin, her husband, Floyd Williams, a little son, two

brothers and four sisters to mourn her loss. She also leaves an aged grandfather and grandmother, Mr. and Mrs. Nimrod Sharp of War Eagle. She was laid to rest with loved ones at War Eagle Monday, April 7th. [Rogers Democrat 4/10/24]

WILLIAMS, Jesse Dale - {from Centerton} Rev. W.J. LeRoy was called to hold the funeral services of little Jesse Dale Williams, infant child of Mr. and Mrs. Jannie Williams of Shubert, Nebraska last Tuesday afternoon at Hiwasse. Burial at Mt. Pleasant cemetery. [Benton County Record 9/26/24]

WILLIAMS, Mrs. Jess - {from Clantonville} Jess Williams received a message Friday telling him his wife was dead in Illinois where she had gone a short time ago. She fell a victim to that dread disease, T.B. She leaves three small children. Mrs. Similar cares for the young baby, Mrs. Shipley has the next size little girl, while she took the oldest child, a little boy, with her. [Rogers Democrat 12/4/24]

WILLIAMS, W.T. - W.T. Williams, the real estate man who was injured a week ago when struck by an automobile on Walnut street, died last evening at 5:30 at the Love Sanitarium of heart failure. Mr. Williams was down town the first of the week and it is thought his weakness, as a result of the shock and the exertion, was too much for him and was the cause of the sudden collapse yesterday noon when he became unconscious in his little office on South First street. He was taken at once to the Sanitarium but failed to rally and passed away as stated. Mr. Williams has no relatives here but an effort was being made last night to get in touch with a brother and sister in Ohio. He had lived here for a number of years, having built a home on North C Street. Part of the time he has lived there alone with few if any intimate friends. For a number of years he occupied a small frame building in the street at the corner of Main and Cherry and was known as "Williams, the Rent Man." [Rogers Democrat 3/27/24]

W.T Williams passed away last night about 5 o'clock. He was taken ill yesterday morning while in his office and went to Dr. Love's Sanitarium where he became unconscious but rallied for a time and conversed with the Doctor and Mrs. Love, then passed into a state of coma and died. He is about fifty years old and has been in the real estate business here with a small office on South First street for several years. He built a nice bungalow on his farm near W.B. Starks about a year ago and most of the time he has rented the place and boarded with his tenant. Very little is known here of his private life or business affairs. He has a brother in the east who has been advised of his death and no arrangements will be made for his funeral until he is heard from. His death was due to heart trouble, to which he has been a sufferer for several years. [Rogers Daily Post 3/27/24]

The body of W.T. Williams, the real estate man who died at Love's Sanitarium Wednesday night after a few hours illness, was shipped last night to Vincennes, Ind. upon the instructions of a brother who lived in Cincinnati, Ohio. J.W. Bryant, who had charge of the arrangements, states that no other information came, neither age or birth and practically nothing can be learned as he lived a quiet life, apparently having few close friends. [Rogers Daily Post 3/28/24]

WILSON, Mrs. F. Ed - {from The Siloam Springs Daily Register, March 7th} Mrs. Ed Wilson, whose home was five miles west of Maysville, died at the City Hospital last night as the result of burns received yesterday afternoon. She was burning brush in a field on their farm while her husband was plowing some distance away. Her clothing became ignited and before the flames could be extinguished the woman was terribly burned on her body and face. Mrs. Wilson was about 40 or 45 years old and the mother of four children. [Rogers Democrat 3/13/24]

While walking across a field that had just been swept by a fire, the clothing of Mrs. F.E. Wilson, the wife of a farmer living west of Maysville, caught fire from burning embers and soon was a mass of flames. The unfortunate woman screamed for her husband who was ploughing in a field near by but he could not reach her quickly enough to save her. She was so badly burned that she died a few hours after. She leaves two children, one four years old and another aged 10, her husband and friends and relatives to mourn her death. [Benton County Record 3/14/24]

WILSON, Willie - {from Elm Springs} Willie Wilson died one day last week and was buried in the Elm Springs cemetery. [Benton County Record 4/18/24]

WOLFE, J.J. - From the Grainfield {Kan.}Cap Sheaf, published by Fred I. Wolfe, we learn of the death of his father, a former Gravette citizen. The report in part says: "Mr. J.J. Wolfe, formerly a citizen of Grainfield and one of the early settlers of Gove Co., having taken up the white man's burden here in 1885 and braved the storms of the elements and times, passed away at his home in Longmont, Colo. Sunday, January 27th, 1924 after a brief illness of two weeks. On Sunday, January 13, 1924 he suffered a stroke of paralysis which terminated in his death last Sunday. Mr. Wolfe was 73 years, 2 months of age; he leaves to mourn their loss six children, 4 sons and two daughters; 6 brothers and 3 sisters; a large number of other relatives and a host of friends and neighbors in Colorado, Kansas, Iowa, Nebraska, Illinois, Missouri and Arkansas." [Gravette News Herald 2/8/24]

WOOD, C.D. - {from Decatur} C.D. Wood, an old resident of this section, died at his home west of Decatur Monday at the age of 72. A general breakdown of his system followed by an illness of a year or more caused his death. He was buried in the Decatur cemetery Tuesday. Besides his widow he is survived by two sons, Bob and Ralph Wood of Decatur and their daughters, Mrs. Millie Clark of Decatur, Mrs. May Randalls in Illinois and another married daughter in Detroit. [Benton County Record 6/6/24]

WOODARD, A.H. - A.H. Woodard, the oldest resident of Pea Ridge, died at his home in that place on Friday, February 22, 1924. Had he lived until next July he would have been 92 years old. His wife passed away about four years ago. Funeral services were held Saturday afternoon at the M.E. church, Revs. Lark and Carnahan officiating. Burial was made at Buttram's chapel. Mr. Woodard was born in Alabama in 1832. He was an old Confederate soldier and came to Pea Ridge from Charleston, Ark. about 20 years ago. He is survived by two sons, Z.Z. and E.L. Woodard of Pea Ridge and one daughter, Mrs. Nellie Sanders of Proctor, Okla. [Benton County Record 2/29/24]

WOODRUFF, Albert Henry - {from Monte Ne} We are very sorry to report the death of Albert Henry, little son of Walter Woodruff and wife, who died Saturday night and was buried in the Frisco cemetery. Funeral services were conducted by the Rev. Ness of Springdale. We all sympathize with the bereaved family. [Rogers Democrat 1/17/24]

WOODRUFF, Mrs. Walter {O'Brien} - {from Monte Ne} We are very sorry to report the very sudden death of Mrs. Walter Woodruff who died in Washington county at the bedside of her ill father, Mr. O'Brien, who was a former citizen of Rogers and is nearing his 95th birthday. She leaves a husband and five sons, a father and several brothers and sisters to mourn her death. The family have our sympathy. [Rogers Democrat 10/2/24]

WOODS, Minerva - {from Pea Ridge} Word was received here Saturday that Aunt Minerva Woods died at Wichita, Kan. Friday. [Benton County Democrat 2/14/24]

WRIGHT, Elizabeth McDonald - {from Sulphur Springs} Mrs. Elizabeth Wright died at the home of her daughter, Mrs. Blanche Odle of Southwest City, Mo. Wednesday, June 4 at the age of 84 years. Mrs. Wright came to Sulphur Springs from Texas about 15 years ago. She has been an active worker in the local chapter of the Eastern Star and of the Baptist church of which she has been a member for several years. She is survived by two daughters and one son, Mrs. Etta Johnson of Sulphur Springs, Mrs. Blanche Odle of Southwest City, Mo. and Joe McDonald of Idaho. A host of friends extend their sympathy to the bereaved ones. [Benton County Record 6/13/24]

WRIGHT, Mrs. J.A. - Mrs. J.A. Wright, aged 63, died at her home in Cave Springs Saturday, November 8th, 1924 after a lingering illness. The funeral services were held at the home Sunday morning at 11:30 and interment was made in the city cemetery at Bentonville Sunday evening. She is survived by her husband, J.A. Wright, of Cave Springs and five children, Mrs. Albert Beard of Iowa, Mrs. C. Horton of Hiwasse, L.A. Wright, Hiwasse, C.D. Wright of Cave Springs and Wesley Wright of Wenatchee, Wash. [Benton County Record 11/14/24]

{from Cave Springs} Mrs. J.A. Wright, aged 63, who died at her home in Cave Springs on November 8th, is survived by her husband, J.A. Wright, of Cave Springs and five children - Mrs. H.M. Horton of Hiwasse; Mrs. W.F. Beard of Vancouver, Wash.; Pete Wright of Cave Springs; Luther Wright of Garfield and Thos. W. Wright of Pocatello, Idaho. [Benton County Record 11/21/24]

1924

YOUNG, W.H. - {from Sulphur Springs} W.H. Young, aged 40, formerly of Noel vicinity, was burned to death last Tuesday night. He had tramped here from Haynes, Ore. on business and had camped in Dog Hollow. He went to sleep by a campfire and his clothing caught fire. Instead of jumping into the creek he ran to the home of Mrs. Williams, a widow, who wrapped him up and called a doctor. Young dictated a letter to his mother and died the next morning. [Gravette News Herald 3/7/24] [Benton County Record 3/7/24]

1925

AARON, George - {from Pea Ridge} Funeral services were held at the M.E. Church Sunday afternoon for George Aaron. [Benton County Record 1/23/25]

AARON, Joe - {from Prairie Creek} Oscar Aaron, Mrs. C.D. Conley and Mrs. L.J. Conley received the sad news of the death of their uncle, Joe Aaron, who lives near Springdale, on Sunday afternoon. Sunday, a week before, they attended the funeral of their uncle, George Aaron, of the same place. Both were buried at Elm Springs. We sympathize with them in the loss of their uncles. [Rogers Democrat 1/29/25]

ACKERMAN, George - George Ackerman, a Bentonville resident some 30 years ago, died at Mt. Pleasant, Ill. on Sunday. He was a single man and about 68 years of age. He leaves two sisters in this city, Mrs. C.J. Eld and Miss Kate Ackerman, and another sister, Mrs. Nancy Jouenck, of Tipton, Ia. [Benton County Record 9/11/25]

ALLEN, Mary C. - {from Gravette} Mrs. Mary C. Allen, an old and highly respected citizen, died at her home in Gravette October 8. Burial in Mt. Enterprise cemetery October 9th. She was the mother of Luther Allen, carrier on Route 3 out of Gravette. [Benton County Record 10/16/25]

ALLRED, John W. - John W. Allred, a well known citizen of this section, died at the home of his daughter, Mrs. Marion Hegwood, in Rogers on Sunday morning at the age of about 85 years. He was buried at the Martin cemetery near Larue the following day. Besides his daughter, Mrs. Hegwood, he is survived by Malcolm Allred of Rogers and John W. Allred, Jr. of Larue. Mr. Allred came to Benton county in 1881 and located on the White river, near Larue, where he lived until recently. [Benton County Record 3/13/25]

ALLRED, William H. - W.H. Allred, for many years one of the best known citizens of Walnut township, died Sunday in Rogers at the age of 84 years, seven months and 28 days, at the home of his daughter, Mrs. M.S. Hegwood, on North 2nd. He was laid to rest in the Martin cemetery at Larue Monday March 9th, his old friend and neighbor, Rev. G.C. Bland, conducting the services. W.H. Allred was born in Randolph County, North Carolina June 11, 1840. He moved to Benton county in 1881, arriving here when the Frisco railroad had just reached Seligman on its way south. He located in Walnut township, near Larue, where he lived until two years ago when he sold his farm and had since made his home with his children. He professed a hope in Christ when a young man following the plow. He was married to Martha Ann Moon March 28, 1867. To this union were born three children: J.W. Allred of Larue, and Z.M. Allred and Mrs. M.S. Hegwood of Rogers, who were present at their mother's death March 31, 1888. They were also at the bedside of their father at the home of Mrs. Hegwood where he passed away Sunday. In 1893 he was married to Mrs. Mary Pittillo, who, after being afflicted 18 years, passed away March 27, 1919. Mr. Allred is also survived by sixteen grandchildren and seventeen great-grandchildren. He was a faithful husband, a kind and loving father. He showed a great patience in his aged years, always kind and never a murmur escaped his lips. He was honored and loved by all who knew him. [Rogers Democrat 3/12/25]

William H. Allred, aged 80 years, died Sunday afternoon at the home of his daughter, Mrs. Marion Hegwood, in Rogers after a short illness. He was buried Monday near his old home at Larue by the side of his wife who died a few years ago. Besides his daughter he is survived by two sons, Malcolm and John W., the former living at Rogers, the latter at Larue. [Benton County Democrat 3/12/25]

{from Glade} We are sorry to relate the death of W.H. Allred who died March 8th. He was 84 years old. Mr. Allred moved from North Carolina to this state some 40 years ago and has lived in this part of the country ever since. He was a prominent and well known settler of Benton county. He is survived by three children, J.W., M., and Mrs. Ellen Hegwood. He was laid to rest in the Martin cemetery. The funeral services were conducted by the Rev. G.C. Bland. The bereaved family have the sympathy of the entire neighborhood. [Benton County Democrat 3/12/25]

ALMINDINGER, infant - {from Hiwasse} The infant child of Mr. and Mrs. Roy Almindinger which died Sunday was buried the following day. [Benton County Record 6/5/25]

AMMONS, Martha Caroline SUMNER - Simple and beautiful were the funeral services for Mrs. W.E. Ammons which were held at the family home west of Bentonville at 2:30 o'clock Wednesday afternoon. The Rev. A.W. Henderson, pastor of the Presbyterian Church, read the impressive passage from the last chapter of Proverbs and a prayer was made by the Reverend W.C. Wheat. Mrs. Ammons passed away on Tuesday morning at 10:00 o'clock after suffering over a year with mortal illness. Nearly a hundred automobiles made the funeral cortege to the cemetery where interment was made in the mausoleum. Martha Caroline Sumner Ammons was born in Mississippi October 13, 1869. Her forebears were pioneers of renown, the town of Sumner, Miss. being founded by and named for the grandfather of Mrs. Ammons. Her youth was lived in her native state and on September 30, 1886 she married William Erwin Ammons, who is also a native Mississippian. To them were born four children, one daughter having died in infancy. The other children survive and are W.L. Ammons and Jess Ammons, sons, and Miss Ruby Ammons, daughter. Her husband, five grandchildren, seven brothers and two sisters, also survive her. In early life Mrs. Ammons united with the Baptist church but after her marriage she joined the Presbyterian church with her husband. The Ammons family came to Bentonville in 1910 and have since made their home here. [Benton County Record 12/11/25]

AMMONS, Mrs. Will {ELAM} - The funeral of Mrs. Will Ammons, who had died Saturday at Tipton, Okla. from uremic poison, was held Monday morning at the Baptist church, conducted by the Rev. R.L. Keen. Interment was in the Centerton cemetery. Deceased was the daughter of Mr. and Mrs. Lucius Elam of Centerton and the wife of Dr. Will Ammons, a chiropractic physician who has been located at Tipton, Okla. for the past year, moving there from Southwest City, Mo. where he opened offices following his graduation. Mr. Ammons operated a mill here several years ago, being associated with his father-in-law in business. Two children also survive the mother, a boy aged 4 and a girl of nine years. [Benton County Democrat 4/30/25]

ARDEMAGNI, Michael - Springdale, Dec. 5.- Michael Ardemagni, twenty-five years old, son of Felix Ardemagni, mayor of Tontitown, died at six o'clock Saturday afternoon from injuries sustained when a team he was driving ran away and a wagon wheel crushed his body. No definite reports were received here concerning the accident. Ardemagni is said to have been driving a young team of horses which became uncontrollable. He is thought to have been thrown from the wagon and one of its wheels crushed his body. It is thought the funeral will be held at Tontitown Sunday. The family is one of the best known in Tontitown and the father is one of the recognized grape authorities of Northwest Arkansas. [Rogers Democrat 12/10/25]

ARMSTRONG, Taylor - Taylor Armstrong, aged 18 years, son of Mr. and Mrs. W.N. Armstrong, died at the family home here today shortly after noon. He had been an invalid for nine years. The boy's father, Mr. Armstrong, is proprietor of the Armstrong electric shoe shop and moved his family here from Oklahoma a year or more ago, where they have made many friends and acquaintances who sympathize deeply with them in their sorrow. Besides his parents, Taylor is survived by two sisters and two brothers. Funeral services will be held at four o'clock Friday afternoon from the Baptist church. [Benton County Democrat 1/29/25]
The funeral services of Taylor Armstrong, the 18-year-old son of Mr. and Mrs. W.L. Armstrong who died suddenly on Thursday afternoon of last week, were held Friday at the Christian Church and were conducted by Rev. Stephen A. Morton and Rev. Luther Smith. Interment was made in the city cemetery. Besides his parents the lad is survived by two sisters and two brothers. [Benton County Record 2/6/25]

ARMSTRONG, Wayne - Wayne Armstrong, the fifteen year old son of Mr. and Mrs. W.M. Armstrong, died Tuesday evening, November 3, 1925 following a short illness. He suffered a stroke of paralysis when seven years old which badly crippled him. The past eight years he has spent in a wheel chair. He was a bright, cheerful boy and while he could not play with other children he enjoyed watching nearly as well. He was born in Pawnee Rock, Kans. in 1910. Besides his parents he is survived by one brother, Don, and two sisters, Alma and Lois Armstrong. Funeral services, conducted by Rev. J.M. McMahen, were held at the Baptist church Thursday morning with interment in the city cemetery. [Benton County Record 11/6/25]

1925

ARNEY, Fred - {from Monday's Siloam Springs Register} Fred Arney of Neiscoop Prairie, west of here, was stabbed and fatally wounded at his home last night about ten o'clock by his brother-in-law, Geo. Bayes, following an altercation of some kind of which the details are lacking. Arney was cut only once by Bayes who used a butcher knife, cutting him in the leg, severing the femoral artery. Arney died almost immediately. Bayes remained on the scene for some time following the killing but owing to the excitement little attention was paid to him. He afterwards left and posses are scouring the country side in an effort to apprehend him but so far without success. Arney is survived by his wife and several brothers and sisters of whom Miss Nell Arney of this city is one. [Rogers Democrat 3/5/25]

ASHTON, Beulah - Mrs. S. Nighswonger received a message Saturday telling of the serious illness of her little seven year old granddaughter, Beulah Ashton, of Wichita, Kansas. Mrs. Nighswonger left in the early afternoon on the bus for Joplin and caught the night train out for Wichita. A message was received from her early Monday morning stating the little girl had passed away. Mrs. Nighswonger will remain in Wichita for several days. [Gentry Journal-Advance 12/25/25]

ATKINSON, Jim - Jim Atkinson, aged 68 years, died at his home in the Fairmount neighborhood last Tuesday of pneumonia and was buried Wednesday at 10 o'clock. Carpenter Bros. had charge of the funeral. [Gentry Journal-Advance 3/20/25]

ATKINSON, Mrs. R.M. {FUNCHESS} - The sudden and unexpected death of Mrs. R.M. Atkinson which occurred at 1:30 o'clock this morning at her home here, removed from prominence one who has been an active element in social, literary and community life here for a long period of years. Mrs. Atkinson became ill at 12:30 o'clock and summoned her daughter-in-law, Mrs. R.M. Atkinson, Jr. Dr. Charles Hurley was summoned immediately and found Mrs. Atkinson in an unconscious condition. Dr. Atkinson, Mrs. Atkinson's son, was out on a professional call at the time and reached home shortly afterwards. Mrs. Atkinson's death has been attributed to a heart attack. She suffered a similar attack several years ago, it is said, but had not been subject to any in two years. Mrs. Atkinson is survived by her son and daughter, Mr. and Mrs. R.M. Atkinson, and a sister, Mrs. J.C. Hennon. [Benton County Democrat 8/25/25]
Mrs. R.M. Atkinson, mother of Dr. R.M. Atkinson, died suddenly at the family home in this city shortly after one o'clock Monday morning at the age of 63 years. Death was due to heart failure. Funeral services were held on Wednesday afternoon at the M.E. Church, South, the Rev. H.C. Hoy of Cape Girardeau, Mo. conducting the services. Mrs. Atkinson was a member of the Study and Shakespeare Clubs and president of the latter organization for many years. Mrs. R.M. Atkinson was born in Mississippi on August 19th, 1862. When a small girl her parents, Dr. and Mrs. B.P. Funchess, moved to Eastern Kansas, where she grew to womanhood, attending

Highland University, Kansas and the Gulton-Trueblood School of Expression in Kansas City, Mo. For several years she taught school in Dallas and Crockett, Texas. At the latter place she met and married R.M. Atkinson. In 1901 Mr. Atkinson and family came to Bentonville where he engaged in the wholesale grocery business. In her girlhood the deceased united with the church and remained a consistent, active member until the day of her death. Her life may be summed up in two words - Service and Devotion. Her work in this church and in literary and social circles is familiar to all. Aside from home duties she found time to coach students in Latin and English, drill students in high school plays and devoted much time to landscape painting, of which art she was very fond. When failing health compelled her to give up many of her activities she held with all her strength to the Women's Missionary Society of which she was president. At 1:15 a.m. on August 25th, 1925 she was called to answer the final summons, leaving to mourn her loss her only son, Dr. R.M. Atkinson, and his wife, Mrs. R.M. Atkinson; one sister, Mrs. J.C. Hennon; several nieces and nephews and a host of friends. [Benton County Record 8/28/25]

AUSTIN, Elizabeth Louella COWGUR - Elizabeth Louella Cowgur was born at Sherman, Texas Nov. 6, 1859. Died at her home near Cottage Grove {Gravette, Ark.}, April 11, 1925, being aged 65 years, 5 months and 5 days. She came to Arkansas with her parents in her childhood and settled near Bethel where she attended school and church. It was there she first met her companion who survives and deeply mourns her departure. Oct. 15, 1876 she was married to Elige Austin. To this union was born ten children, six of whom survive: John of Gravette; Straud of Kansas City, Mo.; Mrs. I.W. Hopkins, Sulphur Springs; Mrs. L. Rodgers and Mrs. H.L. Fair, Gravette; and Mrs. W.H. Mount of Pea Ridge. She professed faith in Christ at the Bethel church in a meeting conducted by Rev. Pierce Merril in 1890 and joined the Baptist church soon after and lived and died a faithful and loyal member to that day. The funeral, which was largely attended, was held at Bethel April 12, conducted by Rev. J.A. Scoggins, assisted by Rev. W.H. McCarroll, after which the last sad earthly journey was begun, led by the pall bearers, followed by six of her granddaughters as flower girls. And there beneath the spreading oaks in the silent grave was tenderly placed the last earthly remains of mother, undisturbed in the last deep sleep that knows no waking until the trumpet of God shall sound and the dead shall come forth. Her husband and children. [Gravette News-Herald 5/1/25] [Benton County Record 5/1/25] [Benton County Democrat 4/16/25]

AUTREY, baby - {from Monte Ne} We are sorry to report the death of Robert Autrey's baby who died last week. It was buried in the Frisco cemetery. We all sympathize with the bereaved parents. [Rogers Democrat 6/25/25]

AVERY, C.W. - C.W. Avery, local insurance man, committed suicide in New Orleans last Saturday night. The suicide was caused by morbid melancholia insanity, caused by worry over financial troubles, it was said, in a note left by the man following his taking bichloride of mercury. Avery disappeared from Bentonville about three weeks ago and besides one letter from Memphis, nothing had been heard of the man until the news of his death from New Orleans. The man, it is alleged, was in financial straits with an insurance company that he was connected with here. About three weeks ago, leaving word that he was going to Fort Smith on business, Avery left for Memphis. Nothing was heard from him for several days until word came from Memphis that he was there. This was the last message that was received from him except a farewell letter written upon his death bed. The man had lived here for about fifteen years and was well known throughout this section of the country. He left about two years ago and only recently moved back from Fayetteville. He married in Fayetteville only about three months ago. Though facing a financial shortage it is believed officials of the insurance company were not preparing to take steps to make a charge against him but were preparing to assist him. The continual worry over this trouble, it is believed, caused a temporary melancholy insanity that led to his leaving and later to his self-destruction. For some time Avery had carried the poison, it is said, planning his death. Burial took place in New Orleans. He is survived here by his wife and two step-daughters, Pearl and Joe Alen Avery. [Benton County Democrat 10/20/25]

BAGGETT, Josephine - Fayetteville, Jan. 1.- Little Josephine Baggett, 5-year-old daughter of Joe Mock Baggett of Prairie Grove and granddaughter of Mrs. J.J. Baggett of this place, was burned to death Wednesday. The little one had been playing in the yard and is thought to have poured oil on a smouldering trash pile. [Rogers Democrat 1/8/25]

BAKER, Charlie - {from Cloverdale} Mrs. Dean received a telegram announcing the death of a nephew, Charlie Baker, who was operated on at a hospital in Trenton, New Jersey for appendicitis. A second operation was performed and septic poison had set up and he passed away and was buried at Trenton. He spent some of his boyhood days in Rogers. His mother is buried in the Rogers cemetery. He leaves a father and brother, a wife and two small daughters. He served in the late war and spent several weeks in France. [Rogers Democrat 2/5/25]

BAKER, J.C. - {from Clantonville} J.C. Baker, who has been sick at his daughter's home in Fayetteville for some weeks, passed away Saturday at 5 o'clock p.m. He had Bright's disease, with other complications, and his age was enough advanced to be against his recovery. Mrs. Baker stayed with him till the last and his children accompanied his body to its last resting place at Hoisington, Kansas by the side of his former companion, while Mrs. Baker returned to her children. Mr. Baker was a pleasant man, a good neighbor, straight in his business. He will be missed from among us. While he has not taken an active part for some time on account of his declining health we realize a good man is gone. [Rogers Democrat 8/13/25]

1925

BALCH, Wm. Henry - Wm. Henry Balch, age 80, died in Decatur on Saturday, June 20. Funeral services were held from the Methodist church Monday and the remains were laid to rest in the city cemetery. [Gentry Journal-Advance 6/26/25]

BALL, B.H. - B.H. Ball, a Siloam Springs attorney who was on his way to Battle Creek, Michigan for treatment, died at Kalamazoo, that state. [Rogers Democrat 7/2/25]

BALL, Henry Spencer - The many boyhood friends and schoolmates of Spencer Ball and friends of the Ball family here were shocked late Friday to learn of his accidental death which had occurred that afternoon at Muskogee, Okla. while working in line of duty as an employee of the Oklahoma Gas and Electric Co. He was a member of the crew employed in handling and repairing the high tension lines and while working on a pole Friday afternoon slipped and fell across the wires. He was cut loose by a crewmate working with him but death was instantaneous. Henry Spencer Ball was born at Colby, Kan. December 27th, 1892, his death occurring April 3, 1925 at the age of 32 years, 3 months and 7 days. Coming to Bentonville with his parents and brothers and sisters when quite small, he lived here until 15 or 16 years of age, attending the Bentonville schools and has often since visited with friends and relatives here. On October 18, 1914 he enlisted at Cheyenne, Wyo. in the United States Marine Corps. During the World War he served overseas with the 16th Company, 5th Marines, of the Second Division, as gunnery sergeant, four of the boys of this family serving with America's overseas forces and another brother, Frank, being in training camp when the armistice was signed. He was a member of the International Brotherhood of Electrical Workers, Local 384, Muskogee. That he was a conscientious worker and stood high in the regard of his superiors on the work and his fellow-workers is shown by the fact that ten of these came to Bentonville to attend his funeral, while of the immense number of floral tributes heaped about the casket, the greater part were from those who had worked side by side with him. Mr. Ball is survived by one sister, Miss Eunice L. Ball of Muskogee and six brothers: Rex H. and Harry E. of Muskogee; Ted J., Fort Worth, Texas; Benton, Birmingham, Ala.; John H., Hoxie, Ark. and Frank P., Wichita Falls, Tex. These were all here for the funeral except Frank and John Ball. Mrs. Rex H. Ball, Mrs. Harry E. Ball and Mrs. Benton Ball were also here. His parents and two other sisters, Mrs. R.C. Whayne of Bentonville and Mrs. Fred Hinde of Madison, Kan. died several years ago. Funeral services were held Monday afternoon at the Whayne residence conducted by Rev. J.L. Evans of the M.E. church, South and interment made in the family lot in the Bentonville cemetery. [Benton County Democrat 4/9/25] [Benton County Record 4/10/25]

BARNETT, D.L. - D.L. Barnett, well known to a number of Gravette people, died of paralysis on February 12 at the home of his son, Rev. Ira Barnett, at Riverside, Calif. The body was brought back to Warren, Mo. for burial. Mr. Barnett will be remembered as the father of Mrs. M.G. Stackhouse, formerly of Gravette. The Barnetts are related to the L.B. West family. [Gravette News-Herald 2/2/25]

BARRON, Kate MILLS - Mrs. Kate Barron, former resident of Benton county, died in Springdale on April 2nd at the age of 53 years. She is survived by eight children, one of whom, Mrs. Ruby Piercy of Osage Mills, lives in Benton county. Mrs. Barron was the daughter of Mr. and Mrs. B.F. Mills. Funeral services were conducted at the home by Rev. F.A. Bradshaw, pastor of the Hazel Valley Presbyterian church in Vaughn, with interment in the Barron cemetery. [Benton County Record 4/10/25]

BEANER, Ethel ROBINSON - Mrs. Ethel Beaner, daughter of Mr. and Mrs. John Robinson, was born July 27, 1889 at Robinson, Ark. and died August 3, 1925 aged 36 years and one week. The funeral services were conducted by Rev. Chas. Sherman of Prairie Grove Tuesday afternoon at 3 o'clock at the White Oak church house, interment being in White Oak cemetery. It was so arranged that following deceased into the church and cemetery, her Sunday school class, all girls, came close behind, carrying many beautiful flowers, speaking in a way, of their love and appreciation for so loyal and faithful a teacher, whose influence and teaching would not soon be forgotten. She united with the M.E. Church in early life and lived a sweet Christian life. On Friday of last week Mrs. Beaner picked a small boil or pimple on her lip, causing blood poisoning which took away the life of a young and happy wife and mother. Dec. 20, 1908 she was married to Will Beaner and to this union four children were born, Evelyn, Doyle, Lester and Francis, all surviving except little Doyle, who passed away some few years ago. Others surviving are a devoted husband, kind father, Uncle John Robinson of Siloam Springs, one brother, Clifford Robinson, also of Siloam Springs and an only cousin, Rosa Griffith, of Robinson. [Benton County Record 8/14/25]

BEAVER, J.L. - J.L. Beaver, age 57 years, died early Tuesday morning in the Siloam hospital. He is survived by one son, Marion, who is employed at the depot here. Funeral services were held near Cassville, Mo. in Corinth cemetery Wednesday in charge of Carpenter Bros. Deceased leaves a large circle of friends here and in Missouri to mourn his going. [Gentry Journal-Advance 5/1/25]

BELL, Lois - Heart broken because her family objected to her sweetheart, Cloe Drain, Lois Bell, aged 17 years, daughter of Mr. and Mrs. J.F. Bell at the Parkdale Addition, committed suicide here Thursday morning by drinking carbolic acid. The young girl drank the poison at 8:30 o'clock and died at 9:30 without having spoken. She left a note which is in the possession of Drain and the contents of which have not been made public, according to information from her brother. Funeral services were held this afternoon at Dowel's Chapel. The deceased is survived by her parents, four brothers and six sisters. The girl's father and sweetheart are said to be employees of the Silgo Lumber Company. The father's objection to the girl's lover are said to have culminated in the former whipping the girl who threatened suicide if her father attempted to enforce his orders thru such punishment. [Rogers Daily Post 7/24/25]

BELTON, Mrs. William M. - Mrs. William M. Belton died at her home Thursday morning at 11:40 a.m. following a stroke of paralysis. Immediate medical aid was summoned but Mrs. Belton passed away before the physician arrived. She had been stricken with paralysis once before but survived it. Funeral services for Mrs. Belton will be held Saturday afternoon with the rector of the Winslow Episcopalian church officiating, at the M.E. church, South. She is survived by her husband and one son, Sidney. She lived three miles east of Bentonville. Mrs. Belton was a devoted member of the Episcopalian church. [Benton County Record 12/11/25]
What is home without mother? This question was made to answer on last Thursday at the 11 o'clock hour at the W.M. Belton home when God in His goodness and mercy called Mrs. Belton home after a second stroke of paralysis. She was taken very suddenly and before Dr. Pickens could reach her after a hurried call, she had quietly and peaceably passed on. The pen cannot praise her enough. She was loved by everyone and always helped the ones that needed help spiritually or financially. She was a faithful member of the Episcopalian church. Just a short time ago she looked on the face of her oldest son, Percy, the last time this side of the silent river, and said "good-bye son, for a little while," and the shock was so great and sad that she never entirely overcame it. Interment was made in the City Cemetery at Bentonville Saturday after a brief service by the minister from Winslow, Ark. [Benton County Record 12/18/25]

BENBROOK, Ben - Mr. Ben Benbrook, father of R.C. Benbrook of our city, died at his son's home last night. While the elderly Mr. Benbrook had not been in extra good health for some time he has been fully as well as usual during the past few weeks. Sunday he was at church and Wednesday evening he attended the mid week church service. Last night he retired as usual and as he slept his spirit took its flight to God. Funeral arrangements have not yet been definitely made but the family will probably leave with the remains at 5 o'clock Sunday afternoon, going to the old family home at Calico Rock for the burial. [Rogers Daily Post 4/18/25]

BENTLEY, John Richard - John Richard Bentley was born in Bentonville, Ark. Feb. 15, 1871 and died in Gentry, Ark. Dec. 1, 1925. He was the son of Robert W. and Fanny Bentley, who after the birth of "Dick," located in Louisiana, Mo. where he lived until the age of 16 when he entered the employ of the famous Stark Nursery Co. and remained in their employ 23 years. Always a lover of trees, there was no knowledge of practiced nursery work which he did not know and was always ready to give and receive of his wonderful science. He was married to L. May Post June 3, 1903 at St. Louis, Mo. and she is left to mourn his departure. He came to

Gentry in the spring of 1917 and took charge of the Miller orchard and by his effort has made it one of the noted orchards of Benton county. He had been ill some two weeks and after his recent trip to Kansas City where he consulted doctors as to his serious condition, was confined to his bed until his death. He is survived by his widow and two sisters, Mrs. T.A. Harpole of Elsbury, Mo. and Mrs. Hattie Boyd of Louisiana, Mo. and a brother, Albert Bentley of Farmington, Ark. and a host of friends mourn his loss. The funeral was conducted by Rev. R.L. Hughes and the remains were shipped Wednesday night to his old home in Louisiana, Mo. for burial. [Gentry Journal-Advance 12/4/25]

BEVERLY, Andrew B. - Andrew B. Beverly, an old and highly respected citizen of Gravette, died at his home on West Main Street Saturday, April 4, aged about eighty-four years. Mr. Beverly had been ill for some time from a complication of diseases. Mr. Beverly was born in Kentucky in 1841, coming to this community from Pittsburg, Kansas about twelve years ago. His wife died about five years ago. For some time he has made his home with Mrs. Belle Clarry. He has no relatives so far as can be learned. Mr. Beverly was a veteran of the civil war, having served in the Federal army. The funeral was conducted Sunday afternoon by Rev. Lark of the M.E. Church, South and Mr. J.W. McAllister. Interment was made at the Dow cemetery by the side of his wife. [Benton County Record 4/10/25] [Gravette News-Herald 4/10/25]

BISHOP, son - {from Lowell} The young son of Mr. and Mrs. Bishop died Saturday following an illness of typhoid fever. Funeral services, conducted by Rev. Joe English, were held Sunday afternoon at the Baptist church. [Benton County Record 11/20/25]

BLACKBURN, George A. - George A. Blackburn died Friday, March 6th at his home, 1810 Michigan Avenue, Joplin, Mo. at the age of 78 years, two months and 24 days. Funeral services were held at the residence of Rev. E.W. Love of the Bethany Presbyterian church Saturday, March 7th at 2:00 o'clock and services were held at the cemetery by the Masonic order of which he had been a member for many years - in fact, ever since he was 21 years old. Surviving Mr. Blackburn are his wife, Mrs. Susan Blackburn; two sons, Frank Blackburn of Racine, Mo. and Ward Blackburn of Joplin; and seven daughters, Mrs. Delbert Buttry of Muskogee, Okla.; Mrs. Homer Yeager of Tahlequah, Okla.; Mrs. Belle VanDover of Joplin; Mrs. Robert Morris of Atlanta, Ga.; Mrs. E.L. Walker of Paris, Ark.; Mrs. W.M. O'Bryan of Bluefield, West Virginia; Mrs. C.A. McAdory of St. Louis; one brother, P.W. Blackburn of Monte Ne, Ark. and one sister, Mrs. Kate Reynolds of Texas. Mr. Blackburn was born at War Eagle in Benton county in 1846 and lived in that part of the county until he moved to Joplin a few years ago. He was a cousin of the late ex-State Senator J.A.C. Blackburn of this city and has many relatives in this county. He was a member of Col. Brooks Regiment, Co. B, in the Confederate army. [Rogers Democrat 3/19/25]

1925

BLACKBURN, Mrs. Ottie - {from War Eagle, for last week} The friends of Mrs. Ottie Blackburn will be grieved to learn of her death on Christmas eve after an illness of several weeks. She leaves a husband and a two month's old baby. We deeply sympathize with the bereaved husband in his hour of sorrow. [Rogers Democrat 1/8/25]

BLACKWELL, C.P. {Polk} - Polk Blackwell, known to many of the older residents of Bentonville, died Wednesday at his home in Grand Junction, Colorado following injuries received last Friday when he was struck by a steam ditching machine in Palisades, Colo. where he was engaged in putting a sewer system in that city. Mr. Blackwell was born in Trinidad, Colorado but lived here in his younger days. He left Bentonville about 30 years ago and has been engaged for some time in the contracting business. He was about 55 years of age and is survived by his widow and three sons. Mrs. K.C. Campbell is a sister of the deceased. Mrs. Campbell received a message Wednesday announcing the sad news but the full particulars of his death were not given. His leg was struck or mangled in the ditching machine and the loss of blood was so great that it caused his death. [Benton County Record 10/23/25]
One of the largest funerals ever held was of the late C.P. {Polk} Blackwell of Grand Junction, Colo. who recently died in that city and was buried there. The deceased was the brother of Mrs. Kit Campbell of Bentonville. At the funeral the Masonic Temple was filled and many persons were turned away. Mr. Blackwell spent much of his life in the building of the west and friends from all of western Colorado attended the funeral. Blackwell was born in Fort Stanton, New Mexico in 1870. He moved to eastern Colorado in 1885 to the town of Norwood. Later he became interested as a builder and erected the town of Vanadium in San Miguel County. In 1901 he moved to Grand Junction, where he engaged in the business of contractor and builder. Many monuments of his work stand in that city, works that were designed and erected by him. Mr. Blackwell was considered by the citizens of his city as active, public spirited and representative of the highest type of citizenship. For more than thirty years Mr. Blackwell was eminently identified with the Masonic order and had reached the highest orders in the work. In Grand Junction the Masons of that town expressed that deepest indebtedness to their brother for the building of the Masonic Temple. In the dedication services of the building, in 1923, the deepest appreciation of the lodge was expressed to Mr. Blackwell for his tireless efforts and zealous management of the building. Blackwell is survived by his wife and three children and sister, Mrs. Kit Campbell. Many people in Bentonville were acquainted with Mr. Blackwell and regret to hear of his death, the death of a man who was beloved to all who knew him. [Benton County Democrat 11/10/25]

BLAKE, Bertha Jane CURTIS - Funeral services for Mrs. Bertha Jane Blake, wife of the late T.T. Blake, who died at her home Wednesday morning,

May 6th, 1925, aged 71 years, seven months and seven days, were held Thursday afternoon at the M.E. Church, South which was filled to overflowing with friends come to pay last tribute of respect and love. The services were conducted by the pastor, Rev. J.L. Evans, who spoke especially of the inspiration Mrs. Blake had been to him during their brief acquaintance by her ever ready cheerful optimism and faith. Members of the local chapter order of the Eastern Star attended the funeral in a body. Interment was made in the family lot at the Bentonville cemetery beside her husband and other members of her family. A daughter of Mr. and Mrs. John N. Curtis, pioneer settlers in this section, Mrs. Blake was born in Bentonville Sept. 29, 1853 and spent her entire life here with the exception of some 10 or 12 years. In 1875 she was married to T.T. {Taylor} Blake, a young man who later became prominent in the affairs of Benton county, serving as sheriff and in other capacities. He died here March 18, 1920. For many years Mr. and Mrs. Blake operated the old Southern hotel here in Bentonville and also the Hotel Massey for a time and under their management these hostelries attained a wide and enviable fame for hospitality and service. Few women ever enjoyed so great a number of friends and acquaintances as Mrs. Blake, for beside her intimate friends and neighbors, there were hundreds more who had come to know her when stopping at the hotels and whose hearts had been warmed by her genuine friendliness, motherly sympathy and hospitality. She is survived by three sons, Julian T. of Tulsa; Finney C., Okmulgee, Okla. and Carlos D. of Texas; and four daughters, Mrs. Wallace D. James of Joplin; Mrs. Arch Wright of Fayetteville and Misses Flora and Bob Blake, Bentonville, and nine grandchildren. Another daughter, Mrs. Will Wood, died a few years ago. She is also survived by one brother, P.P. Curtis, of Bentonville who remembers her not only as a sister but as a mother as well, their mother having died when she was hardly grown and he only a few years of age. To him she gave, insofar as possible, the loving care that only a mother can give. [Benton County Democrat 5/14/25]

Mrs. Bertha C. Blake passed away peacefully at the family home in Bentonville early Wednesday morning, May 6th, 1925 following an illness of many months. She had been gradually sinking for the past two weeks. Funeral services were held at the M.E. Church, South the following afternoon. Three sons, Julian Blake of Tulsa; Finney Blake of Okmulgee and Carlos Blake of San Antonio, Texas and four daughters, Misses Flora and Bobbie Blake, of the home; Mrs. Arch Wright of Fayetteville and Mrs. Wallace James of Joplin, survive her. She also leaves one brother, P.P. Curtis, of this city. Mrs. Blake was one of the oldest living residents of Bentonville and was born here in 1854. She was the daughter of Mr. and Mrs. John N. Curtis. She was married to Taylor T. Blake in Mt. Vernon, Mo. Mr. Blake was sheriff of Benton county for many years. The two for a long time were host and hostess of the Southern Hotel and the fame of Mrs. Blake's fine cooking was known far and near. Since the death of Mr. Blake she has lived quietly with her two daughters in Bentonville. [Benton County Record 5/8/25]

BOLCH, William Henry - W.H. Bolch, for 50 years a resident of Decatur community, died at his home southwest of Decatur Saturday, June 20 at the age of 80 years. Mr. Bolch homesteaded the farm where he died in 1875. He was a member of the Methodist church for more than 40 years. For 30 years he served as Justice of the Peace for Decatur township. He is survived by his wife, five sons and twenty-six grandchildren. [Gravette News-Herald 7/3/25]
In the presence of a host of friends who had gathered from miles around to pay their last tribute to an honored and respected pioneer of Decatur community, services were held at the Methodist Church at 3:00 Sunday afternoon. A mixed choir from the Baptist and Methodist churches furnished the music and Rev. W.C. Savage conducted the service. Interment was made in the Decatur cemetery beside his wife and daughter. William Henry Bolch was born at Hickory, Catawba county, North Carolina April 28, 1845. He spent his early life in North Carolina and when but a youth served bravely in the Confederate army. Following the war he crossed over into Tennessee where he located at Greenville and married Miss Susan J. Malone December 28, 1869. To this union were born one daughter and five sons. In 1872 he moved his family to Craighead county, Arkansas and located at Jonesboro. After his residence there he came to Benton county and homesteaded 160 acres of government land, upon which he built his home. For thirty years he held the public office of Justice of the Peace and ever after he was known affectionately to his people as "Squire." His wife died June 24, 1911. He married the second time to Candace Harmend of Hickory, North Carolina in 1916. He was a member of the Methodist Episcopal Church and a member of the local Masonic order. During February of this year Mr. Bolch suffered a siege of pneumonia and since that time his health has failed him. He died shortly before 5:00 o'clock Saturday afternoon, June 20, 1925. Besides his widow he is survived by his sons, C.A. Bolch, Miami, Okla.; I.J. Bolch, Kansas, Okla.; J.E. Bolch, Baxter Springs, Kansas; G.A. Bolch and H.C. Bolch, both of Decatur, all of whom were with their father at the time of his death. [Benton County Record 6/26/25]

BOOTH, Mr. - General E.E. Booth of the U.S. regular army and stationed at Ft. Riley, Kansas, was in Bentonville Tuesday on his way home after a useless search for his father's grave, located at or near Elm Springs. His father died in December 1884 when General Booth was but a boy of 13 years. Together with his parents they were returning overland by wagon from Texas to the north. Near Elm Springs the father became ill, died and was buried in Elm Springs. General Booth, with the aid of Riley Ritter of Bentonville, who formerly lived there, searched in vain for the last resting place of the general's father. [Benton County Record 5/15/25]

1925

BOSSE, Mrs. Harold - Mr. and Mrs. S. Bosse received the sad news Monday morning of the death of their daughter-in-law, Mrs. Harold Bosse, who died Sunday afternoon in St. Louis. A day old baby survives her. Mrs. Bosse left that night for St. Louis. [Benton County Record 5/15/25]

BOWAN, Jack - {from Hiwasse} Mr. and Mrs. P. Whyle were called to Joplin Sunday by the death of their little grandson, Jack Bowan, son of Mr. and Mrs. Ray Bowan. [Benton County Record 10/23/25]

BOYD, David L. - David L. Boyd was born on July 11th, 1842 and died on July 4th, 1925 at the age of 82 years, 11 months and 23 days. Uncle David, as he was commonly known, had for some years made his home with his nephew, E. Piercy of Osage Mills, and where he was residing at the time of his death. He was married in January 1868 to Margaret Wilkinson who preceded him to the better world ten years ago. He came to Arkansas from Missouri in the year 1867 and had lived here the remainder of his life. He was an ex-Confederate soldier and was most loyal to his post of duty at the time of the Civil War. He is the last of an old family, his brothers and sisters all having preceded him to the Great Beyond. He leaves to mourn their loss a number of nieces and nephews and other relatives. He was converted at the age of 42 years and united with the Missionary Baptist Church and was a faithful member at the time of his death. He was laid to rest in the Temperance Hill cemetery on Sunday, July 5th. Rev. Rice of Springdale had charge of the services. Six great-nephews acted as pallbearers. [Benton County Record 7/10/25]

BOYER, J.L. - C.W. Boyer received a telegram Saturday announcing the death of his brother, J.L. Boyer, at Redfield, South Dakota. Mr. Boyer and wife spent last winter here and at Siloam Springs and will be remembered by many Rogers people. They had expected to come again this winter but could not because of poor health. C.W. Boyer could not go to the funeral because he, too, has been in poor health for some time. [Rogers Democrat 3/12/25]

BRADY, W. Tate - W. Tate Brady, 55 years old, of Tulsa, Okla. and who with his family has been a frequent visitor in Bella Vista, killed himself at his home in Tulsa last Saturday night. Morbid melancholia caused by continual worry over the death of his son, Dave Brady, who was killed in an accident at the University of Virginia this spring, is said to be the cause for his suicide. Mr. Brady, who was very prominent in Oklahoma state and national politics, and a civic leader of Tulsa, often visited at Bella Vista. His son, David Brady, who was killed in an accident in Virginia, and another son, Henry Brady, were visitors last summer at Bella Vista; and this year a younger son, Haskell Brady, spent several weeks visiting here. The death of Mr. Brady is regretted here by his many friends in Bentonville and by the many people of Bella Vista who knew him; especially Tulsans who looked upon him as one of the leading men of their community. [Benton County Democrat 9/1/25]

1925

BRAZIL, Mrs. L.P. - Mrs. L.P. Brazil, mother of G.L. Brazil who operates the grist mill on North Arkansas Street, died this morning at the home of her daughter, Mrs. Mary Cox, west of Avoca. Mrs. Brazil has been confined to her bed for the past week with heart trouble. The body will be shipped back to Wheeler county, Texas for burial. [Rogers Daily Post 7/18/25]

BREEDING, baby - (from Maysville) The Breeding baby, who was burned so seriously, died Friday morning and was buried in the Tinnin cemetery. The family has our deepest sympathy. [Benton County Record 7/3/25]

BREZIL, Mrs. - (from Mountain View) Mrs. Brezil died Sunday morning at the home of her daughter, Mrs. Mary Cox. She had been sick for several days with heart trouble which caused her death. She has one son, George Brezil, of Rogers and one son and three daughters in Texas. She was taken back to Texas for burial. Mrs. Brezil was a very kind and sweet woman and friends of the family extend sympathy to all the children. [Rogers Democrat 7/23/25]

BRIDGFORD, Benjamin Franklin - Benjamin Franklin Bridgford was born May 31, 1852 in Monroe county, Missouri and grew to manhood near Sante Fe, that state. Later he moved to Oklahoma and came from there to Arkansas in 1906. He was united in marriage to Cora McCarey December 23, 1884. To that union was born a little daughter who departed this life when an infant, his wife passing away a few months later. He was united in marriage to Mrs. Mary Massie in 1908. To this union was born a son, Leon Maurice, who died when three years of age. He made the confession and was baptized into the Christian church when he was about 18 years of age. He was 72 years, seven months and seven days old at the time of his death. He was a member of Triumph Lodge, No. 16, Knights of Pythias of Missouri. He was loved by all who knew him and besides his wife, is mourned by three sisters, two brothers and a host of friends. [Rogers Democrat 1/15/25]

(from Cloverdale) Mrs. Verna Young came down from Kansas City to be at the funeral of her stepfather, B.F. Bridgford; who was stricken with paralysis Sunday, January 4th. He was taken to the home of his brother-in-law, Brinson Dean, where medical aid could be reached more readily and where he passed away on the 7th and was laid to rest in Rogers cemetery. [Rogers Democrat 1/15/25]

BROADHURST, Dora Ford - Dora Ford Broadhurst, wife of T.E. Broadhurst, formerly of Pea Ridge, died at her home near Rocky Comfort, Mo. Wednesday, June 17th of apoplexy. Mrs. Broadhurst was 44 years of age and apparently enjoying the best of health until the day before her death. She complained of sick headache on Tuesday and the following day at 11 o'clock she was stricken and fell on the porch and never regained consciousness. She passed away at 8:15 p.m. The funeral services were held at the Presbyterian church at Rocky Comfort and she was laid to rest in the cemetery there. She leaves to mourn her loss a husband, four children, three girls and a boy; three sisters and one brother, all of whom were present at her funeral except the one brother. She leaves a host of relatives and friends who will feel the shock of her sudden death. [Rogers Democrat 6/25/25] [Benton County Democrat 6/25/25]

BROWN, son - {from The Springdale News} The 8-year-old son of Mr. and Mrs. Frank Brown, residing southwest of Springdale in the vicinity of Harmon, was almost instantly killed Tuesday afternoon when his body was crushed between a wagon and house. Mr. Brown owns a mare which has the habit of beginning to back every time she is harnessed up and Tuesday afternoon when she was hitched to the wagon the little son of Mr. Brown was hanging on the back end of the wagon. The animal began backing, catching the lad between the wagon and a house standing near. He was dead almost by the time assistance reached him, being badly crushed. Funeral services were held Wednesday, burial being in the neighborhood cemetery. Deceased was a grandson of Jeff Brown, for years one of the leading residents of that vicinity. [Rogers Democrat 7/16/25]

BROWN, Lenna - Lenna Brown, 11 year old daughter of Mr. and Mrs. Curt Brown whose home is in Mason Valley, died in Rogers of typhoid fever Friday. A fight was made by physicians to save the life of the little girl who was taken to Rogers for treatment by Miss Ruth Beall, executive secretary of the Benton County Tuberculosis Association. Miss Beall secured the financial aid of the business men of Rogers and Bentonville in attempting to save the life of the child. There is much pathos in the story of this little girl's death, as many other members of her family who survive her are also ill. The funeral of the girl was held in Mason Valley. [Benton County Democrat 9/15/25]

{from Centerton} Lennie Brown, the thirteen-year-old daughter of Mr. and Mrs. L.C. Brown, living near Eagle Corner, died at a hospital in Rogers following an illness of typhoid fever and pneumonia. She was buried the following day in the Coffelt cemetery. Both Mr. and Mrs. Brown are also quite ill, the former having had tuberculosis for over a year. [Benton County Record 9/11/25]

Miss Lennie Brown, daughter of Mr. and Mrs. L.C. Brown, was born Dec. 14, 1913 and died Sept. 9, 1925 at Rogers, Ark. She professed faith in Christ April 3rd. Funeral services were conducted by Rev. Morton of Bentonville. She was an active Sunday school worker in the community where she lived but on Sept. 9th God called her home. The remains were laid to rest in the Coffelt cemetery Sept. 11th. Those left to mourn her loss are her parents, one sister and one brother. The family have our sympathy. [Gentry Journal-Advance 9/25/25] [Rogers Daily Post 9/10/25]

BROWN, Oliver - A family feud between the Brown and Ogdon families broke out Tuesday at Pettigrew, Madison county and Oliver Brown, aged 35, was killed. It is reported that six Ogdon brothers fired on Brown, who was alone. Twenty-seven bullet holes were found in the dead man's body. [Benton County Record 7/24/25]

BROWN, Paul Lester - Paul Lester, 16 day old son of Mr. and Mrs. Ralph Brown, was taken sick on Thursday of last week and died Friday, Dec. 26, 1924 at the home of Mr. Brown's sister, Mrs. Charles Steincamp. The funeral was conducted Saturday by Rev. W.H. McCarroll and interment was made in the I.O.O.F. cemetery. Sympathy is extended the young parents and other relatives. [Gravette News-Herald 1/2/25]
Ralph Brown, who is employed in Kansas City, arrived last Thursday on account of the illness of his baby son. Miss Tippie Edwards, the baby's aunt, was also down from Kansas City attending the funeral. Mr. Brown and family and Miss Edwards returned to Kansas City this week. [Gravette News-Herald 1/2/25]

BROWN, S.F. - Rev. S.F. Brown passed away Wednesday morning at 2 o'clock at the home of his daughter, Mrs. Arthur Woodward, after an illness of several weeks. Funeral services were conducted from the Methodist church Thursday morning at 10:30 o'clock by Revs. Villines and Sherman, and interment was in Gentry cemetery. [Gentry Journal-Advance 3/27/25]
Rev. S.F. Brown was born near Wytheville, Va. June 26, 1854. His father was a farmer and a man of splendid Christian faith. As a result, very early in life Rev. Brown was converted and joined the Methodist Episcopal church, South, the church he loved and served until the day of his death. Finishing high school with honors he went to Weaverville College, N.C. and took up the study of medicine but after a short time he felt so strong the call to preach that he turned his attention to theology and at an early day was licensed to preach. He graduated from Weaverville College in 1877. Shortly after his graduation he met Miss Eugenia F. Brown, to whom he was married Sept. 30, 1879. To this union two children were born: Ernest H. Brown, deceased, and Mrs. Eula L. Woodward of Gentry, Ark. Also reared an orphan boy, S.C. Brown, now of Osceola, Ark. After spending some ten years in the local ranks Rev. Brown moved to Arkansas in the year 1887 and immediately was admitted on trial in what was the old White River conference. His first appointment was Wheatley and he served with credit the following charges: Brinkley, Lagrange, Boydesville, Swifton, Alicia, Nettleton, Osceola, Luxora, Marion, Manilla, Reno, Biggers, Black Rock, Gentry, Springtown and Decatur. Because of failing health he asked and was granted the superannuary relation, hoping to in a short time regain his health and take regular work. Three years later when it was found that his health continued to fail he was granted the superannuate relation. His was a long and useful life, some 38 years in the ministry. As his pastor I found him a source of great help. Brother Brown has gone home. On the early morning of March the 25th God called for him. He walked with God and is not because God took him. Floyd G. Villines, P.C. [Gentry Journal-Advance 4/17/25]

1925

BROWNING, George - George Browning, a well known resident of the Decatur neighborhood, died last Wednesday following a stroke of paralysis. Mr. Browning was a resident of this section for nearly 40 years and was about 70 years old. Funeral services were conducted by the Rev. A.W. Crowley with interment in the Falling Springs cemetery. Two sons, Will and Sam Browning, and two sisters, Mrs. W.H. Box and Mrs. L.P. Gortney, survive him. [Benton County Record 11/13/25]

BROWNING, Thomas - Thomas Browning, a well known and highly respected farmer, died at his home east of Hiwasse, near Condit, Saturday evening after an illness of some time. Funeral services were held from the home with interment in the Coffelt cemetery. Besides his widow he is survived by one daughter, Mrs. George Maples, of Pea Ridge and one son, Will Browning of Hiwasse. [Benton County Record 1/16/25]

BROYHILL, George - {from Decatur} George Broyhill, a well known farmer living west of town, died on March 4th of pneumonia resulting from an attack of the flu. He was a brother of Paul Broyhill and was about 60 years of age. A wife and two grown children survive him. Burial was made in the Falling Springs cemetery. He was an old resident of this section and had lived here over 40 years. [Benton County Record 3/13/25]

BRUNER, Bertha - {from Gentry} Mrs. Bertha Bruner, age 70 years, died at the home of her sister, Mrs. A. Bolin, October 8 after a long illness. Interment was made Friday in the city cemetery. Mrs. Bruner was born in Germany and was a graduate of the Berlin Conservatory of Arts. [Benton County Record 10/16/25]

Mrs. Bertha Bruner died at her home in northwest Gentry Thursday. With her sister, Mrs. A. Bond, she had made her home here a number of years. She was a native of Germany, being born in Berlin seventy years ago. The sister here is the only known relative. Funeral services were held Friday afternoon conducted by Rev. R.L. Hughes and burial made in the city cemetery. [Gentry Journal-Advance 10/16/25]

BULLEN, Wm. G. - {from Vaughn} F.A. Bradshaw was called to Lincoln on Sunday afternoon to preach the funeral service of Wm. G. Bullen of that place. Burial was had in the Cane Hill cemetery. [Benton County Record 9/4/25]

BURCH, Alford - {from Stony Point} Word came to relatives last week of the death of Alford Burch at Atchison, Kansas on last Tuesday. He did quite a bit of work around the lime kiln during the time of its operations here. [Rogers Democrat 11/5/25]

BURCHER, James C. - James C. Burcher, an old time resident and merchant of Gentry some 8 years ago at the Brogdon corner, died last Tuesday morning, the 17th of November and was buried on the 21st in East Iola, Kansas cemetery. The deceased was 69 years and 9 months of age. His son, Charley, of Kansas City, was there to attend the funeral. [Gentry Journal-Advance 12/4/25] {from Gentry} J.C. Burcher, formerly a grocer and resident of Gentry and who moved to Iola, Kans. about three years ago, died at his home in that city last Wednesday. Death followed an illness of a number of months. [Benton County Record 12/11/25]

BURNETT, Jerry - {from Hiwasse} Curt Banks was called home from Tulsa, where he has been working, by the death of his grandfather, Mr. Burnett, close to Pea Ridge. We all wish to extend our sincere sympathy to Mrs. F.H. Banks in her bereavement. [Benton County Record 6/12/25] Jerry Burnett died at his home near Jacket, Mo. June 6th, 1925 at the age of 70. Mr. Burnett was one of Benton county's native sons and was born in Pea Ridge in 1854. He is survived by seven grown children: Joe and Leroy Burnett of Jacket; J.E. Burnett of Grove; Reuben Burnett of Afton; Natt Burnett of Webb City; Mrs. F.H. Banks of Hiwasse and Mrs. J.C. Neehan of Anderson, Mo. He had been a member of the Christian church for over 30 years. [Benton County Record 6/19/25]

BURRIS, Burt - Several from here attended the funeral of Dr. Burt Burris at his home on Flint creek Sunday afternoon and later burial was made in Siloam cemetery. The funeral oration was delivered by Rev. W.T. Farley of Siloam and a Gentry choir furnished the music. The funeral was under the auspices of the Masonic lodge. [Gentry Journal-Advance 7/3/25]

BURROW, James Wesley - James Wesley Burrow died suddenly at his home in Decatur Sunday night about 8 o'clock. He was 64 years of age and had lived in or near Decatur all his life. Funeral services were held Monday afternoon and burial was made in the Decatur cemetery. [Gentry Journal-Advance 10/16/25}

BURROWS, James W. - {from Decatur} In the death of James W. Borrows, who died on October 11th, Decatur loses its oldest resident for Mr. Burrows was born here sixty-four years ago, long before a town here was thought of. He had lived here practically all his life. [Benton County Record 10/23/25]

BUSHONG, Samuel - {from Hiwasse} Word was received by Mrs. E.A. Stanley of the death of an uncle, Samuel Bushong, of Orange, Calif. He was 83 years and 18 days old. Death was caused by a complication of diseases and old age. [Benton County Record 1/23/25]

BUTTRAM, Madge Louise - Madge Louise Buttram, the ten months old daughter of Mr. and Mrs. L.H. Buttram, died Friday afternoon at the home in Bentonville after an illness of but a week. Funeral services were held Sunday afternoon with burial at Buttram's Chapel. The bereaved ones have the sympathy of their many friends in their hour of sadness. [Benton County Democrat 10/13/25]

BUTTRAM, Mary Josephine - Mary Josephine Buttram, the sweet little daughter of Mr. and Mrs. James Buttram of Pea Ridge, is missed by her little playmates, Sunday school classmates and friends. On the 13th of February the school children had a Valentine party at the public school and they stopped by to show little Mary Joe, as they affectionately called her, their valentines. Filled with glee she ran into the kitchen to show them to her father and mother and accidentally stumbled over a boiler of hot water that had just been taken off the stove and received burns that caused her death March 1st. On Monday afternoon at Buttram's Chapel, where she was a faithful little Sunday school pupil, many friends and relatives gathered to show their love for Mary Joe. Mr. Giles told how faithful she was to the Sunday school. Her pastor, the Rev. W.T. Bone, and Rev. J. Wilson Crichlow, told of the beauty of her short life. Then her body was laid to rest by the side of her little brother, James, and the mound was covered with beautiful flowers. Her stay with us seems entirely too short - from June 16, 1921 to March 1, 1925. J. Wilson Crichlow. [Rogers Democrat 3/19/25] [Benton County Record 3/6/25]

BUTTRAM, William Dottry - William Dottry Buttram was born on January 3, 1839 in Meigs county, Tenn., died July 29, 1925. He came to Arkansas when a young man and was married to Miss Josie Patterson in the prime of manhood. To this union was born seven children. Three have passed on to be with God. He was converted when a young man and united with the Methodist Church, to which he was faithful and true until the end came on July 29 at 12:45 o'clock. God saw fit to call his companion from this world to be with Him in heaven in the year 1896. A happy home circle was broken. Brother Buttram was again married to Miss Mattie Hileman in the year 1900. This was a happy union until death again came and called for Brother Buttram. The church has lost a faithful member. Uncle Dot, as he was known by that name, will be missed by everyone who knew him. He leaves a faithful wife and two sons and two daughters and a host of relatives and friends to mourn his death. The funeral service was conducted by the pastor, assisted by Rev. J.E. Vinson of Texas and Rev. A.E. Carnahan, pastor of the Presbyterian Church of Pea Ridge. The funeral service was at the Buttram Chapel Church at 2:30 o'clock Friday afternoon, July 31. After a service that touched all those present he was laid to rest in the Buttram Chapel cemetery. Before a large congregation of friends and loved ones he passed away, but his influence for good will still be felt in the community. His Pastor, Willie Thomas Bone. {"Uncle Dot" was one of our oldest citizens, being 86 years, 6 months and 26 days old. His children surviving him are Mrs. Lee Pounds of Claridian, Texas; Mrs. Orvil Buttram of near Texarkana; Mrs. Tim Rice and John Buttram, both of Brightwater.} [Benton County Democrat 8/11/25]

BUTTRY, Madge Louise - The infant daughter of Mr. and Mrs. L.H. Buttry lingered but a few months before she was transferred to the home eternal. Madge Louise was the name given her. She was born December 22, 1924 and went to the sunshine of the better world on October 10, 1925. She was a beautiful babe and until the unrelenting clutches of disease seized her, gave evidence of growing into a vigorous child. In the presence of a multitude of friends and with floral tributes banked about the little white casket, the funeral rites were said by Rev. Joe M. Tyson, pastor of the Church of the Nazarene, and her little body was laid to rest in the Buttram Chapel Cemetery to await His coming. She is survived by a little twin brother, an elder brother and sister and the parents. [Benton County Democrat 10/20/25] [Benton County Record 10/16/25]

CADY, George Byron - G. Byron Cady died at 6:15 Tuesday evening at the home of his parents, Mr. and Mrs. W.R. Cady, just southeast of Rogers. He had been failing rapidly for several days and his death was not unexpected by the family and intimate friends, although Byron himself refused to give up hope for recovery until the last. He was kept alive for several weeks almost solely by his determination to live and he was continually making plans for the coming summer, but the ravages of disease were too great to be overcome. Funeral services will be held this afternoon at the Presbyterian church at 3:00 o'clock and will be conducted by the pastor, Rev. Ben. H. Moore. Services will be conducted at the Rogers cemetery by the Masonic order and the Knights Templar. Mr. Cady had been troubled with poor health for several years but it was not until the first of the year, 1924, after he went to Chicago for an operation, that he became bedfast. After his return to Rogers a year ago he was able for a time to get about in a wheeled chair, but later in the summer had to spend most of his time in bed. In the fall he was taken to Tucson, Arizona by his brother, Howard Cady. Something over a month ago the physicians at the Tucson hospital notified the family that he was losing ground and advised that he come home. His father went after him and since his return he had been at the Cady home. While the friends of Mr. Cady are glad that his long months of suffering are over, they deeply regret his untimely death, for Rogers has lost one of its deservedly popular and most promising young men. Most of his forty years were spent in Rogers - and he had "made good" in every way. It is not easy for the Democrat editor to write these lines for his heart is sore at the loss of a tried and true friend of more than a quarter of a century's standing. For some six or seven years the writer and Byron were editors respectively of the Rogers Democrat and the Rogers Republican and during that entire time there was never a serious disagreement or the slightest break in their friendship. Only a couple of weeks ago the Democrat told of the resignation of Mr. Cady as postmaster of Rogers, enforced by his continued illness and absence from the office, and gave a detailed sketch of the many improvements initiated by him during his service in that position. We are glad that he was able to read and enjoy that little tribute for it was honestly earned and he was entitled to know that our people thoroughly appreciated his continued efforts to improve the local postal service. Byron Cady was a man with real executive ability and much talent and had his physical resources been equal to the demands all too generously made upon them he would have gone far in his chosen profes-

sion - that of newspaper worker. At the time when he had a firm grasp upon the rounds of the ladder of success as managing editor of the Waco {Texas} Morning News, he was compelled, because of ill health, to give it up and retire to the farm and orchard here as a member of the firm of W.R. Cady & Sons. In 1917 he was a member of the Rogers Rotary Club under the classification of "Cooperage," one of the activities of this family combination of business men. When he became acting postmaster of Rogers May 16, 1921, followed on June 1st of that year by his appointment as postmaster, he threw himself into the work with all the intense enthusiasm that he had always given to his work and we fear perhaps the indoor work and the long hours given to the study of the needs of the office and the patrons it served, was the immediate cause of the trouble that was finally diagnosed as tuberculosis of the spine, although there have been other complications that hastened his death. George Byron Cady was born in Springfield, Mo. Sept. 15, 1885 and was the oldest son of Mr. and Mrs. W.R. Cady of this city, Mr. Cady being at that time in the railroad service out of Springfield. Byron graduated from Rogers Academy in the class of 1903 and at once took over the management of the Rogers Republican, which had been bought by his father, then postmaster here several years earlier, and with which Byron had become well acquainted. After the sale of the Republican in 1907 Byron went to the Springfield Leader-Democrat and a year or so later became a member of the staff of the El Paso Daily Herald as railroad reporter. From El Paso he went to the San Angelo Standard and then a year or so later he went to Waco to the work previously mentioned. He was married to Miss Vivian Kruse of Rogers September 4, 1917 and to them was born one son, Jim, who is seven years old. They made their home on the Cady farms on the corner south of his father's place until he returned from the hospital a year ago when they moved to the Wing place on West Poplar. In addition to his parens, his wife and his young son, Mr. Cady is survived by his younger brother, Howard B. Cady of this city, and numerous other relatives. [Rogers Democrat 5/21/25]
{Shorter notices were found in The Benton County Record of 5/22/25, The Benton County Democrat of 5/28/25 and The Rogers Daily Post of 5/20/25}

CALLIS, Polly - "Aunt Polly" Callis, long a resident of Centerton, died at the home of her son, Bone Callis, Monday afternoon. Burial will take place Tuesday afternoon in the Gamble cemetery. She is survived by two sons, Bone and John Callis, both of Centerton. She has lived in Centerton for many years. She was the wife of the late William Callis. Aunt Polly had been in ill health for a long time and very little hopes had been held for her recovery. Her death brought great sadness to many people of Centerton, who had known her for such a long time. She had always been very active in religious work until her recent long illness. [Benton County Democrat 10/13/25]
{from Centerton} Mrs. Charles McKissick and James and wife came over

from Big Cabin, Okla. Tuesday to attend the funeral of her mother, Mrs. Polly Callis. [Benton County Record 10/16/25]

CAMERON, Mrs. Dan {McCARTNEY} - Mrs. Dan Cameron, 28 year old daughter of Mr. and Mrs. W.M. McCartney, the local chair manufacturer, died this morning at the Lutheran Hospital in Denver following an illness of several months. Mrs. Hattie McGivins, a younger sister who lives in Picher, Okla., was with her at the time of her death. [Rogers Daily Post 5/28/25]

CAMPBELL, A.B. - {from Gravette} Notice has been received of the death of A.B. Campbell, a former well known Gravette citizen. He died December 10th at Canyon, Utah. He was about 80 years old and leaves a widow and one son. [Benton County Record 12/25/25]

CARDWELL, W.A. - W.A. Cardwell, one of Benton county's highly respected citizens, fell from the barn loft at his home south of Springtown on Monday of last week and was fatally injured. Physicians were called at once and upon examination it was found that his lungs were so injured by the fall that there were no hopes for his recovery. He passed away on Thursday evening. He was 74 years of age. Besides his widow he is survived by seven children, Walter, Jake and Bert Cardwell, who live in Oklahoma, and Mrs. Cal Guthary and Mrs. Tom Dellinger of Logan; Mrs. Wm. Holbrook and Mrs. Jason Guthary, also living in Oklahoma. All of his children were at his bedside when he died. While here Mrs. Holbrook lost her eyesight and was taken home in a serious condition. Funeral services were held at the Fairmount church, Rev. Willie Downum officiating. He was laid to rest in the presence of his old friends and neighbors. He professed faith in Christ when a young man and has been a member of the M.E. Church all his life. He also served as a deacon in his church for a number of years. [Benton County Record 6/12/25]

CARL, Tom - {from Decatur} Word was received here last week that Tom Carl, son of Mr. and Mrs. H.C. Carl, had been shot and killed at Auburn, Cal. The deceased was about 45 years of age and was born and brought up here. [Benton County Record 1/23/25]

CARSON, W.H. - Word was received last week of the recent death of W.H. Carson at the home of his daughter, Mrs. D.E. Henderson, at Sioux City, Iowa. Mr. Carson, who was past 80 years of age, was buried by the side of his wife at Sloan, Iowa. The Carsons and Hendersons lived east of Rogers a number of years ago on the road to the Ozark school house and are well remembered by many of the people of that neighborhood. [Rogers Democrat 3/5/25]

CHAMBERS, Pearl - The burial of Pearl Chambers, who died last week in New Mexico, was held in Centerton Sunday. The deceased was a former resident of Centerton, having moved to New Mexico about a year ago. She had been in ill health for some time. The body was accompanied to Centerton by Albert Chambers, her father, who is also a former resident of Centerton.

Mrs. Chambers was unable to attend the funeral on account of illness. She is survived in Centerton by Mrs. Ruth Bailey, her sister. A brother, Rex Chambers of Joplin, attended the funeral. [Benton County Democrat 10/13/25]

CHILSON, W.H. - Prof. D.M. Greer with his mother, Mrs. L.C. Greer, and his son, David, driving overland, left Tuesday for Henrietta, Texas, called there by a wire telling of the death of W.H. Chilson, brother-in-law of Mrs. Greer, which occurred that morning. Prof. Greer and his son will return immediately but Mrs. Greer will remain indefinitely. They arrived in Henrietta Wednesday afternoon. [Benton County Record 6/19/25]

CLARK, Lulu COOPER - The remains of Mrs. Ernest Clark, who died at her home in Slaton, Texas June 25, were laid to rest in the Mt. Pleasant cemetery Monday afternoon. Mrs. Clark was the youngest daughter of Mr. and Mrs. Dave Cooper and was born and reared and lived most of her life in this community. Her aged mother, her husband, son and sister, Mrs. J.L. Buxton, and Mr. Buxton and nephew, Ray Hubby, accompanied the corpse from Slaton. Elder C.M. Day conducted the funeral services. [Benton County Democrat 7/2/25]

Funeral services were held at the family home near Hiwasse on Tuesday afternoon, June 30th, 1925 for Mrs. Ernest Clark, daughter of Mr. and Mrs. David Cooper, who died on Thursday of last week at her home in Slater {sic}, Texas, after an illness of several months. She was about 30 years of age. Besides her parents she is survived by her husband, a small son and several brothers and sisters, including Mrs. John R. Duty of Rogers. She was born and grew to womanhood near Hiwasse. The funeral was conducted by Rev. Day, pastor of the Christian church. The body was brought from Rogers by Undertaker A.D. Callison and was accompanied by six car loads of relatives and friends. Interment was made in the Mt. Pleasant cemetery. [Benton County Record 7/3/25] [Rogers Daily Post 6/29/25]

Funeral services were held Monday afternoon at the Mount Pleasant cemetery near Hiwasse for Mrs. Lulu Clark, wife of Ernest Clark and a sister of Mrs. John Duty of this city. Mrs. Clark died June 25th at Slaten {sic}, Texas after a long illness. The deceased was a daughter of Dave Cooper of Hiwasse and is survived by her husband and one son. [Rogers Democrat 7/2/25]

CLARK, R.C. {Bob} - Springdale, Dec. 25.- R.C. {Bob} Clark, 53 years old, one of Springdale's best known business men, died suddenly of heart disease Thursday night at 8:30 o'clock at his home on North Thompson street. He was alone at the time, Mrs. Clark having gone to the First Baptist church to attend the Christmas exercises. Shortly before he died Mr. Clark called Dr. J.E. Martin over the telephone, telling him that he was having a little trouble with his heart and as he was alone, requested the doctor to come up and see him. Dr. Martin went immediately and when he reached the Clark home he found Mr. Clark seated in a rocking chair, dead. One foot was on the foot-rest of the stove, showing that he died without a struggle. He was about his business as usual at the Famous Hardware company all day Thursday, apparently in his usual health, but had complained of slight illness the day before. His last words over the telephone to Dr. Martin did not indicate anything serious. The death of Mr. Clark came as a shock to the community. He was universally liked. He had served as president of the Springdale community club and was one of the vice-presidents at the time of his death, and also a member of the city council. He was chairman of the committee that staged the grape festival in Springdale last August and much of the success of the affair was ascribed to his enthusiasm. He was a charter member of the local Rotary club and took an active part in all civic affairs. Mr. Clark was born in Tennessee April 28, 1873 and at an early age moved with his parents, Mr. and Mrs. J.M. Clark, to Boone county, this state. When he was 14 years old the family moved to Madison county, locating near Hindsville, and here he spent his early life. In March 1907 he entered business in Springdale as a member of the Famous hardware company and has been active in the affairs of that company since. [Rogers Democrat 12/31/25] [Benton County Democrat 12/29/25]

CLARK, Sarah O. - Miss Sarah O. Clark, a sister of Rev. T.B. Clark, pastor of the First Christian church, died at 3:15 this morning at 516 Spring Street at the age of 21 years, nine months and 17 days. Death was the result of tubercular trouble with which she had suffered for several years. Miss Clark came to Rogers from El Paso just three weeks ago today. Miss Clark was a native of Arkansas, having been born near Jonesboro. Funeral services will be held at the Christian church this afternoon (Thursday) at 2:00 o'clock and will be conducted by Rev. W.W. Phares. [Rogers Democrat 4/23/25]

Miss Sarah Clark, sister of Rev. Tom B. Clark, passed away this morning at her home on Spring St. at the age of 23 years. Miss Clark was a victim of flu five years ago which later developed into tuberculosis and had been in a sanitarium in San Angelo, Texas. Mr. Clark wished to have his sister near him and thinking this climate might prove beneficial he brot her here a few weeks ago. The change seemed to make a decided improvement but last night after having passed a comfortable day she began sinking and died a few hours later. The funeral occurred this afternoon at the Christian Church at 2 o'clock conducted by the Rev. Phares. The interment was made in the city cemetery. Rev. Clark and Mrs. Clark have the sympathy of every one in Rogers in this loss which came so unexpectedly and only three weeks ago Mr. Clark returned from the funeral of his brother. Many members of the Kiwanis club, of which Mr. Clark is a prominent member, attended the services today. [Rogers Daily Post 4/23/25]

(This item was written by a friend. We have included only any additional information.) Miss Sarah O. Clark was born near Salado, Ark. July 22, 1905 and died at Rogers, Ark. April 23, 1925. Being left an orphan at 12 years of age her brother, Rev. T.B. Clark, has been more than a brother to her for many years. Funeral services were conducted at the First Christian Church at Rogers at two o'clock Thursday afternoon, April 23, Wm. Washington Phares of Dallas, Texas officiating. [Rogers Daily Post 4/24/25]

CLARK, Will, Jr. - {torn item} Will Clark, Jr. of Riverton, Kans., a nephew of J.H. Peel of this place and a former Bentonville boy, died last Friday evening at Joplin, Mo. after an illness of some weeks, ______ about 40 years. Interment was made at Wichita, Kan. where Mr. Clark and his wife had formerly lived and where they have a child buried. Will Clark was a son of Mr. and Mrs. Will Clark, who formerly _____ here, and was born at the old ______ Hotel, where the Hotel Massey now stands, where his grandparents ______ lived and where his father was ______ . In early manhood he left Bentonville and later became associated with the Empire Electric Company ______ of the largest power companies in the country and at the time of his death was head electrician of ____ power site at Riverton, Kan., ______ one of his brothers is also employed. Besides his father and stepmother, who live at Spokane, Wash., he is survived by two brothers, Bob Clark of Riverton, Kan. and Chas. Clark of Spokane, Wash., and two sisters, Mrs. John Bryan of Tulsa and _____ other married sister who was formerly Miss Bess Clark of this place. [Benton County Democrat 5/7/25]

CLAYBOURNE, Mr. - {from Highfill} Mr. Claybourne passed from this world on Monday night a little past midnight. He was an old soldier and a highly respected citizen. He had been an invalid for a great many years and a constant sufferer. No matter how severe his pain he was always cheerful and loved to talk of the war. He was a firm believer in God and was anxious to be called home where there would be no suffering or sorrow. Brother Brogan of Healing Springs conducted the funeral services which were held at the family residence and the body was laid to rest in the Highfill cemetery. [Benton County Record 4/10/25]

CLAYTON, Ollie - Miss Ollie Clayton was born in Texas March 12, 1888 and departed this life February 15th at 7:30 a.m. in Rogers. She has been afflicted for some ten years. She was converted some three years ago and united with the First Christian church. She remained faithful until death claimed her. She bore her afflictions cheerfully and would talk with her Master. She leaves to mourn her loss a mother, a sister and six brothers. Only the sister was by her side when she died. She leaves also a host of friends. Funeral services were conducted Sunday evening at 4 o'clock at the Rogers cemetery by Rev. J.W. Crichlow of the Central M.E. church. Callison Undertaking Co. was in charge of the body and both rendered fine service. The remains were laid to rest in Rogers cemetery. [Rogers Democrat 2/19/25]

Ollie Clayton, who had suffered with tuberculosis for a period of ten years. died Sunday in Rogers at the home of Mr. and Mrs. Burdick where she had been cared for. The funeral was held Sunday afternoon and interment made in the Rogers cemetery. The tubercular patient had been absolutely helpless for several years but had borne her suffering patiently. [Benton County Democrat 2/19/25]

CLEMENT(S), John - {from Cave Springs} John Clements, a well known citizen of this place, died Monday night of pneumonia. Mr. Clements was sick only a few days. He leaves a wife and nine children and at this time three of them are ill with pneumonia. Lloyd, the first to take the disease, has been seriously ill but is better now. Mrs. Clements has the sympathy of the entire community in her bereavement and trouble. The body of Mr. Clements was buried in the local cemetery. [Benton County Democrat 1/22/25]

W.A. Clement and his niece, Marie Clement, attended the funeral of his brother, John Clement, at Cave Springs Tuesday afternoon. [Benton County Record 1/23/25]

John Clement, a well known carpenter of Cave Springs, died Monday night, January 19th, 1925 of pneumonia, after an illness of about a week. Funeral services were held Tuesday afternoon with interment in the Phillips cemetery. Besides his widow he is survived by nine children. He is also survived by four brothers - W.A. and Burton Clement of Bentonville; L.A. and Charles Clement of Dawn, Mo.; and one sister - Mrs. Ida Leach of Fredonia, Kansas. [Benton County Record 1/23/25]

{from Hebron} Death took away another useful life when John Clement answered the call Monday night at 10 o'clock at the age of 54 years. His going leaves a wife and eight children and most of the children are small and solely dependent on his work for maintenance. He was one of the most honest, upright, noble men we have ever known. He was a good carpenter and hundreds of buildings in the country are monuments to his handiwork. When not otherwise employed he was pruning apple trees and was an expert at the job. He never asked exorbitant prices for his labor, was always reasonable in his dealings; always doing the meek and humble things of life; never out of humor or worried, and ever had a cheerful "Hello" for his many friends - and everyone was his friend. Funeral services were conducted at the Apostolic church Tuesday at 2:00 o'clock and the body was interred in the Phillips cemetery. [Rogers Democrat 1/22/25]

CLOUD, Isabell FULLER Rinard - Mrs. Isabell {Fuller} Cloud was born April 21, 1848 and departed this life at the home of her daughter, Mrs. R.L. Notson, the evening of May 8, 1925, aged 77 years and 17 days. When she reached womanhood she was married to Shadrach Rinard, a minister of the Christian church, who is the father of Mrs. Notson. Two daughters preceded her in death, leaving but one surviving child; one died in childhood and Mrs. May Hall of Salina, Kan., who also died at Mrs. Notson's home in Oklahoma 15 years ago. Her first husband passed away several years ago. She was married to William Cloud in Indiana some years later. Mrs. Cloud united with the Christian church early in life and died in the faith of that denomination. She has made her home the past two years and over with her daughter at this home. Being in feeble health during this time and bedfast for the last six months, she received the very best care her daughter could give her. She is survived by several grandchildren and great-grandchildren and one daughter, Mrs. R.L. Notson. Sunday afternoon, Mother's Day, funeral services were held at the Notson home, attended by a large number of sympathizing friends and neighbors, conducted by Rev. D.F. Lillard, pastor of the Gentry Baptist church. After the services the casket was borne to the Gentry cemetery near the home where she died and there she was tenderly laid to rest to await the resurrection morn. [Gentry Journal-Advance 5/15/25]

CLOUSTON, Gary Nellette TULLY - Mrs. Charley Clouston died at an early hour yesterday morning at her home at Nellette Ranch, ten miles southeast of Rogers. Her condition had been very critical for several weeks and her death hourly expected for some time. Only unusual vitality with a tenacious desire to recover kept her alive so long. Funeral services will be held at the Presbyterian church of Rogers Friday afternoon at two o'clock, conducted by the pastor, Rev. Ben H. Moore. The body will be placed in the Bentonville mausoleum, waiting later arrangements as to the final resting place. Mrs. Clouston came to Benton county from St. Louis some fifteen years ago and bought the property on White river that has since become the Nellette Ranch, famous thruout the country as the home of one of the finest Island Jersey herds in the Southwest. Mr. Clouston, who was in business in St. Louis, spent only a portion of his time here in the early years of the making of the Ranch and the management was in the hands of Mrs. Clouston and her manager, Larry Palm. When in the last days of her illness Mrs. Clouston desired to see the famous Nellette Ranch Jerseys, which were being shown at the various Missouri fairs and which had already won many honors, they were brought home from Carthage Sunday. Mrs. Clouston was born at Salem, Ill. and was 48 years old. Her maiden name was Gary Nellette Tully. She married Charley Clouston in 1893 and most of their life, before she came to Northwest Arkansas for her health, was spent in St. Louis. They had no children. A nephew, Frank Tully, lived with them at the Ranch. Mrs. Clouston was a big hearted woman with many splendid qualities and the spirit of kindness, charity and helpfulness were perhaps best known in her own neighborhood where she was for many years the guardian saint of the sick and needy on every possible occasion. She will be missed by an unusually large circle of friends and acquaintances, both here and abroad. [Rogers Democrat 9/10/25]
{from Rogers} The funeral of Mrs. Nellette Tully Clouston, prominent throughout this section as the founder of the famous Nellette Ranch, who died at her home near Rogers Wednesday morning following a long illness, was held from the First Presbyterian church at Rogers Friday afternoon.

The body was placed in the Bentonville mausoleum where it will remain until a place of burial has been selected. She is survived by her husband, Charles Clouston and two nephews, Frank and Harry Tully of Philadelphia. Mrs. Clouston was a second cousin of the late William Jennings Bryan. Throughout northwestern Arkansas Mrs. Clouston was noted for the famous ranch she founded eight miles east of Rogers and which is famed for its progressive stock raising methods. Mrs. Clouston moved to Rogers from St. Louis fifteen years ago following the advice of physicians. She had practically regained her health until the last illness. Loved and greatly admired in Rogers was Mrs. Clouston for her philanthropic work. She was a leader in the community and her loss will be greatly felt. After establishing the Nellette Ranch she stocked it with registered cattle, imported from the Isle of Jersey. One herd was brought from the Missouri fair where they were on exhibition last week, that the owner might get a farewell look upon her prize winning herd. She also had a kennel of English bulldogs, one of which was her constant companion until its death last month. Hundreds of tourists visited the ranch annually where they were always welcomed by the owner. [Benton County Democrat 9/15/25] [Benton County Record 9/11/25]
{Excerpts from an eulogy} Married at the age of sixteen on Jan. 10, 1893 at the home of her brother in Salem, Ill., Gary Nellette Tully, to Charley Clouston, her home life has been ideal, the devotion between the two has been noted. There were no children: they have had two nephews, Frank and Harry Tully of Philadelphia, in their home. Mrs. Harry Miller of Siloam Springs is a niece and there is another nephew, Thomas Jean Osborn, of Beaver Falls, N.Y., besides some second cousins, one of whom was the late William Jennings Bryan. [Rogers Daily Post 9/9/25]

COLCORD, Mrs. Clay - {from Gravette} Clay Colcord of Chicago, whose wife died there on December 8th, is here with his four motherless children who will be cared for by his mother, Mrs. I.A. Colcord. [Benton County Record 1/2/25]

COLE, William M. - William M. Cole, for fifty years a resident of the Centerton community, died at his home four miles northwest of Centerton on Tuesday morning, September 29th, 1925 at the age of 76 years. He had been ill for the past six weeks, having suffered a general breakdown. William Cole was the eldest of a family of five children and was born in Hickory county, Mo. on January 25th, 1849. His parents, Newton C. Cole and Candace Brashears Cole, had come to Missouri from Tennessee. When a child of five years he moved with his parents to Barry county where they settled on a farm on Big Sugar west of Seligman and where he grew into manhood. His home was but a few miles from the battle fields during the Civil War and the rumble of cannon and the curse of war were black marks on his childhood memory. The Cole farm and home were constantly trespassed upon by both armies and the Coles fed Union men and

Confederates alike. He was but 12 years old at the time and when the bushwhackers and the hangers on were menacing the country around, William Cole and two other persons drove a herd of horses of blooded stock to Dardanelle, Ark. for their safety. The one horse that was left on the Cole farm was taken by one of the armies and served some rider in the battle of Pea Ridge. On January 25th, 1872 Mr. Cole was married to Miss Margaret M. Easley. To this union were born three daughters. He became a member of the Primitive Baptist Church in November 1874. He came to Arkansas in 1875 and homesteaded 160 acres of government land in Benton county on which he has lived the remaining fifty years of his life. He is survived by his widow, who is an invalid, and two daughters: Mrs. E.P. Woods and Mrs. G.D. Allen of Leach, Okla.; one sister, Mrs. M.L. Seamster, and five brothers, Joe Cole, Jasper Cole, Jim Cole, John Cole and Robert Cole. [Benton County Record 10/2/25]

COLLINS, baby - {from The Springdale News} The year old son of Rossie Collins of Combs, Madison county was found dead in bed Wednesday morning of last week. During the night some time it had gotten the cover wrapped around its neck in some manner, choking to death. [Rogers Democrat 6/11/25]

COLLINS, Nancy E. WALKER - Nancy E. Walker, daughter of Jesse and Jane Walker, was born Oct. 15, 1854 near the old Thornsberry camp ground and died April 5, 1925, aged 70 years, five months and 20 days, at her home near Robinson. The funeral services, conducted by Rev. J.A. Leach of Siloam Springs, were held Sunday afternoon at the Stanfield cemetery where interment was made. She was married to Jim Riley Collins Nov. 7, 1872. To this union four children were born, one dying in infancy, and a married daughter, Catherine Hodges, passed away on Dec. 5, 1904. A devoted husband, two children, ten grandchildren and seven great grandchildren, three sisters and two brothers are left to mourn her departure. The children are: Otis Collins and Mrs. Abbie Holland. Grandchildren: Mrs. Audie Thompson, New Mexico; Clyde Holland, California; Lester Holland, Kansas; Mrs. Irene Abercrombie, Robinson, Kans.; Misses Beulah and Cleo Holland, Cave Springs, Ark.; Neta and Walter Holland, Thornsberry; Mrs. Nona Locke, Wichita, Kans.; and Carl Collins, near Robinson. Her sisters: Mrs. Mary Sheffield, Westville, Okla.; Mrs. Ann Bolton, Grove, Okla. and Mrs. Jim Walker, Tolola, Okla. and John Walker, Neosho, Mo. She also leaves many other relatives and friends who will mourn the loss of one whom the Reaper has gathered as his own. She was baptised into the Church of Christ when about 17 years of age, having lived a true, Christian life for the past 53 years. There is nothing I can add about her life except what is already known to those of her acquaintances, as she was personally known and loved by everyone, having spent nearly all of her entire life within one mile of her birthplace. She was indeed a loving wife, tender mother and good neighbor. [Benton County Democrat 4/9/25]

COLVILLE, Mary LOONEY - Mrs. Mary Colville died Thursday at Holdenville, Okla. at the home of her daughter, Mrs. Lucy Horne. Mrs. Colville was 86 years old and was reared in this county, near Colville. Her husband died about three years ago. Besides Mrs. Horn, Mrs. Colville is survived by three other daughters, Mrs. Samuels of Springdale; Mrs. Sallie Boydstun of Larue and Mrs. Emma Lynch of Clifty. She is also survived by one brother, Mart Looney of this city. [Rogers Democrat 3/19/25]

COOK, Fred - The car of the youthful bandits was taken to the United Garage and while examining it Tuesday a half a gallon jug of whiskey was found hidden in the battery box underneath the car. Deputy McAllister took the jug to Bentonville Tuesday and turned the same over to Sheriff Gailey. The car was riddled with buckshot and bullets and the windshield shot to pieces. It looked as if a machine gun had been turned loose on it. About 30 shots were fired by the officers and bandits. Perry's coat was grazed by one of the first shots fired by the robbers. He promptly dropped to the ground and shot from that position. Fred Cook, aged 19, was shot and instantly killed and Brooks Goodpasture, 26, and C.M. Bullock, 20, captured in a gun fight with Deputy Sheriff Ern McAllister and H.E. Perry on the state highway in Gravette about 12:15 Monday morning, after robbing the Cook Drug Store in Noel, Mo. about an hour previously. The robbers, who claim Edgerton, Mo. as their home, only secured 15 cents for the midnight adventure, Mr. Cook having a short time before removed about $300 from the cash register and hidden it. After the hold-up the bandits left town in their Ford at a rapid rate and headed south. Phone messages were sent to nearby towns asking the officers to be on the lookout for the robbers and arrest them. Ern McAllister, night watch at Gravette, who is also a deputy sheriff, and H.E. Perry, the proprietor of a cafe in that town, stationed themselves on the highway just north of Main Street. Two cars were halted but neither contained the desired parties. The third car refused to stop when ordered and its occupants opened fire on the officers. McAllister, who was armed with a shotgun loaded with buckshot, and Perry with a big German Luger pistol, returned the fire. In the fight Cook was shot in 2 places and died almost instantly. The other two robbers then surrendered. They were armed with two Colts and one Iver Johnson revolver. Sheriff Gailey and Deputy Fields arrived a short time afterwards and made the run from Bentonville to Gravette in 30 minutes. Goodpasture and Bullock were brought back and placed in jail. Sheriff Ray Smith of Pineville was notified and he and his son came after them about 11 o'clock Monday morning. As the robbery was committed in Missouri they will be tried in McDonald county court. The body of the dead bandit was taken to Rogers where Coroner Callison held an inquest. Mr. Callison notified the dead young man's father, George Cook, in Edgerton, Mo., who wired to have the body shipped to Edgerton. While here neither Goodpasture or Bullock would talk. [Benton County Record 6/26/25]

1925

COON, Vida D. LOONEY - Vida D. Looney was born Sept. 24, 1897 in Madison county, Ark. near Canuck postoffice. She died October 10, 1925 at her home in Henryetta, Okla. at the age of 28 years and seventeen days. When a child she moved with her parents to south of Rogers where she made her home for several years. At an early age she professed faith in Jesus Christ and united with the Baptist church at Pleasant Grove and since had lived a devoted life for her God and family. June 14, 1916 Miss Looney was married to Arthur O. Coon and to this union were born two children, Harry and Bernice, who survive her as do also her husband, her mother, Mrs. R.N. Looney of Lowell; four sisters, Mrs. Effie C. Clark and Mrs. Maggie B. Cowan of Lowell; Mrs. Etta Adams of Gresham, Oregon and Miss Addie Looney of Tahlequah, Okla. and one brother, Elmer T. Looney of Portland, Oregon. Besides her family and relatives she leaves many friends to mourn her loss. Mr. Coon and family have made their home in Henryetta, Okla. for the past six years. Those present at her bed-side were her husband, children and mother. Burial was made at Henryetta. [Rogers Democrat 10/29/25]

COOPER, children - Word was received here Monday of the death of the four young children of Mr. and Mrs. Zack Cooper near Joplin when they were cremated in the burning home. Mrs. Cooper is a daughter of Mrs. Tina Hathaway of Rogers and is best remembered here as Bell Hathaway. Her mother lives just north of the Robinson lumber yard on the east side of the Frisco, but was not here when the word of the terrible tragedy came, having gone to Bella Vista to help care for some sick there. A sister, Mrs. Pearl Goodhart of this city, has been in the State Hospital at Little Rock for some months. Mrs. Cooper used to have several brothers here, Joe Hathaway having been with the Famous Bakery for a number of years. Another brother was with the Rogers Light Co. but they are all in other states now. The following story of the fire and death of the children is taken from yesterday's Joplin Globe: A single casket and a single grave will receive the bodies of Dorothy, Mary Belle, Cecil and Jack, children of Mr. and Mrs. Zack Cooper, who perished Monday in a fire that razed their home two miles northeast of Chitwood. A coroner's jury attempted to learn yesterday afternoon at an inquest how the fire occurred and why the eldest of the children, 6-year-old Dorothy, could not escape, but no one knew. The jury formally announced: "Death was caused by being burned to death in a burning building." Testimony offered showed that Mrs. Cooper had gone over the hill 300 yards away to cut some wood and had been at a neighbor's house about an hour before she learned that her children had been burned to death and her home was in ruins. The roof had fallen in before a neighbor, G.A. Sansom, saw the smoke from the dwelling. He was helpless to aid the children and went to tell the mother. It was the conjecture of the jury, although no formal report was made, that the fire broke out in the roof, destroying the upper story of the house first. A flue ran through the center of a large upstairs room. Mrs. Cooper had to be supported to the stand to testify. Her replies to questions were mechanical. She seemed not to hear the voice of Coroner R.M. Stormont as she replied, "Yes, sir;" "No, sir," or "I don't know." When asked if she had locked her children in the house when she left she answered that she had not, adding that neither door had a lock. She had no idea how the fire started she said. The four torsos and the charred body of a faithful family dog were found huddled together when undertakers arrived on the scene. The three youngest children had been asleep in bed and it is believed that Dorothy, becoming frightened, ran to her brothers and sister and covered them and herself with a quilt, too frightened to act. Mary Belle was 4 years old, Cecil was 3 and Jack was 2. The father is employed at the Butte-Kansas mine. There are two other children, Sammy, 9 years old and Veda, 7, who were at school. Funds were being subscribed yesterday to provide for the burial and to aid in relieving the stricken family. [Rogers Democrat 1/29/25]

COOPER, Mrs. G.W. - Mrs. Herb Lewis and W.C. Cooper received word from their father, Elder G.W. Cooper, Cleveland, Oklahoma announcing the death of his wife - their stepmother - which occurred on Saturday, May 30th, 1925. Mrs. Cooper was advanced in years and had been sick nearly a month. The elder Cooper is in his eighty-second year. [Gravette News-Herald 6/12/25]

COPATCO, M.M. - M.M. Copatco of Gentry died here at one o'clock this morning, aged 78 years, having been brought to Bentonville about a week ago suffering from mental trouble and to be under guardianship of the county judge's office. The deceased had lived near Gentry for a number of years and owned a 40-acre farm and home there. He is also said to have had about $300 on deposit with the bank at Gentry. He came to this section from Illinois but nothing definite is known as yet as to his people there as he seems not to have been in touch with any relatives he may have had. The body is being held at the Kerr & Callison undertaking establishment here awaiting possible instructions from relatives with whom the authorities are trying to get in touch. [Benton County Democrat 3/12/25]

M.M. Copatco, living about two miles north of Gentry, died in Bentonville on Wednesday night. For the past week he has been a ward of the county while waiting to be taken to the State Hospital for Nervous Diseases at Little Rock. He became insane over religious matters and was taken to the County Home. He grew worse and Judge Edwards had him brought to Bentonville where he was placed under the care of a guardian. He has lived near Gentry for the past 15 years and owns a good 40-acre farm. He is not known to have any immediate relatives. Some time ago Mr. Copatco made a request of Frank Mitchell and George Jenkins that when he died they would see that his remains would be placed beside his wife and relatives in Chicago. This wish Mr. Mitchell and Mr. Jenkins will faithfully carry out. [Benton County Record 3/13/25]

CORDELL, Jane - Miss Jane Cordell, who recently died at her home in Santa Ana, California, willed $100 to the Hebron church south of Rogers and $100 to the Hebron Cemetery. The Cordell family lived in this community years ago and several members of the family are buried at Hebron. [Benton County Record 12/4/25]

CORTIANA, Natatia Rosy - Natatia Rosy Cortiana, six years old, daughter of Mr. and Mrs. Domenic Cortiana of Tontitown, was killed Thursday afternoon of last week when she fell from her father's truck, the rear wheel passing over her body and crushing it. She lived only a short time afterward. She was born in Tontitown and funeral services were held Friday morning with burial in the Tontitown cemetery. [Rogers Democrat 6/4/25]

CORY, Abigail JAMES - Abigail James was born Feb. 10, 1847 in Hannibal, New York. She was united in marriage March 14, 1870 to James Cory at Hannibal. To this union was born four children: Arthur Cory of Tulsa, Okla.; Henry Cory of Brazil, Indiana; Roy Cory of Fayetteville and Walter Cory of Stroud, Okla. She is also survived by ten grandchildren. Her husband died at Springdale in July 1917. She died Friday, Sept. 25 and was buried in the National Cemetery at Fayetteville on Saturday, Sept. 26th. Funeral services were conducted at the M.E. Church, South of which she had been a member at different times for the past 35 years. Services were conducted by the pastor, Rev. Wade. [Rogers Democrat 10/8/25]

COVEY, Joseph P. - Joseph P. Covey, one of the early settlers of Gravette community, died at his home in Los Angeles, Calif. on Thursday, April 16. Mr. Covey was the oldest member of the Covey family of which R.W. Covey of Gravette is the remaining member and was aged about 85 years. Joe Covey was the owner of Oldtown and plotted the town of Nebo which postoffice was succeeded by Gravette. He moved to Southwest City in 1881 and a few years ago to California. He was a Confederate veteran, having served thru the entire war and participated in five battles. [Gravette News-Herald 4/24/25]

COVEY, Lola Vernie - Lola Vernie Covey, wife of Sherman Covey, died at her home southeast of Gravette on Thursday, March 5th, aged 26 years, 10 months and 13 days, the result of flu. Besides her husband she leaves four small children. Mr. Covey is a distant relative of the Coveys of Gravette. The burial was in charge of Undertaker Tom Haywood. Funeral was conducted by Rev. Scroggins of Decatur and interment made at Bethel cemetery Sunday. [Gravette News-Herald 3/13/25]
{from Decatur} Mrs. Sherman Covey, living north of town on the Jack Gordon farm, died on Friday, March 6th of influenza. She was about 26 years of age and is survived by her husband and four children, the youngest a babe of nine months. She was buried in the Bethel cemetery. [Benton County Record 3/13/25]

COWAN, Miles - {from Lowell} The many friends of Miles Cowan were grieved to hear of his death last Friday at the home of his son, Demp Cowan, west of town. Burial was in the Pleasant Grove cemetery. Uncle Miles was one of our oldest citizens, having lived here a greater part of his life. He was the father of Demp Cowan and Mrs. Byron Jones of this place. [Rogers Democrat 2/5/25]

COWDEN, Clarissa C. WILLIAMS - Clarissa C. Williams was born in Benton county, Arkansas on July 13, 1855 near Bentonville. She was married to Henry Cowden in the year of 1880. To them were born five children, two boys, Robert of Highfill, Ark. and L.D. of Healing Springs, and three girls, Mrs. Della Evans of Bentonville, Ark., Mrs. Maggie Downum of Oklahoma City, Okla. and Mrs. Minnie Mason of Highfill, Ark. They made several trips to Texas and it was while in Texas and the children very small that Mr. Cowden passed away. They returned to Benton county, Arkansas and moved to their old home where they remained for a number of years, the place that Mrs. Dr. Hubbard now occupies. Mrs. Cowden was the daughter of David and Margaret Williams, pioneer settlers of Tennessee. She was converted at an early age and joined the Missionary Baptist church at Old Temperance Hill. She lived a devout Christian life. She was confined to her bed on Nov. 26, 1916 and died at the home of her son, Robert Cowden of Highfill, on January 17, 1925. Mother Cowden, as she was known by all, was loved and respected by everyone who knew her. She was greatly afflicted but was a patient sufferer for seven long years. She was so kind and cheerful that it was a great pleasure to sit by her bedside and talk with her. Bro. E.F. Rice, the pastor of the Baptist church, conducted the service. A Friend. [Benton County Democrat 2/5/25] [Benton County Record 2/13/25]
{from Highfill} Mother Cowden passed away at the home of her son, Robert Cowden, on Saturday, January 17th, 1925 at about 6 o'clock in the evening. The funeral services were held at the Baptist Church at 11 o'clock on Monday and she was laid to rest in the Phillips cemetery by the side of her little niece, Reba Cowden, daughter of L.D. Cowden. Brother Rice, the pastor of the Baptist Church, officiated. Everyone who knew her could not help but love her. She had been in constant pain for a great many years and her suffering had been beyond words; although no matter how severe her pain she always had a smile and kind words for everyone who went to see her. Her children were all present at the funeral. [Benton County Record 1/23/25]

CRABTREE, Vinia MOLDER - Mrs. Vinia Crabtree, wife of C.H. Crabtree, died at the family home 8 miles northeast of Bentonville at noon Wednesday, Jan. 28, aged 79 years. Death followed a stroke of paralysis of early Saturday morning. Funeral services were held Thursday afternoon at Pea Ridge by the Rev. Mr. Carnahan of the Presbyterian church and interment made in the Pea Ridge cemetery. Besides her husband she is survived by one son, T.W. Crabtree, of Route five, Bentonville and two daughters, Mrs. Ida A. Greenlee, Ozark, Ark. and Mrs. M.A. Freeman, Tulsa, Okla. She was also related to the pioneer Blevins and Ricketts families. [Benton County Democrat 1/29/25]

Mrs. Vinia Crabtree, wife of Caleb Crabtree, died at her home on The Bella Vista-Pea Ridge road near the Stroud spring, Wednesday after a lingering illness. She is survived by her husband, one son and two daughters. Mrs. Crabtree was born in Illinois in 1846 and has lived on the place where she died for over 40 years. [Benton County Record 1/20/25]
Mrs. Vinia Crabtree, wife of C.H. Crabtree, died a week ago at her home a few miles east of Bentonville following a stroke of paralysis. She was 79 years old and her entire life had been lived in Benton county. She was a daughter of Moses Molder who came to Benton county from Tennessee. Funeral services were held Thursday afternoon at Pea Ridge and were conducted by Rev. A.E. Carnahan of the Presbyterian church. Burial was in the Pea Ridge cemetery. [Rogers Democrat 2/5/25]

CRAIN, Charity Susan GARRETT - Charity Susan Garrett was born in Bedford county, Tenn. on Oct. 15th, 1846. In 1848, 12 years before the Civil War, she came with her parents to Benton county where they settled near what is now known as Wager. She lived the greater part of her life in this section. When the family located there the settlements in the county were but few and miles apart. In 1879 she moved to Springtown where she lived for two years then moved to Texas in 1877. In 1880 she returned to the old home place where she spent the remainder of her life. She was married on July 22nd, 1879 to Thomas Jefferson Crain who departed this life 17 years ago. To this union was born four children. One died in infancy and one daughter, Mrs. Martha Reams, died some years ago. She passed to her reward on November 28th, 1925 at the ripe old age of 79 years, one month and 13 days. She was the last survivor of a family of nine children. She leaves to mourn her loss one son, Albert Crain, and one daughter, Polly Crain, ten grandchildren, a number of other relatives and a host of friends. Funeral services were conducted at the home on Sunday, November 29 at 2 p.m. by Elder W.H. Sears and she was laid to rest in the cemetery near by. [Benton County Record 12/4/25] [Rogers Democrat 12/3/25]

CREAMER, A.M. - {from Gravette} A.M. Creamer, living on the Ed Buck farm, died Saturday and was buried Sunday. [Benton County Record 12/4/25]

CRITTENDEN, Ada LEWIS - Mrs. Ada Crittenden, daughter of William Lewis, died at the residence of the latter last Friday morning, Feb. 13, 1925 at the age of 24 years. Mr. and Mrs. Crittenden and children came in from Oklahoma a few days previous because of her failing health, being afflicted with tuberculosis. She was the eldest child of Mr. Lewis and besides her husband and three small children, leaves two sisters, Alma and Dessie Lewis, and one brother, Oral Lewis. The funeral was conducted at the home Saturday by Rev. M.R. Lark and burial was in Mt. Pleasant cemetery. [Gravette News-Herald 2/20/25]

CROW, J.L. - Paul N. Crow was called back to Crossett, Ark. Saturday night on account of the serious illness of his father, J.L. Crow, who suffered

a stroke of paralysis some days ago. The elder Crow died Sunday morning before Paul arrived at the home. Paul's many Gravette friends sympathize with him in the loss of his parent. [Gravette News-Herald 5/29/25]
{from Gravette} Paul Crow, of the Ideal Drug Store, was called to Crossett, Ark. Saturday night on account of the death of his father. His father died at 2 o'clock Sunday morning. [Benton County Record 5/29/25]

CROWE, William - Another pioneer is gone. William Crowe died February 5th, 1925 at the home of his daughter, Mrs. G.N. Vanhorn, west of town. He was born in Belmont, Ohio August 18, 1838 and had reached the age of 86 years, 5 months and 13 days. Mr. Crowe united with the Christian church in 1865. He was married to Susan Meyers in 1861. To this union two children were born, Mrs. M.B. Vanhorn of Gravette and Wallace Crowe of Anderson, Mo. His wife died in 1865. Mr. Crowe was married again in 1871 to Mariah Harrion. To this union were born five children, four girls and one boy: Alice Cook, Springdale, Ark.; Olive Cowart and Pearl Kelley of Gravette; John Crowe of Hiwasse and Iva Manos, deceased. Mr. Crowe has been making his home with his children. He leaves 48 grandchildren and 20 great-grandchildren. The funeral was conducted by W.A. McDonald on Friday and interment followed at the Russell cemetery. [Gravette News-Herald 2/13/25]

CURTIS, Millie - Mrs. Millie Curtis, living near Prairie Grove, died last Tuesday from burns received while lighting a fire in the kitchen stove. In some way her clothing caught fire and she jumped into the rain barrel to extinguish the flames but she was too badly burned to recover. [Benton County Record 6/5/25]

DARBY, Mary Lucette - Mrs. Mary Lucette Darby died on Monday noon, July 20th at her home at 1110 South Fourth street after a serious illness of several months at the age of 52 years and eleven months. Funeral services were held at Central M.E. church Tuesday afternoon at 4:30 and were conducted by the pastor, Rev. J.W. Wilcoxon. Interment in the Rogers cemetery. Mrs. Darby was born at Summerville, Shelby county, Tenn. and she was married there to Will Darby in December 1897. To them were born three children, Mrs. Lloyd Patterson and Will and Dillard Darby, all of Rogers. Mr. Darby died December 14, 1912 at Booneville, Ark. and the family came to Rogers from Memphis some ten years ago. Mrs. Darby had visited in Rogers shortly after her marriage with her husband's mother, Mrs. H.H. Darby, and had liked this town so when she was looking for a location in which to raise her young family she decided to come here. She was a woman greatly beloved by her friends and acquaintances and her death is a great loss, not only to her immediate family but to the entire community. Mrs. Darby is survived by a sister in Memphis and by a sister-in-law, Mrs. E.R. Dickinson, of Blytheville, Ark. who arrived Monday noon just a few minutes after Mrs. Darby's death and she is still here with the sons and daughter. [Rogers Democrat 7/23/25]

1925

DAVENPORT, James H. - {from Decatur} James H. Davenport, a well-known and highly respected citizen, died at his home in Decatur Thursday, September 18th, 1925 at the age of 57 years. He had been ill for nearly two years. Funeral services were held at the Methodist church Friday afternoon with Rev. Sherman of Prairie Grove, assisted by Rev. Lark and Rev. J.A. Scoggin, conducting the services. Interment was made in the City cemetery and the I.O.O.F. lodge, of which he was a member, held services at the grave. Mr. Davenport is survived by his wife, two daughters, Mrs. William Bryson and Mrs. Mary Nell Guthrie, and one son, Charles Davenport. [Benton County Democrat 9/22/25]
{from Decatur} The funeral services of J.H. Davenport at the Methodist Church last Friday was largely attended. The services were conducted by Revs. Sherman, Clark and Scroggin. The family, Mrs. Davenport, Mary and Charles, left Sunday morning for a trip to Wayne, Okla. with Mr. Davenport's brothers. [Benton County Record 9/25/25]

DAVIS, Alex - Alex Davis, an inmate of the County Home, and father of Lem Davis, died at that institution Monday. A stroke of paralysis and injuries received before he was stricken led to his death. [Benton County Record 7/3/25]
Lem Davis of near Centerton who has been creating considerable notoriety around Bentonville the past month and who has been spending his vacation in jail laying out a fine for carrying concealed weapons, has left for parts unknown. It happened this way: Lem's father died Monday and after begging Sheriff Joe Gailey long and earnestly that he be allowed to attend his father's funeral, and Joe having a warm spot in his heart, he relented and let him out upon a solemn promise to return after the funeral. Freedom was so sweet to him that he forgot to go to the county home to see his dead parent or even to attend the funeral. He also neglected to call and see his wife. The two have had considerable marital difficulties of late and it is reported that she has sued for divorce. If Lem is gone for good the taxpayers will save considerable court costs later. [Benton County Record 7/3/25]

DAVIS, Mary C. Allen - {from Gravette} Mrs. Mary C. Davis died at her home in West Gravette Thursday of last week. She was about seventy years of age. She was the mother of Luther Allen, carrier on Route 3 out of Gravette. [Benton County Record 10/16/25]

DAVIS, Nettie WOMACK - Mrs. Nettie Davis, wife of J.T. Davis, died at the family home west of Centerton on Sunday evening, July 12th, 1925 at 8 o'clock following a stroke of apoplexy. She was 55 years of age. Mrs. Davis' death was a shock to the entire community. She had been in apparently good health and Sunday morning, with her husband, attended services at the Community Church in Centerton. Just as the services were about to close Mrs. Davis was stricken with apoplexy. Medical aid was summoned and as soon as she was able she was taken to her home. She died a few hours later. The shock was so great to Mr. Davis that he collapsed and for some time it was thought that his reason was impaired. He is still suffering from a nervous breakdown but is improving. Mr. Davis is one of the best known men in this section. The funeral services, which were held Wednesday forenoon, both at the house and at the Community Church, was one of the largest ever held in Centerton. Rev. E.L. Boyles, assisted by Rev. Mr. Keen, conducted the services. Interment was made in the Centerton cemetery. Mrs. Nettie Davis was born in March 1870 at the old Womack home south of Hiwasse, now owned by Loyd Keith. She was the daughter of William and Elizabeth Womack, old pioneer settlers. In 1886 she was married to J.T. Davis and has lived at the family home west of Centerton for 26 years. Besides her husband she is survived by four children, Orville Davis and Mrs. Everett Harrell of Centerton; Mrs. Beulah Story of Hope, Ark. and Everette Davis, residing in Northern California; also by three brothers, Richard and Frank Womack of Centerton and A.O. Womack of Decatur; also by one sister, Mrs. Elmer Johnson of Centerton. Mrs. Davis was a woman of splendid Christian character, a gentle wife, loving mother and esteemed by all. [Benton County Record 7/17/25]

DAWSON, Sarah E. - Mrs. Sarah E. Dawson passed away at the home of her son, W.P. Dawson, in Gentry last Sunday morning at 4:30. Deceased was 86 years and 7 days old and had lived in this town for a number of years. Another son, G.D. Dawson of McAlester, Okla. came here to attend the funeral of his mother which was at Mt. Vernon, Mo., the old home of deceased, at 2 o'clock Tuesday afternoon from the Christian church of that city of which she was a member. The remains were laid to rest by the side of her husband, Isaac B. Dawson, at Mt. Vernon, who passed away several years ago. Carpenter Bros. had charge of the body and the trip was made by automobile. [Gentry Journal-Advance 1/16/25]
Mrs. J.A. Kyte of Hawkerville, Okla. came in Monday to attend the funeral of her aunt, Mrs. Sarah E. Dawson. [Gentry Journal-Advance 1/16/25]

DAY, Mrs. Alfie - {from Tuck's Chapel} The funeral of Mrs. Alfie Day was conducted by Rev. Renfro Monday afternoon. She was laid to rest by the side of her husband who died several years ago. Mrs. Day lived for several years in this neighborhood but later moved to near Avoca. She made her home with her daughter, Mrs. Bob Stephenson. We extend sympathy to the children in their hour of sorrow. [Rogers Democrat 6/25/25]

DEAN, James - Died, May 4th, 1925 at the home of his daughter, Mrs. Kermer {sic}, southeast of Bentonville, with whom he had made his home for several years, James Dean, aged 64 years. "Uncle Jimmie," as he was known, suffered a stroke of paralysis about a week ago from which he never recovered. Funeral services were held at the home on Tuesday morning by Rev. J.M. McMahen of the Baptist Church at Bentonville. Interment was made in the Twelve Corner cemetery on Pea Ridge. Mr. Dean was a native son, being born on Pea Ridge in 1861. He is survived by several children. [Benton County Record 5/8/25]

Uncle Jimmy Dean, who was living with a daughter, Mrs. H.H. Kehmeier, southeast of Bentonville, died Monday May 4, after a short illness. Death resulted from paralysis and apoplexy. Deceased was born in Benton Co. on Feb. 23, 1851 and had spent practically his entire life here except for a short time in Texas. In 1868 he was married to Miss Caldona Carden and to this union 8 children were born, one son dying in infancy. He is survived by 4 sons and 3 daughters: Oscar Dean of Atlanta, Kan.; Morris and Jasper Dean, Bentonville; Henry Dean of Nester, Cal.; Mrs. Pearl Threet, Mrs. Bertha Johnson and Mrs. Nettie Kehmeier, all of Bentonville. Also by 3 brothers and a sister: Calie and Albert Dean of the same place and Hulen Dean of Springdale, Ark. Uncle Jimmy was a member of the Baptist church and funeral services were at the home by Rev. J.M. McMahen of that faith. Interment was in the Twelve Corners cemetery by the side of his wife who died in 1919. Rev. John Hall conducted the services at the grave. [Benton County Democrat 5/14/25]

DEAN, Susan - {from Bestwater} Mrs. Susan Dean died Saturday, September 26th, 1925 at the home of her son, Clarence Dean, of Garfield, Ark., with whom she had been visiting since her illness several weeks ago. She was buried Sunday afternoon at the Tucks Chapel Cemetery by the side of her husband, Jot Dean. Mrs. Dean was a member of the Methodist Episcopal Church at Bestwater and will be {the last line or two of this item was obliterated during the microfilming process.} [Benton County Democrat 10/6/25]

DEARBORN, Frederick R. - Capt. Frederick R. Dearborn was born in Saratoga, N.Y. Feb. 15, 1837 and died at his home in Gentry, Ark. Aug. 28, 1925, aged 88 years, 6 months, 13 days. He removed to Wisconsin where he enlisted at the beginning of war in Co. C, 7th Reg., Wis. Ironclad Brigade, serving as orderly sergeant and lieut. until Oct. 22, '64, when he was commissioned as Capt. of Co. D, 7th Reg., Wis. He married Miss Helen Strunk July 17, 1865 and to this union was born 6 children, 3 of whom, Jay, Elenor and Frank are deceased. He came to Arkansas in 1906 and resided 2 years on his farm northeast of town, since when he has lived in town. His wife having died 9 years ago, his daughter, Mrs. Elmer Barrett, came to take care of him and faithfully has completed her work. Friday night, Aug. 22, he was taken with an attack of heart failure and altho he appeared to recover, grew steadily worse until at 7 a.m. on the 28th he was not, for God had taken him. He leaves to mourn his departure 3 children: Mrs. Elmer Barrett, Geo. Dearborn, who came here from California on a visit a few days before his father's attack; and Chas. Dearborn of Arlington, Cal. Also 12 grandchildren and 4 great-grandchildren. The funeral was held from the Congregational church Saturday, Aug. 29th, where a host of friends gathered and with floral offerings sought to show respect to one of whom no word of reproach could be uttered. [Gentry Journal-Advance 9/4/25]

1925

DEGAN, Elby - Elby Degan, a farmer of near Hartwell, Madison county, died suddenly of heart failure while plowing one afternoon last week. He was working alone and it is not known how long he had been dead when his body was found by some member of the family who went to the field to ascertain why he had not returned home at the close of day as usual. [Rogers Democrat 4/30/25]

DERRICK, W.L. - A message to Mr. and Mrs. W.H. Crayton Tuesday announced the death of W.L. Derrick at Madill, Okla. that day. Mr. Derrick will be remembered by many here as having spent several weeks here last year when his sister, Mrs. Nancy Givens, was suffering from injuries sustained when hit by an auto. Mr. Derrick was a very likable gentleman and the friends he made here will learn with regret of his death. [Gravette News-Herald 3/6/25]

DICKERSON, Flora C. HUNTER - Flora C. Hunter was born on Feb. 27, 1875 in Johnson County, Ark., near Yale postoffice. Died Oct. 4, 1925 at 11 a.m. at her home near Cave Springs, Ark. at the age of 50 years, 7 months and seven days. At the age of eighteen Miss Flora professed publicly her faith in Jesus Christ and united with the Protestant Methodist Church at Mulberry Hall and ranked with the most loyal members of that church. August 18, 1895 Miss Flora C. Hunter was united in marriage to John F. Dickerson and to this union was born five children, three boys and two girls, namely: Kimbrel Dickerson, Lillie D. Dickerson, Joe B. Dickerson, Iris Dickerson and Haskell Dickerson, and two grandchildren, all of whom survive her and she leaves a devoted husband, John F. Dickerson, also four brothers: John M. Hunter of Stilwell, Okla.; William M. Hunter of Abilene, Texas; Benjamin F. Hunter of somewhere in Texas; Pat E. Hunter of Coal Hill, Ark.; and also five sisters, Mrs. Mary E. Killian of Diboll, Texas; Mrs. Hannah Lamb of Healing Springs, Ark.; Mrs. Sarah Cornett of Houston, Texas; Mrs. Lou Hill of Ozark, Ark. and Mrs. Christian Kiser of Dermott, Ark. Besides her husband, children and relatives she leaves a host of friends to mourn her loss. Burial was made Friday in the Yale cemetery. [Benton County Record 10/16/25] [Benton County Democrat 10/13/25]

DODGEN, Fay - Miss Elizabeth Wasson received a message Sunday telling that her uncle, Fay Dodgen, had been killed in an automobile accident at Tulsa Saturday evening. She, accompanied by Mr. and Mrs. Hugh Carl, attended the funeral at Ozark, Ark. Tuesday. [Gentry Journal-Advance 10/30/25] [Benton County Record 10/30/25]

A message here Saturday night from Tulsa announced the death by accident of Fay Dodgen, a former Gentry man. A car in which he, with another man, was returning from work, was hit by a Frisco train, killing him instantly. He went to Tulsa 6 or 8 months ago from Springtown where he made his home. His wife passed away about 6 months ago. He was a nephew of W.B. Dodgen of Springtown. Funeral services were held Tuesday at Ozark where burial was made. [Gentry Journal-Advance 10/30/25]

DOKE, Fannie Iris McPHETRIDGE - Mrs. Fannie Iris Doke, wife of W.J. Doke, passed away at the family home on West Twelfth street at 8:30 Tuesday morning. Death came suddenly and unexpectedly, even to the physician and family, and although Mrs. Doke had been in feeble health for two years and it was known that she had been suffering from illness for several days, her death came as a profound shock to the entire community. Mrs. Doke was born at St. Joseph, Mo. April 24, 1865, the family afterwards making their home at Plattsburg, Mo. where she was married to Mr. Doke on Dec. 1, 1886. Mr. and Mrs. Doke and their only child, Eugene M. Doke, moved to Bentonville in July 1893, living here since. Besides her husband and son she is survived by two grandchildren and by one sister, Mrs. W.S. Herndon of Plattsburg, Mo.; two brothers, W.R. McPhetridge, Pittsburgh, Pa. and O.W. McPhetridge, Las Vegas, N.M., and a half-brother, Roy F. McPhetridge, Wichita, Kan. He and Mrs. Herndon arrived here Tuesday night. Funeral services will be held at the Christian church this {Thursday} afternoon, conducted by the Rev. Stephen A. Morton, pastor, and Dr. J.P. Pinkerton, former pastor and an old and greatly loved friend of the Doke family. Interment will be in the mausoleum. [Benton County Democrat 5/14/25]

In the presence of hundreds of sorrowing friends funeral services were held Thursday afternoon May 14th at the Christian church for Mrs. Fannie Iris Doke, wife of W.J. Doke, president of the Benton County Hardware Company and manager of that firm's local store, who passed away at 8:30 o'clock Tuesday morning, May 12, 1925 at the family home here, her sudden death, which followed several months of failing health, coming as a profound shock to the entire community and to a host of other friends. The services were conducted by the Rev. Stephen A. Morton, pastor, and Dr. J.P. Pinkerton of Warsaw, Mo., a former pastor of the local Christian church, an intimate friend of the Doke family for many years. The Rev. C.D. Purlee, of the Siloam Springs Christian Church, also assisted in the simple and impressive rites. Only two songs were used, "Beautiful Isle of Somewhere," sung by Mrs. Rex W. Peel of Oklahoma City, and "The Christian's Good-Bye," sung by Miss Sarah Frances Cloe, Bentonville. Fannie Iris McPhetridge was born at St. Joseph, Mo. April 24, 1865, the family later moving to Plattsburg, Mo. At Edgerton, Mo. on December 1, 1886 she was married to William J. Doke and they began together their journey through life which to the hour of her going was one of constant companionship. Mr. and Mrs. Doke and their only child, Eugene M. Doke, now manager of the wholesale department of the Benton County Hdwe. Co. at Muskogee, Okla., came to Bentonville in July 1893. From that day the family has been prominently identified with the affairs of the community and active in every movement for the betterment of their adopted town, county and state. Mrs. Doke became a member of the Christian Church in 1883 and was ever a faithful member of that denomination. Besides her husband and son and two grandchildren, Dorothy and W.J. Doke II, Mrs. Doke is survived by one sister, Mrs. W.S. Herndon of Plattsburg, Mo., three brothers; W.R. McPhetridge, Pittsburgh, Pa., O.W. McPhetridge, Las Vegas, N.M. and Roy F. McPhetridge of Wichita, Kans. [Benton County Democrat 5/21/25] [Benton County Record 5/15/25]

DONNELLY, Jack - Jack Donnelly, a resident of Decatur for nearly 30 years, died last Saturday at the home of Mr. and Mrs. N.S. Heaslet in Decatur where he had made his home for the past few years. He has been paralyzed for some time. He was a member of the Masonic and Odd Fellow orders, which had charge of the funeral. Interment was made in the Decatur cemetery. He is survived by one son, Will Donnelly of Decatur, and one daughter, Mrs. Paschal Lefors of Willows, Cal. He was born in Ohio about 75 years ago. [Benton County Record 4/24/25]

DOUGLAS, Sarah Emily MORRISON - Another of the county's respected and beloved mothers in Israel is gone as death has claimed Mrs. Sarah Emily Douglas. Mrs. Sarah Emily Douglas was born Feb. 22nd, 1841 about three miles south of where the town of Highfill now stands. She passed away Thursday evening, Nov. 12, 1925 at the home of her son, Marion Douglas, on North Main street, Bentonville, Ark. She was the daughter of Milton and Rebecca Morrison, those sturdy pioneers that emigrated to this country from Tennessee in 1838. In 1865 she was married to Thomas H. Douglas and to this union was born seven children. Five sons and two daughters, five of whom are living - Milton and Morrison Douglas, prominent farmers in the Highfill neighborhood; Marion Douglas, present circuit clerk of Benton county; Marshall Douglas, president of the Liberty Life Insurance Co. of Muskogee, Okla. and Mrs. Ella Douglas Mitchell of Gentry. Mrs. Douglas professed faith in Christ at the Thornsberry Camp Ground some 50 years ago and joined the M.E. Church, South at Highfill of which she was a member until her death. Services were conducted by the Rev. J.L. Evans, pastor of the M.E. Church, South and interment was had at the Douglas cemetery near Highfill on Saturday morning, near where she had spent her childhood, where she had grown to womanhood, where she had married and reared her children - in short, where she had spent the years of her long and useful life. She has gone from us but not forever for some sweet day we shall meet again. W.A. Burks. [Benton County Record 11/20/25] [Benton County Democrat 11/17/25]

DOWNUM, Mary C. - Mrs. Mary C. Downum passed away last Monday morning at the home of her daughter, Mrs. W.D. Dellinger of Logan, at the age of 79 years. Funeral services were held from the Methodist church at Elm Springs Tuesday afternoon and burial was made in the Elm Springs cemetery. [Gentry Journal-Advance 10/9/25]

DUGGER, infant - {from Pea Ridge} The infant of W.L. Dugger of Pittsburg, Kansas was brought to Pea Ridge for burial last Friday. [Benton County Record 4/17/25]

DUNAGIN, John Riley - J.R. Dunagin, a long-time resident of Gravette and widely known throughout Benton county, died suddenly on Wednesday night, April 15th, 1925. The flu, followed by a complication of diseases which he was unable to overcome, was the cause of his death. Mr. Dunagin was one of Benton county's native sons and was born in the northeast part of the county. His father, J.R. Dunagin, Sr., was a Baptist preacher in the days of the old circuit riders. Besides his widow he is survived by one son, Albert Dunagin of Gravette and a daughter, Mrs. W.O. Maxwell. Mr. Dunagin was a good friend and neighbor, a kind father and highly esteemed by all who knew him. [Benton County Record 4/17/25]
John Riley Dunagin was born on Roller's Ridge, Benton county, Ark. March 7th, 1852, the son of Rev. Jasper and Susan Dunagin, his father being a pioneer Baptist minister. Died at his home in Gravette, Ark. April 15, 1925, age 73 years, one month and eight days. December 18, 1873 he was married to Miss Sarah Stokes. To this union were born four children, two dying in infancy. Besides his companion he is survived by two children, A.P. Dunagin of Gravette and Mrs. W.O. Maxwell of La Junta, Colo., three grandchildren, Robert Maxwell, David Lee and Mary Lou Dunagin; three sisters, Mrs. Stokes of Muskogee, Okla.; Mrs. Jordan of St. Louis and Mrs. Threet of Texas, one brother, W.D. Dunagin of Texas; two nieces, Mrs. F.M. January of Gravette and Mrs. Snodgrass of Pineville, Mo. and one nephew, J.W. Seamster of Rogers. At the age of 15 years he was converted and united with the Missionary Baptist church, at the time of his death having been a member of that church 58 years. He has been a deacon in the church for the past 30 years. While a young man he was engaged with his father and Dr. Mitchell in the mercantile business at Rogers. He assisted in incorporating that town and was one of the first council. Later he went to Avoca, Benton county, and engaged in the mercantile business. He came to Gravette in 1893. Here he served several times on the city council, also as mayor and a member of the school board. The funeral was conducted at the Baptist church at 10:30 a.m. Friday, April 17 by Revs. I.M. Phillips of the Baptist church and M.R. Lark of the Methodist church, South. Interment was made in the I.O.O.F. cemetery. [Gravette News-Herald 4/24/25] [Rogers Democrat 4/23/25] [Rogers Daily Post 4/18/25]

DUNCAN, G.W. - {from Hiwasse} The many friends of Mrs. Will Belew extend to her their sincere sympathy in the sickness and death of her father, G.W. Duncan, of Row, Okla., who died Monday night. Funeral services were held Wednesday afternoon and burial was made near Maysville. [Benton County Record 2/13/25]
{from Hiwasse} Mr. and Mrs. Will Belew and Elmer Duncan were called to Oklahoma last week on account of the sickness and death of Mrs. Belew's and Mr. Duncan's father. [Gravette News-Herald 2/20/25]

DUNKEE, Mary K. - That the last wishes of Mrs. Mary K. Dunkee, who died in Siloam Springs last Friday, might be carried out, the Pyeatt

Undertaking Co. of that city took the body of Mrs. Dunkee to Virden, Ill. where it was placed by the side of her husband in the cemetery there. The round trip, according to the speedometer on the hearse, was a little over one thousand miles and was made in 48 hours. This is believed to be the longest motor hearse drive ever made in the west. [Benton County Democrat 8/5/25]

DYER, Bert - {from Gravette} The body of Bert Dyer was brought to Gravette Thursday for burial. He died in Kansas City Tuesday. [Benton County Record 11/13/25]

EAGLESFIELD, Eli C. - Eli C. Eaglesfield was born at Binghampton, N.Y. March 21, 1851 and passed away at the home of his son, Perl E. Eaglesfield, in Joplin, Mo. Jan. 17, 1925 at the age of 73 years, 9 months and 27 days. Mr. Eaglesfield was a trainer of race horses and was hurt internally while in a race last August which was primarily the cause of his death, though paralysis hastened the end. About five weeks ago his son, Perl, went to Springfield, Ill. and brought his father to Joplin, where he was most tenderly cared for. His son, Ralph, and wife were also with him during these last anxious weeks. Mr. Eaglesfield was the son of Susan Simmons and John George Eaglesfield. When about 21 years of age he was converted and joined the church. In 1881 he was married to Celestia A. Newell, who died in Gentry in February 1902. To this union were born five children: Mrs. E.R. Maxson of Milton, Wis.; Guy E. of Bisbee, Ariz.; E. Ralph of Timpas, Colo.; Perl E. of Joplin, Mo. and Mrs. Tacy Kerr of Milton, Wis. There are also left ten grandchildren. Mr. Eaglesfield was a man of most excellent character and will be remembered and mourned by many friends. He came to Gentry in 1901 and lived here about fifteen years. Many friends remember how he had to be both father and mother to his children after the death of his wife and they can also recall how nobly he fulfilled his mission. The farewell service was held in the Seventh Day Baptist church in Gentry Sunday afternoon, Jan. 18. As Pastor Severance was away on a missionary trip Rev. Mr. Hughes of the Congregational church conducted the service and the remains were laid to rest by the side of his wife in the Gentry cemetery. [Gentry Journal-Advance 1/23/25]

EDDY, Elizabeth - A message was received here Tuesday morning announcing the death of Mrs. Elizabeth Eddy in New York City. Mrs. Eddy had visited here on several occasions, the guest of her sister, the late Mrs. A.M. Evans. No details of her illness and death were stated in the telegram received by Marion Wasson at the bank. [Gentry Journal-Advance 10/9/25]

EDMONSON, Highfill - Walter Edmonson, residing near Vaughn on the Bob Rife farm, has received the sad intelligence that his brother, Highfill Edmonson of Big Creek, Cal., was drowned near that place on Monday. He had been in California for the last three years. The body will be sent back here for burial and will arrive in Gentry some time Saturday and will be taken to the paternal home, R.D. Edmonson of Springtown, and from there will be buried Sunday afternoon in the Barron cemetery near Vaughn. [Benton County Record 7/31/25]

EDWARDS, Virginia Juanita - The home of Mr. and Mrs. Fred Edwards was saddened last Friday when Virginia Juanita, their little 9 year old daughter, passed away after a long illness. Funeral services were held Saturday afternoon at 3 o'clock and burial was made in the Flint Creek cemetery by Carpenter funeral directors. [Gentry Journal-Advance 9/25/25]

EICHER, Mary L. HOLLAND Smock - Mrs. Mary L. Eicher, wife of J.R. Eicher, died at the family home a mile northeast of Bentonville at 4:15 o'clock Tuesday afternoon, death resulting from an attack of food poisoning. Mrs. Eicher was taken suddenly and critically ill about 4 o'clock Monday morning following a neighborhood dinner of noon Sunday at the home of Mr. and Mrs. W.E. Lollace. Of the twenty guests attending the dinner seven were taken sick about the same hour as Mrs. Eicher but none of the others are reported to have been so seriously affected. Doctors are said to be undetermined as to the exact food causing the trouble and to be of the opinion that it may have been a peculiar combination of other foods with homemade "chow-chow" pickle. The latter is said to have been used, however, by one of the families almost daily without any ill effects. Mrs. Eicher was born at Owensboro, Ky. Oct. 4, 1861. Her girlhood days were spent in that state where she was married to a Mr. Smock. To them were born four sons and one daughter. The daughter died several years ago and is buried at Salina, Kan. The four sons, Walter, Elza and Albert Smock, all of Salina, Kan. and Claud Smock of Topeka, Kan. are expected here for the funeral. Mr. and Mrs. Smock moved from Kentucky to Northwest Nebraska where he died. After her husband's death Mrs. Smock moved with her children to Salina, Kans. and there later met Mr. J.R. Eicher to whom she was married March 29, 1915. Mr. and Mrs. Eicher moved to Goodland, Kans., living there until they came to Bentonville in 1922, buying the Giles property northeast of Bentonville and making this their permanent home. Mrs. Eicher became a member of the Methodist church when a small child, being a member of that organization around 60 years. She and her husband soon became a real part of the community in which they lived and she will be sadly missed by her neighbors and a great number of other friends and acquaintances. Funeral services, conducted by the Rev. A.O. Fortune of the Bentonville M.E. Church, will be held at the home at 1 o'clock Friday afternoon and the body will be taken to Salina, Kans. for interment. [Benton County Democrat 3/19/25]

Following a thirty-eight hour illness of ptomaine poisoning, Mrs. J.R. Eicher died at her home in the Valley View community at 2:15 on Tuesday afternoon, March 17th, 1925. Mrs. Eicher had been in very good health and on Sunday had been a participant in a dinner party at the home of one of the neighbors. About midnight Sunday Mrs. Eicher first felt the effects of the poison, which could not be warded off or overcome. Mrs. Eicher's maiden name was Mary Holland and she was born in Owensburg, Ky. in 1861. She married Mr. Eicher about seven years ago and has been a resident of Bentonville for four years. With her husband, J.R. Eicher, she is survived by four sons, Walter Smock and Ezra Smock, both of Salina, Kansas; Albert Smock of Bridgeport, Kansas and Claude Smock of Topeka, Kansas. Funeral services were held at the home at 1 o'clock this {Friday} afternoon and the body will be shipped to Salina, Kansas for burial. [Benton County Record 3/20/25]

ELDER, Martha Ann - J.S. Elder received word Tuesday evening of the death of his mother, Mrs. M.A. Elder, at her home at Jonesboro, Ark. and by driving by auto to Monett, caught the night train for Memphis. Mrs. Elder was 91 years old and when Mr. Elder saw her only two weeks ago she was in quite good health. Mrs. Elder lived in Rogers for a number of years with her daughter, Miss Sue Elder, moving to Jonesboro some six or seven years ago. She was a woman of many splendid qualities and is lovingly remembered by a large number of our citizens. [Rogers Democrat 4/2/25] [Rogers Daily Post 3/1/25]

Martha Ann Elder, mother of J.S. Elder of this city, fell asleep at her home in Jonesboro March 30 at the ripe old age of 90 years. Besides her son, J.S. Elder, she is survived by two other sons, T.J. and H.A. of Jonesboro, and two daughters, Mrs. A.C. Broadway of Little Rock and Mrs. Sue Strickland, who was her mother's constant companion, the two never having been separated more than a day or two since Mrs. Strickland was born. Six old friends acted as pall bearers with 9 honorary, all old friends, at the funeral conducted at the home of T.J. Elder. Rev. J.W. Dollison, her pastor, conducted the services and the interment was in the city cemetery. "Mother" Elder was well known by the older citizens of Rogers, having lived here for several years with her daughter, Miss Sue, in a little cottage at the corner of Fourth and Chestnut streets – a home provided by her son that she might linger near him in comfort. [Rogers Daily Post 4/7/25]

ELLIOTT, W.A. - {from Hebron} W.A. Elliott died at his home in Rogers Monday of last week and was buried Tuesday afternoon. Mr. Elliott had lived in our community for a number of years and had a host of friends who attended his funeral. He was 63 years old and had been a member of the Baptist church for years. He was a man of honesty and uprightness and will be missed in his family of six sons and one daughter and wife, but as Mr. Elliott had been a sufferer for almost two years with cancer we feel that he is at rest and hope the family will receive comfort and consolation from the Master who doeth all things well. [Rogers Democrat 3/5/25]

ELLIS, Perry Camby - Perry Camby Ellis, a former resident of Bentonville and well known by people here, died at his home in Quincy, Ill. on Saturday, February 14th, 1925 at the age of 57 years. Funeral services were held the following Tuesday at the family home in Plattsburg, Mo. and interment made in the Green Lawn Cemetery there. He is the son of the late Rev. J.W. Ellis, who for four years was pastor of the Christian Church in Bentonville. Mr. Ellis was a newspaper man on Kansas City papers, including the Kansas City Times, Kansas City Journal and Kansas City Post; also on the St. Louis Dispatch. For twelve years he wrote for the Quincy Whig. In 1911 he founded the Mississippi Magazine which he published seven years. Mr. Ellis is survived by his mother, Sallie Breckenridge Ellis, and one brother, J. Breckenridge Ellis, the author, both of Plattsburg, Mo. [Benton County Record 2/27/25]

ELLISON, Emily - Miss Emily Ellison was born March 17, 1850 at Marine Ill. and died December 25th at her home in Rogers at the age of 74 years, nine months and eighteen days. While a resident of Marine she united with the Presbyterian church but attended the First M.E. church after coming to Rogers. For 35 years she had resided here and in her own quiet way made her home her cherished spot. She was the oldest of nine children. Those living are: Mrs. Frances Booth of St. Louis; Mrs. Ida Saunders, Rogers; Mrs. A.J. Baker, Joplin; August Ellison, St. Louis; and Will Ellison, Colorado. The nieces and nephews in Rogers include: W.E. Saunders, Mary Saunders, Harley Saunders, Mrs. Ora Chapin, Mrs. O.C. Thompson and John Wilson. A fine spirit of unselfishness marks her closing career in that while she was very desirous that her sister, Mrs. Ida Saunders of Rogers, might have a very merry Christmas, she herself suffered the stroke that brought grief and sorrow into so many lives. Funeral services were conducted on Saturday, December 27th at the residence by Rev. Richard C. Lucke, pastor of the First M.E. church. Interment was at the Rogers cemetery. [Rogers Democrat 1/1/25]

ENGLAND, Sallie - Mrs. Sallie England, a full-blood Cherokee Indian, died at her home south of Grove last Friday at the age of 110 years. She was probably the oldest person in Oklahoma. She is supposed to have been born in 1815. When the government removed the Cherokees from their home in 1836 to their new home in the Indian Territory, Sallie came with them. She and her husband were allotted 140 acres of land on Honey creek and on this homestead she has lived for nearly 90 years. [Benton County Record 1/30/25]

ENGLES, Isabella Kinnibrug - Mrs. Isabella Kinnibrug Engles, aged 90 years, died at her home near Farmington in Washington county on Wednesday of last week. Mrs. Engles was a true Arkansawyer. Her entire life of half a score less than a century was spent within a radius of 200 miles from her birthplace. She had lived for 61 years in the house in which she died. Her father, who was an early settler of that section, became particularly well known by the fact that before the Civil War he freed not only his own slaves but also purchased those belonging to his sister and giving them employment when freed. Six grandsons served as pallbearers at her funeral. [Benton County Record 3/6/25]

ENGLISH, Joseph - The funeral of Joseph English, veteran Confederate soldier, was held at the Wardlow cemetery in Avoca last week. He was the father of O.A. English of Centerton with whom he had been making his home for several years. The deceased soldier was born in Searcy county, Arkansas in 1836. After the Civil War he moved to Avoca where he made his home until moving to Centerton. Mr. English enlisted in the Confederate army at the outbreak of the war, serving the entire time until peace was signed. He took part in the battle of Pea Ridge, Wilson's Creek and the siege of Vicksburg. He is survived by a son, Mr. O.A. English, and wife, granddaughter, Evelyn, and daughter, Mrs. Lee Griggs of Joplin. [Benton County Democrat 9/15/25] [Benton County Record 9/11/25] [Rogers Democrat 9/10/25]

EVANS, William Andrew - William Andrew (Dick) Evans was born Feb. 28, 1851 and died Feb. 3, 1925 at his home 2½ miles south of Cave Springs. Funeral services were held at the Baptist church of Cave Springs. Interment was made in the Phillips cemetery. The services were conducted by Rev. Henry of Elm Springs. "Uncle Dick," as he was called, came with his parents from Missouri at the age of four years. Benton county has been his home ever since with the exception of two years spent in Texas. He was married to Martha Pace in the year 1871. Unto this union was born eight children, Edmond dying in infancy and a daughter, Mrs. Pearl Shook, nine years ago. He is survived by his wife and six children, James T. of Bentonville; Mrs. Maggie Smith of Healing Springs; William, J. Frank and Susie Shook, all of Cave Springs; and Mrs. Della Williams of Sardis, Okla. There are thirteen grandchildren and one great-granddaughter and three brothers and one sister: Mrs. Martha Brown of Hightop neighborhood; Jesse of Vaughn; George and Jeff of Mason Valley, who survive him. He was converted four years ago and joined the Spring Creek Baptist church. He was an earnest Christian, having all faith in "The Old Time Religion" of which he loved to sing. [Benton County Democrat 2/12/25] [Benton County Record 2/20/25]

FAGALA, Mr. - Mr. Fagala of Cave Springs has received word that his brother, who has been sick the past year at his home in Texas, was dead and a funeral notice published by a Texas paper was received also. Quite an article was published that had been written by his brother before he died, thanking all his family for their kindness and bidding his friends and relatives farewell. He also expressed his hope for the great eternal blessings. [Benton County Record 9/4/25]

FAGAN, Asa B. - Word comes to old friends here of the death of Asa B. Fagan at St. Charles, Ill. where he moved about 14 years ago. The Fagan family lived in the Jackson house, corner of 7th and Walnut, for some time. The children will be remembered as Julia, Ellen and Virginia and two boys, Arthur and Paul. Upon the election of Wilson as president Mr. Fagan was appointed post master at St. Charles, a position which he held for nine years. Mrs. Fagan will, no doubt, continue to live in their old home as Ellen and Virginia both live at home, the two boys are in business in Chicago while Julia married a prominent young lawyer of Geneva, Ill. At one time Mr. Fagan owned two or three farms in this county bit it is thought he had disposed of them. [Rogers Daily Post 8/13/25]

FAIRALL, Wm. W. - Wm. W. Fairall departed this life March 5, 1925 at his home at 3017 Gillham Road, Kansas City, Mo. at the age of 67 years. Prior to his coming to Kansas City he lived in Gentry, Ark. and was at one time mayor of Gentry and also justice of the peace. He often expressed the wish to see his friends once more. He leaves to mourn his loss a wife, Mrs. Mattie L. Fairall, also 3 children by a former marriage, 1 daughter and 2 sons. [Gentry Journal-Advance 3/13/25]

FARLEY, Mrs. John - Mrs. John Farley, 86, died last week at her home near Siloam Springs where she had lived for more than 50 years. She was an aunt of Rev. W.T. Farley of Siloam Springs. [Rogers Democrat 2/12/25]

FARLEY, Mrs. W.T. - {from Siloam Springs} Mrs. W.T. Farley, a well known resident of this city, died Monday night at the age of nearly 70 years. [Benton County Record 10/16/25]

FARR, Denzel D. - Denzel D. Farr, a well known farmer living between Cave Springs and Elm Springs, committed suicide early Saturday morning by shooting himself in the temple with a 22 calibre rifle. The deed was committed about 4 o'clock that morning by the fireplace in the Farr home after he had passed a restless night. Mr. Farr was considered well to do by his neighbors and his business affairs are said to be in good shape. He was very fond of his wife and family, it is stated, and there were no domestic troubles that are known of. It is said by his friends that his worries were over trivial matters which he had allowed his mind to magnify. Funeral services were held Sunday with interment in the Elm Springs cemetery. Mr. Farr was about 35 years of age and besides his widow is survived by one daughter and five sons; also one brother, Earl Farr, living in that vicinity. [Benton County Record 1/2/25]

FARRAR, Densil D. - D.D. Farrar, a prominent and highly respected farmer living between Cave Springs and Elm Springs, shot himself in the temple with a 22 caliber rifle about three o'clock last Friday morning and death resulted shortly thereafter. Funeral services were held for the unfortunate man Saturday afternoon. There is no reason known for the act of Farrar. It was known he was worrying over some recent business affairs but it was a state of mind rather than business misfortune according to friends. Mr. Farrar was the owner of a splendid farm near the Little Osage and well fixed financially. He was 35 years old and had six children. It is said he had been bothered with restless nights. When not able to sleep he would sit by the fire. That Friday night he had been particularly restless and had spent the fore part of the night sitting up. When his wife asked him if he was ill he replied that he was all right and told her to go to sleep.

Reassured, Mrs. Farrar retired and went to sleep. About 4 o'clock Farrar stretched out on the floor, placed the muzzle of a 22 caliber rifle to his temple and pulled the trigger. The rifle was found by his side. Mr. Farrar had a wide circle of friends in Washington and Benton counties and was known as a good husband and father, always considerate of his family. His father was formerly in business in Springdale. Mrs. Farrar was a Pattishall before her marriage, her family being one of the pioneer families of the community and highly respected. They have the sympathy of the entire community in this bereavement. [Benton County Democrat 1/1/25]
Densil Farrar, son of Mrs. Ola Farrar Holland, living between Cave Springs and Elm Springs, ended his life Saturday morning about three o'clock by placing a 22 target rifle against his temple and sending a bullet into his brain. No one seems to know the exact cause of the deed unless he became suddenly deranged. He had talked the day before about a span of mules he had sold and thought he was in bad circumstances. His brother, Earl, had been with him until ten o'clock Friday evening and had no idea there was such a thought as suicide in his mind. He was only 37 years of age and had always been in the best of health. He was an upright young man and leaves a wife and five children, two of them grown. Besides his mother, Mrs. Holland, he leaves one brother, Earl, and one sister, Mrs. Mina McVey. Tragedy visited the Farrar home ten years ago when his sister, Miss Alta, a lovely 18 year old girl, was killed by being thrown from a buggy. She was out driving with friends and the team ran away. Fifteen years ago his father, French Farrar, fell from a large barn they were building and later died from injuries received. Mr. Farrar resided two and one-half miles south of Cave Springs on the farm where he was born, one of the best farms in the neighborhood. Funeral services were held at Elm Springs Sunday afternoon and a large crowd of friends and relatives were there. Everyone extends sympathy to the grief stricken family. [Rogers Democrat 1/1/25]

FISHER, infant - {from New Hope} A family by the name of Fisher from western Oklahoma moved into the house on the place known as the Widow Bayles place a week or two ago and Sunday night their little baby girl, five months old, died and was buried at Pleasant Grove cemetery at 2:30 Monday afternoon. This family is in very destitute circumstances, having lost three crops in succession in Oklahoma and Mr. Fisher is in poor health and has been for more than a year, but there are two boys and two girls large enough to work and they hope to be able to get work here in the fruit. The neighbors here have all been very kind to them in trouble as is the Arkansas custom and anyone needing help in harvesting their fall crops might do well to give them employment. There is no need for anyone to go hungry here if they are willing to work. [Rogers Democrat 8/20/25]

FLOYD, James - James Floyd, 5 year old son of Mr. and Mrs. Sam Floyd, was almost instantly killed at 2 o'clock Saturday afternoon when struck by a Ford coupe driven by W.E. Spiva, credit man for the Joplin

Supply Co., Joplin, the accident occurring on the state highway three miles north of Bentonville. The child's parents have been at Lawrence, Kan. where the father was working and he and his sister, aged seven, have been staying with their grandparents, Mr. and Mrs. J.T. Floyd, tenants on the farm of Mrs. J.D. Bryan, at which place the accident occurred. The little fellow and his sister had started across the highway and he is said to have run ahead of her into the path of the car. The driver swerved to the opposite side of the road in an effort to miss the child but the fender struck him, throwing him under the car, one wheel passing over his chest. He died within 20 minutes, without regaining consciousness and before a physician could get to him. The accident was witnessed from a distance by a road crew working on the highway. Coroner Callison made an investigation at the scene of the accident shortly after its occurrence, interviewing the driver of the car and others. He expressed the opinion that Spiva had done everything that he could to avoid the accident and that no blame should be attached to him. After having done all he could for the child and immediately following the little fellow's death, Mr. Spiva drove into Bentonville and reported the accident to Sheriff Gailey, the two going back to the scene of the accident and going over the ground in company with Coroner Callison, Whitley Kerr and other persons. The coroner considered an inquest unnecessary as did the little fellow's grandfather. However Spiva later gave bond for his appearance here Saturday, June 13th, when it is said a formal hearing will be held to establish as a matter of public record his innocence or guilt of any criminal carelessness. Before leaving last Saturday Mr. Spiva arranged to take care of all expenses connected with the funeral. James is survived by his parents, grandparents, and one sister, Goldie May. A younger brother died during the past year at Springdale. Funeral services were held at the New Home church Monday afternoon, conducted by Rev. Joe Tyson, pastor of the local Church of the Nazarene, and interment made in the New Home cemetery. The parents arrived Sunday. [Benton County Democrat 6/4/25] [Benton County Record 6/12/25] [Rogers Daily Post 6/8/25]

FORD, Charles Simon - {from Fairview} Charles Simon Ford was born February 9, 1891 at Seligman, Missouri and died February 26, 1925 at his home near Lowell at the age of thirty-four years and fifteen days. Funeral services were held at Tuck's Chapel Friday afternoon and were conducted by Rev. E. Rice of Springdale. Charles' mother died when he was four years old. He leaves his father, Reuben Ford, a step-mother, four brothers and two sisters: Dallas Ford of Lowell; Ernest, Woodrow, Henry, Pearl and Dorothy Ford, all by his bedside when death came. Also a host of friends to mourn his death. Charles was a good friend to everyone he knew and will be missed. He served ten months in the late war, going over seas, serving as a private in Company M, 147 Infantry, while there contracting the disease which later caused his death. He has been an invalid more than two years. [Rogers Democrat 3/5/25] [Benton County Record 3/6/25]

FORD, John Harris - John Harris Ford was born in Cannon county, Tenn. Sept. 9, 1846 and died in Fannin county, Texas on January 22, 1925 at the age of 79 years. He was the youngest son of that early pioneer couple, most generally known as Uncle George and Aunt Jane Ford, and moved with them to Benton county when he was a small boy. He grew to manhood here and in 1872 was united in marriage to Rebecca E. Long who preceded him in death 16 years ago. To this union were born nine children: Mrs. Wiley Edens, Glade, Ark.; Monroe Ford, San Bernardino, Calif.; Mrs. Leonard Williams, Durant, Okla.; W.R. Ford, Tom Bean, Texas; Harvey Ford, White Wright, Texas; Jimmie Ford, who died in infancy; Mrs. Willis Poe, Garfield, Ark.; Mrs. Charlie Rayon, Hominy, Okla. and Albert Ford, Sand Springs, Okla. Together with the children he leaves one brother, Uncle Billy Ford of Garfield and a host of relatives and friends to mourn his departure. Since the death of his wife he had made his home with his son, Harvey, and moved with him to Texas about eight years ago. He united with the Christian church and was baptized June 10, 1920. Uncle John, as he was generally known, had gone through this life with afflictions, being totally blind for about 30 years, but we can truthfully say that he bore his afflictions almost uncomplainingly. And with a ready store of wit and humor he ever tried to make life pleasant for his family and all his associates. He had cultivated his natural instincts and could perform many kinds of work although he was totally blind and has traveled many miles of rough winding road alone, and so keen was his sense of hearing he would readily detect any familiar voice and when you met him on the road or elsewhere and spoke to him he met you with a quick response, at the same time calling your name. To know him was to love and respect him and we are glad to say through gratitude and respect to his son Harvey and wife that they were attentive and watchful to the end, providing all his wants and needs, and then finally complied with Uncle John's last request by bringing his body back and burying him beside his loving wife in Blalock cemetery. Funeral services were held at Walnut Hill and were conducted by Rev. J.H. Martin of Rogers. A large crowd of relatives and friends attended to pay their last respects and after the services his body was taken over the same road which he had traveled so often in his youthful days, by the old homestead, and laid away to await the morning of the resurrection. A Friend. [Rogers Democrat 1/29/25]

FORD, Mrs. - {from Central} Ray Ford and wife were down from Monett last week and spent Wednesday night at the J.W. Pratt home and attended the funeral of the former's brother's wife, which was held at Walnut Hill Thursday of last week. [Rogers Democrat 5/28/25]

FORD, Mrs. H.J. - Thursday morning in answer to a wire Funeral Director J.W. Bryant went to Garfield to take charge of the body of Mrs. H.J.{?} Ford who had died at Cypress, Texas the day before, being brought here to be buried at Walnut Hill. The Ford family are among the old residents of Benton County, H.G.{?} Ford being one of the second generation. [Rogers Daily Post 5/22/25]

FOUST, J.S. - Rev. J.S. Foust, pastor of a church in Prairie Grove, was found dead last Friday with a bullet hole through his head. It is believed that he was accidentally killed by the premature discharge of his gun while out hunting that afternoon. He was discovered later in the day with his dead body lying over a hollow log. From his position it is thought he had been looking into the log in search of a rabbit and in some way the gun went off. He was very popular in Prairie Grove and his tragic death caused a pall of sorrow over this little town. He was 39 years of age and unmarried. The body was sent back to his former home in Gaston, Ind. for burial. [Benton County Democrat 11/24/25]

FOWLER, Elmer B. - Elmer B. Fowler was born near Decatur Nov. 22, 1905 and died April 18, 1925, aged 19 years, 4 months and 26 days. The funeral was conducted by Brother Jeff Finch at Bethel, south of Gravette, and the body laid to rest in Bethel cemetery. He leaves to mourn the loss his mother, father, three brothers and a host of relatives and friends. He was converted in a meeting at Bethel in 1923 conducted by Brother and Sister Ralph Fetters and Sister Anna Waldrip, and baptised the same day by Brother Kilmer. Elmer was an excellent character, loved by all who knew him. He was sick thirteen days from measles followed by pneumonia. His trust was in the Lord during his illness and he was reconciled to God's will. A Friend Who Loved Him. [Gravette News-Herald 5/8/25]

FRITTS, Claude - Fayetteville, Sept. 12.- Claude Fritts, aged 26, died at the City Hospital Saturday afternoon from injuries suffered when his car collided with an automobile driven by Dr. P.L. Hathcock. The accident occurred Saturday at noon. There were no pedestrians near when the car collided and it is not clear whether both swerved to avert a collision and hit the curb. Dr. Hathcock was uninjured and examined the young man at once but after a brief examination said he did not see how Fritts could live. Dr. Hathcock was with the injured man when he died. Fritts' principal injury was concussion of the brain, though he suffered other injuries. It is believed that he was thrown from his car, a cut down racer, and struck his head on the curb. He did not regain consciousness after the accident and physicians declared it futile to perform an operation in an attempt to save his life. Another occupant of the Fritts car, George Pool, age 19, was uninjured. Both Fritts and Pool are employees of an ice company here. [Rogers Daily Post 9/14/25]

FULBRIGHT, Beulah - Miss Beulah Fulbright, aged 20 and a student of the Bentonville high school, died Sunday evening, Feb. 8th at 6 o'clock at the home of her parents, Mr. and Mrs. O. Nossaman, southeast of Bentonville. Her death resulted from influenza and at the time of her death and just prior to it other members of her family were suffering from the same disease. She had lived here only a year or so but during that time impressed herself so favorably upon the minds of all who knew her that she will long live in their memory and hearts as one who refused to be conquered by adverse circumstances; as one striving daily not only to better her own condition and that of her immediate family, but insisted on carrying her part of the burden no matter where her lot might fall. She had won the sincere liking and respect of her schoolmates and teachers alike. At the funeral services at the M.E. Church, South Monday afternoon, conducted by the Rev. J.L. Evans, the Girls Glee Club of the high school sang and the entire student body and all members of the faculty were in attendance. Besides her mother and step-father, she is survived by one sister, Miss Eula Fulbright, also a member of the B.H.S. junior class, her step-brother, Roscoe Nossaman, and other relatives who do not live here. Interment was made in the City cemetery. [Benton County Democrat 2/12/25]

FUNK, Mehetibel "Mamie" - Mehetibel Funk was born March 29, 1867 in Carroll county, Mo. and died at the old family home Jan. 6, 1925 aged 57 years, 9 months and 7 days. She came to Arkansas with her parents when but a girl and with them settled on the farm which has been the family home since that time. "Mamie," as she was known to all her friends, was the oldest of a family of ten children, eight of which are still living, as follows: Melvina Reed of Alpena Pass; Mrs. Jennie Stroud Jenson of Pullman, Wash.; Mrs. Bettie Hart of Veleta, Kan.; Mrs. Mary Knot and Chas. Stroud of So. Bend, Wash.; Melvin Funk and Martin and Oliver Funk of this place. Since the death of their parents Mamie had lived with and been housekeeper for her brother, Oliver Funk. She became a member of the Methodist church at an early age. She was a quiet, retiring, gentle, home-loving soul, kind to everyone with whom she came in contact. For a number of years she had been in ill health but was a patient sufferer. [Benton County Democrat 1/15/25]
Mamie Funk, aged 57, passed away Tuesday morning, January 6th, at the old Funk farm. She had been suffering from a complication of diseases for about two years but was confined to her bed only about two weeks. Surviving are three sisters, Mrs. Flora Reed, Alpena Pass, Ark.; Mrs. Effie Jenson, Washington and Mrs. Mary Knott, Washington, and four brothers, Oliver Funk, Martin Funk, Charlie Funk, Washington, and Melvin Funk, Montana. Funeral services were held at 3 o'clock Tuesday from the home and interment at Mt. Pleasant cemetery. [Benton County Record 1/9/25]

GAMBLE, Mollie Virginia HARDY - Mollie Virginia Hardy was born on Pea Ridge November 22, 1868 and passed away at her home near Centerton Monday, March 9, 1925, aged 56 years, 3 months and 17 days. She was married to John R. Gamble on October 31, 1890 and to this union were born eight children, four boys and four girls, two of the boys having preceded the mother to the Great Beyond. She is also survived by three brothers and two sisters, all of whom were present at the funeral service. She leaves as well a host of others who mourn her loss for she will be

greatly missed within her circle of friends. She was cheerful all through her illness and when the end approached she asked of her family that they not mourn for her going as all was well and she was ready to respond to the call. Early in life she had united with the Presbyterian church and throughout her life continued a faithful church attendant. Funeral services were conducted Tuesday morning at the Centerton Community church, Pastor A.L. Boyles of that church and Rev. F.A. Bradshaw of the Vaughn Presbyterian church officiating. The church was filled with a host of friends who attended the last rites and there were many beautiful floral gifts, tokens of the esteem in which she was held by her many friends. Interment was in the Centerton cemetery. [Benton County Democrat 3/12/25]
Mrs. Mollie Gamble, wife of John R. Gamble, living northwest of Centerton, died on Monday morning, March 9th, 1925 after a long illness. She was 57 years of age and had spent her whole life in Benton county. Funeral services were held at the Community Church in Centerton on Tuesday morning with interment in the cemetery at that place. A large host of friends and relatives, including all her children, were present to pay their last respects to this good woman who had been a cheer and comfort to her family and neighbors. Rev. E. Boyles of Centerton and Rev. J.T. Evans of Bentonville conducted the services. Besides her husband she is survived by two sons, Willie Gamble of Forrest City, Mo.; and Luther Gamble of the home, and four daughters, Ethel, Artie, Alta and Beth Gamble, all of whom live at home. Three brothers, Mack and Wes Hardy of Pea Ridge, and Earl Hardy of Bentonville, and two sisters, Mrs. Lizzie Gamble of Fort Smith and Mrs. Minnie Harris of Pea Ridge also survive her. Mrs. Gamble was born on Pea Ridge in November 1868 and was the daughter of Jake and Artie Hardy, pioneer settlers of Benton county. In 1890 she was married to John R. Gamble. After their marriage they moved to their farm in the Marr's Hill neighborhood which has since been their home. [Benton County Record 3/13/25]

GAMBLE, Mrs. P. - Mrs. P. Gamble, 60 years old, died at the home of her sister, Mrs. Will Holland, southwest of Centerton, about three o'clock Wednesday morning. Mrs. Gamble had been ill about a year. Her home is in Southwest City, Missouri. Funeral services were held at the Gamble cemetery where burial was made Thursday afternoon. [Benton County Record 10/30/25]

GASTON, Joe N. - Joe N. Gaston, a well known resident of this section of the country, died at the Hurley sanitarium in Bentonville Wednesday evening, Nov. 18, 1925. He had been sick 5 weeks. Death was due to blood poisoning caused by a carbuncle on his neck. He was 68 years old. Funeral services were held the following day with interment in the Hebron cemetery east of Cave Springs. He is survived by one son, Wm. Gaston, and two daughters, Mrs. Sadie Shaffer and Mrs. Martha Crawford, all of Cave Springs; also by three brothers of Rt. 5, Bentonville; Henry and Wm. Gaston of Cave Springs {only two named}, and two sisters, Mrs. M.W. Barnes of Rogers and Mrs. A.M. Barnes of Cave Springs. Mrs. Gaston died about thirty years ago. For the past few years he has made his home with his son, William, near Cave Springs. Mr. Gaston was born in Monroe county, Tenn. in 1857 and came to Benton county in 1882 and located where the town of Rogers now stands. In fact he helped clear the timber from the new townsite. Later he bought a farm near Colville where he lived for many years. [Benton County Record 11/27/25]

GATTON, Joe - Joe, the 7 year old son of Mr. and Mrs. Bob Gatton, died at their home in Baxter Springs, Kan. last week and the body was brought to Gravette Friday morning and conveyed to Mt. Pleasant for funeral and burial. Rev. W.H. McCarroll conducted the services. The little fellow had been afflicted with heart trouble for some time. [Gravette News-Herald 4/10/25]

GAY, Vernon - Vernon, the year-old son of R.V. Gay and wife of Springdale, died Sunday in the hospital at Fort Smith Christmas Day. The child swallowed a piece of peanut candy, which became lodged in its windpipe. Local efforts to relieve the child failed and he was taken Saturday to Fort Smith where physicians operated upon the throat but were unable to save its life. [Rogers Democrat 12/31/25]

GETTS, John Wesley - John W. Getts, who has lingered several weeks, a victim of Brights disease, passed away Tuesday morning, March 24, 1925 at the residence of his daughter, Mrs. W.W. Pearson, to whose home he was removed when he became seriously ill. John Wesley Getts was born in Tippecanoe, Indiana Nov. 7, 1861. He moved with his parents to Lamar, Mo. in the fall of 1877. Was united in marriage with Sarah Hartman July 4, 1881. To this union one child was born, Mrs. Aura Pearson, now of Gravette. He leaves his wife, one daughter and one brother, E.V. Getts of Purcell, Mo. John Getts, as the writer knew him, was a man of sobriety, integrity and honor and was true to the cause he represented. For many years he had been custodian of Gravette school house and grounds and was held in high esteem by the people, the faculty and the hundreds of pupils to whom he was endeared, and everyone is going to miss him deeply. Mr. Getts was a member of the Presbyterian church and his funeral will be conducted this Thursday, 2 p.m. at the Presbyterian church by W.H. McCarroll, to be followed by interment in the I.O.O.F. Cemetery. Condolence to the family. [Gravette News-Herald 3/27/25] [Benton County Record 4/3/25]

GIGER, infant - {from Centerton} The infant daughter of Mr. and Mrs. Roy Giger was laid to rest here on Tuesday. Rev. W.J. LeRoy conducted the funeral services. Our sincere sympathy goes out to Mr. and Mrs. Giger. [Benton County Record 8/14/25]

GILBERT, Harris McCager - H.M. Gilbert, one of Benton county's pioneers and well known throughout Benton county, died at his home at

Decatur on Friday, January 23rd, 1925 at the age of 73 years. Funeral services were conducted by Rev. Finch at the Cottage Grove church Saturday and interment was made in the Word cemetery. He was the son of Harris Gilbert, who emigrated from Tennessee to Arkansas several years before the Civil War and located at Bentonville where he followed the trade of blacksmith. This was at the time when Bentonville was a log cabin village. On October 5th, 1855 the oldest son, Harris McCager Gilbert, was born, who lived practically all his life in Benton county, except two years spent in Missouri during the Civil War. He was married to Alice Cherry on May 1st, 1871. After spending a couple of years near Caverna mill they located on a farm near Decatur, where they have lived for over 50 years. His main occupation was that of farmer and he lived an active, useful life up to the time of his last illness which occurred three weeks before his death. Mr. Gilbert lived a devoted Christian life for a number of years. He was a friend to everybody, a loyal citizen, and one who held the respect of all who knew him. He will be greatly missed, not only by his family, to whom he was greatly devoted, but by his church and community in general. He is survived by a wife and five children, a brother and three sisters, besides a number of other relatives to mourn their loss. We extend our most heartfelt sympathy, though their loss has been Heaven's gain. [Benton County Record 2/6/25]

{from Decatur} H.M. Gilbert died at the home of his daughter, Miss Addie Gilbert, local postmistress, in Decatur on Friday morning, January 23rd, after a lingering illness. The funeral services were conducted by Rev. Jeff Finch of Gravette at the Dorsey church north of Decatur. Interment was made in the Word cemetery. Mr. Gilbert was an old resident of this section and was highly respected by all who knew him. [Benton County Record 1/30/25]

{from Gravette} H.M. {Punch} Gilbert, an old and highly respected citizen, died at his home south of town Friday. Mr. Gilbert had been a resident of this community a long time. [Benton County Record 1/30/25]

GILLIAM, Eugene Bailey - E.B. Gilliam, retired orchardist, cotton planter and merchant, and well known in this section and in eastern Arkansas, died here Thursday night, April 16, at 1:20 o'clock, aged 75 years, six months and 13 days. Death followed a week's critical illness and resulted from complications following several years suffering from rheumatism. Eugene Bailey Gilliam was born in Davies county, Kentucky, near Owensboro, October 3, 1849 of a southern pioneer family. When a young man he came to Arkansas and became a prominent citizen of Jackson county with large plantation and mercantile interests at Swifton where he lived until moving with his wife and other members of the family to Bentonville in 1910. Mrs. Gilliam died here on April 19, 1923. Coming to the Arkansas fruit region Mr. Gilliam bought two apple orchards near Bentonville and although he had had no previous experience in the commercial production of apples a persevering application to his new problems and the same characteristics and energies of mind and body that had made him successful in the growing and marketing of cotton and stock and in the mercantile business in his old home county, made him in a position of prominence and respect in his new environment. His liking for and faith in his new home, Bentonville, were also shown by his investments in residence and business properties in the town where he and his family were soon looked upon as a permanent part of the community life. He had been a member of the Christian church since early in life and a member of the Masonic order from his early manhood. He was regular in his attendance at church services until ill health made such attendance impossible. Mr. Gilliam is survived by one daughter, Mrs. Corilla Clymer of Detroit, Mich. and six sons: Otis E., Westville, Okla.; John M., Bellingham, Wash.; Robert L., Bentonville; Embra B., Detroit, Mich.; Paul E., Bentonville and Leon T., Marshall, Mo. and by ten grandchildren. The daughter and all the sons except John M. and Leon T. were here at the end and for his funeral. He is also survived by a brother, Robert L. Gilliam of Owensboro, Ky. who was here for the funeral. A step-daughter, Mrs. J.D. Ashley of West Plains, Mo. and two of her children were also here, coming to Bentonville several days before because of Mr. Gilliam's critical illness. Funeral services were held at the Gilliam home on West E street Saturday afternoon, conducted by Rev. Stephen A. Morton, pastor of the Christian church. Interment was made in the family lot in the City cemetery. [Benton County Democrat 4/23/25] [Benton County Record 4/24/25]

GILLIAM, Ollie HOLLOWELL - Funeral services for Mrs. Ollie Hollowell Gilliam, wife of J.B. Gilliam of Kansas City, Mo., who died in a St. Louis hospital Thursday, May 14, were held here Sunday afternoon at the home of her sister, Mrs. Chas. W. Foster, and family on East C street. While in St. Louis for a few days visit with her son, Volney Gilliam, a student of architecture in Washington University, Mrs. Gilliam suffered an acute attack of appendicitis, an ailment with which she had suffered at times for a number of years. She was rushed to the hospital for immediate surgical attention but her death occurred shortly after the operation. A daughter of the late Mr. and Mrs. O.P. Hollowell, who were among Bentonville's respected citizens, Mrs. Gilliam was born here on March 31, 1882 and lived here until her marriage on Dec. 21, 1903 to Mr. Gilliam who is now superintendent of the car department of the Frisco railway company with headquarters at Kansas City. She was a member of the Kansas City chapter, No. 381, Order of Eastern Star, a sister member of that chapter coming here to attend her funeral, which was also attended by members of the local chapter in a body. She is well remembered by many girlhood friends in the community. The funeral services were conducted by the Rev. J.L. Evans, pastor of the M.E. church, South, assisted by the Rev. W.C. Wheat, and attended by a great number of friends and acquaintances. Besides her husband and son Mrs. Gilliam is survived by two brothers, Ed P. Hollowell of St. Louis and Jim Hollowell of Chicago; three sisters, Mrs. W.H. Maples of Fort Smith, Mrs. Chas. W. Foster, Bentonville and Mrs. J.P. Moore of Laurel, Mont. Interment was made in the Hollowell lot at the Bentonville cemetery, the services at the grave being in charge of the local chapter of the Eastern Star. [Benton County Democrat 5/21/25]

GILMORE, Leon - Leon Gilmore, 20-year-old son of Mrs. M.C. Gilmore, was almost instantly killed Tuesday noon at their home in the northeast part of town by the accidental discharge of his shot gun. Young Gilmore had been hunting and when he stepped upon the porch of the home is supposed to have stumbled or attempted to set the gun down. The porch was being refloored and instead of getting the butt of the gun on a board, it slipped through to the ground. The hammer of the gun must have caught on the edge of the board for an examination shows the firing pin to have been deeply driven into the shell. Most of the load of shot struck him in the lower part of the abdomen, while part struck him in the left wrist and arm, and also in the face. No one saw the accident but O.F. Day, who was working on the house, heard him cry, "I'm shot," and as he ran around the house to investigate saw the boy step off the porch and run out the front way, trying to make his way across the street to the residence of Dr. Geo. M. Love. Dr. Love had heard the shot and glanced out of the window just in time to see young Gilmore start across the street and then crumple face down as he reached the center of the road. He went to him at once but the boy never spoke again and died within a very few moments. Young Gilmore was the only child and with his mother and grandmother had lived here for eight years, coming here from Red Oak, Iowa eight years ago. He attended Rogers high school and also the John Brown College at Siloam Springs. He worked for a time for the Rogers Daily Post and more recently for the Small Electric Co. He was a likeable young fellow and his untimely death was not only a great blow to his mother and grandmother but to the entire community as well. Funeral services will be held this afternoon at 2:30 at the Church of Christ and will be conducted by Rev. A.A. DuLaney of the First Baptist church. Interment in Rogers cemetery. [Rogers Democrat 1/22/25] [Benton County Democrat 1/22/25]

GLADDEN, E.J. - {from New Hope} E.J. Gladden, 62 years old, was found dead in his bed Monday morning by his brother, C.W. Gladden, with whom he made his home in the New Hope neighborhood. It is supposed his death was the result of an overdose of medicine he was taking for heart trouble. Coroner Callison was called but no inquest was deemed necessary. Mr. Gladden was born in Grandville, Pa. Oct. 3, 1863 and is survived by a sister, Mrs. Alice Phillips of Grandville, and a brother, Charles Gladden. Funeral was held Tuesday, conducted by Rev. J.T. Willcoxon, pastor of the Central Methodist church. [Rogers Democrat 9/24/25] [Rogers Daily Post 9/21/25]

GLEAVES, Earl - Earl Gleaves, 17 year old son of Mr. and Mrs. Gleaves who live in the west part of town, died in North Dakota Monday night. The remains are expected to arrive here Thursday night or Friday for burial. [Gentry Journal-Advance 9/18/25]
The remains of Earl Gleaves, who died in North Dakota, were brought home Tuesday evening and burial was made in Springtown Wednesday. [Benton County Record 9/25/25]

GLENN, Mary - Mary Glenn, the eight-year-old daughter of Mr. and Mrs. John Glenn, living in the south part of town, died Saturday. The body was interred in the Zion cemetery in Washington county Sunday. [Benton County Record 7/31/25]

GODLEY, Julia - Mrs. Julia Godley died last Friday at the home of her son, Will Godley, on South Second street, after a long illness at the age of 77 years. Funeral services were held Sunday afternoon at the First M.E. Church of which she had been a faithful and loyal member for many years, and were conducted by the pastor, Rev. E.C. Wardlow. Interment was in the Rogers cemetery by the side of her husband who died here eighteen years ago. The Godley family came to Rogers in 1899 and she had lived in or near Rogers since that time. Mrs. Godley was a woman of many splendid qualities and was held in high esteem by a large circle of friends. She is survived by five children: Mrs. N.G. Stine of Glasco, Kansas; Mrs. Seymour Alford of Fort Worth, Tex.; Mrs. A.E. Montgomery of Florence, Colo.; Chas. Godley of Huntington Park, California and Will Godley of Rogers. [Rogers Democrat 11/12/25]

GOETLILY, Carl - Carl Goetlily of Decatur passed away June 4 at the age of 54. Funeral services were held from the M.E. church June 6 and burial was made in the Decatur cemetery. [Gentry Journal-Advance 6/26/25]

GORSLINE, Mrs. - {from Decatur} Mrs. Gorsline died Monday evening after a long illness. She was buried in the Decatur cemetery the following day. She is survived by her husband, Rev. Gorsline, a retired Methodist minister. [Benton County Record 9/11/25]

GOUGE, Josephine P. - Josephine P. Gouge died at her home March 6, 1925. She had patiently borne several years of affliction and death came when Jesus saw it was enough. She leaves an aged husband and 7 children and other relatives and many friends to mourn her loss. She was buried Sunday morning in the Flint creek cemetery. [Gentry Journal-Advance 3/13/25]

GOULD, Harriet A. - Mrs. Harriet A. Gould, formerly of Rogers, passed away Sunday morning, October 11, 1925 at the residence of her daughter, Mrs. W.A. Brouse, of Blackwell, Okla., aged 83 years. Remains were brought to Rogers Monday for interment beside her husband, Mr. B.W. Gould, who passed away some nine years ago. Mrs. W.A. Brouse, Mrs. Pearl Hughes and S.W. Gould accompanied the remains. Funeral services will be held at the Presbyterian church parlors at 2:30 Wednesday afternoon, Rev. Moore in charge. Interment will be made in the Rogers cemetery. [Rogers Daily Post 10/13/25]

GRAHAM, Louise - {from Lowell} Louise, two and one-half year old daughter of Elbert Graham and wife, died November 3d at their home in the southwest part of town. Funeral services were conducted at the home Wednesday afternoon by Rev. English and burial was in the Wilson graveyard northeast of Springdale. The little girl was the youngest of the family of six children and a great favorite at home and with everyone who knew her, which was shown by the many beautiful floral offerings. The many friends of Mr. and Mrs. Graham extend heartfelt sympathy to them in their sad hour of bereavement. [Rogers Democrat 11/12/25]

GRAHAM, Mrs. Earl - {from Lowell} Lee Graham and wife received word last week of the death of the wife of their son, Earl, at her home in Emmett, Kansas. [Rogers Democrat 3/26/25]

GRAHAM, Ruby - {from The Prairie Grove Herald} Miss Ruby Graham, who has been ill with pneumonia the past few days, died Tuesday afternoon. Funeral services were held Wednesday in the Methodist church with the Rev. Sherman in charge. Interment was made in the Wedington Gap cemetery Wednesday afternoon. Miss Graham was stricken with pneumonia two weeks ago while teaching school. Her condition had been serious during the entire illness but on Sunday the nurse, who had been secured, was discharged and she seemed out of danger. Hopes of recovery were strong when on Monday afternoon her heart weakened. Before medical assistance could be given she had succumbed to death. Besides a large number of friends, those surviving her are W.R. Graham, her father, Viola and Mildred Graham, sisters; and Earl and Russell Graham, who are her brothers. [Gentry Journal-Advance 2/6/25]

GRAHAM, Wesley - Wesley Graham, a well known pioneer citizen of Springdale, died last week at his home northeast of Springdale at the age of 67. [Rogers Democrat 4/23/25]

GRAMBLING, Alexander - The funeral of Alexander Grambling, who lived a few miles north of town, will be held at Tuck's Chapel at 2:30 this afternoon. [Rogers Daily Post 8/4/25]

GRAMLIN, Henry Alexander - Henry Alexander Gramlin was born near Milan in North Missouri October 17, 1863. In 1872, when a child of eleven years, he came with his parents to Arkansas and with the exception of two years, Benton county had since been his home. January 31, 1886 he was united in marriage to Miss Jennie Garrett. To this union three sons were born, all of whom were at his bedside when the call came. In 1893 he was converted and joined the Christian church. In 1913 he renewed his membership in the Christian church at Avoca. He departed this life August 3, 1925 at the age of 61 years, ten months and sixteen days. Funeral services were held at Tuck's Chapel Tuesday, August 4th, conducted by Rev. A.J. Deason and Frank Easley. Interment in Tuck's Chapel cemetery.

He leaves to mourn his loss a wife, three sons, four small grandchildren, one sister, one brother, and a host of friends - and his friends were numbered only by his acquaintances. [Rogers Democrat 8/13/25]

GRAMLING, John Thomas - John T. Gramling of Avoca, postmaster, merchant and many years well known citizens of the east end of the county, died Tuesday night just before midnight after a long illness. Mr. Gramling had been in poor health for many years but for a year past had been confined to his home most of the time, his daughter acting as postmaster. The funeral will be held this afternoon at Tuck's Chapel at 2:00 o'clock and will be under the auspices of the Odd Fellows of Avoca and Rogers, to which order he had belonged most of his life. We are unable to secure an obituary for this issue but we understand that Mr. Gramling was 67 years old and had lived at Avoca almost since the location of the town. He was Frisco agent there before going into the mercantile business. It was nearly 30 years ago that the Democrat editor made his first acquaintance of Avoca and in those days the entertainment of the stranger was looked after by John Gramling, Hunter Peel, Bob Allen and Dr. Munce Rice - and they did a good job of it, too. And many times since then it has been the pleasure of the writer to listen to the whimsical comment and original philosophy of Mr. Gramling. His death will be regretted by everyone who has known Avoca and its people. He is survived by his wife and two children, Harry Gramling and Miss Annie, both of Avoca. [Rogers Democrat 12/10/25]

John Thomas Gramling was born at Milan, Mo. March 25, 1859 and passed away at his home in Avoca, Ark. on Tuesday, Dec. 8, 1925 at the age of 66 years, eight months and thirteen days. Mr. Gramling came with his parents to Arkansas when a boy about fourteen years of age and has from that time made his home in Benton county. On June 21, 1885 he married Miss May Stephenson and to this union was born three children, two of whom, with their mother, are left to mourn their irreparable loss. Mr. Gramling was an elder in the Christian church at Avoca, becoming a member of that church in early manhood. Burial was made at Tuck's Chapel on Thursday, Dec. 10th and the general esteem in which he was held was shown by the very large attendance at the funeral. Mr. Gramling was one of Avoca's real pioneers and served the community in many public positions. Many years ago he was Frisco agent at Avoca; he was for a number of years a justice of the peace, notary public, school director, and for several years had been postmaster. He was a member of the Odd Fellows fraternity; also of Modern Woodmen brotherhood. Besides his immediate family and relatives Mr. Gramling leaves a host of friends who had learned to lean upon him as a wise counselor; and a truly trustworthy advisor in matters pertaining to everyday life in his home vicinity. His memory will long live in the hearts of those who knew him best. A Correspondent. [Rogers Democrat 12/17/25]

GREAVES, Earl - The remains of Earl Greaves arrived from North Dakota last Tuesday night and funeral services were held Wednesday afternoon. The sympathy of the entire community is extended to the parents and other members of the family who are left to mourn his untimely passing. [Gentry Journal-Advance 9/25/25]

GREEN, John - {from Walnut Hill} The body of Uncle John Green, who was 74 years old and had lived in Benton county 55 years, was brought from Neodesha, Kan. and buried at the Snodderly Graveyard Monday afternoon. Six of his nine children were present. A short service was conducted by G.W. Williams and some excellent songs were rendered by the Providence class. [Rogers Democrat 7/23/25]

GREEN, Lloyd - Lloyd Green, aged 17, son of Mr. and Mrs. Grover Green of Lincoln, was drowned in Lincoln Park lake, Lincoln, Washington county, on Sunday afternoon. Funeral services were held Monday morning at 10 o'clock, conducted from the home by Rev. Hugh Armstrong. Young Green and a friend, Harry Routh, were swimming in the lake when Green, who could not swim, found himself in deep water and became frightened. Routh, who was also an inexperienced swimmer, attempted to save his friend and finding this impossible, cried for help. The boy had gone down for the third time when Dr. C.S. Crockett, Fayetteville, and S.P. Mann, Tulsa, Okla., one of the Lincoln Park orchestra, dived for the body. It was located by Mann on the bottom of the lake at a depth of 15 feet. The drowning is the first in the new resort lake and stopped all pleasure for the day. Green is survived by his parents, by three brothers and by one sister. [Benton County Record 7/31/25]

HALL, Mrs. I.R. - Mrs. I.R. Hall died last week at her home in Bentonville at the age of 80 years. She had been a resident of Bentonville for 40 years. [Rogers Democrat 8/13/25]
{from Morning Star} The father and mother and a brother of I.A. Hankins visited him several days, having been called here by the death of Mrs. I.R. Hall. [Benton County Record 8/14/25]

HALL, Mrs. Z.G. - {from New Hope} Word has been received of the death of our old friend and neighbor, Mrs. Z.G. Hall, at the home of her daughter, Mrs. Josephine Farmer, Washington, D.C. on August 22nd where she and Mr. Hall had gone for a visit with their daughter. She was ill when she reached Washington and lived only a week after reaching there. Her body was taken back to Stroud, Oklahoma, where they have lived for a number of years, and was laid to rest there August 26th. Her friends here and in Rogers will be very much grieved to hear of her death as they lived for many years just south of Rogers where they owned and operated a dairy. Her friends were numbered by her acquaintances as she was a woman of many fine qualities. She and Mr. Hall had expected to visit in Rogers this fall on their way back to Oklahoma. She leaves besides her husband, six children, all of whom grew up in the New Hope neighborhood and we certainly all sympathize with them in their great sorrow. [Rogers Democrat 9/3/25]

1925

HALL, Simon - Simon Hall, the eight-year-old son of Mr. and Mrs. S.J. Hall of Fairland, Okla. died in Gravette late Sunday afternoon from injuries sustained a few hours before in an automobile wreck that happened about 3:30 p.m. about three miles east of Gravette. Mr. and Mrs. Hall, son and daughter, were returning home from a visit in the county with relatives and as they were rounding a sharp curve near the Frisco crossing the radius rod became disconnected, causing Mr. Hall to lose control of his car which plunged off the state highway and dropped about 35 feet to the bottom. The little boy was seriously injured and Mr. Hall and daughter were also injured. A passing car took the injured ones to Gravette where medical aid was given as soon as possible. The boy failed to survive his injuries. An ambulance from Fairland came Monday and carried the unfortunate family home. [Benton County Democrat 11/24/25] [Benton County Record 11/27/25]

HANCOCK, Columbus - The death sentence which was pronounced in the Benton circuit court this week {for the murder of L.M. Stout} brought the fact to mind that this is the second time such a sentence has been pronounced in this court since the Civil War. The first crime for which a life was forfeited occurred just fifty years ago next month. On the night of August 4th, 1875 Columbus Hancock was murdered in White's Hollow in the White river country near the Madison county line by means of a knife. Girsham Hoytt and Cornelius Hammon were charged jointly for the murder and were indicted at the fall term of court that October. When the trial came up Hoytt asked for and was granted a change of venue and was tried in the Washington county circuit court at Fayetteville. He was acquitted. In the Hoytt case the defendant was represented by James H. Berry and R.W. Ellis of Bentonville and J.D. Walker of Fayetteville. The state was represented by Col. S.W. Peel, prosecuting attorney at that time. During this time J.M. Pittman was circuit judge of this judicial circuit. John Black was circuit clerk of Benton county and John W. Simmons held the office of sheriff and Syl Lee was his deputy. Hammon was tried in the Benton circuit court. The state was represented by Col. S.W. Peel and the court appointed John C. Peel and E.P. Watson to represent the defendant. The jury, of which John W. Floyd was foreman, returned a verdict of guilty of murder in the first degree and Cornelius Hammon was sentenced to be hanged on the 14th day of January 1876. The case was appealed to the Supreme court and that tribunal refused to grant a new trial and affirmed the decision of the lower court. A petition was then circulated and presented to the governor asking that the death sentence be commuted to life imprisonment. A.H. Garland was governor at that time and he refused to interfere with the carrying out of the death sentence. Before the day set for the execution arrived people began pouring into town from more than 50 miles around and were camped at almost every available spot. The morning of the 14th witnessed, possibly, the largest crowd ever assembled in Bentonville. The execution took place at the scheduled time about a half mile south of town, a short distance south and west of the old Dr. John Smartt home. [Benton County Record 7/24/25]

HARMON, Jessie Bell - Miss Jessie Bell Harmon, only child of J.H. Harmon and wife of Grove, Oklahoma, died March 23d at Paris, Texas after an illness of several years. The body was brought to Rogers for burial March 25th in the city cemetery, services being conducted at the grave by Rev. J. Wilson Crichlow. The Harmons were former well known residents of Rogers and Miss Harmon was born in Rogers August 28, 1897. While in Rogers Mr. and Mrs. Harmon were guests at the home of Mrs. A.Y. Tribble. [Rogers Democrat 4/2/25]

HARRIS, J.H. - {from Rogers} J.H. Hams {sic}, age 36 years, died Monday. Besides his mother, Mrs. W.A. Harris he is survived by three brothers, Tom, Clyde and Will Harris, and one sister, Miss Bessie Harris. He has been a sufferer of a form of paralysis for the past 17 years. [Benton County Record 10/16/25]

HARRIS, Judson, Jr. - Judson Harris, Jr., son of Judson Harris and wife of Siloam Springs, died a week ago at the government hospital at Fort Bayard, New Mexico and was buried Sunday at Oak Hill cemetery, Siloam Springs, with full military honors by the local post of the American Legion. [Rogers Democrat 2/5/25]

HARRIS, Julia Laura ANDERSON - Funeral services were held Sunday afternoon at the Baptist church in Bentonville for Mrs. Julia A. Harris, a well known resident of Bentonville. Just 81 years from the date of her birth until she was laid to rest was the span of her life. During her lifetime she saw the infant State of Arkansas pass through its early hardships that were the lot of pioneers, through the dark days of war and privation, until it finally took its place among the great states of the Union. Julia Anderson Harris was born on the old Barraque plantation near New Gascony, Jefferson county, Ark. on Jan. 16th, 1844. She was the daughter of Dr. Richard S. Anderson, one of the pioneer physicians. He sometimes traveled 50 miles on horseback to see a patient. A grandfather, Antoine Barraque, was one of the early French settlers in that part of the state who came to America after the banishment of Napoleon to St. Helena. He was a soldier and officer under the "Little Corporal" and fought in the great battles of Marengo, the bridge at Lodi and at Austerlitz. He also was one of the Old Guard in its disastrous march to Moscow. M. Barraque came to Arkansas in 1816 and named his new home in Jefferson county, New Gascony, after his old province in France. He died in 1858. During the Civil War she married Captain W.D. Harris, an officer in the Confederate Army. In the early '90s the Harris family moved to Fayetteville and a few years later moved to Bentonville. Captain Harris died about 12 years ago. Surviving her are two sons - Frank P. Harris of this city and Robert C. Harris of St. Louis; also by four daughters - Misses Laura, Alice and Rowena Harris of the home address and Mrs. F.C. Holland of Lake Village, Ark. Funeral services were conducted Sunday afternoon by her pastor, Rev. J.M. McMahen, in the presence of a congregation of friends that filled the church. [Benton County Record 1/23/25]

Mrs. Wm. D. Harris, one of the beloved women of our city and member of a pioneer Arkansas family which was identified with the early history of the state, died at her home Friday afternoon after a brief illness. Funeral services, held at the Baptist church Sunday afternoon by the pastor, Rev. J.M. McMahen, were largely attended. Julia Laura Anderson Harris was born Jan. 18, 1844 in Jefferson County, Arkansas and died Jan. 16, 1925, her funeral being held on her eighty-first birthday. Her father was Dr. Richard Cuthbert Anderson, pioneer Arkansas physician. Her grandfather, Antoine Barraque, who came from France in 1816 and on whose plantation near New Gascony in Jefferson county she was born, was an officer under Napoleon Bonaparte and came to America after the fall of Napoleon and after the confiscation of his own estate. The family was one of influence and its members, related by blood and marriage, were leaders in the affairs of the communities in which they lived. She was married July 18, 1861 to William Daugherty Harris, who died here thirteen years ago. Having grown up on a southern plantation and having had a part in the stirring events of the war and reconstruction periods, this Daughter of the Sixties, who was the wife of a Confederate soldier, was throughout her life interested in the perpetuation of the ideals and traditions of the old-time South. Mrs. Harris moved from South Arkansas with her husband and family to Fayetteville and a few years later to Bentonville where she has since resided. With husband, sons and daughters always interested, like the mother, in the church, the school, and all organizations devoted to the advancement of the community of which they were a part, this home of culture and refinement, over which Mrs. Harris presided, has been for many years one of the most prominent and influential in this community. The Benton County Democrat, with which her son, Frank P. Harris, has been identified for some years, joins in the expression of sympathy for this family whose members have so devotedly and so tenderly cherished their home and their mother for so many years. In her early girlhood she had joined the old Coliseum Baptist church of New Orleans and at her funeral her pastor paid tribute to her lifelong devotion to her church and made special mention of the valuable work, directed for so many years by her daughter, Miss Laura Harris, in the Sunday school of the local Baptist church. She is survived by two sons, Robert Cuthbert Harris of St. Louis and Frank P. Harris of Bentonville; and by four daughters, Mrs. Frank C. Holland of Lake Village, Ark. and the Misses Laura, Rowena and Alice Harris of Bentonville. Another son, William Frederick, and a daughter, Sarah Gertrude, died in childhood. She is also survived by one brother, Fred T. Anderson of Memphis, an artist, who is now in Rye, New York; by one sister, Mrs. Hortense Ferguson of Los Angeles, and a cousin, Miss Elmira Carson of Hensley, Ark. Interment was made in the Bentonville cemetery by the side of her husband. [Benton County Democrat 1/22/25]

HARRIS, Mary - Mrs. Mary Harris died Thursday at her home west of Rogers and the funeral was held Friday at Oakley's Chapel. The family came here about a year ago from southern Arkansas. She is survived by her husband and six children - a daughter and five sons. [Rogers Democrat 11/19/25]

HARRIS, Mrs. Jack - {from Oakley Chapel} Mrs. Jack Harris, who has been very low for the past two months, passed away at her home Thursday night and was laid to rest in the cemetery here Friday. Brother Campbell conducted the funeral services. Mr. Harris and family have the sympathy of the entire community. [Benton County Record 11/20/25]

HARRIS, Mrs. S.D. - {from Droke} Died, at her home near Droke on Friday, November 13th, Mrs. S.D. Harris, after a long illness extending over the summer and fall. She was about 48 years old and leaves her husband and six children besides many friends to mourn her loss. Funeral services were held at Oakley Chapel on Friday afternoon with burial at that place. [Benton County Record 11/20/25]

HARRIS, N.F. - N.F. Harris, an old citizen of the Beaty community, died at his home Friday, October 21, age 71 years, two months and fourteen days. He was born and reared on Pea Ridge. He was well known as a singing teacher. He has one brother in Bentonville and four sons in or near Gravette. [Benton County Record 10/30/25]

HARVEY, Frankie - {from Garfield} Little Frankie Harvey, infant son of E.H. Harvey and wife, was born February 12, 1925 and died March 22nd, 1925. Age one month, ten days. [Rogers Democrat 4/2/25]

HASTINGS, Richard T. - {from The Lawton {Okla.} Constitution} Richard T. Hastings, 79 years of age, passed away this morning at his residence, 910 Sixth street, following a short illness. Mr. Hastings was born in Benton county, Ark. February 17, 1846. He and family came to Oklahoma in 1901, homesteading a farm near Frederick. The family moved to Lawton in 1919. He is survived by his wife, 4 daughters, Mrs. John R. Carl, Mrs. Henry Jesse of Lawton, Mrs. Bertha Peters of Frederick and Mrs. Hi Pemberton of Amarillo, Tex. and 3 sons, Ollie F. and Henry of Lawton, and Dee of Wichita Falls, all of whom are now here to attend the funeral. The sisters of Mr. Hastings, Mrs. James Edwards of Decatur, Ark. and Mrs. Belle Parker of Monroe, Wash. will be unable to be here. C.D. Camp, a brother of Mrs. Hastings, and other relatives will arrive tonight and tomorrow morning to attend the funeral which will be held at the residence Wednesday afternoon at 5 o'clock. Rev. C.H. Painter, Baptist missionary for Comanche-Cotton counties and a long time friend of the family, will conduct the funeral services. Burial will be made in Highland cemetery. The services at the grave will be in charge of the Masons of which he was a member for 60 years. The wide circle of friends mourn with them in the loss of this husband and father. [Gentry Journal-Advance 7/24/25]

HASTINGS, Temp - A message was received in Gentry telling of the death of Temp Hastings at Drumright, Okla. He was a brother of Mrs. Belle Gholson and was formerly a resident of Gentry. [Gentry Journal-Advance 6/26/25]

HAWKINS, Ann - {from The Huntsville Record} "Aunt Ann" Hawkins, aged about 81 years, died Tuesday morning at her home three miles east of Huntsville. The deceased, who was a daughter of Matthew Hawkins, one of the very early settlers of this section, was born and lived her entire life on the farm where she died and which she owned and operated since the death of her father several years ago. She never married and lived alone much of the time since her father's death. It is said that in all her long life she was never farther than thirty miles away from her home. She was of extremely penurious habits and though residing on and operating a productive farm on War Eagle, spending but little of the income from it she denied herself many of the common comforts of life and was content with less than the ordinary household accommodations and conveniences when she could have had a mansion for habitation furnished with every modern luxury, if she possessed all the gold and other money she is reputed to have accumulated and hoarded up somewhere - and that somewhere is what is now concerning her heirs who are having a search made of the old home premises for the pot or pots of gold she is believed to have buried. County Judge Chas. King, County Treasurer Frank Murphy and Everett Spurlock were agreed upon by the heirs as a committee to conduct the search for the hidden money. Up to Wednesday evening the searchers had found $2,640.05 hidden in various places in and under the house and it is believed that still more will be "dug up" before the search is abandoned. Of the money found, $1,700 was in gold, the balance in currency and silver. The money was contained in cans and old purses and even some of the cans had been buried so long they were rusted and rotted. Aunt Ann is reported to have said a short time before she died when asked where her money was hidden, that there was a lot hidden but it would never be found. In addition to the money she kept buried about her home she had about $4,000 deposited in the First National Bank of Huntsville and it is reported that she is believed to have several thousand dollars in a bank elsewhere. About $7,000 in Confederate currency was found during the search. This she must have kept just for the memories it brought back to her of the Civil War through which she passed and in which many of her people were enlisted in the Southern army. Of no value whatever, this Confederate money, yet to Aunt Ann it was worth just as much as the good money with which it was hoarded. She did not spend either. [Rogers Democrat 9/10/25]

HAYES, Bessie - Mrs. Bessie Hayes, the wife of Ed Hayes, died at the home near Robinson on Monday of last week. She was buried on her birthday and only lacked one day of being 33 years old. [Benton County Record 4/17/25]

HAYNES, Bob - John Reamer of McDonald county, Mo. is in the Pineville jail charged with killing Bob Haynes. It is reported that Reamer shot Haynes by mistake and intended to shoot Roy Baker, whom he thought reported him to the officers for operating a still. The shooting took place near the Reamer home close to Arnett, Mo. Reamer, after his arrest for moonshining, was released on bond furnished by Haynes. A few days later he secured a Winchester and shot Haynes. He made his escape but was captured a few days later. [Benton County Record 3/20/25]

HAYS, J.P. {Buck} - J.P. {Buck} Hays passed away very suddenly at his home near Elk Horn Tavern on Saturday morning, October 10, 1925. He was born in Tennessee in 1857 and came to Arkansas when only a year old and has since lived here. He was married to Mattie A. Heath November 4, 1881. To this union four children were born, all of whom survive him and are: Mrs. O.T. Vandegriff of Picher, Okla.; Lena, Harold and Virgil at home and three children by a former marriage: Mrs. Leslie Massie of Sarcoxie, Mo.; Mrs. Pearl Vandegriff of Picher, Okla. and High Hays of Rogers. Interment was made in the Pratt cemetery Sunday afternoon at two o'clock. Funeral services were conducted by Bro. Renfro of Avoca and the Masonic and Odd Fellows orders. [Rogers Democrat 10/15/25]
{from Bestwater} Again our community was saddened on October 10th, 1925 when the sudden death was reported of another of our pioneers, Mr. Buck Hays, who has been our blacksmith for a great many years. His word and his presence will be missed by all who knew him. The Free Masons and Odd Fellows lodges had charge of the last sad rites of laying him to rest in the Pratt cemetery Sunday afternoon, Rev. Renfro of Avoca making a short talk to the large crowd present. [Benton County Democrat 10/20/25]
{from Garfield} Friends of "Buck" Hays were shocked to hear of his death Friday. Mr. Hays has operated a blacksmith shop in and around Garfield for many years. He had just finished telling the children that he had not been in better health for many years when he gasped and died without a struggle. Interment was in Pratt cemetery. [Rogers Daily Post 10/13/25]

HAYS, Mrs. J.P. - Mrs. J.P. Hays died very suddenly Tuesday morning of heart trouble at the home of her daughter, Mrs. Geo. Tripp. Funeral services were conducted yesterday afternoon at 2:30 at the home of her son, Robert Hays, on North B street. [Rogers Democrat 6/11/25]
{from Pleasant Hill} Mrs. Hays died last Tuesday, the 9th, at the home of her daughter, Mrs. Tripp, after several months illness, at the age of 70 years. Interment in Rogers cemetery Thursday. She leaves seven children, three sons and four daughters, to mourn her passing away. They are: Mrs. George Tripp, Mrs. Harry Weaver and Bob Hays, all residing here; Mrs. Joe Hathaway and Miss Nola Hays of Wichita, Kan.; Bert Hays of Arkansas City, Kan. and Vol Hays of Western Kansas. [Rogers Democrat 6/18/25]

1925

HAZLE, Mrs. A.A. - {from Gentry} Mrs. A.A. Hazle died Monday from an attack of pneumonia and was buried Tuesday at Fairmount. Mrs. Hazle has been an invalid for years. [Benton County Record 3/13/25]

HEAGERTY, Mahaley Caroline TURNER - Mrs. J.W. Heagerty, a native daughter of Benton county, died at the family home six miles southwest of Bentonville on Friday, September 25th, 1925 at the age of 63 years. She was born near Springtown and spent her entire life in Benton county. Mahaley Caroline Turner was united in marriage to John William Heagerty on February 20th, 1881. To this union were born four children, all girls. Two are now dead - Nannie, the oldest, died at the age of four years; Pearl, the youngest, died January 30th, 1920, aged 23 years. She is survived by her husband, William Heagerty, two daughters, Minnie Heagerty and Mrs. Nora Ritter; two grandchildren, Maurice and Neva Ritter; one sister, Mrs. Mary Parks; two half-brothers, Jack and Philo Buck. There are many other relatives and friends left to miss her. Over thirty years ago she made public profession of her faith in Christ and united with the M.E. Church. Her Christian life has been true and steadfast. But it has been her home life and mother love that will always be remembered. Seven years ago last January she was afflicted by a severe stroke of paralysis, from the effects of which she never recovered. Three months ago her last illness began. She bore this as best she could. Friday at 4:10 p.m. the all-wise and loving Father of the Universe saw fit to grant her request and took her home where there is no suffering or sorrow. Her plans had all been made by herself and have been carried out as she requested. She asked for a simple burial service. [Benton County Democrat 10/6/25] [Benton County Record 10/2/25]

HEMPHILL, Emma Celena ROBINSON - Mrs. Emma C. Hemphill died at her home, No. 2712 Federal Drive, Tulsa, Okla. at 10 o'clock Monday morning, October 19th at the age of 65 years, six months and 17 days. Her maiden name was Emma Celena Robinson and she was born at Wiota in Cass county, Iowa April 2, 1860. She gave her heart to God early in life and united with the M.E. church of Wiota. She was married March 8, 1883 to F.M. Hemphill, also of Wiota, and in the spring of 1898 they moved to War Eagle, Benton county, Ark. where she was a devoted member and earnest Christian worker of the M.E. church of that place. In 1920 the family moved to Tulsa. At the time of her death she was a member of the Second Presbyterian church of that city and was active in church work. She is survived by her husband, F.M. Hemphill, two sons, F.R. and E.R. Hemphill, both of Tulsa; two daughters, Mrs. J.S. Fogle of Rogers and Mrs. J.T. Powell of Rogers and also eight grandchildren, who with a number of friends and relatives are left to mourn the loss of a faithful Christian wife and a loving mother. Funeral services were held at the Second Presbyterian church at Tulsa at 3:00 p.m. Tuesday, the Rev. W.H. Murphy officiating. Interment was at Rose Hill cemetery. [Rogers Democrat 10/29/25]

HENDON, Jennie Nora ENGLAND - Mrs. Jennie Nora Hendon, who with her husband had been visiting her parents, Mr. and Mrs. E.R. England, near Shady Grove, died Wednesday, Dec. 31 following a few days illness. Besides her husband she leaves four children. Funeral arrangements have not been completed. [Gravette News-Herald 1/2/25]

HENRY, Asa B. - Asa B. Henry, a native son of Benton county, died Monday morning, Nov. 2, 1925 at his home in Bentonville at the age of 68 years. He has been in ill health for the past five years and quite seriously for several months. Funeral services were held at the Baptist church Tuesday afternoon in the presence of a large number of loving friends and relatives. The pastor, Rev. J.M. McMahen, assisted by Rev. Stephen A. Morton and Rev. O.M. Campbell, conducted the services. Mr. Henry was born on what is now the Jeph Shores farm, four miles south of Bentonville, May 3, 1857. In early manhood he married Sophronia Lewis, daughter of Mr. and Mrs. Sam Lewis. Shortly after his marriage he bought a farm on Trout Branch west of Bentonville where they resided until about six years ago when they moved to town. Mr. Henry was highly regarded as a friend and neighbor and his acquaintance was an extensive one. Besides his widow he is survived by one son, Sam Henry of this city, Mrs. Maud Gregory, also of Bentonville and Mrs. Daisy McCauley of Tulsa. [Benton County Democrat 11/3/25] [Benton County Record 11/6/25]

HENRY, T.N. - T.N. Henry, who lately traded his hotel at Pineville for a farm near Southwest City, Mo., was killed by lightning one night last week. He was in his barn at the time. A mule was also killed. [Gravette News-Herald 5/1/25]

HICKMAN, Anna B. WALKER - Mrs. Anna Walker Hickman, wife of J.C. Hickman, died at the family residence in Bentonville, Ark. at 12:20 o'clock a.m. Monday, March 9, 1925, aged 53 years and four months, her death following a long period of ill health. Having lived in Bentonville for more than 20 years and the greater part of the remainder of her life having been lived in the Pea Ridge section, she had in the Bentonville and Pea Ridge communities a great number of acquaintances and life-long friends to mourn her going and whose sympathies go out to the husband and sons and other relatives in their loss. Miss Anna B. Walker was born at Pea Ridge, Ark. November 9, 1871. Her childhood days were spent on Pea Ridge. At the age of 21 she was united in marriage to Mr. J.C. Hickman. They made their home in the Pea Ridge community until 1903 when they moved to Bentonville where they have lived continually with the exception of sixteen months which were spent in Batesville, Ark. To this union two children were born, J.E. Hickman of Fort Smith and Fred Hickman of Bentonville. Mrs. Hickman was converted early in life and has lived a consistent Christian life ever since. At her conversion she joined the Presbyterian church but later joined the Baptist church of Bentonville. She was a true and loving wife, a good and faithful mother. Besides her

husband and two sons, she leaves two sisters and three brothers, Miss Docha Walker, Mrs. J.D. Lasater, W.A. Walker, S.C. and R.H. Walker, all of Pea Ridge. Funeral services were held at the Methodist Episcopal church in Bentonville Tuesday morning, conducted by the pastor, the Rev. O.A. Fortune, and interment made at the Pea Ridge cemetery where many of her relatives rest. [Benton County Democrat 3/12/25]
Mrs. Annie V.{sic} Hickman, wife of James C. Hickman, died at the family home in Bentonville on Monday, March 9th, 1925 at 12:20 a.m. Mrs. Hickman had been ill for a number of years from a complication of diseases. She was 52 years old. Funeral services were held at the M.E. Church on Tuesday morning with interment in the Pea Ridge cemetery. Rev. O.A. Fortune, her pastor, conducted the services. Besides her husband she is survived by two sons, J.E. Hickman of Joplin and Fred Hickman of Fort Smith. Also by three brothers, S.C. Walker and R.H. Walker of Pea Ridge and W.A. Walker of Rogers; and two sisters, Miss Docia Walker and Mrs. Misha Lasiter, both of Pea Ridge. Mrs. Annie V. Hickman was born on Pea Ridge in 1872 and was the daughter of Nack {sic} and Martha Walker who were among the early settlers in that section. She spent all her life in Benton county. In 1893 she married J.C. Hickman, son of another family of pioneers. Mr. and Mrs. Hickman moved to Bentonville about 20 years ago where they have since lived. She leaves a host of friends and a large number of relatives to mourn her loss. [Benton County Record 3/13/25]

HICKMAN, Jane WALKER - Mrs. Jane Hickman died Sunday at her home at Bentonville and funeral services were held at Pea Ridge Tuesday. Mrs. Hickman was a sister of W.A. Walker and an aunt of Mrs. Will Putman, Mrs. Edwin Jackson and Berry Walker of Rogers. [Rogers Democrat 3/12/25]

HINER, Robert Kindred - {This obituary is a little garbled. Copied as printed.} Robert Kindred Hiner was born in Seattle, Wash. January 12, 1905 and died in Rogers Saturday afternoon, March 14th after having suffered with pneumonia for two weeks. His funer- Hospital by Drs. Moore and Ellis. We Church Sunday afternoon, after which his body was tenderly laid to rest in the Rogers cemetery. The many people who attended the funeral and the beautiful floral offerings show the high regard in which the choice young man and Mr. and Mrs. Davis are held in this city. Robert, or Bob as he was affectionately called by his many friends, was a young man active and full of promise and had just reached the age of twenty years, two months and fourteen days. At the time of his illness he was working for the Ewalt Motor Company of Springdale. Prior to that time he had lived here and was a member of the Young People's Class of the Central Methodist Church. Among his many good characteristics must be mentioned the love that he felt and daily expressed for his mother. Mrs. Davis and Robert were close companions as well as mother and son. In this age when boys are so often forgetful it is refreshing indeed to find a son so thoughtful. Robert is survived by his mother, Mrs. Will G. Davis of Rogers;

his father, Charles L. Hiner of San Francisco, his grandmothers, Mrs. Eva Hiner of San Jose, Calif. and Mrs. Elizabeth Kindred Bell of Kansas City, Mo.; two uncles, Ben and Frank Hiner and an aunt, all of California; his stepfather, Will G. Davis of Rogers; his aunt, Miss Addie J. Brook of Wichita, Kansas and a great-aunt, Mrs. A.B. Craven of Kansas City, who came immediately upon receipt of the sad message. To all these the friends extend heartfelt sympathy. [Rogers Democrat 3/19/25]

HISER, infant - {from Maysville} The son of Mr. and Mrs. R.S. Hiser died last Wednesday morning at the age of five months and 28 days. [Benton County Record 1/9/25]

HOLCOMB, Eva - Mrs. Eva Holcomb died at her Bentonville home on Nov. 30 at the age of 51 years. Mrs. Holcomb was married to Albert Holcomb in 1891 and to them were born six children, all of whom with her husband survive her. The Rev. Tyson of the Nazarene church conducted the funeral services which were held Monday. [Benton County Record 12/4/25]

In loving memory of Eva Holcomb, born June 19, 1874 and departed this life Nov. 30, 1925, aged 51 years, 5 months and 11 days. On March 1, 1891 she was married to Albert Holcomb. To this union six children were born, all of whom with her husband, survive. She also leaves two brothers and two sisters. She was beautifully converted in early life and joined the Church of the Nazarene where she lived a consistent life. Devoted to her church and family, the minister, during her active life, always found a hearty welcome in her home and her efforts were tireless in aid of every department of her church work. The funeral services were conducted at the Church of the Nazarene which was packed with friends and loved ones to pay the last respects to this noble character. The pastor, the Rev. Joe Tyson, preached the funeral and spoke in a very impressive manner of the many beautiful traits of Mrs. Holcomb. She was laid to rest to await the coming of our Lord. [Benton County Democrat 12/8/25]

HOLLOWAY, Sidney Mandy - Died, at the home of I.T. McAdams, Sidney Mandy Holloway, wife of the Rev. James A. Holloway, after a long suffering of ten weeks, patiently enduring her affliction until the 13th day of March she went to sleep in the arms of Jesus. She was laid to rest in the Mount Pleasant cemetery near Hiwasse and the funeral services were conducted by Rev. Tillman of Springdale, Ark. She leaves to mourn her loss a husband and four daughters: Mrs. Mary Brown of Decatur, Texas; Mrs. Dora Gracey, Fort Worth, Texas; Mrs. Belle Edwards, Dodge, Okla. and Mrs. Clara McAdams, Vaughn, Ark., and a host of grandchildren. [Benton County Democrat 3/19/25]

HOLLY, Elizabeth Jane - Mrs. Elizabeth Jane Holly died at the home of her son, E.A. Holly, on Thursday, January 15th, 1925 at the age of 73 years. She had been an invalid, more or less, for the past 20 years and almost helpless since breaking her hip some three months ago. Funeral services were held at the home on Friday, the Rev. A.W. Henderson officiat-

ing. Interment was made in the city cemetery by the side of her husband who died Sept. 10, 1922. Elizabeth Jane Holly was born in Indiana in 1851. Later she moved with her parents to Iowa where in 1877 she was married to A.J. Holly. They moved to Benton county in 1888 and located northwest of Bentonville in the Miller neighborhood where she made her home until about six years ago when she moved to Bentonville. The family helped to organize and build the Presbyterian church in the Miller settlement and the deceased was one of its active members. She is survived by three sons - Don, Eugene and Elgin, all of Bentonville. Also by two sisters - Mrs. Julia Wyatt of East Mineral, Kansas and Mrs. Mary Shefle of New Mexico. [Benton County Record 1/23/25] [Benton County Democrat 1/22/25]
Mrs. Julia Wyatt of East Mineral, Kansas who has been here through the illness and death of her sister, Mrs. A.J. Holly, returned to her home Tuesday. Mrs. Wyatt is 93 years old and is quite active for one of her age. She made the trip unattended. [Benton County Record 1/23/25]

HOLT, Mrs. Joe - Mrs. Joe Holt, a pioneer resident of this section, died Sunday of heart failure at her home two miles east of Decatur. She was 72 years of age. She is survived by one daughter, Minnie, of the family home. Her husband passed away about 14 years ago. She was laid to rest Monday beside her husband in the Bethel cemetery. Mrs. Holt was born in Georgia and came here with her parents about 50 years ago and located on what is now known as the Bridge's farm. Later she married Mr. Holt and lived practically all the time since then on the place where she died. The surviving daughter has the sympathy of the many friends of both of them. [Benton County Record 7/3/25]

HONEYCUTT, infant - {from Osage Mills} The four months old son of Mr. and Mrs. Jack Honeycutt, living west of Osage, died on Thursday morning of last week and was laid to rest in the Temperance Hill cemetery at five o'clock p.m. of the same day, Rev. Wm. Sears having charge of the services. The heartbroken parents have the sympathy of the entire community in the loss of this little babe. [Benton County Record 9/25/25]

HORNSBY, Ewell - Ewell Hornsby died at his home in Bentonville at 8 o'clock Tuesday morning at 50 years of age. Funeral services will be held some time on Wednesday. Mr. Hornsby was born in Bolivar, Tennessee in 1876. He grew into manhood at this place and followed the occupation of farming. About 14 years ago he came to Bentonville where he has lived since that time. About nine years ago he contracted tuberculosis which disease he was never able to overcome. He failed rapidly in health the past three or four weeks. The morning of his death he did not complain but when he went into his mother's room he was suddenly stricken and died before the physician could reach him. Mr. Hornsby is survived by his mother, Mrs. Matilda Hornsby of Bentonville; three sisters, Mrs. Fannie Stallings of Bolivar, Tenn., Mrs. Julia Clark of Los Angeles, Calif. and Mrs. John Davis of Bentonville, and two brothers, Joe Hornsby of Stillwell, Okla. and

J.A. Hornsby, living south of Bentonville. [Benton County Democrat 12/29/25]

HOWARD, Ellis - The funeral of Ellis Howard of Lowell was held yesterday afternoon. Interment being in the Rogers cemetery, the services being in charge of the Odd Fellows. All of Lowell seemed to have been in the procession, it being one of the longest ever seen here. [Rogers Daily Post 5/20/25]

HOWELL, John W. - Judge John W. Howell, for eight years postmaster at Hot Springs, died, at his home in Siloam Springs where he has resided for the past 12 years, on Tuesday of this week. He was 85 years old. The body was shipped to Hot Springs for burial. Judge Howell was a native of Illinois and served in the Union cavalry during the Civil War. Besides serving as postmaster in Hot Springs he was also a U.S. commissioner there for several years. He served two years as county judge of Garland county. [Benton County Record 1/30/25]

HOWRY, W. Ellis - {from Lowell} W. Ellis Howry, a pioneer citizen of Lowell, died Sunday morning at his home in the south part of town at the age of 68 years, nine months and nine days. Funeral services were conducted Tuesday afternoon at the Presbyterian church by Rev. Bates of Fayetteville. Burial was in the Rogers cemetery and the services at the grave were conducted by the Odd Fellows. Mr. Howry was a native of Benton county and was well known here and had a host of friends which was shown by the large crowd which attended the funeral. He was married to Rebecca E. Thornsberry on September 1, 1888 and to them were born three children, all of them living: Carl Howry and Pearl Howry, both of Tulsa and Mrs. Earl E. Vinson of Fort Worth, Texas. He was a devoted father and husband and a good citizen and will be greatly missed in the home and community. [Rogers Democrat 5/21/25]

HUDSPETH, Mattie BRITT - Mrs. Jas. Hudspeth died Tuesday evening at her home on East Cherry street. Death was the result of tuberculosis, contracted while caring for her son, Wilbur, who is ill with the same disease at a government hospital at San Antonio. Mrs. Hudspeth spent some time at San Antonio but it was too late to to bring relief. Funeral services will be held this afternoon at Oakley Chapel at 2:30, conducted by Rev. J. Wilson Crichlow. The maiden name of the deceased was Mattie Britt and her mother, Mrs. Sarah A. Britt, 89 years old, is still living. Mrs. Hudspeth is survived by her husband and six children - Charley, Lillie, Lela and George of this city; Mrs. Dessie Niles, who is here from North Carolina, and Wilbur, who is at San Antonio. She is also survived by six brothers - Geo., Jas., Lee and Hugh Britt of Rogers; Napoleon Britt of Chickasha, Okla. and Arch Britt of Okmulgee, Okla. [Rogers Democrat 3/5/25] [Benton County Record 3/13/25]

HUNSAKER, John S. - Following an illness of several months, J.S. Hunsaker, one of the best known citizens of Decatur, died at the home of his daughter, Mrs. Opal Gammon, on Friday, July 3, 1925. Funeral services were held Sunday afternoon with the Rev. C.D. Purlee of Siloam Springs and the Masonic fraternity conducting the services. He is survived by his widow, five sons, Moses, John, Henry, Leslie and Logan and one daughter, Mrs. Opal Gammon. John S. Hunsaker was born in Liberty, Ill. in 1850, later moving to Gravette and from there to Decatur. He has been a resident of Decatur for 35 or 40 years. For a long time he was employed by the U.S. government as a gauger for the Bentonville, Gravette and old Flatt distilleries. When they went out of existence he entered the real estate business. His many friends will miss him greatly. [Benton County Record 7/10/25]

HYATT, Margaret Virginia - Margaret Virginia Hyatt, the nine-year-old daughter of Mr. and Mrs. Charlie Hyatt of Bentonville, died at her home about six o'clock Tuesday morning. The child had been ill with fever for the past five weeks and was unconscious during that time. Pneumonia set in Monday with which the little girl had not vitality to withstand. Funeral services will be held at the Presbyterian Church, in whose Sunday school Virginia was an interested member, at 10 o'clock Wednesday morning and interment will be made in the city cemetery. [Benton County Democrat 9/29/25] [Benton County Record 10/2/25]

HYLTON, Tommy Louise - Tommy Louise, the six day old infant daughter of Mr. and Mrs. L.C. Hylton of Springtown, died Wednesday. Funeral services were held Thursday and burial made in the Springtown cemetery. [Gentry Journal-Advance 10/16/25]

HYRE, L.M. - {from The Gentry Gazette} L.M. Hyre, brother-in-law of the editor, destroyed himself Sunday morning by firing a bullet into his brain. He had suffered from neuritis about six years ago but thought he was entirely free from it, yet a week before the tragedy it came upon him again and he had apoplexy with it so that his condition seemed unendurable and in a moment of aberration he discharged the shot that released him from pain and suffering. Mr. Hyre was 61 years old and besides the wife leaves a daughter. The body was taken to Illinois for burial. [Rogers Democrat 10/22/25]

IDEN, John S. - J.S. Iden, 78 years old, died at the home of his son, Phillip Iden, in this city Friday at noon after a long illness. His body was taken to Monett, Mo. Saturday and buried in the family lot beside his wife who died in that city in 1915. Mr. Iden was born in Owen county, Indiana April 4, 1843 and married Mary Sanders in 1872 at Bourbon, Ind. in 1873. To them were born nine children, only three of which survive their father: Charles Iden, who lives at Crocket, Mo.; Phillip Iden in Rogers and Jay B. Iden of Kansas City, Mo., the latter being managing editor of the Kansas City Packer. Mr. Iden came to Rogers in the early '90s from Western Iowa and was engaged in painting for a number of years. Later the family moved to Monett where they lived until after the death of Mrs. Iden when he returned to Rogers to make his home with his sons. Mr. Iden had been in poor health and unable to work for some years. He was a man of education and in his younger days taught school. He was a Socialist but was never a radical and wrote often for newspapers along political and scientific, especially astronomy, lines. [Rogers Democrat 9/24/25] [Rogers Daily Post 9/19/25]

{Written by Jay B. Iden of Kansas City at the death of his father, J.S. Iden of Rogers} John S. Iden was born in Owen county, Ind. in 1847 and died in Rogers, Ark. Friday, Sept. 18, 1925. We who knew him best will remember him as a just man. From early boyhood he seemed always to be flung out on the pioneer line and he knew much of hardship. Even his birth occurred shortly after the family had moved into Owen county. There pioneer conditions became unbearable and there was return to Ohio. Following that his father with two brothers, all with their families, went into Northern Indiana and settled in the swamps on the county line between Kosciusko and Marshall counties. The farm was covered with big timber which had to be removed before a farm could be made. The timber, much of it, was sold to the Pennsylvania railroad in the days when cord-wood was used for fuel in engines. Ague was common and the family suffered much. In the midst of the struggle the mother died. John S. Iden, being the eldest of the group had much of the care and responsibilities of the household. It is an interesting fact that in the midst of this struggle the entire family found time to acquaint themselves with the best of printed matter. They were able to attend only the district school but early in life were to be found teaching in the neighborhood. They were useful in community development and the introduction of better livestock and a community fair started by the several Idens in existence and known as the Marshall County Fair. One brother, the late J.W. Iden, was teaching school at the age of sixteen and later became a lawyer, practiced at Parsons, Kansas where he had taught school and where for years he was president of the schoolboard. The writer cannot recall the date of John S. Iden's marriage but his wife was a school teacher. The two launched out rather happily, with a thriving photography business picked up somewhere along the way, supporting them handsomely. But the panic of '73 took that business, creeping up on a young man not yet acquainted with the trickeries of fate. It was this rather tragic fact, no doubt, which led Mr. Iden to become a student of economics. There was not a phase of the money question he had not studied with the thoroughness of the most profound scholar. In his idle time he produced landscape painting of more than ordinary quality, did them with the few colors and tools at hand. There was a house under a hill where the family lived in those days and it is remembered that in the periods when living was hardest one saw there the best of the world's literature which was bread and meat to Mr. Iden and which had a profound and good influence on his children. Early recollections are of world topics being discussed there in scholarly language, by both father and mother. The Bible he knew as the average man knows his daily newspaper and could discuss it with the best. He had a love for trees and flowers and grass. Wherever he paused he usually planted a tree, made a flower bed and sowed some clover seed. At that time the black lands of Iowa were calling and Mr. Iden heard and went out into Harrison county, settling at Logan. The writer drove through that county not long ago and was shown a little weather-beaten school house under a hill where he had taught. He was told of county records in the court house, said to be the most accurate and displaying the finest penmanship of any records in the building, which he had made while working in a county office. Out in that new country babies came, and went. Five died in infancy. Winters were long and cold and work was not plentiful. Ill health came into the family and life dropped into that steady grind of meeting emergencies, that condition with which many of us are acquainted. Mr. Iden found work as a painter. And still the artist and the scholar persisted in him. He was known for the neatness of his handiwork and his fair dealing. In 1904 the family climbed into a covered wagon and drove to Rogers, Ark. It was an unfortunate fact the move was made when still another panic was being felt, the panic of 1893. There he engaged in the painting business and continued his interest in studies of all kinds. We last remember him asleep over a magazine. In 1900 he moved to Monett and with his son, Fred Iden, deceased, bought the Monett Leader from George Callaway. He was able to hold the paper about three months. He then took up the paint brush again and that was his chief vocation until he got too old to work. When the Socialist movement was at its height he thought he saw some relief in that for the troubled condition of the country and threw himself in the work wholeheartedly. He published for a time a small magazine called the "We're Here." The office was in the Westbay building on East Broadway. Shortly after the death of Mrs. Iden, which occurred in Monett, he went to Kansas City. But he was no longer able to work. He lived in Kansas City awhile, going later to the old home in Indiana and to Michigan. But he soon returned to Rogers, Ark. where he had lived for the past five years and where he died at the home of his son, Philip Iden. He is survived by three sons, Philip Iden of Rogers, Ark., Charles Iden of Crocker, Mo. and Jay B. Iden of Kansas City. We like to remember that he was held in high esteem by those who knew him well, he was kind and generous and always honest and fair. His life was humble but with the humbleness of grass roots and clover blossoms and the high tossing elm limbs; he tip-toed heights unknown to many and was capable of soaring into mighty realms of thought. But his mental wings grew weary, his body exhausted and he sleeps. [Rogers Democrat 10/1/25]

INNES, infant - {from Highfill} The infant child of Ed Innes died on Monday and was buried on Tuesday in the Springtown cemetery. Rev. Chastain conducted the services. [Benton County Record 4/3/25]

JOHNSON, David A. - After several months illness David A. Johnson died at the home of his daughter, Mrs. Winnie Robbins, in Bentonville Thursday morning, Mch. 12, aged 69 years, three months and five days. Mr. Johnson was born on Pea Ridge, east of Bentonville, Dec. 7, 1855 and lived the greater part of his life in this section where he was widely known and respected. In 1886 he was married in Stone county to Miss Ellen Trimble who now survives him. He had always been a farmer and only gave up his farm work and farm home a few months ago, being overtaken by ill health, and with Mrs. Johnson moved to Bentonville to make their home with their daughter, whom death some months ago had deprived her of her husband, the late Albert Robbins. For many years he had been a member of the Methodist Episcopal church. Besides his wife he is survived by a son and daughter, Theo Johnson, and Mrs. Winnie Robbins, both of Bentonville, two brothers, Armstrong {Tobe} Johnson, Bentonville and John Johnson, Rogers, other relatives and many friends. Another daughter, Miss Nola Johnson, died several years ago. Funeral services will be held from the Methodist Episcopal church Friday afternoon, conducted by the pastor, Rev. O.A. Fortune, and interment will be in the Buttram Chapel cemetery near Pea Ridge. [Benton County Democrat 3/12/25]
Mrs. A.R. McClure, Mr. and Mrs. Leslie Fawver and T.L. Trimble returned to their home in Seligman, Mo. after attending the funeral of their brother-in-law and uncle, D.A. Johnson. [Benton County Record 3/20/25]

JOHNSTON, Samuel R. - S.R. Johnston, who with sons conducted the Gravette broom factory, is dead. Everyone will remember him as a fine type of citizen and will regret to hear of his passing. The Wayne County {Iowa} Democrat, of Corydon, published the following obituary: Samuel R. Johnston was born in Logan County, Ohio January 12, 1848 and died in Corydon, Wayne County, Iowa March 27, 1925. On April 16, 1874 he was united in marriage to Miss Rosa French and to this union were born eight children: Mary Alice Davis, who died two years ago; Roy F. Johnston of Fremont, Nebr.; Walter J. Johnston of Denver, Colo.; Lillie Johnston, who died in infancy; Grace McIntire of Corydon, Iowa; John R. Johnston of Topeka, Kans.; Ellen White of Clio, Iowa and Pansy Phillips of Kansas City, Mo. Early in life he united with the United Presbyterian church and always remained loyal to that church, though of late years, having lived where he could not attend services with that denomination, he had his membership in the M.E. church. Shortly after marriage he and Mrs. Johnston came to Iowa and practically all their married life was spent in this state. For 35 years he has been afflicted with partial blindness and for months past his health has been failing. During his long illness his companion of nearly 51 years was constantly by his bedside and all was done for his comfort that loving hearts and hands could do. Services were held among his friends at Clio by Rev. Cunningham and his remains tenderly laid to rest in the Clio cemetery. [Gravette News-Herald 4/17/25]

1925

JOLLY, Frederick - {from Pleasant Hill} Frederick Jolly was born in Osage county, Kansas Nov. 2, 1875. Came to Benton county some eight years ago. Was one of a family of 11 children, joined the Spanish American Army in 1898, serving his country for several months. Was united in marriage to Mrs. Ida M. Osborn Sept. 1921. He departed this life July 5th, 1925, age 40 years, 8 months and 23 days. Funeral services were held at the First Baptist church at Rogers Monday, July 6th at 3 p.m. by Rev. A.A. DuLaney and Rev. A.J. Deason. Interment in Rogers cemetery. He leaves to mourn his loss a wife, three sisters and four brothers. His father, mother, two sisters and one brother preceded him in death. He had been in poor health for some time but his condition was not considered serious until a week before his death. Our sympathy is extended to the bereaved. [Rogers Democrat 7/23/25] [Rogers Daily Post 7/6/25]

JONES, George W. - Following several months of ill health, George W. Jones died at his home on West Eighth street at three o'clock Saturday morning, April 18, aged 32 years, six months and 14 days. A son of Mr. and Mrs. D.C. Jones of this place, Mr. Jones and his family had come to Bentonville a few months ago from their Texas home hoping the Ozark climate would benefit his health. Mr. Jones was born at Western Grove, Ark. June 4, 1892. On July 20th, 1913 he married Miss Rosetta Heffley of Whitesboro, Texas. To them were born three children, Fayma, Darrel and Floyd, all of whom survive their father. Besides his wife, children and parents he is survived by four brothers: James Jones, Kansas City, Mo.; Lem Jones, an employee of the Doke Motor Co. of this city; Arthur and Howard, also of Bentonville; and four sisters: Mrs. Lum Heffley, Coalgate, Okla.; Mrs. Manson Criner and Mrs. Hobart Criner, both of Mt. Judea, Ark. and Miss Bonnie Jones, Bentonville. Another brother, Floyd Jones, died some years ago. Funeral services, conducted by the Rev. Stephen A. Morton, pastor of the Christian church, were held at the home Sunday morning, attended by many friends. Interment was in the Bentonville cemetery, the grave marked by many floral tributes to his memory. [Benton County Democrat 4/23/25] [Benton County Record 4/24/25]

JONES, Lewis Swart - Died, at his country home five miles south of Bentonville, Ark. on Friday, July 10th, 1925 at 9 o'clock a.m., Lewis S. Jones, after an illness of two weeks. Lewis Swart Jones, son of John Clark Jones and Asenah J. Swart, was born at Deep River, Iowa on June 24th, 1880 and at the time of his death was 45 years and 16 days of age. When but a small child he moved with his parents to Audubon, Iowa where he resided until 1894 when, with his parents, he moved to Bentonville in November in which vicinity he had lived the remaining years of his life. In 1906 he was married to Gertrude Hays, also of Bentonville. To this union were born four children - Florine, Francis, Robert and Josephine - all of whom are at home. In 1903 he professed faith in Christ as his personal Savior and united with the Pleasant Site Missionary Baptist Church, remaining a faithful member until his death. Besides his wife and four children he leaves to mourn his going three sisters and one brother - Mrs. H.W. Gipple of Bentonville; Mrs. G.G. Lewis of Tulsa, Okla.; Mrs. Villa Pratt of Centerton and James F. Jones of New Norway, Alberta, Canada - all of whom were present at his bedside when he passed to the Great Beyond. Funeral services were conducted at the Baptist Church at Bentonville by Brother McMahen at 3 o'clock p.m. on Saturday, July 11th, 1925 after which he was laid to rest in the city cemetery beside his father and mother. Lewis S. Jones was a man of upright character, a man loved and respected by his fellowmen, as was shown by the many beautiful floral tributes sent in loving sympathy to the bereaved family. Written in loving memory by his sister, Villa Jones Pratt, Centerton, Ark. [Benton County Record 7/17/25] [Benton County Democrat 7/16/25]

JONES, Mary - {from Valley View} Mrs. Mary Jones died Saturday afternoon at 6:30 and was laid to rest Sunday afternoon at Pea Ridge. [Benton County Record 2/20/25]

KERR, Hoover - {from Hiwasse} C.H. Kerr and son, Warren, received a message Monday of the death of their son and brother, Hoover Kerr, in Iola, Kansas. They left Monday night for Iola. [Benton County Record 3/13/25]

KETNER, Thomas B. - Funeral services were held at the cemetery on Monday morning, May 25th at 10 o'clock for Thomas B. Ketner, who died at Garber, Okla. on May 22nd, 1925. Rev. O.A. Fortune of the Methodist church gave a short life history and the choir of that church sang several hymns, the United Daughters of the Confederacy assisting in the service. The casket was draped with the flag of the Confederate States and covered with flowers. Interment was made in the mausoleum beside his wife who died about seven years ago. Thomas Ketner was born near Jasper in Marion county, Tennessee Feb. 14, 1841. In that country he grew into manhood and married, making his home there. In 1861 he enlisted in the Confederate Army in Tennessee and was engaged in active service under General Lee for three years. He served in the infantry and was in the cavalry troop commanded by Jeb Stewart. Two years after the Civil War he moved to Texas and located at Mineral Wells, residing there for 25 years. He also lived a number of years in Hemphill and Randall counties in that state, after which he came to Bentonville. He has resided here about 25 years. He was a member of the Masonic Order but not affiliated with the local lodge. He had gone to Garber to visit his nephew, E.B. Harris, where he died suddenly. He is survived by his only child, Mrs. E.T. Harris, of Snider, Texas; E.T. Harris, her husband, four grandchildren and two great-grandchildren. Mr. and Mrs. E.T. Harris, Mrs. E. Brune of Tonkawa, Okla. and Mr. and Mrs. C.B. Harris of Garber, Okla. came Sunday to attend the funeral and returned to their home Tuesday. [Benton County Record 5/29/25] [Benton County Democrat 5/28/25]

KEY, Bonnie BURKS - Mrs. Bonnie Key, wife of Lloyd Key, died last Thursday night at Dallas, Texas, the result of injuries received three weeks previous. She was playing with a child on the floor and her dress caught fire from an open gas fireplace, burning her quite severely before the flames could be extinguished. The wounds did not heal readily and resulted in blood poison. The body was taken to Muskogee for burial as it is the home of her mother, Mrs. Wm. Burks. Mr. Key's father, Jove Key, of Rogers was called to Muskogee to the funeral which was held Sunday and Lloyd returned to Rogers with him Tuesday. Mrs. Key, whose maiden name was Miss Bonnie Burks, was born at War Eagle, this county, and is a niece of Mrs. C.A. Rice and Mrs. Arthur Ragsdale of this city. She had visited here often and was known to many of our people and her untimely death is a great shock to them and has saddened the Holiday season for the family. [Rogers Democrat 12/24/25]

KILLOUGH, Goldie - Miss Goldie Killough, the daughter of Mr. and Mrs. J.S. Killough, died at her home on East A Street, north Sunday morning at 10 o'clock. Funeral services will be held at the home Friday afternoon at 2:30. Reverend Stephen A. Morrow {sic} will conduct the services. Interment will be made in the city cemetery. Miss Killough was born in Bentonville September 23, 1902. She grew up here attending the grade and high schools, the latter from which she graduated in 1921. She has been a member of the Christian Church since childhood. Her death followed an illness of four months. Besides her parents she is survived by two brothers, W.R. Killough of Santa Ana, California and W.E. Killough of Bakersfield, Cal., who is on his way to Bentonville. The family has the sincere sympathy of the entire community. [Benton County Democrat 10/6/25]

W.E. Killough of Santa Ana, Calif. is visiting his parents, Mr. and Mrs. Killough. He was called home by the death of his sister, Miss Goldie. J.S. Biggs and son, Fay, of Springfield, Mo. and Mr. Y.T. Buck of Delaney, Ark. were also here to attend the funeral. [Benton County Record 10/16/25]

KINCAID, L. Clifford - L. Clifford Kincaid died Monday morning, May 25, at the home five miles west of Centerton, following an illness of typhoid fever. The funeral service was conducted at 3 o'clock Tuesday afternoon from the home, conducted by Rev. E.L. Boyle of the Community church, assisted by members of that choir. Interment was in the Gamble cemetery. Mr. Kincaid was a native of Illinois, being born in that state on November 15, 1867. At the age of seven years he had moved to Kansas where he grew to manhood, living there for 22 years. He came to Arkansas in 1896 and had since made this state his home. In November 1892 he was married to Miss Helen Sprague and to this union seven children were born, one of whom, Jessie L., died on Sept. 8, 1905. He is survived by six other children and seven grandchildren. The sons are, Frank W. Kincaid of Hill, N. Mex., Jewett R., Orla W. and Bertie L. The daughters are Eunice A. and Gertie, all of Gravette, which has been the home post office of the deceased for the past 25 years. [Benton County Democrat 5/28/25] [Benton County Record 5/29/25]

KINNEY, Mrs. Frank M. - Mrs. Frank M. Kinney, a resident of Gravette for nearly 30 years, died Sunday night at the age of about 60 years. Funeral services were conducted by the Rev. C.D. Purlee of Siloam Springs at the home Monday afternoon. Interment was made in the Odd Fellows cemetery. Besides her husband she is survived by two sons and three daughters. [Benton County Record 7/3/25]
Mrs. Frank Kinney, who died Sunday night at Gravette, was one of the old settlers of that neighborhood. She was a sister-in-law of Mrs. Willis Miller of Vaughn. [Rogers Democrat 7/2/25]

KNOTT, Jimmy - Jimmy Knott, 7-year-old son of Mr. and Mrs. Jim Knott, Jr., died Wednesday afternoon following an accident Wednesday morning in which he was struck by a Ford coupe driven by C.H. Alspaugh who was driving south on A street below the Massey hotel at about 8:30 in the morning. The child's death is a tragic one in which the entire community is grief stricken. The lad had left the home of his grandmother, Mrs. Ara Dickson, whom he dearly loved and with whom he spent the greater portion of his time, to take a parcel of garments to the Coulter home on A street to be laundered. The child delivered the package and left the home to go on to his school work. He was crossing the street below the Coulter home when the accident happened. The tragedy apparently was one resulting from a combination of circumstances over which no control could be had. Two cars were driving south on A street as Jimmy left the Coulter lot to cross the street. He evidently saw the first but failed to note the coupe and stepped in front of it in crossing over, possibly to join a small girl who was probably a classmate. The driver of the coupe had noticed the girl on the right side of the street and had a premonition she might cross and was watching out for her and failed to see Jimmy approaching from the left and the coupe ran him down, striking in such a way as to fracture his skull on top and at the base. A party of traveling men from Kansas City saw the accident and came to the aid of Mr. Alspaugh and the boy was brought to the medical offices of Drs. Lindsey & Pickens for first aid treatment. However, medical aid was without avail and no surgical skill could give relief, the child's vitality gradually ebbing until 2 o'clock when the end came. Mrs. Elizabeth Temple, home demonstration agent, and Mr. Alspaugh were on the way to Siloam Springs and she had turned the car to him to drive when they started from their offices only a few minutes earlier. Both Mr. Alspaugh and Mrs. Temple are grief stricken at the tragedy, over which they had no control, and remaining with the lad until the end along with the immediate members of his family. Jimmy Knott was a favorite with his many friends and belonged to one of the best known pioneer families of northwest Arkansas. He is survived by a younger brother, Dickie Knott, his parents and his grandparents, Mr. and Mrs. J.C. Knott, Sr., and his maternal grandmother, Mrs. Ara Dickson. Funeral services will be held this {Thursday} afternoon at 3 o'clock at the home of Mr. and Mrs. J.C. Knott, Sr. on East Thirteenth street, conducted by Rev. A.W. Henderson, pastor of the Presbyterian church. The interment will be in the City cemetery. [Benton County Democrat 1/15/25] [Benton County Record 1/16/25]

KNOX, A.H. - A.H. Knox, aged 54, who moved here in the early fall from Colorado, met accidental death last Friday while chopping wood on the Burton Clements place north of town. A tree which he and J.S. Killough, a companion, were felling, struck him in such manner as to fracture his skull and death resulted within an hour. Knox and Killough, who was his neighbor, had been working in the timber together throughout the winter. Knox was inexperienced and Mr. Killough directed the felling of trees. The two had cut down a big oak tree, which in falling had lodged in a small hickory tree. They were sawing down the hickory to release the oak and had completed the work and Knox used his axe to strike the last blow which would cause the tree to fall, as had been planned by Mr. Killough. As the tree started to topple Killough warned Knox to be careful as the tree was falling and Knox, looking up, became confused evidently and instead of stepping away from danger, stepped into the path of the falling tree, which struck him on the head and shoulders and pinned him to the ground. Mr. Killough succeeded in lifting the tree from his body and administering first aid by which Knox regained consciousness. He then hastened to the Clements house a half mile away to call assistance as he realized Knox was in critical condition. Aid came at once and the injured man was taken to town for treatment, but died on the way. The Knox family had planned to settle here and had contracted to buy a farm and were preparing to complete the financial transfer at an early date. The deceased is survived by a widow and 3 children, a boy of 6 and two girls several years older. He also is survived by one sister and two brothers who came here from Buffalo, Okla. for the funeral services which were conducted Sunday afternoon by the Rev. S.A. Morton of the Christian church. Interment was in the city cemetery. [Benton County Democrat 1/8/25] [Benton County Record 1/9/25]

KONTZ, Vida LOONEY - {from Lowell} Friends were grieved to learn of the death of Mrs. Vida Kontz at her home in Henryetta, Oklahoma. Mrs. Kontz was formerly Miss Vida Looney, daughter of Mrs. Jane Looney, and before her marriage lived near Lowell. The mother and a sister, Mrs. Will Clark, attended the funeral. [Benton County Record 10/23/25]

KOST, David L. - D.L. Kost died in his home in the south part of town early last Friday morning He had been an invalid for a number of years and was one of Gentry's oldest inhabitants. His wife passed away a few months ago. He leaves a son and daughter to mourn his going. Funeral services were held last Sunday from the Congregational church conducted by Rev. R.L. Hughes and burial was made in the City Cemetery. [Gentry Journal-Advance 7/31/25]

David L. Kost was born at Mt. Vernon, Ohio February 18, 1835. He passed away at Gentry, Ark. July 25, 1925. He was 90 years, 5 months and 7 days old. Mr. Kost taught school when 17 years old and graduated from the law college at Oberlin, Ohio when he was 21. He served in the Civil war as secretary to the general of the 65th Ohio, Company H, was in several battles where he contracted an abscess caused by extreme exposure, and was discharged after 11 months service. He was 1st commander of Harker Post 104. Mr. Kost went to Gallatin, Mo. in 1864 and started the newspaper, "The North Missourian," and practiced law. He was sent to the state legislature once, the state senate twice. He came to Gentry in 1894 and spent 9 years on a farm near town. Besides taking care of the duties on the farm he was the editor of Gentry's second newspaper. He moved to town in 1912 where he spent the last 12 years of his life. He was converted in early life and lived a consistent Christian until the end came. He was one of the charter members of the Congregational church, had also been superintendent of the Sunday school for 8 years. He was always present at the regular services until the last few years when ill health prevented his going. His wife preceded him in death only a few months ago. They have both left us for a higher realm while their bodies sleep side by side in our beautiful cemetery. He is survived by four children: Paul and Victor of Chicago, Byrdie of Cleveland, and Nona May of Gentry. Nona May has been his faithful aid and companion all these years and we are sure there will be a starry crown awaiting her on high. Funeral services were conducted at the church at 3 p.m. by the pastor. Interment was made in the Gentry cemetery by Pyeatt Undertakers. Contributed. [Gentry Journal-Advance 8/7/25]

KRUSE, Will H. - Word was received here Monday evening by relatives of the death of Will H. Kruse at his home in Minneapolis after an illness of several months. His sister, Mrs. M.V. Deason, and a brother, Ed J. Kruse, both of Rogers, left that night for Minneapolis, where it is presumed he will be buried. Mr. Kruse is also survived by his wife and a daughter, Miss Elsa, who were with him at Minneapolis; by a brother, Henry Kruse, a newspaper man at Vinton, Iowa, and two sisters, Mrs. L.E. Scriber and Mrs. J.C. Huber of Rogers. Mr. Kruse was 65 years old and a native of Ohio. Mr. Kruse was chiefly responsible for the operations on the old Kruse place in the southwest part of Rogers known as the "Kruse Gold Mine." The first work done on the so-called mine was in August 1902 and it has been pushed with varying degrees of activity ever since. The buildings were destroyed by a wind storm last summer but have been rebuilt on a smaller scale this fall and winter. [Rogers Democrat 12/31/25]

LANDERS, Florence Loretta WOODS - Mrs. Newt Landers died Tuesday morning at her home at No. 110 North Fourth street in this city after a long illness, the result of tuberculosis. She had been very low all fall and her death was not unexpected. Funeral services were held at the First

Baptist Church yesterday afternoon at 3:00 o'clock and were conducted by the pastor, Rev. A.A. DuLaney. Burial was at the City Cemetery. Florence Loretta Woods was born northwest of Rogers June 23, 1877 and was a daughter of Robert Woods, one of the pioneer settlers of that part of the county. She was 50 years, five months and eight days old at the time of her death and most of her life was spent in and near Rogers. She married J. Newton Landers in February 1896 and to them were born three daughters. Mabel, the oldest child, died in Texas at the age of seven and Opal, the youngest, died in Rogers at the age of four. She is survived by her husband and by one daughter, Miss Hattie Landers of this city. Also by three brothers: Bert Woods of Coffeyville, Kansas; J.N. Woods of Carthage, Mo. and Herbert Woods of Fellsmere, Florida. Mrs. Landers was a member of the Baptist church, holding her membership in the church at Pleasant Hill, north of Rogers, but attending here so long as her health allowed. She was also a member of the Daughters of Rebekah. [Rogers Democrat 12/3/25]

LANE, William Henry - William Henry Lane was born in Northeast Missouri Oct. 24, 1863. Departed this life May 4, 1925. At the age of 16 years he moved with his parents to Benton county, Ark. When he was 20 years old he joined the Missionary Baptist church. Was married to Charlotta Heather Dec. 20, 1884. To this union was born six children: Robert E., Mary May, Ambrose, Charley, Ray and Claude. Charley preceded him in death in 1901. He leaves to mourn his death his faithful wife, 5 children and 7 grandchildren; also one step-daughter, Mrs. Julia Trammel. He was a loving husband, a kind father and was prepared to go home and be at rest with loved ones over there. The funeral services were conducted by Rev. Fleer at Cross Roads and his remains laid to rest in Flint cemetery southwest of Gentry. Written by Chas. Linton. [Gentry Journal-Advance 5/15/25]

LAUBER, Mary - {from Monte Ne} Mrs. Mary Lauber died Sunday, June 7th after a long illness. She was 75 years old and had lived here for more than thirty years. She was a good mother, a kind friend and neighbor and was loved by all who knew her. She leaves four sons and one daughter and nine grandchildren. She was buried in the Stanley cemetery and the services were conducted by Rev. DuLaney, pastor of the Baptist church at Rogers. The family wishes to thank everyone who assisted them in the illness and death of their mother. [Rogers Democrat 6/11/25]

LEACH, Clarence - Clarence Leach, 27, died at the home of his parents, Mr. and Mrs. Dan Leach, west of Bentonville Tuesday night from injuries sustained on Thanksgiving night when he fell under a truck. Leach, with a group of men, was sitting on the back of the truck, his banjo in his hands, when he fell from the truck near the Mort Lincoln orchards. His raincoat caught on something and he was dragged a considerable distance. The other persons did not miss him from the truck or thought he left voluntarily. He was picked up by a passing motorist in an unconscious condition. Funeral serices were held Thursday afternoon, the Rev. Joe Tyson having charge of them. Interent was mae in the emetery here. He is survived by his parents and several brothers and sisters. [Benton County Record 12/18/25] [Rogers Democrat 12/24/25]

LEE, infant - {from Walnut Grove} The infant baby girl of Mr. and Mrs. Tom Lee was buried Wednesday at the Hickman cemetery. [Benton County Record 12/25/25]

LEFORS, B.P. "Buck" - B.P. Lefors, one of the pioneers of Gentry, died on Thursday night, August 6th, 1925 at the home of his daughter, Mrs. Charles Hardcastle in Siloam Springs where he had been taken for medical treatment. Mr. Lefors had been in ill health for some time and has been gradually sinking for the past few months. Funeral services were conducted from the home in Gentry on Saturday by the Rev. Mr. Hughes of that place. The funeral was one of the largest ever held there. Interment was made in the Bozarth cemetery. He is survived by his widow and six children, all of whom were present at the services. These are Frank, Sherman and Earl Lefors of Gentry and Don Lefors of Williams, Cal. and Mrs. Sam Peek of Decatur and Mrs. Charles Hardcastle of Siloam Springs. [Benton County Record 8/14/25]

Another old resident has been called to his home on high where the supreme architect presides. Bro. B.P. Lefors, who was known by all as "Uncle Buck," has been an advisor on political and financial affairs of this community for many years, having seen Gentry grow from a heavy timbered land to its present beautiful city. Preaching services were conducted at his home by Rev. L. Hughes. Bro. Lefors was a charter member of Bloomfield Lodge, F.A. Masons. His remains were laid to rest by Gentry Lodge, No. 222, F.A. Masons, Bro. O.E. Ramsdill officiating. Funeral was in charge of Carpenter Bros. A Masonic Brother. [Gentry Journal-Advance 8/14/25]

LEMMING, Will D. - {from Fairview} Will Lemming of Pocatello, Idaho, a brother of Mrs. Morris Johnson and who grew up in this neighborhood and married a neighbor girl, Dora Horsley, met a violent death last week. An automobile accident was the cause. The car ran into a river and turned over, pinning him underneath. [Benton County Record 3/20/25]

{from The Pocatello {Idaho} Tribune, March 9, 1925} W.D. Lemming, Pocatello taxi-cab driver and owner, met death by drowning some time last night when the enclosed Buick sedan in which he was riding crashed through the wooden barrier on a bridge across the Snake river, a mile northwest of Blackfoot. The car fell into deep water and was completely submerged. The body of Lemming was recovered at 1:00 a.m. today but up to the time of going to press workers at the scene of the accident had been unable to raise the automobile completely out of the water. The Tribune received first news of the accident in Pocatello and immediately communicated with Mrs. Lemming who lives at 889 East Clark street. She stated that her husband had left Pocatello Sunday evening at 5 o'clock with two passengers for Blackfoot and when he did not return home she became worried. Lemming left a hotel in Blackfoot about midnight, according to the information received here. The two passengers he brought from Pocatello were not with him when he left Blackfoot. The accident occurred on the road to Aberdeen and no reason is known why Lemming should have taken this road. The accident occurred on the east side of the bridge about forty feet from the end. It appears that the car scraped along the wooden railing before breaking through. It is thought the machine was traveling at a high rate of speed. When it crashed through the bridge it fell some distance from the bridge into the middle of the river channel. News of the accident was telephoned the office of the sheriff and identification of Lemming was made from a name on a letter found in one of the pockets of the victim and from an Equitable Savings Loan receipt book. The family had resided in Pocatello twenty-one years, coming to this city from Rogers, Arkansas. For five years Mr. Lemming was employed by the Short Line as engineer. He is survived by his wife and the following children: Thelma, Herbert, Howard, Harold, Beulah and Teddy. The body was brought to Pocatello this afternoon and funeral arrangements will be announced later. ***** The above clipping was brought to the Democrat office by Mrs. M.C. Johnson, sister of the deceased, who was a son of the late Joe Lemming, for many years one of the best known residents of this section, living southwest of Rogers. Mr. Lemming was a brother of Rev. Lee Lemming. There are a number of other brothers and sisters but none of them are now living in Arkansas. The deceased was born in Kansas but came to Benton county when a small child and lived here until he went to Pocatello. [Rogers Democrat 3/19/25]

LEWIS, John Wilson - John Wilson Lewis, a former member of the Bentonville city council, died at his home on B street, N.E., aged 71 years, death resulting from heart trouble. He was ill Saturday morning but seemed entirely recovered in the afternoon and came down town on business, the heart failure which caused his death occurring after he had retired. A native of Missouri, Mr. Lewis was born in that state Nov. 24, 1853. He came to Bentonville about seven years ago from Winfield, Kans. where he had lived for a long time. He bought property here and later married Mrs. E.H. Jacobs of this place. The respect of his townsmen for his good citizenship, integrity and business acumen was evidenced in their selection of him as a member of the town's governing body. He is survived by his wife, three sons, and a step-son, Reybourn Jacobs, a student in the University of Arkansas, who was called here by Mr. Lewis' death. Two of his sons, J.L. and Tom Lewis, of Mounds, Okla. were also here and a sister of Mrs. Lewis, Mrs. Cave, of Liberty, Mo. Another son living at Winfield, Kan. was unable to be here. Funeral services were held at the family home Tuesday afternoon conducted by Rev. J.L. Evans of the M.E. Church, South and interment made in the City cemetery. [Benton County Democrat 2/19/25]

John W. Lewis, a retired farmer, died at his home in Bentonville on Saturday evening, February 14th, heart trouble being the cause of his death. Funeral services were held at the home on Tuesday afternoon at 2:30 and interment was made in the city cemetery. Mr. Lewis was born in Platte county, Missouri on November 24th, 1854. When about seven years old he moved with his parents to Kansas where he spent most of his life. He was married to Kate Stevenson who died in February 1916. He moved to Bentonville from Winfield, Kansas. On June 7th, 1919 he was married to Mrs. Lucie Jacobs, widow of the late E.H. Jacobs of Bentonville. Mr. Lewis was a member of the Methodist Episcopal Church, South and has many friends in Bentonville. Besides Mrs. Lewis and her son, Reyburn Jacobs, he is survived by three sons - Fred Lewis of Winfield, Kansas; John Lewis of Vinita, Okla. and Tom Lewis of Mounds, Okla. [Benton County Record 2/20/25]

LEWIS, Rosamunde COOPER - Mrs. Rosamunde Lewis, wife of Herb Lewis, for many years publisher of the Gravette News-Herald, died Wednesday, October 21, 1925 in Los Angeles, Calif. where she was visiting her children. She died of peritonitis after an illness of but three weeks. Mr. and Mrs. Lewis left in their car about a month ago for a visit with their children in Los Angeles and shortly after arriving there Mrs. Lewis was taken ill. Burial will be made in Los Angeles. Mrs. Lewis was born about fifty years ago in what is now Delaware county, Okla. She was the daughter of Mr. and Mrs. G.W. Cooper, an early day preacher. About thirty years ago she was married in Southwest City to Mr. Lewis. They came to Gravette shortly afterward, which place has since been their home. Besides her husband she is survived by four children: Wyric Lewis of Sulphur Springs, Ark. and Frank, Jesse and Sadie Lee of Los Angeles. Mr. Lewis has the sympathy of not only the people of Gravette but of the whole of Benton county in his bereavement. [Benton County Record 10/23/25] [Rogers Daily Post 10/24/25]

LINDSEY, Felix G. - Judge Felix G. Lindsey died Monday, June 29 at 10 a.m. at the home of his son, Vol T. Lindsey, in this city, aged 63 years, four months and six days. Judge Lindsey's death resulted from diabetes following a prolonged illness which made him an invalid in the last few months. He was born at Stockton, Cedar county, Mo. February 23, 1862 and moved to Sulphur Springs, Ark. with his parents in 1867 where he spent his formative years. He married Miss Emma Strain in Sedan, Kan. on Sept. 3, 1885 where he and his wife continued to make their home for many years. Three children were born to them, two sons, Vol and Grover, of this place, and a daughter, Virgie E., who died in infancy. In March of 1893 he removed to Bentonville and began the practice of law, first as a law partner of Attorney W.D. Mauck and later as a member of the law firm of McGill and Lindsey, a partnership which continued more than 20 years and was ended only with the decision of Judge Lindsey to discontinue his private practice and enter the service of the state. In 1917 Mr. Lindsey was appointed to the position of state fire marshal by Governor Brough. The business-like methods which he adopted in the handling of this important position won him re-appointment under succeeding governors Thomas C. McRae and Tom Terral. Judge Lindsey had been a prominent member in the Masonic fraternity for many years. In 1911 he was honored by election as Grand Master of Arkansas Masons, a position his close friend, Storm O. Whaley, now occupies. At the conclusion of his service as Grand Master he was selected as Orator of the Arkansas grand lodge. He was also a member of the Eastern Star order and the knights of Pythias. The latter organization provided a special guard of honor at the funeral which was held at the home of his son, Vol T. Lindsey, in Bentonville. Besides his wife and two sons, Judge Lindsey is survived by four sisters, Mrs. W.H. Thomason of Nowata, Okla.; Mrs. Mary Hood, Glenrose, Tex.; Mrs. Al Majors, Bentonville; Mrs. John McDonald of Sulphur Springs and two brothers, B.F. Lindsey of Grove, Okla. and G.W. Lindsey of Sulphur Springs. [Benton County Democrat 7/2/25] [Benton County Record 7/3/25]

LITTLE, Nannie - Mr. and Mrs. J.T. Elms attended the funeral of his niece, Mrs. Nannie Little, at Summers, Ark. last Thursday. [Benton County Record 2/13/25]

LOONEY, Bob Terry - {from The Pierce City, Mo. Leader} Bob Terry, little ten year old son of Mr. and Mrs. Y.C. Looney of Raton, N. Mex. and grandson of Mr. and Mrs. Robert Brashear of this city, passed away Thursday, March 12th at his home on 619 south 6th street after an illness of five months. [Benton County Democrat 3/26/25]

LOWE, Mary MURPHY - Mrs. Mary Lowe died on March 21st at the family home in Huntsville at the advanced age of 90 years. She was the daughter of Governor Isaac Murphy, the eighth governor of Arkansas. [Benton County Record 4/3/25]

LUCAS, Harrison - Harrison Lucas, living on the old Bella Vista-Hiwasse road in Tanyard Hollow, died Sunday at the age of 84 years. He had been a resident of this section for over 30 years. Death was due to pneumonia following a 3 week's illness. He was an old soldier and served in the Confederate army in his home state of Kentucky during the Civil War and was a member of Co. B, Fifth Ky. regiment. Funeral services were conducted by Rev. Stephen A. Morton of the Christian church with interment in the Dug Hill cemetery. He is survived by two sons, Luther Lucas, living near Bella Vista and J.P. Lucas of Rosalia, Kansas; and three daughters, Mrs. Hugh Roughton of Hiwasse; Mrs. Mary Edgar of Beaumont, Kansas and Mrs. Emmet Petty of Oklahoma. [Benton County Record 3/6/25] [Benton County Democrat 3/5/25]

LUCKEY, May Matilda MYERS - Mrs. T.B. Luckey died at her home south of Gravette Saturday, March 28 after a brief illness of pneumonia, age 65 years, one month and twelve days. May Matilda Myers was born in

Madison county, Iowa February 16, 1860. She was married to T.B. Luckey in 1880, coming with her husband and daughter to Arkansas about six years ago. Mrs. Luckey was a devout member of the Brethren church. She is survived by her husband and a daughter, Mrs. Grace Bray, who made her home with her parents. Also by six brothers and three sisters: Dr. Mark M. Myers of San Francisco, California; Rev. B.F. Myers of Annona, Iowa; W.D. Myers of Long Beach, California; Miles Myers of Washington state, Isaac Myers, state representative of Lamar, Colo. and James Myers of Billings, Montana; Miss Jennie Myers of Waukee, Iowa, Mrs. F.M. Blair of Oskaloosa, Iowa and Mrs. C.A. Blair of Grinnell, Iowa. Mrs. C.A. Blair and husband being present for the funeral. The funeral was conducted at the home Monday, March 30th by Rev. McCarroll of the Presbyterian church. Interment was made in the I.O.O.F. cemetery. [Benton County Record 4/3/25]

LUCKEY, Mary Malinda MYERS - Mary Malinda Myers was born in Madison County, Iowa Feb. 16, 1860; died at her home near Gravette, Ark. Sunday morning, March 29, 1925. She was the daughter of Michael M. and Nancy Jane Myers. March 7, 1880 she was united in marriage to T.B. Luckey who with the daughter, Mrs. Grace Bray, and two grandchildren, survive. She was the second in a family of eleven children, all of whom are living except the youngest brother. They are Mrs. Geo. Myers, Waukee, Iowa; Dr. Mark Myers, Santa Ana, Calif.; J.M. Myers, Billings, Mont.; J.H. Myers, Lamar, Colo.; Rev. B.F. Myers of South Dakota; Miles Myers, Scota, Wash.; Mrs. F.M. Blair, Oskaloosa, Iowa and Mrs. C.A. Blair, Grinnel, Iowa, who with her husband attended the funeral. At the age of sixteen Mrs. Luckey united with the church of the Brethren and has lived a faithful Christian life. Quiet and unassuming, never thinking of herself, giving her life for her family - a good wife and mother has gone to her reward. Funeral services were conducted from the home Tuesday afternoon by Rev. McCarroll and interment in I.O.O.F. cemetery. [Gravette News-Herald 4/10/25]

LYNN, Emily S. DICKSON - Mrs. Emily S. Lynn, daughter of E.J. and Sophia Dickson, was born near Bentonville, Ark. on August 26th, 1842 and passed away at her home in Buffalo, Ill. at 4:30 p.m. on Thursday, August 6th, 1925 at the age of 82 years, 11 months and 11 days. She had been ill for several months from heart trouble. Mrs. Lynn was of Scotch ancestry. She was converted at the age of 16 years at a Methodist camp meeting in Thornsberry camp ground in this state. In May 1867 she was united in marriage to R.P. Lynn and settled in Buffalo Heart Grove, Ill. To this union were born seven children, two of whom died in infancy, and Sophie, Emily and Robert after reaching maturity. Mr. Lynn died in 1882. In 1884 Mrs. Lynn and family moved to Buffalo, Ill. where she lived until her death. She is survived by two daughters, Mrs. Katherine Robinson of Springfield, Ill. and Harriet, who lived at home with her mother; also by a sister, Mrs. Vaughn, of St. Joseph, Mo. [Benton County Record 9/4/25]

McCANON, F. - The many friends of Mr. F. McCanon will be sorry to hear of his passing away at his home, Des Moines, Ia. the 6th. At one time he lived in Bentonville and made many friends while among us. The Sunday school class he taught at the Methodist Episcopal church while here remembered him so kindly. They feel the loss of a good friend and their sympathy goes to those who are left. [Benton County Democrat 2/26/25] [Benton County Record 2/27/25]

McCLURE, Mrs. L.E. - Mrs. L.E. McClure died Monday night at her home north of Rogers, the result of a stroke of paralysis on last Friday. Mrs. McClure was 62 years of age and the family had lived here about four years, first in the Pleasant Ridge neighborhood and then moving to a farm north of town. [Rogers Democrat 7/2/25]

McCONNELL, Albert P. - Albert P. McConnell died at his home four miles northwest of Gentry on Thursday, February 5th, 1925. Funeral services were held at the Falling Springs church and interment made in that cemetery. He is survived by his wife, a daughter, Mrs. John Peterson of Decatur and two sons, William McConnell and Claude McConnell, both of Westville, Okla. Mr. McConnell was born in Michigan in 1850 and has traveled broadly over the United States in search of a climate which could benefit his health. Nearly 44 years ago he made the trip overland with a wagon and team from Missouri to the West Coast and settled in the State of Oregon. A few years later he made the return trip. He has located in 26 different places in the country where he made his home for a few years. He settled northwest of Gentry in 1904. Mr. McConnell has become well known during his residence in this community and was a highly respected citizen. [Benton County Record 2/13/25]

McCOOL, John Jacob - John Jacob McCool, a well known and respected resident of the Pea Ridge section, died at the home of Walter Goff, west of the town of Pea Ridge, at 11 o'clock Monday night, aged 70 years. Mr. McCool was a native of Coffee county, Tennessee but had been a resident of this section practically all of his life and had a wide circle of friends and acquaintances. He is survived by two sons, Jim McCool of Denoy, Okla. and Bill McCool, Pittsburg, Kan.; and two daughters, Mrs. Willis Keen and Mrs. Frank Crabtree, both of near Pea Ridge, and a number of other relatives. Funeral services were held Wednesday afternoon at Pea Ridge by Rev. W.T. Bone, assisted by Rev. Joseph Price. Interment was in the Pea Ridge cemetery. [Benton County Democrat 5/14/25] [Rogers Democrat 5/21/25]

John McCool, aged 69 years and a resident of this county for nearly 40 years, died at the home of his nephew in McDonald county, Mo. Monday. He was buried on Pea Ridge Tuesday. Two sons and two daughters survive him. [Benton County Record 5/15/25]

McDANIEL, Andrew Lafayette - Andrew Lafayette McDaniel died at 8:25 Tuesday night at his home four miles southwest of Rogers. He had been in poor health for some time but his condition had been considered serious for only the last three weeks. Funeral services were held yesterday afternoon at 3:00 o'clock at the Pleasant Grove Baptist church where Mr. McDaniel had been a member for many years and were conducted by Rev. A.A. DuLaney, pastor of the Rogers Baptist church. Interment was in the Pleasant Grove cemetery. Mr. McDaniel was born November 29, 1856 in Benton county and was 68 years, one month and 15 days old at the time of his death. He died on his farm, which was a part of the old original homestead taken by his father when the former came here from Tennessee some seventy years ago. He was married Dec. 22, 1887 to Miss Julie Ann Smith of Lowell, who survives him. To this union was born ten children, nine of whom are living: Ernest McDaniel of Healing Springs; Will and Jasper McDaniel of Rogers; Wesley McDaniel of Seattle, Wash.; Austin McDaniel of near St. Louis; Asberry McDaniel, Lowell and Winfred and Guy McDaniel at home, as is also a daughter, Miss Fannie. Mrs. Bessie Fagala died two years ago. Mr. McDaniel is also survived by two brothers, one in Oklahoma City and another near Tahlequah, and by four sisters, Mrs. Abe McGarrah, Mrs. Margaret Pitts, Mrs. May Jane Archey and Mrs. Armiza Keeling, all of Rogers. The deceased was one of the best known men in his neighborhood and stood high in the esteem of all as a good citizen, husband and father and his passing is regretted by a large circle of warm friends. [Rogers Democrat 1/15/25]

{from Fairview} Andrew McDaniel died at his home five miles southwest of Rogers on Tuesday and was buried in Pleasant Grove cemetery Wednesday afternoon. Mr. McDaniel was 68 years old, having always lived in Fairview School District and on the same farm. He has eight grown boys and all of them attended the funeral. One of them, Wesley McDaniel, came all the way from Seattle, Wash. [Benton County Record 1/23/25]

McGARRAH, infant - {from Monte Ne} We are very sorry to report the death of an infant son of Mr. and Mrs. Oscar McGarrah last week. Interment in the Frisco cemetery. [Rogers Democrat 5/21/25]

McGEE, George - George McGee, formerly of Gravette, died Tuesday while driving from Welch, Okla. to his home at Miami, the result of heart trouble, it is stated. Senator Austin, who helped his daughter, Mrs. Clarry, move to Commerce was in Miami Tuesday and was told that Mr. McGee was returning from a visit with his brother at Welch and parties on the road saw him fall forward on his steering wheel. Realizing his condition he shut off the gas and the car rolled off the road and stopped. After telling that he was sick and stating where he was going, he died. Mr. McGee was the son-in-law of "Parson" McCraw, a pioneer citizen of Eldorado township who died here some years ago. The funeral was held at Miami Wednesday. He leaves his wife and several children. [Gravette News-Herald 6/12/25]

McKENZIE, David Calvin - David Calvin McKenzie was born on Aug. 26th, 1838 in York District, South Carolina and died at the family home two miles west of Centerton on Saturday night, March 14th, 1925. Death was due to kidney trouble and the flu. He served as a Confederate soldier during the Civil War, professing faith in Jesus during a battle but never united with any church. Funeral services were held Sunday afternoon at the Community Church in Centerton and his body was laid to rest by the side of his wife in the Gamble cemetery northwest of that place. Mr. and Mrs. McKenzie are survived by four sons - Charles, George and John McKenzie, who live west of Centerton, and John C. McKenzie, of Hollister, Idaho; also by three daughters - Mrs. Mary Boyd, living southwest of Bentonville; Mrs. Emma Osborne of Jerome, Idaho and Mrs. Annie Stone of Tekoa, Wash. Another daughter, Mrs. Ellen Womack, died in May 1920. They also have 21 grandchildren and 17 great-grandchildren and a host of friends to mourn their loss. [Benton County Record 3/20/25]

McKENZIE, Mr. and Mrs. D.C. - Within the week this section has lost two of its oldest and most highly respected citizens in the death of David Calvin McKenzie, aged 84 years, and his wife, Mrs. Nancy Jane McKenzie, aged 79. Their deaths resulted from influenza and pneumonia and occurred at the old family home west of Centerton. Both had been critically ill for some days, Mrs. McKenzie passing away Thursday night and Mr. McKenzie late Saturday. Mrs. McKenzie's funeral was held Saturday morning at the Centerton Community Methodist church, the pastor, Rev. Boyles, conducting the services. Funeral services for Mr. McKenzie were held Sunday. Both were interred at the Gamble cemetery near Centerton. Mr. and Mrs. McKenzie were natives of Georgia. They settled in Arkansas early in their married life and were residents of this vicinity for a great number of years. Of their eight children, seven of them survive. [Benton County Democrat 3/19/25]

The closing chapters of a long and eventful married life extending over a period of nearly 60 years ended last Saturday by the death of Calvin McKenzie, who had lived in the vicinity of Centerton for 57 years. Two days previously his wife, Nancy J. McKenzie, preceded him to the grave. In less than 50 hours the light of these two pioneers went out. [Benton County Record 3/20/25]

McKENZIE, Nancy Jane ALLISON - Nancy Jane Allison was born on November 14th, 1845 in Alabama. On the 20th of December 1866 she was married to Calvin McKenzie. She died on March 12th, 1925 at the age of 79 years, three months and 28 days. She was afflicted with a cancer and died from pneumonia following the flu. She professed a hope in Jesus in her early days and united with the Methodist church. Funeral services were held at the Community Church in Centerton on Saturday afternoon, the Rev. E.L. Boyles conducting the services. Interment was made in the Gamble cemetery. [Benton County Record 3/20/25]

McKINNEY, Tommie JEFFERSON - Mrs. Tommie McKinney, beloved wife of J.H. McKinney, died suddenly at the family home two miles east of

Bentonville at seven o'clock on Wednesday morning, September 23rd, 1925 of hemorrhage of the brain. Mrs. McKinney was ill but a few hours. She was in Bentonville on Tuesday afternoon and when she retired that night seemed perfectly well. About 12 o'clock she was stricken and never regained consciousness. She was about 49 years of age. Besides her husband she is survived by a daughter, Fay, a student in the Bentonville school. She is also survived by one brother, Jim Jefferson, of that neighborhood, and four sisters - Mrs. Kate Roberson of Tulsa, Okla.; Miss Lizzie Jefferson of Bentonville; Mrs. Fannie Woods of New Mexico and Mrs. Ella Mills of Tulsa, Okla. She also leaves a large number of relatives and friends to mourn her departure. Mrs. Tommie McKinney was the daughter of Mr. and Mrs. George Jefferson, Sr. and was born on the old Jefferson homestead east of Bentonville on November 2nd, 1876. Her entire life was spent in that neighborhood. On February 26th, 1900 she was married to J.H. McKinney, a resident of that neighborhood, at the home of Rev. Peter Carnahan, the officiating minister. Funeral services were held at the family home at 2:30 Thursday afternoon, the Rev. J.L. Evans officiating. [Benton County Record 9/25/25]
The funeral of Mrs. Tommie Jefferson McKinney was held from the family home at 2:30 p.m. Thursday afternoon. The death of Mrs. McKinney occurred Wednesday morning. The Reverend J.L. Evans officiated at the funeral services. Mrs. McKinney was a native of Benton county, having been born here November 2nd, 1876. Mrs. McKinney joined the Cumberland Presbyterian church at Mt. Eden when 16 years of age and later became a member of the M.E. Church, South in Bentonville. February 22nd, 1900 she was married to John McKinney, to which union three children were born, Fay, and one son and daughter who died several years ago. She is survived, besides her husband, by four sisters and one brother, Jim Jefferson of Bentonville; Mrs. Clint Woods of Flora Vista, New Mexico; Miss Lizzie Jefferson, Mrs. R.H. Mills and Mrs. W.T. Roberson of Tulsa, Okla. [Benton County Democrat 9/29/25]

McNEIL, John Harris - John H. McNeil, 36 years old, died Monday at the family home in the southeast part of Rogers after a long illness. He had been slowly sinking for some time and his death was not unexpected. Funeral services were held Tuesday afternoon at the Baptist church and were conducted by the pastor, Rev. A.A. DuLaney. Interment was in the city cemetery. John was born here and his life was spent in Rogers and on the farm southeast of town. He is survived by his mother, Mrs. W.A. McNeil, his sister, Miss Bess McNeil, and 3 brothers, Will, Tom S. and Dr. Clyde McNeil, all of Rogers. [Rogers Democrat 10/15/25]
John Harris McNeil died yesterday at the home of his mother, Mrs. W.A. McNeil, aged 36 years and 16 days. He had been a sufferer of progressive paralysis for 17 years. He leaves to mourn him his mother, sister Bess and three brothers, Will, Tom and Clyde, all well known in business circles.

The funeral was held at the Baptist church this afternoon, Rev. DuLaney officiating. Interment in Rogers cemetery. [Rogers Daily Post 10/13/25]

McQUEEN, Mr. - {from Oak Hill, for last week} Miran Hull received word from his sister that Mr. McQueen had died. Mr. and Mrs. McQueen used to live here about ten years ago. Leaving here they moved north of Rogers on Sugar Creek where they lived several years. They were near Mt. View, Mo. when he died. Mrs. McQueen and relatives have the sympathy of our community. [Rogers Democrat 11/12/25]

MAHANAY, Marian M. - M.M. Mahanay died at his home in Oldtown Monday night following a few days of sickness from pneumonia. He was aged about 87 and was one of a type of sturdy pioneers of this region, few of whom remain with us. Mr. Mahanay had resided here the greater part of his life and was a character who was everybody's friend. Until a few days ago he made frequent trips up town. A host of people regret his passing. He leaves his aged companion, one son, Estel Mahanay of Gravette, and three daughters, Mrs. Ollie Busey, Pittsburg, Kan.; Mrs. Eva Nitchman, Gravette and Mrs. Mable Longan, Morrison, Okla. Another son, Garland, died a few years ago. The funeral was held at the home Wednesday afternoon, conducted by Dr. W.A. McDonald, followed by interment in the I.O.O.F. cemetery. The Masons had charge of the burial. The bereaved family have the sympathy of everyone. [Gravette News-Herald 1/2/25]

Bro. Marian M. Mahanay was born in Jackson county, Tenn. June 19, 1837 and died at 8:15 p.m. December 29, 1924, aged 87 years, 6 months, 10 days. He moved from Tennessee to Cascade county, Mo., coming to Washington and Benton county, Ark. in 1868. Here he married Susan Snider. Nine children were born to them, five of whom survive: Estel Mahanay of Gravette; Mrs. Olive Busey and Mrs. Ida Bailey of Pittsburg; Mrs. Eva Nitchman of Gravette and Mrs. Mabel Longan of Morrison, Okla. The wife also survives. Bro. Mahanay spent the most of his life here except for 15 years in Texas. He was made a Master Mason at old Bethel Lodge July 8, 1870 and was an honorary member at the time of his death; and one of the oldest members. He was a faithful father and husband, grateful to his God and fraternal to his fellowmen. The funeral was conducted Wednesday, Dec. 31 by Dr. W.A. McDonald, the Masons participating, and burial following at the I.O.O.F. cemetery. [Gravette News-Herald 1/9/25]

MAHANEY, John C. - John C. Mahaney died Monday at 7:00 o'clock at the age of 67 years. Funeral services were held Tuesday at 2:00 o'clock at Ozark school house, east of Rogers, and were conducted by Rev. R.M. Thompson and Rev. T.B. Clark of the First Christian church. John C. Mahaney was born in Kentucky but was taken to Mt. Vernon, Ill. when a child and there grew to manhood. Mr. Mahaney's parents moved to Benton county about forty years ago where they have since made their home. Mr. Mahaney lived for many years on White river where he was always a welcome guest in every home. He was married to Miss Annie Cook in 1889 and to this union were born four children of whom three daughters are living: Mrs. Pearl Day, now at Claremore, Okla.; Mrs. Mary Key, who lives on White river, and Mrs. Winnie Martin of Rogers, who has so faithfully and tenderly cared for her father during his long, painful illness. He leaves also two sisters, Mrs. Dollar and Mrs. Burdick, who live in Rogers, and five grandchildren. Mr. Mahaney was a kind, helpful neighbor; always ready to lend aid wherever it was needed. His dealings with his fellowman was in accord with the Golden Rule. He leaves many friends who mourn the loss of one whose whole life was that of honest good to all his associates and neighbors. [Rogers Democrat 3/19/25]

MAPES, Novella - Novella Mapes, 25 year old daughter of Duffey Mapes of Bentonville, commercial photographer, died in Wichita Falls, Texas Saturday night after swallowing a portion of a two-ounce bottle of carbolic acid. The girl died about 25 minutes after taking the poison. Mr. Mapes was notified of the girl's death and left immediately after receiving the wire Sunday. The girl left a note addressed to her sweetheart telling of her eternal love for him. Her roommate and a man were in the room at the time the acid was taken and in attempting to prevent her taking the poison were burned on their hands and faces from the contents of the bottle................ Her father recently moved to Bentonville and resides on East Twelfth Street. He is a commercial photographer here and for many years was engaged in the same business at Wichita Falls. He is very well known here. [Benton County Record 11/27/25]

MARR, Virgil - {from Centerton} The body of Virgil Marr, accompanied by his father, Frank Marr, arrived on the morning passenger train Saturday. Funeral services followed at the Community Church and in the absence of the pastor Rev. O.M. Campbell of Bentonville conducted the services. Interment followed in the Centerton cemetery. Virgil died suddenly near Gallup, New Mexico on Tuesday, August 18th, 1925 while on an automobile trip with his father. They left here about six weeks ago and drove to California and were returning to Colorado for his health. Virgil, who was rapidly regaining his health, did most of the driving. When about 40 miles out of Gallup, New Mexico he complained of being ill and grew worse. A passing tourist went to Gallup for medical aid but he died twenty minutes later. Death was due to acute indigestion. Virgil Marr was born in Marionville, Mo. in 1906 and was 19 years old. Later he moved with his parents to Gravette where his father engaged in the canning business. He graduated from the Warrensburg high school and planned to take an electrical course in college next year. Mr. Marr, who also lost his wife recently, has the heartfelt sympathy of his many friends here and in other parts of the county. [Benton County Record 8/28/25]
Frank Marr arrived on Saturday morning's train with the remains of his son, Virgil, who died near Gallup, New Mexico. Mr. Marr and two sons, Clarence and Virgil, had been taking a pleasure trip. Clarence had left

them and had gone to begin his school in Minnesota, Mr. Marr and Virgil coming on home. They ate dinner at Gallup and drove 32 miles. Then Virgil said he was ill and would have to stop. He only lived about 20 minutes after getting out of the car. His death was caused by acute indigestion. Mr. Marr could not get in touch with the two boys but the two girls, Miss Ruth and Miss Mabel, were here visiting relatives. Virgil was a member of the Methodist Church and rarely ever missed a service of any kind. We shall miss him; but we know that God doeth all things well. Virgil's mother died on Nov. 11th. She was a sister of Mrs. Hugh Goode and the Womack brothers. [Benton County Democrat 8/25/25]

MAXFIELD, Hannah Medaline BURGESS Gibson - Mrs. Edd Maxfield, more familiarly known as "Aunt Med," died at the family residence in Cave Springs on Saturday morning, August 15th, 1925 after an illness of only two days. However, she had been in failing health for the past year or more. Aunt Med, whose maiden name was Hannah Medaline Burgess, was born in Tennessee in 1837. In 1853 she was married to James Gibson, who died during the Civil War. To this union was born three girls and one boy. After the Civil War she was married to Edd Maxfield, who survives her. Her son, Wilse Gibson of Tulsa, Okla. and his two sons, Gus and Carl, and her granddaughter, Mrs. May Roark of Healing Springs, were with her during her illness and at the time of her death. Besides her husband, son and the grandchildren mentioned Aunt Med leaves eighteen grandchildren, forty-one great-grandchildren, one great-great-grandchild and seven nieces to mourn her loss. Aunt Med professed faith in Christ when she was fifteen years old and has since lived a devoted Christian life. Funeral services were conducted at the residence and cemetery on Sunday afternoon by Brother Brogan of Healing Springs. Burial was made in the Thornsberry cemetery. The bereaved family has the sympathy of the entire community in their sorrow. [Benton County Record 8/21/25]
{from Vaughn} Mr. and Mrs. A.M. Smith, Mrs. Sarah Parker, mother of Mrs. Smith, and Mrs. Ola Crittenden attended the funeral services at Thornsberry Camp Ground Sunday afternoon of Mrs. Edd Maxfield, an aunt of Mrs. Parker. [Benton County Record 8/21/25]

MAXWELL, J. Henry C. - With a feeling of sincere regret the many friends of Rev. J.H.C. Maxwell learn of his death in a hospital at Kerrville, Texas. Rev. Maxwell and wife spent the month of June visiting with the father, Leander Maxwell, and an older sister north of Rogers on Sugar Creek. During his visit Henry, as he was known in the neighborhood, was in the best of health and no one could suspect that so soon an announcement of his death would appear. During his boyhood Henry attended school at Pea Ridge and began a medical course of study which he later abandoned to enter the ministry where he served for more than a dozen years. At the time of his decease he was a member of the Central Texas Conference of the M.E. church, South, stationed at Poteet, thirty miles southwest from

San Antonio. On July 1st he and Mrs. Maxwell and single daughter, Miss Karin, drove some seventy-five miles to Kerrville to visit relatives and the day after their arrival was attacked quite severely with appendicitis. Though serious his condition was not at first thought critical however an operation was performed on July third and at that time it became apparent that he had little chance for recovery. He passed away at 2:30 a.m. Thursday of last week, surrounded by his wife, Miss Karin and an older daughter, Mrs. Bonnie Lee Rogers and husband, at Secor Hospital in Kerrville. W.T. Maxwell was called from Kerrville by long distance telephone Monday and left on Frisco No. 3, arriving several hours after his brother had died. A younger brother, John D., passed away in 1916 and was buried in the Hickman cemetery just north of the Maxwell homestead. Of the family of Leander Maxwell, Mrs. Belle Baldwin, Mrs. I.C. Casey, Mrs. E.B. Mayhew and W.T. Maxwell survive. [Rogers Democrat 7/16/25]

MAXWELL, Lou M. - Miss Lou Maxwell passed away at her home on the Osage, about six miles south of Bentonville, at ten p.m. Sunday, Dec. 13th. She had been in poor health for years but had seemed no worse Sunday when death suddenly took her. Funeral services were held for her Monday with the Rev. Brogan of Cave Springs in charge and were largely attended. Interment was made in the Hebron Cemetery near Colville. Miss Maxwell was born on Oct. 18, 1856 and lived all her life on her father's farm near Cave Springs. She was the daughter of Mr. and Mrs. Jim Maxwell who settled their farm in the very early days of Benton county. The family has always owned and lived on the homestead. Her brother, Jim, died in 1921 and since that time Miss Maxwell had lived alone until a short time ago when Miss Maggie Richardson of Gentry went to be with her. She was a member of the Methodist church but in later years had attended the Church of Apostolic Faith at Cave Springs. Though having no immediate relatives Miss Maxwell leaves a host of distant relatives and friends in this county and elsewhere. Among them is W.T. Maxwell of Ft. Smith who owned land north of Bentonville for several years. Mrs. I.C. Casey of Bentonville, Tom Maxwell of Gentry, Mrs. Richardson of Gentry and Leander Maxwell of Pea Ridge, are also related. [Benton County Record 12/28/25]

MAYFIELD, Elizabeth Larrine - Elizabeth Larrine Mayfield died Monday at the home of her parents, Mr. and Mrs. J.L. Mayfield, near Buttram Chapel at the age of 13 years and 10 months. She has been ill for some weeks from a complication of diseases following the flu. Besides her parents she is survived by two sisters and a brother. Funeral services were conducted Tuesday afternoon at Buttram Chapel by Rev. J.W. Critchlow of Rogers and Rev. Bone. The deceased was loved by all who knew her and she leaves a host of friends and relatives to mourn her loss. [Benton County Record 3/27/25]

MAYFIELD, Elizabeth Lorean - Elizabeth Lorean, daughter of Jas. and Nannie Mayfield, was born May 23, 1911 and departed this life on

March 24, 1925. She was better known as Bess and was loved by everyone who knew her, for she was such a sweet, kind character that it seemed to be her delight to make others happy. When eleven years of age she was converted and united with the Methodist church, South to which faith she was true until the end. The funeral service was conducted by her pastor, assisted by Rev. J. Wilson Crichlow of Rogers, after which her remains were laid to rest in Buttram Chapel cemetery where members of four generations of her father's people sleep. Her Pastor, Willie Thomas Bone. [Rogers Democrat 4/2/25]

MAYFIELD, Elizabeth Lorine - Died, Bess Mayfield, early Tuesday morning, March 24, 1925, aged 13 years and 10 months. Interment was made at the Buttram Chapel cemetery same afternoon at 3:30 o'clock. The death angel has again entered our community and taken from Mr. and Mrs. James Mayfield their daughter, Elizabeth Lorine, aged 13 years and 10 months. Bess, as she was known, was a child with a sweet and happy disposition, giving promise of exceptional intelligence and had arrived at an age where she made herself a source of joy in the home. [Benton County Democrat 4/2/25]

MEAD, C.W. - Mr. C.W. Mead, 72 years old, died last night at 8:40 at the home of Roy G. Brooks, northwest of town. Mr. and Mrs. Mead came from Los Angeles to Arkansas for Mr. Mead's health and had just been here two weeks. They have a son, R.W. Mead, who has just located here southwest of town and Mrs. Mead is the mother of R.G. Brooks and C.V. Brooks, both of Route 2, Rogers. Burial was this afternoon at 3:30. [Rogers Daily Post 4/23/25]

MEANS, Katie THOMPSON - Entered into rest Tuesday morning, May 19th, Katie Means, wife of Claude Means, daughter of Mr. and Mrs. Jeff Thompson. Born November 28, 1899 in Maries county, Mo., she came to Arkansas with her parents and resided near Monte Ne. At the age of fifteen she was united in marriage to Claude Means. To this union was born three children, one of whom died in infancy. Besides the two children and her husband to mourn her loss are her aged parents, three brothers and three sisters. Burial was in the cemetery at War Eagle beside that of her little one. [Rogers Democrat 5/28/25]
{from Monte} Our community was very much shocked to learn of the death of Mrs. Claude Means on the 19th of May. She died very suddenly of heart failure. She was 26 years old and leaves two small children. She was buried at War Eagle. We all sympathize with the bereaved family. [Rogers Democrat 5/28/25]

MEEKER, Jane C. - Mrs. Jane Meeker, aged 57, of near Decatur, died at the Siloam Springs hospital at 6 o'clock on the evening of Feb. 7, 1925. All of her children were with her at the time of her death. Mrs. Meeker was one of the best known school teachers of Benton Co. She began teaching at 15 years of age and taught for some years and for the last 15 years she had

taught continuously. She leaves to mourn her loss an aged father and six children: Mrs. J.D. Simpson of Fayetteville; Mrs. L.C. Carn of Siloam Springs; Mrs. Donald Van Sickle of Earlton, Kan.; Mrs. Jack Davenport of Keifer, O.; Nelson Meeker of Decatur and Orville Meeker of Centerton. Funeral services were held at the Baptist church in Decatur Monday morning at 11 o'clock, conducted by the pastor, Rev. John Scoggins. Interment was made at the Springtown cemetery. Besides a large crowd of friends from Decatur and other neighborhoods there were present from Centerton a number of close friends of her son, Orville Meeker, who is an instructor in the Centerton schools. [Benton County Democrat 2/12/25]
Mrs. Jane C. Meeker, a well known school teacher of Benton county, died following an operation at the City Hospital in Siloam Springs on Saturday evening, February 7th at 6:45 o'clock. Mrs. Meeker was a native of Ohio and was born in Belpre on July 5th, 1867. When a young girl she came with her people to Decatur which was then known as Corner Springs. Here in this vicinity she grew to womanhood and married John Meeker, making their home some miles east of Decatur. Her husband died about 15 years ago and since then Mrs. Meeker has become an efficient teacher and has taught in many different parts of the county. She leaves four daughters: Mrs. S.T. Corn, Mrs. J.C. Simpson, who live near Siloam Springs; Mrs. Don Van Sickle, Earlton, Kansas; Mrs. C.R. Davenport, Wynnewood, Okla.; and two sons, N.J. Meeker, Decatur and Orval Meeker, who is an instructor in the Centerton school. Funeral services were held in Decatur at 11 o'clock Monday morning and interment was made in the Decatur cemetery. Many people came from over the county to pay their last respects to this friend and teacher, many of whom she had instructed during her years of teaching. Mrs. Meeker was a noble woman with a character of power and influence to overcome obstacles and to be victorious in the face of defeat. The friends and neighbors extend their sincerest sympathy to the children in the loss of their mother. [Benton County Record 2/13/25]

MIDDLETON, Columbus - Columbus Middleton, Confederate veteran and prominent citizen of this section for 60 years, died at the old family home near Bentonville Friday, May 8, 1925, aged 86 years, one month and 25 days. Funeral services were held from the home Sunday afternoon conducted by Rev. F.A. Bradshaw, pastor of the Presbyterian church at Vaughn, assisted by Rev. J.L. Evans of the M.E. Church, South, Bentonville. A great number of friends and acquaintances from the entire countryside, including many from Bentonville, Rogers and other county towns, gathering there to pay this last tribute of respect to his memory. Interment was made at the Hart cemetery, southeast of Bentonville, where sleep his parents, other relatives and many of his old friends. Columbus Middleton, a son of Mr. and Mrs. H.L. Middleton, was born in McMinn county, Tenn. on March 13, 1839. In 1851 the family came to Arkansas, settling on the Illinois river in Benton county. Later the elder Middleton decided to take his family back to the old home in Tennessee, returning via the Missouri route. Rumors of the approaching war between the North and South halted them in Greene county, Mo. where they located until the war clouds should pass over. The war coming on, however, Columbus Middleton enlisted in 1861 in the Southern army as a member of a Greene county, Mo. company of Gen. Price's division, serving throughout the war and fighting in some of the more decisive battles, including those of Wilson Creek, Pea Ridge and Vicksburg. Captured at one time by Northern troops, he was held for some time in the Rock Island prison. He proved himself a loyal soldier of the cause he had espoused and after the close of the war turned to the building up again of his own fortunes and those of the South. In 1866 he again came to Benton county with his parents and others of the family and from that time was a resident of this section until his death. The home where he died was a part of the 600 acres purchased by his father the second time he moved his family to Arkansas. In 1867 Mr. Middleton married Mrs. Minnie Maxwell and to them were born six children, two of whom died in infancy. He is survived by his wife, two sons, Frank and Sam, and two daughters, Mrs. W.K. Rife and Miss Flora Middleton, all of Bentonville and by six grandchildren and two great grandchildren. One of the former is Mrs. Richard C. Meade of Philadelphia, who was among those from a distance here for the funeral, who, having lost her parents in infancy, was reared by Mr. and Mrs. Middleton as their own child. He is survived also by three brothers, Joe and Lee Middleton, Bentonville and Alexander Middleton, Springfield, Mo. and two sisters, Mrs. Anna Cook, Bentonville, widow of the late Taylor Cook, and Mrs. T.A. Nicholson, Springfield, Mo. [Benton County Democrat 5/14/25] [Benton County Record 5/15/25]

MILLER, Sarah Smith Cunningham - Mrs. Sarah Miller died at her home near Hiwasse on Wednesday, November 25th, 1925 at the age of nearly 91 years. She was one of the oldest residents of that section and has been a member of the Baptist church for 49 years. Probably no woman in Benton county had as many grandchildren as Mrs. Miller. Seventy-eight of them survive her, including 20 grandchildren, 41 great-grandchildren and 17 great-great-grandchildren. Mrs. Miller was born in Tennessee in 1835 and was married to Charles Smith in 1855. She leaves two sons, W.D. Smith of Temple, Texas and E.T. Cunningham of Guthrie, Okla. and one daughter, Mrs. Tom Spiva of Bentonville, Route 3. [Benton County Record 12/4/25]

MILLS, B.F. - Rev. Mills, retired Methodist minister and farmer, died at his home south of Vaughn on Friday, May 22nd, 1925 at the age of 81 years. Death was due to a complication of diseases following an attack of the flu about nine weeks ago. Rev. Mills was born in Haywood county, Tenn. on April 15th, 1844 and came to Arkansas about 1870. He came to Benton county in the year 1892. He was married to Miss Jennie D. Revely in 1866. To this union ten children were born, eight of whom are living. They are W.W. Mills of Stillwater, Okla.; R.H. Mills of Tulsa, Okla.; Mrs. Clemmons of Clarksville, Ark.; Mrs. Hale of Phoenix, Ariz.; A.W. and Dick Mills of near Vaughn and Mrs. Kerr and Mrs. Bright. Brother Mills had been a member of the church for 57 years. He had been a local preacher in the Methodist Episcopal Church, South for about 35 years. He had been active in church work until the past few years. His hearing being so bad it made it impossible to do the work. The funeral services were held from the Methodist Church at Centerton and he was laid to rest in the cemetery at Centerton. A.M. Campbell, Pastor. [Benton County Record 5/29/25]

MITCHELL, Ivy Frank - Ivy Frank Mitchell died early last Monday morning at the home of his parents in the south part of town of pneumonia. Funeral services were held from the Methodist church last Wednesday afternoon, conducted by Rev. Villines and burial was made in the city cemetery. Many relatives and friends were present and the floral offerings were very beautiful. He leaves his parents, one son, two sisters and two brothers and a large circle of relatives and friends to mourn his going. [Gentry Journal-Advance 1/2/25]

MITZLER, Jack - {from Lowell} Jack Mitzler died Sunday morning, November 15th at 8:30 o'clock after a lingering illness with typhoid fever. The older brother was just recovering from an attack of the same fever. Funeral services were conducted by Rev. English at the Baptist church and burial was in the Pleasant Grove cemetery. Heartfelt sympathy is extended the family in their sad hour of bereavement. [Rogers Democrat 11/19/25]

MOOMEY, O.H. - O.H. Moomey, age 66 years, died last Saturday morning at his home four and one-half miles northwest of Decatur. He had been ill a long while with heart disease. The remains were shipped by the Carpenter Bros. undertakers Sunday to his old home in Mason City, Neb. and were accompanied by his wife and one son, who survive him. [Gentry Journal-Advance 8/28/25]

MOORE, James G. - James G. Moore was born Oct. 17, 1887 in Bonham, Texas and died Nov. 6, 1925 in Henryetta, Okla. He is survived by his wife, Mrs. Gladie Moore and a brother, John Moore, of Muskogee, Okla. The remains, accompanied by his wife and her sister, Mrs. Hattie Harper, and his brother, John Moore, of Muskogee, arrived here last Sunday night and funeral services were held Monday afternoon from the Baptist church, conducted by Rev. Riene Dilworth and burial was made in the City Cemetery. The sympathy of the entire community goes out to the young wife who is remembered here as Miss Gladie Griner, daughter of Mr. and Mrs. W.W. Griner of this city. [Gentry Journal-Advance 11/13/25]

MOORE, John Goodrich - J.G. Moore, an old pioneer settler and Confederate soldier, died at the home of his daughter, Mrs. Walter Harris, on Tuesday, April 7th, 1925 after a long illness. Funeral services were conducted by Rev. O.M. Campbell on Thursday, April 9th from the Harris home and interment was made in the Barron cemetery near Vaughn. Mr. Moore

was born in North Carolina and soon after the Civil War came to Benton county and settled on the farm where Syl Rife now lives, west of Osage. In 1883 he was married to Miss Mary E. Heagerty, to whom eight children were born, all dying in infancy except Mrs. Harris. Mr. Moore had been in ill health for some time and was recently taken to the home of his daughter where he died. In youth he united with the M.E. Church. He was a Mason of many years standing and members of that order assisted in the funeral services which were largely attended. A sister, Mrs. M.C. Lewis, of Kansas was present at the funeral. [Benton County Record 4/10/25]
John Goodrich Moore was born on Sept. 4th, 1845. Died on April 7th, 1925. His birthplace was Iredell county, North Carolina, eleven miles from Statesville. In 1867 he came to Arkansas and settled on what is now the S.G. Rife farm. Later he moved to the present home place where he had lived since. The last year of the Civil War found Uncle John {as he is now known to so many of us} serving with the Confederate Army. He was in several battles. His record as a soldier and also as a man and citizen, has been one strong for his convictions and always doing what to him seemed right. On November 25th, 1883 he was married to Mary Elizabeth Heagerty. To this union were born eight children, seven dying in infancy. He is survived by his wife, Mary Elizabeth Moore; one daughter, Inez Harris, and her husband, Walter Harris; two grandchildren, Leon and Lee Harris, one sister, Mrs. Myra Lewis, of Kansas City. There are many other relatives and a host of acquaintances who also mourn his passing away. If Uncle John could have stayed until September he would have been 80 years old. It seems useless for anyone to try and tell of those years when he has lived them so well. He professed faith when but a boy in North Carolina. However he did not take an active part in church and Sunday school work until after he was married. Then he united with the M.E. Church and has always been steadfast, loyal and untiring in his Christian life. His last two years were ones of breaking health and his last months filled with intense suffering. At 2:30 a.m. Tuesday the summons came. The pain wracked body is at rest and his soul at peace. [Benton County Record 4/17/25]

MORRIS, Mary Kathrine - {from Gravette} Died, Thursday, October 15, 1925, Mary Kathrine Morris, two year old daughter of Mr. and Mrs. J.P. Morris. Little Mary Kathrine had been sick for some time and her death was not unexpected. Funeral was conducted Sunday, October 18th from the home, Elder C.D. Purlee, pastor of the Christian church of Siloam Springs, in charge. Burial was at the I.O.O.F. cemetery. [Benton County Record 10/13/25]

MOSIER, Charles A. - Charles A. Mosier died at his home in the valley northeast of Gravette Sunday evening. For three months he has fought a battle with pneumonia, during which time an operation on his lungs was performed. He seemed to be rallying but succumbed to a bad heart attack. Charlie Mosier was a fine citizen, American every inch, and a man whom everyone admired. He came to Benton county at the age of 18 and had resided on the farm where he died ever since, and was nearing his 70th birthday. His first wife died some years ago. Three of six children by this union survive: James Mosier, Mrs. Lou Eldridge and Miss Byrd Mosier. He also leaves his second wife and many other relatives. The funeral was held at the Baptist church below Sulphur Springs Thursday. [Gravette News-Herald 4/3/25] [Benton County Record 4/3/25]

MURDOCK, John H. - John H. Murdock died at the family home northwest of Cave Springs on Friday morning, September 4th, 1925 at the age of 67 years. Mr. Murdock had been confined to his home for about two years on account of ill health, his death being caused from pneumonia. The funeral services were held at the family home on Friday afternoon. Rev. Henry of Elm Springs conducted the services. Interment was made in the Phillips cemetery. Mr. Murdock was born in Ripley county, Ind. on May 22nd, 1858. He confessed faith in Christ and joined the Baptist Church and was baptized in 1875. He moved to Benton county, Ark. and joined the church at Cave Springs. He was married to Barbra P. Phillips in 1880. To this union were born nine children, five girls and four boys. Three boys and four girls are still living and all are Christians. Besides his wife he is survived by seven children - Mrs. Nannie Fagala, Mrs. W.E. Rozar, Mrs. Lige Allen, C.O. Murdock and C.R. Murdock, all of Cave Springs, Ark.; Mrs. Homer Scoggins of Highfill, Ark. and J.E. Murdock of Belton, Mo. Also two brothers and three sisters - C.A. Murdock of Avon, South Dakota; S.E. Murdock of Lisle, Mo.; Mrs. Anna Hughes of Omaha, Neb.; Mrs. Nellie Phillips of Cave Springs, Ark. and Mrs. Ola Holland of Elm Springs, Ark. Also 29 grandchildren and a host of friends. Mr. Murdock was a man of upright character and was loved and respected by his fellowmen and was a kind and loving husband and father. [Benton County Record 9/11/25] [Rogers Democrat 9/17/25]

MYERS, "Bony" - {from Centerton} News was received recently of the death at the soldiers' home in Indiana of "Bony" Myers, former well known resident of this community. Mr. Myers is survived by one son, Harry, of Baxter Springs, Kan. and has a daughter living at Peru, Ind. [Benton County Democrat 4/9/25]

NABLET, Philo - {from Monte Ne} We are very sorry to hear of the death of Philo Nablet at the Love Sanitarium Sunday night following an operation for appendicitis. He leaves three children, his wife having died several years ago. [Rogers Democrat 5/28/25]

NANCE, William L. - W.L. Nance, best known in Rogers as "Bill," died last Friday in a government hospital at Legion, Texas, the result of tuberculosis contracted as a member of the A.E.F. during the World War. The body arrived in Rogers Tuesday evening and funeral services were held Wednesday morning at Oakley Chapel where he was buried by the side of his parents, the Hon. R.L. Nance and wife. The William Batjer Post,

American Legion, attended in uniform and Mr. Nance was given a military funeral, assisted by Rev. Ben H. Moore, pastor of the Presbyterian church. William L. Nance was born in Rogers, the youngest son of R.L. Nance and wife, and at the time of his death was 29 years, eight months and four days old. All of his brothers and sisters were here for the funeral and are: Mrs. A.M. Harding of Fayetteville; Mrs. Bonnie McBrinn and Mrs. M.G. McGee of Oklahoma City; R.S. Nance of Oklahoma City; Hon. John W. Nance of Rogers and James C. Nance of Walters, Okla. Bill was among the first American troops to land in France and served in the A.E.F. for twenty-two months. He returned to this country broken in health and most of his time since then had been spent in government hospitals. [Rogers Democrat 2/26/25]

NASH, Bobby SIMPSON - Word was received by Mr. and Mrs. Jim Cain of the death caused by appendicitis of Mrs. Darrel Nash at Tulsa, Okla., which was a shock to her many friends here who remember her as Miss Bobby Simpson. She was employed here for a number of years at the Mutual Aid Union, also at the Benton County Hardware Co. She made her home for some time at the O.F. Chapin home. She was married to Darrel Nash, a Rogers boy, two years ago at Tulsa and his numerous friends extend sympathy. Mr. and Mrs. Cain and their son, Will and wife, left at once to attend the funeral. [Rogers Democrat 6/25/25]

Friends were grieved today to learn of the death of Mrs. Darrell Nash of Tulsa, Okla. who is well known in Rogers as Bobby Simpson, for several years an employee of the Benton County Hardware Company and before that of the M.A.U. The message came at midnight to Mr. and Mrs. Jim Cain whose son Clessan married a sister of Mrs. Nash with whom the Nashes made their home. Mr. and Mrs. Cain, accompanied by Mr. and Mrs. Will Cain, left immediately for Tulsa. Mrs. Nash was one of the most popular girls in Rogers. She made her home for four years with Mr. and Mrs. Ora Chapin, coming here from Stuttgart, Ark. where she has a mother, several brothers and two sisters. Her father died New Years Day. Her marriage to Darrell Nash, son of Mr. and Mrs. Fred Nash, then of Rogers, two years ago, was of unusual interest, the wedding taking place in Tulsa with the honeymoon spent among their friends here. The cause of her death was from appendicitis two or three years ago. An operation was performed at that time but she never fully regained her health and a few days ago another one was deemed necessary as a last resort but evidently that also failed in results. No word has been received as to the funeral arrangements nor where the interment will take place. The Daily Post joins with the many friends of Darrell Nash in his great sorrow. [Rogers Daily Post 6/19/25]

NEALE, James - James Neale, 83 years old, died last week at Tontitown where he had lived for 20 years. He was station master there when the Felker railroad was operating to that point. He was born in England in

1842. He was a Catholic and a news item mentions that an Irish, a German and an Italian priest officiated at the funeral. [Rogers Democrat 4/23/25]

NICHOLS, Leona - Bentonville friends and acquaintances learned with deep regret of the death of Miss Leona Nichols which occurred Tuesday morning at the home of her parents, Mr. and Mrs. J.O. Nichols, near Hiwasse. Although it was known that her condition had been critical for many days it was hoped that after her four months of suffering and the determined fight she had made with every possible help of parents, family and physicians, she yet might recover. {The notice in The Record mentions that she had had an operation for appendicitis on Nov. 28 and had never fully recovered. Ed.} Miss Leona Nichols was born January 26, 1909 near Hiwasse and died Feb. 10, 1925, aged 16 years and two weeks, her death coming as a great grief to all those whom she had been associated with in school and elsewhere. Besides her parents she is survived by one brother and one sister, Lloyd and Velma Nichols, her grandmothers, Mrs. Mary Nichols and Mrs. J.D. Bates, and a large number of other relatives among them her aunt, Mrs. Bert Douglas of Bentonville and her cousin, Miss Agnes Nichols, of the Benton Co. Hdwe. Co. office, Bentonville. Funeral services, conducted by the Rev. S.A. Morton of the Christian church, Bentonville, were held Wednesday afternoon, Feb. 11th at 1:30 o'clock at the Mount Pleasant church near her home and interment made in the Mount Pleasant cemetery where beautiful flowers mark her resting place. [Benton County Democrat 2/12/25] [Benton County Record 2/13/25]
Mrs. Bert Douglas attended the funeral of her niece, Miss Leona Nichols, near Hiwasse Wednesday. Others from here who attended the funeral were Misses Agnes, Eva and Edith Nichols and Florine Todd, cousins of the deceased, Mrs. Reed Adcock and Rev. Stephen Morton and son, Craig. [Benton County Record 2/13/25]

NIPPER, Mrs. W.M. {Schmidt} - The will of Mrs. W.M. Nipper was filed at Fayetteville a week ago and it began with these words, "I will my soul to God and my son to His keeping." All of her property went to her son, Frank M. Schmidt. [Rogers Democrat 7/16/25]

NOBLETT, Philo - {from Pleasant Ridge} Philo Noblett died Monday at the Home hospital in Rogers after an operation. He has been known in this vicinity for some years where he has lived ever since the first of the year. He was operated upon on his thirty-sixth birthday. He leaves four children, a sister and brother. The remains were laid to rest beside his wife in Highfill cemetery. [Rogers Democrat 5/28/25]

NULL, Mary RECHER - In the death of Mrs. Null, mother of J.W. Null, living three miles west of Bentonville, Northwest Arkansas lost a character whose life contains many interesting incidents and who was a personal acquaintance of many historically known characters. Mrs. Null, who was Mary Recher before her marriage, was born in Hagerstown, Maryland February 12, 1838. She was married to Jacob Null near the close of 1864. In 1887 she moved to Kansas. In 1901 the Nulls moved west of Bentonville where they have resided since. One of the many interesting incidents of Mrs. Null's life was a dinner she prepared for John Brown and his four men the night Brown marked his name in the history of the civil war, the night of the immemorial raid he made on Harper's Ferry, October 16, 1859. The men ate with Mrs. Null and in her home they prepared the raid that was one of the beginnings of the strife between the North and the South. The men were especially thankful to Mrs. Null for her hospitality and blessed her for the aid to them. During the three days battle at Gettysburg she sat on the slopes of the Blue Ridge Mountains and heard the roar of the guns and the continual fire of the artillery. Sitting there in hearing distance of the cannonade, praying that her friends and kinsmen might be saved and that the dreadful disaster of the country would be soon stopped; listening to the dreadful battle and praying only as a woman can, that the conflict would soon end. Toward the end of the battle when the small arms were brought into play, as the hopes of the Confederacy advanced toward the impenetrable heights held by the Union men; the great advance of Pickett's men that blasted the chances of the South, Mrs. Null listened to the fire that sounded to her life a terrific hail storm in the distance. In the summer of 1881 the Greeley Artic Expedition was made. The expedition began with 25 men of which 16 starved, one drowned, and one was shot for stealing supplies. Only seven survivors were left wandering in the wilds of the arctic country. Howard Ames, a sergeant in the United States Army, was placed under Captain Schley who was dispatched to the north to find the expedition that had been lost for many weeks. Before making the start Ames presented Mrs. Null with a beautiful deep blue water set of five pieces. Mrs. Null kept the present intact through all the years and still had it at her death. Mrs. Null was a cousin of Giser, known the world over for his invention and promotion of the Peerless Engines and Separators that are used extensively in the country and was the first engine to separate the wheat from the chaff. The shops are located at Waynesboro, Pennsylvania and does an extensive business. Mrs. Null was a very intelligent woman up until her death, accurately telling of incidents of the Civil War and able to discuss any topics of the day. She was a strong Christian character and possessed a sterling personality. Before her death she expressed a desire to enter into the rest of God and willingly met the end. [Benton County Record 11/6/25]

NULL, Mary Magdalene RICHER - Mrs. Jacob W. Null died at the home of her daughter, Mrs. Katie L. Baker, northeast of Centerton, Thursday, October 22, 1925 at the age of nearly 88 years. She had been in ill health for some time and blind for the past five years. Funeral services, conducted by the Rev. E.L. Boyles, were held from the Baker home Friday with burial in the Centerton cemetery. Mary Magdalene Richer was born in Frederick county, {no state given} and was married to Jacob W. Null at the close of the year 1864. They moved to Kansas in 1887 and later to Benton county in 1901 where they have since resided. She joined the church in early womanhood and was a member of the Centerton Community Church. Besides her husband she is survived by two married children, Mrs. Katie L. Baker and James W. Null, both of the Centerton community. [Benton County Democrat 10/27/25] [Benton County Record 10/30/25]

OAKES, infant - The two-weeks-old infant of Mr. and Mrs. Oliver Oakes, living near Dug Hill, died Saturday from pneumonia. Funeral services were held at the home Sunday and interment made at Dug Hill cemetery. [Benton County Democrat 1/29/25]

OLDHAM, Eliza HUNT - Mrs. Eliza Oldham, wife of C.L. Oldham, died Monday, April 13, 1925 at the farm home west of Gravette at the age of 58 years, 7 months and 9 days. Mrs. Oldham has been seriously afflicted for some time and her death was not unexpected. Mrs. Oldham was a daughter of Thomas Hunt and was born in Missouri. The funeral was conducted at the home Wednesday by Rev. Scroggins. The body was conveyed to Springfield, Mo., former home of the family, for interment. Sympathy is extended the husband and all bereaved ones. [Gravette News-Herald 4/17/25]

OSBORN, Mrs. John - Mrs. John Osborn died at her home near Siloam Springs at the age of 70 years. She is survived by six children. Funeral services, conducted by Rev. F.A. Bradshaw, were held at Vaughn on Wednesday, December 31st. Interment was made in the Barron cemetery. [Benton County Record 1/2/25]

OWNBEY, Andrew C. - {from Hiwasse} Andrew C. Ownbey, aged 62, died at his home in the Mt. Pleasant neighborhood Wednesday, June 24, 1925 following a long illness. Burial was made in the Mt. Pleasant cemetery the following afternoon. [Benton County Record 7/3/25] [Gravette News-Herald 7/3/25]

PARISH, Mrs. C.H. - Mrs. C.H. Parish passed away at her home on Nelson avenue at noon last Tuesday after a lingering illness. She had been confined to her bed since early last fall, suffering from ailments superinduced by asthma. The funeral will be held Thursday afternoon at 2:30 and burial will be made in the city cemetery. [Gentry Journal-Advance 1/23/25]

PARKER, Nannie - {from Eagle Corner} Nannie Parker died February 3rd-after a lingering illness of almost two years. She was laid to rest in the Coffelt cemetery. Bro. Clarence Coffelt officiated. [Benton County Record 2/13/25]

PARKINS, J.W. - {from The Gravette News Herald} J.W. Parkins was born in Smyrna, Ohio March 3, 1868; died at his home in Oklahoma City, Okla. on Monday, Sept. 7, 1925, aged 57 years, 6 months and 4 days. At the age of sixteen he went with his parents to the state of Kansas and when about twenty years of age he came to Arkansas with his parents, settling at Maysville, Benton county. He was married to Anna Thompson December 7, 1895. To this union was born two daughters, Mrs. R.M. Dague and Miss Jennie Parkins, both of whom live in Oklahoma City. Following his marriage he lived in Gravette until about nineteen years ago when he removed to Rogers, Benton county, where he was employed at his trade of plumber and sheetmetal worker by E.C. Lone. He went to Oklahoma City seven years ago where he has since lived, working as a foreman of sheetmetal construction for a large contractor. [Rogers Democrat 9/24/25]

PARMENTER, Sidney B. - Sidney B. Parmenter, age 36, died at the home of his sister, Mrs. John B. Gann, Wednesday afternoon at 2:30. He is survived by a wife and two children and other relatives. Funeral services were held Thursday afternoon at the home at 2 o'clock and burial was made in the City Cemetery by the Carpenter Bros. Funeral Directors. [Gentry Journal-Advance 8/21/25]

PARRISH, Mrs. S.E. {Harper, Redman} - Mrs. S.E. Parrish was born in Jefferson county, Indiana Jan. 8, 1856 and died Jan. 20, 1925. At the age of 17 she joined the Congregational church. She was married to Jas. M. Harper Sept. 24, 1874 and joined the M.E. church to be with her husband in church affiliation. To this union were born three children, one daughter, who died in infancy, and two sons, A.C. Harper, who resides at Stilwell, Okla. and James A. Harper, who lives at Tulsa, Okla. After Jas. M. Harper died she married Jas. M. Redman. To this union was born a daughter who died Oct. 5, 1908. She was married to C.H. Parrish Nov. 3, 1917. Her husband and two sons were present at the funeral services. Her life was a benediction to all who knew her. Funeral services were conducted by the pastor, F.G. Villines, and S.F. Brown. Signed, S.F. Brown. [Gentry Journal-Advance 1/30/25]

PARROTT, G.H. - The body of G.H. Parrott, 36 years of age, arrived in Springdale the last of the week for burial. He was conductor with the C.B. & Q. railroad, making his home at Beardstown, Ill. He died of injuries received in a railroad accident. His mother, Mrs. Susan Parrott, lives at Springdale. [Rogers Democrat 4/2/25]

PATTERSON, Napoleon Bonapart - {from Cloverdale} Again our hearts have been made sad when God called from us a loved one, Mr. N.B. Patterson. He answered the call Sunday evening at 7 o'clock May 31, 1925 at the age of 73 years, 9 months and 27 days. Uncle Bone, as he was known, will be greatly missed in this community. He leaves to mourn his departure one son, John Patterson, three daughters, Mrs. Farmer Miller, Mrs. Albert Graham and Miss Dove Patterson, with whom he lived. All were at his side when death came. He also leaves a brother and a host of friends. The funeral was held Monday afternoon at Pleasant Hill under the direction of J.W. Bryant and services were conducted by Rev. Renfro and Rev. Hendrix. Interment was made in the Rogers cemetery by the side of his wife. [Benton County Democrat 6/4/25]

Napoleon Bonapart Patterson, better known as "Uncle Bone," was born in

Medford county, Tennessee Aug. 5, 1851, departed this life May 31, 1925 at the age of 73 years and 26 days. He had been a patient sufferer for several weeks but the kindly ministration of friends and loved ones made his last days easier to bear. He was married to Mattie S. Huffman Dec. 12, 1878 and to this union was born three children, Mrs. Albert Graham, Mrs. Farmer Miller and John J. Patterson, all of whom are still living and were at his bedside when he passed away. The mother of this family died Aug. 6, 1889. He then married Polly Ann Cox and to this union was born two children, one dying in infancy and the other, Dovie, with whom he made his home. He came to Benton county with his parents when only 2 years of age, settling on Pea Ridge. Another of our old landmarks has been felled by the grim reaper, Death. He will be greatly missed for he was a kind friend and loving father. [Rogers Democrat 6/11/25]

PATTISHALL, Jim - Jim Pattishall, aged 72 years, died last Saturday morning at ten o'clock at his home in Cave Springs after being ill but four days with pneumonia. Funeral services will be held Wednesday in order that his daughter who lives in Oregon may arrive to attend. He leaves four daughters, Mrs. Clarence Langley, Mrs. Burr Atkinson and Mrs. Walter Boyd {only three named}, and a son, Oscar, as well as his widow. [Benton County Record 12/25/25]

PATTON, Franklin Pierce - Entered this life July 24th, 1884. Entered into eternal life August 8th, 1925, Franklin Pierce Patton, son of James M. Patton, deceased, and Harriet Patton. Husband of Dennie Shepherd Patton. Father of Gladys, Mildred, Jewell and Ruth. His marriage occurred November 24th, 1909. Mr. Patton entered Sunday school as a small boy and in early youth was converted and united with the M.E. Church, South at Buttram's Chapel. From that time on he was noted for his piety, his activity in Sunday school work and his interest in the religious welfare of his community. He served his church as steward for fifteen years or more and during that period he also served in the Sunday school as superintendent, choir leader, faithful and efficient teacher of the Men's Bible class. Aside from his church activities Mr. Patton was a successful farmer and public school teacher and as such was highly esteemed by his pupils. Besides his wife, daughters and mother he leaves two brothers, Thomas and Boyd Patton, three sisters, Mrs. Z.B. Sims, Mrs. Harry Rice and Mrs. Henry Taylor, and other relatives to mourn his loss. Funeral services were conducted at Buttram's Chapel by Rev. W.T. Bone, his pastor, and Rev. Wilcoxon of Rogers Central Methodist Church, South in the presence of a large concourse of relatives and friends who gathered to pay their last tribute of respect to one whom they loved. [Rogers Democrat 8/27/25]

Frank Patton, a well-known resident on Pea Ridge, died at his home near Elkhorn Tavern on Saturday, August 8th, 1925 following an illness of about six months. Death was due to tuberculosis. He was about 40 years of age. Funeral services, which were held Sunday at Buttram's Chapel, was one of

the largest ever held there. Rev. Bone, assisted by Rev. Crichlow of Rogers, conducted the services. Besides his widow he leaves four daughters, the eldest of whom is sixteen, and a large number of relatives and friends to mourn his death. Mr. Patton was born on the old Patton homestead near his present home about 40 years ago. He was the son of Mr. and Mrs. J.N. Patton and had spent practically his entire life in that neighborhood. He was a member of the M.E. Church and for fifteen years faithfully acted as superintendent of the Sunday school at Central. He was also a justice of the peace and a school director. He was a broad-minded man and a friend and worker for better schools and communities. [Benton County Record 8/14/25]
{from Walnut Grove} Miss Anna Patton and her brother, Ernest Patton, and his family attended the funeral of Mr. Patton's cousin, Frank Patton, at Buttram's Chapel Sunday afternoon. [Benton County Record 8/14/25]

PAYNE, infant - {from Decatur} The infant of Mr. and Mrs. Lon Payne died Saturday. [Benton County Record 4/24/25]

PECK, Joshua Taylor - Joshua Taylor Peck died at the home of his daughter, Mrs. Dick Johnson, No. 725 North A street at 9:30 Tuesday morning. Death was the result of kidney trouble. Funeral services were held at the Johnson home Wednesday afternoon at 2:30 and were conducted by Rev. T.B. Clark of the First Christian church. Mr. Peck was born at Terre Haute, Ind. January 15, 1837, being 88 years, one month and two days of age at the time of his death. He was married to Miss Belinda Miller March 19, 1872 and to this union were born seven children. Three died before reaching man and womanhood. Besides his wife he leaves Mrs. Myrtle Lowry and Mrs. Dick Johnson of Rogers; Mrs. W.C. Campbell of Osawatomie, Kansas and Jim Peck of Neodesha, Kansas. Mr. Peck and family moved to this state 46 years ago and for the last 28 years he has been a resident of Rogers. He was known in the early history of Rogers as a stock buyer and was one of the leaders in the up-building of the town when it was begun. He was converted at an early age and was ever ready to do his duty as a Christian. To know Mr. Peck was to know a man held in high esteem by his friends, for his friends were numbered by his acquaintances. In business he was a man at any angle you looked at him. In his church he was a devout Christian gentleman and in his home a devoted husband and a loving father. To those in distress or need he was ever ready to help. In the death of Mr. Peck Rogers has lost one of its best citizens, the family a guiding hand and the friends a hearty welcome to his home. [Rogers Democrat 2/19/25]

PENDLEY, John - John Pendley, well known in the Gravette community, died at the County Home at 5:30 o'clock on Wednesday afternoon. Pendley was taken ill earlier in the day at the Beckett home north of Gravette where he had been staying but was brought to the County Home where he might have better care. An operation was found to be necessary but before this could be done the unfortunate man died. [Benton County Record 8/28/25]

PERRY, D.H. - {from Healing Springs} Mr. and Mrs. Brogan were called by long distance telephone to the bedside of Mrs. Brogan's father, D.H. Perry, at Johnson, Ark., who has been seriously ill for some time. Mr. Perry died on Wednesday, the 13th. [Benton County Record 1/23/25]
{from Rocky Comfort} Mr. and Mrs. Brogan attended the funeral of Mrs. Brogan's father which was held at Shady Grove cemetery near Springdale last Wednesday. [Benton County Record 1/23/25]

PERSON, R.C. - Mrs. A.M. Sherril received a message from Seligman last night informing her of the death of her uncle, R.C. Person. The Post carried an item a few weeks ago telling of the death of Mrs. Pearsons(?). They formerly lived southeast of Rogers. Mr. Piersons(?) worked all day yesterday apparently in his usual health but at suppertime was taken with a hemorrhage of the lungs which caused his death in a short time. [Rogers Daily Post 10/24/25]

PERSONS, Nannie - {from Osage Mills} R.A. Sikes received the sad news Sunday of the death of his sister, Mrs. Nannie Persons, of Seligman, Mo. Mrs. Persons had been in poor health for some time. Mr. and Mrs. Sikes attended the funeral at Seligman on Monday. We extend our heartfelt sympathy to them in this sad hour. [Benton County Record 9/25/25]

PETERSON, Mrs. - {from Valley View} Mrs. R. Ericson received the sad news of the death of her mother, Mrs. Peterson, of Nebraska which occurred on December 27th. [Benton County Record 1/9/25]

PETERSON, Mrs. O.T. - Word came this week of the death in Wichita, Kansas of Mrs. O.T. Peterson. Mrs. Peterson left here four or six weeks ago with her husband to make their home in that city. She had been in ill health for some time and the change was made to benefit her health. News of her death comes with much sorrow to her friends in this community. [Gentry Journal-Advance 10/30/25]

PHILPOT, Leta - {from Cave Springs} Miss Leta Philpot, after a lingering illness of several months, died Monday morning at the home of her father, Alex Philpot, who lives about two miles west of Cave Springs. Funeral services were held at the Phillips cemetery on Tuesday afternoon where interment was made. Surviving are her father, little sister, Guernie, and three brothers. [Benton County Record 1/2/25]
Miss Leta Philpot of the Osage community died Monday morning as the result of tuberculosis and from which she had been a sufferer for several years. [Benton County Democrat 1/1/25]

PICKENS, Robert Addison - Robert A. Pickens, pioneer, Confederate veteran, Mason, and one of the best loved and most highly respected citizens of Benton county, died at his home here Monday morning, aged 82 years. The enviable place held by Mr. Pickens and his family in the love and esteem of the people of Bentonville, Pea Ridge and throughout this section, was shown in the great number of friends, including Confederate veterans, who gathered in tribute to his memory on Wednesday afternoon when his funeral was held here at the Presbyterian church and interment made in the city cemetery. The impressive funeral service was conducted by Rev. A.W. Henderson, pastor of the Presbyterian church, assisted by Rev. J.L. Evans of the M.E. Church, South and by the Rev. Peter Carnahan, who, in spite of advanced years and failing health, beautifully eulogized the life of his old friend and comrade of the Confederate Army. Following the eulogy the Rev. Henderson read the following biographical sketch: Robert Addison Pickens was born at Richmond, Bedford county, Tennessee Nov. 27, 1842 and died at his home in Bentonville at 11:45 Monday morning, Jan. 19, 1925, aged 82 years, one month and 23 days. He was the son of Samuel and Susanna Morrison Pickens, natives of Tennessee who left that state in October of 1852 and located at this county at Pea Ridge, March 17, 1853. Three families of relatives, the Pickens family, the family of an uncle, Rev. Addison Morrison, who was a pioneer Presbyterian minister, and the family of William Morrison, came to Arkansas together and were members of the large group of Benton County pioneers who came from Tennessee, whose sturdy, honest qualities and whose interest in education, religion and good citizenship, made the community formed by them at Pea Ridge one of the most prominent and influential settlements in the state. The names of some of these pioneer families who came from Tennessee and which are well known in this section are Pickens, Hickman, Miser, Rice, Gamble, Patton, Patterson, Etris, Harston, Hardy, Burns, Dickson and Knott. They were families of influence in Tennessee and practically all of them were of Revolutionary and early colonial ancestry. Some affiliated families settled at Cane Hill in Washington county, which like Pea Ridge, in early days became a center of culture and learning. The homestead established by the Pickens family on Pea Ridge was the home of Mr. Pickens from the age of eleven years, when he arrived in Arkansas, throughout his long life with the exception of the time he lived in Bentonville. He lived here during his two terms as sheriff and on his retirement from active affairs in 1920 moved here. His parents died at the old family home before the war and are buried on Pea Ridge. Mr. Pickens was a Confederate soldier, having enlisted at Bentonville in Co. F, 15th Northwest Arkansas, of which Captain Thompson, and later Captain Etris, was in command. The late James and Robert Hickman, honored citizens of this community, were members of the same company. He took part in the battle of Pea Ridge, the battle of Iuka, Miss. and the siege of Vicksburg. After the siege of Vicksburg he was paroled and returned home but later became a member of Hawthorn's brigade of Churchill's division and took part in the battle at Mark's Hill and other engagements in south Arkansas, the last being Jenkins Ferry. After his discharge at the close of the war he returned to Pea Ridge. Mr. Pickens was a successful farmer until his health necessitated his retirement from active affairs some years ago. He has been for the past eighteen years a director of the Benton County National Bank of this city. He was elected sheriff and collector in 1900, serving two terms from 1900 until 1904. The family has always been interested in education and all other matters looking to the advancement of the community. His uncle, the Rev. Addison Morrison, pioneer Presbyterian minister, was instrumental in the establishment of an academy at Pea Ridge which became known in the early days of the state as a seat of learning and culture. The parents of Mr. Pickens were Presbyterians and he was brought up in that faith. In youth he joined the Cumberland Presbyterian church and he and Mrs. Pickens have always been faithful and influential members of the church, he being for many years a ruling elder. On Dec. 28, 1871 he was married to Miss Martha Alice Harston, daughter of Robert H. and Nancy Stroud Harston, who, with five sons and two daughters, survives him. His children are Dr. E.A. Pickens of Grove, Okla.; Dr. R.O. Pickens of Bentonville; E.C. Pickens of Bentonville; Mrs. L.E. Miller of Dallas, Texas; Dr. Wm. A. Pickens of Bentonville; Mrs. James McKinley of Tulsa; and Hunter C. Pickens of Dallas. A son, Dr. Lon O. Pickens of Ashland, Okla. and a daughter, Grace Pickens Broyles of Rudy, Ark., died in 1911. Mr. Pickens is also survived by a brother, Captain Cyrus L. Pickens, and a sister, Mrs. Mary Etta Pickens Miser, both of Pea Ridge, and 16 grandchildren, one of whom, Grace Pickens Broyles, has made her home with her grandparents since the death of her mother. [Benton County Democrat 1/22/25] [Benton County Record 1/23/25]

PICKRAN, Narcissus - Mrs. Narcissus Pickran, who for two years made her home at the County Home, after a few days of illness on October 1st, 1925 bade her friends a good-bye and went to be with her Lord whom she loved so tenderly. Grandmother Pickran was a most devout Christian and everyone who came and talked with her left feeling her influence and was constrained to live as she seemed to. She always had a word for her Christ who had done so much for her. Grandmother was 86 years and five months of age. She will be missed by those who knew her best. Rev. Joe M. Tyson conducted her funeral, assisted by Mrs. J.W. Centers. [Benton County Democrat 10/6/25]

PLUMLEE, Omer - Harrison, July 31.- Homer Scroggins and Omer Plumlee were killed and Ike and Jim Plumlee, brothers, were seriously, perhaps fatally, injured as the result of the premature explosion of a charge of dynamite on Hilltop road, near Harrison, early this afternoon. Several score of farmers witnessed the tragedy as the Hilltop road is a community road and is being built by labor supplied by farmers. How the accident occurred still remains a mystery for those who know how it really occurred are either dead or so seriously injured that they are unable to give an account of the tragedy. However it is known that the men were blasting a small stump that obstructed the right of way. The general belief is that the tragedy was caused by a poorly constructed fuse, which exploded the dynamite before the man had an opportunity to seek shelter. [Rogers Democrat 8/6/25]

POE, Ed - {from The Cassville Democrat} Ed Poe died at his home in Exeter last Thursday at the age of 45 years. He had engaged in business at that place but was forced to retire a short time ago on account of declining health. He leaves a wife and two children to mourn his passing. The remains were taken to Garfield, Ark. for interment. Mr. Poe was a good man and had many friends in his home town. [Rogers Democrat 10/29/25]

POLLOCK, Nancy Samantha LOCKE - Mrs. F.M. Pollock was born Dec. 20, 1852 and died at Rogers, Ark. June 14, 1925, aged 72 years, 5 months and 24 days. She was married February 9, 1871 to F.M. Pollock, who, with two sons, J.A. Pollock and J.F. Pollock, both of Rogers, four daughters, Mrs. Lee Williams, Newberg, Mo.; Mrs. Stanley Hoy, Lusk, Wyoming; Mrs. Belle Bradin, Omaha, Neb., and Mrs. Clarence Hampton, Bakersfield, Calif., survive her. The last three named could not be here. They came to Arkansas about 1876 and by this long residence here the deceased and her family became widely known and is one of the oldest residents. Mrs. Pollock had been an invalid for many years, also losing her sight many years ago and to add to these afflictions she fell early last winter and broke a hip, thus making her a helpless sufferer. Funeral services were held yesterday afternoon at the home on the east side at 2:30 and were conducted by Rev. J.T. Willcoxon, pastor of the Central M.E. church, South of which the deceased had been a member for many years. Burial was in Rogers cemetery. [Rogers Democrat 6/18/25]

Nancy Samantha Locke was born in Bedford County, Tennessee and died at her home in Rogers June 14, aged 72 years, 5 months, 24 days. She was married to F.M. Pollock February 9, 1871. To this union were born seven children, six of whom are living. They are Mrs. Belle Bredin, Omaha, Neb.; Mrs. Hattie Hampton, Bakersfield, Calif.; Mrs. Lee Williams, Newberg, Mo.; Mrs. Stanley Hoy, Lusk, Wyo. and John and Jim of Rogers. Mr. and Mrs. Pollock moved to Rogers in 1878, forty-seven years ago, and were prominent in the building of Rogers, Mr. Pollock having laid the first stone and the first brick in the town. Four of their seven children were born here and raised to manhood and womanhood. "Grandma" Pollock, as she was affectionately known, was stricken with blindness 28 years ago but this did not interfere with her household duties, her home was a model of neatness and all these years she did her cooking. She was the victim of a fall last October and broke her hip. From this she became bed-fast and suffered much until death released her. Mrs. Pollock was known as a good neighbor, helping those in need and encouraging those who needed help. She was an exemplary wife and an excellent mother. The funeral arrangements will not be made until the arrival of Mrs. Bredin from Bakersfield{?} who is expected to reach here Wednesday. Mrs. Williams came last week. The other two daughters will not be able to come. The services will be held

at the home in the south part of town. Rev. J.T. Willcoxen will preach the sermon. [Rogers Daily Post 5/15/25]
The funeral of Mrs. F.M. Pollock was held yesterday morning at the family home, Rev. Willcoxen conducting the services. The profusion of flowers attested the esteem in which the family, which are among the pioneers of Rogers, is held. The daughter who started Saturday from Bakersfield, California Saturday arrived here today at noon, having been detained 12 hours behind a wreck. Since no word was received from Mrs. Hampton it was thought she had changed her mind about coming. [Rogers Daily Post 6/18/25]

POTTS, Wayman - Wayman Potts, age ten years, son of Mr. and Mrs. Marion Potts of Spring Valley, Washington county, was instantly killed Sunday morning on the Jasper road south of Harrison when a truck in which he was riding toppled over a 75 foot bluff. The child's body is said to have been ground almost to a pulp, but three other passengers, the elder Potts, Gulley Pigg and Jim Phillips, all of Valley Springs, were unhurt. The wreck was viewed by several Fayetteville parties making the trip to Diamond Cave who found the three men hysterical and unable to give a coherent account of the accident, details of which were secured later by telephone. The remains of the child and the men, including the bereaved father, were taken to Harrison by a passenger automobile. Potts, Sr. is an employee of the state forest service reserve and with his son had started for one of the forests where they and Phillips had expected to camp. The truck was loaded with supplies and corn. The great weight caused the vehicle to topple over the bank when the driver went too near the edge of the bluff. The truck was wrecked. [Benton County Record 7/10/25] [Rogers Daily Post 7/8/25]

PRESTON, T.T. - Rogers relatives received word Friday of the death of T.T. Preston at Lawrence, Kansas after an illness of some months. Funeral services were held at Lawrence Sunday and the body then taken to the former home of the deceased at Corning, Iowa for interment. The deceased is survived by his wife and three sons. Mr. Preston was a resident of Rogers some fifteen years ago, being associated with E.W. Homan in the laundry business. He married Miss Virgie Puckett of Rogers, a sister of Miss Grace and Will A. Puckett of this city. Mrs. Preston will remain in Lawrence, at least until after the close of school this spring. [Rogers Democrat 2/5/25]

PREUS, Frank - Frank Preus, who had been ill for several weeks and was taken to Fayetteville for an operation, died there Saturday night and was buried at that place Sunday. Mr. Preus will be missed by Rogers citizens as he conducted a shoe shop here for a number of years. [Rogers Democrat 6/18/25]

PRICE, Edith May ENFIELD - Mrs. Oscar Price died Monday, January 19th at her home southwest of Rogers in the Oak Hill neighborhood, at the age of 39 years, seven months and twenty days. Funeral services were held Tuesday, conducted by Rev. A.A. DuLaney of the First Baptist church of Rogers. Edith May Price, daughter of Eli and Sarah Enfield, was born May 9, 1885 in Lyons, Kansas and was united in marriage to Oscar Price July 30, 1903. To them were born seven children of whom two died in infancy and five are living: Oscar Price, the oldest son, is in California, and Archie, Geneva, Gladys and Violet were at the bedside of their mother. Besides the five children she leaves two brothers and three sisters. Her husband passed away about five years ago. In her young life she gave her heart to God and united with the Baptist church at Hutchinson, Kansas. [Rogers Democrat 1/22/25]

PROPHET, Samuel J. - Samuel J. Prophet died at his home three miles west of Pea Ridge on February 12th, 1925 at 10 o'clock a.m. at the age of 83 years, two months and two days. He was born in McMinn county, Tenn. on December 10th, 1841 and moved to Missouri in 1852 and from there to Arkansas in 1900. He professed religion when 12 years of age and united with the M.E. Church, South and was a faithful attendant of the church of his choice as long as he was able to go. He has been afflicted for several years and bore his affliction as one who has the blessed assurance of a perfect day. On November 17th, 1865 he was married to Margaret Thurman. To this union was born eleven children, six of whom have passed on before. His life-long companion and three children were with him when the end came. He leaves his wife, five children, ten grandchildren and a host of friends who will greatly miss him. Funeral services were held at the home on the 13th at 1 p.m., conducted by Rev. Bone, and the body was laid to rest in the Pea Ridge cemetery. [Benton County Record 2/20/25]

PRUES, Frank - Frank Prues, who has been ill for some time and who recently underwent an operation in the City Hospital at Fayetteville, died Saturday night and was buried at that place in the Catholic cemetery. Mr. Prues, with an aunt who kept house for him, came to Rogers several years ago. He has conducted a shoe shop ever since coming to this city and will be greatly missed by his many patrons. [Rogers Daily Post 6/15/25]

PRUITT, Harrison - {from Centerton} Harrison Pruitt, an old resident of the Vaughn community, died at the home of his daughter, Mrs. James Harrel of this place, late Tuesday night. Funeral services were held on Wednesday afternoon with interment in the Barron cemetery. [Benton County Record 9/11/25]

PRUITT, W.R. - W.R. Pruitt, aged 75, died Monday at the home of his daughter, Mrs. Walter Dillo, in the Miller neighborhood northwest of Bentonville. Funeral services were conducted at the church Tuesday by Rev. O.A. Fortune. He is survived by the married daughter with whom he made his home. He has been a resident of this community for nearly 25 years. [Benton County Record 2/13/25]

PRUITT, William Campbell - William Campbell Pruitt died Monday, Feb. 9th at his home near the Miller school house northwest of Bentonville, aged 70 years, one month and eight days. Funeral services, conducted by Rev. O.A. Fortune of the Bentonville M.E. Church, were held Tuesday afternoon and interment made in the Miller community. [Benton County Democrat 2/12/25]

PURCELL, Mrs. - {from Pea Ridge} Funeral services were held at the M.E. Church Monday afternoon for Mrs. Purcell. [Benton County Record 1/23/25]

PURYEAR, Sophia CARY - {from Hiwasse} Mrs. J.H. Puryear, living near Mt. Pleasant, passed away Wednesday, January 7th. Heart trouble was the cause of her death. She is survived by her husband. [Benton County Record 1/16/25]

Mrs. Sophia Puryear, wife of John Puryear of Hiwasse vicinity, died at her home on January 7, 1925, aged about 73 years. Mrs. Puryear, formerly Sophia Cary, was born in Illinois Jan. 31, 1852. She was married to Mr. Puryear in 1877 in Missouri. They had no children. Mrs. Puryear leaves, besides her husband, two brothers, J. and T.F. Cary of Illinois, a nephew, J.C. Cary, and two nieces, Mrs. H.L. Davidson and Mrs. G. Gatton, and other relatives. Burial services were held at Mt. Pleasant at which place the body was laid to rest. Mr. Puryear, left alone, is selling his property this week, today, at a public sale and will reside with his nephew, Jesse Puryear. [Gravette News-Herald 1/23/25]

PYEATT, Elizabeth J. PAYNE - {from Fairview Chapel} Elizabeth J. Payne, born Aug. 4, 1854 in East Tennessee, died March 14, 1925. She moved to Arkansas with her parents in 1875; was married to W.A. Pyeatt in 1882. She is survived by one son, Henry Pyeatt of this place, also two brothers and two sisters and other relatives. She had been a member of the Methodist church since girlhood. [Gravette News-Herald 3/20/25]

QUEENE, John - While stripping the soil from a gravel pit on the R.R. Turner land two miles west of Grand River bridge on Friday the workmen unearthed what proved to be the remains of a man. G.P. Stone brought the relics to town with a view to getting some light on the matter. In the meantime Will Ballard, who has lived all his life in the vicinity, came forward with the statement that the grave was that of a man named John Queene, who died 55 years ago of pneumonia and at his request was buried at the place described. As usually happens when burial is outside of regular cemeteries, this unmarked grave was, in the course of time, forgotten, and many years ago a house was built directly on the grave. This house was removed in order to get it out of the way of the gravel haulers. [Benton County Democrat 8/18/25]

RAKES, Irene MARTIN Webb - The burial of Mrs. D.C. Rakes was held Friday afternoon from the family residence south of Bentonville, interment taking place in the Hart cemetery. The Rev. Taylor of Garfield officiated at the services. Mrs. Rakes, who was 90 years old, died on Thanksgiving Day at her home. Mrs. Rakes, who was Irene Martin before her marriage, was born in Carroll county, Va. on October 2nd, 1835. She married at a young age to Enoch Webb also of Carroll county. To this union three boys and two girls were born. Enoch Webb was killed in the early part of the Civil War through which Mrs. Rakes spent the entire time near the actual fighting. In 1866 she married D.C. Rakes in Carroll county. To them five boys, Albert, John, Joe, Asa and Rush were born, and one daughter, Mary Wallace, who now lives in Cave Springs. The family came to Arkansas in 1906, settling near Centerton where they have all lived. Mr. Rakes died in April of 1921. Mrs. Rakes joined the Trinity Baptist Church over fifty years ago and since that time has been a goodly worker in the church and a profound Christian. Mrs. Rakes was known for her Christian kindness and was loved by her co-workers. For some time previous to her death Mrs. Rakes was in failing health and the end had been looked for for some time. The entire community mourns the death of the woman and offers the deepest sympathy to her sons, all five of whom live in or near Centerton. All of the children by her first marriage are living in Virginia excepting one son, who resides in Ohio. [Benton County Record 12/4/25] [Benton County Democrat 12/1/25]

RAND, Stephen Leander - {Credit for this item was not given.} Stephen Leander Rand, only son of the late Stephen and Susan Watson Rand, was born at Highland, Wisconsin, November 3, 1852 and passed away at the home of his friends, Mr. and Mrs. O.U. Sisson, in Chicago while there on a visit, on Friday, February 20, 1925. He and his wife had come two weeks previous on a visit from their home in Gentry, Ark. He was married June 10, 1884 to Virginia A., second daughter of the late Mr. and Mrs. Wm. A. Pierce at Mineral Point, Wis. The only near relative to mourn his going is his wife as there was no family. In April 1913 he moved from Chicago to Gentry, Ark as he owned an orchard there and as an orchardist had made a success of it. Burial was at Mineral Point, Wis. Tuesday afternoon, February 24 at 2:00 p.m. from the Congregational church, Rev. Norman Henderson of Madison, Wis. assisting the pastor of the church at the services. Burial was at Graceland cemetery. [Gentry Journal-Advance 2/27/25]

RAY, Tom - Tom Ray of Marble, Madison county, died a week ago at the age of 71 years, most of his life having been spent in the community where he died. [Rogers Democrat 11/26/25]

REED, E.T. - E.T. Reed, age 78 years, died at his home near Gentry on Thursday, June 25, 1925. Mr. Reed was born in Knox county, Ohio, moving to this community in March 1919. He is survived by his widow, Mrs. Annie Reed, and 13 children by a former marriage. His son, E.T. Reed, Jr. of Thomas, Okla. was with him during his last sickness and death and accompanied his remains to Nevisville, Iowa for burial. Mr. Reed was a trainer and fancier of fine horses. The big black horse that was owned and driven by him was left to Marion Wasson, president of the First National Bank. [Gentry Journal-Advance 7/3/25]

REED, Ira - {from Highfill} Courtland High, telegraph operator at Joplin for the Frisco, came in Thursday for his grandmother, Mrs. Ira Reed, who will make her home with him since the death of her husband who died at the Mallory farm. [Gentry Journal-Advance 2/27/25]

REED, Jake - {from Cave Springs} Jake Reed, who has been an invalid for years, died at one o'clock Friday afternoon. Funeral services were held at the Elm Springs cemetery where the burial was made Saturday. Quite a number of people from Cave Springs attended the funeral and the sympathy of the entire community is extended to the family. [Benton County Record 7/3/25]

REYNOLDS, Edward J. - {from Springtown} The funeral of Uncle Ed Reynolds, conducted by Rev. Masters at the Baptist church, was attended by a large crowd. Interment was made in the Springtown cemetery. [Gentry Journal-Advance 5/1/25]

Edward J. Reynolds was born June 11, 1858 in what was then Caufman county, Texas. He died April 16, 1925 in Benton county, Ark. where his home had been since childhood. He was married December 12, 1878 to Miss Louisa A. Garrett, who survives him. To this union were born 10 children, seven of whom live to mourn his loss. The other three died in infancy. He professed a hope in Christ at the age of 12 years and soon afterwards united with the Baptist church at Springtown. He was ordained to the work of the gospel ministry March 10, 1895 in the church at Cross Roads, of which he was then a member. He became a member of the church at Shady Grove at the time of its organization and his membership was in this church till the time of his death. [Gentry Journal-Advance 5/15/25]

RICE, J.R. - {from The Springdale News} J.R. Rice was killed about ten o'clock Wednesday morning a short distance south of Sonora, being run over by a wagon heavily loaded with wood, drawn by a pair of burros. The accident was witnessed by a daughter of Calvin Johnson who was working in a field near by. Mr. Rice was placed on a cot and lived about an hour and a half after being injured and died just as the attending physician and friends carried him to the store at Sonora, having been semi-conscious and suffering intensely. The wheels of the wagon passed over his body, crushing his ribs. Burial was Thursday morning in Bluff cemetery. Mr. Rice was a well known character around Springdale, owning nothing but his wagon and a pair of burros, old and tired, but never owning defeat in spite of the fact that one hand was off at the wrist. No one can vouch for his age though he must have been between 75 and 80. In all kinds of weather one could see him, whip in one hand and the reins to his team of burros wrapped around the stub on his other arm, and a load of wood in his wagon, always industrious. He lived to himself and whether he has a living relative remains to be learned. Two letters were found in his shack, both from his brother in Iowa, one dated January 1918 and the other in February of the same year. Efforts are being made to ascertain his whereabouts. It is thought Mr. Rice, in guiding his team down the hill, was making an effort to hold them back as he walked beside the wagon when his foot slipped, throwing him under the wheels. All Springdale and vicinity will miss the familiar sight of the elderly little man with the team of burros that had been on the streets and roads for so long a time. Mr. Rice formerly resided on the Becker property at the foot of the mountain east of town but about two years ago he moved on the old J.W. Grider place, one and one-half miles southeast of Sonora. [Rogers Democrat 7/30/25] [Rogers Daily Post 7/24/25]

RICH, Chas. O. - Chas. O. Rich was born at Fort Scott, Kansas and departed this life October 30, 1925 at 3:00 o'clock a.m. at his home near Avoca. He was united in marriage to Miss Maude M. Rowe August 12, 1899 and to this union were born eight children - four boys and four girls, two of them preceding him to the great beyond. He leaves to mourn his loss a wife and six children; a mother, eight brothers and one sister and a host of friends. The last few weeks of his life he suffered much but always enjoyed having the saints to pray with him. Funeral services were held at the home October 31st. Interment in the McDaniel cemetery. C.B. Huff. [Rogers Democrat 11/5/25]

{from Mountain View} Charlie Rich was born in February 1874 and died October 30th. He leaves a wife and six children: Mrs. Ethel Bradley, Floyd Rich, Zola May, Arthur, Burley and Hazel Rich, a mother and eight brothers and one sister. The children were all present at the funeral save Miss Hazel who is in Oklahoma and did not get the telegram in time to come. Bro. Ben Huff preached the funeral sermon and he was laid to rest in the McDaniel cemetery. Mr. Rich had lived in Rogers several years but had traded his property there for a small farm here. Mr. Rich had not been in good health for a long time. He had a nervous breakdown this fall from which he never recovered. Friends extend sympathy to Mrs. Rich and family in their hour of sorrow. [Rogers Democrat 11/5/25]

RICHARDSON, mother - {from Gentry} J.E. Richardson received a message Friday evening telling of the death of his mother at Olathe, Kansas. [Benton County Record 2/13/25]

RIDER, Barney - {from Central} Barney Rider died February 23rd at Baxter Springs, Kansas and the body will be brought back here and buried today {Tuesday} at Buttram's Chapel. [Rogers Democrat 3/5/25]

RIGGS, James M. - James M. Riggs died Monday, November 23d, at his home at No. 122 North Fourth Street. Funeral services were held Tuesday afternoon at the Methodist church at Springdale where the deceased lived before coming to Rogers and the sermon was preached by Rev. J.T. Willcoxon of Rogers. Burial was in the Bluff Cemetery at Springdale. Mr. Riggs was 70 years old in September and was born in Montgomery City, Mo. He was married December 27, 1882 to Miss Anna Etta Smith and their early married life was spent in Vandalia, Mo. Mr. Riggs is survived by his wife and six sons: R.E. Riggs, Pocahontas, Ark.; H.S. Riggs, Wellington, Texas; and W.R. Riggs, C.S. Riggs, J.B. Riggs and G.M. Riggs, all of Rogers. [Rogers Democrat 11/26/25]

ROBBINS, Charles Hurley - Charles Hurley Robbins, son of Neely and Martha Robbins, was born in 1896 at the old Robbins home 1½ miles east of Bentonville, Ark. and died January 31, 1925 at Mills, N.M., age 29 years. He and his wife and two children went to New Mexico last August for his health. With a change of climate he seemed better for awhile but about two months ago he again began to fail rapidly. He is survived by four brothers, Floyd of Gravette, Will and Earl of Bentonville, Ark. and Preston of Cyclone, Mo. Hurley was cared for in his last days by J.O. Baker, an old friend who moved to New Mexico a few years ago from Jane, Mo. He was laid to rest in the Mills cemetery. [Benton County Democrat 2/5/25] [Benton County Record 2/6/25]

ROBBINS, Charles Lester - Charles Lester Robbins died at his home in Bentonville on Sunday evening, November 29th, 1925 of heart trouble after an illness of nearly one year. He was 47 years old. Funeral services were held at the M.E. Church, South on Tuesday afternoon, the Rev. Stephen A. Morton officiating. The funeral was largely attended. Besides his widow, Mrs. Lulu Robbins, he is survived by one son, Sherman Robbins, and two daughters, Frances and Virginia, also by his mother, Mrs. N.H. Robbins, two brothers, Homer and Henry Robbins, all of Bentonville and a sister, Mrs. G.C. Lipscomb, of Polytechnic, Texas. Charles L. Robbins was born on the old family homestead east of Bentonville on April 26th, 1878. He had lived in Bentonville and vicinity all his life. On November 25th, 1904 he was married to Miss Lulu Kate Howard, daughter of Mr. and Mrs. J.W. Howard. Both families were prominent pioneers of this section. [Benton County Democrat 12/1/25] [Benton County Record 12/18/25]

ROBBINS, John - {from Highfill} John Robbins, brother of Jack Robbins, passed away on Sunday morning at seven o'clock. He had been operated on for appendicitis about a week ago at a hospital in Rogers and it was thought he was doing as well as possible until a few days prior to his death. His home is in the Oak Grove neighborhood. Burial was made at Elm Springs on Monday. [Benton County Record 9/18/25]

ROBERTSON, John - John, the 8-year-old son of J.A. Robertson, Jr. and wife, died last Thursday morning the result of an attack of typhoid fever with which he had been afflicted for several months. Funeral services were held at the Church of Christ Friday afternoon. The boy was thought to be improving and the sudden death came as a great shock to the family, relatives and friends. [Rogers Democrat 7/9/25]

A shock came to the many friends of the J.A. Robertson family this morning when word was sent of the death of their eight year old son, John, which occurred this morning at 7:30. John and his eleven year old brother, Jack, have been the victims of typhoid fever for more than eight weeks and while Jack is gaining rapidly it was thought that John had passed the crisis and was on the road to recovery. This morning about three o'clock he was given some nourishment and turning over dropped off to sleep. At three-thirty he awoke with convulsions and passed away a few hours later. The funeral will be held tomorrow afternoon at the Church of Christ. Besides his parents he is survived by one brother and other relatives among whom is Miss Bert Robertson who has spent every night for two months caring for the little fellow who made such a game fight to get well. [Rogers Daily Post 7/2/25]

ROBINETT, John - {from Clantonville} John Robinett was born July 23, 1851, died April 22, 1925. In 1876 he was married to Ellen Forgey. Lived on his farm three-quarters of a mile north of Clantonville most of his life. To this union were born two children, Effie and Maggie, the latter, Mrs. Maggie Roller, having departed this life two years ago. Effie still lives, working in Kansas City for some time. His first wife having died in 1878 he was married to Diana Williams in 1879. And to them were born six boys and two girls. Two boys, one an infant, and David, 21 years old, preceding their father to the Great Beyond. Michael and Della live in Kansas City and the remainder, Winter, Oscar, Charlie and Etta live near the old home place, all are married except Winter. Uncle John, as all know him, left a large circle of friends to mourn his departure. He was of a jolly disposition, had nothing displeasing to say of anyone and his many friends and relatives will miss him. He had a complication of diseases, some of them being Bright's Disease, lung trouble and flu. The funeral was preached by Rev. Monta Taylor at the home and his body was laid to rest in the Roller cemetery. Much sympathy was extended to him and family during his sickness and a large crowd of sympathizers gathered at the home and accompanied the body to its resting place. [Rogers Democrat 4/30/25]

ROBINSON, Allen - Allen Robinson died last week at Huntsville at the age of 77 years. He was the father of Mrs. G.W.R. Keck, who lives southwest of town. [Rogers Democrat 1/1/25]

RODMAN, Mrs. W.C. - R.C. Benbrook and wife went to Harrison the last of the week, called by the death of Mrs. R.C. Rodman, mother of Mrs. Benbrook. Interment was at Calico Rock. [Rogers Democrat 9/24/25] [Rogers Daily Post 9/18/25]

ROGERS, Betty Lou - Betty Lou, little 4 year old daughter of Mr. and Mrs. Auda Rogers, passed away in a Joplin hospital Tuesday, June 22. She had never enjoyed good health during her brief stay in her home. All that could be was done for her but God called her to be with Him. Funeral services were held Tuesday afternoon and burial was made in the city cemetery. Mr. and Mrs. Rogers and the little children are left to mourn her going. [Gentry Journal-Advance 6/26/25]

ROLLER, infant - {from Clantonville} The infant son of Mr. and Mrs. Marshall Roller was laid to rest in the Roller cemetery Saturday. Mrs.

Roller's mother, Mrs. Pendergraft, from Seligman, is remaining with her during her sickness. Marshall arrived home Sunday from Picher, Okla. where he has been employed. [Rogers Democrat 7/9/25]

ROLLER, G.W. - G.W. Roller died February 22nd at his home at Seligman at the age of 81 years. He fell several weeks ago and had been confined until the day of his death. [Rogers Democrat 3/5/25]

ROLLER, J.V. - {from Clantonville} It is with great sorrow that we report the death of J.V. Roller, living about 1/4 mile south of this place. He fell suddenly Monday evening and the doctor was called and pronounced it a broken blood vessel. He died suddenly. Was buried in Missouri in what is known as the Pad Roller cemetery Tuesday evening. Funeral services were preached at the home by Rev. Monta Taylor. [Rogers Democrat 8/20/25]

RONE, Wiley - {from Decatur} Wiley Rone died suddenly on Thursday, March 5th, 1925 of apoplexy. That morning he was perfectly well and worked in the woods helping his brother-in-law, Rev. John Scoggin, saw wood. Just before noon he complained of feeling poorly and went home. He grew worse and died suddenly. He was about 55 years old and is survived by a wife and several relatives. [Benton County Record 3/13/25]

ROSE, R.E. - Springdale, July 17.- R.E. Rose, 14 years old, son of Mrs. Minnie Rose of Wichita Falls, Texas, was badly scalded on the body from neck to waist Tuesday afternoon when a gallon bucket of hot water exploded, quantities of the water and steam penetrating his outer clothing and underwear and almost cooking the flesh underneath. Mrs. Rose, who is the wife of a railroad man in Wichita Falls, Texas, arrived in Springdale Monday evening and with her four children registered for room and board at the Commercial hotel. Tuesday afternoon the Rose boy wished to demonstrate to Mrs. Langford's son, Lonnie, 14 years old, how to make a steam engine with a gallon bucket filled with water, one small hole in the lid and a fire underneath. Mrs. Langford had discouraged the idea of the prank but the boys were eager for the experiment and hid themselves beneath a bridge back of the hotel with the explosion as a result. [Rogers Democrat 7/23/25]

ROSS, Wells A. - W.A. Ross died at his home at Wichita, Kansas Monday, March 23d after a brief illness of only ten days. The body arrived in Rogers yesterday morning accompanied by Mrs. Ross, Lloyd Ross and family and Mrs. J.F. Taylor of Fort Scott, Kansas. Funeral services were held at the First Methodist Church at 3:30 and were conducted by the pastor, R.C. Lucke. Interment in city cemetery. Wells A. Ross was born in Pennsylvania December 6, 1852 and was a son of the late Rev. J.A. Ross, who died here two years ago. He married Julia A. Lester in Ohio in 1878 and to them were born four children, three of whom are living - Frank W. Ross and J.A. Ross of Conneaut, Ohio and Lloyd Ross of Wichita, Kansas. Mrs. Ross died in Ohio in 1891. After the death of his wife Mr. Ross and son, Lloyd, came west and lived in Kansas and Louisiana before locating in Rogers in 1906.

Since that time he has lived in Rogers and Wichita. He was married Sept. 4, 1910 to Mrs. Sarah A. Taylor of Rogers who survives him. He is also survived by his sister, Mrs. T.A. Winkleman of Rogers. By occupation Mr. Ross was a carpenter and contractor. He was a member of the I.O.O.F. and the Encampment, holding his membership at the time of his death at Ashtabula, Ohio. His membership in the Canton was in Wichita. He was a member of the Methodist church from his youth and served as a supply preacher at several points. He was an exemplary citizen where ever he had lived and was ever held in high esteem by his friends and associates. [Rogers Democrat 3/26/25]

ROTRAMMEL, Henderson - {from High Top} Mr. and Mrs. Jake Holland and Mr. and Mrs. Walter Cox attended the funeral of Mrs. Holland's uncle, Henderson Rotrammel, at Mt. Pleasant Monday. Mr. Rotrammel died in the Hospital for Nervous Diseases at Little Rock last week. He had been there for almost three years. [Benton County Record 9/11/25]

ROULHAC, J.P.G. - {from Pea Ridge} Prof. J.P.G. Roulhac, Jr. received a message Sunday morning stating that his father, J.P.G. Roulhac, had just passed away at Phoenix, Arizona where he and his wife were spending the winter. The body will be brought back to Fayetteville for burial. Mr. Roulhac was about 78 years old and had lived on his farm near Greenwood for 25 years. He retired from his farm about a year ago and moved to Fayetteville. His widow and nine children survive him. [Benton County Record 1/16/25]

J.P.G. Roulhac, 78, died recently at Phoenix, Arizona and the body was brought back to Fayetteville for interment. He was the father of Prof. J.P.G. Roulhac, Jr. of Rogers. [Rogers Democrat 1/22/25]

ROYAL, Mrs. Charles - Mrs. Charles Royal, aged 28, and her mother, Mrs. H. Carmen, of Goodman, Mo. were almost instantly killed and Mrs. A. Lanke of Kansas City, a daughter of Mrs. Carmen, badly injured when they were struck by a Hudson car driven by Doyle Phipps of Fayetteville. The accident happened Monday night as Phipps, accompanied by Fay Reed and Edgar Summers of that city, was returning home from Kansas City. The three women were walking along the highway toward their home when they were struck by Phipps' car which, it was estimated by witnesses, was traveling at least 40 miles an hour. Mrs. Royal's husband, who was walking a short distance ahead of the women, said that he did not notice the approach of the car until it struck them. Mrs. Carmen's body was badly mangled and Mrs. Royal was run over by the car. Mrs. Lanke was dragged about 30 feet by the car and was badly bruised. She may recover. Phipps was arrested for manslaughter and taken to the Pineville jail where he was released on a $4,000 bond. Feeling runs high in Goodman over the tragedy. Goodman is about 20 miles south of Joplin on the Bentonville-Joplin highway. Phipps is noted for being a fast driver and was recently publicly scored by Herbert R. Wilson, state highway commissioner, for driving from Little Rock to Fayetteville at an average speed of 50 miles an hour. He was later fined $100 and costs for this offense in Van Buren. [Benton County Record 7/31/25]

RUTHERFORD, Mrs. Rufus - {from Highfill} Mrs. Rufus Rutherford passed away at the home of her son, Tom Rutherford, on Tuesday evening, Jan. 21st at about 4 o'clock. The funeral services were held Wednesday afternoon at 2 o'clock at the Baptist church in Springtown. She was laid to rest in the Springtown cemetery. Bro. Reynolds, her pastor and a life long friend of the family, conducted the services. [Benton County Democrat 2/5/25] [Benton County Record 2/6/25]

SAFFER, C.L. - C.L. Saffer, a former Bentonville resident living on East Eleventh Street, died at his home in Bunker Hill, Ill. on Friday, June 12th. Funeral services were held in Bunker Hill Sunday afternoon at 2 o'clock and burial was made in the cemetery there. He is survived by his wife and an adopted daughter. [Benton County Record 6/19/25]

SCHAUM, Jacob - Jacob Schaum, a resident of Bentonville for 34 years, died at his home near Park Springs suddenly on Saturday, May 23rd, 1925 at 1:15 o'clock. Funeral services, conducted by Rev. A.W. Henderson, were held at the Presbyterian Church Sunday afternoon and interment made in the city cemetery. He was born in Notzinger in the Kingdom of Wittenburg, Germany on Aug. 16th, 1845. He came to America in 1868, coming to Illinois, where he settled at Brighton in Macoupin county. That same year he united with the German Methodist Church. In 1872 he was married to Miss Emma McMinamie. To this union was born 4 children, one of whom died in infancy, a son died in young manhood and a daughter who also died in early life. Mrs. Schaum died in Brighton, Ill. in 1882. He was married the second time to Mrs. Anna Urbach in St. Louis in 1890. Five children were born to this union, one of whom died in infancy. Mr. Schaum moved his family to Arkansas in 1891 and purchased land in the Miller neighborhood northwest of Bentonville where he lived before locating in Bentonville. He united with the Presbyterian church in the Miller neighborhood and transferred his membership to the local church. He is survived by his wife, Mrs. Annie Schaum and 5 daughters: Mrs. Anderson, Greenville, Ala.; Mrs. Rex Chambers and Mrs. George Rakes of Bentonville; Miss Louise Schaum, Joplin, Mo.; Miss Lora Schaum, Fort Smith, two step children, Mrs. Jess Crabaugh, Bentonville; and Gus Urbach, Kansas City. Also a sister in Germany, one brother in Eustis, Nebraska and ten grandchildren. [Benton County Record 5/29/25] [Benton County Democrat 5/28/25]

SCHELL, Mrs. S.J. - {from Pea Ridge} Mrs. S.J. Schell, who lived four miles north of Pea Ridge near Jacket, Mo., died last Saturday, leaving besides her husband, five children, two of whom are twins four weeks old. [Benton County Record 3/6/25]

SCROGGIN, Grandma - {from Eagle Corner} Grandma Scroggin, who died suddenly at her home Wednesday morning, Sept. 23, was buried at the Coffelt cemetery Sunday afternoon. Bro. Rice of Springdale preached the funeral sermon. Her sons, Allison of Highlands, Calif. and Granville of Fredonia, Kans., came home for the funeral, and her sister, Mrs. Perryman of Tulsa, was also present. [Benton County Record 10/2/25]

SCROGGINS, Mrs. Wiltz - {from Vaughn} Mrs. Wiltz Scroggins of near Eagle Corner, who died Tuesday night, was buried at the Coffelt cemetery Sunday afternoon, Rev. Rice of Springdale conducting the service. [Benton County Record 10/2/25]

SCROGHAM, W.G. - W.G. Scrogham, well known citizen of Bentonville, died at his home on West Eighth street this {Thursday} morning at 1:30 o'clock, aged 53 years, death resulting from a stroke of paralysis suffered late Sunday afternoon, Jan. 18. Mr. Scrogham, who was a carpenter and contractor, moved to Bentonville with his family about five years ago from Texas. He had lived also in Oklahoma. Since making their home in Bentonville Mr. and Mrs. Scrogham and children have made a host of friends who deeply sympathize with the family in its great loss. Besides his wife Mr. Scrogham is survived by two daughters and two small sons and other relatives in Kentucky, Texas and other states. Mr. Howard of Lexington, Ky. was called here several days ago on account of his son-in-law's serious illness. Funeral services will be held Friday afternoon at 2:30 o'clock at the Christian church, conducted by Rev. S.A. Morton and interment made in the city cemetery. [Benton County Democrat 1/29/25]
W.G. Scrogham, who was stricken with paralysis on January 18th, passed away early Thursday morning at his home in the north part of Bentonville at the age of 57 years. Funeral services will be held from the home Friday. Besides his widow he is survived by two sons, Howard and Marion, and two daughters, Eva and Blanche Scrogham. Mr. Scrogham was born in Kentucky and came to Bentonville from Shawnee, Okla. He was a carpenter by trade and considered one of the best in the city. [Benton County Record 1/30/25]

SEAMSTER, Robert Asbury - Robert Asbury Seamster of Graham, Tex. died at the home of his brother, Alvin Seamster, near Bentonville last Monday afternoon, Feb. 16, 1925, his death following an illness of six months, during which time he had come back to the old home near Bentonville, hoping that the higher altitude and climate of the Ozarks might aid in his recovery. A son of M.L. and Nancy J. Seamster, pioneers of this section, he was born near Beatie, Benton Co., Ark. Sept. 25, 1881 and died at the age of 43 years, four months and 22 days. Until stricken last September with the illness that finally resulted in his death he is said to have been unusually healthy and active. For the last year or more he had been living in Oklahoma and Texas but has in this county a great number of friends and acquaintances who deeply regret his death. Besides his parents he is survived by a son and a daughter, one sister, Mrs. A.M. Crouse of near Centerton and seven brothers: John W. and Attorney Lee Seamster,

Fayetteville; Marion of Miami, Okla.; Bert of Veteran, Wyo. and Roy, Alvin and Jess Seamster, Bentonville. There are a number of other relatives, among them Dr. Lee Seamster of Minerl Wells, Texas, who cme to Bentonville several days ago. The parents, sister and all brothers except Bert Seamster were here for the funeral. Among other relatives coming here for the funeral were Mrs. Lee Seamster, Miss Leona Seamster and Floyd Seamster, all of Fayetteville. Funeral services, attended by a large number of relatives and friends, were held Tuesday afternoon at the Mt. Pleasant church near Hiwasse and the old Seamster home, conducted by Rev. Stephen A. Morton, pastor of the Bentonville Christian church. Interment was made in the family plot at the Mt. Pleasant cemetery beside a brother who died some years ago. [Benton County Democrat 2/19/25]
Robert Seamster, son of Mr. and Mrs. M.L. Seamster, living northwest of Centerton, died at the home of his brother, Alvin Seamster, in this city on Monday, Feb. 16, 1925 at the age of 43 years. Death was due to abdominal dropsy, from which he had been suffering for the past year. Funeral services, conducted by the Rev. S. A. Morton of Bentonville were held at the Mt. Pleasant church south of Hiwasse on Tuesday afternoon in the presence of a large number of friends and relatives. Robert Seamster was born west of Gravette on September 25th, 1881. He grew to manhood in this vicinity and a few years ago went to Texas and later to Oklahoma. When taken ill he was brought home that he might have the loving care of his aged parents and their children. Besides his parents he is survived by two children, one sister, Mrs. A.M. Crouse of Bentonville, Route 3, and seven brothers - John W. Seamster, Fayetteville; Marion Seamster, Miami, Okla.; Roy Seamster, Bentonville; Bert Seamster, Veteran, Wyo.; Lee Seamster, Fayetteville and Alvin and Jess Seamster of this city. [Benton County Record 2/20/25]

SELLERS, William C. - William C. Sellers, a prominent and well known citizen of Benton county, died at the home of Dr. J.T. Powell in Gravette where he was taken for treatment for tetanus on Monday morning, March 17th, 1925. About 10 days ago Mr. Sellers ran a sliver in his thumb but paid little attention to it, thinking the thumb would fester and the sliver would work its way out. The thumb became more troublesome and the hand swelled. Last Friday tetanus set in and he was removed from his home in Maysville to the home of his old friend and family physician, Dr. J.T. Powell, in Gravette. But the disease was too far advanced to be checked and he died 4 days later. Friends and relatives from far and near were present at the funeral Wednesday afternoon. It was the largest attended funeral ever held in Maysville. Rev. Grover Scales, pastor of the Baptist church at Grove, conducted the services. Interment was made in the Maysville cemetery. Besides his widow, Mrs. Lydia Sellers, he is survived by his aged mother, Mrs. Joel Sellers, aged 84, and four brothers, Hugh Sellers of Grove, Okla.; Dr. R.L. Sellers of Westville, John and James Sellers, who also live in Oklahoma; also by two sisters, Mrs. Will Wells of Maysville

and Mrs. Fannie Perry of Miami, Okla. Mr. Sellers was born southeast of Maysville in 1860. His parents, Mr. and Mrs. Joel Sellers, came to Benton county from Tennessee about 70 years ago and were among the pioneer settlers of that section. Wild and woolly were those early days around Maysville which was then one of the most important trading posts in Northwest Arkansas. In 1886 he married Miss Lydia Peppers at that now forgotten town of Eldorado. While Mr. Sellers was always a stock man and one of the best judges of the value of stock in the county he also ran a drug store in Maysville for over 15 years, selling the same about 20 years ago. Mr. Sellers was a good business man and through careful investments became one of the richest men in Benton county. Besides being one of the heaviest stock holders in the Bank of Gravett he also owned from 10,000 to 15,000 acres of land in Oklahoma. He was a quiet and unassuming man and lived the free and outdoor life of his ancestors. He was a splendid citizen and one who will be greatly missed by the citizens of Maysville and his friends elsewhere. [Benton County Record 3/20/25]
{from Decatur} W.C. Sellers of Maysville died last week of lockjaw. Mr. Sellers was a cousin of C.S. Hedges, our druggist. [Benton County Record 3/20/25]
Will C. Sellers, prominently known throughout this region, died at the home of Dr. J.T. Powell Monday forenoon, March 16, 1925, the result of tetanus. Mr. Sellers had recently recovered from pneumonia and about two weeks ago got a splinter in one of his fingers. When badly infected he came to Gravette last Saturday with B.F. Tanner for treatment. Dr. Powell, finding Mr. Sellers' condition serious, took him to his, the doctor's, home where everything was done that medical skill possesses to relieve him but the patient gradually grew worse until death came. William C. Sellers was born at Maysville in 1860, a son of the pioneers, Joseph and Martha Sellers, and was aged 65 years. He was married to Miss Lydia Pepper in 1886. There are no children. Besides his mother, now aged 81 years, and the wife, he leaves four brothers, Dr. R.L. Sellers, Westville, Okla.; J.H. Sellers, Afton, Okla.; Hugh A. Sellers, Grove, Okla.; John Sellers, Tahlequah, Okla.; and two sisters, Mrs. Fanny Perry, Grove, Okla. and Mrs. Will Wells of Maysville, Ark. Mr. Sellers was very widely known in Arkansas, Oklahoma and Missouri as a banker and stockman. He probably owned more real estate than any man in all this region, covering practically all of Wet Prairie and about 10,000 acres in all. He was connected with Gravette banking interests. The funeral was held on Wednesday, March 18th at 2:00 p.m. at Maysville, the services being conducted by J. Grover Scales, pastor of the Baptist church from Grove, Okla. Many relatives and a large concourse of friends attended the obsequies. Those bereaved have the sympathy of a host of friends. [Gravette News-Herald 3/20/25]

SETSER, Dan M. - Dan M. Setser, a former resident of Benton county, died at his home in Tulsa, Okla. on January 10th, 1925 at the age of about

68 years. He is survived by his widow and several grown children; also by four brothers - Manuel Setser of Gravette; David, George and John Setser of near Decatur. Mr. Setser was born in Benton county, southwest of Gravette, and lived in that section about 50 years. At one time he owned the land that is now the west part of that town. For about 20 years he taught school in Benton county, teaching in Gravette, Word, Decatur, Springtown and other places. He also served one term in the Arkansas legislature as a representative. He left Arkansas about 18 years ago and went to Texas. Later he moved to Tulsa, which has since been his home. He was instructor in penmanship in the Tulsa schools. Mr. Setser was well known to many of the older residents of Bentonville and throughout the county. [Benton County Record 1/23/25]
Dan M. Setser, one of Gravette's former prominent and highly respected citizens, is dead. The News Herald has no particulars regarding Mr. Setser's death other than that it occurred on Saturday, Jan. 10th, 1925 at his home in Tulsa, Okla. Mr. Setser was a native of Benton county and resided here for many years. He made an early record as a public school teacher and a fine penman, being associated with the noted George Wear of Texas whose copy books are used in schools all over the nation. Mr. Setser was a devout church member and a citizen whose influence was ever for good. He served Benton county very ably as a member of the lower house of the Arkansas Assembly perhaps 25 years ago. He belonged to one of those sturdy pioneer families who helped to develop this region. At Gravette he still has two brothers, John H. and Emanuel H. and one sister, Mrs. I.R. Garman; also two brothers, Dave and George, near Decatur. He leaves a wife and {if remembered rightly} two sons and a daughter at Tulsa. There are many of Dan Setser's friends at Gravette who will regret to learn of his death. He, however, has earned a great reward as a faithful, conscientious American, Christian citizen. [Gravette News-Herald 1/23/25]
{from The Tulsa World} Dan Setser, 72 years old, well-known schoolmaster in Tulsa county, died Saturday night at his home at 327 South Vieter. He had been ill only a week. Last Friday he suffered a stroke of apoplexy. Mr. Setser was well known throughout the county. He has taught in many of the county schools and served as superintendent of penmanship in the schools here. He came to Tulsa about 18 years ago from Benton county, Arkansas where he had taught school for a number of years. Because of his advanced age he retired six years ago. He was a member of the First Baptist church and the Business Men's Bible class. Besides his widow he is survived by one daughter, Mrs. A.J. Sumner, and three sons, Harold Setser, W.A. Setser and Herman Setser, all of Tulsa. [Gentry Journal-Advance 1/23/25]

SHARP, Nimrod - {from War Eagle} We are sorry to report the death of Nimrod Sharp occurring last week at the age of 80 years. Mr. Sharp was a good neighbor and a kind friend to all. His friends are many and he was held in high esteem by all who knew him. He leaves an aged wife, two sons and three daughters to mourn his loss, to whom we extend sympathy. [Rogers Democrat 8/20/25]

SHERRELL, Grandma - {from Lowell} Grandma Sherrell died at the home of her son, Emmett, in Lowell on Saturday night. Funeral services were conducted at the cemetery on Sunday afternoon by a minister from Rogers. Interment was made at Rogers. [Benton County Record 1/23/25] [Rogers Democrat 1/22/25]

SHIBLEY, John - John Shibley was born January 22, 1849 at Carlysle, New York. He was the son of Samuel P. and Mary Elizabeth Shibley. At the age of six years he came with his parents to Adair county, Missouri, at which place he grew to manhood. He was engaged in agricultural pursuits for a number of years. At the age of 34 he entered Rush Medical College, Chicago where he graduated in the class of 1886. The following June he was united in marriage to Josephine Jones. To this union there were born two children, Maun Lillian and Ralph Emerson. He practiced medicine for a period of 30 years, during which time he was also interested in banking and agricultural pursuits. He became a member of the Masonic Order when a young man and advanced in the work to the 32nd degree. He lived a devoted and prayerful life. He united with the Congregational church within the last year where he took an active interest in christian work. He was ever charitable and kind to all and devoted to his family. He departed this life November 25, 1925. He leaves to mourn his departure his wife, Josephine Shibley; two children, Maun L. Wilson of Gentry, Ark. and Ralph E. Shibley of Guthrie, Okla. and two grandchildren, John Stewart Wilson and John L. Shibley; two brothers, David H. of Montana and George of Green City, Mo. Funeral services were held from the Congregational church Friday morning, conducted by the pastor, Rev. Hughes, assisted by the Rev. Dickey and burial was made in the City Cemetery by the Masons. [Gentry Journal-Advance 12/4/25]

SHIELDS, Naomi - {from Gravette} Naomi Shields died at the home of her parents, Mr. and Mrs. G.C. Shields, Tuesday afternoon after a lingering illness. [Benton County Record 11/6/25]

SHIELDS, Norma Lena - Norma Lena Shields, the eldest daughter of Mr. and Mrs. G.C. Shields, died at the family home near Gravette on Tuesday, November 3rd, 1925 at the age of 12 years. Funeral services were held at the M.E. Church in Gravette, the Rev. M.R. Lark conducting the services, assisted by Rev. and Mrs. W.H. McCarroll. Interment was made in the Odd Fellows' cemetery following the services. Besides her parents she is survived by five brothers, a sister and a grandfather, as well as a large number of relatives and friends to mourn her loss. Relatives from a distance who attended the funeral were: Mr. and Mrs. John Duncan, Mrs. Lizzie Crissman and son of Bower Mills, Mo.; Mr. and Mrs. Lee Duncan of Row, Okla. and Fred Shields of Rogers. [Benton County Democrat 11/10/25]

1925

SHOCKLEY, Susan Ella Jane HARDWICK - Mrs. Joe (Ella Hardwick) Shockley, who has been battling for life since she underwent a serious operation some weeks ago, died Tuesday morning at her home on Railroad street. She was about 42 years of age. Mrs. Shockley grew to womanhood in Gravette and enjoyed a wide acquaintance. She leaves one sister, Anna, and two brothers, John and James Hardwick. Mr. Shockley, who was employed in Alabama, arrived this Thursday morning and the funeral will be conducted at the M.E. church by Rev. Lark at 2 p.m. Friday and burial will be at the I.O.O.F. cemetery. [Gravette News-Herald 1/2/25]
Miss Susan Ella Jane Hardwick was born near Sulphur Springs, Ark. Sept. 5, 1883; died at her home in Gravette Dec. 30, 1924 at the age of 41 years, 4 months, 25 days. She was married to Joe Shockley Sept. 19, 1917 at Fort Smith, Ark. at Mrs. Bassham's residence. (Mr. Shockley is employed by the Texas Rode (sic) Co. He asked the company to stop work five minutes during the funeral. They wired back they would shutdown all evening.) Sister Shockley was converted four years ago. She lived a constant Christian life and was a member of the Church of God. She bade loved ones and friends farewell and went to join her father, mother and brother who preceded her to the glory world. She leaves to mourn their loss her husband, Joe Shockley; one sister, Mrs. Anna Starch; two brothers, John and James Hardwick; two sisters-in-law, six nieces,3 nephews and a host of friends. The funeral services were conducted by Rev. Lark, assisted by others, at the M.E. church Jan. 2, 1925, to a large sympathizing congregation. Sister Shockley was loved by all who knew her. Interment was made in the I.O.O.F. cemetery. [Gravette News-Herald 1/16/25]

SHOUP, John, Jr. - John Shoup, Jr., 4-weeks-old infant son of Mr. and Mrs. John Shoup, died at the family home on East Fifteenth street at 11:30 o'clock Monday night from bronchial pneumonia. Besides his parents he is survived by one brother and two sisters. Funeral services were held Wednesday, conducted by Rev. Joe Tyson of the local Nazarene church and interment made in the City cemetery. [Benton County Democrat 1/12/25]

SLUSHER, Mrs. Jesse - Mrs. Jesse Slusher of Madison county was instantly killed a week ago when the auto in which she was riding was overturned, her neck being broken and her skull fractured. The other occupants of the car, which was driven by the husband of the deceased, were only slightly injured. The accident occurred on the Eureka Springs road six miles north of Huntsville. The Slusher family had just recently returned to Madison county from Wyoming and were returning from Eureka Springs where they had gone to purchase household goods, preparatory to going to housekeeping. There were eight persons in the car when it overturned, five of them children, and it was remarkable that only one person should have been fatally injured. [Rogers Democrat 12/10/25]

SMITH, Charles E. - Charles E. Smith died Friday morning at his home west of Oakley Chapel on the Bentonville highway west of Rogers where he had lived for many years. Mr. Smith has been in poor health for several years but few knew that his condition was serious and the word of his death came as a great surprise to his friends in all parts of Northwest Arkansas. The morning of his death he was able to be up and had even been out on the porch but came back in the room, laid down and quietly passed away at the age of 78 years, ten months and 3 days. Funeral services were held Sunday afternoon at Oakley Chapel, being conducted by Rev. Womack and Rev. Campbell, in the presence of a large number of friends and relatives. He is now at rest in the little Oakley Chapel cemetery where for fifty years he had assisted in the same service for scores of friends and relatives. Mr. Smith was born near Fulton, Hempstead county, Ark. March 6, 1846. He came to Benton county about 1872, settling in the neighborhood where he lived until his death. He married Miss Addie Oakley May 15, 1873, member of one of the largest and best known pioneer families of this section, who survives him as do also six children - Mrs. Alva Dodson of California; Mrs. J.C. Bell of Rogers and Miss Belle Smith, who lives at home; also three sons, Eugene Smith of Pine Bluff, who was home for the funeral, and Jim and Joe Smith, the latter living at Leesburg, Florida, and Jim was on a visit in that state. Two grandchildren, Carl and Kenneth Doescher, sons of a daughter, Mrs. Carl Doescher who died some years ago as also did her husband, live in the Smith home. A brother, R.A. Smith of Oronogo, Mo. was here for the funeral and he also has a brother, Joseph E. Smith at Nashville, Ark. By the death of Mr. Smith Benton county loses one of its best citizens and one of the pioneers in the small fruit industry in this section. Back in the days when the Rogers Shippers Union was the model co-operative shipping organization of the Southwest and David Wing, R.P. Owens, W.A. Miller, J. Alvin Dickson, Newt Woods and others of our early citizens were members of the Board of Directors, Mr. Smith was one of the active members and served on the Board for many years in various capacities. He was progressive in his ideas, conservative in his speech and always optimistic as to the future of Northwest Arkansas. Mr. Smith was always an active church worker and served as superintendent of the Oakley Chapel Sunday school for more than forty years, only retiring when his health would no longer permit regular attendance. [Rogers Democrat 1/15/25] [Benton County Democrat 1/15/25] [Benton County Record 1/16/25]

SMITH, J.A. - {from Centerton} J.A. Smith, 80 years of age, who has been making his home with his son, Henry Smith, died last Thursday. He leaves two sons and a married daughter in California. Funeral services were held on Friday last with burial in the Barron cemetery. [Benton County Record 1/2/25]

SMITH, Malinda - Mr. and Mrs. J.W. Ryan were called to Green Forest, Ark. last week Wednesday on account of the death of Mrs. Ryan's mother, Mrs. Malinda Smith of that city. Mrs. Smith was born and reared near Harrison and was aged 72 years. Six other children survive. The funeral was held at Green Forest on Friday, Feb. 27 and interment made in the Pickens cemetery. [Gravette News-Herald 3/6/25]

SMITH, Mary A. - {from Silent Grove} Mrs. Mary A. Smith, 91 years of age, died Saturday afternoon at the home of her son and daughter-in-law, Mr. and Mrs. George Smith, with whom she had made her home for a number of years. Burial was in Silent Grove cemetery Sunday afternoon conducted by Rev. Joe English of Lowell. Deceased was a native of Tennessee, born Jan. 18, 1834 and had spent the past 41 years in this community. Her husband died some years ago. She is survived by four daughters, five sons and a number of grandchildren and great-grandchildren. Six children preceded their mother in death. The children present at the funeral were Mrs. Julia McDaniel of near Rogers, Mrs. J.W. Pogue of Springdale, John Smith of Springdale, James Smith of Texas and George Smith. Those unable to be present were Billie Smith of Goad Springs, who was very sick with the flu, Grant Smith of Pocatello, Idaho and two daughters who reside in Tennessee. The deceased had been a member of the Missionary Baptist church for a number of years. Just before the end came she bade her loved ones goodbye and told them she was going home to be with Jesus. [Benton County Democrat 4/2/25]

SMITH, Mrs. J.G.W. - {from Lowell} Lowell friends were shocked Tuesday when a telegram came telling of the death of Mrs. J.G.W. Smith. She had gone to Tennessee to spend the winter with relatives. Death was the result of pneumonia fever. Mrs. Smith was loved by all who knew her. She was always thoughtful and considerate of anyone in need of help and her many deeds of kindness will be remembered here by all. [Rogers Democrat 2/26/25]

SMITH, Sarah F. - {from The Little Rock Democrat, April 23} The grandmother of Mrs. W.R. Mayer, 806 Park avenue, and the aunt of Mr. Mayer, died within three hours of each other Wednesday night it was learned yesterday. Mrs. Sarah Smith, aged 82, grandmother of Mrs. W.R. Mayer, died at her home, 806 Park avenue at 6:45 p.m. Less than three hours later Mr. Mayer received word that his aunt. Mrs. Augusta Mayer, aged 58, had died at a local hospital. Mrs. Smith is survived by two daughters, Mrs. J.L. Shinpaugh and Mrs. John Stalcup, both of Rogers, and a son, George Smith of Springfield, Mo. The body was sent to Rogers last night by P.H. Ruebel & Co. where services will be held Friday morning. Burial will be at Rogers. ***** The body of Mrs. Smith arrived in Rogers Friday morning, accompanied by her daughter, Mrs. Shinpaugh. Mrs. Shinpaugh and mother have been living in Little Rock since last fall. A grandson of Mrs. Smith, Joe Shinpaugh, also lives in Little Rock and has charge of the laundry department at the Deaf-Mute school. [Rogers Democrat 4/30/25]
Mrs. Joe Smith, mother of Mrs. John Shinpaugh, died in Little Rock this morning. The body will arrive in Rogers Friday morning. Funeral services will be held at the home of Mrs. J.B. West at 307 East Walnut Friday

afternoon at 2:30. Burial will be in the City cemetery. [Rogers Daily Post 4/23/25]

SMITH, W.H. - W.H. Smith was born October 23d, 1842 in Washington county, Arkansas and died April 16th, 1925 at his home near Highfill. Early in life he was united in marriage to Miss Jane Morrison and to them were born four sons and one daughter, Allie and Wicks of Highfill; Britt and James of Fayetteville; Mrs. Wm. Holland of Tahlequah, Okla. Funeral services were conducted by F.A. Bradshaw at the M.E. church at Thornsberry Camp Ground and interment in the cemetery at that place April 17th. [Benton County Record 4/24/25]

SMITH, Wilbur - {from Walnut Grove} Wilbur Smith died Sunday in the hospital at Rogers following an operation on Thursday and was buried Monday at Pea Ridge. Rev. Bone conducted the services. [Benton County Record 6/19/25]

SMITH, Wilburn - Wilburn Smith died yesterday morning at the Home Hospital following an operation for appendicitis. He was 52 years old and had lived for several years three miles southwest of Pea Ridge. He leaves besides his wife, five children. The funeral was conducted this afternoon by Rev. Bone with interment at Pea Ridge. [Rogers Daily Post 6/15/25]

{from Pea Ridge} Wilburn Smith, living about three miles south of Pea Ridge, died at a hospital in Rogers Sunday following an operation Thursday. Funeral services were held Monday afternoon, Rev. Bone officiating and burial was made in the Pea Ridge cemetery. He was nearly fifty-three years of age and is survived by his widow and five children. [Benton County Record 6/19/25]

SOWERS, Jno. - {from Decatur} Jno. Sowers, aged 82, one of the oldest residents of Sulphur Springs, died last week. The body was sent to Palmyra, Mo. for interment. He is survived by his wife, Margaret Sowers, of Sulphur Springs and three children who live away. [Benton County Record 12/11/25]

SPARLING, Laura Emely - {from Rogers} Mrs. Laura Sparling, the third member of this family to die within the past six weeks of pneumonia, was buried on Tuesday of last week. On March 14th her husband died of the same disease and a week later his brother passed away. She was 79 years of age. [Benton County Record 5/1/25]

Laura Emely Sparling was born Nov. 19th, 1846 in Belleville, Ill. and died April 20, 1925 in Rogers, Ark. Mrs. Laura Emely Sparling passed away at the home of her son, J.M. Sparling, of this city where she had been staying since the death of her husband on March 14, 1925. Mrs. Sparling was 79 years old and is survived by four children and one adopted daughter. Mrs. Sparling was very patient during all her sickness of a month and thirteen days and through the death of her husband and brother-in-law who died within a few days of each other. Funeral services were conducted by the Rev. Rich. C. Lucke, pastor of the First M.E. church, yesterday afternoon. Interment in Rogers cemetery. [Rogers Daily Post 4/22/25]

SPARLING, Samuel - Sam Sparling, who had lived here for many years, died Saturday at his home on Arkansas street and was buried Sunday in the Rogers cemetery. Rev. R.C. Lucke conducted services at the graveside. Death was the result of pneumonia. [Rogers Democrat 3/19/25]
{from Rogers} Samuel Sparling, age about seventy years, and Robert Hines, twenty, both died of pneumonia within the last few days. [Benton County Record 3/20/25]

SPARLING, William B. - {from Rogers} W.B. Sparling, age 80 years, died Sunday from the effects of flu. [Benton County Record 3/27/25]
William B. Sparling, 80 years old, died Monday at his home on Arkansas street. He was a brother of Sam Sparling, who died a week or so ago. [Rogers Democrat 3/26/25]

SPIVA, Sarah - {from Marr's Hill} Mrs. Sarah Spiva passed away at the home of her daughter at 11 o'clock a.m. on November 25th. Funeral services were held on Thanksgiving Day and interment was made in the Gamble cemetery. Grandma was 90 years of age. She suffered bodily affliction but she bore it patiently, no one ever hearing her murmur or complain. [Benton County Record 12/4/25]

STABLER, Jarrett Wesley - Jarrett Wesley Stabler died at his home at 1021 West E. street Sunday morning, aged 82 years, four months and ten days, death following an illness of some weeks from which his many friends and acquaintances had hoped that he was gradually recovering. Born at Shrewsbury, Penn. Sept. 21, 1842, Mr. Stabler later became a resident of Illinois and was married to Miss Anna Yeargain at Quincy, Ill. Jan. 2, 1868. To them were born six children, three boys and three girls. He and his family moved to Kansas in 1872, residing in that state for 30 years. In 1902 he moved his family into what was then the Indian Territory, living there when Oklahoma became a state. In 1920 the Stabler family moved to Bentonville, Ark., Mr. Stabler dying here Feb. 1st, 1925. During their four years residence here Mr. Stabler and his family made a host of friends who remember him as an ideal citizen, husband, father and grandfather, a consistent Christian and a man of likeable personality. Mr. Stabler was a veteran of the Federal Army, having enlisted in Company E of the 84th, Illinois regiment and serving through the entire War between the States. At his funeral a group of Union veterans, who like Mr. Stabler, have long made their homes here, attended in a body. At a very early age he became a member of the Christian church and remained faithful to the end, serving for many years as an elder of that church. Besides his wife he is survived by a daughter, Mrs. W.E. Knox, of Bentonville and two sons, Will C. Stabler of Newton, Kansas and George C. Stabler, Geronimo, Okla., his granddaughter, Miss Jarrett Knox of Bentonville and other relatives. Funeral services, attended by many friends, were held Tuesday afternoon, Feb. 3rd from the Christian church, conducted by his pastor, Rev. S.A. Morton, assisted by Rev. J.M. McMahen of the Baptist church, and interment made at the City cemetery. [Benton County Democrat 2/5/25] [Benton County Record 2/6/25]

STAFFORD, Susanna FLEMING - {from The Lawton Constitution} Mrs. B.S. Stafford died at her home one mile west of Lawton Tuesday afternoon. Mrs. Stafford had been in failing health for several months but she was seriously ill only a short time. Susanna Fleming was born May 2, 1860 near Manhattan, Kansas. She was married to B.S. Stafford July 7, 1888. Besides her husband she is survived by three daughters, Mrs. Oliver Layne of Heavener, Okla.; Misses Lilly and Mary Helen Stafford of Lawton; two sisters, Mrs. J.T. Edwards of Ponca City, Okla.; Mrs. J.M. Nunelly of Petaluma, Calif.; and a brother, E.F. Fleming of Liberty, Mo. The immediate family were at her bedside when she passed away. Neither the sisters nor her brother were able to attend the funeral. Early in life Mrs. Stafford was converted and united with the Baptist church of which she as a faithful and devoted member for over fifty years. The funeral services were held at the Baptist church, conducted by Rev. A.M. Brown, assisted by Rev. J.T. Stephens, long time friends of the family. Mrs. Stafford had a charming personality and a wide circle of friends who sincerely sympathize with the family in their loss. The Misses Lilly and Mary Helen Stafford are teachers in the Lawton high school. The high school teachers attended the services in a body in honor of their fellow teachers. [Gentry Journal-Advance 1/23/25]

STANLEY, Mrs. James - J.S. Elder received word from Mrs. Elder that her sister, Mrs. James Stanley, living in North Little Rock, had died and was buried today at 10 o'clock at the First Baptist church of that city. [Rogers Daily Post 6/12/25]

STANTON, Mary C. PRICE - {from New Hope} Mrs. Enos Stanton died at her home Saturday morning at 3 o'clock and while it had been known for several days that her condition was very serious, the announcement Saturday morning that she had passed away came as a shock for she was one of the best known and best loved women in our community. Mary C. Price was born April 22, 1885 at Rogers and died January 17th at the early age of 39 years, eight months and a few days. She was united in marriage to Enos E. Stanton September 14, 1908. To this union were born three children. The oldest, Enos Hallie, died February 26, 1920 and Schooley and Larry will miss the loving care of their mother just when they need it most. She professed religion in 1903, uniting with the First Christian Church of Rogers and was baptized June 21, 1921. Besides her heartbroken husband and two sons, there is left to mourn her untimely death her parents, Mr. and Mrs. Balim Price, and three brothers, Hal, Fred and Don Price, with a host of other relatives and friends. Her funeral was held Sunday afternoon at the home under the direction of J.W. Bryant and the services were conducted by Rev. T.B. Clark, pastor of the Christian church of Rogers, and were attended by a large crowd of weeping friends and neighbors. Mrs. Stanton was a leader in everything that stood for the upbuilding

of school and church and was never happier than when doing a kind act for the sick or poverty stricken. She was one of the most active members of the New Hope Sunday school and we feel that the King's Daughter's class has suffered an irreparable loss in her death. Also the Fairview school district; in fact, we can think of no woman who would be missed so much both at home and abroad as Mrs. Stanton. [Rogers Democrat 1/22/25]
{from Fairview} Mrs. Enos Stanton suffered from appendicitis last week. The attack was sudden and violent and much medical aid was given but to no avail. She died Friday night and was buried Sunday in the Rogers cemetery. A large host of relatives and friends paid her their last homage. Two boys, ten and twelve years old, and her husband survive. We extend our sympathy and solicitude. [Benton County Record 1/23/25]

STATER, Mary SINKS - Mrs. Mary Stater, aged 76, died at the home of her daughter, Mrs. T.W. Nelson, Wednesday morning at 2 o'clock, June 9th, 1925, following a stroke of paralysis which occurred a week ago. Funeral services were held at the home Thursday morning at 10 o'clock, conducted by Rev. S.B. Clark, pastor of the First Christian Church of Rogers. She is survived by two daughters, Mrs. Budie Schader of Rogers and Mrs. T.W. Nelson of Bentonville and one son, O.W. Stater of Oklahoma, who were with their mother when she died. Mary Stater {nee Sinks} was born in Fairfield, Iowa in 1849. She spent her youth there and married S.O. Stater in November 1869. The Staters lived a few years in Fairfield and then moved to Kansas City, Mo. where they made their home for 12 years. They also lived in parts of South Missouri and came to Rogers, Ark. from Kansas City about seven years ago. Mr. Stater died two years, two months, two days and two hours before his wife. Burial was made in the Oakley Chapel cemetery. [Benton County Record 6/12/25]
{from Droke} V.A. Stater, who was called here by the illness of his mother, Mrs. M.E. Stater, left Sunday for his home in Oklahoma City. [Benton County Record 6/19/25]
The funeral of Mrs. Stater who died yesterday at the home of her daughter, Mrs. Nelson near Bentonville, took place this morning at the home with interment in Oakley's Chapel, Rev. T.B. Moore conducting the services. Mrs. Stater was the mother of Curry Stater who runs a garage on West Walnut Street. [Rogers Daily Post 6/11/25]

STEELE, William Volney - William Volney Steele, son of Marion DeCalb and Francis S. Steele, was born February 2, 1856 at Powhattan, Lawrence Co., Arkansas. Was married to Laura E. Railey August 2, 1884. To this union was born seven children, Francis E., Marion Railey, Raphael William, James DeCalb, Mancil Arthur, Thomas Price and Miss Laura Fay Steele. He is also survived by two brothers, also a number of other relatives. Brother Steele was converted very early in life and joined the M.E. Church So., living a loyal christian life. He was one among the first to settle in this community we now call Gentry. He was a charter member of the Methodist church of this place and lived to see this congregation that was at the beginning only a struggling handful, grow to be one of the strongest in this part of the country. God called in the early morning of May twentieth and brother Steele went home to be with Him and loved ones gone before. Funeral services were held from the Methodist church Thursday afternoon, conducted by Rev. C.H. Sherman, a life long friend, and Rev. Villines, his pastor. Services at the grave were under the auspices of the Masons. He was also the oldest Odd Fellow here, having been given a gold medal by this order as being its oldest member about three years ago. The remains were laid to rest beside his wife who passed away in 1918, surrounded by a host of relatives and friends. He leaves five sons and two daughters: Price of Kansas City; James D. and Dr. Ralph of Siloam; Ray and Author {sic} and Mrs. Francis Fears and Miss Fay Steele of Gentry; and a sister, Mrs. Lucy Wasson of Springtown, besides a large number of relatives to feel his loss. [Gentry Journal-Advance 5/29/25] [Rogers Daily Post 5/23/25]

STEPHENS, J.B. - Word was received the last of the week of the death of J.B. Stephens, a former well known Rogers citizen who died January 14th at Aurora, Mo. and was buried there the following day. Mr. Stephens had been in poor health for a number of years but had been confined to his bed only a short time. Mr. Stephens and wife lived in Rogers until about six years ago, moving to Aurora to be near the daughter, Mrs. May Siceluff. Mr. Stephens was connected here with the old Rogers Milling Company for a number of years. A son, John Stephens, is a well known passenger conductor on the Frisco Central division. [Rogers Democrat 1/22/25]

STEVENS, Joe - The remains of Joe Stevens, who died last week in Little Rock, were brought to Gentry and laid to rest beside his father, who passed away a few weeks ago. We did not get an obituary. We understand Mrs. Stevens will make her home with Rev. and Mrs. H.C. Griffin on Flint. [Gentry Journal-Advance 5/1/25]

STEVENS, M.C. - Rogers friends received word last Thursday morning of the death of M.C. Stevens at the home of his daughter, Mrs. Mary Jones, in Tulsa. Burial was at his old home at Vineland, Kansas where he had been living since leaving Rogers several years ago. Mr. Stevens, who was at the time living in Rogers and engaged in the lumber business, was four years ago stricken with paralysis. For several years he was quite helpless and was at the home of a brother in Vineland. During the past year he had greatly improved and until a month before his death was driving a truck between Vineland and Kansas City. When his health failed again he went to Tulsa where he died. Mr. Stevens was for several years superintendent of the Presbyterian Sunday School of this city, an officer of the church and one of the most active members. He was one of the promoters of the Kansas Club of Rogers for he was a native of that state and lived there many years. Mr. Stevens was 57 years old and is survived by his wife and 1 daughter. [Rogers Democrat 12/24/25]

STEVENSON, H.N. - H.N. Stevenson, a brother of A.W. Stevenson of the Gentry meat Market, died very suddenly Wednesday morning at 4 o'clock. Deceased had been sick for several days but it was not thought he was in a serious condition. Funeral will be held today and burial in Webb City, Mo. [Gentry Journal-Advance 4/10/25]

STEWART, Jerusha Celia - Mrs. Jerusha Celia Stewart died Sunday, July 19th at her home at 212 North Eighth street at the age of 83 years and one month. Mrs. Stewart had been in poor health for some time but the immediate cause of her death was a stroke of paralysis suffered a week ago. She was a member of the Presbyterian church and the funeral was held at the Presbyterian church Tuesday afternoon at 2:30 o'clock, being conducted by the pastor, Rev. Ben. H. Moore. Burial was in the Rogers cemetery by the side of her husband, H.C. Stewart, who died here December 6, 1912. Mrs. Stewart was born at Westfield, Chautauqua county, New York June 19, 1842. She was married to Henry Clay Stewart November 7, 1860 at New Oregon, Iowa. Two children, a daughter, Jessie, who died here November 7, 1903 and a son, W.H. Stewart, who has lived here with his mother for the last six years, were born to them. A granddaughter, Mrs. Ruth C. Price, of Pharr, Texas was raised in the home of her grandparents and has been with her for several months past. Another grandchild, Lloyd E. Stewart, lives in Minneapolis. H.C. Stewart and wife came to Rogers in 1894 and for a number of years lived on their farm just southwest of town. After the death of her husband in 1912 Mrs. Stewart bought the home on North Eighth where she died. [Rogers Democrat 7/23/25]

STOKES, Boyce - Boyce, the 13-year-old son of Mr. and Mrs. Robert Stokes, was accidentally killed last week, Thursday morning, Feb. 12, 1925 near their home at Duncan, Okla., being run over by a heavy truck. Boyce was a member of the Boy Scouts, some 35 of whom had been out to a weinie roast, and were returning to their homes. Boyce and another boy, riding on the running board of the truck, fell off, he falling under the truck and one wheel passed over his breast. He died before the party reached town. The sad hearted parents and a number of other relatives arrived here Friday night, accompanying the body which was conveyed to Maysville on Saturday for burial. Rev. W.H. McCarroll conducted the funeral services and interment was made in the Tinnin cemetery. His father, Robert Stokes, was reared in the vicinity of Gravette and Maysville and Mrs. Stokes is one of the well known James family of Maysville. They have numerous relatives and a host of friends here who deeply sympathize with them in their untimely bereavement. [Gravette News-Herald 2/20/25] [Benton County Record 2/20/25]

STONE, Bill - Bill Stone died at his home in this city Saturday after a long illness at the age of 54 years, four months and two days. Funeral services were held Monday at the Holiness church on the east side. Mr.

Stone is survived by his wife and one son. He had lived in Rogers for a good many years. [Rogers Democrat 7/23/25]

STOTTS, Chas. - {from Lowell} Mrs. L.P. Davis attended the funeral of Chas. Stotts in Huntsville last Monday. He died in San Francisco after undergoing an operation for appendicitis. He is a brother of Mrs. Frank Barr of Fayetteville and spent his childhood days in Arkansas. [Rogers Democrat 7/9/25]

STOUT, Louis Mauker - More than 500 people were present at the funeral of L.M. Stout at Sulphur Springs Monday afternoon. The services were held in the big tabernacle in the park. Not only were the business houses in that city closed out of deep respect for their fellow townsman and friend, but all the banks in Benton county closed that afternoon and most of their officers were present at the funeral. Great masses of flowers lined the speaker's platform, the gift of many friends far and near. Rev. W.M. Runyan, pastor of the Community church in Sulphur Springs in his address paid a flowing tribute to the life and character of the man whose candle was snuffed out so quickly and so tragically. Following the services, the funeral cortege wended its way to the Butler creek cemetery where the remains were laid to rest and the newly-made grave was banked high with flowers he loved so well. Louis Mauker Stout was born in Farmington, Ill. Dec. 24, 1865 and died in the Freeman hospital in Joplin, Mo. Friday, June 12, 1925 from bullet wounds inflicted by Oklahoma outlaws who had robbed the Bank of Sulphur Springs the previous day. When a child his parents moved to Indianapolis, Ind. where they lived until he was15 years of age. Then the family moved to Sedan, Kansas where he remained until nineteen. Ill health compelled him to go to Colorado where he spent two years. Regaining his health he joined his parents in Sulphur Springs who had previously moved to this place. A little later he left home to become a mail carrier in Kansas City, Kansas. Here he met and married Mary B. Holmes. To this union two daughters were born, one dying in infancy, and Henry Stout who now resides in Los Angeles and was unable to attend the funeral. Continued ill health compelled Mr. Stout to return to Sulphur Springs. In 1897 his engineering work took him to Osborn, Mo. where he met Bessie Fay McGuire and they were married in Pineville, Mo. on November 8th, 1898. They took up their residence in Sulphur Springs and lived here continuously except for six years spent in Bristow, Okla. Four children were born to them, Richard David Stout and Louis Hibler Stout, of the home, and Mrs. Louise Hilboldt of Lanagan, Mo. and Mrs. Nona Lester of Gravette. Besides the wife and children he is also survived by two brothers, David E. Stout of Neosho and Dick Stout of Perma, Mon.; also by two sisters, Mrs. Clara V. Heckman of Sulphur Springs and Mrs. Etta Spahr of Pearson, Iowa. [Benton County Record 6/19/25] [Gravette News-Herald 6/19/25]

STRAIT, Ellen - {from Decatur} Mrs. Ellen Strait died at her home east of town on Saturday afternoon from measles and flu. She leaves five little children, her father, two sisters and a brother to mourn her loss. [Benton County Record 3/20/25]

STRINGFIELD, P.A. - P.A. Stringfield passed away at his home in Danville early Friday morning and was buried at that place. He will be remembered by a number of old friends here having lived at War Eagle for a number of years. He is survived by his wife, a daughter, Mrs. Minnie Carr, and a son, Clyde C. Stringfield. [Rogers Daily Post 8/31/25]

SULLIVAN, Dennis - The death of Dennis Sullivan at 4 o'clock Sunday afternoon removes from prominence one who has been for years a distinguished element in Benton county affairs. Sullivan, who was 84 years of age, died at the home of his son-in-law, Bob Bright, in the Morning Star district. Mr. Sullivan's burial rites were solemnized at 3 o'clock yesterday and interment took place in the beautiful Hart cemetery. Sullivan was born in Ireland 84 years ago and emigrated to this country when a child. For fifty years he has lived on one farm in this county and has been prominent among those who have hewn Northwest Arkansas from a wilderness and made it into a productive section. Sullivan is survived by two sons and two daughters. [Benton County Democrat 8/4/25]

SWIFT, infant - {from Pea Ridge} The infant son of Mr. and Mrs. Jack Swift of Okmulgee, Okla. was buried at Buttram's Chapel cemetery Monday with services conducted by Rev. A.E. Carnahan, pastor of the Presbyterian church. Mrs. Swift is best remembered as Addie Ottinger. [Benton County Record 12/18/25] [Rogers Democrat 12/17/25]

TAYLOR, Betty Lorene - {from Providence} Betty Lorene, daughter of E.P. and Nettie Taylor, was born in Kansas City, Mo. October 21, 1924, died March 18, 1925, age 4 months, 27 days. A short sweet life budded on earth to bloom in heaven for of such is the kingdom of heaven. The funeral services were held Friday at Bestwater then the little body was taken to Tuck's Chapel and laid away to await the resurrection. [Rogers Democrat 3/26/25]

TAYLOR, Charles H. - Eureka Springs, July 24.- Mrs. Jim Tucker was seriously injured here Thursday afternoon about 5 o'clock by Charles H. Taylor, who after shooting Mrs. Tucker went into the attic of the Ward cottage and fired a bullet into his heart. No reasons for the shooting were given. Taylor was the owner of the Ward Cottage and Mrs. Tucker and her three children were living in an apartment there. Taylor also owns the Chautauqua Hotel here. According to witnesses of the tragedy Taylor came out on the front porch of the Ward Cottage and after a few words with Mrs. Tucker drew a 38 automatic pistol and shot her in the left side, the bullet coming out her back. He then ran to the attic and when local officers arrived they found him in the attic with a bullet hole in his heart. Taylor came here over a year ago from Kansas City and little of his past is known here. Mrs. Tucker has been a resident here for several years and her husband is a fireman on the Missouri, Kansas and Texas railroad. Mrs. Tucker is in a local hospital, reported to be in a serious condition. Taylor's wife at Parsons, Kansas was notified Thursday night and will arrive Friday. [Rogers Daily Post 7/24/25]

TAYLOR, Gladys Irene FAIR - Mrs. Earl Taylor died at her home near Elm Springs Tuesday, Sept. 15 at 7 o'clock p.m. Funeral services were held at the Methodist church at Elm Springs Wednesday afternoon at 2:00 o'clock, conducted by Rev. Bert Henry. Interment in Elm Springs cemetery. Gladys Irene Fair Taylor was born in Benton county, Ark. March 1, 1895 and died Sept. 15, 1925. She was married to Earl Taylor May 29, 1919. To this union one child was born. She was converted at Elm Springs in July 1914, joined the Baptist church at Spring Creek Aug. 1921 and lived a devoted Christian life until death. Besides her husband and daughter she leaves a father, mother, four sisters, four brothers and a host of relatives and friends to mourn their loss. [Benton County Democrat 9/22/25]

TAYLOR, John V. - Another old Gravette citizen died Wednesday night. J.V. Taylor, aged 82, passed away following an attack of flu which led to heart trouble. Mr. Taylor has been a resident of Gravette for the past 25 years and was an old Union soldier. He is survived by his widow. [Benton County Record 4/17/25]
John V. Taylor, who died at his home in Gravette last Wednesday night, April 15, 1925, was about 83 years of age and was a native of Ohio. He came to Gravette nearly 30 years ago and had been one of our substantial citizens. He was engaged in the shoemaking business the most of the time. He was unassuming and a character in whom everyone found a friend. He united with the Christian congregation here and had been a deacon for some years. His first wife died in June 1910 and their only daughter died two years before, in 1908. Besides his present companion and step-son, Robert Cole, he leaves half sisters and brothers and other relatives in Ohio and one sister in Arkansas. The funeral services were conducted at the home Friday afternoon by Rev. W.H. McCarroll. Mr. Taylor was a veteran of the Civil war, U.S. Army, and six veterans of the Blue and the Grey were honorary pallbearers. The interment was made in the I.O.O.F. cemetery. A good, conscientious and loyal citizen is laid to rest. [Gravette News-Herald 4/24/25]

TAYLOR, Mrs. M.I. - Mrs. W.W. Williams received the sad news of the death of her mother, Mrs. M.I. Taylor of Temple, Texas which occurred after a brief illness Monday, January 12th. Less than a week ago she also lost her brother, F.C. Taylor of Santa Ana, Texas who died suddenly Saturday, January 10th. [Benton County Record 1/16/25]

THOMAS, Justin Walter - Justin Walter Thomas, formerly of Kansas City but who for ten years resided near Osborne in the northeast corner of Benton county, passed away in St. Johns Hospital, Springfield, Mo. Thursday, November 19th. He was born February 15, 1870 at Hennepin, Ill. and was the youngest son of James W. and Louise Forbes Thomas. He is survived by one sister, Mrs. E.N. Snell of Marionville, Mo. and two brothers, H.S. and R.E. Thomas of the home. Funeral service and burial was in the family plot at Windsor, Mo. Saturday, Nov. 21st. [Rogers Democrat 11/26/25] [Benton County Record 11/27/25]

TINER, Albert - Albert Tiner was born in Brightwater township, Benton county, Ark. August 20, 1872 and died Tuesday, September 1st at the age of 53 years and eleven days. He was converted at the age of 20 and united with the M.E. church at Brightwater in which he led a life the church was ever proud to point to. He was married in 1906 to Miss Minnie Younce of Pineville, Mo. and to this union was born one son, Preston Tiner. Mr. Tiner was born, reared and lived on the same farm for fifty years and where his father, Bennett Tiner, lived for 80 years. The Tiner family was one of the pioneer families of Brightwater township and were noted for their quiet life and love of home and neighbors. In the passing of Albert Tiner the Sugar Creek valley lost a man who came as near living up to the Bible command, "As much as lieth in you, live peaceable with all men." Having spent his entire life here, save a few months in Colorado, his acquaintance with the older residents was extensive and their respect for him was shown by the large crowd of friends and a host of relatives who gathered Wednesday, Sept. 2nd at the Liberty Cemetery to pay their last respects to his memory. All of his sisters were present at the funeral: Mrs. Nannie Parker, who helped so faithfully his wife and son to wait upon him; Mrs. Crinda Ruddick of Garfield; Mrs. Betty Roberts of Springfield, Mo.; Mrs. Dea Lawrence of Keifer, Okla.; and one brother, Tilf Tiner, was present. Sam Tiner of Wichita, Kan. and Billy Tiner of Los Angeles, Calif. were unable to be there. Rev. Bone, pastor of Brightwater church, conducted the funeral services, assisted by George Williams, who made a short talk on the life of the deceased. We join with a host of friends in extending love and sympathy. [Rogers Democrat 9/10/25]

TINKER, Martha ELDRIDGE - {from Gentry} Mrs. Martha Tinker died at her home west of town Sunday evening. Burial was made Tuesday. She leaves three children and a large number of other relatives. [Benton County Record 6/5/25]

Mrs. Frank Tinker passed away last Sunday morning at her home ¾ of a mile west of town. She had been in failing health for some time, due to old age, being in the eighties. She was confined to her bed only one week. She leaves 3 sisters; Mrs. Eliza Londagin of Gentry; Mrs. Sarah Hastings of Oklahoma and Mrs. Lon Crumley of near Fayetteville; and two brothers, Wm. and John Eldridge of Gentry, 2 half brothers and a half sister, besides a number of children and grandchildren. Funeral services were held at the home Wednesday afternoon, conducted by Rev. Lillard, and burial was made in the Bloomfield cemetery. [Gentry Journal-Advance 6/5/25]

TINNER, Albert - {from Bestwater} Our community was very much saddened last Wednesday, September 3rd when the Death Angel came to claim our friend and relative, Mr. Albert Tinner. The body was laid to rest in the old Liberty cemetery. Mrs. Lawrence of Oklahoma, Mrs. Jodie Roberts of Springfield, Mo. Mrs. Arch Blancit of Garfield, Mrs. Jim Pollick of Rogers and Mrs. Nannie Parker, all came to attend the funeral of their brother, Mr. Tinner. Also three sisters and a niece and nephew of Mrs. Tinner and Mrs. J.H. Buttram, came from Rocky Comfort. Singing by the Taylor quartet and services conducted by Rev. W.T. Bone and Prof. Williams. [Benton County Democrat 9/8/25]

TINSLEY, C.W. - C.W. Tinsley died January 25th at his home in Rogers on North Third street at the age of 70 years. Funeral services were held Friday at the First M.E. church and burial was in the Rogers cemetery. [Rogers Democrat 2/5/25]

TOMPKINS, Carrie - Mrs. Carrie Tompkins, a former resident of Gravette, died in Kansas City, Mo. on Wednesday, Jan. 28, 1925 at the age of 79 years at the home of her daughter, Mrs. C.F. Longbine, 3833 E. 17th St. She leaves, besides her daughter, one son, W.A. Tomkins; two granddaughters, Mrs. Bessie Stillwell and Mrs. Homer Stratton, and a great-granddaughter, Mary Elizabeth Stratton, of Kansas City; and one sister and three brothers at Fayette, Mo. Funeral services were held at the Longbine home in Kansas City Thursday evening and the body was accompanied to Gravette Friday by Mr. and Mrs. Longbine. Services were conducted here at the Baptist church and interment made in the I.O.O.F. cemetery beside the grave of Mr. W.G. Tompkins who died here in 1915. [Gravette News-Herald 2/6/25]

TORBETT, Sue - {from Maysville} We regret to learn of the death of Mrs. Sue Torbett which occurred at the home of her daughter, Mrs. J. Parmley, Wednesday, March 11, 1925. She leaves a host of relatives and friends to mourn their loss. [Gravette News-Herald 3/20/25]

TOWNSEND, Mrs. Jeff - {from Lowell} Mrs. Jeff Townsend died on Friday of last week after a lingering illness. Funeral services were conducted at the Presbyterian church by Rev. Bates of Fayetteville. Burial was in Pleasant Grove cemetery. She has been sick for several years but was always kind and patient through all her sufferings. She leaves a husband and three daughters to mourn her loss. [Rogers Democrat 5/21/25]

TRAMMEL, Rena - {from Walnut Hill} Miss Rena Trammel was born in Tennessee July 30, 1838. She died June 22nd, being 86 years, ten months and 23 days old. Aunt Rena, as she was called, spent the greater part of her life in Benton county where she made a friend of all with whom she had any length of association. She remembered her Creator in her earthly days and lived a very pure, pious life. Yet she never united with any particular church. She lived for many years with her sister, Mrs. Joe Moore, and called that home, but did many years of service in Rogers in the early days of that city. She was longer in the Jones Hotel in Rogers than any other person who ever worked there. Since the death of her sister and in her declining years she has been cared for by her nephews and their families, who live east of Avoca. She had never married and had no family of her own, yet no one could have been better cared for in her old age than was Aunt Rena. Her life was spent in the service of the needy about her and a tale of distress and woe would take from her the last penny or the rest of many nights. She was laid to rest beside her eldest sister in the Snodderly cemetery. A short service was conducted by George Williams who remarked that he was burying the last caretaker of his infant and childhood days.- Written by request. [Rogers Democrat 7/2/25]

TUCKER, Paris - Paris Tucker, 76 years old, died last week the result of injuries received a few days previous when he fell from a telephone pole. He was assisting in repairing a telephone line between Huntsville and the McConnell chapel community. He had lived in Madison county seven years and for four years had been manager of the farm of Dr. Fred Youngblood. [Rogers Democrat 12/17/25]

TUGGLE, Mrs. - {from Springtown} Mrs. Tuggle, who died at the home of her daughter, Mrs. Will Phillpot, near Row, Okla. was buried in the Springtown cemetery Monday. Funeral services were conducted by Rev. Sturdy, evangelist, who is engaged in a revival meeting here. [Gentry Journal-Advance 2/27/25]

TURLEY, Sarah - {from War Eagle} Grandma Turley died last week and was laid to rest in the Sharp cemetery. She leaves a daughter, Mrs. Phillips, and a host of friends who grieve her departure to whom we extend sympathy. [Rogers Democrat 8/27/25]

{from Rogers} Mrs. Sarah Turley, one of Benton county's pioneer women, died at the family home east of War Eagle on Tuesday at the age of about 80 years. She had lived in that section all her life. [Benton County Record 8/21/25]

Another old pioneer passed away yesterday afternoon when Mrs. Sarah Turley died at her home near War Eagle nearing the 80th milestone of life of which the entire span was spent in this section of Arkansas. She was in her usual health when she went to the spring to get a pail of water. Returning she sat down on a chair and immediately passed away in the presence of her only daughter, Mrs. Phillips, and a grandson. Besides these two named she is survived by two grand daughters: Mrs. Eulalia Plunkett of Fort Smith and Mrs. Tom Mulos of Rogers who is now in St. Louis with a sick baby and unable to attend the funeral held this afternoon. Tom Mulos accompanied his sister-in-law to War Eagle this morning. The farm upon which Mrs. Turley has lived all her life is partly in Benton county and the rest in Madison county, necessitating trips to two county assessors to pay the taxes. The Looneys are distant relatives of the deceased. [Rogers Daily Post 8/19/25]

TURNER, James Blair - James Blair Turner, who resided at Gravette for some years with his brother, Chas. V. Turner, died at the latter's home in Rockford, Ill. on Friday, Feb. 27th, 1925 at the age of 76 years. Mr. Turner leaves two other brothers, Will and Robert, of Chicago. The Rockford Star contained an interesting sketch of "Uncle Blair," who was a printer of the old school. His funeral was conducted by Rev. G.D. Heuver at the Third Presbyterian church of Rockford and burial was in Greenwood cemetery. [Gravette News-Herald 3/13/25]

TWEEDY, William M. - William M. Tweedy, 82 years old, died recently at his home near St. Paul, Madison county, where he had lived since he was three years old. [Rogers Democrat 2/5/25]

VAN DEVENTER, Mrs. J.B. {HENDREN} - {from Gravette} Mrs. J.B. Van Deventer, a former resident of this place, died at Los Angeles, California July 8, following an operation. She was a sister of Mrs. W.H. Austin and N.B. and E.L. Hendren. Mrs. Austin left at once to attend the funeral which was held Monday. [Benton County Record 7/17/25]

WALDRIP, Bud - Uncle Bud Waldrip died suddenly last Sunday night at the home of a neighbor in the Elm Springs community while attending cottage prayer meeting. He had just finished a short talk and while taking his seat he suddenly fell over dead. He was the last of the Waldrip family and brother of Mrs. J.M. Mobertson, deceased, of Springdale, the mother of Mrs. Alice Beard, postmistress of Gentry. He had made his home with his son, Rufus Waldrip, near Cave Springs for a number of years. Burial was made Monday afternoon at Elm Springs and was largely attended by many old friends who are left to mourn his sudden passing. [Gentry Journal-Advance 10/9/25]

WALKER, Arthur - Arthur Walker, 30 years old, was killed instantly late yesterday from a shot fired by federal prohibition agents when Walker refused to surrender to officers who found him operating a still near War Eagle Creek in Washington county. Prohibition Agents S.M. Gurley and R.N. Wilson with Deputy Sheriff Lem Guinn came upon Walker and Riley Clardy operating a 25-gallon and a 22-gallon copper pot. According to the officers the two men refused to put up their hands and drew their guns instead, firing upon the raiding officers. The first shot fired by officers killed Walker, Clardy then surrendered. The prohibition officers found four 60-gallon barrels of mash, five half gallon jars of alleged moonshine whiskey and a 60-gallon cooler. Walker is survived by his wife and one child. [Rogers Daily Post 10/15/25]

WALKER, Mary Ann JEFFERIES - Mary Ann Jefferies was born in Bedford County, Tennessee the sixth day of September 1844. She moved with her parents to Arkansas some time before the civil war. December the 12th, 1860 she was married to J.R. Walker who preceded her to the other world. In early life she gave her life to God and united with the M.E. Church, South. Her life was such as became a Christian. She was devoted to her church and to her family. She died at the home of her son, Horace Walker, October the eighth, 1925. She lived to the ripe age of 81 years, one month and two days. She leaves to mourn their irreparable loss, four children: Mrs. John Burnett, Mrs. George Burnett, Mrs. Emery Chiles and Mr. Horace Walker; also three sisters, one brother, 13 grandchildren, three adopted grandchildren and ten great-grandchildren besides other relatives and friends. Mother Walker leaves to her children the heritage of a good name and they know where to find her. Her body was laid to rest in the cemetery at Elm Springs, where sleeps the husband, to await the resurrection morn. W.E. Bishop. [Benton County Record 10/16/25]

WALLS, Rachel MOULDER - {from a correspondent in Tulsa} Rachel Moulder was born at McMinnville, Tenn. Dec. 2nd, 1828. She was converted at the age of 20 years, joining the Methodist church in 1867. In 1852 she was married to Charley Walls. To this union were born three children: Mrs. Tom Williams and Mrs. Janie Phipps of Tulsa; and Media, who passed beyond a few years ago. There are seven grandchildren and seven great-grandchildren surviving her. Her family moved from Tennessee to Missouri and from there to Rogers in 1853. She lived near Rogers for 65 years. She was a true Christian and loved by all who knew her. She passed away on Jan. 28, 1925. The funeral was held at the Nogales Avenue Baptist church and she was laid to rest in Rosehill cemetery at Tulsa. [Rogers Democrat 4/23/25]

WALTERS, Oscar Perry - Oscar Perry Walters, 40 years old, who had been teaching school near Watts, Okla., died last week in the hospital at Siloam Springs of bronchial pneumonia. He had just a day or two previously been elected principal of the Siloam Springs High School for next year. [Rogers Democrat 4/9/25]

WARD, Mary MOORE - Mary Moore Ward, the eldest daughter of Mr. and Mrs. Joseph Moore of Bentonville, died in a hospital in New York City where she had been an invalid for the past year and four months, on Friday, April 17th, 1925. Besides her parents she is survived by her husband, Nelson O. Ward, of Ridgewood, N.Y., a sister, Miss Hattie Moore of Kansas City and a brother, Carl Moore of New York, the three latter who were with Mrs. Ward when she died. Mrs. Ward was born in Avoca, Iowa in 1872 and came with her parents to Arkansas in 1893. She was a natural born musician and was a skillful player of the piano and violin and was a splendid vocalist. She was on the stage for seven years. Funeral services were held at Ridgewood and interment was made in the cemetery there. [Benton County Record 4/24/25]

WARE, Mary L. - {from Gentry} Funeral services were held last Friday for Mrs. Mary Ware. The remains were shipped to Pittsford, Mich., her former home, for burial. She was about 70 years of age and died from a stroke of paralysis. She is survived by one son here, Ben F. Ware, and two sons in Kentucky. [Benton County Record 10/2/25]

Mary L. Ware was born at Waldron, Mich. June 9, 1846. Died at Gentry, Ark. Sept. 23, 1925, aged 79 years, 3 months and 14 days. The deceased was married to Albert Ware in 1863 and to this union 3 children were born; one daughter and two sons. The husband and daughter preceded her to the other world some years ago and in 1917, because of her failing health, she was brought to Arkansas by her sons and has lived in this state eight years. She has been a member of and an active worker in the United Brethren Church for many years and died secure in that faith. She is survived by two sons, two grandsons, three great-granddaughters and four great-grandsons. [Gentry Journal-Advance 10/2/25]

WARREN, Charlie - Mrs. J.T. Perry left Wednesday for Muskogee, Okla. after she had received a telegram announcing the death of her brother, Charlie Warren, in that city. The deceased, according to Mrs. Perry, was an ex-soldier who had seen war service in France and had been ill some time. Mr. J.T. Perry received an equally as tragic telegram almost concurrently with Mrs. Perry. His mother in Prague, Okla. is ill and is not expected to live. Mr. Perry also departed Wednesday. [Benton County Record 8/21/25]

WASSON, Abner G. - In the death of Abner G. Wasson Gentry loses one of its most prominent citizens. For over twenty years he ranked among the leaders in all public enterprises. The store of Wasson, McGaugh & Co. was known far and wide and drew a large business from Oklahoma. The funeral, which was held Saturday afternoon, was one of the largest ever held in Gentry. Mr. Wasson was born in Elm Springs sixty-two years ago and moved to the new town of Gentry when it was established by the townsite company of the Kansas City Southern, who had just completed their road to this point. He has been in ill health for over a year, suffering from cancer of the stomach, which finally resulted in his death. He is survived by his widow, Mrs. Mamie McGaugh Wasson, and a son, Leon Wasson, living in Butler, Mo. [Benton County Record 10/23/25]

A.G. Wasson died at his home in the northwest part of Gentry last Thursday night of cancer of the stomach. He had been sick for a number of months and had been a patient of Mayo Bros. in Rochester, Minn. All that could be was done but he passed peacefully away, out of his suffering that he had borne so patiently. He was only 62 years of age and should have had many useful years ahead of him. He was a native of Washington county but the last thirty years of his life was spent in Gentry where he established the first store in Gentry, remaining an active business man until just a few years ago when he retired to a private life on his farm near town. At the age of 25 years he was married to Miss Mamie McGaugh and to this union three children were born, two of whom died in infancy. He was connected with the local bank from its establishment, being vice president until the time of his death. He had long been an active Mason, being a past Grand Master. Funeral services were held from the Methodist church conducted by Rev. Villines of the Methodist church and Rev. Lillard of the Baptist church. The services at the grave in the City Cemetery were in charge of the local Masons, assisted by the Decatur Lodge. The funeral was largely attended, there being many relatives and friends coming from Springtown, Decatur and Siloam Springs. He is survived by his widow, Mrs. Mamie Wasson, a son, Leon, of Butler, Mo., three sisters, Mrs. Mary Reed of Cave Springs, Mrs. Sara Greathouse and Miss Belle Wasson of Portales, New Mexico, and a brother, John Wasson of Elm Springs. [Gentry Journal-Advance 10/23/25] [Benton County Democrat 10/20/25]

WATSON, Mary Josephine - Mary Josephine Watson, the beloved daughter of Mr. and Mrs. E.P. Watson, Jr. of San Diego, Cal. and granddaughter of Col. and Mrs. E.P. Watson of Bentonville, died on Friday, September 25th, 1925 in a Los Angeles hospital following an operation for a tumor on the brain. She was seven years of age. Burial was made in San Diego, Cal. and Mrs. Watson visited their son and his family two years ago and became very much attached to their little granddaughter. [Benton County Record 10/2/25]

WAYLAND, Grace Maud CAPPLE - Grace Maud Capple, born near Walnut Hill, Ill. February 19th, 1884, aged 51 years, 2 months and 13 days. She met and married J.E. Wayland May 21, 1902. To this union were born nine children, all of whom are living. Mrs. Wayland was converted at the early age of 14 and united with the Methodist Episcopal Church, South. She was a wonderful woman - she loved her home, her husband, her children. She was devoutly religious, finding her faith in God sufficient in every trial. She was not afraid to go while she would like to have tarried here for a while in order to help keep back the evils of this present life from the little nest. Committing all these interests to His eternal care she heard the call and went home. [Gentry Journal-Advance 5/8/25]

WAYLAND, Susan Bell PRICE - Susan Bell Price was born February 27, 1854 at Fayette, Mo. The early part of her life was spent in this state. On April 9th, 1872 she met and married Wm. James Wayland. This proved a happy marriage. To this union were born five children, one daughter dying in infancy and four sons, three of whom are living, one having died at the early age of 22. Grandma Wayland was converted early in life and united with the Methodist Episcopal Church, South. It was her wonderful faith that sustained her during the trying times of the early days. Perhaps no one has had so trying an experience as she, being left a widow with a house full of little ones looking to her for support. Many times the wolf stood very near the door but her faith in God proved the anchor sufficient for her soul. She suffered no one knows how much for months before she died. But in spite of all she continued so thoughtful for others, never growing impatient. [Gentry Journal-Advance 5/8/25]

WEATHERS, Irbert - Irbert, 6-year-old son of Virgil Weathers of Kingston, Madison Co., was choked to death one day last week by swallowing a piece of lead pencil. [Rogers Democrat 12/17/25]

WEBBER, Minnie TURNER - Word has been received of the death of Mrs. Charles Webber in Hollywood, Cal. on December 8th. She was known to the older residents here as Miss Minnie Turner. She was married to Mr. Webber about 20 years ago. [Benton County Record 1/2/25]

WEEKS, infant - {from Central} A daughter was born to Durward Weeks and wife Sunday night and it being dead, was buried at the Pratt cemetery Monday afternoon. The parents certainly have the sympathy of this community in the loss of this little one. [Rogers Democrat 1/8/25]

WELLS, Josephine HULL - Mrs. A.H. Hull received a message announcing the death of her sister-in-law, Mrs. E.T.C. Wells, which occurred Saturday, May 23, 1925 at the hospital in Iowa where Mrs. Wells has been taking treatment since leaving Gravette. Miss Josephine Hull was born at Wellington, Iowa where she grew to womanhood and met and married E.T.C. Wells. There are six children: Arthur of Davenport, Iowa; Earl of Portland, Ore.; Marcus of Bisbee, Ariz.; Miss Hermia of Chicago, Ill.; Mrs. Opal Frye, Cranston, Iowa and Mrs. Lillian Johnson, Mason City, Iowa. Mrs. Wells was a sister of the late Dr. A.H. Hull and another brother, C.C. Hull of Wellington, Iowa survives. Mr. and Mrs. Wells came to Gravette several years ago and Mr. Wells died here at the farm home south of town which was still the property of Mrs. Wells. She had been in failing health for some time. The funeral and burial were at her old Iowa home. [Gravette News-Herald 5/29/25]

WHAYNE, Malinda Jane HOARD - Mrs. M.J. Whayne, widow of the late I.W. Whayne, died at the family residence in Bentonville at 6:50 o'clock Friday morning, May 1, 1925, aged 75 years, 7 months and 13 days. Death occurred only a few hours after an attack of heart trouble with which Mrs. Whayne had suffered for many years. Malinda Jane Hoard was born at Maysville, Mason county, Kentucky Sept. 18, 1849, the daughter of a pioneer Kentucky family. It was in the closing days of the War Between the States when this young couple, like many thousands of others through the South, started to build a home amidst the devastation of the war-torn Southland, and through their lives sturdily maintained faith in themselves, their people and their land. The Whayne home has always been typified by its unequaled hospitality and a veritable host of people, living and dead, could testify to unforgettable kindnesses and courtesies shown them by members of the Whayne family in health and happiness, in sickness, trouble and death. No more staunch Southerner ever breathed than "Uncle Buck" Whayne, and his bride of the sixties was just as firm in her love of and faith in the South. Mr. Whayne died Dec. 29, 1902. In early childhood Mrs. Whayne became a member of the Primitive Baptist church and remained true to this church until her death, often going many miles to attend its services. Her life was an exemplification of faith, hope, charity and hospitality, mother's love and a friendliness for all with whom she came in contact. The Whaynes moved to Bentonville in 1882. All the children have been reared here, the lives of all the family becoming a part of the life and progress of the community. Mrs. Whayne is survived by two sons, R.C. Whayne,

Bentonville and Will Whayne of Independence, Kan.; three daughters, Mrs. R.G. Macon, near Ketchum, Okla.; Miss Lydia Whayne and Mrs. Bert Riddle, both of Bentonville. A son, Mark Whayne, died a few years ago. She is also survived by eight grandchildren and one great grandchild. Funeral services, attended by a great number of friends, were held at the Whayne home on East Eleventh street Saturday afternoon, conducted by the Rev. Oliver Koons, pastor of the Primitive Baptist church at Little Flock. In respect for Mrs. Whayne, a member of the city council, the city officials attended the funeral in a body. Interment was made in the family lot at the Bentonville cemetery by the side of her husband and other members of the family. [Benton County Democrat 5/7/25] [Benton County Record 5/8/25]

WHITE, Amanda YORK - Word has been received here of the death of Mrs. Amanda White June 16th at Banner, Okla. at the age of 40 years, two months and nine days. Her maiden name was Amanda York and she lived in and near Rogers until going to Banner, Okla. where she married Edd White and she had since made her home there. She leaves to mourn her loss a husband, six children - four boys and two girls. Also three sisters, Mrs. Gertrude Boggess of Lawson, Mo.; Mrs. Anna Smith, Blair, Okla.; Miss Millie West of Banner and three brothers, James and Mont Wells of Banner, and Elige of Washington. [Rogers Democrat 7/9/25]

WHITE, Ford - Ford White, formerly of Sulphur Springs, died at Anderson, Mo. May 8, aged 82 years. [Gravette News-Herald 6/5/25]

WHITTINGTON, William Wesley, Jr. - William Wesley Whittington, Jr. was born March 28, 1880 at Peoria, Ill. While in his infancy the family moved to a farm in Lyons county, Kansas where they resided for 13 years. William's education was begun at that place. The family then moved to Pawnee, Pawnee county, Okla. where he finished his education and grew to manhood. Two years previous to his death William, with his mother, moved to a farm near Highfill, Ark. where they resided until his death Feb. 16, 1925. William was afflicted with asthma at the age of eight years and suffered constantly until his death. In the last few years he suffered with heart trouble but bore his suffering patiently until the end came, which was not altogether unexpected but a great shock to the family. William was united with the Christian church and baptized in 1923. He was dearly loved and cherished by all who knew him. Those left to mourn his death are: his father and mother; one brother, John H. Whittington of Kansas City, Mo.; six sisters, Mrs. Verdie E. Shrack, Gentry, Ark.; Mrs. Jennie M. Fisher, Fruithurst, Ala.; Mrs. Ida E. Ballard, Kansas City, Mo.; Mrs. Mary E. Philiber, St. Louis, Mo.; Mrs. Maude E. Morgan, Waco, Texas and Mrs. Gertrude H. Foster, Muskogee, Okla. [Gentry Journal-Advance 2/27/25]

WILDER, Mr. - {from Hebron} Mr. Wilder, who has lived on the Goode farm for the past six months, died last week and was buried at the Larue cemetery east of Rogers. He was an old man and leaves a large family, very needy of this world's goods. [Benton County Record 11/6/25]

WILLIAMS, baby - {from Clantonville} The little baby of Jess Williams, who Mrs. Simlar was caring for, passed away Monday and was buried Tuesday in the Walden cemetery. [Rogers Democrat 1/22/25]

WILLIAMS, Mrs. Alf - Fayetteville, Dec. 8.- Mrs. Alf Williams of Fayetteville, died in Los Angeles Monday afternoon according to information received here. The body will be brought here for burial, arriving Friday or Saturday of this week. Funeral services will be held Saturday, either from the home or from the Central Presbyterian church. Burial will be in Evergreen cemetery. Mrs. Williams, who was 70 years of age at the time of her death, was a pioneer resident of Fayetteville and active in local work. She had spent the greater part of the time in California for the past several years but spent a part of each year with her son here. Surviving are her husband and four children: Mrs. Charles Healy of Rochelle, Ill.; Mrs. Wallace Wood of Los Angeles; Hosea L. Williams of Fayetteville and Roy W. Williams of Los Angeles. ***** Mrs. Williams was a sister of Mrs. John Felker of Rogers and was well known here. [Rogers Democrat 12/10/25]

WILLIS, Nancy Evelyn - Mrs. Nancy Evelyn Willis, age 65, mother of Mrs. Frank Parker, died at the Parker home Sunday morning. She had been ill for some time. [Gentry Journal-Advance 6/26/25]

WINKLEMAN, John - The many friends here of Mr. and Mrs. Chas. Winkleman of Fayetteville will regret to hear of the death of Mr. Winkleman's father, John Winkleman, in Kansas City Monday night. Mr. Winkleman was an old settler of Washington county, having moved there in 1888 and is well known in this section of the country. His funeral was held in Fayetteville Wednesday afternoon. [Benton County Record 9/4/25]

WOLFE, Bill - Bill Wolfe, sentenced to the state penitentiary for burglary at the last term of circuit court in Benton county, died at the penitentiary hospital Saturday morning as the result of wounds inflicted by officers. In company with four other convicts Wolfe attempted to escape from the convict farm a few days ago and L.B. Hartshorne, one of the five, was wounded and captured. Another was later captured and Wednesday night of last week Wolfe and D.A. Daniels, another of the convicts, were discovered as they were attempting to cross the Saline river bridge on the Sheridan-Fordyce road. Both men, it is said, attempted to draw guns when the officers opened fire, killing Daniels and wounding Wolfe so seriously that he died. [Gentry Journal-Advance 9/18/225]
The remains of Bill Wolfe, escaped convict who was killed in a gun battle with officers and who died in a Little Rock hospital last week, arrived here last Saturday and were taken to Cherokee City for burial. His mother made the request that he be brought there to be laid away. [Gentry Journal-Advance 9/25/25]

WOLFENBARGER, Della - Mrs. Della Wolfenbarger of near Mason Valley died Sunday morning, July 26, after an illness of several months. She is survived by her husband and five or six children. Funeral services

were held Tuesday afternoon and burial was made in the Coffelt cemetery. [Gentry Journal-Advance 7/31/25]
{from Highfill} Mrs. Charles Wolfenbarger passed away at her home east of Highfill Sunday morning at about eleven o'clock. She had been very sick for several months and suffered terrible agonies. Her children were all at her bedside except Pearl and Opal who had just recently returned to their duties in Chicago, Ill. They were called home and got here Monday night. The funeral was held Tuesday afternoon from the church at Mason Valley. [Benton County Record 7/31/25]

WOODS, Mary V. TROUTT - Mrs. Mary V. Woods, one of the oldest residents of this section, died at the family home two miles west of Bentonville late Sunday afternoon, July 26th, after an illness of nearly 10 months, following a stroke of paralysis. Funeral services were conducted from the home Monday by Rev. A.W. Henderson, pastor of the Presbyterian church. The body was laid to rest in the Centerton cemetery by the side of her husband, T. Allen Woods, who died on August 20th, 1921. The funeral was largely attended. Mrs. Woods was the daughter of Mr. and Mrs. J.L. Troutt and was born near Huntsville, Ark. on November 23rd, 1840. With her parents she moved to the vicinity of Bentonville in 1843 or 44, where she grew to womanhood. On her 19th birthday she was married to Allen Woods, the son of Samuel Woods, another pioneer family in this section who located here in 1840. No children were born to this union. Mrs. Woods has lived continuously on the old homestead for 66 years. Mrs. Woods dearly loved her home and rarely left it. It is stated that she has not been off from it for 25 years. She became converted early in life and joined the old Cumberland Presbyterian church in Bentonville. [Benton County Record 7/31/25]
Miss Margaret Woods of Port Arthur, Texas was called home the last of the week by the illness and death of her aunt, Mrs. Allen Woods. [Benton County Record 7/31/25]

WOODY, Mrs. Merritt - Mrs. Merritt Woody, well known here and who left here 3 years ago for Mt. Vernon, Wash., died on the 30th of November last and was buried on the 2d day December. The deceased was 76 years of age. [Gentry Journal-Advance 1/16/25]

WOOLWINE, E.A. - E.A. Woolwine, retired farmer and well known resident of Benton county for the past twenty-five years, died at the home of his son, D.P. Woolwine, east of Centerton, Wednesday, Jan. 21, aged 91 years, one month and 11 days. Mr. Woolwine was born Dec. 10, 1833 at Newcastle, Clark county, Ohio and moved with his family to Benton county, Arkansas 25 years ago, coming here from Kansas. He was a good citizen and earned the respect of all who knew him wherever he lived. He is survived by two sons and two daughters, D.P. Woolwine, Centerton, Ark.; J.R. Woolwine, Cripple Creek, Colo.; Mrs. Ely Morgan, Bentonville; and Mrs. Mary Gaasch, Denver, Colo. He is also survived by a number of grandchil-

dren. Funeral services were held at the Centerton Community church Thursday morning, Jan. 21, 1925, conducted by the Rev. Boyles of the Centerton Church. Interment was made in the Centerton cemetery by the side of his wife who died October 8th, 1923 while they were making their home here at Bentonville. [Benton County Democrat 1/22/25]
E.A. Woolwine, one of the oldest residents of the Centerton community, died at the home of his son, D.P. Woolwine, northwest of town, about 8 o'clock Wednesday morning following a week's illness of pneumonia fever. He was a little over 91 years of age and had been a resident of this neighborhood for nearly 25 years. Funeral services were held at the home Wednesday with interment in the Centerton cemetery. The funeral was largely attended. Rev. E.P. Boyles of Centerton and Rev. Joe Tyson of Bentonville conducted the services. Mr. Woolwine was born in Dayton, Ohio in 1833 and came from Kansas to Benton county in 1900. He is survived by two sons - D.P. Woolwine of Centerton and J.R. Woolwine of Cripple Creek, Col.; also by two daughters - Mrs. Ely Morgan of Bentonville and Mrs. Mary Gaarsch of Denver, Col. Mrs. Woolwine died about a year ago. [Benton County Record 1/23/25]

WOOTEN, Napoleon Bonaparte - N.B. Wooten, a resident of Benton county for nearly 50 years, died at his home in Burgin Valley, eight miles west of Decatur, Wednesday morning, Oct. 25, 1925 following a short illness. He was 80 years of age. His widow and one son, John Wooten, survive. Funeral services were conducted by the Rev. F.A. Bradshaw Thursday afternoon at the Barron cemetery where he was buried. The Masons of Centerton and Vaughn had charge of the funeral. Napoleon Bonaparte Wooten was born in Tennessee in 1845. The Civil War broke out when he was about fifteen years old. He joined Wheeler's famous cavalry in the Confederate army and was in active service until the close of the war. His parents then moved to Illinois; from there to Missouri, after which they came to Benton county where they located near Osage Mills. In 1892, when 47 years old, he married Miss Maggie Osborn. The wedding took place in Bentonville. About 40 years ago he moved to Burgin Valley which has since been his home, During Pierce Galbreaith's term as sheriff of Benton county, he served as his deputy for four years. His life will long be remembered as that of a model citizen and one who was always ready to stand for the right in any cause. [Benton County Democrat 11/10/25] [Benton County Record 11/6/25]

WORTHY, Marvin Leslie - {from Hebron} Death winged its way in our circle and acquired the life of one of our dear little school boys, Marvin Leslie Worthy, the 13-year-old son of Tom Worthy and wife and we all bow in grief for he was such a sweet boy and he looked forward to the last day of school and on Saturday before he died his parents took him to Rogers and bought him his first pair of long pants to wear on that occasion, but God willed it otherwise and he was buried in the lovely suit. He was stricken with pneumonia the following Sunday and grew rapidly worse. Everything was done to save the precious life by doctor, nurse and friends and we hope some day to understand the work of our creator. Just one month before his father was critically ill with pneumonia and his life was despaired of and Marvin so faithfully did the chores and everything he could to help out. The only ones at his home are his mother and father and the father was unable to attend the funeral, having pneumonia again, his little sister, Maxine and brother, Carroll; grandparents, J.D. Brown and wife, and several aunts and uncles. The funeral was conducted at Hebron Tuesday morning at 10:00 o'clock by Rev. Campbell. [Rogers Democrat 3/26/25]

WRIGHT, infant - {from Vaughn} The infant daughter of Mr. and Mrs. Wilt Wright was buried at the Barron cemetery on Wednesday afternoon, August 26th, with Rev. F.A. Bradshaw conducting the service. These parents have the sympathy of the entire community in this time of sorrow. [Benton County Record 8/28/25]

YOCUM, Ella HALEY - Miss Ella Haley was born near Marble, Ark. Oct. 13, 1889. She was converted and united with the Christian church in 1903. Was married to George Yocum on August 25th, 1906. She departed this life Oct. 20th at the age of 36 years and seven days. Funeral services were held at Tuck's Chapel Oct. 26th, Rev. T.B. Clark, pastor of Rogers Christian church, holding the service. She leaves to mourn her death a husband, an aged father, one sister, five brothers and a host of other relatives and friends. Her sister, Mrs. W.L. Brown, and Oliver, Will and Leonard Haley reside hear Ash Grove, Mo.; John and Henry near Berryville, Ark. The father and the three brothers from Missouri were at her side when the great call came. One other brother, Henry, attended the funeral. Mrs. Yocum had been in failing health for several years. Her condition became serious some sixteen months ago. Her attending physician advised her to go to New Mexico and they stayed there five or six months but as her condition became worse they returned to Rogers. Everything was done that human hands could do but God in His infinite wisdom called her home. By a Friend. [Rogers Democrat 10/29/25]

YOKUM, Ellen - Mrs. Ellen Yokum, 37 year old wife of George Yokum, died Tuesday afternoon and was buried yesterday at Tuck's Chapel, Rev. Tom B. Clark holding a short service at the Chapel. Mrs. Yokum was born near Berryville and has been the victim of tuberculosis. She spent some time in New Mexico but her condition did not improve so with her husband she returned to Arkansas. Besides her husband she leaves an aged father and four brothers and one sister. Especially sad is the fact that the sister's husband died the night following the death of Mrs. Yokum in the afternoon. The entire party who came here to attend the funeral left last night for Ashgrove, Mo. to attend the second funeral in the family. Among the old friends from Rogers who went to Tuck's Chapel was Mrs. Chas. Gundlach who has known the invalid many years. [Rogers Daily Post 10/22/25]

INDEX

1923–1925

www.ingramcontent.com/pod-product-compliance
Lightning Source LLC
Chambersburg PA
CBHW060127280326
41932CB00012B/1448
* 9 7 8 0 7 8 8 4 0 4 3 0 6 *